"Wise parents will treat expert advice the same way they would follow the wisdom of Aunt Minnie or Grandma Ellen – they must correct for personalities. Advisers have their own character, quirks, perspectives, and biases." Eyer[1]

Many 'experts' on parenting and children write as if what they say is based on solid scientific knowledge. This is generally hogwash![2] I love the science of psychology and have been reading it (along with psychiatry, sociology, anthropology, etc.) for 45 years. But the science of psychology is not yet at a stage where it can tell parents how to parent. We may be guided and influenced by research and theories, but when people have attempted to base parenting advice on a particular theory the results are often disastrous. And much of the research is dubious and open to alternative interpretations[3]. So you may want to know a bit about me so you can judge my ideas and evaluate my '*character, quirks, perspectives and biases.*' If you don't want to know where my quirks come from then this is one of the sections you can skip (though I may sulk).

I was born in Glasgow, Scotland, in a proudly working-class family of Irish immigrants. I was a mildly obnoxious teenager in the sixties. This time and place coloured my view of the world, though I've been forced to rethink much of the hippy-era stuff. Glasgow was a rough place and I grew up with a fair amount of violence and abuse. Unusually for that time, my parents never smacked us and there was no violence in my home (not even between brothers and sister, although my brother and I did use my sister's dolls for target practice with an air rifle… sorry). There was plenty of violence on the streets and schoolyards, and even more in the classrooms where our teachers physically abused us on a regular basis.

I loved science and just happened to be interested in psychology when it was time to apply for University. I was more interested in animal behaviour than human at first (perhaps that's why I work with adolescents) but I drifted into social work. I've been working with families and young people for over forty years in a variety of health and welfare roles: psychologist, social worker, family therapist, youth worker, residential worker. I've also taught on social work, counselling, welfare and family support courses as well as giving numerous workshops on violence to parents and other topics. I've been a foster parent and have one son in his early twenties. He plays in a 'Death Metal' band so obviously I've been a failure as a parent. The number of troubled families I have dealt with is in the thousands. As they are all different, I never stop learning. I've a degree in psychology and two in social work, but I think my experience is worth more than my qualifications.

Lots of things in my career happened by accident. I believe this is true of many people's lives and this means that we cannot predict how any individual will turn out.

I first became interested in family violence in Yorkshire, England in the 1970s. A colleague asked me to help out with some voluntary work, which involved recreational activities for the children from a large women's refuge. He quietly withdrew leaving me to take from five to twenty children of various ages swimming once a week, accompanied by two or three student volunteers. I did this for three years without anyone drowning (scary to think that no one ever mentioned insurance). It was surprising I lasted so long as the clique of workers and volunteers who ran the refuge proudly referred to themselves as 'radical lesbian-separatist-anarchist-feminists'. It took three years before they apparently realised that I was a man (the kilt must have fooled them) and they then banned me (along with anyone else cursed with a Y chromosome) from having anything to do with the organisation.

At the same time that I was volunteering at the refuge I worked as a social worker, which included quite a bit of child protection work. With hindsight it's surprising just how separate the two activities were, but back in the seventies, and for most of the eighties, the effects of domestic violence (DV) on children was just not on the radar; no research had been conducted and nothing written about it. We were aware of DV but it wasn't seen as directly relevant to the children in the families unless they were also physically abused.

Around that time I became a specialist worker with the intellectually disabled and their families, again by chance. My team leader had mistakenly thought I was interested in what we then called 'Mental Handicap' rather than 'Mental Health' and gave me *all* the relevant cases for almost two years until I noticed that no one else seemed to be doing this work. By then it *was* an interest and when a specialist position came up, I was persuaded to take it. I worked intensively with people with intellectual disabilities, and their families, for several years. Disability remains a big interest and I now see lots of kids, and adults, with various disabilities, especially autism.

The early nineties found me counselling families in Melbourne, Australia, in a low-income, multi-cultural area (where I still work). I happened to have four families at the same time, all consisting of sole mothers with sons aged eleven to thirteen who were in some way being abusive towards them. I realised one day that I was hearing similar things from them and saying similar things to them. It seemed logical to get them together and all four were enthusiastic. We were joined by a fifth mother whose fifteen year old daughter was beating her up. We called ourselves the MAAD group, for Mothers against Adolescent Domination. I like this title but can't use it as it excludes fathers.

This got me interested in violence towards parents and I looked for any literature on the subject. I was surprised to find how little had been written about it. There were thousands of articles and hundreds of books on domestic violence and even more on child abuse but only about twenty articles on violence to parents and (until 2004) no books. I was even more surprised that much of what was written assumed that parents who were being victimised by their children were authoritarian, aggressive or abusive, in other words that they deserved it! This was definitely **not** what I was seeing! This seemed unjust, misguided and a clear case of blaming the victim.

Around the same time, I also began facilitating a group for men who perpetrate domestic violence (called the "*Men's Responsibility Group*") which I did for over twenty years and still do. I was interested in various aspects of family violence including the effects on children of exposure to domestic violence. I soon realised that many of the young people (almost half) who were being abusive to their parents had themselves been exposed to domestic violence (invariably the abusive father was no longer in the home). At first I saw violence to parents, as most people still do, as a child behaviour problem rather than as a form of family violence (it is, of course, both). I also avoided calling the children's behaviour 'abuse' for quite some time.

Over the past twenty-three years, I have kept simple records of the characteristics of families where children are abusing parents, four hundred and eighty families so far. Over the past thirteen years, I've run and developed a group program for parents, called *"Who's in Charge?"* I see both parents and their aggressive children in counselling. I give regular talks to workers and parents on violence to parents. I've studied the research literature and written a Master's Thesis on this. I've been invited to talk on this subject at conferences in Australia, England, Ireland and Spain. Not bad for a sole worker without any organisation or funding! Through my website I've had contact with parents and workers from all over the world concerned about the rising tide of parent abuse.

Of the four hundred and eighty in my sample, I've personally worked with over three hundred and fifty of these families containing five hundred and fifty parents. Besides these parents, I've met several hundred other parents who didn't quite fit into my sample or on whom I didn't have enough information to include them. All in all I have met well over six hundred abused parents and about three hundred of the children who were abusing them, many of whom I've got to know well. I often meet their brothers and sisters and sometimes other relatives.

Makes me tired just to think about it!

I sometimes have to try hard not to think about the weight of tragedy and hurt that this represents. What keeps me going is a sense of humour and the fact that I've been able to help many of these families. There is a lot at stake. It's more than just a year or two of misery for entire families. These young people put themselves at risk in many ways, some of which might have lifelong effects, and by practicing being an abuser they are making it more likely that they are going to abuse their partners and/or children in the future.

Although I now work in private practice, most of my sample has been through welfare agencies or community health services and my private customers are totally or largely paid for through Medicare (no one pays more than Aust$15 per hour and it's a free service for anyone who isn't working or is on a low wage). Since I work in a working-class, multi-cultural area, my sample is definitely not biased towards middle class clients. Private practice here in Australia is rather different to the UK or America as it's a free service to anyone not working or on a low wage. Some people appear to think I am not critical enough of the parents I work with and would like to believe I have a nice middle-class clientele so they can cling to their parent-blaming theories. Overall my clientele are anything but middle class, though I've stated that I see more abused parents who are middle class *than I would expect*. I've never implied that these problems are a purely middle-class issue – far from it.

This book is based more on my experience than on the literature or on theory. Although I've spent a lot of time studying the literature, it hasn't had a big influence on the way I work. Very little is of practical use (when I started there was *nothing* practical) and it's still full of contradictions and prejudices, especially rampant parent blaming.

Eddie Gallagher

"WHO'S IN CHARGE?"

WHY CHILDREN ABUSE PARENTS, AND
WHAT YOU CAN DO ABOUT IT

AUSTIN MACAULEY PUBLISHERS™

LONDON • CAMBRIDGE • NEW YORK • SHARJAH

ISBN 9781787101005 (Paperback)
ISBN 9781787101012 (E-Book)

www.austinmacauley.com

First Published (2018)
Austin Macauley Publishers Ltd.
25 Canada Square
Canary Wharf
London
E14 5LQ

Acknowledgements

I'd like to thank the many parents I've worked with who, despite extreme stress, were often keen to educate others and spread the word about violence to parents. I owe a debt to the workers who have helped me develop the Who's in Charge? group over the years (such as Libby, Carole and Cathy to mention only a few). My wonderful wife has edited and critiqued many drafts of this book.

Contents

Optional Chapters

Introduction

"Parenting: part joy and part guerrilla warfare." Edward Asner

Children are pushing, punching, swearing at and defying parents in a way that was almost unthinkable in the recent past. They are smashing things, putting holes in walls, making threats to kill, spitting on parents and using various forms of emotional and psychological abuse to control or disempower them. Knives are being brandished at parents and at brothers and sisters, sometimes by children as young as six. In my counselling practice and the parent groups I run, I've dealt with over five hundred of such families over the past two decades. It appears to be happening all over the Western world. Though it's far from being rare, it's emphatically **not** normal adolescent behaviour. My guess is that about one adolescent in twenty is seriously abusive to a parent, which makes over two million just in English speaking countries. But this is a guesstimate as we don't really know the incidence. And it could well be rising. It's not only stressful, depressing and downright dangerous for other family members but these young people are themselves at risk.

This book will attempt to explain why this is happening. It has to do with factors in modern society, in families, and in individual young people. It really can happen in the best of homes. It's important that parents let go of some of the unhelpful, undeserved guilt in order to deal with the problem realistically. There is a lot of ground to cover but we will get to some practical suggestions for parenting defiant and violent children. It's also important to raise the profile of this issue as parents are still often met with disbelief and confusion when they try to get help.

"This isn't life in the fast lane, its life in the oncoming traffic." Terry Pratchett

About this book

This book is aimed primarily at parents of children who are abusing them, or are beyond their control. Most of the young people will be teenagers but it's just as useful for parents of younger or older children. I hope many parents will read it before their situation has got out of hand. It will thus be of interest to those who want to prevent such problems from arising, to professionals who want to help such parents, or to anyone who wants to understand this disturbing modern trend.

If you are the parent of a child who is beyond your control or abusing you (the two often go together and one leads to the other), what you probably want are *simple* guidelines as to what to do. I could write such a book, but I haven't. Such a book would be glib, simplistic and wouldn't fit most people's actual situations.

"For every complex problem there is an answer that is clear, simple, and wrong." H. L Mencken

I'm not going to tell you exactly what to do, because every child is different, every parent is different, every family is different, every environment is different, and environments are changing rapidly enough to make our heads spin. Plus there are also moral (rather than scientific or technical) judgments to be made that only you (and your partner if you have one) should make.

So if you expect *simple* instructions on what to do you might be disappointed. This book is not going to give easy-to-follow guidelines which can sort out every difficult child. I'm assuming you are not a silly person so if it were simple you wouldn't need a book, would you? Anyone who says they can *guarantee* results with such difficult teens is a charlatan.

Your attitudes are every bit as important as the techniques you use. So before getting to some concrete advice (and even then, it's flexi-concrete), we will be looking at a number of topics such as parent blaming, guilt, modern parenting, how you understand your child's behaviour, what part does his or her personality play, how has society contributed to this problem, and some ideas such as entitlement, respect, self-esteem and what gives children power. All of these are important to go over before we look at consequences and how to actually deal with a teen terrorist. There are also a large number of related issues, such as anger, communication, depression, ADHD, Autism, past domestic violence, relating to an unsupportive ex, drugs, etc. These are optional chapters you can skip if they don't apply to you. So don't be scared by the length of the book. No one has to read all of it.

When I say 'mothers', 'fathers' or 'parents' this includes carers who may be adoptive parents, foster parents, grandparent carers, and stepparents. This book is just as relevant for them, but there are too many different patterns to discuss them all in detail.

Exercises

There are a small number of exercises dotted about the book. Please don't skip these and if possible compare notes with your partner or do them together.

Case examples

None of the examples of violent children are wholly fictitious but none are recognizable. A few of the examples are composites of several similar families. Not only have all names been changed but often other details have been altered to ensure privacy. Where emails from parents are included, the parent gave permission for this but details and names are changed.

Endnotes

I think it's important to give the sources of studies and quotes even though they are of little or no interest to most readers. Also I need to show off how much I've read in producing this book. References are exiled to the endnotes, which also contain more technical comments which will probably only be of interest to professionals or academics. The numbers that indicate comments, not just references, are underlined. Feel free to completely ignore these.

Start Box

Notes on language

I make no apology for often referring to the parent as 'she' and to the aggressive young person as 'he'. Well, maybe a very mild apology. Mothers make up about three-quarters of abused parents and boys make up two thirds of the aggressive young people. Though I certainly don't want to give the impression that only mothers are abused or that girls are never violent, it gets tiresome saying 'he or she' all the time. Dealing with an aggressive girl is not much different to dealing with an aggressive boy and most of what I say is just as relevant to fathers as to mothers. There's a chapter focusing on violent girls.

As this is a book for the general public I have tried to avoid jargon and to make it readable, even though there are some complicated topics covered. This has meant some minor compromises on language. The following explanation is aimed particularly at some professionals who may be critical of using ideologically unsound or academically shoddy language. I'm not against being Politically Correct in language but it comes second to clear communication.

"Domestic Violence", or DV, is the term I'm going to use for what is also called "wife battering", "intimate partner violence", "wife abuse" or even (very confusingly) just "family violence*". I'm not including violence to parents under this term, though logically it's both violent and domestic (in fact more often domestic than adult DV).

One criticism of the term DV is that it's gender neutral. Most DV takes the form of men abusing women and I understand feminists objecting to gender neutral terms when over 80% of it is male to female violence. However, I also come across a small number of families where men are abused by their female partners and slightly more where the violence appears mutual and reasonably equal (and I think this pattern is increasing). It's not right to exclude these and pretend they are either not violent or not abusive. The 'domestic' in DV is also a bit misleading because it happens both before marriage and very often after separation. Even the word 'violence' can be misleading as DV involves a range of behaviours designed to control and repress the other person, with actual hitting being the tip of an iceberg of abuse and control. But though 'Intimate Partner Violence' or "Partner Abuse" are better terms, they are less familiar than DV.

Significantly, there is no generally accepted term for children's violence to parents. This shows how little attention the subject has received until very recently. None of the major databases of academic literature even includes it as a sub-

---

* I hate the recent trend to use the term 'family violence' to mean adult domestic violence as not only is violence to parents excluded but so is child abuse, elder abuse and sibling abuse.

category (making literature searches tricky). Different authors have used a surprising variety of terms such as "violence towards parents", "abuse of parents", "parent assault", "battered parents", "filial violence", "child-to-parent violence", "parent directed aggression". The possibilities are almost endless. The most often used term is "parent abuse". In my academic writing, I use the term Child to Parent Violence, or CPV, but in this book I will use "violence to parents" or "parent abuse" as the mood takes me. I might even throw in the odd 'victimisation of parents' or 'parent bullying' for variety. 'Adolescent Violence in the Home', or AVITH, seems to be becoming popular in Australia. Since most adolescent violence in the home is directed at brothers and sisters rather than parents, this is not a good term if the focus is on violence to parents. It's also misleading to include the word 'adolescent' when it frequently starts before, and doesn't end with, adolescence.

The note above about DV not just being about physical violence applies just as much to child to parent violence. Although we are certainly **not just** interested in physical violence, this is one common, clear and dramatic form of victimization of parents. When we broaden definitions of 'abuse' to include all forms of verbal abuse, contempt or disrespect we get into territory where the majority of teenagers nowadays might be considered occasionally abusive. I don't think this is helpful as the situations we are concerned with are quite different to run-of-the-mill disrespect and occasional insolence or defiance. It's the abusive relationship, or the fact of a child being beyond control, that is of importance rather than any particular behaviour. I talk about physical violence to parents quite a lot and it features highly in my research, because this shows that we are not just talking about normal adolescent rebellion. But it's definitely **not** just physical!

An interesting indicator of attitudes is shown by the fact that 'child violence' often means violence **towards** a child rather than violence **by** a child. This could perhaps be explained by the fact that 'child abuse' is such a familiar term. However, the term 'parent abuse' usually means exactly the same thing, i.e. abuse *by* a parent not abuse *of* a parent. Remarkably, this clumsy grammar can even be found when children's violence *to* parents is the topic[4]. Similarly, and bizarrely, 'parent victimisation' usually means victimisation *by* the parent, not *of* the parent, and has been used in this way even when the topic under discussion is children's victimization of their parents![5]

Here is a definition of "Teen domestic violence" from the internet: "violence or threats of violence *towards* a romantic partner or a household member *who is a teenager.*"[6] Can you imagine "male domestic violence" being defined as violence *towards* a male?

These abuses of language clearly demonstrate just how pervasive is the assumption that young people are victims!

What to call children who abuse parents is also difficult. I've found many professionals object to calling them 'difficult'. I think this is another indicator of parent blaming as they want to emphasise the relationship with the parent and that it's the parent who is not coping. But parents know perfectly well that some children are *difficult* from the word go and others are easy (see section on personality). Some easy children become difficult adolescents. Being 'difficult' isn't a permanent condition or a diagnosis. In fact, it's far worse to give a scientific sounding mental health label (such as "Oppositional Defiant Disorder" or such) than it is to call a child 'difficult'. So I make no apology for occasionally using this term.

I try not to call a child 'an abuser' even if they are doing a lot of abusing. It isn't grammatically or logically wrong, just not very helpful.

End Box

Violence to Parents – An Overview
Which Children, Which Families?

"Today has been horrendous and I am now wishing I was dead. I am too soft with him and he always gets his own way. Today he has kicked, thumped and battered me. Today I had to get out of the house so I did, he proceeded to lock the door behind me. All I did was sit over in the park, cried, thought, cried, thought and cried some more" Parent from Holts[7] research.

"Most observers hardly seem to notice that modern children are different; they are too busy commenting on – and blaming – the parents." Cable[8]

There have always been some children who hit parents. Until recently these were overwhelmingly toddlers. It appears that in the past, and in other cultures to this day, this was dealt with in a firm manner by the adults concerned. Some cultures dealt with it harshly, even brutally, others dealt with it lovingly and patiently, but the important thing is that it was dealt with *firmly*. Disrespect for elders was discouraged by the wider society, not just by the parents. My reading of the history of families and children tells me that adolescent children were very rarely violent to a parent in the past. My travels, reading about other cultures (Anthropology), and talking to people from all over the world suggests that it's still very unusual in non-Western cultures. Violence to parents is mostly new and largely a Western problem.

Although any hint of actual violence to parents by youth is incredibly rare in the past, for at least a thousand years people have been saying that the current crop of young people are worse than previous ones. For centuries, some people have been crying wolf about feral kids, lack of respect for authority, and the fall of civilization as we know it. The popular press regularly claims that the world has gone to hell in a hand-cart pushed by surly, nasty, ill-mannered youth.

On the other hand, and possibly as a reaction to all this bluster, it's quite unfashionable in academic or liberal circles to suggest that young people today are any different to young people in the past. Any such claims tend to be dismissed as sensationalist scaremongering. But the fact that people have been crying wolf does not make us immune to wolves. Kids *are* different today in important ways. There have been dramatic changes in children in the Western world over the past few decades.

Respect for age and authority are at an all-time low and children are disrespecting parents and teachers far more than in the past. Assaulting parents and teachers is the extreme of this wider trend.

The first studies of violence to parents date back to the late 1970s. I was a social worker then and am confident that such violence was very unusual behaviour. I can think of three such cases in fifteen years as a social worker in Yorkshire. In all of these cases, the children were removed from home as being 'beyond control' (which seldom happens today in most places). Since the seventies, there have been about one hundred articles worldwide looking at violence to parents (including some in Spanish, French, Japanese and a few in other languages). This may sound like a lot but it is tiny compared to research on other forms of family violence, on which there are thousands of papers just in English. Most of the studies of violence to parents were small and limited. There are also major problems with much of the research, as with a lot of research on family violence. I'm not going to go into the technicalities[2] but a lot of surveys on family violence come to rather strange conclusions. One reason for this is that people are neither honest nor accurate when you ask them about violence within the family, especially about their own violence. It's also difficult to make a simple definition of abusive violence so other kinds of violence (self-defence, play, expressive violence, trivial incidents) routinely get included, greatly muddying the waters. The most important result of this is that a great many survey studies apparently show that women are just as violent as men, and girls as violent as boys. This is nonsense, but since the surveys look scientific, and the stats are confusing, many people believe this. These surveys also suggest that most violence is two-way. Many people know enough about adult domestic violence to dismiss such findings. They know that men far more often abuse women than vice versa and that most domestic violence is not mutual violence (even if abused women do sometimes fight back). With violence to parents, however, few people have the experience to judge such findings and many people are quite willing to believe that girls are as violent as boys and that it's mainly mutual violence. Believing the few surveys which suggest that mutual violence is the norm is easy, since blaming parents and seeing children as victims are such common attitudes.

I don't want anyone reading this to lose sight of the fact that there are real human beings involved. So let's have two typical examples, many more are dotted about the book.

Two examples
Jason
Louise separated from her husband after several years of domestic violence and since then has been bringing up her three children on her own with occasional interference and verbal abuse from their father. Her oldest son, Jason, was six when his father left. A rather serious, moody child, he was very angry following the separation and often lashed out at his mother and at his brother and sister. Louise felt guilty that she could not cope with his behaviour and also guilty about what he had gone through. Louise now wishes she had taken his behaviour more seriously early on, but she firmly believed he would grow out of it. She felt a lot of sympathy for Jason's hurt and anger, which made her feel sorry for him even while he was being aggressive towards her. Her ex had been such a keen disciplinarian that she over-compensated and was a bit too soft with the kids. The other two

children are fine behaviour-wise (though the youngest is very nervous) but Jason slowly got worse until Louise became afraid of him. He was close to being expelled from school as he was constantly disrespectful to teachers, especially female teachers. Louise says if she had not got counselling for herself and Jason when he was thirteen he could not have continued to live at home. She was so desperate that she even considered sending him to live with his father, which would not have been a suitable environment (he's a heavy drinker). Luckily Jason (at age thirteen) responded well to counselling – for him part of the motivation to change was that he really did not want to be like his father (despite clearly copying some of his behaviour). Louise simultaneously became a lot firmer with Jason, using withdrawal of privileges whenever he was abusive towards her or violent to his brother and sister. It took a while but now that Jason is seventeen they have a good relationship and Jason's behaviour is 'not great, but acceptable'. He hasn't been violent for the past two years.

Pete

Marge and Trevor are both health professionals and both very dedicated parents. They have three children, all of whom are 'A' grade students and all are well behaved at school. Their oldest daughter is now at University. The middle child, Pete, has always been somewhat overactive and incredibly stubborn. In the past year, since turning fourteen, he has escalated from occasionally swearing at both parents to pushing and threatening them. These blow-ups can happen over trivia but are usually centred on Pete not getting his own way. Marge says she is not so soft that she gives in to his demands when he is abusive (Trevor is not so sure that this is true) but she admits that she was 'tiptoeing around him' more and more and so he was getting an indirect reward from his behaviour. She gets teary admitting she feels afraid of her son, she finds this very sad, but also very embarrassing. He also appears to enjoy the feeling of power from openly defying and abusing his parents. Though he'd pushed and grabbed her a number of times, Pete punched his mother only once and did appear to be genuinely shocked and guilty about this. Trevor is not afraid of Pete but is afraid that he will lose his own temper and Pete has threatened to 'dob them in' to Child Protection if Trevor ever hits him. Pete has goaded Trevor and they think Pete would be pleased if Trevor ever lost his temper enough to hit him. Given Trevor's professional position, a complaint to Child Protection could be very damaging. As they were afraid to leave Pete at home only one of them (Marge) could attend the *Who's in Charge?* group but she discussed the session with Trevor and he read all the handouts. The ideas they have picked up appear to be slowly working. They don't believe they were much different from many middle-class parents but they realise that they need to be a lot more firm and consistent with Pete than with their other children.

Jason and Pete illustrate typical examples of the two most common *types* of families in which I find violence to parents. The first is a single mother, or Mom plus step-dad, where there has been past Domestic Violence. The second is a family with no prior violence who are often caring, child-focused parents and just one difficult child who becomes abusive towards one or both parents. Both examples are fairly typical, and not too extreme. Both had happy endings, which is certainly *not* always the case.

My 'Clinical' sample

I've been keeping simple statistics on families I come across where a child is abusing a parent for over twenty years. My sample now stands at four hundred and eighty children. In almost all of these cases (88%), the child has physically abused one or both parents. I don't include any who have *only* been verbally or emotionally abusive unless they have also made serious threats or damage property. This is **not** because verbal and emotional abuse is not important, but because things become fuzzy and confused if definitions are too wide. It's difficult to know where adolescent rebellion or disrespect ends and abuse begins. It's called a 'clinical' sample because these are all parents who were looking for help and came to an agency I worked for, to me as a private therapist in the past few years, or to a group for parents. I've never actually been based in a *clinic* as such and I try hard not to be *clinical* in my approach. I don't include those children I see who are under eight or over eighteen. The fact that they came for help obviously introduces biases. It's not a *random* sample of abused parents, but since some people are always going to deny abuse, especially their own, and others refuse to take part in studies or surveys, *no* sample in family violence research is ever really random.

When my sample was under a hundred I used to be a bit apologetic as I had no way of knowing if the families I was seeing were at all representative. I'm now a lot more confident that my sample of families gives a reliable picture for several reasons:

- Basic statistics such as number of boys and girls, number of fathers and mothers, number of two parent and one parent families and number with past domestic violence are generally similar to other studies in various countries and with varied selection methods.
- Many things have either held constant (e.g. around half have past DV) or have changed systematically over time (number of girls has slowly crept up, from a quarter to nearly a third).
- The type of family and young person has not differed noticeably whether they came to me via a welfare organisation, a community health service, private practice or by parents attending a group (including groups I was not running).
- There may be biases emerging because I have a reputation for working with violence to parents, hence I get some of the worst cases passed on to me but also people who work in the welfare field sometimes search me out if they are having family problems themselves (not at all rare). However, I have data (with names removed) from other people running *WiC?* groups and I haven't been able to see any major differences. For example, just as many parents who work in the helping professions attend groups run by others as those run by myself. One clear bias in recent years is that my interest in autism means that I get more of these children referred than do other workers.
- On a number of variables boys and girls in my sample are quite similar which suggests that sample biases can't be extreme.
-

I don't think my sample is any more biased than any other and it's far bigger than most.

Gender of young person

In my sample there are 31% girls and 69% boys. This is very similar to studies in a number of countries[10]. This gender ratio is the same in sole parent and two parent families and, surprisingly, the same in those families where there has been past DV or where there has not. I saw a gradual increase in the number of girls for many years, but they are not in danger of catching up with boys and this increase seems to have levelled off.

I have no doubt that males are more aggressive than females generally and I am sure this is partly genetic and partly environmental. There is no known society where females are more violent than males, but the overall amount of aggression varies tremendously from society to society. If this is of interest to you, there's a chapter on girl's violence.

Gender of abused parents

There is no doubt that more mothers are abused than fathers. Overall in my sample, three-quarters of parent-victims are mothers and a quarter fathers. One reason for this is that sole mothers, especially those who have been subject to DV, are particularly at risk. However, even in just the two-parent families only half of the fathers are victims, while virtually all the mothers are abused. In two-parent families, the gender ratio of victims is thus the reverse of the gender ratio of victimisers, one-third male and two-thirds female.

The simplest explanation for this is that mothers are weaker than fathers. This, however, is only part of the story as a great many children abuse parents who are physically far stronger than themselves. When girls are violent to a parent in a two-parent family, they are *just as likely* to abuse their fathers as are the boys. It doesn't make a lot of difference if you are bigger and stronger if they are willing to be violent but you are not (see chapter on Power). I've met several big strong men being abused by little girls of twelve or thirteen. The fathers won't hit their daughters but the daughters have no qualms about hitting them. This may sound trivial, or even amusing, but it's far from being funny if you are getting medical attention because your little princess stabbed you with scissors.

Although a fair number of fathers are abused, a fact minimised by some writers, it's also true that even in the families where both parents are being abused, mothers tend to cop more abuse than fathers and they usually suffer more psychologically. One reason for this is that mothers spend more time with their children (currently three or four times more[11]) and take more responsibility for child rearing. So it's far more likely that it will be a mother who is arguing with a child about things like getting up, doing homework, doing chores, and turning off the computer. Some fathers find it easier to opt out when the going gets tough and can distance themselves physically or emotionally, in a way that few mothers can.

A few writers have tried to make out that parent abuse is *primarily* gender based violence. This is blatantly not the case. Half of all families where there is violence to parents have either a girl as perpetrator or a man as victim (51% in my sample). The difference between boys and girls in violence to parents is smaller than the difference between boys and girls in violence generally. Gender is one part of the equation, an important part, but not of *primary* importance. This is different to adult family violence where gender is of central importance.

Why are mothers more often the victims of children's violence?

The following are not necessarily in order of importance.

1. Mothers spend considerably more time with children than do fathers in most homes.
2. They take more responsibility for children's lives than do fathers. When fathers are with children they are more likely to play with them and are less involved with chores, clothes, school and social life. Thus men are less likely to be in conflict over the day to day trivia around which many arguments revolve. The *more* neglectful the father the less likely they are to be abused.
3. Children, boys and girls, are generally more intimate with mothers than with fathers. Children tend to abuse the person they are most attached to.
4. Mothers are more likely than fathers to adopt the principles of intensive parenting, i.e. they are more often child-focused, indulgent and self-sacrificing.
5. Children are far more likely to have seen their mothers being victimised in the past.
6. Mothers are about eight times more likely to be sole parents than are fathers.
7. Mothers are physically less strong.
8. Even taking physical size and strength into account, mothers are less likely to be physically aggressive and intimidating. Many women are bullied by children who are far weaker than them yet they do not retaliate. This also applies to some men, but women are less likely to fight back.
9. Women have generally lower status in our society than men, so some children have less respect for them (this can apply to girls as well as to boys).

It's important to realise that abuse is about respect not about love. Many children love their mothers more than their fathers, but they take them more for granted.

Most of the above are social factors which are changing over time. I've seen an increase in the number of fathers being abused by children over the past twenty years[12]. Fathers are spending more time with their children (though still not as much as mothers) and they are taking more responsibility for parenting than they did in the past. Intensive parenting ideals started with middle class mothers[13] but have filtered down to lower class mothers and to some fathers, though fathers are not even close to doing as much parenting as mothers. What's more, there is no society where fathers do as much child caring as mothers[14] and in most societies they don't do as much child care as do grandmothers.

"It seems that every joke or hackneyed stereotype about lazy, self-serving men might be true. Of course a great many men are wonderful fathers, exceptionally

hard workers and tremendous partners, but it remains stubbornly the case that most fathers do less, often much less, than most mothers do toward the wellbeing and success of the family." Brooks[15]

Age

The average age of the young people when they were referred was thirteen years and a few months. Since most had been violent to parents for at least a year, the age when it starts is pre-teen in the majority of cases. It's not just a teenage phenomenon and is not necessarily about puberty or adolescence either. It tends to get slowly worse over a number of years. Often there is a sudden deterioration when the child is around thirteen or fourteen. This is mainly because they get bigger, stronger and more adult looking, and research suggests that conflict with parents generally increases around this age. We also tend to react differently to the same behaviour in an adolescent compared to a pre-pubescent: they look more like adults and we expect more from them. Young people also venture forth into the outside world and start making bad connections: they may become sexually active and this can distance them from parents. The age for sexual experimenting and dating both seem to have got younger recently. I have also recently seen many thirteen year olds who are experimenting with drugs, about two years younger than this behaviour usually stated twenty or thirty years ago.

I've mentioned that toddlers hit parents fairly often, but this is not the same as violence to a parent in an older child. It usually stops if dealt with firmly. But in recent years I have seen children as young as six deliberately abuse their parents in a clear attempt to control them and a few parents whose teenagers are abusing them, tell me it has been going on pretty much since infancy. Other children are well behaved during primary school and go downhill fast around the time of starting high school. Parents often mention starting high school as a turning point, which might suggest that it's a social change not a part of puberty.

Some children do stop. A small number grow out of it, or their parents manage to regain control. Other children leave home, voluntarily or otherwise, between sixteen and twenty. Sadly, I come across a few children still living with, and still abusing, their parents in their twenties and thirties.

I hope to research what happens to children who abused parents in their teens when they are in their twenties over the next year or two and interviews with them will be the basis of a future book.

Family type

In my sample, 53% of the families are headed by a sole mother, 4% have sole Dads and 44% are two-parent families. Over a third of these two-parent families have a stepparent, so overall only about a quarter of the families are intact (both birth parents). Stepfathers are less likely to be abused than are birth fathers, contrary to most people's expectations. In two-parent families in my sample, 64% of birth fathers are abused but only 43% of stepfathers, again demonstrating that it's not about lack of love.

There is a chapter on family types but as we shall see, style of parenting is far more important than type of family.

Past Domestic Violence

Being a sole parent appears to be a risk factor *in itself*, they are about twice as likely to be abused by children when the effect of past DV is removed. However, the risk is far greater for those sole parents who have experienced domestic violence and/or where there is ongoing conflict between the separated parents. Often the sole parent is being systematically undermined by their ex – this is just as big a factor for the children as having seen their mother being abused.

In my sample, around half of the families have experienced past domestic violence (47%). While in the sample as a whole there are almost equal numbers with and without a history of DV, among sole mothers 61% have past DV. The rate is almost the same for blended families as for sole mothers (58% of blended families have past DV, almost always from the birth father). Out of the fifteen sole fathers I've dealt with, two had been physically abused by their wives.

The typical situation is that a mother is abused by her child's father, they separate, and later, sometimes many years later, the child becomes abusive towards the mother. It makes less difference than most of us would expect if the mother has re-partnered or not. Let me make it very clear that it's not the abusive parent who is targeted by the child, this is *very* rare. It's the mother who has been victimised by her husband who is then re-victimised by a child.

The child abusing a parent following DV is not necessarily a boy. In my sample, girls have *exactly* the same rate of past domestic violence as have boys.

It's true that the most common pattern in violence to parents is a boy abusing his sole mother following domestic violence. However, this makes up only a quarter (24%) of my sample and to ignore abused fathers, girls as abusers, or the many families where there has been absolutely no previous violence is to take a very distorted view. Some workers are obsessed by the intergenerational transmission of violence. Intergenerational violence and abuse are important but to assume that all violence has been passed down the generations does a great disservice to the many families where this is not the case.

Chapter 29 goes into this important topic in more detail. Be thankful if it's one you can skip!

Social class

Those research studies that have looked at social class and violence to parents have had rather confusing results. A number of studies find that social class makes no difference to the incidence of violence to parents. This would be interesting in itself since social class, poverty, and parents' education all have a *big* effect on *every* other kind of family violence. Although wife assault, child abuse, sibling abuse, and elder abuse are all found across the class spectrum, there is no doubt that they are all more common among those in poverty and less common in the middle and upper classes[16]. Other kinds of violence, such as violent crime, delinquency and bullying of other children, are also found **far more often** in poorer homes. Not only is this **not** true for violence to parents, but a number of studies suggest that this is actually reversed, with middle class homes being *more* likely to experience violence to parents[17]. No other form of family violence or abuse shows such a pattern in even one of the hundreds of studies I have seen.

Since DV *is* related to lower social class and DV is often associated with violence to parents, it would make sense if studies found more violence to parents in the lower social classes. A few studies do, especially criminal justice studies and some welfare agencies see mostly such families. However, it appears that there is also an opposing tendency for middle class children to abuse their parents *more often* than lower class children, counteracting the effect of past DV. In some samples, this balances out but in others there are more middle-class parents being abused. The reason for this counter-intuitive effect will become clear when we discuss parenting styles. But, not to keep you in too much suspense, the simple answer is that modern, indulgent, intensive, parenting is more common among educated parents and this is a major risk factor for violence to parents[18]. Parent education appears to be the key factor not income or neighbourhood.

Related to this and perhaps more surprising, I've also found consistently that a disproportionate number of parents abused by their children work in the helping professions – teaching, welfare and health. These make up just over 20% of my sample of four hundred and eighty! This is far more than I see among my clients for any other type of problem (the overall bias in my counselling practice is towards the poor rather than the rich). Parents who work in helping roles are more likely to be democratic, child-focused parents.

Labels

The majority of the children I meet have been assessed at some point. Parents are often desperate for help and want to know what is wrong; 40% have had some kind of formal diagnosis. The most common in Australia is ADHD, with around 20% of the children having this diagnosis. Very few have any form of real 'mental illness' and the other 20% who have some kind of label have a wide variety of conditions, mostly mild and not necessarily related to the violence to parents. Some have a mild disability, with autism (6%) and mild learning difficulties (also 6%) being the most common. Since these are special interests of mine, this is probably more than would be found in other samples. A small number have depression (2.5%), epilepsy, eating disorders, obsessive compulsive disorder or another anxiety disorders. Others have a diagnosis which is largely, or entirely, based on their bad behaviour, such as Oppositional Defiant Disorder or Conduct Disorder. Since these are based on the bad behaviour, they tell us nothing of interest about the behaviour (more on this later). About 1% have what would be considered a serious mental illness in an adult, which is not much higher than we might expect by chance. This is probably a slight underestimate as some children with a serious mental illness may be referred to psychiatric services and not find their way to me or to a *Who's in Charge?* group. There are certainly a number of adult children with serious mental illness who are abusing their carers. However, I have no doubt that the great majority of the children who abuse parents are **not** mentally ill.

I've been able to compare my sample with samples in both America and Spain[19]. While the three samples were surprisingly similar in terms of gender, family type and past DV, when it came to labels they were very different. Many of the American children who were abusing parents were diagnosed as having bi-polar disorder[20]. Not one child in my sample, I'm glad to say, had this diagnosis. In Spain, there was no mention of bi-polar and very little ADHD (2%) but

'Intermittent Explosive Disorder' was quite popular. I haven't yet come across a child with this diagnosis in Australia. Unfortunately the new diagnostic bible (the DSM5) released in 2014 has something very similar, *Temper Dysregulation Disorder*, so that having tantrums can now be regarded as a 'mental illness' in a child! This makes me want to scream and throw a tantrum!

The reality is that your child's diagnostic label (or lack of) will have *more* to do with where you live, when he is assessed (since they change over time), and which professionals he happens to see, than it does with anything that may actually be wrong with him. Don't take labels too seriously!

Some facts about children who abuse parents

- Two-thirds are boys and one third girls.
- Almost half have been exposed to domestic violence.
- Half have had no prior exposure to family violence.
- *Most* do not have any relevant diagnosed condition.
- *Very few* have what would be called a 'mental illness' in an adult.
- Many have high self-esteem (though some have low).
- More likely to be the first born child in the family.
- Many are only violent within the home. Others are also violent in school or in the community. A minority (though quite a large minority) get in trouble with the law for other reasons than violence to parents.
- Few have been abused, apart from the emotional abuse of exposure to domestic violence.

What sort of person gets abused by their own child?

When parents come to a *Who's in Charge?* group for the first time, they have often not met any other parents with similar problems. They have absorbed some of the parent- blaming myths and hence may expect the other parents to be losers or bullies. They often comment that they are just a normal cross-section of parents (though by that stage a few are very cross); but parents abused by their children are not entirely typical. There are an above average number who are nice, kind, loving people. They score highly on Conscientiousness and Agreeableness on personality tests. There are also a few who are difficult, annoying or silly but that is true of any group of people (such as psychologists for example). There are a few parents who are angry, aggressive individuals (and these are very noticeable) but far more who are placid or passive, or at least they were placid before a teen terrorist was unleashed in their home.

There is a tremendous range of people abused by their children. In countering the myths that these parents are either cruel and controlling, or stupid and pathetic, I can run the risk of making it sound like they are saints. They are certainly not all saints (though a few probably qualify) but the majority are decent, well-meaning, loving parents. Many have made mistakes, but so have we all (see chapter on Perfect Parents). Some are wracked with guilt because they have once or twice fought back or they yell back when being yelled at. Most of the guilt is unwarranted. One of the aims of the first part of this book is to reduce the unhelpful guilt, which greatly gets in the way of assertive parenting.

These parents are not pathetic weaklings who have placidly given in to tiny tyrants and spoiled them rotten. OK, that description does fit a few, but not most. Many are intelligent and have been excellent parents with their other children. They may have even been excellent parents to the problem child prior to them rebelling and may be great parents again after the child settles down (yes, some do). I do think that many of these parents have been 'permissive'. However, they are not permissive in a neglectful way (see chapter on Parenting Style) and many are no more permissive than most modern parents. We are almost all permissive in some ways, by the standards of previous generations and other cultures.

Although they are not all softies, some are. The reality is that parents who are themselves bullies or who are really uncaring tend **not** to be abused by their children. They would either hit back or kick the child out (why would you put up with it if you were uncaring?). Children know this and they know who they can get away with abusing. The fact that girls hit their fathers so often illustrates that these parents are decent human beings. These girls will sometimes say that their father wouldn't take it from a boy but he wouldn't hit a girl – a Chivalry effect. Purists may object that calling this 'Chivalry' is inherently sexist and possibly unscientific. But it fits!

Though you may well need to 'toughen up' a bit, I am certainly not suggesting that you become a bully or neglectful to stop your child abusing you. It's probably far too late for that and the children of bullies do have plenty of problems and may even be more violent overall (towards their brothers and sisters, in school, in the community and to their future spouse and children).

A few surprising facts about parents abused by their children:

- Democratic, indulgent parents are far more often abused than authoritarian or neglectful parents
- Educated parents are somewhat more likely to be abused than less educated.
- Middle class parents slightly more likely to be abused than working class.
- Parents in the helping professions are disproportionately represented as victims.
- In USA, white parents are abused more than black or Hispanic[21]. In Spain, immigrant children are less likely to abuse parents. No data for Australia or England but my experience suggests it's probably similar.
- Parent victims are very rarely perpetrators of DV or child abuse.
- Step-dads are less likely to be abused than birth fathers.
- Preliminary results of my research suggest that abused parents score above average on personality tests on Conscientiousness and (especially) Agreeableness[22].

All this makes nonsense of the common parent-blaming myths. If violence to parents was often a result of the child being abused or was mostly mutual violence, we would expect the parent victims to be more often fathers than mothers, more often step-fathers than birth fathers, less well educated and more often lower class. We would also expect it to be becoming less common as parents hit children a lot less than in the past. All of these are the opposite of what we find, yet the idea that these children are primarily victims and that the parents are to blame remains popular.

Quite clearly the vast majority of parents who are abused by their children are not cruel, neglectful or stupid, though this is how they are often portrayed. On the contrary, they have most often been good, well-meaning parents, often too well-meaning, and too child-focused. And parents reading this book are even more likely to be child-focused and educated. So I make no apology for aiming the book at the majority of guilt-wracked, abused parents who have been good parents. I'm going to pretty much ignore the very small number of abused parents who have been neglectful or aggressive.

A quick summary of 'causes' of violence to parents

I believe that there has been a big increase in Western societies in children's violence to parents in recent decades. Such behaviour never has just one cause but some contributing factors are:

1. Our society has become more individualistic, materialistic and less respectful towards age and authority. This is exaggerated by media aimed at young people and these general social trends affect all of our children and raise the risk of disrespect and abuse.
2. Many parents are more child-focused, indulgent and democratic than previous generations. This intensive parenting produces some children with a high sense of entitlement, who take less responsibility, and may be slow to mature emotionally.
3. Some children with stubborn, difficult temperaments are particularly prone to disrespect and abuse parents. It's the temperament which is important, regardless of whether they happen to fit one of our rather arbitrary labels such as ADHD or ODD. Twice as many boys abuse parents as girls, which is partly to do with temperamental differences and partly with social expectations and socialisation.
4. Women are leaving abusive men more than they did in the past and some of these are later being abused by their children who were exposed to domestic violence and to their mother being undermined.

Is it really increasing?

I am convinced that there has been a real, and quite substantial, increase in violence to parents over the past few decades. I can't prove this because no one kept official records before 2000. To some extent people in some areas have suddenly become aware of it after it has been on the rise for over twenty years. Whether it's still increasing, and what will happen in the future, we just don't know. Many people, including some professionals, remain unaware of how common and serious it is, and this may well affect how people treat parents who have been abused. Parents who are being abused sometimes think they are the only one in this situation and are sometimes still met with disbelief when they try to talk to professionals about it.

Three of the four 'causes' I just listed have been increasing trends over the past half century. Our society has become less deferential to authority or age, parents are more indulgent and child-focused, and women are leaving abusive men in greater numbers. There is no evidence that children's temperaments are changing, though this is quite possible. However, if there have been overall changes in children's temperaments we would expect them to be more violent overall, not just towards parents. With the ubiquity of electronics, mobile phones, and the internet I fully expect that the next generation is going to be significantly different in temperament, and probably not for the better[23].

It's ironic that all of these changes can be seen as positive. I'm glad that we as a society are less deferential to authority than in the past (we children of the '60s have a lot to answer for) although the lack of respect for age is a worry. Less authoritarian, more child-focused, parenting is overall a good thing too and women leaving abusive men is *definitely* a good thing. All of these are examined in future chapters. Even the temperaments that can lead to violence to parents are not bad in themselves and many of these children are interesting individuals with great potential.

Is It 'Abuse'?

A typical incident

Alana and Colby have two children. Colby is a businessman, very involved with his family, but often off on business trips. Alana is an accountant, working part-time from home. She is child-focused, affectionate and an excellent communicator. Chelsea is seventeen, popular, mature and well-behaved at school. Martin is a bright fourteen-year-old. Both children are doing well educationally at private schools. Martin is average in popularity and has some behavioural problems at school.

Martin returned home from school in a foul mood, having argued with a teacher about his uniform. He never swears or raises his voice with teachers but is able to get them quite upset by more subtle forms of disrespect and sarcasm. As he can also be funny and charming, some teachers like him and others dislike him.

Martin got home at four p.m. He threw his bag, shoes and jacket down randomly in the lounge room, grabbed some snacks then went onto the computer in Dad's study and began playing a violent first-person shooter game, Battlescum. At five p.m. Alena asked him to pick up his bag and shoes. He grunted but otherwise ignored her.

At six Chelsea asked him to let her have the computer as she had saved an assignment onto that computer the previous evening.

"You've got your own f**ing lap-top. It's fine for study-stuff. This is the only one fast enough for Battlescum."

"That's yuck!" she said, watching him blow someone's head off on the large screen.

"It's a skilled game. And I'm playing with my tribe, so f**k off." He was playing on-line with a bunch of older kids he'd never met, but whose opinion he cared about greatly. Stopping during an important battle, (and all of them were important), was greatly frowned upon and admitting that your parents had told you to get off was treated with derision.

"I need to do my psychology assignment! You need to get off! I'll give you ten minutes."

Twenty minutes later it was clear he had no intention of getting off and he called her some quite vile names. She responded, "You spoilt little shit! You don't care about anyone but yourself. I'm talking to Mum."

"Crawl away and die, scumbag whore!" he said casually without taking his eyes from the bloody on-screen battle.

Chelsea returned with Mum in tow.

"Martin you've been on here since you got home. You're not supposed to play for more than an hour without a break. Haven't you got homework to do? And I

29

asked you to pick up your bag and shoes. Dinner is in fifteen minutes. After that, no more computer this evening."

"I'm not hungry. Just leave me alone. This is important! We're at a crucial juncture in the game."

"It's just a game. And I don't think you should even be playing this game. It's sixteen plus isn't it?"

"Dad lets me play it. He played it with me."

"You turned the gore off when you showed it to him," said Chelsea.

"You can f**k off, shit-for-brains!"

"Don't you dare talk to your sister like that!"

"She's a f**ing whore and I'm ashamed of her. She's screwing Darren Sygrove. He's a stoner!"

"You lying little turd!"

Alana shooed her furious daughter out of the room. "Martin, this is not good enough! You shouldn't talk to your sister like that!"

"I hate her!"

"No you don't! Ten minutes and you come to eat. If you don't, I'm unplugging the computer."

"Don't you dare! I'm warning you. You'll regret it!"

"How dare you talk to me like that! Just wait till your father gets back from interstate!"

"What's he going to do? Smack my bottom?"

Close to tears Alana retreated to finish cooking. She also phoned her husband who suggested unplugging the computer and banning him from it for a week. Easy to say from inter-state.

There was no response when she called Martin to come for dinner so she went back into the study, feeling panicky and again close to tears. As well as his aggression she was also worried about him not eating properly. She was concerned he might be depressed.

Martin seemed quite agitated, before she could say anything he screamed at the top of his voice. "Leave me alone! Don't you dare touch this computer!"

Alana wondered if the neighbours could hear this and felt a horrible mix of emotions. She was ashamed, scared of physical violence, upset for her son, worried that there was something wrong with him, worried that he wasn't getting his homework done, sad that his sister had to put up with such treatment, and guilty that she couldn't control her own child. She made a move towards the computer with hands trembling and tears welling up in her eyes. Martin jumped up and pushed her towards the door with surprising strength. He was still shorter than her but with an adrenaline rush from anger, he was far stronger. He pushed her out of the door and she fell over in the corridor.

Chelsea had been hovering fearfully at the end of the corridor and ran forward to protect her mother. Martin punched her in the head as she bent over her mother. He shut himself in the study and they could hear him dragging a filing cabinet towards the door. He was screaming, "You're both f**king sluts. I hope you get raped and killed! I don't want to live here anymore. I'll burn the house down."

Alana felt a flash of anger and she rammed the door before he had moved the filing cabinet very far. Chelsea joined in and the two of them pushed the door open.

Alana entered first, only to be punched and kicked by her now raging son. She fled crying. Martin threw a paperweight at the window, cracking it. They could hear him kicking the metal filing cabinet furiously, screaming curses.

Alana phoned Colby but could hardly talk for crying. He phoned the police who arrived a half hour later, an experienced middle-aged policeman and a fresh-faced young policewoman.

To Alana's amazement Martin seemed quite calm when he let the police in to his bedroom. Martin had a fresh bruise on his face. He had done this himself but told the police he wasn't sure if his mother or his sister had hit him or if he'd bumped it in the 'scuffle'.

"It's all a bit of a blur, sir," he said. "I was playing a computer game and I didn't want any food as I was feeling a bit sick. They attacked me and there was a fight. I realise I shouldn't have pushed my mother over. I didn't actually hit her, I don't' think…"

"Your sister says you punched her. She'll probably have a black eye."

"I'm not sure what happened. There were two of them, and they're both as tall as me. I might have hit her. I'm sorry if I did. I'm not a violent person. You can ask my school if you like."

Alana said she didn't want to press charges. The thought of her son having a criminal record was anathema to her.

The young policewoman afterwards made a notification to Protective Services on the basis that there had been an allegation of child abuse.

Next day a very sympathetic social worker interviewed Martin at school and listened to his vague suggestions that his mother was neurotic and that both she and his father drank too much (all gross exaggeration). The school said that Martin could be a smart-ass but was bright and never violent.

Protective Services later gave Alana and Colby a stern warning then closed the case. Next time he got angry and broke something Martin said, "Call the f**king cops, why don't you? Didn't do you much good last time did it? I'll probably get taken into Care, that'll show you! They said you were f**ing pathetic parents, didn't they? They'll probably take Chelsea away too."

Martin never admitted that he'd abused his mother. He saw himself as the victim, though he obviously felt just a little bit guilty. His behaviour was not planned and deliberate, but nor was it really out-of-control either. His parents were bright, capable people and worked together well. With clear consequences such behaviour decreased and had stopped completely by the time Martin went to University. But his addiction to computer games still causes concern.

Similarity to adult partner abuse

I'm often struck by the behavioural similarities between some of the men I work with who abuse their wives and the children who abuse their mothers or fathers. In families where there has been past domestic violence, children might be copying an abusive father, but just as often the similarity is due to similarity in purpose. Both are trying to disempower the victim and get their own way. In both cases, it's largely about power and control, though the teen is often trying to *disempower* the parent rather than *have power over* them. I'm certainly not saying that there is no difference between adult domestic violence and children's violence

31

to parents, there are important differences. However, women who have experienced both forms of family violence often remark on the similarities. They often report flashbacks to their husband's violence when their children are abusing them.

Since the behaviours involved are often very similar and the victims report similar feelings, why is it that domestic violence is universally considered 'abuse' but violence to parents often isn't? I myself avoided the word *abuse* when discussing children's violence to their parents for a number of years. With hindsight, this was a mistake.

What is 'Abuse'?

"*My son is physically and verbally abusing me*" sounds quite different to "*my son has behavioural problems,*" or "*my son suffers from Oppositional Defiant Disorder.*" Those who use such labels are unlikely to say that a child is 'abusing' his parent even if identical (or even less extreme) behaviour on the part of the woman's husband would definitely merit the term 'abuse'. Although people often go to one extreme or the other, the two ways of describing the behaviour are not mutually exclusive. Just because someone, adult or child, has a psychiatric label does not mean that they cannot be abusive. In fact, there are so many psychiatric labels available that anyone with behaviour we don't like can be slotted into one, or more, of them. We could all find ourselves a spot in the weird and wonderful world of the *Diagnostic and Statistical Manual (DSM)*, the bible of psychiatry. Having a label should not lead to any automatic conclusion about whether they are acting abusively, *acting out* emotionally, or doing both (more on this later).

There is still a great reluctance by many professionals to use the word 'abuse' about a child's behaviour. The exception is sexual abuse of younger children by adolescents, which almost everyone would agree was abuse. When sexual abuse is by a pre-adolescent (which appears to be more common recently) this is more confusing. Labelling a child as an 'abuser' would seem far worse than labelling them with one of the pseudo-medical labels. In some ways, calling a teenager 'an abuser' *is* worse than saying they have a 'conduct disorder' and we should avoid both. We should focus on the behaviour and label *it* rather than the individual. Saying that a juvenile thief has a 'conduct disorder' or even 'kleptomania' is far less helpful than stating that he is stealing. People imagine (wrongly) that being a 'kleptomaniac' is something that is out of the individual's control and likely to last, but 'a thief' can choose whether or not he wants to steal. These words tell us nothing about free will and choice.

Professionals tell parents to condemn the behaviour not the child, yet they condemn the child by labelling them rather than labelling the behaviour. Focus on the behaviour rather than the person because these behaviours can change – sometimes overnight. Should it be considered a psychiatric disorder if someone can choose to stop being disordered?

If an eighteen-year-old boy is punching his girlfriend, few would hesitate to declare him an abuser. In fact, a few professionals will demonise such a youth, seeing him as an irredeemable wife basher. Yet the same boy may have hit his mother a year or two earlier and then been regarded as more victim than victimiser. At what point does he move from object of pity to object of disgust?

If you are hoping for a clear definition of what is abuse, you will be disappointed. The word 'abuse' is more of a moral judgment than a precise scientific term[24].

An act may, or may not, be abusive depending on a number of factors. The following exercise is one we use in the *Who's in Charge?* groups. It helps you clarify what *you* consider to be 'abuse'.

Exercise

Look at the list of behaviours below and decide if each one is "abuse" or not, according to your viewpoint. If possible, do this exercise alongside your partner and compare responses and your reasoning. Assume that the children in these examples are developmentally normal (i.e. they don't have disabilities). You and your partner may like to answer the questions separately then compare notes.

Which of the following do **you** consider to be "abuse"?
1. Smacking a three-year-old on the leg for running on to the road.
2. Smacking a seven-year-old for not being able to read.
3. Ten-year-old boy gives his fourteen-year-old brother a black eye in a fight.
4. Ten-year-old accidentally gives two-year-old brother a black eye while play fighting.
5. Ten-year-old deliberately gives his two-year-old brother a black eye.
6. A baby biting his mother.
7. A ten-year-old biting his mother.
8. A ten-year-old saying "I hate you!" to a parent.
9. A parent saying "I hate you!" to a ten-year-old.
10. Ten-year-old calling his mother a "f***ing bitch".
11. Mother calling ten-year-old "f***ing stupid little shit."
12. Parents referring to a young child as "shithead".
13. Sixteen-year-old threatens suicide if he can't get a motorbike.

Having done this exercise with hundreds of parents and professionals, it's interesting to note that the workers are not much clearer than the parents about what constitutes 'abuse' and they have quite similar disagreements. Even family violence and child protection workers are often confused about what they mean by the word 'abuse'.

1. Most people do not consider it abuse to slap a young child if the intention is to prevent them harming themselves. However, a few people do believe that *all* hitting of children is abusive. About 5% of parents and slightly more professionals say that hitting a young child for running on the road is abuse. There has been a huge increase in opposition to hitting children, but the fact remains that the majority of parents (over 75% but dropping) hit their children at some point when they are little.

2. Everyone agrees that hitting a child for not being able to read is abuse, even though the word 'smacking' is often taken to imply that no serious damage is being done. Thus most people justify smacking a child if it's clearly well-intentioned, but see smacking a child for the wrong reasons as abuse.

3. Most people will say that a child hitting an *older* brother is not abuse but quite a few just can't decide, saying, quite logically, that it will depend on the circumstances. A few say it's abuse, but really with this one, even more than the others, it does depend on circumstances. People get confused because it's wrong and violent. But something can be both wrong and violent without being abuse. In recent years, I have come across an increasing number of children abusing older siblings (linked to the erosion of respect for age). If the older child is responsible and non-violent, while the younger one uses violent tactics, the size and age difference may be irrelevant.

4. If a black eye is given 'accidentally', almost everyone agrees that it's not abuse; abuse implies intent. You can't accidentally abuse someone (even though they may feel abused by your being inconsiderate or too blunt). On the other hand, extreme carelessness which causes others injury, may be cause for serious concern if it's repeated. Some parents get confused about something being bad behaviour and it being abuse – most bad behaviour is not abuse.

5. If the same ten-year-old *deliberately* gives his two-year-old brother the black eye, then almost everyone agrees that this is abuse. Interestingly this includes almost all professionals, some of whom would *never* call a ten-year-old assaulting his mother, abuse. However, I've encountered three or four professionals (out of over a thousand) who say that a ten-year-old can *never* act abusively. I think this attitude is actually a bit more common, but these few professionals were brave, or foolish enough, to state this view at one of my workshops!

6. Almost everyone (99%) agrees that a baby biting his mother is not abuse. Babies can't be abusive because they are not seen as having fully formed intentions or being morally culpable.

7. Parents in my groups agree that a ten-year-old biting his mother is abuse. Professionals are much less unanimous, though the majority agrees that it's abuse. When I tell parents that some professionals don't believe that a ten-year-old can be abusive they are horrified.

8. A minority of parents in *Who's in Charge?* groups think that a ten-year-old saying 'I hate you' is abuse. Hardly any professionals call this abuse. For most children saying 'I hate you' to a parent is not abuse. However, if a child is also calling their mother foul names and hitting her, it's reasonable to also consider their 'I hate you' as abusive.

9. The great majority of both parents and professionals say that a parent saying, 'I hate you' to a child is abuse, yet quite a few (including a few professionals) will admit that they've said this or something similar in anger at some point. This illustrates that some types of abusive behaviour are common and, though definitely wrong, don't necessarily indicate an *abusive relationship*. It's important that we look at the context of such behaviour and also make some allowances if they are rare or out of character. This applies equally to a child who occasionally acts this way towards a parent. I don't include a child in my sample if they have only been violent once.

10. **All** the parents in my groups think that a child calling his mother "a f***ing bitch" is abuse and so do the majority of workers. However, I often hear of workers telling parents to ignore their child's swearing, which hardly seems to be taking this form of abuse seriously!

11. Virtually everyone, parents and professionals, agree that a mother calling a child a 'f***ing stupid little shit' is abusive. A few distraught parents admit to having acted this way, sometimes under extreme provocation.

12. There is sometimes debate about parents calling a young child 'shithead' as some will suggest that, though insensitive and not to be encouraged, it might be said in fun or even be an affectionate nickname. Teasing and bullying are not the same things and people may be able to hurl horrible insults at friends and family in fun – context and intention is all important.

13. A child threatening suicide to get his own way always creates debate. Most parents will say that it's probably abuse but a few are concerned that the child might really be suicidal. Professionals are more evenly split. If someone threatens violence, this is abuse regardless of whether they really mean it or how they then act. Similarly, whether or not the child is actually suicidal is not necessarily relevant to whether it's abuse or not. If the child is using emotional abuse to try to get his own way, then he is acting abusively regardless of his real intent or his future behaviour. We generally don't know if he meant it at the time (though often they tell me he had no intention of carrying out such threats) and it's less likely (though unfortunately not impossible) that if he were genuinely suicidal, he would tell us in such a manner. The correct thing to do is to not give in *regardless* of whether he has any intent or not. In the small chance that he was genuinely suicidal, we would be increasing the chances of him acting this way in the future if we reward him. If we don't take the short-term risk in this situation, we are increasing the long-term risk. The same would usually apply if he, or she, were threatening to harm someone else or burn the house down. Giving in to blackmail and terrorism increases the chance of more blackmail and terrorism in the future. If you are in this situation, then getting help, including using the full force of the law or psychiatric services if necessary, is better than giving in and sinking deeper into the trap of the blackmail victim! But there are extreme circumstances where giving in might be the only sensible thing to do.

Can a thrown pillow be abuse?

The difficulty in classifying aggressive acts as abusive or non-abusive is shown by a couple I counselled where a pillow was thrown hard in the other's face, knocking off and damaging glasses. The couple both agreed that this had been an abusive, controlling act of aggression. Yet when we talked about it they revealed that on previous occasions a thrown pillow had been sometimes an angry but harmless gesture (i.e. expressive violence) or else (more often) purely playful (sometimes part of frisky sex-play). In forming an opinion of this, most people might want to know the gender of the two people involved. The default assumption is generally that throwing a pillow is far more likely to be an abusive act for a man than if the woman is throwing it. Is it prejudice that we consider a woman throwing something soft, or slapping a man's face, to be different to a man throwing something or slapping a woman's face? Clearly it's better if we can take all the circumstances into account in each case, but the reality is that, most of the time, there is a big social and psychological difference between a man slapping a woman and a woman slapping a man. The man is far more likely to be trying to control the woman while the woman is more likely to be responding to some form of inappropriate behaviour by the man. The man is unlikely to be afraid and may well find it funny, whereas the woman usually takes it as a threat and feels afraid and humiliated. It's also assumed that in most cases a man's slap will be harder and more forceful than a woman's.

It does violence to the social meaning of the acts to not take context, including gender, into account when looking at violence.

The pillow thrower in the above example was a man. So was his partner.

The most commonly used survey tool for studying family violence asks about things like thrown objects. It doesn't differentiate between a thrown TV and a thrown teddy bear. This is just one reason that gender tends to disappear in surveys of family violence.

Physical abuse

Very young children (two to four) quite often push, slap, punch or kick parents. This is not uncommon and probably happens to some extent in every society[25]. They don't have to learn this behaviour, it comes naturally[26]. In most societies, it's immediately treated seriously and adults make it very clear that this is not tolerable. In many societies, it's met by violence from adult to child but in some it's done assertively but non-aggressively. The important thing seems to be taking it seriously and being very clear about boundaries. Many parents in our weird society have become tolerant of small children being violent towards them. Despite this, most of these children probably grow out of the behaviour, though some give it up then start again around puberty.

Although physical abuse is usually clearer than with other forms of abuse, there are still grey areas. I've heard parents (and wives) say 'he's never hit me', but questioning reveals that he, or she, uses stand-over tactics, pushes or holds them. This is all physical abuse.

Pushing	Slapping	Pinching	Punching	
Pulling hair	Kicking	Scratching	Biting	
Using a weapon	Throwing things	Spitting	Holding	

There are lots of ways of inflicting pain on another person. Some children use a variety of tactics and others stick to one or two. Any attack can vary greatly in amount of force used and can also have very different effects depending on the part of the body targeted. There is a huge difference between a casual punch on the arm, which can sometimes be passed off as playful and a full force punch in the face. A kick in the shin is not the same as a kick in the balls! Within families there are many, many more low-force attacks than brutal, forceful violence. The intention is often to humiliate, disrespect, annoy, frighten, harass or intimidate rather than to inflict injury. It's more about power than about pain. This applies to men who abuse their wives almost as much as it does to youth who abuse parents. This does not, emphatically NOT, make it trivial or unimportant.

I hesitated about including spitting under 'physical abuse' because it's more of an emotional assault and doesn't cause damage or actual pain yet it's a powerful show of disrespect, definitely physical and definitely abusive. Spitting is especially about humiliation.

When people claim that they acted instinctively or that they had no control over their behaviour I sometimes ask why they chose one method of attack rather than others. Often they are quite clear that they would never use certain methods. Within families, violent individuals seldom hit wives or mothers the same way they would hit someone they were in a fight with. Thus few men (though still far too many) punch their wives in the face, though this would often be their first choice of attack in fighting another man. Some children have different 'rules' for how they hit different people. For example, a boy I saw recently said he punches his brother but slaps his sister and only pushes his mother. Such patterns show that there is always some control even in a rage.

Even 'playful' violence can be serious at times. One sixteen-year-old boy used to give his mother Chinese burns on her head, flick her hair to annoy her and hug her uncomfortably tightly. He also played practical jokes on her and used childish insults. He was adamant that he would never hit her and claimed it was all in fun, but she found it intolerable and humiliating and felt it showed a clear breakdown in boundaries and a lack of any meaningful control. Often children claim violence is in fun when it's plainly hurtful or intimidating – a very common strategy when the violence is between siblings.

Physical violence is, understandably, of great concern if there is a chance that someone may be seriously injured, but even without this threat it's often a source of tremendous stress and of emotional hurt.

It surprises me that there have been few serious injuries in my sample. Only two or three parents have been hospitalised, with broken bones, internal injuries or, in one case brain damage (in all the serious cases this had happened before I met them). There is a possibility that someone might be murdered or permanently injured in one of the families I deal with and naturally this worries me. If I were practising in some states in the USA, where many homes have guns, it's *highly* likely that someone would have been shot. Guns are thankfully rare in Melbourne and not one child in the almost five hundred families I've dealt with has threatened a parent with a gun.

Another complication with physical abuse is in deciding when it's self-defence and when it's an attack. It's not unusual for victims to defend themselves but when the perpetrator is a child and the victim an adult, any self-defence may be viewed as child abuse by the authorities. On the other hand, if an adult is attempting to use physical punishment on an older child and they fight back, is this self-defence? How we answer this will depend on our attitude to physical punishment, but often it's not possible to judge whether we are dealing with self-defence or abuse without taking into account the context and past history.

Katarina, a single mother who worked as a carer for the disabled, came to one of my *Who's in Charge?* groups soon after a violent incident involving her fifteen-year-old daughter, Ariana. Ariana had been kicking and punching her mother, as had happened many times. Katarina had at one point grabbed her daughter, who was taller and stronger than her and left some clear finger bruising on her arm. Ariana called the police and accused her mother of assaulting her. Katarina expected support from the police, though she had been putting off calling them, but was stunned and confused that the police were not interested in the bruising she had all over her body. They charged her with assault on her daughter and took out a

Restraining Order against her on her daughter's behalf. Child Protection arranged for Ariana to move to a foster family, treating Katarina as a child abuser. In situations such as this, Protective Services are putting children at greater danger by taking them out of the family and further weakening parental control. Despite the legal order, Ariana phoned her mother almost every day and wanted to meet. Naturally Ariana felt empowered and exonerated by the blame being put on her mother. Ironically, when she first came to the group, Katarina said that the legal order was helping protect her from her daughter, but over the next few weeks she became angry about the injustice of it all. The police eventually dropped all charges, but only after several months of extreme stress and upset for Katarina. Katarina was so confused by the whole thing that she actually asked me if she needed 'anger management' as she should not have become so angry with her daughter that she grabbed her hard enough to leave marks. I told her that she had been far too passive and that some anger about injustice, or about being abused, is not a bad thing.

In many research studies on violence to parents, this would be counted as mutual violence if the parent was being asked and probably as child abuse if the child was being surveyed. A number of such studies conclude that most violence towards parents is mutual – this is certainly not what I have found although occasional self-defence, or even retaliation, is not uncommon. But the majority of parents don't fight back and many have more patience than I would have in their situation.

Verbal Abuse

Whoever first said, "Sticks and stones may break your bones but names will never hurt you," was talking total twaddle!

By far the most common form of abuse of parents is verbal abuse. As with every type of abuse there is a continuum from harmless and humorous to devastating and cruel; there are too many grey areas to give a precise definition. Some writers and researchers simply say that abuse is anything that someone thinks is abuse. This is not helpful since a great many abusers genuinely feel that *they* are the one being victimised. If someone is prideful, highly entitled, touchy and over-sensitive then almost anything can feel like abuse. Is the Paranoid being abused by innocent remarks he misinterprets? *"What do you mean, how am I? Why shouldn't I be OK?"* Such vague definitions mean that almost all abuse can be seen as mutual abuse.

Having someone persistently talk to you in an aggressive, scolding or disrespectful tone of voice can be stressful and hurtful. However, a great many teenagers will at times talk with a nasty tone of voice. They may not be aware that they are doing it and it does not seem appropriate to automatically call this 'abuse' even if the parent finds it hurtful. Not all disrespect is abuse, though all abuse is disrespectful.

Verbal abuse can take a wide variety of forms. Insults may be blatant or subtle, obscene or sneaky, clever or inane, general or personal. Their words may be designed to put you down, to demonstrate disrespect or show disdain. They can be a means of demoralising, dehumanising or just confusing you. Many children play on parent's guilt and insecurity. Using or trying to create guilt is a popular tactic:

"If you hadn't been a shit wife, Dad wouldn't have left us."

"If you didn't drink, I wouldn't have these problems."

"You're a terrible mother. I hate you and wish you'd die. I want to live with Dad/Nan/a foster family."

Children nowadays criticise their parents in a way that was taboo not long ago. It's healthy that children are allowed to express criticism of parents at times. But there can be a fine line between reasonable criticism and criticism that is primarily intended to hurt and disempower.

Children are now exposed to sexual ideas and to bad language at an earlier age than in the recent past and I'm often shocked at ten-year-olds, or younger, calling their mothers 'f**king whores' or "fat c**ts". This can occur in respectable families where they have never heard their parents swear. The child may not fully understand the words he is using and certainly doesn't believe it. The whole point of verbal abuse is that it's meant to hurt the other person. If the parent has a weak point, e.g. if they worry about their weight, the child will use this against them. Sometimes a child will hit on almost the exact words that an absent, abusive father used. The child may have a dim memory of Dad calling Mum a 'fat slut' or he may just know her well enough to know what will hurt.

Disrespect is a crucial factor in abuse of parents. It's both a cause of abuse and showing disrespect can be one of the purposes of the behaviour. Children are increasingly teasing and insulting parents in a way similar to how they tease other children. I talk to a lot of children about teasing in schools and the most popular insults are "gay, fat, retard, loser, whore, bitch, nerd" (the exact words vary from place to place and time to time). Children throw all of these at parents nowadays. So a twelve-year-old girl might call her father 'gay' and her mother 'a fat retard'; 'bitch' and 'whore' are also popular. This would have been unheard of, almost unthinkable, forty years ago. Even the two or three boys I came across who had hit their mothers back in the 1970s didn't call their mothers such names. As a youth, I don't remember anyone using such language about parents even behind their back and swearing at teachers was similarly exceedingly rare (even in Glasgow, where the 'eff' word was used as a punctuation mark).

A very important point is that the names they call you are meant to hurt but the child doesn't necessarily mean any of it. Sometimes these same kids are getting into fights when other kids insult you or their family.

Take it seriously, but don't take it personally.

Verbal abuse is the one form of abuse that **all** these children use. I have not yet met a child who is abusing their parent in other ways who is not at times verbally abusive. Some of the boys don't talk much but they still manage a few choice words.

Once a child starts hitting a parent, making serious threats or destroying property, people may stop taking the verbal abuse seriously. This is a mistake.

I have run behaviour change groups for abusive men for 20 years. In our group, we do not focus particularly on the physical abuse but see the different forms of abuse as part of an overriding pattern of power and control. If the man does not stop the verbal abuse, then sooner or later he will slip over the line into physical abuse again. This applies to children who are abusing parents. Of course it's very important, and urgent, that they stop the physical abuse, but in the long run they have to stop all abuse.

Verbal abuse is also very important psychologically for the victim. Women who are being abused by their partners quite often will say that the verbal abuse is as bad, or worse, than the physical abuse. This may seem surprising. We often tell children to ignore name calling and claim that names can't hurt. It's great if they can ignore it but names can hurt a great deal. I talk to adults (some with conditions such as Asperger's) who were relentlessly bullied at school and some of them recall with horror the nightmare of being put-down and victimised over a number of years. The occasional thump or push is outweighed by the torrent of hateful words. Verbal and emotional abuse can leave lasting scars. Verbal abuse has been implicated in suicides.

On the other hand there is a lot of teasing and insulting, especially between children, which is done for fun. I tease my best friends and am teased by them. It's a sign of belonging, of acceptance and relaxation and can be very funny; it can even be a form of harmless flirting. Sometimes teasing is fun on both sides but at other times, especially for school children, it's simply fun for the teaser but painful for the victim. When children insult or tease parents this can be a sign of a relaxed relationship, a minor sign of disrespect, or a form of abuse. If there have been other forms of abuse, such as physical violence, you may actually need to take teasing and insulting more seriously, not less. Unfortunately I see many families where verbal abuse has escalated to physical abuse (or destroying property) and parents stop taking the verbal abuse seriously enough.

One of the reasons that verbal abuse hurts so much is that it's usually far more frequent than the physical bullying. This applies to school bullies, to domestic violence, and to children abusing their parents. In many cases, physical violence is relatively infrequent but verbal abuse is daily.

Once there has been actual physical abuse the nature and impact of other abuse can change. Threats are obviously quite different if there has been an assault in the past. Verbal abuse also can have more impact when coupled with other abuse and the threat of escalation.

Domestic terrorism

"Terrorism is a form of asymmetrical warfare - a tactic of the weak against the strong – which leverages the psychology of fear to create emotional damage that is disproportionate to its damage in lives or property." Pinker[27]

Like political terrorism, children's terrorism is a tactic used by the weak against the strong. There are other similarities: many parents talk of never knowing when the young person is going to explode and being afraid of what they may be capable of, so they are constantly on edge, forever walking on eggshells.

Another parallel is that if governments give in to terrorists or blackmailers, even occasionally, this makes the tactic far more likely to occur. If it's known that a government will never negotiate with terrorists, then a few nutters may still blow up the occasional building but, importantly, it becomes a futile gesture rather than a useful tactic. Similarly with your child, if they think that you just might give in to their terror tactics they are far more likely to use them. If you *never* give in, this does not guarantee that they will never explode or become violent but in the longer term, it's far less likely that this will become a pattern of behaviour. Most terrorist acts, politically or within families, are not rewarded but even if one in ten produces concessions this may be enough to keep the tactic in play.

If you were assaulted by a stranger, you may be fearful and angry but there are far more emotions involved when the assailant is someone you love, and even more when they are someone you feel responsible for. So a parent abused by a child feels hurt on a more profound level than when the abuse is by someone outside the family. They feel rejected, scorned and betrayed; they feel a sense of loss as they were once close to this person; they feel guilty, embarrassed, powerless and foolish.

Threats

Recently I've been hearing far too often about children waving knives around. Only a very small percentage of these children intend to, or go on to, actually stab someone. This does not mean that it's not serious and even if the knife-waver does not really intend to stab someone, accidents can easily happen in such circumstances. If you choose to call their bluff and assume that they are not going to use the weapon, never say something like, "go on then" or "you haven't got the guts to use it". This can be enough to make them decide they have to escalate the situation to save face or prove you wrong.

Not all threats are this unsubtle. A clenched fist may be a threat, especially if the other person has punched in the past. "I could kill you" may be a very serious threat, but often people saying this, claim that they didn't mean it and didn't expect to be taken seriously. Quite young children are making such threats far more often than in the past.

Threats of self-harm are more complex. If a child says, "I'm going to kill myself, then you'll be sorry!" they probably aren't actually feeling suicidal, yet there is a small, but scary, possibility that they are. Giving in to such threats, or any threat, increases the chances of the threat being used again in the future. In the long run, you could be increasing the risk of suicide by rewarding threats of suicide.

Other forms of abuse

What really hurts, in most cases, is the emotional impact of the blows, words or smashed belongings. All serious abuse is emotional abuse so I'm not giving a separate category to emotional abuse. An abusive relationship always involves some form of emotional abuse. Deliberate humiliation is a powerful form of emotional abuse and much verbal abuse is designed to humiliate and demean.

Some writers have taken the categories of adult domestic violence and tried to apply them to parent abuse. Most are similar but a few just don't translate. Sexual abuse is fairly common when men abuse their wives but extremely rare in parent abuse. Some of the verbal abuse can be shockingly sexual but it's not the same as sexual abuse, it's just a means of showing disrespect and a guaranteed way of

41

upsetting their mother. It also shows sexist attitudes and is a form of gender based abuse, but that is not the same as sexual abuse. I've heard of children grabbing parents sexually or exposing themselves but this has only happened in two or three of the nearly five hundred families I've dealt with personally. Calling mothers "f**ing c**ts", "whores", or even "lesbian" is not at all uncommon but girls appear to do this just as often as boys and younger children don't necessarily know what they mean. They know it hurts and humiliates. They are using sexual language to verbally abuse.

Financial abuse is another common category in adult domestic violence that has parallels in parent abuse, but is generally quite different. Many men control their wives' finances in ways that young people cannot. Children destroy their parents' property and may cost them thousands of dollars. Occasionally this is clearly a deliberate strategy, e.g. when cars are scratched or expensive ornaments targeted. I've had a young person tell me that it just doesn't feel satisfying to break something cheap. More often they smash things without thinking about the cost. Some break their own property more than others. Children often steal from parents but usually the motivation for this is simply financial gain. Drug-addicted young people are particularly likely to do this.

Don't worry too much about these categories. They overlap and terms like Psychological Abuse can sometimes be useful (especially for someone playing mind games) but really this could include almost all abuse. Spiritual Abuse is occasionally included as a separate category but I don't see this as being something distinct (but then I'm not very spiritual).

The word 'abuse' is abused and overused. Something may upset you yet be a sign of the other person's lack of consideration or caring. That is not the same as deliberate abuse. If a husband deliberately doesn't buy his wife a birthday present because she argued with him, that would be abuse. But if he didn't buy her a present because he is a selfish pig, or is autistic and doesn't understand why it's important, or is an absent-minded professor, that isn't actually abuse. A child staying out all night and not telling parents where she is may be devastatingly upsetting for the parents. But she is probably just having a good time and being egocentric. That is bad behaviour (and very serious) but not abuse unless it's a tactic *intended* to hurt or disempower parents.

Start Box

An E-mail

My husband and I have had adolescent trouble since my eldest daughter was thirteen (four years ago). We have four children currently aged seventeen, fourteen, eleven and eight and I seriously felt that I was on my last legs until a very dear friend told me about your website. I live in outback Australia and first looked at your website at work and I couldn't stop crying. Everything that I was reading I had been through and am still going through but on different levels. Your website has given me a source of normality, knowing that other parents have gone through or are going through the same issues that we have faced.

We were a very close-knit family of six, my husband and I hardly ever fought and if we had words it was never in front of the children. My husband doesn't drink and I might have two or three drinks every three months. We don't go out to pubs and clubs, when we do go out our children always came with us. The two girls were involved in acting and singing since they were both very little and my sons play basketball and baseball. Generally I went with the girls and my sons went with their father. Our lives were devoted to all four children. Everything seemed fine until four years ago when my eldest daughter went to high school and developed 'the attitude'. At first we thought it was normal adolescent behaviour as everyone warned us about it, but we were copping a lot of verbal abuse and put downs, saying we were pathetic parents, she was swearing at us, trying to divide and conquer, etc. We tried not to take it personally as we had been advised and we set guidelines, rules and boundaries. But we were dealing with a very intelligent child here, (we found out she has an IQ of 145) and she manipulated us without us even being aware of it. She had been a straight 'A' student but her grades slipped to a D within a year. She got in trouble at school, got suspended several times, lost friends and got into fights. Her behaviour at home was similar and no matter how many times I would ask if she was ok, 'can I help you with anything?' she would just say she hates it at home. Whatever I said she would deliberately go against me. If I said the sky was blue, she'd say it was red just to push my buttons. She started to hang around with the wrong girls and her behaviour became wild, aggressive, extreme and uncontrollable. She started to steal from us and lied constantly. She bullied, intimidated and hit her older brother and ignored her sister (who she seemed extremely jealous of). Her youngest brother she would baby, maybe he didn't appear to be a threat.

She would constantly fight with me, more than with her father, and she was insulting to both of us, particularly in front of her friends when they were over. This vicious constant abuse and lack of respect went on for a year. We would try to get her to see things from everyone's point of view and not just her own. Her behaviour was like a three-year-old's when they don't get their own way. She would say things to her friends about how she hated it at home and how much abuse she would cop from us just to get attention. Sadly, she was using the same stories at school to the authorities to try to justify her erratic and extremely abusive behaviours at school to pupils and staff. She constantly told me that she wanted to leave home, that she hated this place and couldn't stand myself or her father.

Then our worlds came crashing down. I received a phone from the police three years ago stating that I needed to come in to the station as my daughter was in trouble and they needed my assistance. When I arrived I was told that she has made allegations to the school counsellor about me and in particular about my husband. The allegations were that my husband and I were getting drunk and physically and verbally abusing her (how ironic!). She had kept a diary over several months as this is what the school was telling her to do. But when no action was being taken over those allegations she stepped up the ante and made allegations that her father had sexually abused her. They interviewed me and tried to convince me that her father had done this. I knew this wasn't true, but I was told I had to keep an open mind just in case. I felt threatened that they would take all my children away if I didn't. They hadn't interviewed my husband as yet but they were taking an AVO against him restricting him from the house as it was late on a Friday afternoon and they have to take action to ensure that all my children were safe or my children would be removed.

I was in a daze; they are talking about my husband, the father of our children that I had known for twenty-four years. He has never shown any sign of abuse, physically, emotionally, verbally or sexually. After the police officers interviewed my husband, that same Friday night one police officer called me and said she thinks she might have been a bit too hasty in applying for the AVO as they are not sure about my daughter's version. My daughter has always been very convincing and charming; it's part of her manipulating skills.

But the damage had been done. My husband had been forced out of the house legally, my eldest daughter had felt that she was on the right track to divide and conquer her parents. I had to explain to my other children that their father and I are separating as I thought they were too young to handle exactly what was going on, so they were extremely upset. He was out of the house for a total of eight weeks and that is when the real abuse started with her. She had me alone and unsupported and that is where she wanted me. She would call me every name under the sun, tell me that I am a pathetic person and a pathetic parent. She would self-harm herself and pierce her face for my attention. She would run away from home knowing, I would track her down, go to parks and get drunk. She started refusing to go to school and became extreme in everything she did. She would threaten me, saying that she was going to stab me in my sleep. She would constantly undermine me which eventually broke me and shook all of the foundations of the house.

Our daughter eventually told the police that all the allegations she had made were in fact a lie and the court case ($5000 later) and AVO were dismissed. She continued to live at our house but the behaviour continued and once again when she went too far at school she would make another allegation about her father, it would be investigated by the police and Child Protection and dismissed as they could see this pattern forming. This happened over the next two and half years with our once tight knit family being blown apart. At this stage our son had reached high school and was being confronted by kids saying all sorts of things about his father, mother and family. He would stand up to them but he was consistently bullied and bashed by other kids. It got to the point that he was depressed and highly anxious. He began mixing with the wrong crowd, and the wrong girlfriend, and went straight down the path of marijuana and drinking. He would steal from us to support his and his girlfriend's habit. As there was the mixture of depression and drugs his mood was very violent and abusive. He would smash things in the house, graffiti his room and burn holes in the carpet and furnishings. He was selling all his gaming equipment and anything else that he had got for birthdays or saved up with his chores money. When he had nothing left he started stealing his sister's iPods and belongings to sell for drugs. One day I came home from work and he was getting together my PS3 to sell and I went to take it off him and he started pushing me around and threatening me. He ripped the door of its hinges, smashed chairs and pulled shelves down. We called the police and took a protective AVO out on him for all who lived in the house and their possessions. That was very hard to do but we had to as he was out of control. This continued over months but once he broke it off with his girlfriend he started to settle down and the drug intake became less. Unfortunately his depression and anxiety became worse and this wasn't helped that his ex-girlfriend arranged for him to be bashed on several occasions, quite severely.

In the meantime, our youngest daughter has seen way too much for her short life and has become introverted and scared. She very rarely talks unless asked something and if voices are raised slightly she runs and hides, more often than not breaking out in tears and wanting security. She is having trouble sleeping and wants to sleep in our bed with us during the night. Our youngest son is much the same as in he doesn't talk very much but fortunately on the surface it doesn't appear to have affected him too much, but only time will tell.

Now all this was happening while we were still being verbally abused by our eldest daughter. She was consistently running away from home and made more allegations about her father on and off. In fact, I remember seeing her smiling one day at the fact that there is so much chaos in our house, which scared me.

Our eldest daughter's behaviour was snowballing down the line of our children and we felt helpless to stop it as everything we tried she would twist and manipulate and turn it back on us. The only positive thing was that our other children didn't believe what she was saying about her father and myself about the abuse but were picking up her bad habits of abuse.

Then a year ago she went to the police with a mark under her right eye and a mark on the inside of her lip stating that her father had hit her (she had self-harmed before with cuts and bruises, luckily we had taken all this info down). I wasn't home at the time but our son was, all but half an hour and this was the time that she said her father had hit her. The police charged him and I finally told her she had to stay with someone else. I wasn't going to put the family through this again. This is what she wanted, "to get out of this place" so we had to take a stand, she was sixteen at the time. It broke my heart as I love her dearly even with what she has put the family through but I couldn't let her demolish the household. I had to try and salvage the family unit and rebuild. We didn't hear from her for months. I only heard what she was up to through our youngest daughter, the one that she is jealous of and constantly ignored. Our youngest daughter now became very important to her.

Christmas was very hard and I called her to make sure she was ok, but I couldn't let her come back home at this stage. The family was starting to settle down and I couldn't risk it and I truly believe that she hasn't accepted that what she did was wrong. The court case was to be heard a couple of months after Christmas and within that whole time she was still trying to get under my skin. One week she would be pushing my buttons and the next week she would be totally different trying to suck me in. She wouldn't actually admit to me that she lied to the police but she told me on a couple of occasions that she hadn't told the complete truth. Our solicitor called the police officer from the first court case as our witness, as she knows in the first case that she lied and retracted her allegations, and also with the other allegations that they were all false and this was her pattern to get her own way, which was to leave home and justify her behaviour at school. With all this information at hand the court case was dismissed and AVO lifted again as the prosecution felt that she was lying, now with a financial cost of $25,000 and a shattered family.

We have now moved and bought in a different area as my son didn't feel safe in that area anymore after being bashed up so many times defending his father's honour; we were constantly being stopped in the street and asked by our eldest daughter's friend's parents what was going on with her and where is she living. Our youngest daughter's friend's parents stopped letting her friends come over to our house. We couldn't take the humiliation any more.

My husband and I realized what a strong relationship we have, to have gone through all this and still survived. We have created new ground rules for our household and the children are sticking to them, occasionally trying to push the boundaries. Our youngest daughter is being influenced by our eldest daughter now and is starting to verbally abuse us if she doesn't get her own way and refusing to go to school but we are sticking to our guns and not budging, hopefully this will work. So far so good as when she starts to become abusive towards us she is learning that it will not get her anywhere and there are strong consequences in place that will not be broken. Our son is now off the drugs altogether and I have got my boy back but this all started due to him being harassed and bullied at school by the lies his sister told about our family. He is no longer depressed but still suffers with anxiety about leaving the house as he fears he is going to be bashed and is currently being home schooled. We have realized that she will not come back home to live anymore, it took a while and it was very hard to accept but honestly it's the best thing for all. Our family is slowing rebuilding that tight knit closeness again, only this time as a family of five.

Our eldest daughter is now more respectful when she comes over and is trying to get on with us but I still don't think she really understands the full extent of the damage she has caused to our family. Maybe she won't until she has children of her own. We just have to take one step at a time and be sure she also knows the boundaries of the house when she comes and visits.

The most important things that I have learnt is that if you're are consistent, united, set boundaries and show your children that you have unconditional love for them, there is a light at the end of the tunnel.

Your child's life might not turn out the way you thought it would when they first came into the world but you can still have a relationship with them.

End Box

Victim Blaming and Parent Bashing

"The postmodern mother – because her thinking about her child and childrearing is contaminated by a confusion of behavioural, Freudian, and humanistic ideas (i.e. psychobabble) – tends to believe that she is the cause and her child is the effect, that everything her child does or fails to do is the consequence of something she has done or failed to do in his life." Rosemond[28]

We tend to treat all types of violence within the family differently to violence outside the home. We are often less likely to condemn it outright and far more often blame the victims[29]. In the recent past, victim blaming in domestic violence was pretty much given free rein. It was a common idea that women who were beaten by their husbands were masochists who provoked them.[30] It's now rare for women to be seen as staying with abusive men because they *want* to suffer, though they are blamed for being stupid or for not taking the effect on their children seriously enough[31]. But though the myth of masochism is no longer openly acceptable, it's still not unusual for women to be told by therapists that they subconsciously chose an abusive man. Though less common, professionals still occasionally see abused women as provoking the abuse. Attitudes have improved, but blaming the victim in domestic violence is still a concern and many women feel that they are held responsible, especially when children are exposed to DV.

Attitudes to children's violence to parents are about thirty years behind attitudes to domestic violence. Violence to parents is now unique among types of violence and abuse in that blaming the victim is the default mode for most people. Blaming abused parents is the norm not the exception. Parents aren't seen as being masochistic for putting up with it but they are blamed on two levels, historically for having reared an aggressive child and currently for provoking, or not dealing with, the violence.

Devaluing victims generally is so common that it has been suggested that it serves a deep-seated psychological function. It allows us to preserve our belief in a 'just world' [32]. We want to see the world as basically a fair and just place. People don't want to live in a chaotic, dangerous world (i.e. reality) so they invent one that appears to make more sense. Such a world, though fictitious, is a lot fairer than a world in which people are hit at random by illness, accident, tragedy and awful kids! Even when an accident, a random crime or a physical illness happens to someone there are pseudo-scientific theories and mystical ideas (karma) around that reinforce our impulse to blame the victim. One appeal of such superstitious ideas seems to be that nothing is seen to happen by chance and someone can always be found to blame, often the person who is suffering. Perhaps because I've dealt with human tragedies for four decades, I'm forced to conclude that life is not even remotely fair! Many people struggle very hard to avoid seeing this obvious fact.

Unfortunately, this cosily reassuring, naive notion has serious side effects. If we expect bad things to happen to bad people, and good things to happen to good people, then we will have a tendency to assume that people deserve their misfortunes.

"If we could blame the victim for her fate, we could feel safe (and smug). All we had to do was convince ourselves that she did something we would never do. 'She wears short skirts. She walks home through the wrong neighbourhood. She is someone bad things could happen to. Not me. I'm different. So I'm safe.'"
Skenazy[33]

Denigration of victims has been demonstrated in the laboratory, even when the 'victim' has clearly done nothing to deserve their fate.[34] In an infamous social psychology experiment, subjects were persuaded to apparently administer electric shocks to another person. The other person was an actor, but the subjects didn't know that and many delivered what they thought were highly painful and even dangerous electric shocks. Having either seen someone being shocked, or having themselves acted violently towards a victim, many subjects then devalued him or her. They apparently found "*it necessary to view him as an unworthy individual, whose punishment was made inevitable by his own deficiencies of intelligence and character[35]*".

In schools, victims are often devalued by their bullies, and even by bystanders. Bullies may pick on someone randomly, but then they justify their action by seeing the victim as deserving it. Other children also devalue the victim and often the class scapegoat becomes ostracised for no good reason.[36]

When an aggressor feels uneasy or guilty about his or her own behaviour they may be more likely to devalue the victim. Thus an aggressor's guilty feelings about having harmed the victim can actually *increase* their blaming and devaluing the victim. We all tend to make excuses, consciously and unconsciously, for our own bad behaviour[37]. The two main methods of justification are to minimise the behaviour (it wasn't serious) and blame the victim (they deserved it). Both of these techniques serve to make the aggressor feel better and I regularly hear both from violent children. If you are an abused parent, you'll probably find that this sounds all too familiar.

Blaming the victim not only affects how parents are treated by professionals and others but it also plays an important part in ongoing abuse. If people look down on victims generally, they will devalue those who they witness being abused by others within the family. This can apply to a child who has seen a parent abused by the other parent, by a step-parent, or by a brother or sister. Many of the children who abuse their mothers have seen her being abused by someone else, usually their father, an older brother or sister, or both. They lose respect because of this, and then when *they* begin to abuse their mother they lose respect even faster, in a downward spiralling vicious circle. Thus blaming and devaluing victims is one reason why children's abuse of parents often gets worse with time.

It's logical that victim blaming is stronger for the person doing the abusing than for those witnessing the abuse. Abusing one's mother is considered shameful by almost everyone, so children minimise their guilt by devaluing the victim. Blaming the victim excuses our aggression towards others. "She deserved it" minimises guilt and shame. Rehearsing excuses makes us more convinced they are valid and reinforces their effect. This is why certain types of counselling for abusive individuals can make things worse rather than better. If a counsellor believes everything the client says, gives unconditional positive regard and lots of sympathy, many clients will simply rehash and rehearse their victim blaming and other excuses. The more aggressors get to go over their excuses, the more they come to believe their own lies. This is a frequent balancing act for me in counselling. I need to listen to youth I'm trying to engage in therapy, and if I challenge them too much they will simply withdraw, but I realise that their having an audience for excuses and parent blaming is harmful.

Self-blame

Not only do others often blame victims but those who are victimised also blame themselves. This is true even when people are victims of crime by strangers or victims of purely random accidents. The following quote is about crime victims generally:

"The phenomenon of self-blame is one of the most puzzling and disturbingly perverse aspects of victim trauma. Why almost all crime victims should display an overriding tendency to blame themselves and feel guilty for what occurred to them is a mystery that has long puzzled therapists and researchers into victim trauma[38]"

So how much worse is it going to be when someone is assaulted, not by a stranger, but by someone whom they themselves take responsibility for?

One well known family violence researcher suggests that victim blaming is why violence to parents has had such a low profile: *"This is the area in family violence that people want to talk about the least because somehow the victims, the society, and everyone else blames the victim. Somehow it's the parent's fault that the child is beating him up."* Gelles[39]

Victim blaming has become less common in other forms of family violence but is still the norm when it comes to violence towards parents. This is because parents, and especially mothers, are blamed for almost everything. Parent 'bashing' by professionals, the media and the public is rife. It's sad, but understandable, that many mothers have internalised this and bought into the prevalent myths.

"The most poignant instances of mother-blaming within the family are those in which the mother blames herself for whatever goes wrong. Mothers of misbehaving kids blame themselves for 'not setting enough limits' if they are slightly less rigid disciplinarians than average, and if they are slightly more rigid, they blame themselves for 'coming down too hard' on the child." Caplan[40]

Parent Bashing

Mother blaming has been a common pastime for psychiatrists, psychologists, doctors, counsellors, sociologists, therapists, journalists and talk show hosts over the past sixty years. The usual approach is to assume that children are largely, or entirely, the products of the parenting they receive and also that parenting is largely, or entirely, the responsibility of the mother[41]. This is taken to outrageous extremes. Here's an example from "The Mum Factor" by two Australian psychologists:

"In short, the following two realities largely determine our emotional development:
1. *How we were mothered*
2. *How we have responded to that mothering."* Cloud & Townsend[42]

There is no number three! According to these authors your adult emotional life is largely determined by mothering and by your response to mothering. This strange obsession with mothering makes absurdities such as the following possible:

"A therapist tells a sixty-five-year-old man who has recently become sexually impotent that impotence is caused by having had an intrusive, smothering mother during one's childhood." Caplan[43]

The role of the mother is further emphasised by an almost fanatical focus on the earliest years of child development, when mothers are far more important (particularly in our strange society where they are often unsupported and isolated). There is also a general assumption in much of the popular parenting press that most parents are pretty useless unless trained by wise experts, or rather by a particular wise expert as most of the wise experts are quite rude about each other and often dismiss each other's advice out of hand. Frequently parenting experts warn their readers against listening to the experts. They often appear to do this without any sense of irony! I'm also telling you as an 'expert' not to listen to the experts, but at least I appreciate the irony.

It's not just professionals and the media who blame parents. Public opinion polls also find that parents are blamed for the way young people are today. One poll in American found that 83% of people agreed that one of the biggest problems facing families was *'parents not paying enough attention to what's going on in their children's lives'*.[44] As we will see, this is particularly unfair when parents are actually far more involved in their children's lives than in the past. Blaming parents is so much a part of our culture that you might assume that parent blame has always been around, but this is not the case. There are recorded complaints about the current crop of young people since the time of the Ancient Greeks. However, it was not the norm to blame their parents but to blame the young people themselves, society, or inheritance. Even in the first half of the last century, genetic or societal explanations for problems such as delinquency were more common than parent blaming. Our current obsession with blaming mothers stems largely from the influence of two giant egos of the last century: Freud and Hitler. Freud paved the way in the first half of the last century, although genetic explanations still remained more popular. From the middle of the twentieth century genetic explanations went out of fashion, largely due to the thoroughly bad example of the Nazis.

Blame Freud, not mothers!

[Fans of Freud should skip this section… you won't like it!]

Freud was the all-time master of mother blaming and at the forefront of the movement to blame them for everything. To give him his due, he wasn't just negative about mothers but also about fathers and about people in general: "*I have found little that is good about human beings. In my experience, most of them are trash.*[45]" He imagined that he saw in the dreams, free associations and rambling conversations of his adult patients, deeply hidden traces of psychological trauma in the early years of life. He never studied or worked with children and like most men of his era, had little to do with them. Nor did he study parenting but instead based his ideas on talk therapy with a small number of rich, neurotic, middle-class patients, mostly women diagnosed as having 'hysteria' and, on his own wild imagination[46].

That this approach to working out the root cause of problems is *completely* unreliable is shown by Freud's own beliefs about early sexual abuse. At one point he declared that all (not most, but, incredibly, **all**) of his 'hysterical' patients had been sexually abused in their infancy. It's clear that very few, if any, of these unfortunate patients actually remembered being abused but that Freud 'interpreted' their words and memories to reach this conclusion. He bullied some of them into agreeing with him but others valiantly resisted this unsavoury nonsense[47]. Freud found that many colleagues, to their credit, were loath to believe the incredible news that very young children are *routinely* sexually abused by their parents (and these perverts then, more amazingly, stopped abusing them for the rest of their childhood so that they would not remember anything amiss). The fact that *anyone* could believe that sexual abuse of very young children (we're talking babies) is so common shows a paranoid disdain for parents! He then did a complete about face and declared that in fact *none* of them had been abused but instead they were **all** fantasising about being sexually abused! Mind you, he also said that the effect of actually being abused and of having fantasised about it were pretty much the same! Having first invented these tales of sexual abuse and pressurised some confused patients into believing them, he then blamed the patients themselves for fantasising about sex with a parent! His infamous conclusion was that **all** young children must be sexually attracted to their parents!

The idea that young children fantasise about sexual abuse by their parents became central to his bizarre theory of human development. He held that normal development involves an 'oedipal' phase, when all young children are sexually attracted to the opposite sex parent. It's extraordinary that many well-educated people took Freud's erotic fantasies so seriously for so long (and a few still do) especially given that he could hold such extreme but opposite views in a short period of time. This is *such* a warped idea, with no real evidence of any kind, that one must wonder about Freud's mental health. Though there is no evidence that Freud was mad (other than being a bit neurotic and having delusions of grandeur), it's known that he was taking an awful lot of cocaine at the time he developed his wild fantasies about child development. It's a strange and disturbing black comedy involving one of Freud's colleagues called Fliess who was also his personal physician, close collaborator for a time, and was even loopier than Freud.

Fliess believed that the genitals were neurally connected to the nose and that since hysteria has its origins in the female genitals (at the time a quite widely believed bit of anti-female propaganda), he could treat hysteria through the nose! Fliess prescribed Freud large doses of cocaine, to be taken nasally (not then the fashion but based on Fliess' nutty notions on noses and naughty bits). An effect of cocaine seen in some addicts is an obsession with sex, filth and bodily functions. Why Freud came up with such bizarre ideas makes more sense if he was affected by cocaine when he was making up his theory of childhood sexuality. Freud's first published paper had in fact been about cocaine. In this paper, he had argued that cocaine was a wonderful drug which was not at all addictive. This was soon shown to be totally false but for some reason this paper is seldom mentioned by his followers[48].

Just how unscientific and potentially dangerous these ideas were, is shown by the sad story of Anna O, one of Freud's most famous patients. Freud let Fliess perform a totally unnecessary operation on the poor woman's nose! Fliess failed to remove a large piece of gauze and she later began bleeding from her suppurating nose. Freud, in a letter to Fliess, actually suggested that she was doing this hysterically because she was in love with him and did not want to stop therapy. She might have died had she not had another operation to remove the gauze. Freud continued to support his friend despite this gross negligence.

I think this sad, strange story gives a good picture of the arrogance and lack of logic behind Freud's highly influential ideas.

Freud believed that he was not only discovering truths about human development but about human universals. Thus he virtually ignored the importance of culture. He ignored the fact that most societies have not had the same pattern of child rearing as in Vienna and that parents are not exclusive care-givers in most societies (they were far from being exclusive care-givers in Vienna but nannies and servants were easy to ignore). In most societies, other relatives, especially grandparents and older children, do much of the caring for young children and in **no** other society are nuclear families so isolated as they are in ours. There are also societies where fathers don't live with mothers and have very little contact with younger children, so how the oedipal stuff could be a universal is hard to imagine.

One of the things that makes psychoanalysis fundamentally unscientific is that it can 'explain' anything and hence can be neither proven nor disproven. However there are a number of aspects of Freud's theory that should logically be easy to test. For example, breast-feeding should make a big difference to the individual's later personality – it doesn't. Being brought up by one parent rather than two should make a big difference – it doesn't. Having two mothers or two fathers should totally mess up the normal process of development. The evidence from studies of homosexual couples (and from my experience of a dozen or so families) is that their children are pretty healthy and normal. Such evidence is never going to convince **any** psychoanalyst as they go through a cult-like indoctrination process and have a complex magical world view that can explain away anything, even explaining why cynics like me don't believe in it.

The depth of parent blaming plumbed by psychoanalysts has at times l mind boggling! For example, one psychoanalyst speculated that all mot subconsciously want to kill their children and that children subconsciously sense their mother's lethal tendencies, this being the root cause of most problems:

"Perhaps a part of what a person recalls of parental cruelty in childhood is not memory of what the parent actually did but what he sensed the parent was capable of doing. I do not believe that the child attributes to the parent greater potential of destruction than actually exists. As the impulse to murder is almost universal..."
Reingold[49].

Not many (I hope) would support his idea that mothers have a universal impulse to murder their babies (difficult to imagine how this might have evolved), but the idea of subconscious hate and resentment lying behind love and care is a very common theme and many psychoanalysts would have agreed with Reingold that *"a large part of rearing practices and parental acts and attitudes is predicated on hate.[50]"*. This is sadly relevant to the 'iceberg mother' theory of autism which we will discuss shortly.

Mothers have always been considered fair game by psychoanalysts. They can blame mothers for anything whatsoever without worrying about normal standards of proof. Sometimes it's comical: Renee Spitz (who is still often quoted) came out with some wonderfully silly examples: rocking in infants was caused by mothers 'oscillation between pampering and hostility'; faecal play is caused by mother's 'cyclical mood swings' and 'primary anxious over-permissiveness' caused colic![51]

You can probably imagine how parents assaulted by their own children are viewed by those with such a warped world view! Freud, believing that hate lay just below the surface of all family relationships, expected girls to reject their mothers in adolescence: *"This turning away from the mother occurs in an atmosphere of antagonism; the attachment to the mother ends in hate.[52]"*

I'm glad to say that few psychoanalysts have written about violence to parents but when they do, they are in no doubt that parents bring it all on themselves[53]. Since Freud believed that little boys have an unconscious desire to kill their fathers, they would not be surprised by violence to fathers and can easily 'explain' violence to mothers (or girls violence to fathers) as an unconscious reaction to sexual desires.

Though few therapists today take Freud's ideas at face value, a great many still follow one of the many offshoots or derivatives of psychoanalysis. What is more serious is that many ideas with their origin in psychoanalysis have become so widely accepted that they are now sometimes viewed as common sense. Many mental health workers who reject Freud have nevertheless absorbed popular myths derived from his ideas. Thus people come out with vague ideas such as 'depression is anger turned inwards'. This is directly derived from psychoanalytic ideas and is ultimately both un-testable and pretty meaningless. Does it mean that depressed people are going to be more or less angry than others? If someone stops being depressed, do they become more or less violent? Since the 'theory' (if you can call it that) fails to answer such simple questions, it's of absolutely no practical value!

Some other ideas popularised by Freud and his followers (which like many cults quickly fragmented into dozens of warring sects) have been largely discredited yet still persist. One idea which is still very popular is the idea of catharsis, which we shall angrily demolish when we talk about anger.

Some of the common parent-blaming ideas have filtered down in this way, with their psychoanalytic origins obscured. I wish the psychoanalytic stuff was just of historical interest, but it still directly affects how parents are treated by professionals. I have seen psychoanalytic therapists (in Melbourne these are usually psychiatrists) help turn young people against their parents who are clearly being blamed for the young person's problems.

"Unlike con men, the psychoanalysts fervently believed their own patter and ended up bewitched by their own spells… There is a tendency to assign blame where there is only bad fortune. The psychoanalysts gave in to this perennial temptation. In doing so, they caused long-lasting, needless harm to those already bowed low by fate." Dolnick[54]

Toxic Parents?

"In a maddening paradox, the media, often aided by 'experts', idealizes motherhood while it devalues actual mothers. We are regularly scolded and chastised and warned that our smallest mistakes can have negative lifetime consequences for our children…. Leafing through parenting magazines one gets the impression that while motherhood is beautiful, mothers themselves are boneheads in need of constant instruction and reassurance." Levine[55]

Paula Caplan looked at articles published in mental health journals in the 1970s and 1980s and found that in one hundred and twenty-five articles, seventy-two different kinds of problems were blamed on mothers! This included anorexia, arson, bedwetting, poor bowel control, minimal brain damage, schizophrenia, ulcerative colitis, etc.[56].

A central idea popularised by Freud and followers, though not exclusive to them, is that parents unconsciously shape their children's behaviour and personality in the first few years of life. This idea was never based on any reliable evidence or on observable parental behaviour but on guesswork about subtle unconscious motives, inferred originally from what neurotic and suggestible adults said in therapy.

Of course there is no doubt that the first two or three years of life are of crucial importance developmentally. If a child is sick, ill-nourished, neglected, abused or exposed to harmful chemicals in this period, it may affect their brain and body for the rest of their life; these effects are also very important in the womb. However, I've yet to see any clear evidence that what happens psychologically, as opposed to physically, in this period is **more** important than what happens in later years. That's not to say it isn't important, it is. It's just not **all** important. It's complicated because it's almost impossible to separate the physical from the psychological at this stage. If a mother is rejecting the child, there is a good chance she may not have fed the child as well, an increased chance that she smoked or was stressed during the pregnancy, an increased chance that she passed on unhelpful genes, an increased chance that the father was absent or had some kind of problem, and an increased chance of a bad relationship between the parents. The latest fad is to quote brain-development studies based on tiny samples of children exposed to extremes of stress. These are interesting studies but it's a worry that people are basing social policy on such poorly understood ideas. Rather weirdly, brain research has recently been used in an attempt to shore up the sinking ship of psychoanalysis although it has little connection with any of the ideas of Freud or Jung.

The evidence is that people's basic personality is largely genetically shaped and parents' behaviour has a major influence on personality only in quite extreme cases (i.e. mainly if children are abused, neglected or rejected).[57] There have been a great many attempts to find correlations between parents' behaviour and children's resultant personality but they fail to demonstrate any consistent links between the two. As you have probably noticed, brothers and sisters often don't resemble each other in personality. Siblings actually resemble each other in basic personality just as much if they grow up in separate homes as when they grow up together, suggesting that what little resemblance there is between them has to do with shared genes not with parenting. Children brought up in adoptive homes don't tend to resemble their adoptive family in personality (though they do in attitudes and some behaviours). Identical twins reared apart may even resemble each other in personality **more** than those who grow up together. This is because when twins grow up together, as with siblings generally, they often play different roles within the family and may actively try to be different to each other. Thus if one is more talkative the other may get quieter; one is seen as more naughty so the other plays the role of good child; if one is good at sports the other may choose not to compete in sport but become more studious.

Basing ideas about the influence of parenting on what adults say about their childhood in therapy (or elsewhere) is very dodgy indeed. What adults recall about their childhood is partly determined by their present mood and circumstances. One study found that depressed adults recalled their parents negatively when they were depressed but not before or after they were depressed[58]. People who are feeling bad have a tendency to be negative about their families, their memories and everything else. How children in therapy talk about their parents and families can vary dramatically from time to time. While they are at war with their families their parents are awful but when they settle down they suddenly see lots of positives.

> *"The depressed individual comes in the office, is asked, 'So what was your childhood like?' and quite sincerely recalls all the unpleasantness." Dawes*[59]

There is also a tendency in our society to use our upbringing as an excuse for our failings. One study looked at alcoholics whose families had been studied (as part of a larger study) when they were young. Apart from genetic influences, there was no evidence in this study that upbringing was particularly important in who became an alcoholic (this doesn't mean it's never important, it obviously is in some cases). However, those adults who later became alcoholic often provided explanations of their own drinking based on maltreatment and parental pathology[60].

The tendency to recall the negatives if you are depressed, or if you are looking for an excuse, will be *greatly* exaggerated if you are reconstructing hazily-remembered early childhood in conversation with a professional who has negative expectations about clients' families. Since these professionals also see a highly select sample of people, who are more likely to have had bad parenting, such prejudices can persist for decades in the minds of therapists even if they have no real basis in fact. Some therapists hear what they expect to hear, encourage their patients to believe what the therapist believes (this is called having 'insight') and through strongly prejudiced expectations (encouraged by their training and the culture of most professions), they inevitably interpret what patients say to them through further negative filters. There is a tendency for all of us to accept evidence that seems to fit our preconceived ideas while we critically examine any evidence that goes against our theories. Few therapists keep any kind of statistical data on the families they see and their memories are likely to be as biased.

So strong is the belief that troubled adults must have had bad childhoods that people may not be believed if they claim that their childhoods were happy or that they had good parents.[61]

Some therapists not only encourage particular lines of enquiry and negative interpretations from their clients but will actually suggest memories to their clients (as did Freud) or 'uncover' them using hypnosis or related techniques. It's easy to create false memories using hypnosis or guided imagery. Some even believe that they can uncover memories from the first months of life (or past lives)[62].

Freud's persuasion of vulnerable patients that they had been sexually abused by parents without *any* evidence whatsoever, has done immeasurable harm; but so too has his dismissal of actual abuse as a fantasy. For many decades, psychoanalysts dismissed claims of sexual abuse in their patients on the grounds that their unconscious desire to have sex with their parents was responsible for such 'fantasies' of abuse! Then in the late eighties and nineties, there was a horrendous spate of witch hunts (often *literally* witch hunts) when tens of thousands of parents were accused of abuse based on so-called repressed memories 'uncovered' by hypnosis or in similar states of hyper-suggestibility[63].

Looking back, it's hard to fathom that professionals genuinely believed that so many parents were capable of systematic, depraved, incredibly cruel, sexual abuse of their own children; of breeding babies to be human sacrifices; of feeding babies to other children; of microwaving babies (sadly, I'm not making this up); of using advanced mind-control techniques for the purpose of pure evil in a vast paranoid nightmare conspiracy involving doctors, judges, police, priests and politicians! At its worst it was a combination of psychoanalytic psychobabble, B-grade horror movies, and third-rate science fiction! Such ideas were discussed at professional conferences and found their way into respected journals. Many of us were extremely sceptical about all this but most of us (I'm ashamed to say) kept pretty quiet about it when it was at its worst, otherwise we were accused of making light of abuse, of being narrow-minded, or worse. I believe that to understand how such outrageous ideas, such as eating babies, could have taken hold we have to appreciate the depth of prejudice against parents that many of these workers already had[64]. It's rather like some anti-Semites being readily willing to believe the outrageous idea that Jews eat babies when the Nazis told them that this was true.

Twenty years later no one has ever found *any* of the corpses or any concrete evidence of even *one* of these satanic cults yet some professionals still believe in them! And there are still families who have been broken up by hypnotically induced memories of unbelievable, outlandish abuse. A number of people committed suicide when they were caught up in the hysteria.

I am often dismayed by the negative attitudes I encounter towards parents among workers in mental health and welfare. The belief in the intergenerational transmission of abuse (which of course has some basis in fact) is taken to illogical extremes with workers talking as if *every* abuser is an ex-victim and that anyone with any serious problem must have had abusive parenting! Most abusers have more than one victim. Hence, logically, if the majority of victims were to become abusers, the number of abusers would spread like a plague until *everyone* would be an abuser within a century or so. Since this has clearly not happened then either 1) there was far less abuse in the past or 2) most victims do **not** become abusers. Since all the evidence suggests more not less abuse in the past, clearly most victims don't become abusers[65]. The evidence is clear, yet many professionals talk as if the default is for a victim to become an abuser!

Some people do seem to believe that there has been a sudden increase in the amount of abuse. We regularly hear of *epidemics* of child abuse, family violence, violence by girls, bullying, etc. We are having an epidemic of epidemics[*]! Often there is no basis for these claims but equally often they *appear* to be backed up by statistics. On examination, these statistics usually suggest that our societal standards have changed and either more people are seeking help or more are being prosecuted. Statistical increases in various forms of abuse can be a very positive sign, showing increased awareness and that we are taking that form of abuse more seriously. Having said that, I do believe that one form of family violence, namely violence to parents, has increased rapidly in recent years.

Is early mothering crucial?

One of the most popular theories currently among child protection workers and many welfare and mental health professionals is 'Attachment Theory' which is largely based on the ideas of the English psychoanalyst John Bowlby. It certainly contains a core of truth (I don't know *anyone* who doubts that attachment is of crucial importance) but is so vague that it can be (and often is) used to back up almost any opinion or prejudice. Unfortunately, as it's generally applied it can be profoundly mother-blaming. Bowlby believed that infants needed the full-time care of one person for several years or they would be psychologically damaged for life. His ideas were promoted in the 1950s by the British Government which was then keen to get women out of the workforce after their wartime employment. The idea of the full-time, stay-at-home mother has never been the norm in any past society we know of, unless the mother was working from home. The theory seems to take our unique modern way of bringing up children as being not just normal but essential. Bowlby once warned that letting young children stay with grandparents for a week was a bad idea as it would cause insecure attachment[66]. In the same

---

[*] Oops, I just added another one!

interview, he suggested that those who disputed that a mother should be '*devoting herself entirely to her child... may have had poor mothers themselves.*" A wonderful example of blaming mothers for everything, even for those of us who don't blame mothers enough!

Freud's daughter Anna took this idea of one and only one primary attachment so far that she suggested that after a divorce, it was better if children did not see their father at all.[67] Thus attachment theory can be used to deny father's importance or to bolster the need for children to have more contact with fathers after separation (even if the father is abusive). Sadly, because of its focus on very early years and birth mothers, attachment theory is sometimes used to deny the importance of children's attachments, for example attachments to foster parents, grandparents or step-parents.

"Of course, the notion that the normal form of care-giving is exclusive care by the mother is quite wrong... it has always been usual for care-giving to be shared – with grandparents, neighbours, older siblings, au pairs and nannies participating in this role. So far as we know, children cope perfectly well with shared care-giving of this kind." Rutter[68]

In a survey of anthropological data on one hundred and eighty-six non-industrial societies, the mother was judged to be the 'almost exclusive' caretaker in infancy in only five societies (3%). Although mother was the main caretaker in *early* infancy in 60% of societies, that means in 40% the mother was not even the main carer of small babies. When children are past infancy, people such as grandparents, older siblings, etc. were judged to have important caretaking roles in 80% of societies[69]. There is no evidence that mental health problems are any more frequent in the many societies where mothers share the care of infants. In fact, most people assume that mental health problems are **more** common in Western society where mothers are not just the main, or exclusive, carers, but often do this in splendid isolation. In our society, mothers may be the **only** carer through infancy and toddlerhood, a highly unusual, potentially unhealthy, and inherently stressful cultural aberration. The Western way of bringing up children is historically unique, yet it's often treated as if it's not just normal, but the ideal arrangement. Most psychology is based on people who are WEIRD, where this stands for Western, Educated, Industrial, Rich and Democratic[70]. Let's face it, we are all weird!

Perhaps it really does take a village to raise a happy and healthy child? Our new model of child rearing, with a single isolated care-giver (at least for most of the day) focusing their attention almost entirely on a child in a small family is possibly a major reason why our children are so over-entitled and this may be a contributing factor to so many children becoming abusive towards parents.

As some people interpret *Attachment theory* (though it doesn't make clear predictions) it seems that mothers who work are putting their babies at psychological risk. Many studies have looked at this idea and generally the evidence suggests that it partly depends on why the woman is going out to work. If she is forced to work due to poverty and lack of support, then the children will do a bit worse than average (though it's still not devastating and the effect is not predictable for any individual child). If a woman wants to go out to work, the children will do better if she works than if she is forced to stay home when she doesn't want to. Quality of the child care is very important, of course. There is no good evidence that mothers working, or good quality child-care, is at all harmful to children's development. In my experience, mothers who are being abused by their children are slightly **more** likely to have stayed at home with their children than not (when you read the sections on Indulgent Parenting this will make sense).

I'm sometimes asked by professionals in my workshops if I find Attachment theory useful in understanding violence to parents. I don't think it clarifies anything. In my experience, there is no indication that children who abuse parents differ consistently in childhood attachments from their non-abusive brothers and sisters, though there is probably more variation. Some children who are abusing their parents do appear unattached, but if their abusive behaviour stops, the attachment can be strong again very quickly. A few of these children are definitely over-attached, clingy and demanding (which makes sense if they are being over-parented) and others appear to have a pretty normal relationship to their parent-victim most of the time. Sometimes I am amazed that parent and child can still show healthy affection and closeness despite intermittent abuse of the parent.

Abuse is about lack of *respect* not lack of *love,* or lack of *attachment.* There is a relationship between attachment and violence to parents, but it's that overall these children are *more* likely to be violent to those they are attached to. Attachment and respect need not go together. Many children nowadays love their parents but don't respect them. It's also quite possible to respect someone you don't love.

I have worked with a great many children in out-of-home care over the past forty years and those children who have been abused, neglected or rejected by birth parents, are quite often violent to foster carers or residential workers yet they seldom abuse their birth parents. If Attachment theory is going to be applied to violence to parents, it would be in terms of secure attachment being related to child-to-parent violence, an idea I'm sure would not appeal to most attachment theorists! A number of those writing about violence to parents have mentioned attachment theory vaguely without explaining how this applies or how it's useful.

When the therapist of a child who is being violent to a parent focuses on the parent-child attachment, rather than the behaviour, this could make things worse. Be wary of professionals who assume that the troubled relationship between you and your abusive child is the *cause* of the bad behaviour rather than a *result* of it. A great many of the children I see who are abusing parents had solid, secure attachments throughout their pre-teen years. I have also seen many parent-child pairs re-develop close relationships after the abuse has stopped, sometimes almost immediately.

So if you are worrying, or are told, that what happened in your child's early years has directly caused adolescent behaviour problems you should probably leave aside such vague and unprovable ideas while you try to fix the problems in the here and now. If your child was exposed to domestic violence, then what happened in his or her early years probably *does* have *direct* bearing on the behaviour, but even in this case most children exposed to DV don't go on to abuse their parents and counselling about the past abuse, though useful in itself, is not likely to stop the bad behaviour once it has become a habit.

"What we learn from the wealth of research that has been carried out is that babies are not the desperately vulnerable creatures described by [Penelope] Leach. The story of babies' fragility simply does not fit with what we know from careful research. There is no basis, in good research, for a fable that plays so disturbingly with mothers' anxieties and guilts. To suggest that there is does a disservice to all mothers and babies." Scarr & Dunn[71]

Autism and the Iceberg mother

It's now known that autism is a strongly genetic condition[72] and that parenting, even extremely bad parenting, simply could not produce autism without a genetic predisposition. Parenting can be of great importance in whether or not a child reaches his potential but does not appear to be of *any* relevance as to whether or not a child *becomes* autistic. Yet, from the '50s to the '70s a very common explanation for autism was that the mother had sub-consciously rejected the child from birth, causing the super-sensitive little creature to withdraw from the world. The mother need not actually feel any hate or anger towards her child as this could be all subconscious. How scary to think that you *think* you feel love but really you hate your child and have caused a lifelong disability without realising it! How can anyone defend against such a bizarre accusation? A man by the name of Bruno Bettelheim was the best known exponent of this loopy nonsense.

"Throughout this book I state my belief that the precipitating factor in infantile autism is the parent's wish that his child should not exist." Bettelheim[73]

I'm not sure if he coined the awful term 'the iceberg mother' but he certainly popularized the idea. Obviously this links in with the Freudian ideas we've mentioned. There was never a shred of evidence for this flapdoodle. For years, I assumed that Bettelheim was a well-meaning but misguided psychologist. In fact, his biography, *'The Creation of Dr. B'*, makes it clear that he was a dishonest bully who abused the children in his care (physically, emotionally and possibly sexually) as well as emotionally abusing their parents[74]. He was not actually a psychologist, nor a psychoanalyst, as he lied about his qualification when he arrived in America. His books are still widely quoted in psychology and related disciplines.

One commentator (Dolnick) talks of an *"orgy of parent-bashing[75]"* and says that the experts on autism paid almost no attention to what parents of autistic children told them *"after all, they were seen not as authorities but as perpetrators."*[76]

Just how illogical psychoanalytic thinking can become is shown by Bettelheim's explanation of an autistic girl who was obsessed with the weather[77]. He said that the word "weather" contained the unconscious hidden message "we/eat/her" and the girl was *"Convinced that her mother (and later all of us) intended to devour her... she felt it imperative to pay minutest attention to this we/eat/her"* You couldn't make this stuff up! Not so funny for parents in the firing line. In 1986, a third of psychiatrists in the USA and a half in Europe still believed that autism was caused by parents and no doubt there are a few dozy dinosaur docs around who still think so.

The following was written by a doctor who had an autistic child in that era:

"I had more and more the feeling that my wife and I were finding aloofness instead of understanding, coldness instead of warmth, distrust instead of sympathy. Then it became quite clear; to our amazement it dawned upon us that, in the doctor's eyes, we were being held responsible for the children's situation. This was the accepted view, we found, the official doctrine, the only explanation offered and recognized, the sole basis for treatment. Further we soon realised that instead of being anxious and desperate people seeking understanding and help, as I had thought we were, we had become culprits hiding something, people with some dark secret whose words were not a simple expression of the facts but a shield to cover our guilt, a way of concealing the truth from ourselves and misleading others." May[78]

Sadly many parents of disturbed children, not just those with autism, will find the above description very familiar.

You might assume that parents of disabled children will get sympathetic treatment from professionals, unlike parents of badly behaved non-disabled children, but sadly this is not necessarily the case. Parents of disabled children are often viewed with suspicion and are seldom treated as the experts that they are.

The Schizophrenogenic Mother

No, I didn't invent this bit of language abuse! It's a serious piece of jargon, meaning 'inducing schizophrenia' and, sadly, was an outrageous example of parent bashing taken all too seriously not so long ago. This is embarrassing for me as a family therapist as the idea of the schizophrenogenic mother was influential in the birth of family therapy[79].

The idea was that mothers give their children mixed messages, e.g. saying 'I love you' in an angry tone, and that this somehow makes some individuals become psychotic and lose touch with reality. The idea that children are incredibly psychologically fragile came from Freud. Of course communication patterns are going to be a bit unusual for families where there is a psychotic member but, as with the Iceberg Mother theory, it was never based on any meaningful evidence of any kind and is now completely discredited[80]. We don't actually understand what causes schizophrenia. There is definitely a genetic component but most people with the genes to make them vulnerable do not become schizophrenic. In fact, if you have an identical twin who is schizophrenic, you have only a 50/50 chance that you will be too. The child of one schizophrenic parent has a ten percent chance of developing the illness. There is some evidence that extreme stress, such as child abuse, can increase the risk but, surprisingly, the risk of schizophrenia for the child of a schizophrenic parent is the same whether they are brought up by the schizophrenic parent or adopted out. Therapists clung to theories like this despite a complete lack of evidence because of prejudice against mothers.

"One prominent exponent of the schizophrenogenic mother theory noted that many parents of schizophrenic children appeared quite normal. His response was not to question his theory but to marvel at the 'subtle malignancy' of some parents."
Dolnick[81]

Both of these examples have the cart firmly before the horse. Parents' *reactions* to their child's serious problems are seen as *causing* the problem. There are many similar examples where cause and effect is assumed to go from parent to child when the reverse is simpler or more logical. Generally it's no longer assumed that the parents of autistic children or schizophrenics have caused the condition. But people still routinely make that assumption about the parents of children with behavioural problems. There are many other examples where cause and effect are reversed so that parents can be blamed.

Parental monitoring and delinquency

In the many books and articles on delinquency, it's frequently stated that parental monitoring of the young person can help prevent delinquency. The truth appears to be that how well a young person is monitored has far more to do with them than with their parents. It's easy to monitor a cooperative child and almost impossible to monitor the comings and goings of a difficult, defiant teenager. There is a correlation, but cause and effect are the reverse of the traditional interpretation, parents are responding to the young person[82]. I see a great many parents who are trying hard to monitor defiant young people and failing miserably through no fault of their own.

An interesting natural experiment that tests the idea that monitoring teens prevents problems has been given to us with the advent of mobile phones. There has been an amazing increase in the number of teens (and younger children) with a mobile phone over a fairly short period of time. Parental monitoring has become much tighter and many parents now expect to know where their teenage children are every hour of the day. No one seems to be at all surprised that this huge increase in monitoring has made no noticeable difference to delinquency, teenage drinking, drug taking, or underage sex.

Parental depression and child behaviour problems

The many studies of parental depression give another depressing example of putting the cart before the horse. These studies have shown a fairly consistent correlation between children's behavioural problems and parent's depression. Undoubtedly there are *some* cases where a depressed parent has contributed to a child's problems. However, the simpler explanation is that it's depressing to have a difficult child, particularly in our mother blaming culture. When I first ran *Who's in Charge?* groups, I gave participants depression scales. Over half were *clinically* depressed at the start of the group. These questionnaires were too time consuming but we still ask parents at the start of the group if they agree with the statement, "I feel depressed or very unhappy." Seventy percent agree and twenty percent are neutral or unsure, so only ten percent disagree. When children stop being abusive the parent often cheers up remarkably fast! By the two month follow-up to the Who's in Charge? programme only twenty percent agree that they are depressed or very unhappy and fifty percent disagree.

There is a fundamental scientific principle (sometimes called Occam's Razor) that the simplest explanation should be considered first and that we should not make up complicated explanations unnecessarily. Since the children causing the depression is by far the simplest explanation, why is it that the majority of writers assume that the parent has *caused* the child's behavioural problems; the assumption that parents cause children's behaviour and not vice versa is so deep, that most writers are not even aware of it. Prejudice against parents often trumps scientific reasoning.

Blaming the victim in child-to-parent violence

When I first started looking at the sparse literature on violence to parents I was shocked at the parent blaming attitudes, mostly by researchers who had given out surveys but not met these families: that was in the early' 90s. For an unsubtle example of pure prejudice: "*Violence against parents... is usually a response by the child to a consistent pattern of violent parenting*"[83].

Similarly: "*it is important not to focus on the abusing teenager only as a perpetrator of violence but most importantly as a victim of his/her environment which has invariably been abusive*"[84].

In recent years, there is a wider range of opinion about violence to parents but still the general attitude of many academics is that the child must be a victim and that parenting has probably been harsh.

It's true that almost half of the children who are violent towards parents (forty-six percent of my sample) have been exposed to parental violence. Even if this meant that they were retaliating, which it does not, it would still be prejudice to ignore the other half. However, since the parent who has been violent is almost always an absent father while the victim is the mother, this is both unjust and inaccurate even when applied to the half where there has been past domestic violence. The other half has not been exposed to any more violence than the rest of the population. In fact, they have often had less than average exposure to violence. Many come from middle class homes and indulgent parents are less likely than the average parent to have used physical punishment.

Looking at the literature on violence to parents, it's obvious that those who are most into parent blaming are those who have not met the parents. You may be surprised that anyone would write about violence to parents without talking to these parents but this is quite common. Sociologists often study family violence by giving out anonymous questionnaires, either to parents or to young people, asking about violence within the family. Such surveys on adult violence suggest that women are just as violent as men and that most violence within the home is mutual. Those of us with any practical experience of family violence know for sure that this is not true and many workers simply ignore this research, or see it as an anti-feminist conspiracy. Basically, surveys lump together abusive violence with trivial acts of violence, defensive violence, and mutual violence, obscuring differences between males and females and between abusers and non-abusers. In addition, people are not honest or accurate when reporting violence, especially their own, and there are differences between men and women in how they view and recall violence, and in how they respond to such questionnaires.

Surveys of violence to parents also make gender pretty much disappear and make most violence look like mutual violence. Most of the people conducting these surveys, or writing about them, have little or no actual experience of children's violence to parents. But even many of the writers who have first-hand experience, from hands-on research or as therapists, quote surveys selectively. There are three common results of surveys in family violence – this applies to adult family violence and to violence to parents. Surveys suggest:

1. Very high rates of abuse
2. Gender differences are small or non-existent
3. Most violence is mutual violence

A great many writers choose one or two of these and ignore those they don't like. Almost everyone who has written about child to parent violence has accepted the high rates indicated by the surveys. Some writers use the high rates but ignore the findings that males and females are equally violent and don't see the violence as mutual. Other writers accept the gender neutrality but reject the mutual violence findings. A few accept all three. I reject all three.

Most people know that in adult family violence, men are *far more often* the perpetrators but with violence to parents, they have no experience on which to base their judgment. The gender difference in violence is less in children than it is in adults, and the gender difference between boys and girls has decreased in recent years. So it's not *crazy* that some people tend to believe the surveys and either don't know about, or discount, the other evidence. Clinical samples such as mine don't on face value appear to be as scientific or reliable as surveys. Most clinical samples are small (mine is twenty times larger than many) and not random (e.g. all attend a particular clinic). So although dozens of clinical samples, court and police samples and qualitative research samples all suggest that boys are roughly twice as likely as girls to abuse their parents, many reviewers accept some surveys which suggest boys and girls are equally violent to parents. Most evidence is that mothers are far more often the victims but some surveys find little or even no difference.

Parent blaming ideas, and a desire to see violent youth as victims, means that many people are happy to accept any research suggesting that parents are equally violent.

"Violence is used by the child to cope with the hostile and aggressive behaviour of his or her parents... to terminate negative treatment by parents... force them to cease their noxious behaviour toward the child... parents who are demanding and punitive may be forced to retreat... such behaviour serves for the child within a hostile and aversive family environment." Brezina [85]

What is amazing about this is that the writer gave a questionnaire to adolescent boys and based the above orgy of parent blaming on the evidence of just one question! The young people were asked, *"How often do your parents actually slap you?"* All the conclusions about the parents' 'harsh control strategies', their 'hostile and aggressive behaviour' and their 'hitting and slapping' the young person was based on this one question and the researcher did not meet any of the parents, or even ask the young person why their parent had hit them. So if a mother occasionally slapped the face of a boy who was pushing her and calling her a "f**ing whore", he could quite honestly say that she slapped him. Such distortion of the truth is the norm rather than being unusual and in addition, abusers often lie about being hit by their victims.

Though this is a fairly blatant and extreme example, it's not unusual for researchers to simply assume that parents cause their children's behaviour. If a parent uses tougher discipline against a child who is difficult or aggressive, it's assumed that cause and effect is from parent to child. This is despite the fact that a much simpler explanation is that parents have to try a lot harder with difficult children and it would be strange, and very unfair, if badly behaved children were not punished more often than better behaved children.

It seems to me, reading the literature on children's behavioural problems, that shoddy logic slips under editors' noses because prejudice against parents is so strong. Assuming that parents are to blame for children's problems is the default assumption and appears to largely go unquestioned.

Since many researchers, and some of the workers you may encounter, take it as a matter of faith that parents directly cause children's bad behaviour, they often ignore other factors, such as: temperament and heredity, wider society, school, neighbourhood, culture, brothers and sisters and most ignored of all, the effect that children have on their parents. They are thus preconditioned to see parents of difficult children negatively and their belief in a just world is maintained if the victimised parent is seen as somehow responsible. Mothers are blamed for everything anyway so parent blaming and victim blaming become a potent combination. Parents are seen as guilty by implication of either abuse, neglect, or at best, of stupidity. As mothers themselves are often blaming themselves for their child's behaviour, and are thus racked with guilt, it's easy for professionals to maintain this false and unhelpful position, especially when they only see the family in crisis, with parents who may no longer be functioning properly.

"A most distressing characteristic of mother-blaming among mental health professionals is how few of them seem to be aware they do it. Even when therapists are alerted to mother-blaming attitudes and comments, they usually deny that they themselves could do such a thing." Caplan[86]

Effects of parent-blaming by workers in child to parent violence

1. Parents made to feel more guilty thus making them less assertive.
2. Misunderstanding of family dynamics means that advice given to parents encourages passivity and disconnection, when the opposite is needed.
3. Feeds the excuses of the violent child.
4. Reinforces child's negativity about and disrespect for, their parents.
5. Fails to hold child accountable for their behaviour.
6. Parents mistrust workers and become defensive and uncooperative. This reinforces worker's negativity and distrust of parents.
7. Subtly, or sometimes directly, encourages distance between child and parent.
8. Since most children remain with their family, workers feel less hopeful about outcomes as the family is seen as the cause of the problems.
9. Child's deviancy is often underestimated as they are seen as more victim than victimiser, hence violence to siblings and peers not taken sufficiently seriously and child's developing delinquency or substance abuse not given sufficient weight.
10. Self-defence by parents (and especially by step-parents) is seen as abuse, with often drastic consequences for the family.
11. Young person may not respect workers who they view as useful but naive.

A Brief History of Parenting Advice

"Advice given to one generation of mothers was often opposite to that given to the previous generation. One would expect that a mother listening to such advice would have her own 'natural' self-confidence undermined and thus would find her job even more demanding and emotionally taxing." Somerfield[87]

"I tend to praise a lot and try to talk to him like a young adult. This is when I think he sees it as a weakness. I go by all the advice you read on parenting but it seems to backfire."[88]

Parent blaming has become so ubiquitous in our society that we take it for granted. But it's historically new and has little or nothing to do with scientific evidence. Knowing a little about the origins of our society's obsessive parent blaming may be helpful in allowing you to let go of some of your guilt. It may also help you make sense of some of the attitudes you may encounter from professionals, and even from your family and friends.

There have been several excellent overviews of parenting advice (one rather good one is satirically called "Perfect Parents")[89]. They all tell the same sorry tale of arrogant 'experts' peddling their own views as if they were scientific truth. The advice given in days gone by is often laughable and sometimes downright cruel by our standards. Real science has played almost **no** part in the process with authors either reflecting the current societal view or extrapolating wildly from pseudo-scientific theories (such as psychoanalysis). The most famous, and probably the most maligned, is Dr. Spock (not to be confused with the somewhat more sensible Mr. Spock from Star Trek). Much of the criticism aimed at Spock is undeserved. He certainly did encourage parents to be more permissive in the 1950s but in the context of his day this was reasonable. The two other most popular parenting gurus in recent years, Leach and Brazleton, have both been far more permissive than Spock[90].

In the Middle Ages, beating children appears to have been extremely common and parents were often tough and cold towards children by our standards. Yet the few writers from this period encouraged parents to be more strict and less soppy[91] Right up to the Second World War most writers encouraged strict discipline, justified hitting children, and advised minimal attention and affection. 'Experts' in the first half of the last century were into rigid schedules and fierce, obsessive repression of habits such as masturbation and thumb-sucking. The most popular writer on parenting at the start of the twentieth century in America, Dr Holt, asserted that: *"Babies under six months old should never be played with, and the less of it at any time the better.[92]"* Holt's ideas now seem extreme but they were very popular and were given government backing. The US Children's Bureau also advised that, '*The rule that parents should not play with the baby may seem hard, but it is without doubt a safe one.*'

Along the same lines, here is a typical example from Watson in the 1920s (not only a parenting guru but a prominent psychologist and founder of behaviourism): "*Never hug and kiss them, never let them sit in your lap. If you must, kiss them once on the forehead when they say good night. Shake hands with them in the morning.*[93]"

That's probably where you went wrong: you didn't shake hands in the morning!

For Watson, and other behaviourist writers, too much love was seen as a BIG problem. Watson said that mother love was '*an instrument which may inflict a never healing wound, a wound which may make infancy unhappy, adolescence a nightmare, an instrument which may wreck your adult son or daughter's vocational future and their chance for marital happiness*'[94]. He was not talking about mothers withholding their love or being manipulative, but just mothers doting on their children and being normal mothers. It probably never occurred to him that any fathers would be so soppy.

Watson used behaviourist theory to back up his tyrannical pronouncements on parenting but there is no real science behind them and behaviourism could just as logically have been used to suggest that children need lots of play, stimulation and affection. Like too many psychologists he used vague theory to appear to back up his own beliefs and the prejudices of the time. These ideas certainly weren't new but a continuation and exaggeration of advice that had been given in previous centuries.

A reaction against strict, authoritarian parenting was loooong overdue and came to a head around the time of the Second World War. Instead of too much love and attention being seen as a big problem, parents were now encouraged to lavish as much love and attention on their children as was humanly, or inhumanly, possible. The encouragement of *democratic parenting* (a historically novel idea) was rare before WW2[95]. There was a dramatic change in the type of advice given before and after WW2.

Up until WW2 genetic explanations of behaviour were very popular. They were often taken to extremes with delinquency, mental illness, alcoholism etcetera, all being seen as largely due to *bad blood*. The eugenics movement saw bad blood as the cause of most of society's ills. The rise of huge institutions where the mentally ill or disabled could be locked away was largely due to the eugenics movement, largely to stop them breeding. Sterilisation was widely used in these institutions. Parents were blamed for carrying bad genes rather than for bad parenting. Bad parenting was more likely to be seen as a sign of genetic inferiority rather than having a major direct effect on the child.

The Nazis borrowed ideas from the American eugenics movement in justifying the final solution[96]. It's often forgotten that the Nazis began by exterminating unfortunate disabled and mentally ill people before targeting gypsies and Jews. It was understandable that there should be a reaction against fascist racial ideas and this was extended to a reaction against genetic explanations in general. This shifted the balance dramatically in the nature-nurture debate. It became almost taboo to talk of inherited traits or of children's temperament. When I was studying psychology and sociology in the early '70s, you did not dare suggest that a child's behaviour might be related to his or her temperament or that genetics play any part in human behaviour (especially in gender differences – still taboo in some quarters).

"Most educated people have been persuaded to believe in an erroneous and naïve radical environmentalism and, in particular, to attribute all of their personal faults and problems to the way they have been treated, especially in childhood."
Lykken[97]

This historically new idea, that people are as they are *largely* due to early parenting, caught on in a big way. It caught on for historical and political reasons, not because there was any sound scientific evidence for it. With hindsight much of the supposed evidence looks decidedly shoddy[98]. When the influence of temperament and genetics are dismissed, this lends itself to mother blaming since mothers do most of the nurturing.

Psychoanalysts see us all as being neurotic as a result of our early upbringing (pay them lots of money and they'll un-neurotic you, as they did for Woody Allen over a twenty-five year period, before he married his adoptive daughter). Parents were seen as repressing and emotionally abusing their children almost as a matter of course and children are viewed as being incredibly delicate and vulnerable psychologically. Parents were advised not to frustrate or inhibit children. This approach pushed permissiveness in ways that would have been previously unimaginable. For example, children's defiance of parents became seen as healthy and their aggression was something that should not be bottled up but let out. Some of these ideas fitted with hippy-era radicalism, where parents were seen as inherently despotic representatives of a repressive society.

Copyright 2005 by Randy Glasbergen.
www.glasbergen.com

"Discipline and good behavior are the keys to family harmony, so my husband and I do everything our children tell us to."

Parenting gurus made '*the promise that, if a child's early experiences were pleasurable and if he suffered a minimum of frustration and was given a maximum of encouragement and understanding, he would develop into a well-adjusted person.*[99]" The assumption was, and still is for many, that if a child does not grow up well there must be a fault in the parenting they received. This mythology has been incredibly powerful and extremely damaging.

Advice from Parent's Magazine 1950: *'We should feel suspicious of ourselves when we react strongly to something as absurdly simple, for example, as a child calling us names.'*[100]* This article was typical of a lot of advice from the second half of the century. It suggested that the child must be allowed to express their anger and hostility because repressing this would store up later problems. This article actually suggested that a mother getting upset about being verbally abused by her progeny was expressing *'her own fears and insecurities'*.

Benjamin Spock was number one parenting guru of the last century. He used Freud's psychoanalytic theory to back up his liberal approach, but as with behaviourism, the theory is so vague that it could be used to support any approach you like. In recent years, one of its offshoots, attachment theory, has been used to support so-called 'attachment parenting', a scarily over-indulgent form of baby worship, and 'attachment therapy' which is ultra-strict to the point of being abusive and has resulted in at least one death[101]. Spock was definitely in favour of permissiveness about elements of child rearing such as schedules, toilet training, masturbation, play and affection. When it came to discipline he was not at all permissive by our modern standards. He bemoaned the permissiveness of parents and he was rather harsh and distant with his own children[102].

Spock wrote the following in the introduction to his 1957 edition: *"When I was writing the first edition, between 1943 and 1946, the attitude of a majority of people towards infant feeding, toilet training, and general child management was still fairly strict and inflexible... Since then a great change in attitude has occurred, and nowadays there seems to be more chance of a conscientious parent's getting into trouble with permissiveness than with strictness."*

So over fifty years ago, Spock, considered the prophet of permissiveness, believed that the pendulum had already swung too far for many parents. He was shocked to see how widely permissiveness had spread by the Nineties (when he was in his nineties).

In a review of parenting advice, called *The Mechanical Baby*, Daniel Beekman suggests that much of the advice has been arbitrary and it has overall tended to disempower parents: *"the picture of mother and child became one of mother, expert and child, and mothers were often made to feel less competent than authors, no matter how bizarre the writers' ideas were.[103]"*

Reading parenting manuals it's sad, but comical, how often authors have followed a similar pattern:

1. They complain about the amount of 'expert' advice and point out (rightly) that much of it is opinionated nonsense (and I am, of course, doing this too!).
2. They make at least one statement about the danger of permissiveness.
3. They tell parents to have more confidence in themselves.
4. They then erode parents' confidence and generally talk about parents as if they are bad, stupid or both.
5. They stress how fragile children are and how easy it is to screw up your child for life.

6. They encourage permissiveness and disempower parents by taking extreme positions on discipline and attacking almost any form of parental control.

Everyone *says* they are opposed to 'permissiveness.' However, what they call 'permissiveness' may be *very* different to what you call it. Though I'm warning against permissiveness, I am permissive compared to previous generations (if I had my time as a father over again I'd be slightly less permissive than I was with my son). With rare exceptions, the experts, and most professionals, have been far more permissive than the general public since WW2. It's thus no coincidence that I see quite a few professionals who have beyond control children.

"The ironies involved with the myth that mothers need the advice of experts in order to raise children are many. First of all, most of the honest experts freely acknowledge that human behaviour is complex and that they usually cannot explain why a child from a problem-ridden home can turn out fine, but a child who seems to have everything can become a criminal." Caplan[104]

Dreikurs as an example of parenting mis-advice

It would be easy to give outrageous examples from lesser known writers but I'll use another of the most influential writers on parenting of the last fifty years, Dreikurs. Dreikurs had a great deal of influence on professionals and other parenting experts (more than Spock) and was also quite popular with parents (though not nearly as popular as Spock). He is a good example of a lot of mainstream parenting advice, though a bit ahead of his time. He popularised some of the ideas still widely used in parent education and he did have some good ideas.

Dreikurs clearly says that he opposes permissiveness: *"The popular practice of letting children have unrestricted freedom has made tyrants of children and slaves of parents. These children enjoy all the freedom while their parents assume all the responsibilities! This is hardly democracy."[105]*

Writing in the 1960s, he said that children were daring to do what his generation would never have thought to do to their parents... *"The problem is stimulated by the general cultural change which is now taking place. Children sense the democratic atmosphere of our times and resent our attempts at authority over them."[106]*

So far, so good! Dreikurs appears to be warning against the excesses of a democratic approach to parenting and is blaming it on our culture rather than on individual parents. But in fact he was urging more, not less, democratic parenting. He urged parents to *"withdraw from the conflict."* Saying, *"There are always two sides to any unpleasant situation between parents and children. The disturbance is the result of a conflict between two people. If one person withdraws, the other cannot continue. If the parent removes himself from the battlefield, he leaves the child in a vacuum."[107]*

Back then, abuse of parents was still extremely rare, so Dreikurs probably would not have even considered it worth mentioning. Withdrawing from the conflict is advisable for some tantrums and conflicts in early childhood. However, if a child is abusing the parent, or his siblings, withdrawing may make him feel a lot more powerful. If the child is playing up to get a parent to leave him alone, then the parent's withdrawal is a clear victory and reinforces the behaviour. When an older child is abusing a parent, withdrawal may also be sometimes necessary for safety's sake, but it's not good advice overall; it's an occasional necessary evil, not a desirable response. When the home is continually 'the battlefield' where is the parent meant to remove herself to?

Most of the examples that Dreikurs gives are of younger children but there is no hint that different methods might be needed for teenagers (this is true of a great many parenting books) and that to 'withdraw from the conflict' with a child who is heading down the road towards drugs, promiscuous sex or crime may be an utter disaster.

Dreikurs is encouraging parents to give up trying to control children: "*Since democracy implies equality, parents can no longer assume the role of the 'authority'. Authority implies dominance: one individual having power over another. There can be no such dominance among equals. Dominance – force, power – must be replaced with egalitarian techniques of influence.*"[108]

Dreikurs was one of the first of a long line of parenting experts who claim to be opposed not only to harsh or physical punishment but to **all** punishment of **any** kind, including withholding privileges. He is also opposed to using rewards: "*Punishment and reward belong properly in the autocratic social system. Here, the authority, enjoying a dominant position had the privilege of meting out rewards or punishment according to merits.*"[109]

The few quotes above are representative of Dreikurs overall approach, which was followed by many other writers. This is so idealistic and out of touch with what we actually do that it makes most parents doubt themselves and feel guilty and disempowered.

"*Children have gained an equal social status with adults and we no longer enjoy a superior position to them. Our power over them is gone: and they know it, whether we do or not. They no longer recognise us as a superior power.*" [110]

The idea that children truly have equal power to parents is an odd one. If this were true, then obviously we should split our wages equally among all members of the household and allow children to decide if they wish to attend school or not. We should make decisions jointly and if the children outnumber the adults (as they usually did in Dreikurs' day) they could out-vote us consistently, e.g. instead of buying a practical new car they may want a sports car or that we all get motorbikes instead. What if the children decide that the "f" word is acceptable but the words 'no' and 'school' should be banned? We are fooling ourselves if we think children really have equal power and it's scary that anyone would think this was a good idea. Very few of the children I talk to would think it was sensible. If you do have equal power with your children, then something has gone very wrong indeed (which is probably why you are reading this book)!

Dreikurs concludes not that we need to work harder to maintain control but that we should give up what power we do have: "*We must realise the futility of trying to impose our will upon our children.*" However, even in permissive homes with beyond control children, parents still routinely impose their will on their children. If we choose to buy cabbage rather than chocolate, we are imposing our will on our

72

children. If we tell our ten-year-old that they can't stay up all night, or a teen that they can't smoke in their bedroom, we are imposing our will.

The uneasiness about exerting *any* form of power is not confined to the influential writing of Dreikurs but runs through parenting books, psychology, counselling, social work, etc. and has seeped into the minds of a great many parents.

If you haven't read much parent advice, you may be confused about the idea of condemning rewards as well as punishments but this is quite a common theme. Dreikurs sees rewards as just as bad as punishments: *"the system of rewarding children for good behaviour is as detrimental to their outlook as the system of punishment. The same lack of respect is shown. We 'reward' our inferiors for favours or for good deeds. In a system of mutual respect among equals, a job is done because it needs doing, and the satisfaction comes from the harmony of two people doing a job together..."* [111]

So children should be our equals according to Dreikurs! No wonder some modern families get taken over by a diminutive dictator, not content with being treated as an equal but hungry for power and control over the adults. This shouldn't happen according to writers like Dreikurs for the simple reason that children are inherently good: *"Children don't need bribes to be good. They actually want to be good. Good behaviour on the part of the child springs from his desire to belong, to contribute usefully, and to co-operate."* [112]

If you have a particularly difficult child, you may be laughing at the idea that they have an inherent desire to be good and cooperative. This does apply to some children; probably not the majority, but quite a sizable minority (for example those with high traits of agreeableness and conscientiousness). The idea that it applies to most or all children is amazingly optimistic and idealistic. Such a belief is an example of people believing what they want to believe despite abundant evidence to the contrary.

This remarkably idealistic approach to child-rearing is not only confusing but is fundamentally hypocritical. Dreikurs gives examples such as a mother deciding not to buy sweets if a child does not brush her teeth. You agree no doubt that this is reasonable parenting but it hardly supports his suggestion that parent and child are equals! It's hard to imagine the child creating a logical consequence to stop the mother smoking, even though the mother's behaviour is far more harmful and serious than not brushing teeth. "Mum, you know that smoking increases the risk of heart attack and lung cancer. Until you stop smoking I've hidden your car keys so that you will have to get more exercise." Logical, but the fact that it's comical shows that we do not consider children equals and do not want them to have equal power. As a child I did occasionally hide my parents' cigarettes but unfortunately this never made any difference to how much they smoked.

Dreikurs advises parents not to be shocked if a child swears but to pretend they don't know what the word means[113]. There is no hint that the child may be deliberately trying to hurt or control the parent. Ignoring a child in this context is withholding attention but still giving them power and this is *very* dangerous advice. If they actually believe that you don't know what the swear word means, they will think you not just weak but also stupid.

Since it's a central philosophical belief of many parenting advisors that children are innately good, it must be someone's fault if they turn bad. *"It is so much easier for a child to be good that he has no need to be bad unless he has met obstacles in his environment that have caused him to become discouraged and turn to misbehaviour as a way out of his difficulty."* [114]

Thus parents presumably should avoid creating any 'obstacles' and parents are clearly seen as responsible for the child's bad behaviour. So along with the idea that children are inherently good goes the assumption that bad child means bad parent. A related idea is that aggression comes from frustration so children will not be aggressive if we can avoid frustrating them. There is some truth to this *in the short term*. However, by giving in to them and overindulging them, their demands and sense of entitlement keep getting cranked ever higher. The harder parents try not to frustrate their children, the more the children end up frustrated and unsatisfied due to impossible expectations (reinforced nowadays by the massive advertising and media campaign turning children into avid, demanding consumers).

Another common theme in parent advice and psychology is that moral judgments are irrelevant. Dreikurs says, *"Since the child has a purpose in his misbehaviour, moralizing does not change it nor remove the obstacle. It adds to his discouragement."*[115]

Why having a purpose removes any moral considerations is mystifying. A thief quite clearly has a purpose in his behaviour and most violence is quite purposeful. It actually makes more sense to take a moral stand about purposive bad behaviour than about expressive or irrational bad behaviour. Isn't lashing out in a rage *slightly* less morally culpable than deliberately punching someone to steal from them or to control them? This is certainly how our legal system views it. In reality, moral judgment is merely being suspended for children, not for adults, and the reasoning given to support this is just silly.

Dreikus's view of a family democracy is so idealistic that it's scary to imagine *any* real family actually attempting it: *"Even the very young child can participate in the Family Council. Chairmanship should be rotated so that no one 'bosses' the meeting... If the parents see that a course of action is going to be uncomfortable, they still must abide by the decision, bear the discomfort, and allow the natural result to take place."*[116] So out goes the cabbage and up goes the budget for chocolate!

That Dreikurs is advocating permissive parenting rather than authoritative parenting (by most people's definitions) is also very clear in the chapter on children's fighting. He makes a blanket ban on parents interfering in their children's fights, giving an example where one child bites another and stating: *"When we side with the baby, protect the youngest against the oldest, stand up for the seemingly 'abused' one, we reinforce his feeling of inferiority and teach the victim how to use deficiency and weakness to gain special consideration... We can best help them by stepping out of the situation and giving them room... One can, and should, have a friendly discussion about fighting, without the least hint of finger-pointing or of moralizing..."*[117]

So if we are not to use any form of punishment (heaven forbid) or rewards, and shouldn't moralise or get involved when children are violent to others, what are we to do? Apart from examples of using consequences (which look awfully like rewards and punishments but apparently they aren't really) we obviously have to be pretty damn clever to be good parents: *"Proper behaviour must be stimulated, not demanded. However, I can utilize my ingenuity, tact, and my sense of humour to promote willingness."* [118]

Isn't this demanding rather a lot of parents? What if one or both parent is disingenuous, tactless and humourless? Should they be sterilised or is it inevitable that their children will be uncontrollable?

I'd like to stress that I'm using Dreikurs as an example not because he is *particularly* bad but because he was such a well-respected and highly influential writer and is typical of so much of the parenting advice which followed him. Re-reading him now, I find it rather scary that he was so influential, for example in the design of still widely used parenting programmes. If you have done a mainstream parenting programme and wondered why it didn't work for you, or thought that it all seemed a tad over-idealistic, you may have Dreikurs to thank.

In most families, what he is proposing would result in anarchy not democracy! He and many parenting advisers like him were not encouraging Authoritative Parenting as they claimed, but definitely encouraging Indulgent Parenting.

In case you think that Dreikurs is writing a long time ago and that parent advice is more sensible nowadays, let's look at a more contemporary example. It's unusual in that it actually mentions violence towards parents, which very few parenting books do. Unfortunately it treats it as non-serious, obviously thinking of small children hitting parents. It isn't a particularly extreme or bad book. Ironically it's called 'Positive Discipline'.[119]

Quotes from "Positive Discipline"	My comment
"Children aren't born aggressive, but they can become this way when no one asks their opinion or considers their needs.	If children are naturally peaceful, why is hitting extremely common for toddlers in every society. In most societies in the past *no one* asked their opinion yet young children were often less aggressive than are our children.
When parents assume they know what is best for their children, they inadvertently may be inviting a lot of pent-up anger that comes out as aggressive behaviour." p 37/38	If parents don't assume they know what is best for young children, we're in serious trouble! The idea of most young children having "pent-up anger" at parental control is nonsense (probably inspired by Freud's ideas).
"When a child is hitting, usually his or her feelings are hurt. Your child needs help from you but may feel frustrated because he or she isn't getting the help needed.... Perhaps you are overreacting and treating your child disrespectfully out of shame and embarrassment."	So when a child is hitting, you should focus on his or her emotions rather than how their behaviour is affecting you or the victim... and **you** are not being respectful enough to the child!

"Take the child by the hand and say, 'It's not okay to hit people. I'm sorry you are feeling hurt and upset. You can talk about it or you can hit this pillow…'"	Children who hit are not necessarily feeling hurt and upset and may not even be very angry. Hitting other things may be better than hitting people but it does not make anyone less aggressive. Isn't a child being taught to associate anger with hitting? There are no consequences, other than attention, for this child. We'll discuss (and demolish) the idea behind hitting a pillow when we look at anger.
"Ask, 'Would it help you to go to your time-out spot now?'"	This is encouraging wishy-washy and feeble parenting. Any child getting such a weak response from hitting someone is likely to lose some respect for the adult and is not being given a clear message that hitting is not tolerated.
"With children under age four, try giving them a hug before removing them from the situation."	How confusing is this? They hit you (or another child) and you give them a hug *before* removing them!
"When your pre-schooler hits you, decide what you will do instead of trying to control your child."	*Instead of controlling?* Control is exactly what your stroppy pre-schooler needs. If you don't take control, you are doing them a serious disservice (not to mention those they are hitting)!

You may find it hard to believe that this is not a particularly bad or extreme parenting book. The attitudes it demonstrates are quite common among other parenting gurus as well as some welfare workers, psychologists, paediatricians and researchers. I'm a little sorry to pick on such an easy target and obviously the writers mean well (but the road to Hell is paved with good intentions). They are increasing unhelpful parental guilt and if parents followed their advice, this seems likely to make some children's aggressive behaviour far worse. Years of this kind of wishy-washy parenting with a stubborn, difficult child can create teen terrorists who put themselves and other people at serious risk.

Indulgent Parenting has been encouraged by many professionals over the past fifty years. Looking at parent education courses; most of them appear to roughly follow Dreikurs' lead and virtually ban all punishment. Here's an example from Parent Effectiveness Training: *"parents will want to communicate to the youngsters that punishment is not to be used at all any more, even if it is suggested by the kids, as it often will be.*[120]" Note that they are not talking about *physical punishment* but *any* form of punishment!

Here's another fairly random example taken from a typical book about parenting teenagers.

"It hurts and humiliates parents to be put down by foul language. As authoritative parents we can set an example and firm limits regarding tone and language. Statements like these may help:

- *I feel hurt when you use that language or tone*
- *What is behind your anger?*
- *Why are you being disrespectful?*
- *How can we prevent this happening next time we [sic] are angry?"*

Young people are often disrespectful because they do not feel respected by their parents."[121]

I often have parents tell me that they responded to verbal abuse by telling the young person that they don't like that sort of language or that they felt hurt. I usually point out that that is the purpose of verbal abuse. If you say, 'I feel hurt' when they are being outright nasty, you are simply confirming for the young person that they have succeeded in their goal of hurting your feelings.

It's not difficult to see how well-meaning parents using such a modern, irresolute approach might produce some children who become more and more aggressive and less and less respectful towards adults and authority. It's this style of parenting that is particularly common among educated, liberal parents, such as those who work in the helping professions. As I've mentioned before, teachers, nurses and health and welfare workers are over-represented among those abused by their children. Overall a fifth of the children in my sample have a parent working in a caring role. The main reason for this is that they are particularly influenced by sixty years of parenting advice encouraging warm but weak parenting. An interesting irony is that these methods, if not taken to extremes, do actually work well with the majority of children. You probably have one of the many exceptions where modern parenting backfires.

It's interesting to note that most parenting experts have been men and that several have been publicly acknowledged as being mediocre or bad parents. Rousseau, one of the first to encourage permissive, child-focused, parenting, abandoned all five of his infant children to foundling hospitals, in those days often a death sentence. Dr. Spock was a distant and stern father according to his sons[122]. When Bettelheim wrote "The Good Enough Parent" he was bitterly estranged from his oldest daughter[123]. Erik Erikson placed a disabled son in an institution and told his other children that he had died, and was distant and uninvolved with these children too according to his daughter's biography. The son of R.D. Laing, one of the most radical parent blamers ever, had this to say, *"When people ask me what it was like to be R. D. Laing's son, I tell them it was a crock of shit. It was ironic that my father became well-known as a family psychiatrist, when, in the meantime, he had nothing to do with his own family.*[124]"

The other extreme

I may have given the impression in this chapter that all parenting advice since WW2 has encouraged permissiveness; this is not true. There have always been a minority of books pushing for a return to the 'good old days' of harsher discipline.

Many of these are by the religious right and some still support smacking children. The book, 'Dare to Discipline' by James Dobson, first published in 1970, was very successful and went through a great many editions. It's perhaps a good example of how times have changed, as not only does he encourage smacking of children (though even he does not support hitting teenagers), he even suggests pinching their shoulders painfully as an effective discipline method. Furthermore, if they cry for more than five minutes after such torture, they should get more of what made them cry[125]!

There is plenty of ammunition in the Old Testament Bible to encourage Bible-thumpers to be child-thumpers. "Spare the rod and spoil the child" is the best known but there are many others, including the suggesting of the death penalty for cursing a parent[126] – a trifle strict by modern standards!

If I had to choose between the wishy-washy Spockian, child-centred parenting manuals and the bring-back-the-rod type, I'd definitely go for the former. Luckily, we don't have to go to either extreme.

Box

Popular Parenting Myths

Parenting is instinctive.

You get out of parenting what you put into it.

The more you love someone, the more they will love you.

If you do the best you can, your children will respect you for it.

Well-brought-up kids always turn out OK.

People are only ever violent or abusive if they are exposed to this at home.

The nuclear family is the ideal, natural family form.

The first two years are far more important psychologically than later years.

Young children need 100% of your attention and care.

Children need constant adult supervision.

It's very easy to screw up your children without knowing it.

All stress or upset is harmful to children.

Good communication can solve all interpersonal problems.

Punishment is never necessary.

Fathers are always the biggest influence on boys and mothers, the biggest influence on girls.

Children only turn to their peer groups for approval if something is lacking at home.

There is one right way to raise children that will work for all.

Science can tell you how to be a good parent.

Experts know the best way for you to bring up your kids.

Although most parenting advice given in the past was either wrong or harmful, we now know enough to tell parents exactly what they should do for the best.

End Box

Causes, Influences and Explanations

Ralph, a fourteen-year-old boy has kicked a hole in a door in his home. These are some possible explanations different people might come up with (in no particular order):

- Teenage boys have hormonal changes that can result in rages.
- He's always been a difficult child: it's his personality to be oppositional and aggressive.
- He saw his father punch holes in walls when he was younger.
- His mother is over-controlling which makes him frustrated.
- His mother was in his face and he felt cornered and upset, so he kicked the door rather than kick her.
- He's smoking pot, which can make people irritable.
- He has a developmental disorder.
- Such behaviour is far more common among young people nowadays, they have no respect for their parents or for property – they've had it too easy.
- Boys are more aggressive than girls. It's typical male behaviour.
- His parents have spoiled him and he expects to get his own way, throwing childish tantrums if he doesn't.
- His parents don't see eye to eye about parenting and undermine each other.
- He's upset about his parent's separation.
- He's just being a bully, using intimidation against his mother; it's about power and control.
- His father was aggressive and he's inherited similar traits.
- Adolescents today are over-stimulated by the media and electronics. They don't get enough sleep or fresh air. They've been bombarded by advertising making them over-entitled.
- Like many children nowadays he's addicted to computer games, and addicts often get aggressive when someone tries to limit their addiction.
- It's the junk food and chemicals that young people are exposed to nowadays.
- He drank too much red cordial.

It's quite possible that many of these are true. But are any of them 'explanations' for the behaviour on their own? Being a boy is a factor which increases the risk of such behaviour, but most boys don't kick holes in doors. The same applies to *any* of the other explanations.

80

Most of the time we don't look for explanations of our own behaviour or of the behaviour of people around us unless, we don't like it. *Why do you read books? Why do you brush your teeth? Why do you drive within the speed limit?* We take these things for granted so don't seek explanations. We want explanations when things go wrong: someone is drinking too much, worrying too much, kicking doors or hearing voices.

We can divide explanations for bad behaviour into those that focus on the individual, those that focus on the family, or those that focus on the wider society. Any of these could then look at past influences or at factors in the immediate, current situation. There are always lots of possible choices.

An explanation for a husband hitting his wife may look at 'historical' causes: that he had an abusive upbringing; or at current causes: that he is stressed. Both of these causal explanations may seem to excuse the behaviour. They are **not** excuses, but are often used that way.

We can also explain someone's behaviour in terms of its purpose for the individual. A man may have struck his wife because he wanted to stop her questioning him about his drinking. Or more generally because he wanted to show he's the boss. He would say he was violent because she was nagging him or not respecting him.

We tend to explain *our own* behaviour in terms of purpose and situational factors but to explain *other people's behaviour* in terms of what sort of person they are: *I hit him* because he was threatening me; but *he hit me* because he's a violent person. When people explain *their own* aggressive behaviour they nearly always look to the immediate situation and give the other person's behaviour as the 'cause' of their anger and aggression.[127] Violent men or youth often say things like, "*If she didn't make me so mad, I'd never act like that!*" I've heard two young people in the past month say they hit their mother because she was 'annoying'. However, if the behaviour is very serious or there are legal consequences they may then revert to blaming things like their early upbringing or a mental condition.

Explanations based on purpose, or function, are more likely to hold the individual responsible for their actions. It's not that one type of explanation is correct and the other incorrect. Behaviour is never caused by just one thing, so several explanations can all be equally true. What is important is which explanations are useful and which are unhelpful.

When people ask me as a therapist the 'why?' question about someone else's violence, they usually expect a causal explanation (probably based on psychological theory). They are surprised, sometimes disappointed, when I say that he does it to get his own way or because he can get away with it. There is an excellent book about domestic violence called '*Why does he do that?*' The author, Bancroft, basically comes down to rejecting the excuses and saying that men are violent in the family to get their own way, because they like the feeling of power, and because they can get away with it. This also applies to almost all the young people I deal with who are violent towards their parents. I've pinched his title, 'Why does he do that?' for a later chapter.

Explanations in terms of the individual's personality (extrovert, stubborn, pig-headed) are seldom taken as being a complete explanation. Yet once their personality is seen as fitting a known pattern, and given an official label, such as

'ADHD', 'Oppositional Defiant Disorder', 'Asperger's' or some kind of *personality disorder,* then this suddenly seems like an acceptable explanation by many people. It is even treated as if it's a *complete* explanation. If this was logical, then most or all people with that label would behave violently, which is clearly not the case. None of these conditions force anyone to behave in any particular way and most people with these conditions do not behave in the same way, so they are no more an explanation than is being male. If you are interested, there is more on labels later.

The explanations in terms of changes in society are clearly of great importance, especially when the frequency of a particular behaviour is changing over time, as is violence towards parents. Some troubling behaviours have increased dramatically in recent years. For example, many more children are cutting themselves and more youth are carrying knives. It would be illogical to explain such widespread changes in terms of individual children's personalities, yet people blame their individual parents when clearly society has changed. When talking about a particular individual, citing the societal changes can sound a little strange ('I'm a victim of society') and they often get ignored. However, increases in behaviours such as cutting, drug use, or suicide are generally socially transmitted. Professionals are often reluctant to see or discuss such social changes. For example, few workers when they first come to my training sessions agree that the media plays a part in violence to parents. Some people suggest that there has always been violence to parents: we just were not aware of it. Yet looking at the evidence on non-Western societies it seems clear that adolescent violence to parents is an extremely rare aberration except in modern Western society[128]. The next chapter looks at how our modern culture makes violence to parents more likely.

A number of our listed 'explanations' for Ralph kicking the door can be seen as making excuses for him and those that blame his parents are extremely popular among professionals and in our society generally. Professionals often claim they are not interested in blame, while clearly blaming parents. We can't really escape the issue of blame when we are talking about violence and abuse. Ignoring blame when talking about abuse often results in blaming the victim just as much, or more, than the perpetrator. Ignoring blame can also be amoral, making it sound as if abuse is either just a logical choice or that the abuser has no control over their actions. When such reasoning is applied to rapists or child sexual abusers, it rightly makes our hackles rise. But it is applied routinely to young people's violence in the home. Ignoring the question of blame can also be insulting to the perpetrator, treating them as if they are not capable of being moral or making choices, i.e. not fully human.

On the other hand blaming individuals is quite often unhelpful and unproductive. Shaming and blaming publicly hardly ever helps. In my counselling, I try to hold the abusive individual accountable but in a respectful and sympathetic way. If I can make them feel guilty, this is usually a good thing but it has to done subtly and has to come from them. They are often quite ashamed of their behaviour but that does not necessarily relate to feeling empathy for their victim or to taking responsibility.

When you think about it, there is never just one reason why anyone does anything. If your child is behaving like Ralph, then it's partly about the immediate situation and his goals, desires and attitudes, partly about the kind of person he is, partly about your family and the sort of parenting he's had, and partly about the society and culture we live in. Your influence is only ever a small part of this picture. Later we will walk you through an exercise that illustrates this and puts the extent of your influence, and your responsibility, into perspective.

We are going to look at three types of influences on violence to parents in the next few chapters: societal changes, parenting styles, and personality and gender.

Don't you need to understand causes before you can cure?

There are those who believe that before helping an individual or family with their problems, you must do a thorough assessment and work out where the problems originally come from. I don't believe this is necessary or usually helpful. Often the multiple influences that led to a behaviour or relationship problem are so complicated that we can never work them out with the information available. People's memories are not great and are easily distorted by strong emotions. Luckily, we don't have to understand why someone *developed* a behaviour to help them *change* that behaviour. If two thirty-year-olds want to give up smoking, it makes no difference if one started smoking when they were traumatised by exams just as their parents were divorcing, while the second started simply because their new boyfriend smoked. It may be irrelevant to a teenager deciding to give up throwing violent tantrums if they have been doing it since they were a toddler or if they started on commencing high school. What helps eliminate violent behaviours may be pretty much the same whether the child is an over-entitled child in an otherwise healthy family or if they came from a family where there was past domestic violence. Admittedly, the child who has been tantruming for longer and the child who has been exposed to DV are less likely to change quickly, but sometimes they do. As a general rule, if a behaviour or problem started suddenly it's more likely to stop suddenly.

I try to be patient with parents and professionals who believe that they have to 'get to the root cause' of a problem before actually dealing with it. Unfortunately, 'root causes' may remain forever elusive while the problem behaviour gets more and more entrenched, relationships deteriorate and at-risk, out-of-control children develop new problems.

Some of the children I deal with have been traumatised in the past, most commonly by exposure to domestic violence; a small number have been abused themselves. Andrew had been both physically and sexually abused by his father, as well as having witnessed his father abuse his mother. There had been no contact with his father for nine years. Andrew was sixteen when I met his mother, Vera. Her son had hit her many times and hardly spoke to her, except to call her vile names. Vera had been told that Andrew would need extensive therapy to get over being abused before he would be able to stop abusing her. This made her feel even more guilty (if that were possible) and confused her about who the real victim was. The problem was that Andrew wouldn't talk to any professional and I had to work with Vera for a number of months without getting to meet Andrew.

Vera became more determined not to put up with the abuse from her son and eventually took out a Restraining Order against him. Andrew was at first incredibly angry at his mother but he was wary of the police and so did not abuse her for the next two months. He slipped up once and pushed her over. She gave him the choice of either talking to me or being charged. He agreed to talk to me, but only on his own territory, so I did a home visit. Andrew was shamefaced and surprisingly likeable. We had only one useful counselling session: the abuse by his father was not mentioned. Many years have passed since then, with no recurrence of abuse towards his mother. Andrew has a steady job, a steady girlfriend and a very healthy relationship with his mother. It would be five years before he felt able to face a counsellor to talk about his past sexual abuse and he only felt he needed a few sessions. Many workers would assume that Andrew had to deal with his own past abuse before he could stop abusing his mother. The opposite was true: he was stressing himself so much by abusing his mother that there was no way he could face working on his past abuse.

Since then I've realised that past abuse in itself is not a risk factor for violence towards parents, although it often occurs along with domestic violence, which is a definite risk factor. Also it complicates things when it has occurred (the story of 'Peta' in the chapter on girl's violence illustrates this well). I've worked with a great many traumatised individuals over the past forty years, including many victims of sexual abuse, physical and emotional abuse, and neglect. These people tend not to be violent to parents, though some are violent towards foster parents, residential workers or teachers. 'Trauma' has become a bit of a buzzword recently. Unfortunately it is a vague term and can mean almost anything anyone wants it to mean.

Influences and the Slippery Slope

Shit happens! Lots of things just happen. I firmly believe that chance and random factors play a big part in our lives. Thus, although we can always find 'explanations' for why things turned out one way rather than another, these are often simply after the fact constructions – 'just so' stories. If the past was different, we would make up totally different explanations for the same thing[129].

If a child who is abusing a parent is adopted or has lesbian parents, these are quite likely to be seen as an 'explanation' of the behaviour. Yet these are not at all common precursors of violence to parents. Of four hundred and eighty young people abusing their parents only two or three were adopted, and two had lesbian parents. Women who worked when their child was young worry that this has caused the disrespect and anger, yet more mothers of abusive children did not work. If your child was exposed to you being abused (typically by their father), then this *is* a major factor but most other factors may be only a minor influence or not of any relevance whatsoever.

A family is a system. It has parts that mutually influence each other, often in complex ways, over minutes, months and years. There may be millions of interactions. In a complex system, there are processes whereby change might be resisted and dampened down (homeostasis). There are other processes which amplify and magnify change (vicious circles). A simple example is a deteriorating relationship: The husband is beginning to grow tired of his wife. She senses this (perhaps unconsciously) and becomes either more demanding or more distant. Either of these may increase the husband's resentments and make him more grouchy and argumentative. This feeds back into her unease and unhappiness and the relationship steadily decays until it ends in divorce many years later. Having talked to hundreds of people about separation and divorce I think this happens all the time and no one can say when it started the downward spiral.

An adolescent who is straining for more freedom (which may or may not be reasonable) has a father who becomes more controlling and rigid in response. Such young people may move from having a pleasant healthy relationship with parents when aged twelve to total war with them by age thirteen. But such a process may not be at all inevitable. It may have got worse temporarily because the boy's new best friend at High School encouraged him to be rebellious, or because the father was stressed at work and overreacted badly on just one occasion. It may be largely luck how things pan out.

Once a young person begins to abuse a parent, even with mild insults or low-level disrespect, they often lose more and more respect. The relationship deteriorates and positives reduce over time while the negatives increase. This is a slippery slope. It can accelerate greatly when a young person starts staying out more and hanging around with youngsters who are a bad influence. It may dramatically accelerate if they start taking drugs.

The following diagram illustrates a slippery slope and just a few of the common influences which tilt it in one direction or another.

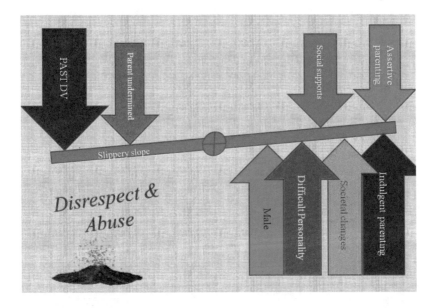

One of the key things to notice is that parenting is just one of a number of influences. When I work with parents I may be able to change their style from Indulgent to Assertive but there is no guarantee that this will always change the young person's behaviour. There are still lots of other influences which we usually have no control over. Some situations have deteriorated to such a point that the young person is not going to let the parent be a parent in the near future. Sometimes the young person leaving home is the best outcome, but in the majority of families, a change in parenting style does make a significant difference. Most parents (about 75%) who complete a *Who's in Charge?* group report that their child is showing less abusive behaviour at the end of the eight week group and there is continued improvement by the two month follow up session.

We are going to look at these factors in the coming chapters. First we will look at the changes in society that have made children less respectful and thus made violence to parents far more common overall. Next we will look at parenting style and family structure, which may predispose some children to violence. We next look at characteristics of the young person: personality, developmental disorders and self-esteem. All three levels, society, family and individual, influence why a child develops these behaviours. There is never one cause but many influences.

The simple concepts of entitlement and the power of not caring will further help you understand this kind of behaviour.

Simply understanding why your child may be behaving this way might give you ideas about how to move things back towards respect, but to back this up there are several chapters looking at how you can alter the consequences of your child's behaviour to be the best influence you can in the future.

The Butterfly Effect

There is a fair probability that a child with aggressive behaviour at age six will have aggressive behaviour at age sixteen. A casual reading of the research or listening to many clinicians talk about children with behavioural problems might make you feel that there is little long-term hope. But the fact that many children continue to have problems hides the crucial fact that **just as many** such children change for the better as change for the worse. Overall the number of violent children and the amount of violence goes down with age so clearly more grow out of violence than get worse.

Why, when, and if, they change may depend on random events. It's not popular to talk about random events influencing us or our children. We humans like to see patterns in things. This is a useful trait but unfortunately we see patterns even when none exist. We don't like to accept our ignorance and most societies have had favourite explanations for things they don't understand. In many societies, things going wrong are blamed on black magic or the will of the gods. In our society, we make up pseudo-psychological explanations for events we don't fully understand or can't explain. The most popular pseudo-psychology has been psychoanalysis which tends to blame things on unconscious processes which are usually traced back to parents and early experiences.

Chance events, even apparently trivial ones, can set someone off on one path or another. Reading biographies backs up the idea that random events can alter lives. If you think about your own life, you will be able to see such forks in the road where things could have gone one way or another. Life is full of fateful forking factors!

A child may improve their behaviour for many reasons:
- ☺ They may improve because they have a particularly good teacher in fifth grade.
- ☺ When they start high school they may just happen to be sitting next to a high status child who takes them into their circle of friends and encourages confidence and a positive outlook.

☺ They may give up the role as class clown when a better clown moves in.

☺ Someone in the family getting ill could lead to them becoming more responsible and maturing.

☺ They may have contact with a strong but gentle uncle or football coach.

☺ They may happen to get caught stealing at age twelve – which could be a turning point for the better as they realise that they don't want to be seen as a thief.

☺ They may discover a talent that gives them an alternative identity to the negative one they were adopting.

☺ Equally, some chance factors can make things worse.

☺ They have acne in adolescence which harms their self-esteem and makes them depressed, irritable and angry.

☺ Being late to reach puberty can have a huge negative effect on some children.

☺ On the other hand reaching maturity early can be a major risk factor for some girls if they start hanging around with an older crowd.

☺ Being bullied or teased when they start a new school can set in play a chain of negative effects.

☺ Failing an exam.

☺ Having a sarcastic teacher.

☺ Finding a group of friends who admire their fighting ability.

☺ Having an admired relative make an off-hand remark that they feel justifies their violence.

☺ Their best friend moves away.

☺ A temporary deterioration in their parent's relationship with each other makes the young person more vulnerable to peer influences and reluctant to be home.

All the events listed above could be crucial in the direction that someone's life takes. These are *noticeable* events but much smaller chance happenings can have a significant effect depending on their timing. The timing of such events is often crucial. A grand-parent dying may not faze a particular child at age eight but may devastate him or her at age twelve. Stress factors tend to multiply in their effects, rather than just add, so if two or more stress factors happen to coincide the result may be dramatically different than if they occur spaced out. Thus the precise timing of events can be crucial. If bereavement happens to coincide with being rejected by a close friend and developing acne, it could trigger an emotional crisis. Most of the teenagers I've seen over the years who have been suicidal have had a romantic relationship or friendship issues play some part. This may be unrequited love that parents don't even know about or breaking up with a boy or girlfriends who they had only gone out with for a week. I became depressed for six months at age sixteen because the first girl I loved ditched me after only two weeks. My parents knew nothing of this. This did me no lasting harm (although I did write poetry for a while), but for some young people such an event could lead to drugs, crime or leaving home. Of course there are almost always other things going on but the immediate cause of the crisis may be small and such effects can have lifelong consequences or even be life-threatening.

The 'butterfly effect' is an idea from Chaos Theory which I believe applies in all families and also to the course of our individual lives. In a complex system, tiny changes can lead to major changes. The proverbial butterfly flaps its little wings and changes a breeze by a tiny amount which leads to a different feedback effect so that a weather pattern builds up rather than dies away. This can theoretically lead to a hurricane. A family is a *highly* complex system involving millions of interactions over many years. In a family, a misheard word or a sidelong glance can lead to an argument between two people. An argument can lead to increased tension, more suspicion or resentment which can lead to either withdrawal or to more arguments. Things can deteriorate between two people (often with other people playing a part in the enfolding drama) over a period of months or years, leading eventually to a variety of crises, or to depression and stagnation. The players in these dramas frequently feel that they have little or no control over what is happening and typically they are largely unaware of how things are changing when they are in the thick of it.

Given how complex and fundamentally unpredictable are most people's lives, I find it surprising that some therapists believe they can work out, using only their clients fallible and suggestible memories, what exactly caused a particular person's life to develop in the way it did.

Box

E-mail from Nathan's mother

I'm so tired and exhausted, I literally don't know where to start, but I really need help in coping with the situation with our son. As Nathan's mum, I've raised him since he was born. I married his biological father and for many reasons, the marriage didn't work out. I was left eight months pregnant with Nathan; I gave birth to him alone and raised him on my own for six or so years, before I met Nathan's stepfather, Steve.

Even when I was struggling financially, Nathan never went without. I didn't allow him to know I was struggling to feed us both from week to week. I studied a degree, I worked part-time and I raised him to be a well-mannered, beautiful boy. I was lucky enough to meet and marry the most incredible man who took on being Nathan's father in every way, both emotionally and financially, and has always regarded Nathan as his own. How rare and special that is. Nathan has known Steve as 'Dad' since he was six years old.

Together, Steve and I have given Nathan a safe, loving, encouraging home. We have sent him to the best schools, involved him with sport, and encouraged him in anything he has wanted to do. He has never wanted for anything. We bought acreage in the hope that he might enjoy a bit of space and thought when he was showing behavioural problems at twelve years old, that such a move might help him somehow.

His biological father has never wanted to know Nathan, never provided for him financially or emotionally, I have never even been given means of contacting him, in the case of an emergency. I have always addressed this issue carefully and lovingly with Nathan. I've been open and understanding and have always reminded him of how special he is and how important he is.

When Nathan was thirteen years old, the year he began high school, things really started to change. He refused to do his homework and would never take any help from either his stepdad or me, despite our offers. If we did try to help him, Nathan would see it as criticism and would take offence. He would rather cheat from the back of the book than allow us to help explain the sums so that he could do it on his own. Any instruction whatsoever seemed to anger him. He began lying - prolifically - about anything and anyone. There was no real way of knowing what was true or not with him. One night when Steve and I were sitting on our bed chatting to Nathan talking to him about his lies, he became so angered he screamed at us, "I'm going to kill you both later".

We have spent the last three years trying to manage Nathan's outbursts which have included physical and verbal threats, abuse, wilful damage to our home, lies, ignoring curfew to the point where he would simply not come home overnight, and in the last six months of living with us, we discovered he was taking drugs and drinking alcohol, activities that were only going to make matters worse.

His aggressive behaviour at home was often out of control, frightening and abnormal. His outbursts were cruel, threatening and occurred weekly. It wasn't just at home, it involved Nathan threatening violence towards others in the community, taking a knife to school and using it against another boy during a scuffle, for which he was suspended, and carrying a knife in his bag to and from his part-time job, which he claimed was for self-defence. In August of last year, he was cautioned by Police after recording sex with another minor on his mobile phone and having shown it to schoolmates. In December of last year I discovered I was pregnant with my second child, we shared the news with Nathan and his behaviour grew worse, creating more and more stress in the home, sometimes not returning home overnight and telling me that my baby would be a down syndrome child or premature, he even threatened to 'bash me in the belly' later claiming that it was a joke.

It was no laughing matter living with Nathan; he was intimidating and frightening. We were fully aware that Nathan's behaviour was not considered normal and we sought help from mental health professionals as well as counsellors and Police.

After another bout of his abuse one day, screaming yelling - often uncontrollably on our verandah at the top of his lungs yelling words like "I'm a victim, I'm a victim", he was bashing up his room yet again, we asked him to calm down. Steve explained to him when he had calmed, that because of his outburst (which yet again was a result of us questioning him because that's all it would take) he was grounded. He seemed to accept this from Steve. He waited until the next morning just after Steve had left for work, and declared to me he was going to the shops to hang out with his friends. At this point in his life, Nathan had refused to return to Year 11 at school, wanting to take a traineeship in a bakery that had been offered to him through the part-time job I had encouraged him to get six months prior - which we supported even though we both secretly wanted him to complete Year 11 and 12. This morning, I reminded him of what his father had said the night before to which he declared we couldn't stop him. I told him calmly that if he leaves and does not respect our home then he should find somewhere else to live - which he did. He packed his things and went to stay with friends (sleeping on their couch). He stayed there a week and lied to the father of the house, went to Centrelink to try to get assistance and came up with a plan to purchase a caravan to live in their back yard. I spoke with the father during this week, at first he was very supportive of Nathan and seemed to be under the belief that a huge row had occurred in our home and that he was happy for Nathan to stay for a few days. After a week, I called the father and he expressed that Nathan had lied to him and that his sleeping on the couch was causing havoc for his family. I asked the father to return our son to us, and he did. Nathan turned up at the front door with nothing but contempt and hatred for us.

We took Nathan to see the psychologist; I talked with him about what is making him so angry, about his drug abuse, alcohol abuse. I was trying to reach out to him. He would only be cruel to me, saying incredibly cruel things to me. I could give you countless examples of the cruel things my son has said to me...but this email would turn into a book, so I won't. Needless to say, he always seemed to take pleasure in mocking me, saying cruel things to me and watching me cry.

After returning home he went to his part-time job, we just tried to maintain that any outbursts in the home were unacceptable. He was on probation at his work. He had gone from a part-time position, to being offered a traineeship (because he was raised so well, he comes across as very well mannered, well-spoken and is quite convincing when he wants to be of course), to the traineeship being withdrawn and his hours being cut back. He was having problems with other employees (very jealous of any praise his female employer gave to another employee) and his employer often communicated with me about her concern. She caught him lying, often he would disappear, he showed her defiance when she tried to direct him to do a task. In other words, his behaviour was deteriorating at his work, in similar ways that we had seen his behaviour deteriorate at school and at home. What underlined all the behaviour problems was simply a refusal to comply with rules and total disregard for authority. His employer, who had given him many chances, had explained to him that he was on probation but that his traineeship was still offered on a part-time basis. He needed to 'earn' back his full-time traineeship.

Within a week of returning home, I had driven him to work. Instead of him returning home on the bus at the time he agreed to, he called hours later claiming to be at a friend's house (the same friend) and asked if he could stay over and watch movies with her and her family. I asked to speak with the father and the father confirmed that he was home watching the kids and that all would be okay for him to stay. I explained that Nathan had work on the next day, the father offered to drop Nathan home in the morning so he could change into his uniform ready in time for work. The next day, they never showed up. I called and the father explained that Nathan had left at 5am from his home, claiming to have had to start work early. We couldn't find Nathan all that day and he kept rejecting our calls to his mobile (which he had often done before during the nights when he hadn't returned home) until he finally called reverse charge to our home phone and told me "mum I'm at the shops, I just need a bed, come and get me - if you don't, I'll sleep on the streets and it will be on your conscience". During that long day, his employer had called wondering where Nathan was. I could no longer 'cover' for him as I literally did not know where my son was. She explained that she could no longer keep employing him, that the traineeship and job was gone. When we picked him up and after talking with him, he explained that he had gone to the shops to purchase a bottle of Vodka. He didn't seem to care that he had lost his traineeship. He was defiant, and full of hate. He screamed profanities at us as we tried to talk to him and denounced his stepdad telling him 'you're not my f***ing father'.

By the week of the 15th February (which was only two weeks later) despite all our efforts, nothing had seemed to have any positive effect on Nathan. We had taken Nathan to a psychologist and psychiatrist appointment on the Monday prior and by Monday afternoon we had a family talk and again explained to Nathan the negative impact of his behaviour on all of us as a family and that if his behaviours continued, he could no longer remain living at home. We told him how loved he was, I asked him if he wanted to study art at TAFE and offered to set up an interview for him to do a course. He had always been a gifted little artist and we had sent him to art classes and bought him all art equipment to help encourage his talent. I thought this might excite him. He seemed mildly interested but I said we would set up a time to meet with TAFE. We asked Nathan to make a commitment to try to behave better, to stop yelling at me, to stop threatening that he was going to live on the streets, to stop his drug taking so that we could stay together as a family. We talked about the option of him living at a youth shelter should his behaviour continue, it was very clearly pointed out to him that we could no longer endure what was going on in our home, particularly as I was pregnant with his brother or sister in my first trimester. Nathan agreed to make an effort. Within four days of this conversation, I drove Nathan to a psychologist appointment. On the way there he was texting his friends. I spoke lovingly about opening up to the psychologist so that it could help him. When he came out he seemed happier, I asked him if he wanted to come see a movie with his Dad and I that afternoon to which he replied 'no, he wanted to be with his friends'. I said okay, dropped him off and agreed on a curfew time for him to be at the bus stop so we could collect him that afternoon. Within twenty minutes of coming out from the movie at around five thirty p.m. we got a call from police. Nathan had set fire to a park bench and had been apprehended. Police told us that at first Nathan claimed to be 'living on the streets'. The police had confiscated his mobile phone and when we looked at it, whilst I was driving him to his psychologist appointment, he had been texting profanities about us and sourcing drugs. When we collected Nathan from the Police station that Friday night, he (as all the other times) showed no remorse for his actions and simply demanded his mobile phone be returned to him. He was not apologetic, he was annoyed at the Police, at us, at his friends, he claimed his commitment to us made some four days prior applied only to behaviour in the home and therefore these behaviours outside of the home 'did not count'.

We finally took Nathan to a Youth Shelter in late February because we could no longer endure his abusive behaviour in our home and he was not going to give us any reprieve. It was a very difficult drive to make but when we arrived, the shelter told us they were 'family focused' and that this time is important 'time out' for us as parents. Unfortunately, those at the shelter have not actively involved us in Nathan's life and of course Nathan has continued to reject and devalue us as a family. They have encouraged him to receive welfare benefits and take himself off our Medicare card, which he has done.

He continues to present to people around him that we have never supported him, have been terrible parents. He has not made any attempt to return home, despite our invitation to him and has been outwardly cruel over the phone when we have called him. He now claims that we sent him to the shelter because of that one incident - setting fire to the park bench - and apart from that he was a good son.

I'm now seven months pregnant and suffering from depression and fatigue. Steve was experiencing chest pains whilst Nathan was living with us and being abusive, now that he is gone, Steve's pains are gone. He's also suffering from depression about all of this, but coping better than I am.

I'm so sorry for the convoluted email, I hope it isn't too long a story and I hope I have made sense. I'm not thinking so straight a lot of the time, I feel so empty and am so tired of the pain and sadness I feel. I am relieved to not be living with such an abusive person in my home any longer, I feel I, Steve and our unborn baby are much safer now and even that thought makes me sad given that I am talking about my son.

End Box

Modern Society – A Toxic Culture?

"Kids Rule!" slogan of Nickelodeon Company.

"In the present era the nuclear family is a site of submerged hostilities as precocious children wrestle with their parents for adult privileges and material goods." Steinberg[130]

When discussing the problems of young people, the focus is often firmly on the family and parenting. Parenting is certainly of importance – this book is primarily aimed at helping you make some adjustments to your parenting to increase your positive influence. However, over-emphasis on the influence of parenting – and some writers and professionals pretty much ignore all other influences – is parent-blaming and guilt-inducing. There is a strong tendency to ignore the huge contribution that the personality and choices of the young person make to behaviour problems. There is also a general neglect, especially in psychology and psychiatry, of the impact of the wider society in which these problems are occurring. If something, whether it's teenage depression, cutting, or violence to parents, is becoming more common generally it makes sense to first ask about changes in society. It doesn't make much sense to automatically assume that parents must have changed their behaviour en masse and this has therefore changed the behaviour of young people.

There has been a big increase in violence to parents and an even bigger increase in petty defiance and disrespect. This **is** partly due to changes in parenting, particularly the move to more indulgent parenting, but I am convinced that it **equally** reflects changes in society. These changes affect all of our children to some extent but have much greater impact on some than on others. Personality plays a big part in how societal changes, or parenting, affect a particular young person and all three interact in complex ways.

Sorry if this is a bit confusing. Neat slogans and formulas may be reassuring but are neither honest nor accurate.

"For every complex problem there is an answer that is clear, simple, and wrong."
H. L. Mencken

What is culture?

If you compare a group of modern day New Yorkers with a tribe living in Papua New Guinea, the differences in culture would be staring you in the face (especially if the latter have those amazing two-foot long penis sheaths). However, the cultural differences between the New Yorkers and Londoners are not so obvious but are still quite real. I moved from Scotland to England when I was twenty and found there were marked cultural differences (for example down south they drank less but cuddled more). Similarly when I moved to Australia fifteen years later I noted many important differences in culture. Australians, however, are not only unaware of most aspects of their own culture but most of them don't even realise they have funny accents! In Britain they are more aware of their funny accents because there are so many different ones.

People tend to only be aware of their culture where there are obvious contrasts to be seen, and with fundamental attitudes and beliefs they often remain completely unaware. The phrase, '*It's a rare fish who knows he's wet*' sums it up well. Unless you are a member of an ethnic minority you probably take most aspects of your own culture so much for granted that they never reach the level of awareness. What we do and how we think, is just 'common sense', 'normal' or 'civilised' to us (this is especially true of many Americans and English). It's thus almost impossible for us to see the contribution that our own culture makes to an individual's behaviour.

Culture is never static. There is an *enormous* difference between the culture of the modern New Yorker and the Pilgrim Fathers who landed there four hundred years ago. But how much cultural difference is there between now and twenty years ago, or between those adult New Yorkers and their children? It has been claimed, and some research supports this, that which generation you belong to is a bigger factor affecting behaviour than which social class or family you are born into[131].

There has always been, to some extent, a separate culture of children. One hundred years ago teenagers didn't have a distinct culture but either adopted adult culture or blended this with children's culture. Children entered the adult world, working full time and sometimes married, before they were done with puberty. One of the unusual things about modern society, that we take for granted, is that adolescents spend little or no time with adults other than their parents or authority figures[132]. 'Adolescence' as a distinct in-between stage of life didn't really exist, *in the way we see it*, until most children started going to school, late in the 19th century or thereabouts. Many societies had an in-between child and adult stage but these were brief and seldom associated with the type of problems we associate with adolescence[133]. From the middle of the last century, teens developed their own culture distinct from both children's and adults, largely driven by media interests, (initially music and movies). This is new. The very words 'teenager' and 'adolescent' are recent additions to the language.

What we are now seeing is the spread of teen culture downwards into childhood and upwards into the twenties. Adolescence is a vague stage of life whose length currently is growing and growing. I've been joking for a while that adolescence now lasts from eight to twenty-eight, but the joke is wearing a bit thin as it gets closer to the truth! Since teen culture has emphasised rejecting authority, being a smart Alec, and being independent of family, the spread of this culture downwards is a worry, and very relevant to some of the problems we are increasingly seeing in twelve and thirteen year-olds.

Media

"The heady cocktail of popular culture that our kids engage in is responsible for everything from their attempts (and successes) to look sexy, to temper tantrums and distorted body image." Brooks[134]
"The average eight to thirteen year old is watching over three and a half hours of TV a day. American children view an estimated 40,000 commercials annually. They also make approximately 3,000 requests for products and services each year." Schor [135]

For her book *'What's happening to our girls?'* Maggie Hamilton interviewed American teenage girls and was struck by how similar their responses were regardless of their background. She says this puzzled her until she realised "*this was due in part to the overwhelming influence of popular culture, which has become the 'super' parent.*[136]" While not agreeing with the term 'super parent' (as I don't think parents have ever had an all-encompassing influence on children), I do agree that the influence of popular culture is growing while parents' influence is shrinking.

Society and 'culture' exert an influence on every individual throughout their entire lives. Traditional cultures consisted of interactions between people that were verbally transmitted and stored in memories, particularly by the elders. The culture our children are growing up with consists far more of various forms of media, with written media, sadly, becoming less important compared to electronic. Our children are immersing themselves in digital media: you could say wallowing in it. And this is changing so rapidly that none of us can keep track. Recently social media has become incredibly important and YouTube videos have become as influential as TV for many young people. These developments are not all bad. I find it amusing that some parents think that watching commercial TV is overall more positive than surfing the web or talking to friends on Facebook. Personally, I think watching TV with ads is far worse than these, and probably worse than playing most video games.

Juliet Schor studied media involvement by American children and concluded that high media use resulted in a variety of problems, including depression, anxiety and low self-esteem. Of particular interest for us was her conclusion that higher levels of consumer involvement resulted in worse relationships with parents[137]. There is also suggestive evidence linking the amount of television children watch with increased rates of ADHD[138]. Another study found the amount of TV watched at age four was related to the child at ages 6 to 11 teasing and bullying classmates. [139]

In her study (of marketing to children, "*Born to buy*"), Schor noted that "*marketers blame parents for the excesses of consumer culture*" and she gives a particularly galling example: '*The reason that there is childhood obesity is because caregivers don't have enough time to spend with their children. So what they're doing is giving their kids 8 hrs of TV a day,*' says Ken Viselman (the producer responsible for inflicting *Teletubbies* on America*)!*[140]

There is little point in my saying anything about particular electronic media as by the time you read this it will be out of date. The rate of change is incredible, and apparently speeding up. This is a problem in itself as it widens the generation gap and makes our children more convinced that we are out of touch. We are out of touch, but our children can't keep up with the rate of technological and social change either. They only try to keep up with what their friends, and the marketers, say matters at the moment.

Social media is a whole new ball game. There's been little research but some suggestions of the harmful effects of social media, which might be very relevant to violence to parents. I've observed that the general level of rudeness and disrespect on Facebook, even among adults, has got worse in recent years. What effect this practice at being nasty, rude, negative and disrespectful will have on developing children over the next decade is scary to contemplate[141]. Cyber bullying is common and creates an opportunity for some children who would not have the nerve, or strength, to be conventional bullies with their peers. Having an audience readily on hand that will support young people in being anti-authority, and support their complaints about parents, is not healthy and social media can put barriers between parents and children. There is evidence that social media use increases narcissism and also makes people more individualistic[142].

Parents can only control what their children are exposed to when they are young. They have less and less control as they get older. Older children view material in other children's homes, on the internet and now on phones and other devices. Technology is fast removing parents' ability to monitor or control their children's expose to media. Putting all the responsibility back on to parents when there are billion dollar industries making material designed to be irresistible to children is really pretty lame!

Despite all this, there is a general reluctance among many professionals and academics to place importance on media in children's problems[143]. If a parent suggests that playing violent video games or listening to Eminem is associated with their violence in the home, they are liable to be dismissed out of hand by many professionals, yet young people themselves make such connections when I talk to them.

Individualism

"Individualism is a powerful ideology. One of its potential end-points has been hostility against families, with parents seen as oppressors and children seen as victims." Paris[144]

A good example of how unaware we are of our own culture is in how much we take for granted the level of *individualism* in modern Western societies. We are more focused on the individual (as opposed to the extended family or communities) than *any* people in history or in *any* other culture today. English-speaking countries have tended to be even more individualistic than other European countries and middle class, educated and urban people are more individualistic than working class, less educated or rural people. Individualism is not only relevant to why more of our children are oppositional within the family, but is also of relevance to the attitudes you may encounter from professionals, who will tend to focus more on the individual than on the family unit. They are thus likely to view your teenager more as an independent individual than as a part of your family and to see your efforts to control your teen as being oppression.

I don't want to get too political but it seems to me that capitalist society is making us more and more individualistic. This is related to increased divorce rates but also to some things that I'd consider very positive, such as later marriage and smaller families. This trend over recent decades means that some of our young people are far more individualistic in their attitudes than are their parents. The phrase 'the me generation' was coined some time ago but as the trend has continued, I'm not sure what our current kids should be called, perhaps 'the me, me, me and sod-the-rest-of-you' generation! The family is certainly not dead in Westernised cultures but its hold on people has definitely become less strong. Since this is a long-term trend it affects people of the older generation too, as they are less likely to have a close-knit extended family and thus less family support than previous generations.

I will say again that there are still a lot of wonderful young people and many are caring and well-meaning. They are not *all* egomaniacs, but *on average* they are probably less family-focused, less interested in collective action of any kind, more egotistical and more self-obsessed. The media and commercial forces encourage this stance – it sells!

Materialism

'Too many companies simply see our children as little cash cows that they can exploit." Hilary Clinton

Our children are the richest generation ever, yet more of them feel poor than in previous generations. The media is largely to blame for this. An American study found that those who watched more TV believed that people in America were richer because TV shows a disproportionate amount of wealthy people[145]. It isn't just those in poverty who now feel poor but children in average homes who are aspiring to Hollywood images and craving the latest gimmicks and gadgets. I had one private schoolgirl say, with a straight face, that her family were 'povs' because they only had a small swimming pool!

Young people feel pressure to have the latest 'in vogue' items. Girls in particular experience feelings of inadequacy and discomfort as a result of 'images of perfection' promoted by advertising… The more consumerist children were…— the more likely they were to be dissatisfied more widely." Mayo [146]

If one of the common results of increased materialism is increased dissatisfaction, generally this is bound to make some children more irritable and critical of their parents. This translates to less respect and, for some children, more conflict. Reduced respect coupled with increased conflict can lead to abuse.

I believe that many of the problems we are seeing in modern children are exacerbated by marketing and materialism. Yet people continue to blame parents for not supervising their children's media exposure. Supervision gets more and more difficult as gadgets proliferate and internet access becomes easier.

Unfortunately, there seems little chance that our politicians are going to do anything about this situation in the foreseeable future as the markets come first.

"If she tired of something, say the TV wasn't big enough, then it would get broken, so she needed a new one." Parent in NZ study of children's damaging of property[147]

Advertising[148]

"Advertising at its best (sic) is making people feel that without their product, you're a loser. Kids are very sensitive to that... You open up emotional vulnerabilities, and it's very easy to do with kids because they're the most emotionally vulnerable.[149]" These are the words of one of the people who have almost free access to our children, the president of an advertising company.

The average child in English-speaking countries watches between 20,000 and 40,000 TV ads per year[150]. In the USA, advertisers spend close to $20 billion advertising to children each year. Since many people now wear conspicuous brand labels (walking billboards who pay for the privilege) and product placement and internet ads are becoming ubiquitous, the total number of ads a typical child is exposed to would be impossible to calculate and may be in the millions per year.

Advertisers' conferences have actually featured sessions called '*The Fine Art of Nagging*'. One marketing expert estimated that children pester parents for stuff about three thousand times a year.[151] So it seems highly likely that part of the increased demandingness and entitlement that our children show nowadays is a result of our consumerist society and the advertising industry. You can hardly expect to relentlessly bombard children with messages to increase demand for products yet not increase demandingness! Yet most of us are so immersed in this barrage of brands and bullshit that we tend no longer to be properly aware of it. We seem to have accepted a society based on waste and greed.

Prosperity

"Prosperity fosters bad tempers." Seneca

The Greek philosopher Seneca, tutor to Emperor Nero, believed that rich people had higher expectations than the poor so they were more often disappointed and hence got angry more frequently. This fits with the idea of Entitlement which we will discuss later. It doesn't fit with ideas that see violence as closely linked to poverty, stress and low self-esteem.

Our children are materially the richest generation that has ever sat on the planet (they sit more than they walk). In terms of comfort, health, housing, clothing, variety of food and amount of entertainment there is simply no comparison between them and earlier generations. Perhaps young Nero had a more luxurious childhood but he didn't have computers, phones and DVDs. Other than the children of emperors, few people in history would have had the material wealth to compare with the children from average homes in the Western World today. Even when parents try not to be indulgent, most children are materially indulged compared to any past generation. It has been claimed that, adjusted for inflation, kids in the past decade in the USA spend *five times* more than their parents did at their age.[152] In some children this adds to their sense of entitlement, making parent abuse more likely. Although some forms of violence are frequently associated with poverty *within* our society it's also found that being rich is associated with a sense of entitlement, less honesty, and less caring behaviour towards others[153]. So Seneca had a point.

We've mentioned that there is evidence that violence to parents is actually more common for middle and upper-class families than for poorer families. Taking a global view, it's *far* more common in rich *countries* than in poor ones. I'm certainly not suggesting that wealth alone is going to make any child abuse their parents but there does appear to be a relationship. You may be indignantly thinking, especially if you are a sole parent, 'we're not rich', but compared to the world as a whole, and to previous generations, you probably are. I'm certainly not saying that poor children can't be abusive to parents too. It's just one factor, but an interesting one that goes totally against what many people believe.

There are even those who think that within Western nations rich kids actually have *more* problems than poor ones[154]. I don't believe this, but it's certainly not true that they are immune to emotional or behavioural problems, including drugs, suicide and eating disorders as well as violence.

Children's expectations have gone through the roof. Of course, some of this materialism comes from parents' direct influence. If parents are spending their lives in hot pursuit of the newer car, smarter home, trendy clothes etc., it is no surprise that their children are even more vulnerable to the pressure to become rabid consumers. But it does not need parents' example for some children to get on the treadmill of rabid consumption.

Disrespect for age and authority

"Children are bombarded from the time they are very small by conflicting and discouraging messages concerning parental authority." Ambert[155]

"The media typically depicts highly empowered children and childlike adults" Schor[156]

I think the film *Home Alone* was one of the first times that the child-as-hero and all-adults-are-idiots theme was made glaringly obvious. It was a funny film. When any one film, show or game is mentioned as a bad example, several objections are usually made:

- One movie/show/game isn't going to change anyone's attitude or behaviour.
- It's not a big deal, it's just entertainment.
- The kids know it's just fantasy.
- It has artistic merit, or it contains a deeper message or moral, or its funny/parody/satire.

- It's up to parents to control what children watch – you can turn it off.

Generally one media item is *not* likely to change someone's behaviour or attitudes (though there have been dramatic exceptions where copycat violence has been carried out) but it isn't *just* one item. Children today view hundreds of thousands of media items, and messages such as 'adults are idiots' are contained in a great many. The impact on attitudes when this is repeated from an early age may be enormous, as it is with commercialisation, materialism, sexualisation and violence.

The fact that it's funny and entertaining does not in any way negate the harmful messages but actually make it *more* powerful and more likely to influence children. There may actually be an attempt at showing deeper morality but this is far less likely to influence than the superficial violence. The claim that it's just satire or parody is also irrelevant when children of various ages are exposed to many such messages over a period of time. Juliet Schor in her study of marketing found a 'pervasive anti-adultism' in adverts aimed at children[157], reinforcing the message of TV shows, cartoons, movies and even recent children and teen literature.

A survey in the UK in 2000 found that 87% of respondents thought that a decline in respect for authority was the most negative development in society. Surveys in America similarly find that a lack of respect is seen as one of the biggest problems for today's young people[158].

"Hollywood, for example, elevates teens at the expense of the adults they undermine, sending the clear message that children can control adults, and those who do are heroes. Insults and put-downs, lying and deceit are portrayed on sit-coms as normal and amusing family behaviour." Cottrell[159]

Lack of respect for adults can be seen as part of a bigger picture of lack of respect for age. Our society treats the elderly as a burden, an embarrassment or an irrelevance. Most societies throughout history valued old people greatly. In any other era or elsewhere in the world, my being called 'grandfather' would be a mark of respect. In Western society it's an insult. In pre-literate societies old people were repositories of knowledge and anyone might consult an old person for the information stored in their brains, with writing this became less necessary. Now with the internet, children don't feel they need to tap the stored information in parent's or teacher's heads. Why ask an adult when you can Google?

"Many children are increasingly insolent, demanding, or hostile towards parents, teachers, adults in general and other children. Even relatively well-behaved kids can be remarkably impolite, self-centred, and rude. In short, there is a visible decline in civility among American kids." Koman & Myers[160]

Sexualisation

"Growing up in a sex-saturated culture isn't something previous generations of girls have had to deal with." Hamilton[161]

Our children, boys and girls, are growing up surrounded by far more sexual imagery and adult concepts compared to previous generations. The contrast in Western culture between now and the recent past is quite dramatic. This is particularly striking because the idea of children's innocence and ignorance about sex is historically, a fairly new one. In most societies today and in Western societies up until about one hundred and fifty years ago children did not grow up ignorant of sex. There was not enough privacy for one thing, and children were not cosseted and protected to the extent they are today. Children were given ale to drink from the Middle Ages until the 18th century; they attended public hangings and adults made little or no attempt to hide sex, death and adult concepts from them. The age of childhood innocence was probably at its height in the first half of the last century. We have moved fairly quickly from a position where children were *unusually* ignorant, innocent, and made to feel guilty about anything sexual, to a society where young children are being actively encouraged (by advertisers, entertainers and peers and occasionally by parents) to be sexual even before reaching puberty. They are bombarded by sexual images and tales of sexual promiscuity. Naturally enough, once they actually do reach puberty more of them than ever before are keen to experiment sexually and straining at the parental leash like hounds on heat.

Early sexual activity either entails secrecy, conflict with parents, or blurring of boundaries. I now often hear about sexually active thirteen-year-olds – which used to be quite rare. Some groups of thirteen-year-olds appear to have exactly the same attitude to oral sex that we had to 'French' kissing!

Some young people have so little respect for parents that they make no attempt to hide their promiscuity from their parents. I've shocked a few mothers by suggesting that their daughter telling them 'everything' was not so much a sign of a close relationship as a sign of disrespect.

Precocious sex can be a major source of conflict between young people and parents. It can also make them think they should be treated as adults and distorts their peer group relationships, often putting them in touch with much older youth and exposing them to bad influences (most notably drink and drugs). Physically, children are reaching sexual maturity a couple of years earlier than they did a century ago (with most of the change in the first half of the last century) which means that they are emotionally less mature when attempting to have serious relationships (this is further exaggerated by our children being slower to take on responsibilities). However, earlier puberty does not appear to be the explanation for the big changes in adolescent behaviour (for sexuality or anything else) in recent decades. There has only been about a six month change in physical puberty in the past fifty years but a shift of three or four years in teen attitudes and behaviour over that time. Adolescence is more social than physiological.

Besides earlier sex, they are also getting into serious boyfriend-girlfriend relationships younger. As with precocious sex, this can put a barrier between parent and adolescent. It can also distort their relationships with other friends and they are too immature to cope with break-ups.

"Girls are being pressured to appear and act sexy, not to encourage or empower them, but because they're easy to sell to. Companies know how much tweens want to be teenagers, and use this to sell the products." Hamilton[162]

Hyperstimulation and sleep deprivation

There are those who believe we are having an 'epidemic' of ADHD and some blame the electronics that our children are exposed to. I'm not convinced there has been a *big* increase in ADHD (rather than in labelling) but I do think it likely that the stimulation of electronics is having some effect on our children. On a simple level, aggression is more likely when people are aroused in some way so when children are hyped up they may be more likely to argue, defy or become violent. Some young people definitely become aggressive and over-aroused after playing video games (not even necessarily violent ones) and I've seen a few cases where this greatly exacerbated violence to parents.

In what was probably the first study of anger in children, back in the 1930s, Florence Goodenough said that *'a child's protest against going to bed may be relatively mild if there is nothing of absorbing interest that he wants to do at the time, or it may be violent and prolonged if being put to bed interrupts an activity that he has set his heart on performing.'* Parents are now competing with a lot more absorbing alternatives to sleep (or homework or chores) than were around in the past.

Children generally are sleeping less and I know of a great many adolescents who stay up very late whenever they get the chance (often till dawn) to play video games or use the internet. Since so many kids have computers, TVs and mobile phones in their bedrooms (BAD idea!), I'm actually surprised that this has not become an even greater problem than it is. I can't see any reason that it won't continue to grow as a problem as games, communications, electronics and wireless connections all get more sophisticated and more addictive.

If you are the parent of a younger child, you should set firm guidelines now (such as no electronics in bedrooms) *before* it becomes a problem. Things are going to get more complicated and more difficult for parents in the years to come.

Media Violence

"By now it is clear to most unbiased expert observers, in fact to anyone without an axe to grind who takes the time to look at the research, that the effect of televised violence is to increase aggressive behaviour in boys and girls." Garbarino[163]

"You consume media. You take it in and it becomes a part of you. The more you see people hurting each other, disrespecting each other, and treating each other poorly, the more that makes its way into your consciousness. That's especially true with the way aggression is generally portrayed in the media – as cool, gratifying, fun and without consequences." Dill[164]

This is probably the most obvious aspect of how media affects our children, and it gets most attention. There are a great many studies that suggest that exposure to violence in the media makes children more aggressive[165]. But I say 'suggest' as it's difficult to prove it conclusively. Children who are aggressive will choose to watch more aggressive content, and irresponsible parents are far more likely to let them do so, so correlations don't conclusively prove anything. However, a number of reports which have looked at all the evidence have concluded that watching violent media and playing violent games makes people more aggressive[166]. One review by a number of experts concluded that "the scientific debate over whether media violence increases aggression is essentially over."[167] I wish it were, but there are plenty of people who debate the link.

Even if there was no evidence that violent media affects children I find it hard to imagine how this could not be so! People know that advertisers are willing to spend billions of dollars to influence our buying habits and even subtle product placement can reap huge rewards. An average American child sees more than two hundred thousand violent acts and sixteen thousand murders on TV by age eighteen[168]. Is anything more heavily advertised than violence? Yet many people choose to believe that this does not influence children! It's appalling that some media apologists will even dredge out the tired and discredited notion of 'catharsis', i.e. the idea that watching aggro can make you less aggressive (see chapter on Anger).

"To win such [modern computer] games one must immerse oneself in the battle-for-survival virtual cosmos and learn to maim and kill all rivals. A mindset of aggressiveness is established, as violence becomes a 'natural' amphetamine, a sanctioned entitlement to 'get high on death' and kill the boredom of the postmodern childhood." Steinberg & Kincheloe[169]

It seems obvious that the fact that children are actually participating in the violence in video games, rather than passively witnessing, makes them potentially more harmful than TV and movies. Of course, the majority of people watching violent films or playing violent video games do not become noticeably more violent, in the short term, but over time it has a significant effect on some children. The effect is usually long-term and subtle, but not always. Some children become dangerously hyped-up after playing these games. One study found that although watching violent TV, movies and playing violent games made people more pro-violence, only playing video games reduced empathy[170]. It worries me that our youngsters will soon be immersing themselves in realistic-looking three-dimensional games where they can kill, torture and even rape. Market forces will dictate that companies keep pushing the envelope into viler, sicker, bloodier terrain. Many parents turn a blind eye to younger children playing MA or even R rated games, so even if you are vigilant, your children may be exposed to this material in friends' homes (or in the other parent's home if you are separated).

There is probably less of an effect from listening to violent, aggressive music than from watching violence or playing video games. It's less likely to make someone violent who isn't that way inclined. However, for one of the *many* young people who *are* inclined to be aggressive, it helps keep them in a state of angry excitation and lowers the threshold for them to act violently. It isn't just violent lyrics, music can be aggressive by its tone and style (even if you can't make out the lyrics). Aggressive music certainly is nothing new and it's comical to look back on some of the scaremongering about rock and roll back in the '50s. I quite enjoyed the aggressive edge of some punk music in the '70s but, like most parents, I find the in-your-face deliberate nastiness of grunge and rap revolting. It's designed to be aggressive and to get the adrenalin pumping. We parents are not meant to like it. For many young people, it's largely harmless but for some it's yet another factor increasing both aggression and negativity.

"You can turn off the song, but you can't turn off your culture" Dill[171]

I find it bizarre that those making money from entertainment and advertising are being allowed to slowly produce media that is bloodier and bloodier and nastier and nastier! Ratings creep means that what used to be an R rating is now an MA and what used to be an MA is now an M (and ratings seem to be more based on sexual content than violence). There does not appear to be any motivation among our politicians to stop this. It's ironic that right-wing politicians, who shout loudest about old-fashioned values, are even more reluctant to interfere with the market to actually protect our children (whether from nasty media or from junk food). Market forces are into giving people, including children, what they want, regardless of whether it's good for them or not. And little boys especially want violence, titillation and toilet humour. Not only TV, film and games, but even literature aimed at the young caters to this trend. Like viewers of porn, what was once shocking and exciting becomes tame and so there is a constant push for more excitement and titillation. Hence ratings creep, and creeping nastiness, continues relentlessly.

I am not suggesting that you now go in with both guns blazing and confiscate all your teenager's violent games, DVDs and rap CDs. This is unlikely to solve anything in the short term (apart from escalate the conflict) but it's something to be aware of in the long term, especially for pre-teens.

The Dark Side!

People have always had a taste for the macabre, violent, scary and weird, as shown by the popularity of horror, crime, war, action violence, mystery, hospital shows and sensationalised news. This applies to adults as well as to young people. We like to be shocked and to feel the rush of adrenalin from vicarious fear, aggression or lust. Unfortunately our young people are getting a large dose of all this while growing up. It means that they are aware of suicide, rape, child abuse, torture, sado-masochism and human perversity at much earlier ages. Not only video nasties (getting rapidly nastier) but the news, mainstream TV, cartoons, comics, video games and the internet all contribute to this. Since there is so much high-level sex and violence (and high-level vileness) around we tend not to take warnings about 'adult concepts' very seriously but these may have a big impact over time. Like porn, the dark and weird quickly gets tame as we are desensitised, and this leads to some people (and merchandisers) wanting to push the boundaries ever further into tasteless new frontiers.

This familiarity with the dark side of human nature can lead to fearfulness and a general level of low-lying paranoia. The world becomes seen as a dangerous, horrible place (our tendency as parents to over-protect reinforces the idea of the world being dangerous and people being untrustworthy). It can also lead to world-weary cynicism at an early age, or in some to obsessions with evil, danger or self-destruction. For most children, the recent craze for vampires is harmless but for a tiny minority, it's linked to a dark and slightly sick view of life.

These cultural influences are so widespread it's difficult to see their effect, and their effect on different young people is quite varied. Not all children become depressed, anxious or aggressive but they are almost all desensitised *to some degree*. Such activities as binge-drinking, taking illegal drugs, cutting, suicide attempts, or suicide and self-harm threats, are all somewhat more likely than they were for previous generations. I can vividly remember being forced into a fist-fight when I was seventeen. When a trickle of blood appeared on the nose of the boy I was fighting I felt immediate revulsion and asked him to stop, suggesting we could call it a draw (he hadn't hit me). If I had grown up with the virtual blood-fest that today's young people experience, it's less likely that the blood would have made me want to stop. Overall, you may be surprised to hear that I don't believe that society in general, or young people in particular, are more violent than in the past. They may even be a bit less violent[172]. However, the type of violence and targets of violence have changed with less fights between evenly-matched peers and more violence towards siblings and parents. Also there does seem to be a slight tendency for violence between young people to be more severe and cruel when it does occur, and I suspect that media desensitisation has something to do with this.

Competition and bullying

The culture of teens, and increasingly pre-teens, has become one of cut-throat competition. Competition to be one of the in-crowd, to look good, to have the latest fashions, to watch the right shows, listen to the right music, to consume and to conform. Not only girls, but recently even pre-teen boys are becoming obsessed with appearance and body image. Despite the huge increase in obesity (yes, it probably is an 'epidemic'), overweight kids are abused more than in the past and odd-looking kids are more often ostracised. Despite far more acceptance of homosexuality than in the past, homophobia is still alive and well and 'gay' (or an equivalent like 'fag') is the most popular insult among younger teens.

This competitive pressure to conform can make some forms of bullying more intense, can make kids feel very insecure (even suicidal or depressed), can harm self-esteem, but it can also lead to arrogance and entitlement among the in-crowd.

Kids who are a bit 'different' (nerdy or effeminate boys, butch or geeky girls, anyone who is too fat, too small, late to reach puberty, too intellectual, freckled or redheaded) seem to be suffering even more than they did in the past as the pressure to conform has intensified. I've seen no evidence that physical bullying is more common than in the past and general teasing probably has neither increased nor decreased overall. However social pressure no longer stops at the school gates - outcasts can be made to feel inadequate, or directly harassed, by electronic means in the evening and weekend, so that some forms of emotional bullying are probably worse.

On the other hand, one positive is that many schools take bullying more seriously than they did in the past. This means that reported statistics on bullying have increased dramatically. It would be very naïve to conclude that this represents a real increase in bullying (but I'm sure someone has declared it an 'epidemic' at some point).

Protecting our children from the toxic culture

These cultural changes are not being shaped by parents, most of whom detest it, but by marketers and entertainers intent on creating teen-zombie-consumer-clones. Thankfully it isn't a coordinated campaign, and some kids fall through the cracks, but it has billions of dollars at its disposal and Western governments have given them practically free access to our children. The rapid change in technology, culture and fashion means that parents' heads are spinning almost as fast as the kids.

We can't keep up! Parents don't know what is right or normal. A recent example, which may sound old hat, or a lost cause, by the time you read this is, should kids have their mobile phones in their bedrooms at night? I feel this is so important that there is a section on it later in the book.

It disgusts me that parents in general are routinely blamed for letting children watch violent or adult-oriented programs when they are up against billion dollar industries making this programming as desirable as possible to vulnerable young minds. It's like the government making alcohol freely available to, and marketed to, underage children then telling parents it's up to them to monitor children's drinking, and that it's entirely their fault if children get drunk or addicted. This is currently the situation we have with fatty and sugary foods.

This is not to say that parents are blameless. I regularly come across tales of young children being allowed to watch completely inappropriate material (especially by irresponsible access fathers, often those who have been abusive).

One simple thing that parents can do is to keep TVs and other electronic devices (especially any with an internet connection) out of children's bedrooms. If your adolescent son has internet in his bedroom, it's 90% likely that he is watching porn. And some of the porn on the internet today is not tasteful nudes but women with gaping vaginas and people copulating, sometimes with objects or animals. We do not want younger children growing up thinking this is normal!

You can, and should, restrict your child from watching things you disapprove of, even though they will still affect your child. When the majority of other children are watching them this is affecting their culture and the behaviour of other children. Unless you want to live in some kind of isolated cult you just can't escape the influence of the media on your children. The Simpsons is a good example. It was considered quite unsuitable for younger children by many parents when it first came out but Bart Simpson ('Bart' was chosen as an anagram of 'brat') has become the wise-ass, anti-adult flag-bearer for a generation and his attitudes affect all of our children whether they watch it or not. It has also become quite tame (compared to things like South Park and Family Guy) in the space of just twenty years.

Children go to friends' homes and watch the things you didn't let them see. This does not mean that you should give up. It's still worth making a point about your disapproval and you will be reducing the extent to which they are exposed. However, technology is making it more and more difficult for parents to monitor their children's viewing. Children can watch every episode of South Park on the internet. And just in the past year or so the internet is available on mobile phones and other devices, which their friends have even if you are sensible enough not to give in.

Parents really do have less and less influence on these things and this trend looks likely to continue.

I've mentioned it, but I'll repeat, how ridiculous I find the excuse that violent, nasty, sexually depraved material only affects a small number of people. Heroin only affects a small number of people but we don't make it freely available. If only one person in a thousand became potentially murderous from exposure to violent porn, this would be good reason to restrict it and even one mass murderer in a million affects all of us dramatically. The effect of all this stuff is going to be very different for different children but there are a lot of vulnerable children.

We as parents can, and should, try to control what our children are exposed to in their early years. Personally I wouldn't let young children watch *any* commercial TV whatsoever (and didn't with my son). I feel their minds are being poisoned by a sea of commercialism twisting them into greedy little consumers. But you probably think this is too idealistic (or loopy) and it's probably far too late for your child by the time you are reading this.

I think parents should be making a point of showing disapproval of some things. But on the other hand I don't think parents should go overboard in trying to ban everything they don't like, especially once your child is a teenager. This is an area where the rights of children and young people may conflict with parent's deeply held beliefs. You may prefer it if your child never watched anything that glorified violence or sexualised females. If so, then 95% of all TV would be out and chances are that your child is going to rebel against you with a vengeance, and possibly leave home at an early age.

It's all about compromise.

Should we be alarmed?

In 2006, a group of over one thousand experts and celebrities in the UK wrote an open letter to the nation stating their concern about modern childhood: *"Our society rightly takes great pains to protect children from physical harm, but seems to have lost sight of their emotional and social needs. However, it's now clear that the mental health of an unacceptable number of children is being unnecessarily compromised, and that this is almost certainly a key factor in the rise of substance abuse, violence and self-harm amongst our young people.*[173]"

Despite all the doom and gloom in this chapter, I don't believe that our children overall have *dramatically* higher mental illness (though depression and anxiety may have worsened somewhat) or that they are beyond redemption. Children are pretty resilient and despite the poisonous culture there are still an awful lot of nice, responsible teenagers around. The following quote sums it up neatly, though with yet another 'epidemic':

"Sadistic video games, lurid rap songs and grotesquely violent movies are everywhere available – even to young children. This debased popular culture may be creating an epidemic of incivility and insensitivity. But there is no evidence of a psychological breakdown described by the child alarmists." Sommers[174]

The hundreds of young people I've dealt with who are abusing parents are not mentally ill but do dramatically show the 'incivility and insensitivity' that these authors mention. They use the phrase *'child alarmists'* to mean those people who are claiming various epidemics of mental health problems. I don't like the sound of being an 'alarmist', but sometimes 'crying wolf' is the only sensible course of action.

After 9/11 the Australian government issued the comical advice that Australians should be 'alert but not alarmed'. We, as parents, certainly need to be alert but I think we actually should be alarmed, as should our politicians. Things are changing so very quickly that no one can possibly foresee how the latest technology or constant changes in popular culture are going to affect the next generation. Is the number of school shootings in America going to continue to rise? (I don't see them doing anything sensible about the number of guns anytime soon)

We can't assume that current trends are going to continue. If they do, then the next generation is going to be even more disrespectful, rebellious, aimless, negative and sexually obsessed and certain types of violence will be even more common, including violence towards parents. I sincerely hope that present trends don't continue but I don't see anyone in power doing anything whatsoever to prevent this happening. Politicians to the right and the left seem to be far more interested in letting big business make profits from us and our children than they are in protecting our children from exploitation.

As I write this, inside me there is a hairy teenager from the 1960s asking if I've just become a grouchy old fogey. I wish it were that simple!

"If we had proper understanding of why society has been so spectacularly successful in making things psychologically worse for children and young people, we might have a better idea as to how we can make things better in the future."
Rutter[175]

Parenting Styles

A major message of this book, and of much of my work, is to challenge parent-blaming. However, this does not mean that parenting is not significant in violence to parents. It's very important, but not in the way that people usually expect.

In order to understand why parent abuse occurs in some families rather than others we need to consider how people parent. Changes in parenting also explain, along with the social changes discussed in the last chapter, why parent abuse has increased greatly in recent decades.

Any attempt to divide people or families into *types* is going to be a simplification and inevitably somewhat artificial. The majority are in the middle on any continuum. The average parent is not significantly high or low on control, compared to the average: that's what average means. This seems blatantly obvious, but you can read a lot of pop psychology that pretends that everyone can be put in a neat box. When we discuss labels you'll see that I'm not keen on pushing people into pigeonholes. This applies to parents as well as individual children.

Parenting is a complicated collection of behaviours, made up of millions of interactions over a number of years. You probably parent different children differently and may vary in style from time to time. You may be soft in some ways and tough in others, affectionate or involved in some ways but not in others. If you have a partner, they will have different parenting styles to each other to some extent. Differences within couples can complement or can clash.

Don't get hung up on which type you are, and remember that parenting type is one *influence* on violence to parents, never *the* cause. It's more likely that certain types of parent are abused by children but it's certainly not impossible for other types.

Having said all that, simplifications are essential if we are going to talk about parenting at all. Most studies identify two main dimensions of parenting[176], though the emphasis varies as do the terms used to describe these dimensions. For violence to parents, the two important dimensions are **control** and **involvement**.

The Control Dimension

The simplest dimension, and quite clearly of relevance to violence to parents, is the amount of control that parents exert (or try to exert) over their children. This varies enormously from family to family, from place to place and time to time.

Overall there has been a trend for parents to be less controlling than the previous generation for the past one hundred and fifty years[177]. Eighteenth and nineteenth century English parents appear to have been particularly high on control, with American parents a little less controlling at that time. The trend for less control has been a long term one. There may have been some slight pendulum swings but the popular idea that each generation rebels against the one before and that things always swing back and forth is largely fantasy. The rate of change speeded up quite dramatically after the Second World War (see section on the history of parenting advice).

There seems to be little argument that parents are overall less controlling now than in previous generations. When I give workshops for either professionals or parents I sometimes ask for a show of hands on whether those present are more or less controlling towards their children than their parents were towards them. Eighty to ninety percent of people say they are less controlling generally than their parents were and of the remainder, half say about the same, so only about one in ten say they are more controlling than their parents were[178].

The first person to discuss these two dimensions of parenting was an American researcher called Diane Baumrind. She talks of parents' 'demandingness' but most of those who have followed have used the simple word 'control.' There is no doubt that we are a lot less demanding than parents were back in the sixties. The word 'demanding' sounds negative, is more often associated with demanding children rather than parents, and it doesn't seem right when what we are *demanding* is basic respect or non-violence. Baumrind clearly saw fairly high control as a good thing, unlike most writers on parenting since then.

'Control' appears simple and self-explanatory, but it isn't really a one-dimensional measure. There are various ways of controlling children, and there is a big difference between using slapping or using persuasion, for example. Parents can be very controlling in some ways but not in others. Though people are far more permissive today about bad language, bad behaviour, toilet training, masturbation, questioning things, religion, manners, etc. they are **less** permissive when it comes to matters of safety. I often meet parents who are wildly over-tolerant about their children being rude and aggressive while at the same time are highly *over-controlling* about the same children taking risks such as playing in the street or climbing trees. As children, my generation had far more freedom in many ways than do today's children. Thus in monitoring children and restricting their movements (or trying to) parents are actually more controlling, which causes conflict and makes children less responsible, but all other ways they are less controlling than earlier generations. This can be seen as an aspect of us being more child-focused. We are not keeping them at home for our sakes (far from it) but for their sakes (often misguidedly in my opinion).

Besides these dramatic changes, over time there are big differences in patterns of control between families, between cultural groups, and even between adjoining neighbourhoods. Some parents are liberal and easy-going about many things but firm and clear about the things that really matter, such as violence and disrespect. Some parents I come across are trying far too hard to control issues such as homework, or who their children associate with, yet are lax about bad behaviour. Parents (and teachers) in the past often turned a blind eye towards violence perpetrated against other children and this is generally taken more seriously nowadays than it was in the past. However, parents in the past took disrespect towards adults far more seriously.

Some of those who write about violence to parents assume that children who are violent to parents are reacting to high control. A few youth workers believe this as it fits with their philosophy. Children who are beyond control or abusive towards parents frequently claim that their parents are too controlling. They may even believe this. Generally they don't want to allow parents to have any control over them, so they may see parents who are actually less controlling than the average as being highly controlling. In a similar way, men who are abusing their partners, and controlling them, often believe that their partners are trying to control them (both the violent men and violent children are operating from a position of high entitlement, as we'll discuss later). It's very seldom the case that parents abused by their children are high on control and most of the children I meet, or hear about, have had modern parents who are relatively low on control (though this does not have to be extreme). For easy children, low control parenting works well, but for difficult children it can backfire badly.

Parents who are low on control, especially control of misbehaviour, respect and imposing expectations of chores and responsibility are more likely to be abused by their children or have children who become beyond control. But this will depend greatly on the characteristics of the individual child and also on the amount of involvement.

The control dimension is easily understood, found consistently in research and articles on parenting styles, and everyone agrees that it's important, though there is little agreement about how much control is ideal. The second dimension is a little more complicated.

The Involvement Dimension

"Parents today spend much more time looking after their children than previous generations. According to a 2006 report from the Future Foundation, the amount has quadrupled in just 25 years, from 25 minutes per day in 1975 to 99 minutes in 2000, and one of the reasons for this is the fear of letting children play unsupervised." Gill [179]

A number of studies have found that parents are spending more time looking after children. This is certainly my experience. Yet many people actually believe that parents are spending *less* time with children, or less 'quality time'.

The second major dimension in parenting described by Diane Baumrind she called 'responsiveness' but it's also called 'support', sometimes 'affection' and sometimes 'attachment' or 'involvement'. I prefer the term 'involvement' as it's hard to imagine parents being over-responsive but easier to imagine parents being over-involved. Also much of what parents do for children is not a *response* to the child but comes from the parents' agenda, even if this is increasingly a child-focused agenda. It's certainly not about 'attachment' and amount of affection varies wildly in different cultures and families and does not appear to be nearly as important as is involvement.

Involvement is less clear than control; it's related both to how much time parents spend with children, what they do for their children, how emotionally close they are, and to how affectionate they are. It's clearly related to child-centeredness and seems to me to be just as important as the control dimension in violence to parents.

Is a parent involved if they are buying their child electronic gadgets (as we almost all do nowadays) so that they are entertained at home rather than going out to play? A common myth is that parents who are 'spoiling' children by buying them stuff are compensating for not being involved in meaningful ways. I do see this pattern in irresponsible access fathers, but it's not a common pattern generally. In fact material indulgence and spending a lot of time with the child often go together as they are both signs of being child-focused. Parents spend *far* more money on their children today than they did in the recent past.

While there is general agreement that parents are less controlling than in the past, there is far more confusion and controversy about how involvement has changed over time.

If you believe the media, there are more neglectful, under-involved parents around, especially mothers, though deadbeat Dads are getting a bit of attention of late. Ironically it has become common for the mass media to blame parents' lack of interest or involvement for a variety of modern problems! The fifties image of a stay-at-home, family-centred, pre-feminist, dutiful mother is contrasted with the wicked, self-centred, career-women or irresponsible, welfare-dependent, sole mothers of today. There are even those that blame the ills of today's children on an epidemic of 'father hunger'.

It's true that there are more women trying to balance the demands of full-time work with family life and men are working a couple of hours longer than a few decades ago. There are more sole parents now than there were a few decades ago. But there were just as many sole parents a century ago as many parents died before their children were grown. Sole parents are not new.

The fifties were a unique decade, the peak for women staying at home and with low divorce. It has given us the model for our 'ideal' family yet the idyllic '50s cornflake-package image of domestic bliss was always an image of middle-class, white America. Lots of mothers worked back then. When they weren't working, they spent more time on household tasks but this was because they didn't have labour-saving gadgets or access to takeaways and pre-packaged food. Stay at home Mums of the '50s and '60s certainly did not spend more time playing with their children, reading to them, or ferrying them around. Playing with children was seen as a rather modern, middle-class idea until fairly recently. When I was a child few parents played with their children. With larger families and far more freedom to escape the family home, we didn't need our parents to play with us and we did not have the expectation that we were going to be entertained by adults or gadgets.

When I was first working with families, back in the '70s, the idea that parents should entertain or educate children was still a middle-class notion but I have seen this attitude spread so that all parents at least pay lip service to these expectations. Parents today are involved in their children's lives in lots of different ways. We possibly have the most child-focused parents ever. Parents now routinely get involved in aspects of their children's lives that were not seen as their responsibility in the past:

- Families are much smaller so individual children get more parental attention overall.

- Parents play more with their children. They stimulate children more from a very early age than parents did in the past. One result of this is that children are brighter than in the past. This may surprise you but in terms of pure IQ there has been a fairly steady increase in children's IQ during the past century. This is seen even before they start school and appears to be due to us generally stimulating our children more. Prior to the Second World War many experts advised parents not to stimulate young children.
- We get involved in our children's schools and education far more than in the past.
- We get involved in our children's social lives, arranging play dates, sleepovers, driving them around. This has become necessary because many children are no longer free to roam and interact with neighbourhood children in the way they used to (and as they still do in non-Western societies).
- Children are more at ease talking to adults and there is less social distance and formality between them and adults. As a child I seldom talked to any adults other than my parents and grandparents and, compared to my generation, today's children are far more confident, articulate and less inhibited. I've seen this change clearly in my counselling over the past few decades.
- Children are seen to have rights and expected to have some say in the family. This is a positive development, but with some negative consequences. It's definitely good that children have more of a voice in their lives, but it's a worry that they now often have a say in such family decisions as buying a car or a TV (according to advertisers, who encourage this).

Overall, parents are undoubtedly more involved, more indulgent, and more child-focused than in the past. Thus we've seen a big increase in the Indulgent Parenting style. This, I believe, is one of the *main* reasons we are seeing more children abusing parents.

The irony of all this is that most of the changes are positive most of the time. Modern, indulgent parenting works well for most children, but you are probably reading this book because you have one of those difficult children for whom it does not work so well. This does not mean you have been a bad parent, been stupid, or have been outrageously over-indulgent. You may have been typical of modern, educated parents but have a child who, for whatever reason, does not respond well to this approach.

Most writers since the last war have encouraged parents to be less controlling **and** more involved. However, you are probably well aware that being low on control causes problems. Everyone acknowledges the fact that *some* parents are too low on control and other parents are too controlling. What is seldom acknowledged is that you can have too much involvement. You can have too much of a good thing in parenting, even if we are talking about responsiveness, stimulation, closeness, even love and affection.

"The expectation of mother-involvement with a child's life has reached a point of absurdity. And I don't believe it is good for either parent or child." Jeffers [180]

With two dimensions it's possible to divide up parents into four general types. This is a useful simplification. By definition most people are average so many parents are actually somewhere in the middle on both dimensions, rather than belonging clearly to one of these four types. So don't worry if this doesn't really fit your type of parenting or you are definite that you haven't been indulgent.

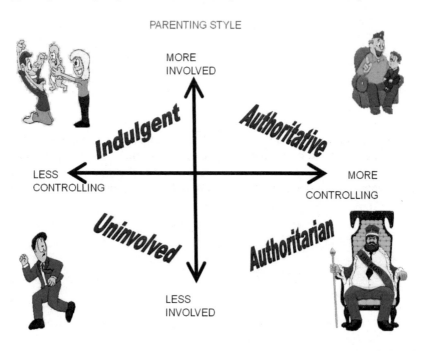

Authoritarian Parenting – strict but distant

Parents high in control but low on involvement are called 'Authoritarian'. These parents are strict and somewhat distant.

By today's standards most parents throughout history were Authoritarian, and this is still true for the majority of parents in the non-Western world. Children are expected to show respect to elders, to obey parents without question, and much of the time to occupy and entertain themselves without troubling adults, or work with or for the parents. Instead of parents acting like children's servants, as is the case today, children were expected to serve their parents. Children were seen but not heard. In the past parents were often dictators; fathers had supreme power in the family, though mothers often ruled within the home. Some were benevolent despots but some were power-mad or cruel dictators. Relations between parent and child were usually more formal (especially with fathers).

Child abuse appears to have been more common in the past than it is now. Commentators in recent years often portray Authoritarian parents as if they are all borderline child abusers, if not actual abusers. It's rather hard to reconcile the view of Authoritarian parenting as being all-bad and seriously damaging to development with the fact that, by our standards, almost everyone in history was brought up that way, including people like Da Vinci, Dickens, Gandhi, Galileo, Churchill, and probably Christ and Buddha. The fact is that the effect of parenting style depends not only on the child in question but on the society in which the parenting takes place. An example is that our children are emotionally affected by physical punishment quite differently to those in societies where it's the norm. If almost everyone is being beaten, it still hurts but it isn't a sign of rejection.

In more traditional societies, compared to ours, parents can be stricter and also more distant from their children without serious ill effects because they share the parenting role with a whole village or tribe. Other adults will not hesitate to pull unruly children into line but will also help them if necessary. Older children and aunts, uncles and grandparents lend a hand with bringing up children and the wider culture is usually pulling in the same direction as the parents, not pulling against them as it does in Western society today. Parenting is shared, not the exclusive burden of one or two parents.

It's interesting that while the experts demonise authoritarian parenting methods, there are examples even within Western societies of immigrant groups whose children have better academic results, better mental health and better behaviour than Anglo children despite their parents using more traditional parenting methods. Diane Baumrind found that Black Ghetto children in America seemed to do better with more Authoritarian parents[181] – in that context more control is needed than in middle class America. Another US study found that authoritarian parenting had a negative effect on white youth but not on Hispanic and Asian.[182]

I see very few authoritarian parents who are abused by their children. It happens, but it's rare and I can confidently say that authoritarian parenting is *not* a risk factor for child to parent violence. When it does play a part it's often because one parent has been authoritarian while the other is indulgent. It's usually the indulgent parent who is abused by the child but a few of these children also abuse the authoritarian parent. These children are likely to be seen by workers as reacting to the controlling parent, but in fact they are reacting to the parents undermining each other, and usually abuse the less controlling, less authoritarian, parent more than the other one.

When most psychologists write about authoritarian parents it's all about how they mess up their kids. For example, "*In adolescence their homes can become war zones as rebellious teens are severely penalized for engaging in the kinds of healthy risk taking that are not sanctioned by authoritarian parents... many children from authoritarian homes, while reasonably conforming and obedient, have low self-esteem, poor social skills, and high rates of depression.*[183]" So why do Western societies have higher rates of most of these problems than do traditional societies? The above quote is actually from an interesting book arguing that affluent kids in America have more emotional problems than less-affluent kids, which is ironic as upper-class parents are overall less authoritarian than poorer parents.

115

I'm certainly not suggesting we should return to authoritarian parenting, but it's unfair and inaccurate to suggest that it's inherently harmful to kids or that we in the West have discovered the secret of good parenting, while everyone else are parenting failures.

"We know the kind of parenting style we are running from – parents who didn't spare the rod or worry about our emotional lives – but we are not quite so sure of what to put in its place" Small[184]

Authoritative parenting – close but firm

It's confusing that this term sounds so similar to the better known term 'Authoritarian' but I haven't found a good alternative[185]. It's no coincidence that it sounds much more positive than the others. This has been held up as the ideal by almost all writers on parenting over the past sixty years. However, many writers use Baumrind's terms but subtly alter the meaning, giving it a quite different emphasis. She has made it clear in some of her subsequent writing that she is keen that parents are in control. She would even consider parents to be authoritative who use a certain amount of physical punishment to control their children[186]. This would be anathema to many parenting experts and professionals who assume anyone using such methods must be Authoritarian, if not abusive. They use her terminology but they play down the need for control. I've even heard the terms Permissive, Authoritative and Authoritarian used as if they were on a continuum of control with Authoritative parents being in the middle rather than being high on control.

Most research on parenting styles concludes that children of Authoritative parents do better on average in school achievement, social competence, self-esteem, mental health and have less behaviour problems. Even when I first read of this research, over thirty years ago, I wondered if this was not mainly a description of stable, middle-class families with intelligent parents. If so, it would be expected that their children do well in our society for all sorts of reasons, not just because of parenting style.

Although on average, in our society, this style of parenting appears to be the most effective for the majority of children there may be some children who it doesn't suit. There is no guarantee that parents won't be abused by their children, or that children won't have other problems, even if they are model parents doing everything according to the book, but being an assertive, caring parent greatly reduces the chances of all sorts of behavioural problems.

Which type of parenting works best is going to depend partly on wider society and culture and also on the characteristics of the child; some children probably do best with low controlling, highly involved parents and a few may do best with Authoritarian parents. Though it's hard to imagine there may even be a few unusual children who thrive with uninvolved parents.

Uninvolved parenting – distant and permissive

The extremes in the other three types of parenting are rare. Sadly, the extreme of the uninvolved parent is not so rare. The ultimate is a totally absent parent, usually (probably nine times out of ten) a missing father rather than mother. It's also not rare (though less common than in the past) for a father (or step-father) to live with children but leave almost all of the parenting up to the mother. Some children do OK with one uninvolved parent, provided the other fills the gaps, but two such parents, or an uninvolved sole parent, are usually disastrous.

While Indulgent parents are also permissive they are close (occasionally too close and over-involved) and caring. Uninvolved parents are not only permissive but neglectful. They may be uncaring but some are caring but irresponsible (or caring and stupid). Some fathers, especially non-resident fathers, love their children but don't really act as parents. One type of uninvolved parent is one who is purely friend and playmate but doesn't try to control or act as a parent in other ways. Thus they may be close and involved in some ways (playing sports or video games, talking to them), and loving in some ways, but not really adopting a full *parental* role. They play with the children (especially with boys if they have similar interests to him) but don't do the harder parenting tasks like nurturing and controlling. As an access parent this may not do much harm but if they are the custodial parent, this can be highly problematic. I've seen teenage children move to such a parent for the fun and freedom but they don't get support educationally and may get into drinking, drugs or delinquency since they lack parental guidance.

Neglectful parents have children with the most problems overall, who are least competent socially and academically, and with the highest rates of anti-social behaviour[187]. Some young people with the most serious, and long-lasting, problems came from homes where there was neglect rather than active abuse. However, although they may be violent outside the home, or violent towards foster carers, aggression towards the neglectful parent is *not* very common. These children don't tend to be highly entitled. Another reason is that if you don't attempt to control a young person there will be a lot less conflict because you don't get in their way. These children may also not feel secure enough to abuse their neglectful parent. They may be desperate for signs of love and caring from their uninvolved parent and they may realize that if they show outright aggression this would lead to complete rejection. I've several times seen young people go to live with uninvolved fathers who then kicked them out (usually back to Mum) the very first time they become aggressive.

Indulgent parenting – close but soft

"Today many children are treated like near equals, possessing rights and privileges beyond those of previous generations. Many parents are actually scared of their kids, and often the children set the rules for the entire household."
Gosman[188]

In the past I sometimes used the term 'democratic' for this type (as have others) but I found that this sounded too positive and hence confused people. Other writers sometimes call them 'permissive' but this doesn't differentiate them from the disengaged/neglectful type of permissive and 'indulgent' therefore appears to be the most appropriate. They are very different to neglectful parents and may not be permissive about everything (they are often over-protective, for example).

Though low on control overall they are usually caring and may be highly child-focused (unlike neglectful parents). Unfortunately, quite a few writers and researchers lump together all those parents who are low on control, combining uninvolved/neglectful with indulgent (hence only having three categories[189]). When they do look at indulgent parents as a separate category, most writers paint a pained and problematic picture. But the reality is that this form of parenting is positive for many children. Overall young people who identify their parents as Indulgent (but this does not mean they really were indulgent), are found to be somewhat more likely to use drugs and to be less engaged in school, but they are highly socially competent, have high self-esteem and are not often into serious delinquency[190]. In my experience, this form of parenting is great for children with easy temperaments and usually works out OK with the majority. It goes badly wrong with stubborn, egotistical, fearless kids (see section on personality) but can also be a problem for some nervous, introverted children who do better with more structure.

When I've given media interviews they often try to get me to use the word 'spoiled.' I resist this for several reasons. One is that when people talk of a child being *spoiled* their emphasis is usually on material over-indulgence. This can be a factor when children abuse parents, but it's not nearly as important as giving children time and attention, and doing things for them and with them. Talk of 'spoiling' also makes people think that Indulgent parents are silly softies who buy their children everything. This is certainly not the case. Many of these Indulgent parents are too intelligent and well-meaning to materially spoil their children. Indulgence in time and attention has been strongly encouraged over the past fifty years by many parent gurus but it can backfire horribly.

"I hate you Dad! All you've ever
done is throw your time and love
at me - you've never given me
enough money!"

A common comment I hear from parents is that, with the gift of hindsight, they tried too hard to be a friend to their children. Being friendly is fine but you can't perform the role of parent and be a friend at the same time. This is rather like my role as a counsellor. I'm sure the majority of my clients would agree that I'm *friendly* but the role of counsellor is not compatible with being their friend. Same goes for the role of parent. Being friendly in the role of parent is not the same as being their friend.

"Children of permissive parents tend to be likable, social, and to enjoy high self-esteem. On the other hand, they tend to be impulsive, immature, and to have difficulty understanding the consequences of their actions. These children tend to be manipulative and have lower rates of academic achievement and higher rates of substance abuse than children from either authoritarian or authoritative homes."
Levine[191]

Though using the term 'permissive' in this quote, Levine is obviously not talking about Neglectful parents but about Indulgent ones. Her description of the children sounds just like a lot of the young people I see who are abusing parents.

Hugh Mackay suggests that modern parents might *"wonder whether they might have indulged their children's wishes to a point which led the children to cling to that most fundamental belief of infancy – the belief that we are each the centre of our own little universe."* Mackay[192]

Here's another quote from Hugh Mackay (a very sensible Australian commentator) who sums it up nicely, *"The Boomers seem able to worry, simultaneously, about their over-parenting and the lack of time they are able to devote to their children. They say they only wanted their children to be happy, yet they admit that they probably put them under too much pressure. They wish their children were not so materialistic, yet they find themselves overindulging them."*[193]

I'm stressing that these categories are simplifications and some parents may be permissive about some things more than others. For the impact on violence to parents, it's a tolerant attitude towards aggression and disrespect that matters most of all.

"If the primary caretaker is generally permissive and 'tolerant' without setting clear limits to aggressive behaviour toward peers, siblings, and adults, the child's aggression level is likely to increase." Olweus[194]

The two dimensions of control and involvement interact in important ways. A study by Robert Hinde looked at British mothers and their four-year-olds. They watched the mothers with their children and also observed the children in pre-school. They measured extent of control and extent of mother's warmth toward the child. They did not find a relationship between either of the two dimensions and the children's behaviour. Neither how controlling they were at home or how involved and affectionate they were predicted how their child behaved in pre-school. However, there was an interesting interaction between the two measures. Mothers who combined *moderate* levels of warmth with *moderate* control had children who were the least aggressive[195]. So too much of either warmth or control, or too little, could increase some children's aggression.

Referring back to the diagram of parenting styles, the risk for violence to parents is greatest at the top left, low control but high involvement. Parents have generally moved in that direction and so more parents are at risk than in the past.

Over-parenting and being Child-focused

Children today may be said to be **over-parented**, not just over-indulged. Over-parenting includes indulgence in time, attention and materials, but also excessive monitoring, excessive emotional closeness and over-protection. Too much of a good thing!

"Over-parenting isn't just bad for kids – it has terrible effects on adults. The disproportionate investment of parental emotions, finances, and time in one's children erodes marital bonds and contributes to a continuing high divorce rate."
Marano[196]

Overall it's positive that *as a society* we are more child-focused than in the past, and a certain degree of child-focus in families is also a good thing. All families should be child-*friendly* but I do not believe that any family should have its *main* focus on the children. This will sound like total heresy to some people.

If a family revolves around the child or children to a great extent, then this is unfair to the adults. The parents may well become dissatisfied and stressed (as a great many are nowadays). Since both parents are seldom equally happy, or equally unhappy, with such a lopsided arrangement this puts pressure on their relationship (possibly leading to divorce). Some children in such families will increase their demands on the parent-servant and they often feel *more* dissatisfied than do children in traditional families. I'm in favour of more equality between parent and child than was the case in traditional families. However, it isn't really treating children as equals when we are excessively child-focused; it's making them our masters. This is not good for them or us.

*"The balanced perspective of authoritative parents is neither exclusively child-centred nor exclusively parent-centred but, instead, seeks to integrate the needs of the child with other family members, treating the rights and responsibilities of children and those of parents as complementary rather than as identical.[197]"*Baumrind

Hugh Mackay talks about the *'Little Emperor'* syndrome, where everything revolves around the whims of a precious child. He points out that one reason for over-parenting and over-indulgence is that we are having fewer children. They are individually more important and valuable to us[198]. Modern life is full of mixed blessings!

Intensive Mothering

Several writers have identified what has been called 'intensive parenting'[199]. This centres on a set of beliefs that are not only modern but until recently were mainly middle class[200]. These mothers believe strongly that parenting should be child-centred, that mothers are inherently better parents than fathers, that parenting is very difficult and demanding, that children need a lot of intellectual stimulation and that parents need expert advice on how to parent. Parents are spending more time interacting with their children despite many of them working longer hours. Such mothers usually fall within the indulgent parenting category and such beliefs would be very common among parents I have worked with who are abused by their children. Some research suggests that such beliefs are associated with stress, depression and lower satisfaction among mothers, which makes sense as such high ideals lead to disappointment and such high demands lead to exhaustion. [201]

Fathers still don't do nearly as much parenting as mothers but they have narrowed the gap in recent years and overall are more child-focused than they were in the past[202]. There still aren't many who would fit the phrase 'intensive fathering', except for a few sole fathers (sole fathers have generally been found to resemble mothers in their parenting).

Parenting Style Changes with Circumstances

"Research has identified links between 'permissive' parenting styles and higher levels of parent abuse (Paulson et al 1990) ... However, it may be a response to a child's difficult or violent behaviour, rather than a cause of it. Indeed, it is very difficult to parent a child authoritatively while feeling intimidated and fearful of them." Holt[203]

We've acknowledged that any classification of parenting style is a simplification. Parents usually vary their style as children mature and may vary between children. Professionals often jump to conclusions. They see a parent who is struggling very hard to discipline a wild teen and assume that this is their typical parenting style when they may be desperately trying to regain control, appearing more controlling than is their preferred style. Other parents react to a particularly difficult child, especially beyond-control teens, by becoming more passive, withdrawing from the field of battle or by becoming more indulgent than usual.

"I was told [by a psychologist] that he was crying out for attention. So I gave him a lot more attention and special treatment. I spent time alone with him leaving the other children out of it. This all seemed to make him worse." Mother of a violent 12-year-old.

I would encourage professionals (and researchers) to take into account how other children in the family are parented before drawing *any* conclusions about parenting style. Unfortunately, prejudice is so strong that when most professionals see that the 'problem child' in the family is treated quite differently to the other children, they then assume that this is *why* he is a problem, rather than assuming that parents are reacting to the 'problem child's' behaviour. I've often heard it suggested that the difficult child is being *scapegoated* within the family (when he's just acting the goat).

Equality in Families and children's rights

Children did not have any rights within the family until quite recently. If you are a parent being bullied by a child, you may view the development of children's rights as wholly negative, but it's great that children do now have rights. They are not our property and we have no right to abuse them, as happened all too often in the past.

It's hard for us to comprehend just how badly children were treated in the recent past. In the UK it wasn't until 1833 that it became illegal to make children under nine work full time. One survey in the late 18th century in America found that 100% of children were hit with a whip or stick, and worse punishments were not uncommon. In New York in 1874, neighbours were moved by the plight of a ten-year-old adoptive girl, Mary Ellen, who was being badly beaten. When they tried to get the authorities to take action they discovered that there was no legislation to protect children so they had to use the law designed to prevent brutality to animals. They had to argue that Mary Ellen deserved protection as 'a human animal'. The same happened in England where the Royal Society for the Prevention of Cruelty to *Animals* was used to protect abused children and the National Society for the Prevention of Cruelty to Children developed from the animal organisation.

There are those who say that children should have *the same* rights as adults. For instance, the influential John Holt, a guru of home schooling, argued in the 1970s that children of 'all ages' should have rights including the right to work, vote, have sex, take drugs and choose their guardian.[204]. Aside from such extreme views, the idea that children should have the same rights as adults is a worry when we look at the rights to self-abuse and gross stupidity that we adults enjoy. Few people think that two-year-olds have the right to stay up all night or that four-year-olds have the right to wander the streets, or that eight-year-olds have the right to drink and smoke, have sex and get piercings and tattoos. Some ten- year-old boys would decide that washing is for wimps and choose to remain dirty and smelly. As an adult I have that right (my wife, friends and clients would, of course, have the right to leave me) but does anyone really believe that children should have such rights?

I'd like to see us get to the stage where all physical punishment of children could be a thing of the past but it will always be necessary to restrain young children, and move them around, against their wishes. This would be counted as violence in adults so if children truly had equal rights, you could not put your three-year-old to bed unless they agree. If you force a non-disabled eighteen-year-old to have a shower or a haircut against his wishes, this would be an act of violence and a clear breach of his rights. But we force eight-year-olds to shower or get haircuts without considering this to be breaching civil rights.

There are those who argue that men and women are fundamentally different and so equality between the sexes is impossible. I don't buy this at all. There are definite statistical differences between men and women but we are not different species or from different planets. On the other hand when it comes to adults and pre-adolescent children, we really are quite different creatures. They are dependent on us and we should be a lot more capable of being sensible and making long-term plans. Admittedly a minority of adults aren't. I had a twelve-year-old girl tell me quite seriously, and apparently accurately, "Let's face it, I'm more mature than either of my parents." But despite a few exceptions, most early adolescents (especially in our society) are not capable of making sensible decisions about their welfare and long-term future. Many of them would choose not to attend school if it was really up to them. It's odd that very few of those who are opposed to parents having power over children are opposed to compulsory schooling, a huge infringement of rights – yet a necessary and sensible one.

We have responsibilities to make some decisions for our children and at times to force our will upon them for their own good. True equality between an adult and a dependent child is not possible. With a man and a woman equality is the ideal which we should be aiming for. With a parent and child equality is **not** the ideal. That does not mean that a move towards more equality is necessarily a bad thing or that parents should be tyrants. There is a happy medium. But where this happy medium lies will vary for different children and changes greatly as they mature.

Children having rights is *only* a problem when they are given adult rights or when they don't respect your rights. In recent years I have seen children actually voicing the opinion that they should have the same rights as their parents; that it's unfair if their parents have more money to spend than them or even suggesting (as one little girl did recently) that if it's legal for parents to slap children then it must be OK for children to slap parents (her parents don't slap her but have grabbed her when she is attacking someone, she counts this as abuse).

The attempt to create equality can create inequality by putting the child in control, which brings us to the idea of the Democratic family. This can be brief as by now you can pretty much guess what I'm going to say.

The Democratic Family

There is no such thing as a truly democratic family, at least if the family contains any dependent children.

A family should be a benevolent dictatorship. In two parent families it should be a 'duocracy', with parents ruling together as equals. It can only very rarely function as a democracy. Every individual would have to be responsible and mature enough to not put themselves or others at any kind of risk, which generally means they are all grown up (although lots of young adults do not fulfil these criteria). Without a leader, or leaders, you either have anarchy or one of the children will fill the vacant leadership role and you get a belligerent, chaotic dictatorship.

So the attempt to create a democratic family often results in either anarchy or a teen tyrant. Some families even elevate a toddler tyrant.

If parents are following the advice of the experts why aren't we seeing the benefits?

Many of those who place so much importance on parenting have been pushing for parents to be less strict, more child-focused and to hit children less. They have blamed old-fashioned parenting practices for a whole host of children's (and society's) problems. There is no doubt that there are less authoritarian parents around and absolutely no doubt that we hit our children *a lot less* than did previous generations.

So if parenting is so all-important in children's development surely we should be seeing a big improvement in children's mental health and behaviour. On the contrary, many people believe that children's mental health has got worse and children are no better behaved than in the past.

Something doesn't add up!

Either:

a) the type of parenting pushed by the experts for the last fifty years is not as straightforwardly beneficial as it has been made out to be,

or

b) parenting isn't as all-important as they claim.

My experience and studies have forced me to conclude that both of the above statements are true. Parenting is certainly important, but not overwhelmingly important, in determining how children turn out and modern democratic, indulgent parenting works very well for some children but is a dismal failure for others. Child-centred parenting is definitely not the panacea that parenting pundits have proposed!

If you agree with the above discussion, you will probably be thinking about how it applies to you and your family. If you have been a modern, indulgent, child-centred parent, do **not** feel guilty about this, and certainly don't imagine that you can now solve your child's problems by going to the other extreme. You may need to become less indulgent, and less child-focused, but becoming authoritarian is not the answer – your child will never accept this and it probably wouldn't suit you anyway. It's quite likely to make things worse.

We simply can't go back to the way our parents parented us. We are in a different cultural context and even if we are comfortable with authoritarian parenting our children won't be.

Box

Dear Eddie,

I sit here in front of the computer reading your articles for the first time, in tears and with a black eye from my daughter's latest outburst. As I read I feel as though you have been living in my house the past years (so many I can't remember). My son aged thirteen and my daughter aged fifteen are all of the young people you describe. They are in every category: victims of domestic violence, under-responsible, over-entitled and living with a parent who is no more than a slave.

You have described exactly how I have parented up until now: I am the text book democratic parent. I treated my children as little adults from the time they were tiny, always explaining my decisions, giving opportunities to negotiate and have given them way too much input into decision making. They have always been able to voice an opinion, even in situations where they shouldn't have been involved (I know that now). My Mum says I have been too good to these children, losing my own identity in the process.

My house is an area of mass destruction not a sanctuary from the outside world. My everyday life is a battle of Iraqi proportions. I am living in a dictatorship where I have had no power at all. I have enabled my children to become tyrants, covering for them and bailing them out of trouble while they abuse me every day. I drive them to soccer, pick them up from school, take them and their friend to the beach, and provide all the finances to maintain their above average lifestyle – the clothes, new surfboards, the latest and greatest of everything. I ask myself 'why?' most days. Is it that I have surrendered and it's just easier to take it, or do I actually believe that I am getting what I deserve (as they constantly tell me)? I have no idea how the last seventeen years have led me here! To the outside world I have a responsible job working with children, I am actively involved in my community, an activist for children's rights to services, and appear to be perfectly sane. Yet I live in chaos that, now that I write it down, seems unbelievable even to me. I have taken today off work as it was all just a bit hard to deal with. I will sit and read your articles over and over again as I am having a window of clarity and need to find an end to the chaos that has become my existence. I don't know if this will even reach you, if it does, great, if not it has still served as the very first time I have acknowledged to anyone the hidden battles I have faced every day for the past long years. Hopefully it will be therapeutic and empowering as I have nowhere to go but up from here. Thank you for listening,

Eleanor

Sent the next morning:

I am amazed how good it has made me feel that the world hasn't come to an end by talking about this problem. I awoke this morning with a feeling of power and the belief that things can change. After my e-mail to you I have also let my family know what has been going on in my life all these years as up until now, they have been getting the edited, glossed over, 'things are OK' version of events. I am hoping that the removal of the unspoken veil of secrecy that has protected everyone from the outside world knowing what goes on behind closed doors, may just tip the balance of power in my favour. In the past twenty-four hours all my siblings have phoned to offer support even though they are geographically removed, they are in shock as to what has been going on.

Regards, Eleanor

End Box

Over-Protection

"By any yardstick, we are raising the most wired, pampered and monitored generation in history..." Honoré[205]

"The generation of young people now coming of age is extraordinarily endowed in material terms – but unusually experience deprived." Marano[206]

In recent years there have been a number of books claiming that parental over-protection is a serious and increasing issue: *"Too safe for their own good," "Free Range Kids," "Paranoid Parenting," "Anxious Parenting,"* to name but a few. Some see over-protection as one aspect of over-parenting generally, of parents being too indulgent and too involved in their children's lives. Others focus just on parents' fearfulness and inability to let children take risks. Despite this new awareness of over-protection, there seems to be no overall change in the trend for more and more protection and greater monitoring of children and young people. So it's important to consider what effect these dramatic social changes might be having on our children.

There have always been over-protective parents. Professionals have long been concerned about a small group of over-protective, neurotic mothers (the focus always on mothers), who were blamed for causing emotional and behavioural problems in children[207]. Overprotective mothers have featured in the psychiatric arsenal of pat explanations for all sorts of problems. 'Over-protection' is often bandied about in such a vague way that it's part of a pattern of blaming parents whatever they do: if you are not monitoring you are neglectful but if you do monitor you are over-protective.

What was a small, deviant group of parents fifty years ago has become the norm in Western society. We now have an entire generation of 'cotton-wool kids' and a vast fleet of 'helicopter parents' who hover over their children (making a lot of noise and ready to rescue them at a moment's notice). The newly wired generation is not only regularly rescued from serious threats (which is a good thing) but also rescued from life's little problems, which is a problem. Children, particularly pre-teens, are given **far** less freedom than in any previous generation (with the exception of children who were working from an early age in the dark days of child labour). The changes have been fast and dramatic.

"Forty years ago, the majority of U.S. children walked or biked to school. Today, about 10% do. Meantime, 70% of today's moms say they played outside as kids. But only 31% of their kids do. The children have been sucked off America's lawns like yard trimmings." Skenazy[208]

126

"The average distance from home British kids are permitted to wander by themselves has fallen nearly 90% since the 1970s." Honoré[209]

Over-protectiveness is an important part of the pattern of Intensive Parenting, which often appears to be involved with child to parent violence.

It's not just parents who have become cautious and risk-averse but society in general. Schools reinforce parental over-protection and routinely expect parents to be instantly available to take over whenever there are problems with their children, behavioural, emotional or minor medical. This puts pressure on parents. Schools have become dramatically more protective and risk-averse than in the past, as have organizations such as the Scouts.

"A culture of risk aversion has encroached into every aspect of children's lives – in school, in social play, in children's clubs and adventure trips and in the wider public realm. Some of this is a consequence of changes in the wider world. Curiously, however, the more obvious threats to children's safety – notably that from road traffic – are not treated with anything like the same degree of obsessive control." Gill[210]

Is the World less safe?

Although parents are aware of being more protective than were their parents, most firmly believe this is justified by modern life being more dangerous[211]. This widespread belief is largely myth. There is no more crime in most areas than in previous generations and most other threats have actually decreased.

"Childhood independence has become taboo, even though our world is no less safe than it was 20 or 30 years ago. The ground has not gradually gotten harder under the jungle gym. The bus stops have not crept further from home. Crime is actually lower than it was when most of us were growing up. So there is no reality-based reason that children today should be treated as more helpless and vulnerable than we were when we were young." Skenazy[212]

"Try as we may, we just can't find much evidence that our kids are more at risk today than a generation ago. Instead, we are seeing what is called 'up-criming,' a phenomenon where our children are more likely than ever before to be charged and tried for adult offences that would have been seen as nothing more than children misbehaving 20 years ago." Ungar[213]

Many people believe we are living in an increasingly violent world even though the evidence suggests the opposite[214]. Although crime statistics have gone up and down over the past few decades, people are (in most places), more likely to report to the police than in the past. In fact, it may be that the safer the environment the more minor crime is actually recorded. I continually hear of schools or parents reporting to the police assaults or damage which twenty years ago they would not have considered nearly serious enough to involve the legal system with. Yet despite this, crime statistics have gone down in many places. Taking reporting into account, it seems highly likely that the real amount of violent crime has decreased overall rather than increased. The media only report unusual events, so when assaults, or even murders, are very common they are not newsworthy. We can thus get the impression of the world being less safe when it's actually safer.

What people fear is not usually logical statistically. Children are most at risk of being hurt or dying in the family car and in the home. Although we are all aware of 'stranger danger' our children are more at risk from people they know rather than strangers. There may be only two or three children a year in your city kidnapped and raped by strangers but this is understandably far scarier than the idea that our child may be hurt or killed in our car, even though this is a hundred times more likely. I'm shocked that many parents let pre-adolescents ride motorbikes, which is definitely dangerous. Even more parents encourage their children to play contact sports where the risk of injury and assault is high, yet they won't let them walk to the local shopping centre where the risk of being assaulted or injured is extremely low. Our children are safer in terms of accidents and health than in the past, so that overall they are the safest generation ever. This has made them more precious and, ironically, made us more risk averse.

Throughout history, and to this day in many non-Western societies, children are given responsibilities from an early age (it's common for six to ten-year-olds to have responsibility for babies and toddlers for example) and what we call adolescents were in the past generally expected to be responsible and productive members of society. Our children are often given no responsibility for anything, not even for themselves, until they are almost fully grown. No one wants to go back to the days of child labour but the example of the past and of other cultures clearly shows that young people are developmentally capable of being far more responsible than we now expect them to be.

Since the world is no more dangerous than in the recent past, and actually far *less* dangerous than it was a century or more ago, are our children less capable than in the past? Yes and no. Our children are physically taller and, as they are healthier and reaching puberty earlier, they are physically stronger than previous generations of the same age (though more are obese). Children are brighter in terms of IQ and are, in many ways, more worldly wise than previous generations. Our children are slightly less likely to be sexually abused because they have far more awareness of what it means than did recent generations. Instead, they now put *themselves* at risk around puberty by a heightened interest in sex, a desire to experiment and a craving for excitement. Ironically, the *only* way in which they are less capable is that they have been over-protected, because we treat them as less capable. Since we expect them to be irresponsible and untrustworthy it's not surprising that more of them meet these expectations. Our lowered expectations of maturity may be another factor contributing to some children showing little or no self-control.

Over-protectiveness can give them power

One of the things that give modern children power over their parents is parental protectiveness. If a child of twelve is throwing a tantrum in the shopping centre, a logical consequence would be for the parent to leave them to make their own way home, possibly giving them bus fare if it's more than an hour's walk. Few parents today are willing to take this risk, even though in most areas in day time the risk is minuscule. So I regularly hear of parents, often with other children in tow, waiting impatiently until their little tyrant has calmed down and deigns to let them give him a lift home. He may continue to verbally abuse his mother in the car, kick the back of her seat while she is driving and punch his little sister. The mother is too afraid to drop him off at the side of the road. The risk in a parent's car for a child who is out-of-control, and who may hit the driver or open the door, must be many thousands of times greater than the risk of them walking home.

I have heard parents in this position say they would like to make the child walk home but will be accused of neglect by the other parent, by grand-parents, or by the authorities. I'm not talking about toddlers here but twelve- year-olds, who should be perfectly capable of using public transport and walking a few miles. A few children who are not afraid of teachers or embarrassment also exert control in school, or on excursions, using similar tactics.

This is just one factor giving children increased power and obviously best against responsible modern parents. Parents who are highly conscientious, with children who are low in this trait, are going to be more affected by this than a less conscientious parent. A highly conscientious, responsible child does not wield this type of power. This ties in with parenting style, and also with the child's personality and to our discussion of power and of entitlement in coming chapters.

Overprotection and Entitlement and Responsibility

Over-protectiveness goes hand in hand with lack of responsibility for many young people. Over-protectiveness is associated with low expectations and infantilisation of adolescents and is often (though not always) associated with an indulgent parenting style. Both lack of responsibility and high entitlement are factors in parent abuse, and they are a particularly bad combination, as we shall see. So although over-protectiveness, in itself, does not cause parent abuse it's not uncommon for them to go together. Additionally, over-protectiveness can be a complicating factor when children are violent in the home or beyond control. Parents are less likely to be assertive because they are so protective and excessive protectiveness gives children additional power.

Monitoring

"Childhood under the constant gaze of adults is a new and growing phenomenon."
Marano[215]

Groups of young people 'hanging around' shopping centres, parks and roaming the streets cause alarm in a way that they did not in the past. Those families where parents don't appear to care what the young people get up to are a highly noticeable minority, more visible now that most parents attempt to monitor their teenagers' movements and keep track of them. Some parents are trying hard to keep track of their children but failing miserably, because the reality is that you can only easily monitor a cooperative child.

It's ironic that for many years it has been stated as a matter of faith that parental supervision helps prevent delinquency, drug taking and early sex. In fact there was never any good evidence for this idea. Parents with good kids find it easy to monitor them and naturally these families have fewer problems, creating reliable correlations between monitoring and low behaviour problems. But this does not mean that increasing the amount of monitoring is going to decrease problems, it can sometimes increase problems. As we've mentioned, the advent of mobile phones has *greatly* increased monitoring for the majority of young people recently but has made no apparent difference to the amount of delinquency, while drug abuse, drinking and precocious sex appear to have grown *somewhat* worse.

"Cell phones keep young people tied to their parents – relying on them for advice, decision making, problem solving, emotional comfort, and sometimes much more – when they should be making their own moves toward independence." Marano[216]

Mobile phones can be very useful and in theory they *could* have made young people more independent, but this does not appear to have happened. Instead, having parents continually on-call has made some young people less responsible. I don't think the new expectation that parents should know exactly where teenagers are and what they are doing every minute of the day is at all healthy. This expectation causes stress more often than it reassures and in many families, it's often is a focus of conflict between parents and youth.

Some adolescents rebel against this stifling form of control but more start to rely on parents to help them out at short notice. This, though sometimes positive, can even lead to some young people taking *more* risks since they expect parents to bail them out of tricky situations when summoned.

Children are spending far more time within the home than in the past. This is partly due to parental paranoia but also due to the entertainment value of electronics. Parents don't let children go out but pre-teen children are accepting this imprisonment with good grace because they have TV, DVDs, computers and a host of electronic gadgets to entertain them. Children are growing up with the expectation that they will be entertained, either by an adult or by a gadget.

Protectiveness and Media Culture

"Night after night, a vision of the world comes into our living rooms and our lives that is sad, sadistic, and totally at odds with the odds." Skenazy[217]

At the same time that our children are being deprived of real-life adventures and experiences, they are being saturated with media coverage of violence, sex, drama, death and the dark side of life. The cartoons, movies, games and books aimed at entertaining them have become more sinister, disturbing and 'adult'. Violence is the most obvious aspect of this but themes of cruelty, despair, madness, suicide and nihilism all add to the world seeming a lot more scary and threatening.

Media, culture, and other influences mean that our children are growing up quicker in some (largely unhealthy) ways while growing up far slower in terms of taking responsibility and being independent. This produces some children who think they know it all, while actually being less emotionally mature and less responsible than previous generations. This is a recipe for disaster! It's perhaps surprising that the majority of our young people are actually doing fine psychologically. However, there is a concerning, and possibly growing, minority of adolescents, and sometimes pre-adolescents, who are depressed, anxious, aimless, sexually precocious, abusing drugs and alcohol, self-harming and prone to suicidal thoughts and threats. The influence of parents has declined as youth culture shaped by and bolstered by commercial media, has become more powerful. Parents are still usually the single (or double) most important influence but they do not (and never did if they are relatively normal) outweigh all the other influences on children's development[218].

This media saturation with the dark side of life is a large part of the reason why parents have become more protective. Both parents and children now see the world as a nasty, dangerous place and see other adults as potential risks rather than as supports or role models. Perhaps it's inevitable when we put such stress on 'stranger danger' that our children will lose respect for adults in general. Is it logical for us to tell children to be afraid of all adults they don't know, yet have respect for adults in general?

Sanitised childhood

"Behold the wholly sanitized childhood, without skinned knees or the occasional C in history! Kids need to learn that you need to feel bad sometimes. We learn especially through bad experiences. Through disappointment and failure we learn how to cope. We learn what we can cope with. It motivates us to change or do better. And we seem to learn more about things through failure than any other way." Marano[219]

Today's children spend far more time around adults than did previous generations. This has created a historically unique situation as children have not usually lived their lives under constant adult supervision. In most societies, children spent much of their day in mixed age groups (older children often baby-sitting the younger ones) roaming around the village or neighbourhood or working in the fields. Our children are now seldom out of sight of an adult.

This change is not all bad; children are brighter and more confident than in the past and the number of fatal accidents has gone down dramatically. However, diabetes, obesity and lack of exercise are frequent downsides to life under adult scrutiny because for many this means a life indoors with little exercise. Health effects of this lifestyle, e.g. obesity and vitamin D deficiency, are on the increase and likely to get worse due to lethargy, diet and lack of sunshine.

Vulnerability

"After literally a lifetime of overprotection, these young adults are overwhelmed by sudden independence. ...take them out of the china cabinet and they break." Skenazy[220]

Children who grow up in today's over-protective environments do not all react the same way. Some survive just fine, a few rebel against intrusive parenting in adolescence, but most are made more psychologically vulnerable than they would have been in previous generations. Parents often comment in my counselling practice that their children can't cope with the real world, over-reacting to frustrations, setbacks or failures. Some children give up easily and can't deal with any failure: sometimes this has a massive impact on their education or employment. This is similar to the fact that children in physically sterile environments don't develop a strong immune system and are more likely to have allergies, asthma and to overreact to infections.

"Parents' desire to protect their children is undoubtedly well-intentioned, but it is likely the single largest factor contributing to the sharp rise in mental health problems among the young and the propensity of today's youth to stay stuck in endless adolescence." Marano[221]

Anxiety

The most obvious and straightforward result of over-protection is an increase in anxiety in children. This can take the form of separation anxiety, school phobia, generalised anxiety, panic attacks and any number of specific phobias. Official statistics on diagnoses certainly suggest a big increase but this is not conclusive proof as rates of diagnoses are very changeable and prone to fashion (some of these changes are deliberately shaped by the drug companies). However, there is reason to believe that some of this increase is real. Many other children do not actually develop an anxiety condition but are generally worried and negative.

Traditionally many 'experts' have blamed children's problems on stress and in some ways children's lives remain quite stressful. What is noteworthy is that major traditional stresses, for example poverty and ill-health, have reduced but this hasn't resulted in any lessening of anxiety and depression. Anxiety and depression are found just as often in affluent families who clearly have less of the traditional stressors in their lives (some even argue they are more common[222]).

These anxiety problems can be confounded in some families by parents not having enough control over their children. In the past if a child had a *mild* school phobia or was developing agoraphobia, parents simply made them go to school, or go out, and in *the majority* of cases they got over it (this won't work for moderate to severe anxiety, but usually it starts off mild). Nowadays a child with mild anxiety about going to school, or going out, may have parents who can't make him do anything, so they avoid facing their fears which get worse. With both school phobia and agoraphobia there is also the problem that home is now a lot less boring than in the past, so motivation to face these fears is lower. Many more children are going to choose to stay home surrounded by exciting electronic gadgets and hooked up to a virtual community of 'friends'[223].

Teenage risk taking, aggression and conflict with parents

"Raised on a pedestal, children come to expect the world to fall at their feet – and get angry when it doesn't." Honoré[224]

Although anxiety is a more obvious result from over-protection, aggression has also long been recognised as a possible reaction. In the 1945 book "Maternal Over-protection", Levy reported the behaviour of twenty children who he judged were over-protected by their mothers and noted that *"their behaviour towards their mother was marked by disobedience, impudence, temper tantrums, excessive demands, and the exercise of varying degrees of tyranny.[225]"* He even mentions a few of the children being physically violent towards their mothers, possibly the first ever mention of violence to parents in psychological literature.

Some over-protected children become aggressive when they encounter frustration or setbacks. Tantrums, meltdowns and violence within the home can all be increased by over-protective, indulgent parenting. Constant monitoring and keeping your children ultra-safe means they are more controlled in some ways but it also makes them demanding as well as giving them opportunities to control parents. If you've come to expect things to go your way, and to expect your servant-parent to be at your beck and call, there is an increased likelihood of aggressive outbursts. At school these children may explode when a teacher does something unfair or when another child teases or taunts them. At home some of these children turn on their parents. It may be that the over-protectiveness is less important than the indulgent parenting that it often goes hand in hand with, but both are often associated with children's abuse of their parents.

Bullying and teasing from other children have always happened (it's probably improved in some schools) but some children are less able to cope with it. Some children react to teasing or social problems by withdrawal but others explode in tantrums or meltdowns (some do both). Sometimes such over-the-top reactions are responses to fairly trivial teasing or inter-personal upsets, or to perceived unfairness. These children are generally less able to deal with frustration than were prior generations. Combined with less respect for authority this can be a dangerous combination at school or at home.

Since these children are inside far more than in the past, there are more opportunities for conflict with parents and also for fights and rivalry between siblings. Some modern homes are emotional pressure cookers with demanding kids trapped with each other and with one or two highly stressed parents. I'm sure I'm seeing more sibling conflict than in the past and one of the reasons for this appears to be that they are stuck indoors together with less opportunity to avoid each other. Brothers and sisters often fight more when parents are around than when they are not (one reason for this is that younger sibs know that the parents will protect them, and the older sib usually gets the blame)[226]. Many parents appear to believe the strange myth that all siblings love each other and that they should therefore be able to play together and be friends. I often hear parents tell children, 'you know you love your brother' when clearly they don't. Sibling rivalry is not inevitable but nor is sibling love.

An inability to cope with life's frustrations and setbacks can have other behavioural consequences besides aggression. Irresponsibility, emotional immaturity and escapism all lend themselves to problem behaviours like delinquency, drug and alcohol abuse, computer addiction, and sexual promiscuity. I'm not suggesting that over-protectiveness *directly* causes these problems. It's not that simple, but over-protectiveness goes hand in hand with a lack of responsibility and an overblown sense of entitlement and these are factors in many adolescent behaviour problems besides violence to parents.

The Effect on parents

Although we should probably be more worried about the effects on children, paranoid parenting certainly isn't good for parents. It contributes greatly to parental stress, depression, ill health and guilt. The lion's share of this stress falls on mothers, of course (should that be lioness's share?), but it also puts pressure on fathers. Fathers have become more involved in child-rearing in recent decades, though still not close to catching up with mothers, who also do more than in the past. Some modern fathers feel guilty too, but guilt has become almost universal for mothers in Western societies, reflecting the impossibly high standards that are being set. Over-protective, indulgent parenting also places stress on couple relationships, not only because of the pressure of time and perpetual motion that over-parenting entails but because emotionally, the parenting part has grown at the expense of the couple relationship, which often becomes almost non-existent, at a time in history when we are expecting more from marital partnerships than people did in the past.

What can you do about it?

Not many parents believe that *they* are over-protective and we all interpret such terms differently. Looking at the advice on the web I came across a site that tells parents not to be over-protective yet begins with the outrageous claim that: "*Today's children require more protection by parents than ever before. Stranger dangers and family abuse are on the rise.*"[227] Reinforcing these myths is hardly likely to encourage parents to be less protective! What these writers consider normal protection I would consider to be over-protection.

It's pointless telling you how much freedom your child should have; it all depends on your child's age, abilities, temperament and the local environment. Nearby suburbs can be quite different and even within the one area, children living in cul-de-sacs often have far more freedom than those on through roads. Standards for different ages vary greatly among different groups and are changing very fast over time.

What it comes down to for you as a parent, is balancing short and long-term risks. Letting your child catch a bus on their own creates a statistically tiny, but real risk *at the time*. Not letting them learn how to be independent can create *far greater* risks but these are not immediate and are hard to predict. In a risk-averse society people tend to go for the greater long-term risks. Ironically, this is even truer of organizations looking after children in residential or foster care (who are often terrible parents).

If you could keep your child permanently indoors in a sterile environment and without any contact with other people, they would be physically very safe *as a child*. Unfortunately, they would have no immunity to any physical disease and have a high chance of developing serious allergies. More importantly, what chance would such a child have of coping with the real world? They would be a neurotic, emotional cripple!

There is good evidence that some exposure to dirt, animals and other children helps strengthen their immune system. Similarly some exposure to stress, failure and life's challenges is probably necessary for healthy emotional development.

Over-protectiveness creates less responsible children, can lead to greater levels of entitlement, stresses both parents and children and, once they reach adolescence, increases conflict between parents and young people.

"A ship in port is safe, but that's not what ships are built for." G. M. Hopper
Free Range Kids website: http://www.freerangekids.com/

Exercise: What do you do for your child?

List *everything* you do or provide for your child: **material** (e.g. buying things for the household, buying things for them, providing home, electricity, phone, etc.), **services** (what work do you do for them daily, weekly, occasionally) **social**, **recreational**, **emotional**, etc. Especially list all *privileges*.
Next mark what services are *optional* (i.e. you could choose not to do or provide them with, without danger or overwhelming guilt)
Finally consider which *optional* services your child **cares about** (at least a little) and mark with a different colour or symbol. You may want to mark how much they care about these things. You may want to refer back to this list when we discuss consequences.

Perfect Parents?

"It's your fault! I wouldn't behave like this if you hadn't spoiled me rotten!"
thirteen-year-old girl.
"I can treat you like shit because you're always there for me!" fourteen-year-old-
boy.

Probably no one uses the phrase 'perfect parent' seriously[228], yet the *idea* of being a perfect, ideal or optimal parent is a very common one. The idea of the ideal parent is implied in many parenting and pop psychology books because the author claims to know **the** best way to bring up a child and usually implies that this would guarantee success.

"We worry that we will scar our children, causing them to spend their adulthood complaining about us to their therapists. Too often, we fear that our children will be traumatised or their spirits crushed if we're not perfect parents." Kindlon[229]

I've met many parents who, although they may joke about the idea, have been clearly aiming to be the perfect parent. This causes tremendous guilt and disappointment because anyone who tries to be perfect at best falls short or, at worst, makes a perfect hash of it. The idea of being a perfect parent is not meaningful, logical, possible, necessary or essential. So let's dissect and deconstruct the idea once and for all then toss it in the metaphorical garbage can with other unhelpful myths.

Here are a few problems with the idea of the Perfect Parent:

1. Our lack of knowledge

We don't know nearly enough about child development and parenting to be at all clear what the perfect parent would be like. The history of advice to parents is full of 'experts' claiming that their theory or research tells us what the best upbringing is for the average child. Outrageously, many authors imply that there is just one ideal way of bringing up *every* child. Most of the past advice (and a lot of the current advice) now looks quite silly and some of it we would now consider abusive. There have certainly been no huge breakthroughs in psychology that suddenly enable any expert to tell us what the perfect environment is for a child to grow up in. Any such formula is based on faith not on science.

2. There is no one natural way to parent

Looking at different cultures, it's obvious that human development is very flexible and there is no type of family or specific parental behaviour that is *essential* for normal development (we'll discuss different types of family in the next chapter and find it makes less difference than you would think). Some form of close attachment to one or more people (preferably more than one), and communication with others, are essentials but how this happens can vary greatly. Humans evolved with children being brought up in dangerous, stress-filled environments where most babies did not survive childhood and parents had plenty of other things to worry about. Mothers were **never** full-time parents (only the very rich could possibly afford to be full-time parents but instead they usually had servants do most of the child care). Whether fathers did nothing, a little, or a lot (usually a little), parenting was also shared with (and occasionally handed over to) older children and other relatives – very different to our way of bringing up children. Polygamy was very common in other societies and extended families the norm in most societies. *Isolated* nuclear families are **unique** to modern society and have *never* existed before. Our way of bringing up children is distinctive in a number of important ways yet some academics write as if the current, Western, isolated, over-protective, two-parent, nuclear family is not just the gold standard *ideal* but they even suggest that it's in some way *natural*! At the same time other academics, and quite often the very same academics, point out that we are having epidemics of youth depression, youth suicide, ADHD, youth violence, etc. etc.

3. The ideal parenting or ideal environment for developing one characteristic won't be ideal for other characteristics

It's simply ridiculous to believe that the ideal upbringing for, say, intelligence will also be ideal for confidence, athleticism, popularity, happiness, spirituality, etcetera. Which of these is the goal for the ideal parent? Clearly if you want your child to grow up to be a Buddhist monk or a harmless hippie you will parent rather differently to those whose aim is a top athlete or ruthless business executive. More broadly than this, is the goal a successful and/or happy childhood or a successful and/or happy adulthood, or some compromise between the two? Obviously some discomfort, such as attending school and brushing your teeth, in childhood is acceptable for the sake of a better adulthood, but where do we draw the line? If we could produce well-adjusted, genius adults at the expense of a really miserable childhood should we do so? Hopefully not.

The Spartans would have thought our qualms were ridiculous. They were willing to inflict suffering and have a fair number of children die to weed out the weaklings and try to produce a master race. We are appalled at such ideas but others might be appalled at our encouraging our children to be highly competitive and acquisitive. We don't want our children toughened up at the cost of even one percent dying, but the attempt to make our children safer has gone beyond what is good for the majority. We drive them around because we are afraid to let them out on their own and close down playgrounds in case one child in a million gets killed on play equipment. Most of us would say that we want them to have a happy childhood yet most parents will force their children to attend a school they don't like if it has better academic outcomes.

The happiest childhood is not guaranteed to produce the best adjusted, highest achieving or even the nicest adults. There will *always* be compromises to make, and these will always be based on value judgments. What are our values in terms of short and long term goals? It used to be assumed that producing good workers and responsible adults was the goal but in recent years many parents pay lip service to the idea of a happy childhood for its own sake. There cannot possibly be a scientific formula for the perfect childhood unless we could clearly define our ultimate goals[230]. So before anyone could say what optimal parenting looks like, they would have to define what are desired outcomes. This is not at all easy to do, and most parenting gurus don't bother, assuming everyone would agree with their vague ideas.

4. Different children have different needs

Children differ **greatly** in personality and abilities from the word go. What is best for a highly active child will not be best for a sedate one; what is best for a nervous, over-sensitive child won't work for a fearless little bruiser; ideal parenting for a very bright child is different to the ideal for a slow learner. I've seen a great many families where apparently the same parenting works well for one child but is a total disaster for another. So *perfect parenting* must differ depending on the child, which means it can never be a simple recipe. Of course every adult is different too and it's really the 'fit', or match, between child and parent that matters. The society they are living in also has to be taken into account; a parenting style that works well within one culture may not work within another.

5. No one is perfect*

Even if we could decide what makes the perfect parent, would it be humanly possible for anyone to actually be such a paragon, or even come close?

There is abundant evidence, from everyday life, and from research, that no parent actually does come close to being perfect. A research study in the USA found that 98% of parents had at some point been 'psychologically abusive' in some way to their children by the time they were six! Were the other 2% perfect, completely uninvolved, or lying in the survey?

6. Would a perfect parent prepare a child for reality

If we knew what was perfect parenting, and some saintly genius was capable of doing the job, would this actually prepare a child for the real world? It's unlikely that the perfect environment is stress free, just as the perfect environment for a child is not sterile and perfectly hygienic.

7. Parenting is just one factor so the outcome would still be unpredictable

Even if parenting was perfect there are so many other factors involved that the outcome for any one child could still never be guaranteed. The idea that parents are practically the only influence on their children is not supported by any evidence I've been able to find. When researchers try to find relationships between parenting and child outcomes, they consistently find that only a small part of the child's personality, abilities or behaviour is predicted by parenting. The only time there are

---

* though I am a perfect example of me

moderate to high correlations between child outcomes and parenting is when parenting is abusive or neglectful – and even then outcomes are variable and not predictable in individual cases.

8.   You are, or you should be, more than just a parent

It's not normal or healthy for anyone to be **just** a parent. Even a doting mother of a young child plays other roles such as daughter, sister, wife, friend, mother to an older child, citizen, etc. and she may soon become a student or worker again without being any less of a parent. There is no good evidence that the children of working mothers are damaged by this[231]. Similarly, the idea that a household needs to be child-**focused**, rather than child-**friendly**, is also a radical new idea which appears to be producing some children who are psychologically at risk for behavioural problems, depression, addictive behaviours and even self-harm and suicide.

Child-focus often breeds *me*-focus!

9.   If perfection is expected, we are all failures

"Our cultural idealization of mothers makes our anger at mother almost inevitable; if you expect someone to be perfect, sooner or later you'll criticize them for having any faults." Caplan[232]

The largely sub-conscious expectation that we should be perfect parents means that parental guilt is almost inevitable. It also gives disgruntled children (of any age) great scope to criticise and to feel hard done-by. It thus adds to parental guilt, making it harder to be assertive and adds to children's sense of entitlement. Both of these increase the risk of violence to parents.

"What happens when we can't be perfect parents? We feel guilty. We think we owe our children everything and we feel bad when we can't provide it. Almost all parents have at one time given into a child or bent a household rule because they felt guilty about something they had done." Kindlon[233]

10. Attempting to be perfect is exhausting

The futile attempt to be a perfect parent means that you are going to be exhausted. It takes the fun out of family life (for you anyway). It places great stress on your couple relationship and increases the chances of not parenting as a team (it's unlikely that both parents are trying for perfection or aiming at the same impossible goals) and can thus contribute to divorce.

"Trying to be perfect is the worst thing you can do to your child. Perfect parents pay a high price in exhaustion for their perfectionism and give their kids a model they can't live up to. Trying to be perfect puts great stress on parents and minimizes the enjoyment of their family-focused time." Small[234]

But some parents do achieve perfection of a kind. A few children, whose parents have *tried* to be perfect, become perfect brats!

"Good enough" parenting

Children need a sense of security and a *reasonable* amount of attention, stimulation and a healthy environment. Most importantly they need to feel loved and valued. If parenting is 'good enough', they will develop normally and how they turn out will have more to do with their own personality, their own choices, and the rest of their world, than it does the behaviour of a parent[235]. Stimulation, attention, praise and love are all *essentials* and a lack of any of these cause serious problems. However, the idea that the more of these things the better the outcome will be just plain silly! Fresh air and vegetables are good for children but forcing them to live in a vegetable garden wouldn't guarantee their health. You can have too much of a good thing, even if the good thing is love, attention, self-esteem or stimulation.

Best parenting possible

We have a responsibility to be good enough parents but **without** sacrificing our own rights and happiness or our other relationships and responsibilities. Keep a sense of proportion, a sense of your own worth and a sense of humour. Your kids won't thank you for trying to be perfect. In fact those parents who try hardest often get the least appreciation from their children. Your children probably won't thank you whatever you do, but they are a bit more likely to thank you for being relaxed, fun, and perfectly human.

"The paradox of parenting is that the pressure to make it perfect can undermine the outcome." Marano[236]

Family Structure

"Never before in human history has any society been composed of so many divergent types of families." Burgess[237]

Some of you reading this will be sole parents. If so, you may well think this is a large part of the problem but the reality is that almost as many two-parent families have similar problems. Those of you in blended families, same-sex relationships, with an adopted child, an only child, a child whose father is dead, or some other family variant, are all likely to assume that this is a highly significant factor in why your child has behavioural problems. If you don't, you may have encountered professionals who think this. It *may* be, but it may be irrelevant or just a small part of the complex array of influences which have shaped your child's behaviour.

All the possible parenting variations are less important than factors such as the child's personality, your parenting style, and environmental factors.

(Thermo)Nuclear Families

The nuclear family has become so taken for granted that many people, including professionals and academics who should know better, talk as if it's the *only* healthy and natural way for human beings to live. As a result of this bias, involved grandparents are often viewed as *over*-involved and close extended family bonds may be seen as a sign of parental immaturity, a lack of independence or a threat to the marital relationship. Sole parents are seen almost inevitably as screwing up their children and step-parents viewed with suspicion. The term 'broken home' has only recently gone out of fashion. Any child not living with their birth parents is seen as being at risk and any problems may be attributed to attachment issues.

"The idealising of the nuclear family in western societies probably reached its zenith in the 1950s when psychologists were prepared to label anyone who did not aspire to this ideal as deviant." McDonald[238]

The *isolated* nuclear family is actually a historically new, probably unique, way for human beings to live. Far from being 'natural' for human beings it's a radical new departure. Nuclear families, a household consisting of two biological parents and their children, have been around for a long time in Europe, (uncommon elsewhere). But they often included other relatives, servants, and lodgers in the household and they were also closely linked to a wider community which included other kin. In other societies there were a wide variety of arrangements. In some, women after marriage went to live with their husband's family and in a few, husbands went to live with their wife's family. A few cultures had separate men's houses and in a great many others there was some form of polygamy, usually one man with several wives (the *majority* of cultures have allowed this). In most societies, mothers were just one carer of children with grandparents, other relatives and older children taking on a great deal of the child care once the child was weaned.

Our isolated nuclear families have become more and more isolated over recent decades. Extended families are now less involved, people are less likely to know their neighbours and the boundary between the family unit and outsiders has become less permeable. This turns many families into emotional pressure cookers. The isolated over-involvement, as we've discussed in previous chapters, puts pressure on couples, increases tension between parent and child, and increases conflict between siblings.

Our indulgent, but over-protective, form of parenting can create more closeness between parent and child, but it gives more opportunities for conflict. Sometimes this closeness prior to adolescence dissolves into conflict around adolescence.

Our society paints an idyllic picture of the cereal-box nuclear family but for many people the reality is far from peaceful. Our modern way of living is certainly not *natural*, not always healthy, and some of our problems with young people stem from this. Thirty percent of the families where children are abusing parents are intact nuclear families. Certainly a minority, but surely a large enough minority to dispel any idea that other family forms are the *cause* of this problem.

Sole mothers

"The debate over whether one parent can raise a child alone diverts attention from the fact that good childrearing has always required more than two parents."
Coontz[239]

It's a common mistake to imagine that single parent families are a new phenomenon. In previous centuries mortality was **much** higher for adults under sixty and since child-bearing years were longer (they started younger and often popped out children up until menopause), there were many more widows and widowers left with children still at home. Many children lost a parent before they were grown. The overall percentage of single parent families dropped from 1900 - 1970 as divorced families increased slightly but widowed families declined more. However, since then there has been a rise in the relative number of sole parent families, from about 10% in the early seventies to around 20% at the time of writing (higher in the USA and the UK than in Australia). You may be thinking: isn't the divorce rate closer to 50%? It is, but the majority of people re-partner so at any one time, 10 to 20% of families have a solo parent.

Though there are more sole parents they are not seen as 'normal' families by society in general. This is important as the stigma attached to sole parenthood may affect children's self-image, lead to lessened respect for the mother, and affect the mother's confidence.

Most single parent families (88%) are headed by a woman and there has been only a slight increase in sole father families.

Despite dire predictions from traditionalists, the evidence is that children in one parent families do about as well on developmental measures as do those in two parent families once parental conflict and economic factors are taken into account. However, there are a number of sole parents who have been abused by their ex, or where one parent has substance abuse or other serious problems, or where there has been a very messy separation. These things can all affect children *dramatically* and so this minority will affect the statistics for sole families generally. But the important fact is that it's the related problems that affect children not the fact of being in a sole parent family by itself.

A consistent finding of the effect of divorce on children is that it's the conflict between parents, before, during and after separation that has the biggest effect, not the fact of separation itself.

"Australian research finds few differences between children of divorced and children of non-divorced two-parent families, and also that adolescents' adjustment is related more to whether they have a good relationship with at least one parent than to whether the parents are together or not." (Eastman, 1989, p101)

If a sole-parent family has been caused by the death of one parent, children do slightly *better* than if the sole-parent family is the result of divorce (provided the death was not suicide or murder). This is further proof that it's not being in a sole-parent family in itself that affects children. My clinical experience suggests that it's often how the child interprets the absence of a parent that is crucial. A child who feels rejected by a father (which can include one who has suicided) may be greatly affected while other children appear much less affected by the absence of a father. Very often loss of a parent is associated with other family problems and this complicates things. Michael Rutter summed it up: *"it's clear that parental loss or separation carries quite mild developmental risks unless the loss leads to impaired parenting or other forms of family maladaptation."* [240]

Fifty-three percent of the families in my sample are sole mothers, and this is roughly similar to studies of violence to parents in other countries. When I first published an article on this subject, I was disgusted that a conservative organisation quoted me on their website with the claim that sole mothers couldn't bring up boys properly without a man on board. They chose not to mention that nearly two-thirds of these sole mothers had been abused by their ex-partners! Far from it being the lack of a man that was causing the problem, it was irresponsible and violent men who were the creating the problems. There's a chapter on past domestic violence later.

In the two hundred plus families in my sample where there has been *no* past DV, about 40% are sole parents, which is twice what we would expect (18% of families in Australia are currently sole parents). Being a sole parent is an influence on violence to parents but no greater an influence than is the child being male. The risk of abuse of parents is far greater if there has been past family violence or if the

143

parent has been undermined in other ways (usually by the child's father but occasionally by other relatives or by an organisation).

Sole fathers

According to some theories it should make a big difference to a child's development if father is the main care-giver, however, the research on sole fathers suggests that "*the most remarkable aspect of findings is how little effect the change appears to have on children*"[241]. A few studies suggest that children, especially boys, do better with sole dads than with sole mums. However, this is not at all a fair comparison as sole dads are a far more selective group. Some of those who become sole dads are exceptionally dedicated while the worst dads are particularly likely to opt out of the care of their children. It's relatively easy for an irresponsible Dad to opt out but there is an awful lot more social pressure on an irresponsible mother to stay involved.

The idea that it's the lack of a man about the house that is the cause of teens turning against sole mothers is not only challenged by the many two parent families where parents are abused but also by the number of sole fathers who are abused. Naturally I've seen a lot more sole mothers abused by their children than sole fathers. I've met sixteen sole fathers who were being abused by a child in their care; this is only 6.5% of the sole parents in my study. But sole mothers are at least eight times more common than sole fathers and are also far more likely to have been past victims of DV. Taking these two factors into account there does not appear to be a big difference between sole fathers and sole mothers in terms of being abused by their children. If we exclude the sole parents where there was past DV, ten percent of the sole parents in my sample are fathers, which is pretty much what we would expect from the current ratio of sole Dads to sole Moms. It's also interesting that the children being violent to sole fathers are quite often daughters (six out of sixteen). Having a man around the house is not a guarantee that there will be no violence towards parents.

The first sole dad I came across who was being abused by a child was a fairly tough, physically strong man who was being hit by his thirteen-year-old daughter. When he told me that his wife had physically abused him I was a bit sceptical at first but both of his children confirmed his story. His wife had been a heavy drug user and had attacked him on a number of occasions and once stabbed him. The fifteen-year-old boy in the family had also been violent towards his father but had stopped by the time I met them. I'll never forget this boy telling me, "I used to think that Dad was weak because he didn't fight back. Now I know he was strong." The sister had seen dad abused by Mum then by her brother and had lost respect (despite choosing to live with Dad rather than Mum).

Blended families

Some of you probably feel as if you and your family have been put through a blender but that's not what 'blended family' means. It refers to families where there is a step-parent and/or step-children. I see a lot of step-families but, for me, the surprising thing about the presence of a step-parent (usually a step-dad) is that it makes so little difference to violence to parents. I see so many of them because many women re-partner after leaving an abusive man.

About two-thirds of the blended families in my sample have had past domestic violence, roughly the same percentage as for sole mothers. The abuser in almost all of these cases was the child's birth father (occasionally a previous step-dad). When a woman leaves an abusive man there is a risk that his children will later become abusive towards her; this is so whether she remains alone or if she re-partners. If the step-father is intimidating, the child will not be abusive towards him or towards the mother when he is around. Thus the presence of a step-dad often *somewhat* reduces the frequency of the child's abuse of the mother but rarely does it stop completely, and occasionally it gets worse. Overall the cases where it helps and the cases where it makes things worse seem to balance out, hence the same rate of past DV for step-families as for sole mothers.

If the mother in a family is being abused by a teenager, a birth father is *more* likely to also be abused than is a step-father. This is the opposite of what almost everyone expects. So it's not usually *because* someone is a step-parent that they are being attacked. It's more accurate that they are being attacked *despite* being a step-parent. When a step-dad is attacked by a teenager, professionals, and sometimes also relatives, often assume he must deserve it or must have done something to provoke it. Of course there are some cases where this is true, but generally it's a very unfair assumption stemming from prejudice. Rather than fitting the wicked step-parents myth, most step-parents who are abused are kind, tolerant individuals guilty only of loving the child's parent. Some even love the child who is abusing them (but there is nothing automatic about love between step-parents and step-children).

On the other hand I do see situations where a step-parent is making things worse. This may be because he is aggressive and provokes the young person. Sometimes a step-parent undermines the birth parent or they openly disagree about parenting. I've seen a few step-fathers who tried to take over and impose their, sometimes quite eccentric, ideas on the family. For example, I've known of two step-fathers who insisted that no one speak at the dinner table! Bullying, violent step-fathers are *less* likely to be abused by the child than are non-violent ones, but the child's mother may still get abused when the step-father is not around.

Occasionally a teenager's bad behaviour is partly motivated by a desire to force the step-parent to leave, and they sometimes succeed in this goal. Teenagers can make life so unpleasant that any rational adult will flee! One mother was told by her two teenage daughters that they could force any man out of the house, and they said they would claim sexual abuse if being violent and obnoxious was not sufficient! Sometimes, as in this case, this is a quite deliberate strategy on the part of the child, but for others the motivation may be largely unconscious. Just because a child likes a step-parent, as an individual, does not mean they want to have a step-parent. Some teens may have mixed feelings when the step-parent does leave. Ambivalence is a pretty common, normal reaction for older children gaining a step-parent.

Step-parents can find themselves in intolerable no-win situations. Seeing your partner being abused in your own home is very upsetting. If you are told that you should not interfere when your partner is being abused (and many are told this),

145

you may feel incredibly frustrated and disempowered. If you feel that your partner is not taking it seriously enough, or is tolerating the intolerable, it can be very hard to stand back and watch. I have a lot of sympathy for step-parents in these situations but many other professionals clearly do not. Step-dads are often assumed to be part of the problem no matter what they do or how hard they have tried, damned if they do and damned if they don't!

The advice given to step-parents generally, especially if the children are older when they join the family, is to leave discipline up to the birth parent. But what if the birth parent has no control over the child or the child is abusing them and others, possibly including the step-parent's children when they come for access visits? No one has to stand back and watch someone being physically abused. A well-meaning step-parent may want to leave discipline up to their partner yet be forced to get involved by other moral, or practical, considerations. Despite best intentions, they can be forced to get involved when someone is being abused. The idea that someone should just stand back and watch their partner be abused is ridiculous! Yet this is the position that the authorities sometimes expect step-fathers to take. Here are a couple of examples.

George was told by Child Protection that he was not to lay a hand on his ten-year-old step-son to restrain him, even if he was attacking his mother, which he had done several times. Their advice to this couple was to take their six-month old baby and leave the house if the ten-year-old was on a rampage. On other occasions Child Protection workers have accused parents of neglect when they have left a ten-year-old alone.

Mario was charged with assault after he manhandled his fifteen-year-old step-daughter, Elise, out of the house to stop her punching and kicking her mother, Trisha. He didn't hit her but quite forcefully removed her. While she was throwing a hysterical tantrum in the street in front of their house, she fell over and bruised her leg. She went to a neighbour and asked them to call the police. She used the bruises on her leg to press charges against Mario and took out an Intervention Order, which said that he was not allowed within five hundred meters of her. Protective Services suggested Mario leave the home so Elise could move back in (she was staying with an aunt), however they backed down when Trisha threatened to go to the media with the story. After a month, Elise let the Intervention Order lapse and she returned home. She still insisted that she was in the right and that Mario was an abuser. She felt she'd been vindicated by the authorities and her parents felt betrayed and abused by the system.

Step-fathers should be able to impose consequences or even physically control the children when they are really out of line. The way to handle this is for the couple to work together (this is crucially important) and mutually agree *very* clear rules and consequences. If these are clear enough, it isn't the step-parent imposing his or her will, but an agreed joint decision. This is crucially important in blended families with difficult children. I considered writing a chapter on step-parents but this book is getting too long and will never be finished if I try to include everything. Sorry!

Adoptive Families

Out of the four hundred and eighty families in my sample where children are abusing parents, only three or four are adoptive families. Yet when a serious problem occurs with an adoptive child it's often automatically assumed that adoption must be the issue; this is illogical. Some children in adoptive families grow up feeling out of place, resentful and different, but these are a small minority and there are a great many happy, well-adjusted adoptive children. Perhaps surprisingly, adopted children grow up to be just as psychologically healthy as non-adopted[242]. The assumption that adoption inevitably leads to a sense of loss is not supported by research, and there are societies where adoption is extremely common and there is no expectation of such a sense of loss[243]. There is even less reason to assume that violence or serious behavioural problems must be the result of adoption[244].

For some children, absent parents are of great psychological importance and they feel a sense of rejection or spend a lot of time wondering about them; for other children it's just not a big deal (some professionals seem to find this very hard to believe and may alienate the child, or parents, by over-emphasising the issue). The reason for the different response is not always obvious unless they clearly are not accepted or don't fit in to the family in some way.

Overall, the evidence is that adoptive parents are better than average in terms of warmth, affection and acceptance. Adopted children are special and often precious to their adoptive parents, who are often child-focused. This could *potentially* lead to greater indulgence and hence to an over-entitled child, possibly increasing the risk of parent-abuse *in a small number* of cases. This applies to children born through assisted technology too (who resemble adoptive parents in their parenting)[245]. It's possible that knowing they are adopted decreases the sense of entitlement of some adoptive children, reducing the risk of violence to parents.

A study from England[246] found that in cases where adoption had broken down, violence to parents was very common and their accounts are quite harrowing. However, the percentage of adoptions which broke down was tiny (3%) even though many were adoptions of older children (far more common in the UK than in Australia). Despite the fact that 97% of adoptions do **not** break down, when there are serious problems it's usually assumed to be due to adoption issues. Where there was violence to adoptive parents: *".... social workers were too ready to label difficulties as attachment disorders before ruling out other possibilities."* [247] Yet despite the common assumption that problems must be due to adoption, when things turned bad, adoptive parents were blamed just the same as other parents: *"There's no acknowledgement of the fact that she is like that because of what happened to her before she came to live with us."*[248]

Violence to foster parents is another greatly neglected topic. It's clearly *very* common but too complicated for me to go into here. It's likely to have some similar issues to abuse of adoptive parents. One major difference is that a child having been a victim of abuse themselves, as opposed to witnessing DV, is a definite risk factor for violence to foster parents. Grandparent carers, especially where the birth parent is irresponsible and undermines them, may be at risk of being abused; another under-researched and neglected group in our society.

One child families

Since indulgent parenting is a significant risk factor for violence to parents, you might assume that an only child will be more likely to abuse parents. There is a common image of the only child as spoilt, over-indulged – a 'little emperor'. Certainly, I've heard a number of abused parents say that professionals have said, or hinted, that the problems are related to a lack of siblings. This image of the spoilt only child is largely myth, with research suggesting that they are not significantly different to other first born children.

I *have* seen a disproportionate number of *first born* children who are abusing their parents. This makes sense in terms of indulgent, child-focused parenting and an overblown sense of entitlement (see also the section on self-esteem). It's certainly possible that these factors would create a bias towards only children but I haven't found this to be very noticeable in my sample. Seventeen percent of my sample are the only child in the family, but this is not too far from their rate in the Australian population (as families get smaller there are far more single-child families around). So if you have an 'only' child who is being abusive towards you, don't listen to anyone who says you should have given them a little brother or sister – if you had they might well be bullying them too! You probably have more invested in this child and may have had a very close relationship before they turned against you, so being abused by your only child can be extra-upsetting. On the plus side, having only one child can simplify imposing consequences.

Birth order

There is quite a bit of rubbish written about birth order. It's certainly true that siblings can have an enormous influence on each other. I've also no doubt that there are *statistical* differences between first born, middle and youngest children but they are not impressive differences and pop psychology massively exaggerates their importance. For any particular individual, birth order is just one among many variables having some influence on personality and behaviour. Making any assumptions about an individual on the basis of this one factor is foolhardy in the extreme and more akin to astrology than science. The arrangement of children in a family is a lot more complex than first, middle and last. Being the first born of two children is different to being first born of three or more. Being a year or two older than the next child is quite different to being five or ten years older. Being an older brother to a girl is very different to being an older brother to a boy. Then there are myriad combinations of personality and abilities; if your older brother is a bully, your childhood will be totally different to the child with a supportive big brother. If two sibs are good at and interested in the same things, they might compete madly and become enemies, or they may become close companions. If they are into different things, they may get on well, or perhaps ignore each other completely. I've mentioned the myth that all siblings love each other, which I've seen disproved many times in both children and in adults.

There is a slight tendency generally for the first born to be dominant and more aggressive, at least in the home (some studies find this only applies within the family but others find it applies with friends too)[249]. Being first born increases the likelihood of violence towards parents. I don't have data on birth order for my entire sample, but 64% of two hundred and seventy-six children who abused parents were first born and they were twice as likely to be the abusive child in the family compared to the last born[250]. There are only very slight differences between middle children and last born in their likelihood to be parent abusers. 'Middle child syndrome' is another popular myth. But I'm a middle child, so perhaps I'm biased.

The fact of first-borns being more often abusive to parents fits with our ideas on indulgent parenting, entitlement and self-esteem, but it's only a tendency so tells us nothing very useful about any particular child. Although it has been reported before, it goes against the common view of these children as being victims with low self-esteem[251].

Siblings play many roles for each other and so the influence can be complex. Here are a few of the roles they may play:

- Playmate
- Source of security or stress
- Social/emotional support
- Bully
- Convenient victim
- Substitute parent
- Positive or negative role model
- Competitor
- Ally against parents
- Source of pride or embarrassment
- Link to other groups of children (other ages, opposite sex)

The roles children play within a family are partly determined by the other children present. A boy with a bossy, domineering older sister may, for an easy life, play the part of amenable follower and this may shape his relations with other people. The same boy with a fearful, quiet older sister may become more confident and develop his own leadership potential. A child with a highly extrovert, life and soul of the party sibling may become more introverted and quiet than he or she otherwise would have been. A child with a bullying older brother could become more nervous and withdrawn, but occasionally more tough and assertive. A child with an older sibling (especially if only slightly older) who is highly successful academically or in sports may feel inadequate and not try in these areas, or may even give up trying to succeed generally. On the other hand, a highly successful and well regarded older brother or sister can be a source of status by association. Other people (including parents) may have higher expectations if an older sibling was successful and this can be either positive or negative for a particular child. I can remember standing up to boys a year or two older than me with the potential protection of my older brother (by four years) as a back-up. I can't recall him actually fighting on my behalf but the threat was often enough. If he had been closer in age to me, we may have been competitors and this would have changed my entire childhood, and probably my personality.

An American researcher, Judy Dunn[252], has studied the effect of siblings on each other and concludes that it's misleading to talk about a family as if it's a shared environment. Each child grows up in a *different* environment to his brothers and sisters because his environment includes his brothers and sisters. The effect of particular parents (as long as they are not too extreme in their parenting, i.e. not abusive or mad) is not great enough to show itself above these other effects.

Homosexual parents

The research evidence on homosexual parents shows surprisingly little overall difference between their children and those with heterosexual parents[253]. This fits with my limited experience of a dozen or so lesbian parents I've encountered over the years (I've no experience of male couples with children). Generally their kids were pretty well-adjusted and having two mothers, or a mum plus a step-mum, is less of an issue for them than most of us would expect, particularly since there is still quite a bit of prejudice against homosexual parents. Most of the lesbian parents I've worked with did not have children who abused them, but three couples did. Currently lesbian parents are more likely to be educated, middle class, less traditional, and child focused in their parenting than are heterosexual parents, and they may view their children as being extra-special. For these positive reasons, they might have a *slightly* higher risk of parent abuse[254].

Although we don't know for sure, I expect that homosexual couples are no more likely to have a beyond control or violent child than anyone else, unless there are factors such as past domestic violence or over-indulgent parenting. However, when there is a difficult or beyond control child, the parent's homosexuality is an issue that an adolescent might then focus on. They may be genuinely upset and confused about it, feel they are not part of a 'normal' family, or they may be using it as an excuse (or any combination thereof).

Anything that lowers a parent's status in the *eyes of the child* can increase the risk of violence to parents, and this has nothing to do with what we as liberal adults may think. This could potentially include parents being obese, poor, disabled, etc.... or gay. See the section on 'respect'. Having a new step-parent can be difficult for any child and if the step-parent is in a same-sex relationship with their parent, this could certainly complicate things, especially if the parent has recently come out as gay. If there is an absent father putting pressure on the child to reject Mum's new partner, this is even more likely to be an issue.

If you are a lesbian parent with a violent or beyond control child, you may well encounter professionals who automatically assume that your sexuality is the central problem, or that the child is experiencing 'father hunger' or an attachment issue. On the other hand, you may also encounter workers who are too politically correct, or embarrassed, to even mention it as an issue. Regardless of our personal views, we should admit that having a gay parent in a society where homophobia is still rife, might really be an issue for some confused adolescents, but it's not a sufficient explanation in itself for violence to parents.

Working mothers

This isn't really a different family type but it fits in here. There are no dramatic overall differences between children whose mothers work and those who stay at home. Girls generally, and boys from lower socio-economic backgrounds, are *slightly* more intelligent if their mothers' work; boys from middle class families are *slightly* less intelligent if their mothers' work, so it has a mixed effect.

An important determinant of whether a mother working outside the home is good or bad is simply: does she want to work? Women who stay home by choice have children who do well, but so do women who choose to work. If you are forced to go out to work against your wishes (for financial reasons), your kids will do a bit less well on average. If you want to work but can't find suitable work, your children will do slightly less well[255]. Having a happy Mum is very good for children.

In terms of violence to parents, I don't have any good data but my impression is that those mothers who are abused by their children were more likely to have been stay-at-home, child-focused mothers. This is probably only one small factor so don't feel guilty if you were a stay-at-home Mum. Overall, I am quite sure mothers going out to work is NOT a factor leading to abuse of parents. A working mother is less likely to have over-entitled children who take her for granted. In fact there is some evidence that *"sons of working mothers appear to have more respect for women than do other boys"* which is going to reduce the risk of parent abuse[256]. Ironically, I have seen a number of mothers who felt compelled to give up work because their child's behaviour was so bad or who felt they could not consider working because their child would sabotage any care arrangements and the school expect the mother to be on hand to deal with meltdowns and suspensions.

Summary

The research is surprisingly consistent in finding that family structures are not all that important in how children turn out. Whether a child is brought up in a one-parent, two-parent, same-sex, blended, adopted or other family configuration is not important compared to things like amount of love and the presence or absence of violence. I know from my work with children that parents' separation can be devastating to a child. However, it's not the fact of separation or whether the child lives with Mum, Dad or a blended family that matters *in the long term,* but the amount of conflict between parents.

All events affect different children in different ways. So if you have a badly behaved child who has an absent father this may be a factor, possibly a big factor, for your child but no one should assume that it *must* be a factor without looking at the individual and their situation. If your child has been exposed to violence from one parent to the other, this is *highly* likely to have had a big impact, though even this does not inevitably make a child violent (see chapter on DV).

Start Box

A lost son

As a single mother of an only child, Harrison, I was planning to be the perfect parent. I was a professional and in my son's early years was self-employed at home. I had read widely on parenting and the early years were idyllic. Harrison was very special to me. However, he experienced bullying for much of his time at primary school and I played an active role in the school, fighting many causes. As Harrison was considered to be a gifted child, he was selected to attend regular gifted programmes. The programme coordinator suggested that I have my son assessed by an Educational Psychologist, who during testing, asked whether he had experienced bullying at school. He explained that it's quite common for a gifted child to be bullied; as his classmates detect that there is something 'different' about such a child. As a result of this information, in an effort to give Harrison more confidence, I ensured that he was exposed to a bigger world and sought to find interests which he could enjoy. I encouraged him to try football, soccer, tennis, judo, scouting and more. He enjoyed music, taking exams for piano and guitar, as well as swimming, sailing and skiing. I raised him in a democratic way, through discussion and seeking his opinions and input and, at the same time, encouraging independence and responsibility. There were boundaries. Often the television set would be wheeled out to the shed when he failed to co-operate or his attitude was unacceptable. I was always available and was the taxi parent, transporting not only Harrison but countless other children to and from activities.

It all began to change when my son turned thirteen. First he became verbally abusive towards me, which then escalated to threats and emotional and physical abuse. Late one night I received a phone call from the parents of a school friend, advising me that he was at their home (he had gone to his room at his usual time and must have left the house after I had gone to bed), a three kilometre walk in the dark. At other times, when he had disappeared, I asked friends and neighbours to help me with driving around the streets at night, searching for him. One evening, while I was watching television, I looked up to find Harrison standing beside the couch, holding a pair of scissors over my head. On another occasion I was preparing our evening meal and looked up to see him aiming a double pointed compass directly at me; he threw pieces of wood through a window while I was in the room folding the washing; he threw cricket balls and rocks at me; he was totally unpredictable. These were all unprovoked, apparently random, attacks. When I tried speaking with him, his eyes appeared to glaze over and I realised that he was in a different space. I installed a chain to my bedroom door, as I feared for my safety. I tried desperately to find help for him and eventually linked him with a Youth Worker. Harrison's main complaint was that he was allegedly being bullied by his schoolmates and also by his teachers; he often refused to go to school. I discussed the matter with the School Authorities and we had several meetings, but to no avail.

One day, after eight months of living this nightmare, there were several Police Officers at my front door. It was claimed that there had been a complaint that I had been abusing my son. I explained that there must be a mistake, because it was the complete reverse. The police claimed that Harrison was covered in bruises. I explained that he often climbed onto our roof and sat there (he knew that it terrified me and I actively discouraged it). He would then lift the roof tiles and access the house through the manhole. He also climbed trees and fences on our ten acre property. The police asked me to accompany them to our local police station and advised that I would be charged with a number of offences. I was put into the back of a Police Van and endured a most uncomfortable journey to the Police Station. At the police station the situation went from bad to worse. I was interrogated, but on legal advice from my Solicitor prior to leaving my home, I answered only the basic questions. At some point, I was advised that Harrison would be removed from my care and placed into Foster Care. I could not believe what was happening. I was asked for my house keys, so that they could take him to our home to collect his clothes and personal possessions. I was absolutely dumbstruck and in shock. I was driven back to my empty home after being detained for approximately five hours.

My nightmare continued. Several days later I was interviewed by an Officer from Child Protection and I invited the youth worker my son had been seeing to attend this meeting at my home. During the Officer's 'cigarette' break, the youth worker said to me that, in his view, the meeting was progressing very well and that the matter should be easily resolved. He also said that the Child Protection Officer had mentioned to him that the bruising on my son was the most minor that she had ever encountered. But the nightmare continued. I attended Court Hearings on twelve occasions over the next eighteen months.

Following Harrison's removal from my care, I was instructed by Child Protection to see a family counsellor, who unstintingly supported and encouraged me throughout the entire horrific process and was able to preserve my sanity. We have continued to remain in contact and she most generously (and unpaid) continues to counsel me from time to time. Relentlessly, I continued to fight for the return of my much loved son through daily telephone calls to Harrison's youth worker at Child Protection, numerous letters to State and Federal Members of Parliament, letters to the Press. I pursued this for over four very long years until, at eighteen, Harrison was released from the System. At my final meeting with Child Protection, I was told that the 'child is always right'. My question to them is, 'regardless of the truth?'

Later, I learned that my son had moved interstate and was at University.

It's now eight years since I lost my son to the System. To this day I do not understand, and can only speculate, as to what happened to my beautiful child. I continue to await his return.

End Box

The Child's Personality

"The consequences of parental practices can only be understood by also taking into account aspects of children's individuality which act as mediators for those practices, ... children with different temperamental characteristics will thus respond differently to similar environments" Schaffer[257].

Which children become abusive or beyond control has *just as much* to do with their personality as it does with family factors or societal factors. Some parents protest that their child's behaviour can't have anything to do with their parenting because they parented their other children the same way, and they turned out fine. It's not so simple! Given similar experiences, the same parents, and similar cultural and social situations there are many families where some kids do well while others are little rat-bags! Exposure to domestic violence is definitely the biggest single factor in children who abuse parents, yet even in these families there are more non-violent children than violent ones.

While there is no one type of personality common to children who abuse their parents, some patterns are more common than others.

From the 1950s until quite recently, it was frowned upon in some circles to talk about children's personality as a cause of their problems. Extreme environmentalism ruled: everything was influenced by *nurture* not *nature*! It's a great pity that the very term 'nurture' in the nature vs. nurture equation emphasised parenting (in particular mothering, since they do most nurturing) rather than the rest of the environment. The '50s was the peak point for the historically new, cornflake-packet, 'traditional' nuclear family. Never before in human history, had there been isolated families with women staying home to concentrate primarily on raising a few children. So environment was taken to be the home and mothers were blamed for children's problems. The huge influence of brothers and sisters was pretty much ignored, along with all the other parts of the environment. The suggestion that any child may be naturally inclined to have problem behaviour was a new taboo.

As most parents know, children pop out with quite different *temperaments*. 'Temperament' means the personality we start off with, before it's shaped by the environment, though the environment of the womb is important even before birth. Some babies are livelier than others in the womb and remain more active throughout their lives. Some babies are excitable and nervous while others are calm and emotionally stable. Some people are naturally amiable and cheerful while others tend to be hostile and surly. Personality certainly can change to some extent over time, but it tends to show quite a bit of consistency. Temperamentally I'm a neurotic extrovert, but my neuroticism has been under control since my teens and my extraversion looked quite different when I was younger than it does now that I'm *almost* middle-aged (I'm in my early sixties but I choose to define middle-age as one year older than me).

The evidence is that personality is largely determined by genetics and parenting, unless it's abusive, has only a small influence. Personality traits are the result of a large number of genes, inherited from both parents and from grandparents and great grandparents. Genes can be randomly shuffled, mutated, and have complex interactions with other genes and the environment. They can also be switched on or off by subtle or random factors, which means that even identical twins can differ in personality.

So if both parents are raving extroverts it's more likely that their children will be extraverted but not at all unusual for them to have an introverted child. This is very important when thinking about personality factors that influence violence. No one directly inherits a tendency to be violent but the odds of developing such behaviour vary a lot and inheritance plays a part in this. But inheritance only ever changes the odds – nothing is ever certain.

Psychologists studying personality in the past few decades have identified five fundamental aspects of personality: conscientiousness, agreeableness, neuroticism, openness and extraversion. These are often called 'The Big Five' personality factors and you can remember them by the acronym CANOE (or OCEAN if you prefer).

Some of these can play a large part in the development of behaviour problems such as violence to parents.

Extraversion/Introversion[*]

This is a fundamental personality trait related to need for stimulation. Extroverts have a high need for stimulation and tend to be (on average) more sociable, friendly, fun loving, talkative, impulsive, adventurous, energetic and assertive; they bore easily. Introverts don't crave excitement and stimulation so much and are more reserved, inhibited, quiet and fonder of their own company. Extroverts are more likely to like jazz than folk music, or heavy metal rather than pop. They are more likely to prefer bright colours over pastels or dull shades. They are more likely to dress extravagantly, while introverts tend to be more conservative about most things. All of these preferences are probabilities that can be reduced or reversed by cultural or environmental influences or counteracted by other personality factors (and this applies to all the other personality traits too).

A common source of confusion is that shy people may be introverts or just nervous (or a combination of the two). There is a big difference between someone who is quiet because they are nervous and someone who prefers to be quiet. Put the quiet person with a group of people who they feel really comfortable with and see if they become extraverted - the true introvert will still be relatively quiet but the neurotic may suddenly become the life and soul of the party. This is a relatively simple example of how the same behaviour may be caused by different personality

---

[*] Note to grammar Nazis: both 'extravert' or 'extrovert' are correct

155

traits and that personality can result in quite different behaviours in different situations.

As with all of these personality dimensions, most people are **not** fully extrovert or introvert but somewhere in between. This is only common sense: most people are not tall or short but of average height and most people are not genius or stupid but have average IQs. Like height, all of these personality traits are determined by a large number of genes and many environmental influences, so people don't clump into clear-cut types. Unfortunately a pseudo-science personality test that slots everyone into either introvert or extrovert remains embarrassingly popular[258].

Children who are outgoing, lively, who crave excitement and are a bit hyper are obviously more likely to cause problems for their parents than those who are quiet and have less desire for excitement. Extroverts are *more likely* to have almost any behaviour problem you can name: crime, drugs, violence, speeding, gambling, etc. Bullies are more often extroverts while their victims are more likely to be introverts[259]. The extreme extrovert may be labelled ADHD (though there is more to ADHD than extraversion) but any highly extrovert child may be 'a handful' at some stage in their development. If high extraversion is coupled with agreeableness you may have a particularly lovable, fun child but if it's linked with low agreeableness, you probably have a difficult child.

Children who abuse parents are more likely to be an extrovert than an introvert. Twenty percent of the children in my sample have ADHD, and these tend to be particularly extraverted. But there are also a number of introverts who abuse parents. Not surprisingly, they are far more likely to only be violent within the home than the extroverts, and some are isolated and don't go out much. Children with autism in particular are often markedly introverted.

It's worth noting that there is certainly nothing inherently bad about being either an extrovert or an introvert. Our society tends to favour extroverts and they are more popular than introverts. Like extraversion, a number of traits that are risk factors for violence to parents are positive in other ways.

Conscientiousness

Those who are highly conscientious tend to be self-disciplined, reliable, responsible and organised. Those low in conscientiousness are less reliable, more negligent and disorganised. Conscientious youngsters are less likely to develop behavioural problems or become wild teenagers (unless they are conscientious members of a gang or the Hitler Youth). Occasionally, conscientious individuals (especially those low in agreeableness) *can* be aggressive or even abusive, if they are convinced they are right and their victim is wrong. Someone can be conscientious but misguided, or even evil (suicide bombers are probably quite conscientious).

I've certainly seen conscientious young people who are abusive at home but those low in this trait are more likely to be difficult and aggressive. Of the thirty young people in my sample who have completed the Big Five personality test, almost all score low, or at best average, on this dimension. Children low in conscientiousness may be academic underachievers and are at increased risk of lying, cheating, stealing, abusing substances and being promiscuous.

Abused parents are more likely to be above average on this trait.

Agreeableness

It took psychologists a long time to include this as a basic personality dimension, possibly because it sounds warm and fuzzy and too much like a value judgment; it is however, fundamental to how we regard people and to how they behave. Agreeable children are generally easy children. They tend to be good natured, polite, co-operative and have empathy for others. They are far more likely to want adults' approval and to behave themselves just to avoid upsetting you. They show more respect for people generally; they may be too nice for our cut-throat society and may be victimised or exploited.

Children who are low on agreeableness are negative towards others, critical, rude and callous. It sounds wrong to say high in *dis-agreeableness* though logically this is the same thing, and if you have such a child you've probably noticed them disagreeing with you quite often. They may be very interesting people, with healthy distrust and cynicism and some are very successful in life. On average, females are higher on Agreeableness than males[260] though there is plenty of overlap.

Personality traits don't cause any particular behaviour on their own but change the probabilities of behaviour in interaction with other personality factors, attitudes, habits and the environment. Past environment is very important in how traits are expressed: someone with an agreeable temperament can learn to be bitter and twisted in an extreme environment and someone with a disagreeable temperament can have these traits reduced by positive experiences. The current environment is also important; a disagreeable person may be nice to others if the consequences of being nasty are sufficiently great to motivate different behaviour, and even the nicest person can become aggressive in extreme circumstances.

Agreeableness shows considerable continuity over time, though as with all personality traits, exactly how it translates into behaviour is complex, variable and changeable. Some agreeable children become far less so during adolescence, which may be a temporary stage or may last into adulthood. Some highly disagreeable people are never violent or abusive and some people who are average on this trait use violence to get their own way. Even the most agreeable individual is capable of acting violently or abusively in some circumstances, but the chances of them doing so are far less. An agreeable personality is one of the strongest factors protecting children from becoming delinquent[261].

My preliminary results suggest that Agreeableness might not be quite as important a factor as Conscientiousness in violence to parents, although most of the children scored somewhat below average. These children certainly are not psychopaths and many of them can be agreeable, considerate and empathic in some circumstances.

Importantly, the parents who are being abused by their children tend to score far higher on Agreeableness than do the abusive young people. In fact of forty parents I've tested only one is below average on this trait and a number have maxed out, scoring the highest possible score for Agreeableness. A few have been apologetic about this, saying things like "People tell me I'm too soft for my own good". This relates to our analysis of parenting styles, to a sense of Entitlement, and to our analysis of Power. Irresponsible, and less caring, children tend to have power over more responsible and caring parents.

Neuroticism

Some people are born nervous, anxious, highly-strung, emotional, cautious and insecure while others tend to be calm, relaxed and more emotionally stable. This is another very fundamental personality trait which is largely inherited and tends to 'run' in the family. It's linked to the reactivity of the autonomic nervous system (which controls the fight or flight reactions which make our hearts race, palms sweat, muscles tense, etc. in readiness for an emergency).

Children who are violent to their parents appear to be somewhat more likely to be at one extreme or the other. Overall (against most people's expectations) I see more children who are violent to parents who are **low** on neuroticism and anxiety. Being *fearless* is a risk factor for all types of violence in youth. This can be shown by something as simple as resting heart rate: children with lower heart rates are more likely to grow up violent than others[262]. This goes against the bullies-are-cowards myth (another comforting belief that makes the world seem a fairer place).

"A child who is relatively fearless from birth is… at risk, and in need of skilful parenting. Not only is he likely to attempt risky things that could get him injured, but he will also be inclined to resist parental discipline. Where the average child will 'do this' or 'stop doing that' at least partly out of fear of the consequences, the relatively fearless child may ignore the injunction, argue, or have a tantrum. Unless the parent has the good sense and the energy to win each of these battles, such a child will learn that resistance or counterattack works, and his undisciplined behaviour will get worse with each such lesson." Lykken[263]

Research has found that fearful children are less likely to have anti-social behaviours overall[264]. A timid child who lives in awe of adults and is afraid to challenge them, is less likely to develop direct opposition to parents and teachers or violence to parents. However this does not mean that it's *rare* for nervous children to be abusive towards parents. It's certainly not rare, but they are a bit less common than the fearless type. They are more likely than the fearless children to only be violent within the home and more likely to only target their mother. They often have highly emotional outbursts of violence, meltdowns, and become very distressed themselves, sometimes in a state of near-panic. Their violence and tantrums may appear more *expressive* and less *instrumental* (see chapter on Anger). They are less likely to be involved in delinquency and substance abuse.

There is a general tendency, particularly among some professionals, to think of violent young people as being depressed and anxious. This is linked to the idea that young abusers are really victims and must be suffering. This is not necessarily so, though some *are* stressed and depressed by the time they come into contact with workers. Sometimes they are stressed because they have made their lives chaotic and unpleasant. Children who are violent within their family stress themselves out and can single-handedly turn a peaceful family into a high-stress war-zone! A few are trying to get sympathy and may portray themselves as suffering victims.

This goes against the common idea that stress is closely related to aggression[265]. Stress can certainly make an individual more or less aggressive or violent *at the time,* but there is little overall association between the two. Stress and strain won't make someone violent if they are not that way inclined. Anxious individuals are overall less violent than non-anxious people, though they experience far more stress. People living in poverty, whether in Western nations or in Third World Countries, are generally no more violent than the more affluent, unless it's a cultural norm for them to be violent. Aggressive people create tension and bad relationships which produces stress. To complicate things even further, some people get a buzz out of fear and stress. Those with extreme cravings for excitement may actually be less sensitive to stress than the rest of us and have to work harder than you or I to get a buzz[266].

Some highly anxious individuals can be very difficult to live with and some are very controlling towards their nearest and dearest. This is especially true of those with obsessive traits or full-blown obsessive compulsive disorders. Such highly anxious individuals may have an extremely high desire to control those around them, so some of their violence may be instrumental and deliberate, even if ultimately motivated by avoidance of anxiety. This is the pattern for many of the autistic children who are violent to parents. There's an optional chapter on Anxiety later.

Openness

The fifth of the Big Five personality traits, Openness, is the least obvious and the least important in the context of violence to parents. It's not about openness to others in terms of communicating your thoughts and feelings or being honest, but about *Openness to Experience*. High scores are linked to imagination, creativity and intellectual pursuits (especially if combined with high intelligence) and to daydreaming and an interest in abstract ideas. Those lower on this trait may be more down to earth, practical and concrete thinkers. Though openness is more obvious in intelligent people, I've worked with people with intellectual disabilities who are open to new ideas and quite thoughtful. Small children are incapable of some kinds of abstract thought but you can see that some are trying to understand and make sense of the world, while others just get on with practical matters and don't worry about life, death and everything.

Those low on Openness may be more stubborn, but those high on Openness may be less accepting of authority. So both extremes *could* play a part in violence to parents for a few individuals even though overall scores appear to be average (this is pure speculation on my part as I'd need to test a much larger sample to show such a connection). As far as I am aware, no one has looked at the personality profiles of children who are violent to parents, possibly because they don't want to look as if they are blaming the young person.

Intelligence

Personality factors are considered to be different to *abilities*, so Intelligence isn't included in 'the big five'. Although we talk about intelligence as if it were a unitary, measurable scale like height or weight (especially when measured as IQ), it's not *nearly* so simple. Statistically, being good at one thing makes it *more likely* that you will be good at another, yet people can be very clever at some things and quite dull at others. High IQ does not guarantee high creativity, high emotional intelligence, or even good common sense (anyone who has worked in a University could give many examples of this). Success in most things depends less on overall intelligence than it does on motivation, other personality traits (such as conscientiousness) and on luck.

IQ scores are a pretty crude measure of intelligence. There are many reasons not to take them too seriously and that is shown here by the fact that teenagers generally do better on IQ tests than anyone else! IQ scores are always adjusted to take age into account. If they were not adjusted, then IQ would increase up to the early twenties then steadily decline with age. This is largely due to the type of tests that are used. On some measures, not given much weight in IQ tests, such as logic and language, middle aged brains do better than younger ones. The main advantage that young brains have is in processing speed[267].

IQ scores are never highly accurate, having a 'standard error' of five points. Motivation and anxiety can greatly affect scores and I've known a number of people be given a label of 'intellectual disability' when this was clearly not correct. IQ is an even less useful and valid measure for people with very unusual personalities or abilities, such as those with any form of autism. [268]

Intelligence, like neuroticism, in children who are violent to parents covers a wide range but seems to be *somewhat* more likely in those who are at either extreme, above or below average.

Overall, low intelligence is strongly associated with increased acts of violence and crime compared to those with average or high intelligence[269]. Of course, they also get caught more often. However, I have seen a great many young people who are of above average intelligence, be violent to their parents. Some are 'A' students and appear to also have high self-esteem (see below) while others are underachieving academically (for a variety of reasons, including the fact that they are uncooperative and disruptive, low on Conscientiousness).

At the other extreme there are a number of young people with intellectual disabilities or other learning difficulties who abuse parents. There are a number of reasons for this, some of which are covered later (see sections on disability and the chapter on autism).

Stubbornness

Stubbornness is not considered to be a fundamental personality trait like the Big Five listed above. It's not often measured or tested and does not play a central part in the labels we give to deviant children (though Oppositional Defiant Disorder has a heavy component of stubbornness). However, it seems to be a consistent feature of the personalities of children who are abusive of parents; in fact it's probably *the* most consistent.

In the *Who's in Charge?* groups I run, I often ask for a show of hands on various characteristics of the participants' children. On average two thirds are male; about a fifth have been diagnosed with ADHD and, about a half are noticeably more active than usual according to the parents. Many say their children are of above average intelligence but a few have learning difficulties. Some are high on anxiety but more are relatively fearless. Some have high self-esteem and others low. There is only one characteristic which almost always produces a unanimous show of hands: "Is your child more stubborn than average?"

160

Stubbornness, or obstinacy, sounds nicer when described as 'strong-willed' or 'tenacious.' Like intelligence, extraversion, openness and fearlessness, being strong-willed can be a very positive trait. These traits (alone or in combination) may become positive with maturity even though they may make a parent's life hell in childhood.

Stubbornness is dangerous in combination with high feelings of entitlement. It's particularly problematic when also combined with low agreeableness and low conscientiousness. It leads to more defiance of adults and greater persistence of bad behaviour. When a confrontation or a tantrum does occur, it persists longer and makes the young person far more difficult to deal with. Their stubbornness reduces the potential power of the parent. Digging in your heels makes you harder to move, literally and figuratively.

I sometimes advise parents that they have to be as stubborn as their child about the things that really matter, but, being stubborn and pig-headed about the small stuff is going to make matters worse. Some parents clash with a child because they are both very stubborn.

Empathy

Empathy is not a fundamental personality characteristic but, like stubbornness, it's a trait that shows considerable continuity and can be very important in behaviour. It's strongly related to Agreeableness, but can vary greatly in different circumstances. It's a common human characteristic to only show empathy to those we see as being 'one-of-us'. If this were not so, there would be no wars or terrorism. For example, many racists, nationalists, and religious fanatics are caring and empathic towards friends and family yet dehumanise strangers or those they see as enemies.

People vary greatly in their general level of empathy for others. Overall women are more empathic than we males, though there are wide variations and much overlap[270]. Though little studied (and very difficult to measure) there are undoubtedly large cultural differences in empathy. There is some disturbing evidence that young people have become less empathic in recent years[271] and this may be linked to an increase in violence to parents. Susan Greenfield suggests that social media may be playing a role in lowered empathy[272]. Being desensitised to violence, by watching violent media or playing violent games, probably helps lower empathy for victims of violence. If she is right, it's likely to get a lot worse!

At one extreme is the psychopath, predominantly male, who feels little or no empathy and can show shocking indifference to other people's suffering. This in itself does not mean that they will *inevitably* be violent or criminal. There still needs to be the motivation to act violently, but when it suits their purpose, the psychopath will feel no guilt or remorse. True psychopathy is thankfully quite rare, but I suspect that there are far more around than is obvious and they crawl out of the woodwork en masse when society rewards the heartless (e.g. in Nazi Germany or Pol Pot's Cambodia). We label criminals as psychopaths but Army Generals and successful businessmen who have no empathy don't get this label. I've heard it suggested a few times that some young people who are treating family members with great cruelty are 'psychopaths' but often they show empathy in some circumstances, and some grow out of such behaviour, so the label is not appropriate and is hardly ever helpful. Actually, I'm not convinced that 'psychopath' should be considered a psychiatric diagnosis. It's not something *they* suffer from and there is no clear dividing line between them and others. It's more a moral judgment than a useful scientific category.

People with autistic traits often have immature and limited empathy and this can contribute to violent behaviour in childhood and adolescence (see chapter on Autism).

Someone with high empathy is *less likely* to act abusively, but empathy is no *guarantee* of non-violence; abusers seem to be very good at switching it off! Many people who are violent are not low in empathy overall but suppress their empathy towards their victims when they act violently. Some have little or no empathy when in a rage but feel guilty and empathic later. A violent child may feel sorry for his mother when she is in pain from other sources but not show any empathy when he himself has inflicted the pain. Some young people appear to have good empathy for their friends, and may be quite caring and nurturing towards them, but don't display this within the family. A few young people appear to show empathy only towards animals or babies.

The ego-centric or narcissistic person is often low on empathy, and this is a common trait in adolescence (at least in our society). There is evidence that narcissism in young people has got worse in recent decades (see section on self-esteem).

Two common personality patterns among children who are violent towards parents

I've only recently been giving young people who are violent towards their parents personality tests in the course of counselling. Numbers are low (thirty) and results are preliminary. Most, though not all, score low on Agreeableness. Even more score low on Conscientiousness. Scores on Extraversion and Neuroticism often go to extremes with two fairly common patterns. Those young people who are introverted appear to be somewhat more likely to be high on Neuroticism. Children on the autism spectrum are the extreme of this neurotic introvert 'type'. The extroverts, on the other hand, are quite often fearless, scoring *below* average on Neuroticism. They also tend to have high self-esteem.

These results appear to fit neatly with the research on 'reactive' and 'proactive' aggression, even though that research did not look at aggression aimed at parents. Nervous, introverted children are more likely to be impulsive and highly emotional when violent, hence 'reactive' or 'expressive' violence. Fearless extroverts are more often 'proactive' or 'instrumental' when violent.[273]

The word 'type' above is in quotation marks because I am not suggesting a *typology*. It's certainly not the case that all children who are violent within the home fit into one of these categories and those who do may not fulfil *all* the criteria. If it doesn't fit your child, don't worry about it. I'm putting it forward to show the range of personality patterns and it may help *some* parents make sense of their child.

Reactive Introverts	Proactive Extroverts
Introverted	Extraverted
Neurotic and anxious	Fearless (low or average Neuroticism)
Often have low self-esteem	May have average to very high self-esteem
Much of their violence appears to be an emotional reaction	More proactive, instrumental aggression
Get very upset and have major tantrums	Sometimes aggressive in a cold and unemotional manner, though can also get into rages
Anger usually a major issue; appear out-of-control	Anger may not be an issue in itself, not out-of-control but controlling
Often a victim at school	May be well behaved or a bully at school
Low popularity, isolated or part of a small low-status clique	May be very popular (one of the in-crowd) or part of a deviant sub-group
Unlikely to be delinquent	May become delinquent outside the home
Unlikely to have drug or alcohol issues	Higher risk for substance abuse and other anti-social behaviour
Often have a mild disability, Autism, or ADHD	Unlikely to have a disability or any meaningful psychiatric label
Often have some learning difficulties	Some are underachievers or uninterested in school. Some are very successful
May be very dependent on parents	May be detached from family and quite independent
More likely to remain at home into adulthood	May leave home when the opportunity arises
More boys fit this pattern than girls	Girls who abuse parents may be *slightly* more likely to be of this type
A minority of children who are violent to parents approximate this pattern	This pattern is more common

Although the Introverted-reactive type are victims far more often than bullies in school, they can become very controlling and bullying at home. Reactive violence may be self-defence (or an overreaction) in school but this is seldom the case with violence to parents – they are too timid to stand up to aggressive adults.

163

Though they start out with expressive, emotional temper tantrums, this can be used to control family members (this doesn't usually work at school, though it may in some junior schools) and over time their violence may improve or else become more controlling and more proactive. Sometimes their attempts to control are directly due to anxiety (particularly common for kids with Autism or Obsessive Compulsive Disorder).

The Extraverted-proactive type may be bullying family members to get their own way or because they enjoy the feeling of power, or they may be disempowering parents in order to have more freedom. Some were difficult from an early age but some only develop aggression in adolescence.

Many professionals wrongly think that most children who are violent within the home are of the first type, expecting anxiety, depression and low self-esteem; thus they often see these children primarily as victims. They may wrongly assume that the child cannot help their behaviour because of a diagnosed condition, believing that they are genuinely 'out of control' rather than controlling others.

The second type often present very well to professionals. Many are articulate and charming with good social skills. They may convince workers and others that they are the victim. I increasingly see such children lie about being victims of abuse. When professionals meet a confident, articulate young person who is being violent to parents they may either assume that the confidence is a mask hiding deep insecurity, or they may assume that parents must be hiding something since an apparently well-adjusted young person can't be abusive.

Start Box

Aaron

Aaron had always been a wild child. He was funny, bright and charming but he was one of those babies who never seemed to sleep and one of those toddlers who bounce off the walls and need constant vigilance. His parents, Beth, a florist, and Frank, an auto engineer, separated fairly amicably when he was four and his behaviour became more overtly aggressive, especially towards his placid older sister. Beth dragged him round to a long list of specialists who gave him various labels but no constructive help. The label that seemed to fit best was ADHD. Somewhat reluctantly, she put him on Dexamphetamine at age eight which helped a little with his ability to concentrate at school. His behaviour continued to deteriorate both at home and at school. The only place he was tolerably well behaved was at Frank's on fortnightly access visits and week-long visits in the vacations.

By the time Aaron was eleven he was being threatened with expulsion from primary school for disruption in the classroom and hitting other children in the playground. His mother decided she could no longer cope. Sending him to Frank's seemed a reasonable solution and for the first few months this went well. However, once the honeymoon period was over, he began defying and verbally abusing his father almost as much as he had his mother. His father lost his temper on several occasions and slapped him. This allowed Aaron to feel that he was in the right and his father was in the wrong. When he was expelled from High School after only one term, a major confrontation with his father ended with Aaron smashing several of his father's antique car models and he was sent back to his mothers in the middle of the night. Soon after this Beth attended the *Who's in Charge?* Group and as a result she became far more firm with Aaron. This seemed at first only to enrage him and for the next few months his behaviour was worse than ever. He struck or pushed his mother on several occasions and terrorised his sister. He was expelled from two more schools for fighting and was charged with shoplifting. He stopped taking the Dexamphetamine but this seemed to make little or no difference to his behaviour although his ability to concentrate in school may have got a little worse. But as he was seldom doing any school work this was not a big deal.

The situation at home came very close to breaking down but somehow Beth hung on and continued calmly applying consequences even though Aaron denied that he cared and tried hard not to comply with any punishment. When Aaron was fourteen he started to show small signs of calming down, at least the periods between rages got steadily longer. He agreed to have counselling and, though his attendance was sporadic, at times he was honest and contrite about his abusive behaviours, though on other occasions he was aggressive and defensive.

An obvious turning point came when he got a part-time job with a local garage (though legally too young to do so) and he seemed to mature overnight. He matured further when he got a steady girlfriend who, although she looked to Beth like an extra in a horror movie, was horrified at the way he spoke to his mother and threatened to hit him if she heard him do this in her presence. He is now sixteen and for the past year there has been no recurrence of the abusive behaviour and he actually managed to complete an entire year at the same school and, though still an underachiever, he scraped a pass. He is soon to start an apprenticeship as a car mechanic and has no problem concentrating on this. His abundant energy, a disadvantage in school, is an asset at work. He is very sociable and popular, with heaps of friends. Aaron now has a good relationship with his mother, though he is less close to his father. He recently made a public apology for 'years of terrible behaviour' to his long-suffering sister on her eighteenth birthday. There wasn't a dry eye in the restaurant.

End Box

Girls Who Abuse Their Parents

"One of the most dramatic changes in the experience of girls vis-à-vis physical aggression is the changing nature of the mass media's treatment of female aggression, from a consistently negative message ('girls do not hit') to an ever more positive message ('girls kick ass')." Garbarino[274]

When I tell people that almost one third of the children who are violent to parents are girls many are surprised, but they may be surprised for very different reasons. Many are surprised that there are *so many* violent girls but almost as many are surprised that there is *any* difference between boys and girls. I've recently given professionals coming to my workshops an attitude questionnaire at the start of the session (before I enlighten them) and to my surprise a little more than half come with an expectation that there are equal numbers of boys and girls being violent to parents. I think this is a worry and may be partly due to the successful campaign by men's rights groups focusing on the fact that women can be violent too.

The evidence from many sources is that almost one third of children who are violent to parents are girls (30% in my sample). Some people claim that violence to parents is 'mostly' boys being violent to mothers. This is certainly the most common pattern, but it's misleading to imply that *most* child-to-parent violence is of this type because in half of these families *either* a girl is the aggressor *or* a father is a victim. Gender issues are important, but nowhere near as important as they are in adult family violence. The single most common situation is where a teenage boy is abusing a single mother after domestic violence, but these are only a quarter of all cases (24% in my sample of four hundred and eighty).

Some people believe that girls are becoming, if they are not already, just as violent as boys. One of the many epidemics we are supposed to be having (part of our epidemic of epidemics) is an epidemic of girl's violence. The gender gap in youth violence has definitely narrowed but is in no danger of disappearing. The difference between girls' and boys' violence is less within the home than it is outside the home. For violent crime and school violence, there is far more than twice as many boys as girls. The proportion of girls in my referrals has slowly increased over the past twenty years, from under a quarter to almost a third, but this appears to have levelled off. In my teen years (half a century ago), I must have seen thirty or forty fights involving boys and not a single one involving girls: now children tell me that girl fights are common, though most say not nearly as common as boy fights. There has been a change in girls' attitudes to violence and I believe, as do a number of researchers, that this has been largely due to the influence of the mass media. Parent still discourage girls from fighting, same as they always have, so this change can't be blamed on parents (boys violence is often blamed on parents socializing them to be aggressive, but society does this even without parents encouragement).

Some people blame feminism for girls' aggression; their reasons are usually misguided or dishonest, yet there is a *tiny* grain of truth in this. Just as, to some extent, the empowerment and liberation of children is related to abuse of parents, the liberation of women has probably played an *indirect* part in increasing girls' violence. I am definitely **not** blaming feminism! I think that the liberation of women has been a really wonderful thing which has benefited all of society, including men and boys… and it still has a long way to go.

It's a sad irony that many of us saw the emergence of kick-ass heroines as a good thing. We cheered for Ripley in the film Alien, one of the first of a new breed of female heroes. The portrayal of women as helpless victims in films up to the seventies now looks pathetic and prejudiced (think of Fey Ray being carried about by King Kong), but an indirect effect of the liberation of women was that the media began encouraging females to be violent. Assertiveness doesn't sell as well as aggressiveness.

To my mind the evidence for gender differences in aggression is overwhelming. Boys have been shown to be more physically aggressive from eighteen months of age[275]. At that age they are twice as likely to hit another child as are girls (and probably twice as likely to hit parents too). The gender gap gets wider in Kindergarten and primary school but doesn't widen any further at adolescence[276]. The gap never goes away during development. This holds up whether we measure children's violence by direct observations in school, by their self-reports, or by parent or teacher reports. Boys are consistently more violent than girls at every age, and in *every* society. Although the overall amount of aggression in different societies varies tremendously, there is no society where females are equal to males in aggression. Nor is there an ape species where females are as violent as males. We are asked by some writers to believe that the clear genetic differences in aggression found in our ancestors have vanished during evolution only to be replaced, in each of the thousands of different societies, by environmental forces making men more aggressive than women[277]. This makes little sense but shows how hard people will try to believe what they want to believe.

Some people really don't want to admit that males are more aggressive than females. Ironically, this includes a few feminists. The politically correct position is that all gender differences are socially created. Others try to explain away differences in abuse by suggesting that males and females just use different tactics. One argument is that females are just as aggressive and abusive as males, but that they use psychological and verbal means rather than physical. A number of studies find that girls indulge in more indirect aggression than boys, gossiping, social exclusion, etc. However, since the behaviour of girls and boys is so different socially, it may be like comparing assaults in soccer to assaults in golf. In addition not every study finds such a difference in indirect aggression and a few have found that boys were more, not less, likely to indulge in indirect, social aggression. Boys are certainly as verbally abusive as girls and in adulthood, men are far more verbally abusive than women. Boys and men also use emotional and psychological means of hurting and controlling others in addition to, not instead of, physical

167

violence. Boys, on average, are not as skilled socially or verbally as are girls of the same age, so they aren't as good at psychological abuse. So while it's true that some forms of social aggression (ostracism, gossip, etc.) are more common for females[278], it's not true that this makes them as aggressive as males.

In most ways the girls who are abusing parents are very similar to the boys. The behaviours involved are more similar than different, despite the girls being physically weaker. They aren't using indirect or social aggression against parents (as female bullies often do in school) but name-calling, hitting and throwing things. They don't damage property *quite* as often in my sample (68% of girls, 76% of boys) but this is the only obvious behavioural difference to the boys. The motivation for the abusive behaviour appears to be very similar, frustration at not getting their own way or attempts to disempower parents. The choice of victim is generally the same, mostly mothers and about half of fathers when they are at home. They are slightly *more* likely to abuse step-fathers than are the boys. I'll list some of the similarities and differences later.

There is no *typical* girl who abuses a parent, but here are a few examples:

Tracey

Tracey is a cute fourteen year-old girl with big eyes and a ready smile. She has a clever and charming way with words and a quirky sense of humour. She wants to be a lawyer and could make a good one. Despite it being our first meeting and the subject of conversation being her violence, she is self-assured and seems quite at ease. She is extrovert, has excellent self-esteem and is low in neuroticism. She finds it impossible not to grin and giggle when her mother tells of her smashing a plate over her father's head. She is less proud of having hit her mother or of having assaulted her little sister but she denies feeling guilty. She hasn't mentioned it to any of her friends but claims that this is because 'it just hasn't come up' rather than from embarrassment. She says her temper isn't a problem *for her* but it is for her parents. Surprisingly, and unusually, she has no real criticisms of her parents and readily agrees that they don't deserve to be abused. My feeling when I get to know the family a bit better, is that she is embarrassed by her parents (they are a bit rough and ready and clearly not as smart as Tracey) but she is too loyal to say this to an outsider. She clearly loves them, but doesn't respect them enough.

I ask what she would do if she were in her parents' shoes. She says she doesn't know. I ask if she would be more strict if she were them. Keeping one step ahead of me she says, "If they get more strict, I'll escalate; it sets me off and they know there will be *consequences*. For every action there is a reaction." I've known a few children who were adept at using consequences against their parents but it's unusual for them to actually use the word.

She claims that the violence isn't a big deal to her. She's not sure if she will grow out of it. "It's just fate. Just the way I am" she says, cheerfully philosophical. She has no problem with coming to counselling but no real goals either and I only see her a few times.

Tracey's mother says that most of the time Tracey is a delightful child who can be cooperative and responsible. It's just the outbursts of violence when she doesn't get her own way that bother them. They have endured her violence for some time but finally called the police when she slammed her sister's head into a table.

As sometimes happens when I'm working with different members of a family, there is an improvement over the next few weeks but I've no way of knowing if Tracey or her parents have made changes, or if she is just maturing. Probably both have made small changes which have resulted in a virtuous cycle. The outlook for a girl like Tracey, with so many positives, is hopeful and it's quite likely she will 'grow out of it'. However, her behaviour needs to be taken very seriously because when a child is distancing themselves from their parents and resisting parental control, they are at real risk of getting into drugs or alcohol and forming liaisons with 'undesirables'.

Liz

Liz was sixteen when I met her. She had agreed through the mother of a friend to talk on video about her violence. She is another attractive, bright, mostly self-assured girl. She says she's been 'feral' since she was little. While Tracey had no serious problems outside the home Liz had plenty. Liz saw her violence as being genetic, coming from her father's side of the family, but she also saw it as childish and was confident she was growing out of it. Unusually, she was more violent to her father than her mother. This was because her mother had "pretty much given up" trying to control her and avoided confrontations. Her father was the disciplinarian, so he was the one who got in her way and tried to rein her in.

Liz's parents are not like the typical parents I encounter who are experiencing violence from their children. She describes her mother as "quiet, a bit of a nerd". Her father however, is a large, tough, aggressive (but likable), tattooed ex-biker with an authoritarian style of parenting. Liz has punched him in the face and tried to stab him. I asked if she was afraid of him. She laughed, "I'm the only one who isn't." I asked what would have happened if she were a boy. "I wouldn't be here if I were a boy. He'd have killed me!" This is probably just a slight exaggeration; her father would have reacted violently to a son but his code of honour prevents him from hitting a girl.

Like many young people I've worked with, breaking free of parental control led to abuse of drugs and alcohol and to dropping out of school. Liz was also in many fights with other girls and now says it was a miracle that she escaped any legal charges. Last year Liz's behaviour was off the planet, "Only the police could control me." At one point she stopped traffic to stand in front of her father's car waving a knife at him. She moved out of home, moving in to a disgusting flat shared by four drug-taking young men. She lasted two weeks and came home with a slightly improved attitude. She said this was a turning point for her but it was the birth of her sister's baby which made her determined to give up violence.

Liz has not been violent for over a year and is getting along well with her parents. She says she's always been close to her father and they clashed so much because they are so alike in temperament. She clearly loves her family, is attending college and is hopeful for the future. It's almost hard to believe that the charming girl I interview could have been an out-of-control 'psycho' not so long ago. Kids like this make nonsense of the idea that such behaviour is a sign of mental illness. It's not much of an 'illness' if you can choose to give it up, is it?

I asked her if she loved her parents even when she was abusing them. "Yes, I never stopped loving them. I didn't think about it, though." As with Tracey it was clearly respect that was missing, not love.

Noelene

In contrast to Tracey and Liz, Noelene is a large, awkward eighteen-year-old with a mild intellectual disability. She is acutely aware of being considered 'disabled' and having attended a special school. Also in marked contrast to Tracey and Liz, Noelene has low self-esteem, though not low enough to make her depressed. Her long-suffering boyfriend does not consider her to be 'disabled' and nor do her many friends. She hits her boyfriend on occasions and Noelene is one of the only young people I've met who are abusive to their father but not at all to their mother. Her explanation for this is very straightforward: Mum wouldn't take it. Mum confirms this in no uncertain terms. I suggest to Noelene that she is taking unfair advantage of the fact that her father and boyfriend are gentlemen. She agrees and seems thoughtful. I see her once more a month later and she and her mother report a big improvement in her behaviour – she hasn't actually hit anyone for a month. I compliment her on her maturity and determination to change (I'm exaggerating her determination but that's the kind of white lie I use to motivate people). Growing out of her violence could have positive long-term consequences since she wants to have children at some point. (I'd be worried if she was planning to have them soon). Interestingly, people with an intellectual disability sometimes respond more quickly to counselling, largely because they are more cooperative and sadly, it can be a stimulating novelty for them to be listened to and taken seriously[279].

Peta

Peta had been sexually abused by her step-father when she was nine. As soon as her mother, Fiona, guessed what was happening, they separated, this despite having no real evidence, and both step-father and Peta denying that anything had happened. It took Peta a year to admit the sexual abuse and there was then too little evidence to prosecute.

One of the alarm signs for Fiona had been that Peta began to have terrible temper tantrums and had gone from being an ideal student to one who would defy teachers and disrupt the class. Surprisingly her behaviour at home remained tolerable but Fiona, with the wisdom of hindsight, says that her own feelings of guilt (completely undeserved) and her natural concern for her abused daughter meant that she altered the way she parented. She became far more indulgent and let discipline slide. She wonders now if this did not contribute to Peta's feelings of insecurity and contribute to the gradual deterioration in her behaviour. Peta began swearing at Fiona on a regular basis from age twelve. Unfortunately (but not unusually), a worker Fiona approached for help told her to ignore the swearing. The worker probably thought that Peta had a lot to be angry about (true) and that swearing at her mother was one way of releasing the anger. Some workers become so fixated on the young person as victim (and Peta clearly was a victim) that they are incapable of dealing with the young person as victimiser. Part of the ubiquitous mother-blaming in the welfare field is a tendency to blame mothers even when fathers abuse children; they are seen as colluding even if they are terrified of the man and they are often assumed to have known about sexual abuse when they had absolutely no idea (people often don't see sexual abuse, even when it's under their nose, because they don't expect it and abusers are very sneaky).

Fiona ignored the verbal abuse and inevitably it got worse. The more Peta got away with, the less respect she had for her mother. She began slapping Fiona when she was thirteen. The same worker who had told Fiona to ignore the swearing now told her to have Peta charged with assault, which Fiona had no intention of doing.

Peta attended a child psychiatrist who prescribed Dexamphetamine despite the lack of evidence that Peta had ADHD. Peta gave them to her friends and on at least one occasion sold them (they are chemically similar to *speed*). She saw a therapist who deliberately avoided talking to Fiona, as there was another worker available to talk to her, and he only worked on what the child voluntarily brought to the sessions. It must make working with teenagers a lot easier if you don't have to juggle loyalty to them with concern for their victims. Naturally, Peta never voluntarily mentioned hitting her mother though she did complain long and bitterly about how over-protective and over-controlling her mother was, rehearsing and rehashing her excuses until she thoroughly believed them herself. This form of counselling, child focused rather than family focused, can do more harm than good for some children.

Peta also began to blame her mother for the sexual abuse (possibly this was as a result of the counselling) and though she was angry at the world in general, Fiona, the safest target, copped the brunt of the bad behaviour. Things took a rapid downhill turn when Peta discovered boys. She was still thirteen but could pass for sixteen. She began hanging around with a group of kids aged sixteen to twenty and became sexually promiscuous. She made no attempt whatsoever to hide this from her now frantic mother and also told her about smoking dope and drinking. Fiona was horrified to find that the authorities (both police and Child Protection) said there was nothing they could do. This was still their reaction when Peta, just turned fourteen, left home for three weeks and was living with three eighteen-year-olds (one girl and two boys). She denied sleeping with either of the eighteen-year-olds and invented an imaginary boyfriend of fifteen (hence safe from prosecution).

Peta was self-harming, cutting her arms and legs. She made light of this and on several occasions did this in front of her horrified mother, sometimes clearly using it to deliberately upset her. She continued seeing therapists of various kinds. One play-therapist had her bury animals representing her step-father and mother in a sand pit and allowed her to 'vent her anger' against her mother on a blow-up dinosaur! Another therapist told Fiona that she should show Peta more love and give her more praise (giving praise to someone who literally spits in your face is not easy – "my, what well aimed spit, my dear!"). Another therapist openly suggested that Fiona had subconsciously been complicit in the sexual abuse, thus implying she had brought all this on herself. When Fiona tearfully and angrily stormed out, the therapist took this as confirmatory evidence of her hypothesis and noted that Fiona had a problem with anger and with control (meaning that she was attempting to be too controlling, not that she had no control). She did get some useful help and advice from a family support worker but overall the system victimised Fiona.

After three weeks away from home, Peta made an effort to improve her behaviour and for a while got on better with Fiona. However, this only worked when Fiona didn't try to restrict her coming and going. Peta at fourteen would go to all night parties or be brought back blind drunk at two in the morning; on one occasion she was dumped unconscious on the front lawn by a car load of laughing teenage boys. At one party she was drugged and raped. After this, Peta took an overdose in a genuine suicide attempt. When Fiona found her unconscious she was momentarily tempted to take the rest of the pills herself and lie down next to her daughter. Though death seemed attractive at that low point, Fiona loved her daughter too much to carry out such a plan and instead rushed Peta to hospital and a stomach pump. Peta was admitted to a psychiatric unit. She was diagnosed at various times with Post Traumatic Stress Disorder, ADHD, Borderline Personality Disorder, Oppositional Defiant Disorder and Conduct Disorder. She also developed an eating disorder and lost a lot of weight.

The next few years continued to be hell on Earth for Fiona, but, agonisingly slowly, things got better. Peta left home at eighteen and moved in with a boyfriend who controlled her every move and eventually hit her. She returned home to Mum and went back to school. The violence towards Fiona decreased and eventually stopped. A side effect of the anti-depressants caused Peta to gain weight, at first this seemed a good thing as she was recovering from anorexia. However, by the time she was nineteen she was overweight and depressed because of this. Gradually she matured and fell in with a good bunch of friends and is now studying art at University.

Peta's story is what many professionals would expect as more typical for violent girls. In my experience, violence to parents that results from the child being abused is not rare but is not all that common either. I've seen more girls like Tracy and Liz than like Peta. However, there may be more girls around like Peta who are treated in the psychiatric or sexual assault services. Their violence to parents may not be taken seriously. It's easy to see Peta as primarily a victim, but it's important to also see her as her mother's victimiser.

Reading their story you can probably empathise with just how awful it all was for Fiona, yet women in her situation, already wracked with guilt, are often treated very poorly by the professionals they have to deal with.

Some likely characteristics of girls who are violent to their parents

- Violence is more 'normal' for boys than for girls. In my sample (and most comparable samples) there are two to three times as many boys as girls who are violent to parents. This is roughly similar to the boy-girl ratios for physical bullying in schools, sibling violence[280] and not too far from the ratios of boys and girls diagnosed with behavioural problems such as Conduct Disorder and Oppositional Defiant Disorder. [281]
- Girls who abuse parents are less likely than boys to be violent outside the home and less likely to be delinquent.

- There is evidence that the gender gap for adolescent violence has narrowed, though there is still a big difference between boys and girls. Crime statistics also suggest some narrowing of the gender gap in recent years, but not all researchers accept that this is a real effect and the gap remains substantial[282]. The ratio for violence to parents appears to be levelling off, but we don't really know what the future holds.

- Although girls are physically weaker than boys, many teenage girls are as strong as their mothers (and a few are as strong as elderly or disabled fathers). Physical strength has little relevance when it comes to threatening people with knives or smashing property and is also of less relevance if the victim is unwilling to use force or violence in retaliation.

- There may be a greater tendency for girls to pick up weapons, especially knives, to compensate for their lack of strength, though in the families I've worked with, they haven't actually used these weapons any more often than the boys.

- There seems to be a *slight* tendency for girls' physical violence to parents to be less severe *on average*, than the boys', though this is not as big a difference as many would expect and may simply be due to them being physically weaker. In fact, of the very small number of parents in my sample who have been hospitalised by their children's violence (causing broken bones and brain damage in a few extreme cases), their attackers have more often been girls. This could just be coincidence, as the numbers are very low, but it does show that girls can be dangerous.

- Girls are quite often more clever at using verbal and psychological abuse than are boys, though this is not a huge difference and in my sample this is not an alternative to physical violence but in addition to it.

- People are more alarmed and shocked by girls' violence and see it as more deviant and concerning, even if the parents are less afraid than when boys are threatening them. It's more noticeable and more memorable than boy's violence and may be referred to helping agencies and the police a bit more often.

- Parents generally worry **a lot more** about beyond control girls than boys. In particular they may be far more afraid of younger adolescent girls leaving home, which can put girls in a powerful position when they don't care if they stay or go.

- Girls' promiscuous behaviour causes **far** more concern than does boys'. This is quite understandable as they can get pregnant, they get raped far more often, and the stigma of being promiscuous is still far greater for girls than for boys (compare 'slut' to 'stud'). The double standard is alive and well, and fully understandable if you are the parent of an adolescent girl.

- Girls are more likely to deliberately use the psychological leverage of putting themselves at risk to gain control over their parents or to disempower them.

173

- Mothers appear to be more likely to have had a very close relationship with their abusive daughter before the abuse started than with their abusive sons.
- Mothers especially are often devastated, distraught and heartbroken by the loss of the relationship and are often frantic with worry about their errant daughters. They are even more likely to be severely depressed and highly anxious than are parents of boys. As far as I can tell this is a reaction to the child's behaviour and I haven't noted any obvious differences between the mothers of abusive girls and mothers of abusive boys.
- Girls are more likely to self-harm than are boys.
- Contrary to most expectations, girls are just as likely as boys to have witnessed their father hit their mother[283]. The idea that children model the same sex parent is exaggerated. They model both parents and also siblings, as well as friends and media personalities (real and fictional).
- Whereas boys who are violent to parents are likely to become abusers in their later relationships, girls seem to be more likely to become victims. We don't know what sort of mothers they become.
- Girls are more likely to grow out of violence somewhat faster than boys. The fact that violence is childish, immature behaviour applies even more to girls than to boys.
- Girls' violence is more likely to lead to them being referred to psychiatric or other services and they are more likely than boys to attend. In my sample girls are less likely to have any diagnoses, but this is largely because ADHD and Autism, the most common diagnoses are far less common in girls.
- Of children who are violent to a parent, girls are *slightly* more likely to abuse their fathers than are the boys. This appears to be simply because they can get away with it; some fathers who would hit a boy, won't hit a girl – it's a chivalry effect. Girls who abuse parents are more likely than the boys to be in a blended family, living with a step-father, and they are considerably more likely to be violent to the step-father than are the boys. This appears to also be the result of a chivalry effect.
- Girls may be somewhat more prone to expressive violence (emotional outbursts) than boys, though they can also be just as deliberately controlling and instrumentally aggressive as boys.
- I've found girls to be slightly less embarrassed by violence to parents than are boys. They may be proud of being able to confront fathers (as are some boys) and many see their conflict with mothers as a fight between two equals or as them standing up to an oppressor. Boys are more often ashamed of violence to a woman.
- Girls are less likely to value aggressiveness and violence generally than are boys but they may confuse their aggression with assertiveness, and being a strong, modern woman with 'standing up for themselves'. Some girls clearly look down on mothers who are submissive and passive (as do some sons). Like boys, they often see themselves as victim rather than as victimiser.

- There may be more girls than boys who have high (but unstable) self-esteem. They are quite often attractive and popular (which also holds for female school bullies) and may more often be extrovert. It may be that a higher level of confidence, or arrogance, is necessary for girls to stand up to adults. Girls' confidence is more linked to attractiveness than is boys' and attractive people tend to be more assertive[284].

So should we parent beyond-control girls differently?

On a number of variables the one hundred and forty plus girls in my sample are very similar to the three hundred and thirty plus boys. Compared to the boys (remembering there are twice as many boys), girls in my sample who abuse parents are:

- Just as likely to be physically violent
- Almost as likely to destroy property
- As likely (maybe *slightly* more likely) to hit Dads
- More likely to hit step-Dads
- As likely to have been exposed to domestic violence
- As likely to have a sole mother
- As likely to be first born

When I meet them, these girls are initially often more cooperative than the boys, and more articulate. Other people are more likely to see them as victims and they seem to be a bit more likely to accuse parents of being abusive to them (a few such accusations are legitimate, some are blatantly untrue, others are exaggerations or twisting the truth). The threat of alleging sexual abuse is a powerful weapon that a few girls wield quite deliberately (two sisters threatened this before even meeting Mum's boyfriend) and this seems to be an increasing trend.

None of the above differences suggest that we should treat girls differently overall to the boys. So there are no general differences in parenting a violent or beyond-control girl as opposed to a violent or beyond-control boy. There are many differences in degree, but they are all individuals and should be treated as such.

Think about how the above factors influence you. Being aware of why you are feeling so powerless can be helpful. Then you need to work out a plan based on the circumstances of *your* child and *your* family. Hopefully the following chapters will help you devise a plan to regain control. Obviously gender will affect this but so will a host of other factors.

Bad Blood and Bad Brains: Blaming Brains, Genes and Labels

"Expert testifies youth killed parents because of 'Adopted child syndrome'" New York Times headline[285]

"When we attribute an action to a person's brain, genes, or evolutionary history, it seems that we no longer hold the individual accountable. Biology becomes the perfect alibi, the get-out-of-jail-free card, the ultimate doctor's excuse note."
Pinker[286]

"I can't help it, I have ADHD" – violent twelve-year-old boy.

This chapter looks at some common excuses and pseudo-scientific 'explanations' for young people's violence. The issues are relevant to all parents even if your child does not have a diagnosed condition. The next chapter goes into labels in a bit more detail.

There is a tendency nowadays to excuse people's behaviour by blaming some vague brain mechanism, hormones, or genetics. Given our current level of knowledge, as *explanations* they are usually weak to useless; as *excuses* they are worse than useless.

If someone's behaviour is beyond the pale, it often makes us feel better if we can see them as 'sick' or 'mad'. It makes us uncomfortable to think that non-crazy people are capable of heinous crimes so we prefer to view them as having wonky brains rather than having freely chosen to do evil. This impulse to explain away evil is exploited, and given a pseudo-scientific gloss, by psychiatry and the legal professions.

We show our strong disapproval of some anti-social behaviour (such as child molestation, sadism or rape) by regarding it as 'sick'. We distance ourselves from such behaviour by labelling perpetrators as *crazy, mad, sick, psycho.*

In complete contrast, seeing some behaviour as an illness can make us more sympathetic: e.g. seeing lethargy as depression rather than laziness. It's common nowadays to regard addictions as illnesses, even though we know it's self-inflicted and that it can be overcome with sufficient motivation. Regarding these behaviours as 'illnesses' usually makes people less blaming[287]. Those who choose to see young people who abuse parents as victims sometimes over-emphasis substance abuse as a cause (see chapter on Drugs).

Thus defining behaviour as 'illness' can either serve to distance ourselves from the behaviour, by viewing them as less than human, or it can serve to make us more sympathetic. But this sympathy often comes at the expense of not regarding them as fully responsible or adult. Abusers themselves, especially child sexual abusers and wife bashers, may be keen to be seen as suffering from an illness rather than as having freely chosen abusive behaviour. In some courts being seen as 'sick', as mad rather than bad, can at times be a matter of life or death! 'Sick' is constantly redefined by the legal and psychiatric professions to include new variations with such notions as 'battered wife syndrome', 'adopted child syndrome', 'Temper Dysregulation Disorder', etc. being added in a fairly ad hoc manner. The number of psychiatric conditions listed in the official 'bible' of psychiatry (the Diagnostic and Statistical Manual, or DSM) has grown at an alarming rate over the past fifty years (from one hundred and fifty to over three hundred) mostly without much evidence that these conditions are in a meaningful way 'illnesses' or even that they make logical sense as categories. What we currently call 'mental illness' is very wide, including serious psychiatric disorders (e.g. schizophrenia and bi-polar), depression (ranging from mild to severe), neurotic conditions (various over-lapping anxiety disorders), disabilities (which shouldn't be classed as mental illnesses), personality disorders (also arguable if these are 'mental illness'), educational problems, anti-social behavioural patterns, substance abuse (including caffeine and nicotine addiction – so every smoker is mentally ill, but you knew that), and also mental conditions resulting from the substance abuse or from brain damage. We are all in this weird and wonderful book somewhere! It's a wild stretch of language and logic to consider all these things to be 'illnesses'!

A few of the categories defy common sense. My favourite is 'Factitious Disorder' which means pretending to be mentally ill. So pretending to be mentally ill is actually a form of mental illness, which means that you **can't** pretend to be mentally ill because you *are* mentally ill by pretending to be mentally ill, which means that you aren't really pretending as you are ill! But what if someone were pretending to have Factitious Disorder? Think about this too much and you *will* go crazy!

Individual psychiatrists may or may not think scientifically about their work (some do, some definitely don't) but at its core, psychiatry is not yet a science. A couple of easily verifiable facts can illustrate this. Firstly, there are no accepted definitions of 'mental disorder' or 'mental illness'. The writers of the various DSMs struggled with it and gave up having any overall definition of what they are classifying. This is a strange state of affairs (a bit like geologists not being clear if they include roads and forests). The second is that not one current treatment in psychiatry was developed on the basis of a scientific theory. The main drugs used were **all** found by accident and most were originally used for other medical conditions. Other treatments such as ECT (shock treatment) and lobotomies were also discovered by accident and trial and error and we still don't know why they (sometimes) work. The talk therapy that *some* psychiatrists use was developed either by psychologists, psychoanalysts, family therapists or social workers – none of the common methods of counselling have their origin in psychiatry.

I'm not just getting at psychiatrists here but also one of my own professions, psychology. Clinical psychology has gotten into bed with psychiatry. Unfortunately psychiatry is already in bed with *Big Pharma*, the Drug Companies.

To take the analogy one step further, Big Pharma is a bloated money-grubbing whore.

The latest version of the bible of psychiatry, DSM5, manages to make matters worse in many ways. Remarkably, it has been soundly criticized by the author of the previous edition DSM-4[288]. Among the brand new illnesses it offers are hoarding and cannabis withdrawal.

Is Family Violence a sign of a disorder?

The idea that most 'wife bashers' suffer from some kind of mental disorder has been generally rejected and is now seen as a cop-out, excusing seriously irresponsible behaviour. Just because an adult is violent or is cantankerous, rebellious or awkward is *not* accepted as sufficient reason to label them with a mental illness. Yet for children we do exactly that, we do it on a regular basis, we do it without any scientific justification, and we do it despite the fact that labelling often has even more serious implications for a child than it does for an adult. As violent and aggressive behaviour is actually **far** more common in children than in adults, it makes *less* sense to see violence as an indication of a mental disorder in childhood than it does in adulthood.

Children who are annoyingly distractible or over-active can be labelled "Attention Deficit Hyperactive Disordered". Children who are persistently aggressive or criminal can be officially labelled "Conduct Disordered" (some of the bad behaviour has to be outside the home). Children who won't cooperate with adults (at home, at school or usually both) can be labelled "Oppositional Defiant Disordered". Children used to often progress from ODD to CD but now DSM5 says that a child can have both labels at the same time. These two labels are simply a medical-sounding description of behaviour and tell us *nothing* whatsoever about what has caused the behaviour or what we should do about it (see chapter on ODD). They can mislead parents, and naïve professionals, into thinking that there is something identifiably wrong with the child and give false hope that the experts can find a 'cure'. There is no 'cure' for these 'illnesses' because they are not in any logical way 'illnesses.' Even as descriptions of behaviour they are not helpful because they are too vague. Since some children can dramatically change such behaviour given a change in their attitudes (I've occasionally seen it happen overnight), or change their behaviour due to a change in the behaviour of those around them (this is quite common), does it make sense to consider these behaviours to be a sign of an 'illness'? Can it be a 'mental illness' if you can choose to give it up?

Temper tantrums as an 'illness'

In the USA there has been a scandalous epidemic of diagnosing children as bi-polar. This seems to be largely an American phenomenon. The US is the only country in the world which allows the drug companies to advertise directly to the public and this has contributed to a number of labelling epidemics (these are real 'epidemics')[289]. Unfortunately, what happens in the USA affects all of us.

178

"Recognizing the catastrophic misdiagnosis of childhood bipolar disorder, they hope to replace it with DMDD, which doesn't carry the same implications of life-time illness and is less likely to be overmedicated with obesity-inducing drugs. This was a silly solution..." Frances[290]

DMDD, or Disruptive Mood Dysregulation Disorder, is the new name for what was being called 'temper dysregulation' and is another way of saying extreme temper tantrums. Frances, author of DSM4, is scathing about this:

"Previously I mentioned a study that found 83% of kids qualify for mental disorder diagnosis by the time they are 21. Now the child researchers have taken it a step further – introducing a new DSM-5 diagnosis that may get the number even closer to 100%. ...the idea of turning temper tantrums into a mental disorder is terrible, however named. We should not have the ambition to label as mental disorder every inconvenient or distressing aspect of childhood." Frances[291]

So all the over-entitled, impatient, egocentric children I deal with who have temper tantrums past the age when we expect them to grow out of it, are suddenly 'mentally ill' and can be labelled with DMDD. Alphabet children can now have even more letters after their names! Don't let anyone fool you into thinking that a label such as this is a real condition or in any way an explanation of anything!

Since the names given to these new disorders are so arbitrary I think I'll call DMDD, Dennis the Menace Dastardly Disruption.

When ADHD was just ADD, I claimed it often stood for "Attends Disabling Doctor".

Jekyll and Hyde – "He must be schizophrenic or something"

Seeing a transformation from a reasonable, likable child to a mad-eyed, maniacal monster can be both scary and puzzling. Thankfully, I don't often get to see these transformations as these children typically reserve them for their nearest and dearest. Just occasionally I get to witness such a monster makeover and it can be truly remarkable! The weirdly different look in their eyes can make one think of demonic possession and want to call an exorcist. It's no wonder that parents both fear and hope that there is some medical explanation for these transmogrifications. They are at once genuinely afraid that their child has a serious mental illness but are also hoping that there is an explanation that relieves them of their illogical guilt by redirecting the blame from nurture to nature. They also have the faint hope that getting a name for their child's condition might lead to a cure. This hope is invariably futile, but at least the child might get a pill to calm them down (and just occasionally this is necessary).

While we remain so ignorant about the workings of the human brain we can't actually rule out that there is some form of disorder contributing to these behaviours, but the evidence suggests that this is very seldom the case.

Consider the following description of these Jekyll and Hyde transformations:

"... mood changes are especially perplexing. He can be a different person from day to day, or even from hour to hour. At times he is aggressive and intimidating, his tone harsh, insults spewing from his mouth, ridicule dripping from him like oil from a drum. When he's in this mode, nothing she says seems to have any impact on him, except to make him even angrier. Her side of the argument counts for nothing in his eyes, and everything is her fault. He twists her words around so that she always ends up on the defensive." Bancroft[292]

The description fits alarmingly well for a great many of the children and young people who are abusing their parents. It probably sounds familiar to many of you reading this. However, Bancroft is not describing teen terrorists and their mothers but adult men and their female victims. We've mentioned that it's generally accepted that men who abuse their wives are **not** psychiatrically ill in any meaningful way (Bancroft is very definite about this; he is describing chosen behaviour). As the motivation and behaviours of adult perpetrators of family violence are often very similar to the motivations and behaviours of teen perpetrators of family violence, why should we assume that mental problems are a cause in one but not in the other? Adolescence and associated hormonal or brain changes do not affect adult abusers so why are they often put forward as 'explanations' when teens behave like this?

Among the nearly five hundred families I've dealt with where children are abusing parents, there have been a small number, under thirty, who had some kind of mental illness. Obsessive compulsive disorder or other anxiety conditions are the most common, followed by depression (See optional chapters on Depression and Anxiety). In my sample there were no more teens with schizophrenia or bi-polar disorder than you would expect by chance (under 1%), though it's certainly possible that a few of these young people will develop such conditions in adulthood.

Although many parents say 'there must be something wrong with him', I can tell them that very few abusive children have been diagnosed with a meaningful mental illness and I honestly can't think of a case where such a diagnosis has actually been a significant help in *stopping* the behaviours. This doesn't mean that it can't happen, or that getting a diagnosis is a waste of time, but don't hold your breath expecting a 'cure' for aggressive behaviour. Medications do sometimes help, but these are based on the behaviour, not on a diagnosis.

When young people do develop a major mental illness this does not often produce violence. It's a dangerous myth that the '*mad*' are often violent. For example, very few adults with schizophrenia are violent in the community, though it's certainly not *un*common for them to abuse their parents if they live with them (another neglected issue).

A large minority of these children do have problems other than their violent and abusive behaviour. By far the most common diagnosis is ADHD (20%); second in my sample is Autism (6%). Which of these conditions is found in other samples of children who are violent to parents will vary greatly, not only because any sample, including mine, will be biased in some ways, but also for the simple reason that all these labels are somewhat arbitrary. The diagnosis of these conditions varies greatly from place to place, and time to time, because the definitions are vague and assessments unreliable. One way in which my sample is definitely biased is in the number of young people with some form of autism. This is another special interest of mine and so I get many referrals of people with autism. Most of these are not violent to parents but since those who are abusive to parents combine my two main specialisms, it's not surprising that they get referred to me in greater numbers.

'ADHD' is a bit different to the labels 'Conduct disorder' and 'Oppositional Defiant Disorder.' With some children there may be a real problem, possibly even a neurological problem and this may justify medication. However, the label describes a wide variety of children with a wide variety of behaviours and gives little or no indication as to how we should treat a particular child. Unfortunately, many parents, and too many professionals, believe that the condition **causes** the misbehaviour. It does not **cause** any specific behaviour any more than **not** having ADHD causes specific behaviour. It does, however, make some difficult behaviour more likely.

If your child has ADHD, Autism, Tourette's Syndrome, Epilepsy or some other possibly genetic condition, you are probably confused about whether this explains or excuses the behaviour. Part of your confusion may stem from professionals you deal with having different views to each other. To get the issue of excuses and explanations into perspective we will take a short diversion to consider a common genetic condition we shall refer to as XDD. You will have come across it, but probably won't recognise this technical term.

A common but dangerous genetic condition

XDD (or X-Deficit Disorder) is a genetic condition consistently shown to increase the risk of violent and anti-social behaviour. Every form of violence and almost every form of crime is several times more common for those with XDD. Overall rates of murder are ten times greater for those with the condition and individuals with XDD show a staggering 2000% higher rate of rape and sexual abuse.

There is no simple cure for XDD. Treatment is controversial and rare. Although some forms of drug therapy are used for youth with XDD this is always justified by a co-existing condition (such as ADHD). Treatment in adulthood is rare and adults with XDD tend to avoid health professionals.

Other common statistical correlations with XDD are: lower empathy, social skill deficits, poorer verbal communication, and an impaired ability to understand or talk about emotions. On average they are somewhat less agreeable than others. Often those dealing with young people who have XDD simply lower their expectations and even anticipate, or excuse, a higher rate of aggression, violence, defiance, disruption, substance abuse and risk taking.

Although all of these problems are clearly statistically related to this condition, we should beware of the prejudice of assuming that all adults with XDD will show these negative traits. You may be surprised to hear that when mature, many make excellent parents, though some shirk their responsibilities, leaving the bulk of the parenting to a parent without XDD.

Before we give up on individuals with XDD it's worth noting that violence in this group decreases with age, though slower than for those without XDD. The rate

181

of violence for these individuals also varies *tremendously* in different cultures (and sub-cultures), so clearly it's affected *as much* by environment as by genetics. Contrary to some prejudiced views, individuals with XDD can be trained. Unfortunately they find ample encouragement for a violent, anti-social, anti-authority lifestyle in our modern culture. Young people with XDD seek each other out socially and often encourage each other in their aggressive, rebellious and risk-taking tendencies. Parents certainly play a part in encouraging or discouraging these tendencies, but often this is a far smaller role than most people imagine.

Despite the consistent relationship between this genetic condition and anti-social behaviour or related personality problems, there are also benefits to this condition. These people are frequently skilled at tasks of a mechanical or programmatic nature; a few even have savant-like skills in mathematics, science or music. The better adjusted are assertive rather than aggressive and some are highly motivated to succeed (at times their economic success is actually aided by their lower agreeableness and ability to disengage from others). There is a movement among adults with XDD to take pride in their condition. Unfortunately this pride is sometimes excessive, verging on arrogance or taking the form of denial. Some deny, in the face of overwhelming evidence, that their condition is even linked to violence and abuse!

I myself have X Deficit Disorder. I inherited this from my father and have in turn passed it on to my son. I am neither proud nor ashamed of only having one X chromosome, otherwise known as being male. On the other hand, those of us with this condition and a tendency to be aggressive, controlling, abusive or irresponsible have a duty to try to overcome this.

It should not need to be said that those with Double-X Syndrome, otherwise known as females, are also capable of violence, abuse and irresponsible behaviour. Almost a third of the young people I have dealt with who are violent to parents have Double-X syndrome.

Other genetic conditions

If you have followed the above argument about the influence of the genetic condition of XDD, I'd like you to now think about the implications for a child with another genetic condition, such as ADHD, autism, a mild learning difficulty or any other. None of these conditions are as unequivocally genetic as is being male and none are so consistently related to violent or anti-social behaviour. Consider ADHD as an example. The question is: if being male is not an excuse why should ADHD be an excuse for bad behaviour?

Boys are twice as likely as girls to be violent to a parent. Children with ADHD may be two or even three times as likely to be violent as those without ADHD. But *most* children with ADHD are not violent to parents.

What is more, a number of these children were given the diagnosis primarily **because** of their behavioural problems. It's circular reasoning to then use it as an explanation of the behavioural problems.

Having ADHD raises the probability of aggression in a similar way that being a boy makes aggression more likely. It's **never** a sufficient cause of violence on its own and other factors are often just as important. A clear example of this is that exactly the same percentage of the children with ADHD in my parent-abusing sample has been exposed to past DV as have those without ADHD (both 48%).

Raging Hormones

"Q: My teenager can say some hurtful things when we argue…
A: Your teenager is hormonally wired to be rude and mean – She is lashing out
and can't really help it."[293]

It's not uncommon to hear such 'explanations' of adolescent behaviour in terms of 'raging hormones' (though not usually 'hormonally *wired'*). More specifically boys' adolescent aggression is blamed on 'raging testosterone'.[294] There seems little doubt that hormonal changes and fluctuations make *some* adolescents more moody, irritable and emotional *at times*. However, there are a number of good reasons why we should be highly suspicious of this being seen as a major contributing factor to the behaviour problems we are concerned about.

- Hormonal changes occur in young people at some point in *every* society, past and present, but non-Western & historical societies have generally had very different adolescent behaviour and don't appear to have had the problems than we are experiencing with adolescents[295].
- All adolescents go through hormonal changes but studies suggest that only about 20% (in Western societies) have serious emotional or behavioural issues.[296]
- The age of becoming rebellious and cantankerous now begins three or four years earlier than it did when I was first working with youth, yet the age of puberty has only changed by about six months. This suggests it's far more social than physiological.
- Children who are late to reach puberty (and its onset varies a lot) are not noticeably more peaceful or obliging than those who are in the midst of these changes. On the contrary, boys who are late to reach puberty often have *more* problems and may be more aggressive in the period when they are physically (and hormonally) lagging behind their peers. Research on girls who reach puberty early suggests that they are at risk of behavioural problems if they mix with older children but not if they continue to hang out with their age-mates.
- There is no clear evidence that adolescents are most difficult at the time when their hormones are either increasing most or at their highest levels. Overall acts of violence are greater long before puberty and violent crime is greater after puberty. Hormones remain high in men into middle age.
- There is a fairly steady decrease in the overall number of violent acts throughout childhood with no obvious increase around the time of puberty. Although there are undoubtedly some children who become violent at adolescence (I've met many) more were violent before puberty (but to other children rather than to adults). Some studies have failed to find any evidence for adolescent-onset aggression, which is odd as it certainly

occurs.[297] However, some children become *less* violent as they mature around adolescence and overall the numbers may balance out.

- Starting high school seems to be a significant turning point for many of those children who become more difficult in adolescence, regardless of where they happen to be in their pubertal development at this time.

- Studies looking at hormone levels and aggression in adolescence have often failed to find any relationship at all or only very weak correlations[298]. Any effect cannot be large or common.

- Although there are some correlations between aggressiveness and testosterone levels, these are small and inconsistent and girls show emotional changes including aggressiveness without surges in testosterone[299]. If testosterone was a significant factor, we would expect a big increase in the *differences* in aggression between boys and girls at puberty as the difference in testosterone increases dramatically. Even the small correlations found are difficult to interpret because competing, acting aggressively, winning, or being dominant all increase individual's testosterone levels. So acting aggressively may be the cause of high testosterone rather than the result of high testosterone.

- Giving a male (human or animal) testosterone generally does not make him aggressive. "On the contrary, it makes him feel great, while putting a chip on his shoulder when he is faced with a rival male.[300]" Thus extra testosterone can increase dominance and competitiveness which may, or may not, lead to aggression.

It's certain that testosterone affects brain development before birth, probably contributing to boys being more aggressive than girls, but this doesn't mean that it's often a *cause* of aggressiveness later, though there are correlations for various reasons. High testosterone does make men more dominant, which has obvious relevance to attempts to control others, and hence to all kinds of family violence.[301]

Violence to parents does quite often start during puberty but I believe this is far more related to social factors than physical ones. It also quite often stops around the time of puberty.

Surprisingly, there has not actually been much research on the effects of adolescent hormonal changes, or other pubertal changes, on children's behaviour. It's quite possible that there is a general connection between hormones and behaviour that we haven't discovered yet but it's unlikely that it's very important. Although it's probably a factor for *some* children *some*times, you probably won't know if your child is being moody or irritable because of hormones or for one of a dozen other reasons. In all likelihood hormones are only ever a small part of a bigger picture. They probably cause irritability and moodiness but don't cause violence or abusive behaviour directly. If someone is willing to be violent or abusive, then being irritable will increase the chances and affect the timing of outbursts but no amount of irritability can force someone to be violent if other factors, such as a difficult personality and negative attitudes, are absent.

In a classic experiment, psychologists injected student volunteers with adrenalin[302]. If they were with someone who acted elated then that's how the adrenalin affected them (this person was actually a stooge, working for the experimenter). If they were with someone who acted fearful, they got anxious and frightened. It's a pretty safe bet that if they were with someone who was acting aggressively they would become more aggro, but the experimenters probably didn't want to risk this. I expect that the effect of hormonal changes on adolescents' moods will be somewhat similar. If your child's friends are lively, enthusiastic and cheerful, then their hormones may make them excitable and happy. If your child's peers are a morose bunch of depressive emos, or a bunch of feral thugs, then their hormones may contribute to their negative emotions. In today's wired world, the 'friends' influencing their moods may be virtual weirdoes from the other side of the world.

Both their brains and their bodies are changing around the same time as their hormones. Over the same period, other people, and society in general, treat them differently because they look more grown up. And they are (usually) interacting with a group of friends who are also all changing rapidly within a society changing faster than would have been imaginable in the recent past.

No wonder they're confused! No wonder you are!

My brain made me do it

My brain is *making me* sit here typing and your brain is *making you* read this sentence. When you feel an emotion the chemistry of your brain changes and if you change the pattern of your behaviour or your typical emotional response, there will be semi-permanent changes in your brain. Our inherited genes interact with each other and with our environment to make any particular behaviour more or less likely. To excuse a murderer or rapist because he has more or less of a particular brain chemical or some minor structural abnormality in his brain, or because he has a particular gene increasing the chance of violence makes no logical sense to me. As we've seen, my Y-chromosomes make me more likely to be violent than someone without this disorder (i.e. a female) but, thankfully, no court considers this a reasonable excuse (though some individual judges or magistrates have excused atrocious male behaviour in terms of 'boys will be boys').

To assume someone is *incapable* of choosing their behaviour because they have autism, ADHD, Tourette's syndrome or a mild intellectual disability is to treat them as less than human! Unless they are *incapable* of understanding what is going on because they are severely intellectually impaired, or are out of touch with reality because they are psychotic, then all adults should be considered accountable for their actions. The logical alternative is that **no one** is accountable for their actions, a position that abolishes morality and treats us all as machines (a position only appealing to some defence lawyers and perhaps a tiny number of eccentric philosophers).

The adolescent brain

There has been some interesting research in recent years showing that the brains of adolescents change far more than we had previously thought. Brain cells and their interconnections multiply and die away at a staggering rate (the dying away part being very important in development), and some parts of the brain do not fully develop until the twenties. This should not have been a surprise, yet not so long ago it was thought that brains were pretty much built in the first few years, then didn't change much and that no new neurons were grown after the first burst of development. This is now known to be quite wrong and lots of evidence has revealed how *plastic* the brain is, even into adulthood. We can grow new neurons and areas of the brain even increase or decrease in size and cell density depending on how much we use them.

What I find odd is that the enthusiasm for the news of massive changes taking place in adolescence hasn't stopped others claiming that changes in the first year or two are permanent and pretty much 'hard wired' for life. Both sets of brain enthusiasts appear to ignore the evidence that brains keep on changing. We do not understand the implications of the changes in adolescent brains yet, but this hasn't stopped all sorts of assumptions being drawn by pop psychologists.

Unfortunately, some 'experts' on adolescence use such pseudo-science to reinforce whatever message they wish to get across, sometimes that adolescents can't help it and should be given more sympathy and longer leashes. 'Explanations' of teenage behaviour in terms of the recent brain research often ignore a few crucial points, very similar to the arguments against hormones being an explanation of common teen behaviour.

1. Adolescent brains have been developing in much the same way for a hundred thousand years but most of the behaviour, attitudes and problems we associate with adolescence are historically new (or occurred at different ages in other societies)[303].

2. In many societies there is no expectation that adolescence will be a time of upset and conflict[304].

3. The majority of adolescents even in Western society don't have emotional or behavioural problems[305]. It's a myth that all adolescents go through a difficult phase and there are those who even think that it's unhealthy if they don't have problems! If it makes people too accepting of adolescent's bad behaviour, or stops adolescents getting the help they need, this can be a dangerous myth.

4. Much of the recent evidence from neurology stresses *neuro-plasticity*. Brains can be amazingly resilient and adaptable. There have been a few cases where children have lost an *entire half* of their brain yet they have largely recovered and are not severely disabled. A one-year-old can have the side of the brain that normally controls language completely removed and still learn to talk, read and write.

5. It's also quite possible to consider the evidence about the rapid changes in adolescent brains and predict that we should be seeing a rapid increase in their intelligence (which we do), but also a rapid increase in responsibility, empathy and social understanding. In Western society we do see such increases in some young people but far less than in other societies. Why so many problems start in adolescence in our society is not *explained* by the fact that brains are maturing. It's true that there is a difference in developmental rate between intelligence and responsibility but this is hardly news and it varies greatly between different children and at different times.

6. Almost *everything* that is said about the underdeveloped teenage brain applies **far more** to children's brains but we don't expect the same problems in children. Any statement about adolescents' underdeveloped frontal cortex, etc. applies *far more* to pre-pubescent and younger children.
7. We don't understand the long-term consequences and implications of these adolescent **brain ch**anges. I have heard people who should know better talk of things being 'hard-wired' during adolescence. Brains cannot be 'hard wired' as brains are not hardware; they aren't software either but squidgy-ware. Patterns (in brains, attitudes, thoughts or behaviours) may last a lifetime but they can sometimes change dramatically. I have met a large number of adults who had wild, wanton teenage years, including some who were deeply into drugs, crime, etc. but who have ended up as responsible, decent adults. Never give up hope because some expert declares that your child has a personality disorder or a 'bad brain'. Brains can be damaged of course and some drugs can do permanent damage, but this does not hard-wire behaviour or attitudes.
8. On average the changes of adolescence are largely positive. By the end of the teenage years, there has been a marked reduction in violence, crime, bullying, etc. and a big improvement in empathy and responsibility. By late adolescence we see more serious mental health problems because these are more common among adults than among children or adolescents. All the mental health problems common in adolescence are either obviously due to the strange, in-between state our society imposes (rather similar to unemployment in some ways) or are the start of adult problems. I can't think of any mental health problems that are specific to puberty or adolescence.

So whether your child has a normally developing adolescent brain or some kind of abnormality this does **not** mean they are mindless machines absolved from responsibility for their actions. They should still be held accountable for the decisions they make. That doesn't mean we shouldn't give them our sympathy or that we should expect ideal or adult behaviour. Giving them some moral leeway is fine – this is what we naturally do with children and young people anyway – but unfortunately some parents, and some professionals, give far **too much** leeway. The evidence of other societies shows clearly that adolescents are capable of taking on adult responsibilities. I have seen dramatic improvements in young people when they take on responsibility, usually by starting work, but occasionally by leaving home or getting into a serious relationship. There is a lot of concern that adolescents in some families having to take on too much responsibility, e.g. when parents have disabilities or serious mental health problems. Some of this concern is warranted but such responsibility can also make for some really great, mature, caring young people.

I have met a number of children who believed, or perhaps pretended to believe, that they could not help their behaviour because of a particular condition[306]. This is a self-fulfilling prophecy. If we don't expect and insist on good behaviour, we are not likely to get it.

Michael was fifteen when I met him and his younger brother Jack, aged thirteen. Michael had believed for many years that his terrible temper tantrums were due to his epilepsy, a belief shared by his family. When I met these two boys, Michael's epilepsy was well controlled by medication and he had not had a single seizure for over two years, and had not had a tantrum for one year. On discussion the following facts emerged:

- Stopping the seizures had at first had no apparent effect on his tantrums.
- He still had epilepsy but no longer had any tantrums.
- His younger brother was having remarkably similar tantrums without epilepsy.

Michael readily accepted that there had never been any real evidence for the idea that his tantrums were caused by his epilepsy. Because he had both of these problems, his family (and probably some of the professionals involved) had simply assumed that they were related. He was relieved. He no longer required an excuse for his tantrums (which he had grown out of) yet the idea that a brain disorder had been making him behave aggressively was scary and sapped his confidence. This belief may well have made the tantrums last for years longer than they need have. Jack soon got over his tantrums when his parents became firmer with him.

There may have been a link between Michael's tantrums and his epilepsy but it was **not** a direct causal link.

"Children who suffer from psychopathology are no less in need of rules and values than are 'normal' children. The opposite actually may be true, for the more chaotic the child's inner world, the greater is the need for an orderly, stabilizing framework." Omer[307]

Adolescent problems are social not due to hormones or brains

What we call adolescence doesn't really exist in non-Industrial societies. There is ample evidence that the problems we associate with the teenage years don't tend to occur in the majority of societies. So it's pretty certain that they are not explained by puberty or by the changes in bodies and brains that are taking place.

There is nothing whatsoever inevitable about adolescent rebellion or mental health problems and even within our society, they are not shown to any great extent in the majority of young people. So don't believe anyone who claims that this is an inevitable result of development or point to unfinished brains as the culprit. In most societies these unfinished brains would be acting very like adults. We infantilise our young people and create a situation where they are separated from adults and pushed into the company of other young people[308].

Bad blood?

As we've seen, the debate about whether our behaviour comes from our genetic makeup (nature) or our environment (nurture), has been dragging on for well over a century with no sign of any resolution. But among scientists there is a general consensus recently that either extreme in the nature versus nurture debate is naïve. There is probably no aspect of our behaviour, emotions or personalities that is not influenced to some extent by **both** genes and environment, yet people still go to one extreme or the other. Thus there are still many professionals who act as if **all** of children's behaviour is a result of how they have been parented (also ignoring the rest of their environment). The denial of the importance of children's inherent temperament makes the blaming of parents pretty much inevitable.

On the other hand, when a child has a label such as 'intellectual disability' or 'ADHD' which is assumed to be genetic, some professionals (sometimes the same ones) go to the other extreme and assume that parenting and the rest of the environment is **irrelevant** to the child's behaviour and abilities. At its worst this is not only wrong but it is also very negative and can lead to hopelessness.

Parenting is *always* of some importance regardless of a child's genetic makeup. A child with a disability may have greatly increased chances of developing certain behaviours and greatly decreased chances of developing others. However, their environment, including both family environment and the wider society, can be crucially important.

There is no gene for violence!
Traits such as impulsivity, irritability, extraversion, agreeableness and adventurousness are all partly inherited. This does not mean that a child will necessarily 'take after' one parent or the other, as genes can be passed down the generations, can combine with each other in new and novel ways, can mutate, and can be expressed or suppressed depending on environmental or purely chance factors. There are probably dozens of genes involved in any personality trait and genes are almost never straightforward in how they translate into personality, abilities or behaviour. We are always talking about probability and potentials. Take height as an example: height is a lot simpler genetically than personality but we would never assume that a tall parent **must** have tall children, though it's more likely that they will. Height is less influenced by the environment than is aggression yet environmental changes have increased average height by several inches in a century.

An inherited temperament can make the chances of being rebellious, criminal or violent more or less likely but **never** makes such behaviour **inevitable**. Inheriting traits that make a child difficult may tend to go with family stresses. Some children with a violent father have inherited some tendencies from him but are also copying his behaviour and attitudes (see section on DV) and are also angry because of the effect he has had on their lives. And though some of their personality traits are inherited from him, just as many come from their mother.

Because something is inherited does **not** mean it cannot be changed. Inherited traits can increase the *likelihood* of behaviours but actual behaviours are chosen, with the choice being influenced by habits, attitudes, relationships, culture, environment and the specific situation.

The Vikings were famous for their violence and warlike nature. Icelanders are of almost pure Viking descent yet have one of the lowest rates of violent crime in the world. Their genes are pure Viking but their environment is totally different. Different cultures vary tremendously in their amount of violence, with no evidence so far suggesting that such differences are genetic. In some cultures children are treated quite harshly by our standards yet grow up to be more peaceful than we are. In other cultures young children are indulged and loved yet grow up to be outrageously violent by our standards. Overall the wider culture appears to be far more important than early parenting in determining aggressiveness. In Modern Western societies, a very important cultural influence is the commercial culture of the mass media – which is reinforced by other children as well as picked up directly. This culture is violent, competitive and anti-social.

"He's just like his father"

I sometimes hear despairing mothers claim that their sons are a carbon copy of an abusive or irresponsible father. The emotional impact of resemblance between a growing child and a hated or feared ex can be intense. If a child clearly looks like his father, we may get used to this and still see him as an individual, but if he begins to look *more* like his father at puberty this may be a shock. Even more intense is when little quirks, such as the way he laughs, speaks, stands or does something, creates an unpleasant association. Such genetic quirks *seem* very meaningful but they are not; they are not necessarily associated with important character traits. He could have one parent's personality to a close match yet look exactly like the other parent, and how he holds his head or scratches himself may be unrelated to either.

If he is behaving like his father in some ways, especially in dramatic ways such as violence, lying, stealing or drinking, then we are likely to see any other resemblances, even trivial associations, as profound and for some women these resemblances can produce flashbacks to previous abuse.

The reality is that most children will have had some contact with their father and so habits may be copied, inherited, or more often are a subtle combination of the two. If a son calls his mother the same insulting names that his father did, this may just mean that they both know her well enough to know how to hurt her. He probably does resemble his father in some personality characteristics. It's unfashionable to admit that the children of violent men are *statistically* more likely to be violent themselves but this is undoubtedly the case, *to a small extent*. Research often fails to take this into account, producing spurious results that suggest that parenting is more important than it actually is[309]. Though there does not appear to be any genes *specific* to being violent, there are lots of traits that increase or decrease the risk of such behaviour. In identical twins, if one is violent it's not inevitable that the other one will be. Children who are adopted are slightly more likely to be delinquent or criminal if their birth parents had a criminal record. However, having a birth parent who was a *violent* criminal does not noticeably increase the chance that they will be *violent* criminals[310]. So it's a slight tendency to be criminal that is inherited rather than a tendency to be violent.

Personality traits are *largely* genetically transmitted (see section on personality) and certain combinations may greatly alter the *probability* of violence. An introverted, agreeable, nervous child is less likely to develop aggressive behaviours than an extraverted, fearless, disagreeable child.

Even if a child were a genetic clone of their parent they could turn out quite different. Identical twins do not have identical personalities even when they grow up at the same time, in the same family, in the same neighbourhood and attend the same schools. There are a number of serious conditions such as schizophrenia and bi-polar disorder which are considered largely genetic, yet if one identical twin suffers from the condition there is only a 50-50 chance that the other twin will develop the same condition.

Even if, by a one in a million chance, a child happened to have *exactly* the same combination of personality characteristics as a parent, there is nothing inevitable about them developing the same behaviours. Personality is not destiny. I have seen a great many young people and adults stop being violent, yet their basic personalities and their genes, do not suddenly change.

Violence is chosen behaviour

Sarah was twenty years old and had recently left a special school. She was classified as 'intellectually disabled' and also thought by her mother and some workers to have a mental illness. Her mother was keen to get a diagnosis as she hoped that psychiatry might cure whatever was causing her to be violent. She was violent to her mother almost daily, ran away from home, had unsafe sex with men (she didn't look disabled), drank and shoplifted. When I talked to her and her mother about her behaviour it all sounded quite controlled to me. Rather than being *out of control* she was *controlling* everyone around her. She was not keen to engage in counselling and would only talk to me for fifteen minutes at a time before declaring that she was too bored to continue.

The third time I saw Sarah, I dared her to keep out of trouble for a week. I didn't think there was any real chance of her doing so, I was just trying to explore the idea that she *could* choose how to behave. She didn't make any promises or even appear to pay the challenge much attention. To my great surprise her mother told me later that she had, for the first time in years, not been violent or abusive for *exactly* one week. At the end of one week she had immediately reverted to her usual behaviour. This shows that even someone with an intellectual disability can choose whether or not to be violent. The fact that it was for *exactly* one week shows clearly that it was a conscious choice to start being abusive again. She didn't return for counselling again and may have found a therapist who would be less challenging.

"In research on self-control, one conclusion stands out over and over again: People acquiesce in losing control. In other words, they let themselves lose control, and they become active participants…. People allow themselves to lose control. And they do so in part because they learn to regard certain impulses as irresistible." Baumeister[311]

More on this in the chapter on Anger.

Labels Are for Tins

"Medical research has made such enormous advances that there are hardly any healthy people left." Aldous Huxley.

One child, by the time she reached thirteen had collected the following labels from different professionals: ADHD, Post-Traumatic Stress Disorder, Oppositional Defiant Disorder and Reactive Attachment Disorder. It's a safe bet that as she travels through her teens she will get some new "diagnoses" (if that is not too grand a word for such a charade). If she had lived in the U.S. rather than Australia, she would probably also have been diagnosed as having bi-polar disorder. She's likely to also acquire Conduct Disorder and at least one flavour of Personality Disorder. None of these really *explain* anything and none tell her unfortunate carers how to deal with her. It's generally a waste of time, energy and resources that so many of those meant to be helping such troubled youngsters, spend their time forcing them into pigeonholes. One function of testing is so that professionals can look as if they are doing something smart and sophisticated. This can contribute to therapy-fatigue and the teen refusing to see any more professionals. It may lead to over-medication and the effect of stigma can be enormous and sometimes lifelong.

I find most psychiatric labels pretty useless in my counselling practice but for a long time believed that psychiatrists themselves found them very useful in prescribing medications. However, even this is doubtful. Allan Horwitz, in the most sensible book on psychiatry I've ever read, argues that this only really applies to schizophrenia and bi-polar in adults and ADHD in children. For all other conditions, the labels are often arbitrary and so arc the drug treatments. Drugs that are 'anti-depressants' are also at times useful in anxiety, addictions, etc. and psychiatrists often decide on a drug then change the diagnosis they give their patient in order to fit the drug of choice. If your psychiatrist wants to try an anti-anxiety drug, then he will diagnose you as having one of the anxiety conditions (these overlap and often occur together so that which one is chosen is pretty much arbitrary). If he wants to give you an anti-depressant, he will diagnose you as being depressed. It's not uncommon that they want to try an anti-psychotic and might record the patient as having 'schizophrenia' or 'schizoaffective disorder' when they clearly do not. Such a stigmatized label can stay on medical records for life. I once worked with a delightful but depressed old lady who had accumulated over a dozen psychiatric diagnoses over the space of forty years. Some of these were ridiculous, some were no longer in use, others were no longer used in the same way, yet they followed her around like a swarm of annoying bugs, making her appear on paper to be someone with serious mental conditions when she actually had good reasons to be depressed and was otherwise smart and sane.

The number of people being given a particular label is greatly determined by the popularity of the drugs. Thus the increase in depression in society over the past twenty years seems to be *largely* determined by the popularity of the new anti-depressants and the vast sums spent promoting them. [312] Some of the 'epidemics' we've been having, such as epidemics of ADHD and depression have been largely produced by the drug companies, who nowadays often find peddling diseases more profitable than peddling cures.

A side-effect of our obsession with labels is the assumptions made about those young people who **don't** get a label. It's often assumed that they were born 'normal' so must have been screwed up by their parents. They may also be denied help by some services because they don't fit one of our arbitrary pigeonholes.

Possessing a label says very little about how much emotional suffering the condition causes the young person or their family. There are some very happy, well-adjusted children with labels such as 'Asperger's syndrome', 'ADHD' or 'Intellectual Disability' and many miserable, violent, self-destructive young people who don't fit one of our current crop of craziness categories. Possession of a label also says little about how difficult the child is for others to manage and live with. I've heard a number of parents over the years admit that their child with Down's Syndrome is easier than their 'normal' child. Some extremely difficult young people don't earn a label while some easy children do. Only about 40% of the children in my sample who are abusing parents have *any* form of diagnosis (and this includes conditions such as epilepsy, dyslexia, etc.). Most had been assessed at some point and a few had been assessed several times at the request of parents desperate for an explanation and help. Of those with a diagnostic label it's rare that they only have one clear label, more often they've had several.

The number of different labels a child has is no indication of how difficult they may be. Let's take two examples, Clara and Myst (they are a combination of several young people).

Myst was only very slightly delayed in her development and her behaviour problems were minimal when she was little. Her mother, however, was convinced there was something wrong by the time she was three and did the round of professionals in a frustrating search for help and answers. Most professionals were reluctant to attach a label to such a young child but at age four she was diagnosed as having ADHD, though this was by a paediatrician known to be rather over-fond of this label. Her mother wisely chose not to give her medication for this. She was also diagnosed as having "PDDNOS". This bizarre label meant "Pervasive Developmental Delay Not Otherwise Specified" and hopefully it will be dead and gone by the time you read this. Myst's mother was understandably baffled by this. Her daughter's delay was clearly not 'pervasive' as she was bright in many ways and only delayed in quite specific ways. Two years later this was changed to "High functioning autism". When she was eight, a different paediatrician disputed the 'autism' label and sent her to be assessed by a psychologist who specialized in attachment issues. She was diagnosed as having 'Attachment Disorder' on the basis of her clingy but conflictual relationship with her mother. Another psychologist two years later added 'Oppositional Defiant Disorder' as she was being difficult for her confused and stressed mother and beginning to defy teachers. Myst's mother became interested in autism again when her best friend's son was diagnosed. She visited a specialist in this field who declared that Myst had 'Asperger's Syndrome.' He said this was the same as 'High Functioning Autism' but less stigmatizing (some specialists insisted the two were different). There had been a steady improvement in Myst's behavioural problems over these years but when she started High School, she was bullied and teased and become occasionally violent both to classmates and then to her mother (mostly pushing and swearing). She was expelled from the private Christian school, which had a low tolerance for problem children, and sent to a specialist unit for children with behavioural problems. She was the brightest child there and for a while her self-esteem improved. Given that she knew she had been given six different 'mental' labels, it's not surprising that her confidence was shaky. At fourteen she got pregnant to a boy at the special school and had an abortion. She was then diagnosed as having 'Depression'. She was no longer physically violent by this time but for a few years her relationship with her mother was distant and strained. She began smoking marijuana and binge drinking. She was caught stealing from a shop and given the labels 'Conduct Disorder' and 'Marijuana Dependence'. She had by now seen so many professionals that it was all a game to her and she became skilled at winding them up or giving them whatever impression she chose to give. Over the next two years she was labelled as having a 'Narcissistic Personality Disorder' and 'Borderline Personality Disorder' (mainly because she was going through a period of cutting her arms). When she was seventeen she fell in love, luckily with a stable and sensible twenty-year-old. Over the next year she settled down and began studying. Now aged twenty, despite having had nine 'psychiatric' labels, she lives with her boyfriend and is going to University. Ironically, she is studying psychology. She's still a bit odd socially and still argues with her mother but they have a good relationship most of the time and, though proud to be an Aspie, she does not consider herself to have a disability.

Clara was also diagnosed with autism. She had clear symptoms and was diagnosed at an early age. No one has ever disputed this. She is severely disabled, needs constant supervision, has some very severe behaviour problems and is extremely difficult to parent. Clara, at twenty, with just one label, attends a special school and is heavily medicated. She is still sometimes violent and self-harming. It's extremely unlikely that she will ever be capable of living independently.

The above stories are two extremes but illustrate a general point that the number of labels a child accumulates may say very little about how bad their problems are. As Myst demonstrates, the less severe and less clear the symptoms, the greater the variety of labels a child can accumulate in our current haphazard system. Children with well-meaning, determined parents may also gather more labels than those with less interested or less capable parents. When parents are **overly** keen on assessments, and sadly there are a few parents who seem to thrive on this stuff, this greatly increases the chances of the child becoming an Alphabet child. On the other hand, children who are brought up in Care or have parents who themselves have severe problems, such as some disabilities, are often scrutinized and assessed more often and they may also gain a dizzying variety of labels.

Not all labels are bad and some can be **very** helpful at times. If you are a parent who has tried hard to obtain a diagnosis for your unusual child, please don't add that to your list of things to feel guilty about! It's perfectly understandable that some parents are desperate to find out what is wrong with their child. Unfortunately a major motivator for this is often parental guilt, which should not be related to whether or not a child fits our current arbitrary categories.

Two illogical ideas about labels are sadly quite common:

a) All labels show a genetic cause or a malfunctioning brain.
b) If a child with bad behaviour problems doesn't have a diagnosis, they must be reacting to bad parenting.

The first idea often leads to parenting and family situations not being taken into account, sometimes even when children have been exposed to domestic violence.

Let's look at some of the advantages and disadvantages of labels.

Advantages of labels:
Can make services available

The main purpose of these labels is to make services available to children with specific conditions. It's sad that this is necessary as in an ideal world, services such as extra educational help, should be based on individual needs not on the child fitting an arbitrary category. I think it's a worry that many professionals (and professional organisations) blithely accept this situation and seldom protest at being forced to stigmatise children in order to get them the help they need. Given the lack of reliability and arbitrary nature of our current labels, this is ultimately not even an efficient way to ration resources. Politicians and bureaucrats try to save money by limiting services to those with a diagnosed condition. Professionals respond to this by expanding the categories to include more children (we've seen this happen dramatically with ADHD and Asperger's). As a parent, don't feel guilty if you need to go down this path to get your child the help they need, just be fully aware of the possible costs.

Since violence to parents is such an extreme and serious problem, it's wrong if services also require the child to fit into one of our current categories in order for them to help the family.

Reassuring to the individual

It can be reassuring to know what is wrong with you. This applies less often to children than it does to adults. Some brighter young people however, have been relieved and reassured to be told that their problems (usually school problems) are caused by Asperger's, ADHD or a specific learning disability. However, most children given pseudo-psychiatric labels, which are seldom properly explained to them, are not at all reassured. In many cases the child does not actually think they have a problem needing a label and one of the main purposes of children's labels is to reassure parents.

May reduce parental guilt

It's sad that so many parents will feel that they must be to blame for their child's behaviour or educational problems unless they get a diagnosis. This is doubly illogical as the fact of having a diagnosis says nothing, in most cases, about the cause of the condition. Some children given labels such as ADHD, and the majority who are given the label 'Reactive Attachment Disorder', have been abused or neglected. A few children who have mild intellectual disabilities, speech problems or other conditions would not have them if they had been better cared for. The fact of labels reducing guilt is particularly illogical in these cases.

Imply understanding (at least by the 'expert')
A diagnosis implies that someone must understand what is really wrong. Yet with our present state of knowledge this is hardly ever true as we don't actually understand even the most common conditions such as ADHD or autism. A diagnosis is not an explanation. Hopefully, in the next few decades, we will bring together new knowledge of genetics and the brain to actually understand the causes of some of these conditions.

Give hope of a cure
Many parents who gain a diagnostic label for a young child are hopeful that there is a cure. It's certainly possible that being told that a child has some form of autism early on can make a *big* difference to that child if they are given the help they need. Knowing that a child has a specific learning difficulty (such as dyslexia) can make a huge difference to their education, provided the school is flexible and supportive. However, we don't actually have any real *cures* for these conditions, just interventions that help with the symptoms.

Useful simplifications in research
In trying to understand the complexity of childhood and family problems, simplifications have to be made. One of these simplifications is to lump together children given the same diagnostic label, despite huge variations in most of these categories. This necessary simplification can obscure what is really going on. For example, the research on ADHD generally doesn't look at the fact that many of these children have been exposed to family breakdowns and violence.

Provide an excuse
Psychiatric labels are used as an excuse in the legal system. This is occasionally appropriate and valid but more often it appears to be a game that solicitors and psychiatrists play which costs millions of dollars and sometimes makes a mockery of justice. Personally I think it's wasteful that so many psychiatrists and psychologists spend time writing reports for the court system.

A bizarre example occurred here in Melbourne when a man who killed his wife was found guilty of manslaughter, rather than murder, on the grounds that *he* was suffering from 'battered *wife* syndrome'. Outside the legal system a label may be used as an excuse by an individual and this may be helpful on occasions. For example, some schools are sympathetic to children who have labels and may not suspend or expel them for behaviour for which they would punish other children. But this is also one of the negatives.

The assessor feels they've done something

Some professionals feel that they have earned their keep if they can provide a plausible explanation even if they can't actually help the child or family. It's easier than therapy and pays better.

Disadvantages of labels
Labels are stigmatising

Even socially and educationally successful teenagers frequently worry about whether they are 'normal'. Such self-doubt and identity crises seem to be worse for today's young people than they were a few decades ago. To complicate things, today's teens often look down on 'normal' or 'average' and want to be *special* in some way, but to be superior, not to have 'special needs'. With a large number of young people we effectively tell them that they are officially below 'normal'.

Although most of the labels we are discussing are not 'psychiatric', in terms of representing a mental illness in any meaningful sense of the word, the child is often seen by a psychiatrist (and some psychologists don't make it clear that they are not 'shrinks'). The child may attend a clinic based in a hospital with words like 'mental' or 'psychiatry' on the door. I've heard brothers and sisters of children with ADHD or a disability say that their sibling sees 'a shrink' or goes to a place for 'mentals'. Generally less than 20% of the children child psychiatry deals with have any condition that would be considered 'psychiatric' in an adult (intellectual disabilities and autism are not considered to be mental *illnesses* in adults).

I will never forget a likable, interesting, very bright boy with 'high functioning autism'. He committed suicide leaving a note which read "I don't want to be autistic anymore." I'd been trying for a few months to boost his self-esteem and make him proud to be an 'Aspie' but I was too late (or not skilled enough) and, according to his parents, he'd had years of interventions that had helped make him feel different and damaged.

Labels give *false* hope of a cure

In physical medicine, gaining a diagnosis is often an important first step towards your doctor or a specialist helping cure the condition; in psychiatry this seldom happens, though a diagnosis may sometimes help find a drug or a treatment that will ease some of the symptoms.

For most of the children's conditions we are interested in there are no cures and often no reliable treatment. ADHD symptoms in some children respond to drugs such as dexamphetamine and Ritalin but there is no way that these should ever be considered *cures*. Sadly, I hear of clinicians who give parents the impression that these drugs will be given for a while until the child improves then they will be taken off the drug. What usually happens in practice is that the child stays on the drug until parents notice a bad reaction or the child refuses to take it any more (often in early or mid teens).

Labels remove responsibility and provide excuses

Occasionally parents **are** partly, or largely, to blame for their children's difficulties. I've worked with hundreds of children who had been neglected or abused, and have been in and out of Care. These are hardly ever among the children who are abusive towards parents, but I see children for all sorts of other reasons. Instability and stress in children's lives can produce behaviour that looks exactly like a child with ADHD. To give these traumatised children who are reacting normally to an abnormal environment, a pseudo-psychiatric label seems cruel and illogical to me. There is nothing wrong with them except their environment and lack of nurturing, yet the labels may let parents (and the system) off the hook.

Both adults and occasionally children, use labels as excuses, which may benefit them in the short term but cause problems in the longer term. I have known adults who stop looking for work because they are told they have a personality disorder, Asperger's or an addictive personality. Many abusive adults (especially sexual abusers) are very keen to get some form of psychiatric diagnosis to use as an excuse for their cruel behaviour. I have known a number of juveniles attempt to justify bullying and violence on the grounds that they have ADHD.

It's generally accepted that giving adult men who abuse their wives a psychiatric excuse is not helpful. However, giving violent teenagers similar excuses is seldom questioned. This reduces the chance that they will take responsibility for their own behaviour. It also confuses their parents, making it less likely that they will be suitably assertive with the young person. It appears to confuse many workers too. Though they should know better, they may assume that the label *explains* the behaviour or that the label implies that the child *can't help* their behaviour. Unless the disability or mental illness is extreme, this is unhelpful rubbish.

Here's the gist of a conversation with an eight-year-old boy with Asperger's Syndrome:

"Do you think it's a problem that you swear at your mother?"

"*No. I do it when I'm mad.*"

"Do you swear at teachers?"

"*Oh, no. I'd get into trouble. I might get suspended.*"

"Do you swear at your Nan?"

"*No [obviously shocked at the idea]. I love my Nan.*"

"Do you swear at your Dad?"

"*No, he's a bit strict.*"

This is not unusual. What is a little unusual about this is his honesty. If his mother was led to believe that his bad behaviour was a result of his Asperger's Syndrome, she would most likely continue being too soft with him and his oppositional and verbally abusive behaviour would be likely to get worse over time.

Agencies which focus on assessments and labelling are in a very poor position to work on chosen bad behaviour. They are going to find it difficult to challenge young people about their violent, criminal or anti-social behaviour because the label gets in the way. Generally violence to parents is not considered as an issue when people write about specific conditions, even when they focus on the child's aggressiveness. For example, a study of aggression in children with Tourette's syndrome mentioned quite an array of violence aimed at mothers (they didn't ask about fathers) yet did not link this to any of the literature on violence to parents, and just assumed that the behaviour must be linked to the Tourettes[313].

Labels imply certainty

These labels sound definite, scientific and imply certainty. This is almost always misleading. These are fuzzy categories. Some children do fit clearly in the middle of the category but many others will be somewhere around the fuzzy boundary, either the boundary with 'normal' or the boundary with another label. Whether they get Label A, Label B or no label may be largely chance, depending on which labels are in fashion, which professional they see, how they present on that occasion and what their parents or teachers say. Often these diagnoses are based mostly on what parents or teachers say to the assessor. What a parent says will depend partly on whether they are positive or negative, good at explaining subtleties, and how good their memory is. For example, a depressed mother will see their child more negatively and focus on their problems more than their strengths. If a parent is angry at their child at the time of the interview, they may be far more negative. If a parent really needs some service or benefit for their child which depends on getting a label, they can hardly be expected to be impartial about this and naturally may exaggerate problems.

These labels are officially changed every so often and I am willing to bet that in twenty-five years' time labels like "ADHD" and "Oppositional Defiant Disorder" will either be radically redefined or obsolete. I included "Asperger's" when I wrote this paragraph only a year ago and it has already gone. I watched the category "Asperger's syndrome" be widened steadily over a fifteen years period and officially there are now far more children with autism than there were just a few years ago. At one time there were over twice as many children labelled "ADHD" in the state of New South Wales as there was here in Victoria. There is absolutely no reason to suspect that children in the two states differed, but the culture of those making the diagnoses did.

Behaviour becomes seen as sickness

There are muscular tics and epileptic seizures which are not under conscious control, but generally most behaviour involves a choice. Some choices may be very difficult. I could choose not to eat for the next week but this would be incredibly difficult and I would need a huge incentive (saving my life would definitely do it and a million dollars just might). For someone with a genuine addiction, choosing not to drink, gamble or take drugs may be almost as difficult as choosing not to eat for a week, as might resisting a compulsion for someone with obsessive-compulsive disorder.

However, even people with obsessive compulsive disorder can resist their compulsions in some situations or for short periods of time. Addicts are not robots either and can make choices. If you offered them a million dollars to stop the addictive behaviour for a month, almost all of them would do so. I often ask young people (and adults) how much I would have to pay them to stop their unwanted behaviour (which may be tantrums, swearing, stealing, staying up all night, getting into their parent's bed, not going to school), money being a simple measure of how hard it would be for them to change for a month. Most young people will say that they could stop being violent for $100, others would need $1,000. A very small number say it would be hard to change the behaviour even for $1,000,000.

Violence and abuse can be habits but are not addictive behaviours even if labels like "explosive personality disorder" are sometimes given to them. Viewing such behaviour as a form of illness is illogical and usually quite unhelpful; it's not a compulsion but a choice.

Labels can be disempowering

"For some people, a label can become the thing that defines them. It can easily lead to what I call a handicapped mentality. When a person gets a diagnosis of Asperger's, for instance, he might start to think, what's the point? Or I'll never hold down a job. His whole life starts to revolve around what he can't do instead of what he can do." Temple Grandin[314]

If someone believes that a label means that they, or someone close to them, has no control over their behaviour, they feel disempowered. The attitude may be "leave it to the experts" and the individual, or their family, may give up trying.

'Cure' can be as bad as original problem

No treatment is without risks. Not so long ago, being 'treated' for autism usually meant incarceration in a horrible, abusive institution. Thankfully, we've made a lot of progress in the past forty years. But labels such as 'autism' still frequently result in over-medication. Obviously any drug that messes with our brain chemistry can do possible harm as well as good, especially in a fast-developing adolescent brain. There has been very little research on the long term effects of the medications we are giving to children to control their behaviour.

There is inevitably stigma attached to *any* therapy or treatment that is targeted at children with problems (rather than given to all children). Any targeted intervention has the *potential* cost of being stigmatising.

Counselling has lost some, but not all, of its stigma. It's an activity with few risks, provided the counsellor is ethical and sensible. Unfortunately there have been a lot of quacks around and some very suspect approaches. The most common risk is that counsellors keep children in therapy for extended periods of time without any visible progress. This may be bad for the child's self-esteem and some develop therapy-fatigue and will refuse to see counsellors when they are old enough to actually profit from the experience. I see counselling as a necessary evil.

Labels imply permanence and hopelessness

Most people believe that conditions such as ADHD, autism and learning disabilities are permanent conditions. This is often because they are seen as genetic disorders but some believe that children are damaged for life by early experiences (usually blaming parents). Such ideas lead to hopelessness, lowered expectations and sometime self-fulfilling prophesies. Young people pick up on others' attitudes even though these are seldom discussed with them. They may sense that they are expected to be disabled for life.

Mild intellectual disability is a good example: intellectual disability is seen as permanent by definition, so most people, including the majority of professionals, expect a lifelong disability. However, the majority of those with an intellectual disability fall into the mild range (defined as an IQ between fifty and seventy, with far more near the top end of this range than under sixty). Most of these don't use any specialist services as adults. Most get married, hold down jobs and merge into the population and are no longer disabled regardless of their IQ[315]. IQ is not an accurate measure but has an error rate of five points generally. For those who have poor communication, poor motivation, severe anxiety or very low self-esteem, the error can increase greatly. Thus someone whose IQ test results are seventy when they are fourteen years old may well score eighty ten years later. But they are hardly ever retested. Even if their IQ is still under seventy the official definition of 'Intellectual Disability' states that there should be impairment in their functioning as well as a low IQ. So if they are living a normal life with no major impairments in everyday functioning, they *are* no longer intellectually disabled, regardless of IQ. Yet the message they receive is usually that they will be disabled for life. Parents who don't accept this may be seen as in denial.

Our current tests for Autism are *far* less reliable than the tests for intellectual disability. It's quite possible that someone who is on the borderline of meeting the criteria when in their childhood or teens will not meet the criteria in adulthood. To say that they 'must still have autism' as many people do, shows that the label is given more credence than it should have. In some settings the traits that classify someone as having Autism, if not too severe, can be useful and can make them highly productive adults.

There is even less probability that ADHD will produce any meaningful *disability* in adulthood. On the contrary the traits that make these children difficult for parents and teachers can be useful in some occupations and many adults with ADHD are successful in their chosen careers (admittedly for a small minority the chosen career may be crime, vice, or drugs).

Medication

"Boys' aggressiveness is increasingly being treated as a medical problem, particularly in schools, a trend that has led to the diagnosing and medicating of boys whose problem may really be that they have been traumatized and influenced by exposure to violence and abuse at home. Treating these boys as though they have a chemical problem not only overlooks the distress they are in but also reinforces their belief that they are 'out of control' or 'sick', rather than helping them to recognize that they are making bad choices based on destructive values."
Bancroft[316]

The number of children in Western countries (especially in America) being prescribed mind-altering drugs has risen dramatically over the past two decades. Various types of medication can temporarily reduce aggressive behaviour and violence. Tranquillizers, anti-depressants or ADHD medication (stimulants such as Ritalin® or Dexamphetamine) may all reduce the likelihood of violent behaviour *to some extent*. It should be appreciated that none of these are in any way 'curing' any underlying condition. It's often wrongly claimed that if ADHD medication works then this proves that the child must have ADHD. This is nonsense. Smoking marijuana makes many people less aggressive while they are high but no one suggests that this proves there is an underlying condition that the dope is treating! ADHD meds improve the school performance of most boys, but all drugs have side effects and costs. I've known children who were constantly subdued and dull unless they forgot to take their meds, when they then became their true, lively, likable, though difficult, selves.

When medication is given for a behavioural problem without any attempt to deal with the young person's behaviour or the parents' handling of this, I believe an injustice is being done which may make things worse in the long term. There is no good evidence that these meds help in the long term[317]. There are several serious problems which can result from the use of medication for behaviour problems:

- It excuses bad behaviour and reinforces the idea that it's beyond the individual's control.
- It confuses parents and can make them less assertive with their child, which may lead to problems later, perhaps when the medication is no longer prescribed or the youth refuses to take it any longer (many children refuse to take the medication once in their teens).
- Taking medication becomes a habit which may lead to increased use of prescription medication in later life.
- It's possible that the habit of taking drugs *may* increase the likelihood that they will take illegal drugs (there is conflicting evidence, some studies find that children who are not given medication for their ADHD are more likely to take drugs, others the opposite).
- There is very little evidence about the long term effects of taking mind-altering chemicals while the brain is still developing. I am shocked that millions of children are being given such medication with little concerted effort to test the long term effects. There are some reports of serious complications (including making behavioural problems worse) due to common prescription drugs given to children but we don't have the evidence to properly judge this. Part of the reason we don't have the evidence is because we are in the ridiculous position of the drug companies, multi-national, profit-making organisations worth billions of dollars, controlling most of the research themselves and the psychiatric profession is in bed with the drug industry[318]. If a drug trial shows the drug has no effect, it usually doesn't get published, creating the misleading impression that drugs such as anti-depressants are far more effective than they really are. This is a sick and insane system!
- Some children see taking medication as proof that there is something seriously wrong with them and they may feel stigmatised and lose self-esteem (though this loss of self-esteem is often balanced or countered for some by improved academic performance or improved relationships). Some children are even told, without any evidence, that they will have to

take medication for the rest of their lives, which emphasises the fact that they are disabled and different!

- Other children sometimes tease children who take medication and teachers may view them as having serious problems. Having 'ADHD' is becoming a school-yard term of abuse, equated with bad behaviour.

- As mentioned in the quote by Lundy Bancroft above, sometimes serious problems with the individual or family are obscured by reducing the symptoms without treating the cause. Children who have suffered abuse or witnessed domestic violence often receive labels such as 'ADHD' or 'RAD' (reactive attachment disorder) though their behaviour may be a perfectly understandable reaction to their situation. I've mentioned that children who abuse their parents and are labelled ADHD are *just as likely* to have experienced past DV as have the children without these conditions.

- A few children may experience 'stimulant rebound' and get more aggressive when the stimulant medication is wearing off. This is common enough that all parents should be warned of the possibility, but few are. Some violent and disturbing behaviour I have seen in a few pre-teen children appeared to be caused by their medication and stopped when they were taken off of it. Unfortunately, there are professionals who would assume that the answer is to increase the medication, or add another drug, and in several such cases parents had to go against medical advice to stop meds which were clearly doing harm.

- Side effects are sometimes serious and obvious but subtle ones may not be noticed. Loss of appetite is a common side-effect of ADHD meds and the effect of this on developing brains in adolescence is not known. The drug companies are not at all likely to fund such research! There is evidence that these medications delay puberty, which can have serious repercussions as children lose status with their peer group when they lag behind in size and development. Anti-depressants often lead to weight gain, which can have serious effects physically and psychologically.

None of the above says medication is **never** justified. A few children experience huge difficulties, make their own and their families lives hell, and have little chance of learning anything in school without medication. However, when medication is offered as a cure for bad behaviour we should *always* think seriously about the alternatives and about the long term implications. I don't believe that these medications should *ever* be given without counselling (for child, parents or both) or other behavioural intervention also being tried.

Box

Suzanne

Susanne is an angelic looking teenage girl of seventeen with a mild intellectual disability. She is exactly on the borderline as regards IQ (seventy) and coped quite well in primary school. She can read and write well and do simple arithmetic. It's worth bearing in mind that she would not have been considered disabled in our society a few decades ago or in any non-Western society today. Mild intellectual disability is not a 'condition' or 'disorder' but just the bottom end of a normal continuum of intelligence. The cut-off point is arbitrary.

Susanne's parents separated when she was eight. She did not see or hear from her father for a number of years and on occasions got either very sad or very angry about this. In the past few years he has made contact and she sees him sporadically. Her mother, Gloria, is a clerical worker and, although she can be very caring and patient, she is tough with a fierce temper and can be stubborn and even verbally aggressive. Suzanne had no behavioural problems whatsoever until she started high school. She was teased and bullied and after six months of this transferred from mainstream to a special school. Suzanne had never mixed with disabled children and was horrified to find herself with 'spastics' and 'Mongols' as she called them. Her behaviour deteriorated rapidly.

Suzanne found that she could get attention outside school from boys, usually much older than her, and she became sexually promiscuous at age fourteen. She also decided that being seen as tough was preferable to being seen as disabled. Frequent fights at school led to fights in the street and then fights at home. Suzanne felt intense anger but did not know who to be angry at. Mum was the safest and closest target.

The conflict with her mother began in earnest when she started staying out late and hanging around with a succession of much older boyfriends. Some of these were clearly breaking the law as Suzanne was then a minor and they were undoubtedly having sex. However, Gloria found that she was helpless to do anything unless Suzanne would give evidence or make a complaint, which she never did.

Gloria says she was too indulgent and permissive for many years. Now that she has started trying to impose consequences on Suzanne, she feels undermined from a number of directions. Suzanne's father gives her money and buys her things without consulting Gloria and has let Suzanne stay overnight without her mother's permission. Thus when Gloria has tried to discipline her daughter by refusing to let her go to a party, her father has let her stay the weekend and drives her to the event. Gloria's own parents also overindulge Suzanne and undermine Gloria. Gloria is very angry at some of the youth workers and disability workers who have been involved (there has been a steady stream of changing faces, mostly very young faces). They have told Gloria that she has to treat her daughter as an adult and has no right to send her to her room (not that she will go anymore), stop her allowance, or prevent her from seeing her friends (latest friend is a forty-five-year-old man whose daughter went to school with Suzanne). Gloria and Suzanne have had wrestling matches and Gloria feels great shame that she loses her temper and screams and yells on occasions. Suzanne has once or twice had slight bruises after these fights, whereas Gloria frequently has bruises and has had cuts, black eyes, and once a broken nose. Suzanne smashes things, but never her own things. Gloria says some of the workers (disability and youth workers) treat her as if she is an abuser and say, or imply, that she should give Suzanne more attention and affection to boost her self-esteem. Gloria finds them condescending and has at times lost her temper with them, convincing them that Gloria is the aggressor, whereas Suzanne to them appears as sweetness personified.

Gloria has had to reduce her hours of work and is on medication for depression and anxiety. She feels her health has been deteriorating. She prays every day that her daughter will mature enough to stop being abusive. Suzanne is twenty, and she is still waiting.

End Box

Self-Esteem

Eddie: "You said your Dad was a loser because he punched holes in walls."
Glen: "Yep, he's a loser!"

Eddie: "But you're copying this, you've punched holes in walls too. Does that make you a trainee loser?"

*Glen: "No, it's different when I do it because **I'm** awesome!"*

Although fourteen-year-old Glen said this with a grin, his mother confirmed my impression that most of the time he really did believe he was 'awesome'.

In my sample of nearly five hundred children who abused their parents there are a few factors, such as intelligence and anxiety, which tend towards either extreme, higher than average in some but lower than average in others. For both of these factors the most common extreme is the opposite of usual expectations: high intelligence being slightly more common than low and low anxiety more common than high. Self-esteem, similarly, can be unusually low or unusually high. It's high, not low, self-esteem that is more common among young people who abuse parents. But it's complicated.

Self-esteem is complicated. It's not a basic personality trait like extraversion or neuroticism; it's far more changeable than these and far more responsive to the environment.

I'm concentrating on high self-esteem in this chapter for two reasons. One is that it goes against expectations and is hence more interesting (no one has written about high self-esteem and violence to parents), and the second reason is that it appears to be somewhat more common than low self-esteem in young people who abuse parents.

Low self-esteem

There is no doubt that some children who abuse their parents have low, sometimes extremely low, self-esteem. However, what is cause and effect is not always clear. Some children have low self-esteem because they feel guilty about their behaviour and have soured their relationships with the most important people in their lives. When they stop abusing their parents, their self-esteem may go up significantly.

A child may have lowered self-esteem for a number of reasons:
- They have some kind of developmental disorder or disability.
- They are failing educationally.

206

- They are being bullied, teased or ostracised by peers.
- They have been exposed to domestic violence.
- They have been rejected, mistreated or put down by a parent or carer.
- They have alienated themselves from their family and are stressed and insecure.
- They feel guilty about their behaviour.

All of these can be associated with violence to parents, especially exposure to DV. So it's not an illogical expectation that many children who are violent to parents will have low self-esteem. I observe many with low self-esteem but they are not the majority. And the last two reasons above are a result of the behaviour rather than a cause of violent behaviour.

In terms of personality in young people who abuse parents, it's often those children who are anxious introverts who have low self-esteem, while the fearless extroverts are far more likely to have above average self-esteem.

I am not making light of low self-esteem. It's a serious problem. At its most dangerous it can be linked to anxiety, social isolation, depression and even suicide. I often focus on this in counselling youth. However, although it's found for the above reasons in many children who are abusive to parents, it's not usually a contributing cause of violence to parents while excessively high self-esteem is an important contributor.

If your violent child has low self-esteem, then by all means try to do something about this. Heaping on praise is not likely to work unless there has been too little praise up till now. Boosting self-esteem might be through counselling but this can be stigmatising in itself. More likely, you can try to boost self-esteem by encouraging the things they are good at and trying to keep them away from those who put them down (this may not be possible if it's a family member). But don't expect that such interventions are going to stop the violence. They may help, but only indirectly.

High self-esteem and violence

It's a common assumption that people with problems have low self-esteem and for many problems this is likely to be true – though that doesn't mean it causes the problems. People with serious physical, mental, social or financial problems all tend to have lower self-esteem. However, for behavioural problems such as violence, abuse and crime, there is no good evidence that self-esteem tends to be low despite this being an almost universal assumption. The belief that people who are violent or abusive have low self-esteem is widespread among writers, professionals, and the public. It's a myth that fooled me for years. There is some evidence suggesting the exact opposite; that violent and abusive individuals tend to have high self-esteem.[319]

"Dangerous people, from playground bullies to warmongering dictators, consist mainly of those who have favourable views about themselves. They strike out at others who question or dispute those favourable views." Baumeister[320]

This is a radical idea for many people and in my workshops it sometimes meets with outright disbelief or even hostility. Someone may object that 'Deep down inside they have low self-esteem.' Since this is true of almost everyone (except psychopaths) it's not really relevant. Or someone will state that people who appear arrogant are covering up low self-esteem. Such ideas are impossible to prove or disprove and hence generally of no practical use. If I talk about 'arrogance', 'pride' or 'narcissism' rather than high self-esteem, no one objects.

"It turns out that deep down inside, narcissists think they're awesome." Twenge & Campbell[321]

High self-esteem contributing to violence is a bit of a worry since there has been a huge push over the past fifty years to raise self-esteem. Parenting gurus, politicians and psychologists (especially pop psychologists) have encouraged us to have high self-esteem and to boost our children's self-esteem to the max!

"Where did this lopsided emphasis on self-esteem, self-regard, self-importance - come from? When did we decide it would be a good idea for children to take themselves so seriously, to believe everything they do is wonderful, and never a word of criticism or correction to be heard? 'Brilliant' we cry, at the drop of a hat, 'gold stars all round!' Mackay[322]

A fairly typical example of attitudes to childhood self-esteem is given in the book *Bully-proof Your Child.* The author states, without feeling the need to offer any proof, that *'Self-esteem is the single most important factor in determining whether your child will grow up to be happy and successful.'* He goes on to give an approving example of meeting a two-year-old child with high self-esteem: *'She looked me straight in the eyes and said confidently: 'I'm gorgeous.' The older girls laughed and said [she] always said that.[323]'* Cute (maybe) in a two-year-old, but if she continues to believe this up to adolescence, she could either come down to earth with a vengeance (which could mean depression) or she might become an arrogant bully.

There has been a steady and impressive increase in self-esteem among young people over the past few decades. *"Almost every trait related to narcissism rose between the 1950s and the 1990s, including assertiveness, dominance, extraversion, self-esteem, and individualistic focus."[324]* In the context of violence to parents, all of these traits are relevant.

There is good evidence that more child-focused parenting, when compared to authoritarian or uninvolved parenting, leads to higher self-esteem in children[325] and so it's not surprising that there has been an increase in children's self-esteem over the past few decades. I am constantly struck by how much more confident and self-assured the children are that I meet today compared to twenty to forty years ago. Self-esteem has risen but it has not been the panacea that pundits predicted. It hasn't reduced mental health problems. On the other hand it may have helped produce what is possibly the most narcissistic, arrogant, self-obsessed generation of young people ever – the Selfie Generation.

I should say again that there are many wonderful young people and I'm surprised how resilient some of them are in the face of a toxic culture. However, there is also a developmental tendency for adolescents to be egocentric and self-obsessed (at least in Western society) and so these traits are exaggerated in the teenage years.

"In the rush to create self-worth, our culture may have opened the door to something darker and more sinister."[326] So say Twenge and Campbell in their book they called, *'The Narcissism Epidemic'*. Yes, yet another epidemic! They don't mention violence to parents but I see some of the darker and more sinister aspects of entitlement and narcissism in some of the young people I work with.

'Narcissism' means self-love. People showing an extreme of self-love may be labelled as having 'Narcissistic Personality Disorder'. I don't find labelling people with some kind of 'disordered' personality to be very helpful, and please don't worry about whether your child fits this label or not – it won't help you deal with it. Many people (including Twenge and Campbell) see narcissism as being different to high self-esteem but the distinction seems to be largely based on a moral judgment, and as far as I am concerned, narcissism is just *excessively* high self-esteem. Too much of a good thing! Many highly successful people: artists, actors, politicians also have sky high self-esteem but if they are socially successful they don't get labelled with a personality disorder. We tend to call high self-esteem *'narcissism'* only when it makes us uncomfortable or when it leads to highly objectionable behaviour. There are people who quietly love themselves but also respect others – good for them! It's really only when high self-esteem goes with a disregard for others that it becomes problematic (as with the balance of Entitlement and Responsibility, see Chapter 25). Those who love themselves but are Agreeable and Conscientious are not likely to be a problem to others, and may be very popular and successful.

It seems clear to me that our modern parenting methods are responsible not just for the rise in positive self-esteem but also the rise in excessive, narcissistic, self-esteem. Idolising children has mixed results. Professor Twenge says that the increase in Narcissism is due to a number of factors, which include celebrity culture, the internet and permissive parenting.

"It seems clear that a person who receives too much adulation is likely to lose the capacity for self-criticism and hence to make inflexible and wrong decisions."
Sutherland[327]

Self-esteem is a very useful concept but it's certainly not a simple one. We talk about it as if it's a unitary, measurable thing, like height, but this is a gross oversimplification. Although overall self-esteem may be high, low, or (more often) in between, someone can have high self-esteem in some ways but low in others. In addition it can be stable or unstable, secure or insecure. Self-esteem is not fixed for an individual and some people can vary greatly at different times or in different situations, in how confident they are and how they feel about themselves. Depression, failure, embarrassment or disgrace can all dramatically lower self-esteem but this can sometimes bounce back quickly. Anxiety also affects self-esteem and this can vary by the hour. Being abused often dramatically lowers self-esteem and this may last for a lifetime – or may recover rapidly. Many of the parents abused by their children who I've worked with were confident people with good self-esteem *until* their son or daughter began abusing them. In the course of the *Who's in Charge?* programme, we often see parents becoming visibly more confident and watch their self-esteem rise dramatically.

I would like to consistently measure self-esteem in the children I work with but so far haven't found a suitable test. Most tests focus entirely on low self-esteem and a few tests measure the other extreme, narcissism. I've given a number of children who abuse parents tests of self-concept and many score high overall, a few score low, and others are clearly high on some aspects of self-worth but low on others[328]. I am not aware of any study that has looked at high self-esteem and child to parent violence; it seems to be assumed that they have low self-esteem by most writers.

Pride is often associated with high self-esteem. It's interesting that we see *pride* as a good thing, but only up to a certain point. Lacking pride in oneself is clearly bad, but excessive pride is a definite problem. Injured pride is a frequent motivator for violence[329].

"To the extent that narcissists believe they are particularly deserving of high status, they will be particularly sensitive to any provocation that threatens that status." Fiske & Tage[330]

This is especially true of *male pride*, often involved in domestic violence. Yet we don't tend to think of self-esteem in the same way as pride, as having a happy medium with both extremes being problematic. They are!

Excessive self-esteem goes hand in hand with pride and both are related to high entitlement, an important factor in violence to parents.

"Villains, bullies, criminals, killers, and other evildoers have high self-esteem, contrary to the comfortable fiction that has recently spread through American culture. ... The people (or groups or countries) most prone to violence are the ones who are most susceptible to ego threats, especially those who have inflated, exalted opinions of themselves or whose normally high self-esteem does occasionally take a nosedive." Baumeister[331]

Unstable high self-esteem

The most dangerous combination appears to be *unstable high self-esteem*, the insecurely arrogant. They may think they are pretty damn special, but their pride is easily challenged and they are often hypersensitive to any slight or insult, the 'ego threats' that Baumeister talks about. For some of the highly arrogant young people I meet, any real or imagined criticism, teasing, joking, or asking them to do the dishes or stop texting in class, can be a blow to their overblown pride. Their egos are large yet fragile. The young people I meet who get into the most fights are those who think that someone looking at them is *'dissing'* them and challenging them to fight. They will make eye contact with strangers and if the stranger doesn't back down (like an animal showing submission), they see this as an affront to their pride and an invitation to violence.

The idea that someone can be genuinely arrogant, yet highly insecure at times, makes sense to many parents living with violent children and some have expressed surprise that they had never thought of this before. They often say things like, 'That's our Timmy to a T'. However, as I've mentioned, professionals are often uncomfortable with this idea, they tend to focus on the insecurity and dismiss the pride and arrogance as being superficial.

For those who are abusive to others, getting caught can dramatically lower their self-esteem. Some studies or accounts of abusers fail to take this into account. Those who are being forced to admit to their abuse (in the legal system or any kind of therapy) may appear to have low self-esteem but they may have been arrogant and self-satisfied for many years until charged with assault or forced to face the loss of their family. Their high self-esteem may crumble in these circumstances but this is not surprising and does not prove that their abusive behaviour was in any way the result of low self-esteem. Even though I am usually meeting violent young people after they have been forced into counselling, and many men attending a behaviour change group accused of family violence, many of them are still prideful. Others are shamefaced at first but quickly reveal arrogance, pride and a sense of entitlement. If I was still convinced that they had low self-esteem, I could easily overlook the pride or dismiss it as false or unimportant. Over time I've been forced to acknowledge that their arrogance has often been part of the process leading to them becoming violent to others.

Biographies of some of the greatest villains who ever lived, Hitler, Stalin and Napoleon, show that they had long periods of thinking they were god-like and wonderful, but also occasional periods of despair and extreme self-doubt[332]. People with bi-polar syndrome often have low self-esteem when in a depressive cycle and may have outrageously high self-esteem when manic. They are *far* more likely to be violent in the manic phase. Depression, often associated with low self-esteem, is not associated with violence[333]. It's absurd that depression is quite often trotted out in the courts as an excuse for violent crime.

The idea that abusers and bullies often have high self-esteem doesn't seem fair. As we have pointed out, people try hard to view the world as a fair and reasonable place, against overwhelming evidence to the contrary. Some of your guilt, confusion and general bewilderment may stem from your deeply held beliefs that good things happen to good people, and that good people have good kids. Sadly, both of these ideas are baloney!

Most group programmes for parents, and parenting manuals, have raising their children's self-esteem as a goal: *"Children need to feel loved. Feeling loved gives children better self-esteem and protects them in times of difficulty. Love and warmth also strengthens relationships and reduces conflict within the family unit."* [334]

Overall these statements are true but they are certainly not always true and the myth that more love, warmth and attention are always a good thing runs through most parenting literature along with the belief that you can't have too much self-esteem. I believe assumptions like this are why parents of abusive children often find regular (non-specialist) parenting classes confusing or even insulting.

I listened to an internationally known speaker recently talking about working with difficult adolescents. He described some very arrogant young people and showed several on video. However, he still seemed to believe that these young people had poor self-esteem, they needed to learn to be assertive, and that their parents were trying too hard to control them. He mentioned that these children often felt as if their parents were 'dissing' them and implied that the parents needed to treat these children with more respect!

"Narcissists also get angry and aggressive when they feel their freedom is restricted – in other words, when they can't do what they want." Twenge & Campbell[335]

Although there is research evidence supporting the idea that violence and abuse *generally* can be linked to high self-esteem, we don't have any hard evidence on self-esteem and violence to parents – it's never been researched. When self-esteem is mentioned in relation to violence to parents in the literature, it's assumed that low self-esteem is the norm. My experience of working with men who abuse their wives and with children who abuse parents, is that both groups are quite often arrogant, prideful and opinionated with an overblown sense of self. Most often, though not always, this overblown self-esteem is somewhat fragile and insecure. Insecure high self-esteem leads easily to injured pride and defensiveness.

The prideful and self-important who are truly secure in their high opinion of themselves don't need to be defensive. Their pride is not easily shaken by real or imagined slights, which they may simply shrug off. They get into fewer fights because they don't feel they have anything to prove.

There has been far more research on school bullying than on children's violence within the home (and it's far easier to observe and to get people to talk about). This research clearly contradicts the common myth that portrays bullies as pathetic failures who are compensating for their inadequacies. Bullies are often popular, are physically stronger than others, on average they are just as good academically as non-bullies and they "often have a relatively positive view of themselves"[336]. Female bullies are often among the more attractive girls.

Many, though certainly not all, of the young people I meet who are violent to parents are confident, opinionated, arrogant and prideful. Some are high achievers in school but more could be if they studied. Academic underachievers are common among them for several reasons: some find it difficult to learn because they think they know it all already; some are low in Conscientiousness; and some are stressed or living a chaotic life due to their own behaviour. I've had a number of such youngsters tell me that they could get A's in school if they chose to, but they aren't trying.

Though I hesitate to mention it, girls who are violent to adults are quite often of above average attractiveness (as with female bullies). A parent in one of my groups first brought this to my attention – he'd been comparing notes with the other parents and asked if all the girls who were violent in the home were attractive. I initially dismissed the idea. However, a female youth worker colleague, who had met a great many of these girls, made the same observation and I then started noticing that many of the girls who abuse parents were pretty little princesses (it's amazing how we can miss the obvious when it goes against our expectations).

"[W]omen who perceived themselves to be attractive – like strong men – were more prone to anger, felt greater entitlement, were more successful in conflicts, and found violence to be more useful after controlling for physical strength."
Marczyk[337]

A mother said to me recently, before I'd met her violent fourteen-year-old daughter, "Unfortunately she's very beautiful!" This mother recognised that this was related to her arrogance and over-confidence. It's ironic that many people picture violent girls as being rough, butch and lacking in confidence. Many people are more comfortable seeing these kids as victims, suffering insecurity and low self-esteem. The fact that pretty, popular girls often bully other girls, and their own parents, also goes against some interpretation of girls' violence, where girls are seen as *primarily* reacting to powerlessness and oppression or are rejecting female roles. This may be true of some girls who join gangs or who are involved in some types of crime, but girls who are violent within the home are just as often among the *more* powerful (both in status and wealth) and are usually no less feminine than other girls their age.

"And if your daughter is a princess, does this mean that you are the queen or king? No – it means you are the loyal subject, and you must do what the princess says."
Twenge & Campbell[338]

I'm not very good at judging if young men are attractive or not, and their social status and self-esteem are less dependent on looks than is the case for teenage girls (though it's becoming more important). However, many of the boys who abuse parents are socially successful (as with school bullies) and some are unusually talented at sport or in other ways.

So our modern parenting and teaching methods, emphasising praise and avoiding any hint of failure or inadequacy, can give children unrealistically positive views of themselves. This is complicated by the fact that an increasing number of our young people compare themselves to Hollywood ideals and internet prodigies rather than their neighbours. Thus some come down with a crash in adolescence and become depressed, others are angry that the world doesn't think they are wonderful, and some are both depressed and angry.

Isn't violence due to powerlessness?

The idea that violence is related to low self-esteem, powerlessness, depression and social inadequacy is very popular, especially in liberal academic and welfare circles. This idea probably makes it easier for some workers to work with violent individuals but it leads to them being seen as unfortunate victims and not being held accountable for their abuse of others.

There certainly **is** an association of violence with low income, poor education, and unemployment. Overall there is definitely more violence among poor and less well educated people within Western society. However, most poor people are not violent and it's not particularly their powerlessness that makes some individuals more violent than others but other factors including social sophistication, responsibility, and the sub-cultural acceptance of violence. As we've mentioned, school bullies are less often marginalised, powerless kids and more often popular, socially powerful ones. They don't tend to have low self-esteem, though their victims do. Men who abuse their wives and children are not less powerful within their home but *more* powerful. Being bullied in their work could make them somewhat worse at home, but so can being in a position to bully others, such as being a boss, a policeman or a security guard.

Some children who bully parents are themselves bullied at school. This is certainly not rare but they are a bit *more* likely to be bullies than victims of bullying (and some are both bully and victim). As I've mentioned, there is no contradiction in being both victim and victimiser – they are roles not identities.

The idea that children who are violent to parents are reacting to feeling powerless is very common in the scant literature on violence to parents, and naturally this idea gets linked to parent blaming explanations. This is close to being the opposite of the truth! On the whole children who abuse their parents are not those who are particularly powerless but those who are **too** powerful. The statistical association between low income and violence holds for men hitting their wives but does **not** apply to young people hitting their parents, who are just as likely to be middle class as working class and as likely to be wealthy as poor. If we looked at violence to parents throughout the world, there would in fact be an extremely strong correspondence with wealth, not poverty, since this form of violence is far more common in rich Western societies than in poor Third World ones. Overall, violence to parents is *far more* common in societies where children are *more* powerful in relation to adults.

Perpetrators of violence do not generally *feel* powerful. The over-entitled would prefer, in most cases, not to have to use brute force to get what they want. It would suit them better if other people would just give in without a fight; and this does often happen. Once someone has a reputation for being dangerous they often get others to acquiesce to their wishes from fear or a desire to keep the peace. For example, parents tiptoe around their violent offspring, wives do the same with violent husbands, and other children often try to appease bullies (sometimes by becoming loyal followers). Violence gets results, at least in the short term. Denying this is yet another way in which we try to preserve the myth of a just world and show reluctance to admit how unfair the world is.

We've mentioned that perpetrators of violence when forced to talk to workers about their behaviour (they seldom do so willingly), are less likely to seem as prideful and arrogant as they would in other circumstances. They also may genuinely believe that they are the real victims. Both adults and youth who are violent within the family may twist things to convince themselves that they are the primary victim. Even if they don't really believe this, they may try to convince others that they are the victim, frequently exaggerating, or blatantly lying about, the other person's violence. False allegations of child abuse are far from uncommon in these families[339] and appear to be getting more common. The excuse that the violent child is really a victim fits neatly with many workers' parent-blaming assumptions.

Just recently a young boy assaulted his mother in my waiting room (she wouldn't buy him a computer game). Although I saw him punch his mother and pull her hair, he made a huge fuss about a tiny scratch from where his mother had grabbed his arm to defend herself. When I asked him to leave the building he phoned his father and said, in an impressively scared voice, that we were holding him against his will. Often I can't even tell if they believe their own tales of victimisation or not. Incidentally, it's been very rare in the forty-one years I've worked with youth for me to see them behave like this, and this has only happened in the past decade – a sign of the continual erosion of respect for authority.

"We must abandon the obsession with self-esteem. Instead of creating well-adjusted, happy children, the self-esteem movement has created an army of little narcissists." Twenge[340]

Box

Steven

Steven's father, Howard, is a graphic artist and his mother, Julia, an accountant. Both are attractive and have lots of friends and many interests. They have had a very good relationship until the past two years. Steven, sixteen, is the middle child of three. His older brother, who is at University, and his little sister are both well-behaved, well-adjusted A-students. Steven too is an A-student and is also an elite athlete. He has seldom had any problems at school bar the odd argument with teachers when he can be demanding and over-assertive, but is not blatantly defiant or rude outside the home. At home it's a very different picture. Over the past two or three years bouts of temper and verbal abuse have increased in frequency, and he has assaulted both parents on several occasions. Steven is over six foot tall and equal to his father (who is certainly no wimp) in physical strength.

Howard was horrified when his son first pushed over Julia and describes alternating waves of fury and grief. Julia persuaded him that it was a one-off and that they should let it pass. Next time Steven flew into a rage he punched his father. Howard says he had not been in any kind of fight since primary school and just 'went to pieces'. Julia and Howard argued for months about whether Steven needed psychiatric help or to be sent away to a residential school [in Melbourne: this option is open to very few families as it's very expensive]. For a long time, they felt the problem was like a huge wedge coming between them. Then, quite abruptly, they started working together and are now closer than they have been in years.

In counselling when Steven admits to his behaviour, he talks quite rationally about the frustrations of being treated as a child when he feels that he is an adult. He clearly resents his parents having any control over him whatsoever. He says he has no intention of taking drugs, doing crime, getting his girlfriend pregnant or putting himself at risk, so why do his parents need to tell him what to do? He admits he gets illogically angry when they give him any commands and he 'sees red' and 'loses it'. Although he admits his behaviour was wrong and says he feels ashamed and guilty, he does not see it as terribly important. He was horrified

215

recently that his parents called the police and they have taken out a restraining order so that he is not allowed to hit or abuse any family member. Steven is astute enough to point out that this is a legal nonsense as these things are illegal anyway. However, he has been behaving far better since the order was taken out.

End Box

"Since when does the princess have to take orders from the chambermaid?"

Respect

"Abuse and respect are diametric opposites: You do not respect someone whom you abuse, and do not abuse someone whom you respect." Bancroft[341]

"Without respect, no sustainable warmth between a parent and a child is possible" Doherty[342]

Growing up in the sixties I did not place much value on respect for authority. Many of the great evils in the world are associated with too much respect for, and blind obedience to, authority. So for most of my career I avoided the word 'respect' because of its old-fashioned, authoritarian overtures. However, I've been forced to acknowledge that respect is a key concept when children abuse their parents and I see signs of disrespect all around.

Few of those who write about child development or parenting teenagers discuss respect, except in terms of parents respecting children. Here's a typical example from *'What to do when your Children turn into Teenagers'* the short section entitled 'Showing respect' is about us showing our teens respect, with this wonderful piece of wish-fulfilment about respect for parents: *"Teenagers respect us if we show them respect in meaningful ways.*[343]*"* Sadly this has only a tiny kernel of truth in it and a huge amount of ideology. Respecting others does overall *increase the odds* that others will respect you, but if you think this is inevitable you are living in cloud cuckoo land.

Although social scientists have been reluctant to use the concept of respect (possibly because they often side with the young person against parents) the general public realise that there is a real problem. In a survey in the UK in 2000, a whopping 87% of people saw a decline in respect for authority as *the* most negative change in modern society[344].

'Respect' is not simple, fixed or one-dimensional. It's one of those concepts we all understand, or think we do, but can't easily define and generally don't even think about except when there is a problem, i.e. a lack of respect.

Respect can mean:

a) Admiration, deference, or reserve based on someone's qualities, position, or age or,

b) Showing others basic courtesy, decency and consideration for their rights regardless of their qualities.

The first of these implies some form of acknowledged superiority as we look up to, or obey, the other person. The second, common courtesy and consideration, should apply to everyone, even those we look down on.

The respect you show a beloved grandmother is very different to the respect you show to your boss. It's common nowadays to deny that respect based largely on fear is 'real' respect but this is largely a moral judgment and it's possible to feel a mixture of both love and fear. If you were to appear in court, you may well feel some fear of the judge but you can still respect him in his role. You certainly don't have to feel any affection for someone to respect them.

Our current Western view of respect for age and position is a weak and much diluted version of the type of respect that was common in our society until recently, and is still the norm in non-Western societies. Subservience to age and authority has been the rule in virtually every society throughout human history. Before the modern democratic era only a few radical intellectuals questioned the idea that some people (including the elderly) are superior to others and should be treated with obedience and deference.

It's hard to imagine that children only a century ago often called fathers 'sir'. 'Sir' gave way to 'Father' which became 'Pop', 'Daddy' and 'Dad'. Now it's not unusual for older children to call parents by their first name[*]. Unfortunately I also regularly hear of children calling their father 'idiot', 'loser' or worse... far worse. When I was at school we called teachers 'sir'. This would be anathema to many of today's students. I grew up in Glasgow in the same era as comedian Billy Connolly and if you've heard his patter you'll know how often he uses the 'f' word. It was like a punctuation mark for many of the kids I grew up with. Yet I can't recall a single student swearing at a teacher. In some schools nowadays swearing at teachers is no longer considered a major offence.

Western society may be unique in largely abandoning this idea of respect for age, and encouraging the belief that we are all equal and should all be treated the same. In practice the elderly are not treated equally but are discriminated against. We've mentioned the fact that to call an unrelated man 'grandfather' in our culture is usually an insult while in other cultures it's a sign of respect.

I'm not suggesting that we should return to Victorian values with high degrees of formality and social distance between the generations. It definitely had a dark side with an emphasis on duty rather than love towards parents.

The two forms of respect cause confusion for modern parents. Parents often vary between asking for: a) respect based on superiority or b) respect or common decency that is due to anyone.

Most of us do not want to return to the fear-filled form of respect which many children had for parents (especially fathers) in the past. Hopefully you don't want your children to fear you. True closeness is impossible when respect is based mainly on fear.

You can't insist that your children love you, look up to you, or hold you in high esteem. But you certainly can, and should, insist that they treat you with the

---

[*] I've made the mistake in recent years of letting my son call me 'Eddie.' I've tried getting him to call me 'Sir Eddie' but to no avail.

basic respect due to anyone. Everyone has worth just by being human. Love need not be related to respect. We feel a lot of love for new babies but we don't really have a lot of respect for them as we wipe their bottoms or have them spew up on our shoulders. We certainly don't have much respect for the obnoxious, drunken teenager who is throwing up on the flower bed, though we still love him (a bit).

When 'respect' is associated with this distant, old-fashioned parenting you may become confused about expecting or demanding it. You would like some kind of obedience but don't want blind obedience. It's perfectly reasonable to expect some compliance from your child but not unquestioning, submissive obedience. People don't want their children to see them as distant, fearful authority figures any more, but they do want basic human respect and to have *some* authority within their own homes. This doesn't even involve treating children as inferiors since you *should* have authority in your own home and this would apply to adult visitors or lodgers.

As noted elsewhere, even democracies need leaders. A family should be a benevolent dictatorship and can only very rarely function as a democracy (every individual has to be responsible and mature enough to not put themselves or others at any kind of risk). Without a leader you either have anarchy or one of the children will fill the role and you will then have a non-benevolent, belligerent, dictatorship.

The past few decades have seen a dramatic increase in low-level disrespect of parents and adults in general, by children of all social classes. This is very obvious to anyone who has had contact with children over more than one decade.

"The general opinion is that, as the proportion of children with diagnosed special needs has increased, so has the proportion that doesn't have a specific diagnosable disorder but are just distractible, impulsive or badly behaved." Palmer[345]

It's clearly no coincidence that there has been just as steady an increase in young people physically, verbally and emotionally abusing parents. The children involved are getting somewhat younger and it's also now spanning the generations. Ten years ago I saw children who abused parents but not grandparents; now they are often abusing grandparents too. Not only are more teachers being abused but even head teachers are becoming victims, something almost unheard of a decade or two ago. I come across twelve-year-olds from good families who have no respect for, or fear of, the police. These children will mock the police while they are being interviewed or when the police are called following a destructive tantrum. Teachers complain that even the well-behaved children argue with them in recent years, which was very rare in the past. Though low-level disrespect and abuse is not the same thing, the two are closely connected as disrespect can slip into a pattern of abuse.

Even between children themselves there is far less respect for age. It used to be that parents could leave a fourteen-year-old to look after a ten-year-old. Now the younger child is likely to refuse to heed the older child and may even attack him or her if he thinks he can get away with it. This not only makes sibling fights and rivalry more common than in the past but it puts a great deal of pressure on some parents, especially sole parents. In all societies, older children have looked after younger ones (in some societies this is **the main** form of child care after infancy) but now many children need constant **adult** supervision. This is historically new and unique and is not only stressful for all concerned but inevitably leads to children being less responsible and independent.

As I've said before, abuse is **not** about the lack of love. People can, and often do, abuse people they love. In fact, the sad truth is that people more often abuse the ones they love most. It may be possessive, demanding and not the kind of love we approve of, and at the point of actual abuse, the love may be forgotten, but it's love all the same. All abuse involves a lack of respect. You won't abuse someone you have respect for, even if you dislike them. Just as men who abuse their partners are often dependent, possessive and demanding, so too are *some of* the children who abuse their parents.

It's a sad irony that some parents have lost the respect of their children through the process of trying to be their friend rather than an authority figure. A few teenagers are good friends with their parents but generally speaking, why would they want a friend of their parent's age? Friendship is notoriously fickle and changeable at this age and can't be relied on. Friends may come and friends may go but a parent is a parent for life. You should be their friend only in so far as this is in addition to, not instead of, being an authoritative parent.

Look at the table below and consider where your problem child falls in their attitude to you.

← Respect		Neutrality	Disrespect →	
regards as superior		regards as equal	regards as inferior	
Esteem	Admire	Indifferent	Condescending	Ashamed of
Honour	Appreciate	Distant	Unresponsive	Detest
Venerate	Approve of	Detached	Uncaring	Hostile
Revere	Obey	Uninterested	Discourteous	Abhor
Be in awe of	Defer to	Remote	Disobedient	Despise
	Look up to	Insensitive	Insolent	Look down on
		Heedless	Disregard	Scorn
			Pity	Show contempt
			Defiant	Disdain
Abuse highly unlikely				Some form of abuse likely

To stop abuse you don't have to get your child to look up to you or admire you. Ordinary respect for a fellow human being is enough; they may still ignore you and avoid you but they won't abuse you.

Very young children often regard parents with adoration and awe; this excessive and unrealistic degree of regard drops off steadily from around age eight and often plummets with adolescence. During adolescence it's not unusual for a teen's attitude to hover around neutrality, with occasional dips into negativity, usually improving again after a period of keeping the parent at arm's length. But we need to remind ourselves that most adolescents do still respect parents and the myth that they all rebel or reject parents is simply a modern myth.

Even neutrality can be a major problem in some cases. If your child is only granting you the same respect as everyone else, then you aren't able to guide them or be a proper parent. A teenager who is neutral towards one or both parents may still go along with requests and rules to ensure an easy life but does not use the parents as a role model or as a source of emotional support. These teenagers may come through this phase okay but some can be vulnerable to negative influences.

When neutrality moves into the realm of disrespect, problems are greatly confounded. A vicious cycle is set in place whereby deteriorating relationships, plus the psychological processes of victim blaming and self-justification, leads to a steady erosion of respect. Disrespect breeds more disrespect. Some young people, over a period of a year or two (typically), can move from having a good positive relationship with a parent, to treating them with complete contempt and raw hostility. It's sometimes hard to believe that these children had a good, secure relationship with their parent in the recent past. For some people, it's also hard to believe that nothing major (such as abuse or mental illness) lies behind such a horrific, tragic transformation. However, I have seen enough cases to convince me that this can happen to the best of parents (though there may be an added stress such as a messy separation, an irresponsible access parent, or a parent with a severe illness or disability).

> *"THESE DAYS we don't take authority very seriously... People no longer unquestioningly do as they are told and those who claim authority without having earned it are rightly treated with derision and contempt. There is much to welcome in this — but at the same time no society can work unless some forms of authority are respected... Even adult authority has been called into question. It is frequently suggested that grown-ups possess no special wisdom and that 'children's rights' should be celebrated. Notice how in almost every new film the special insight and sensitivity of children are favourably contrasted with the inflexibility of their dim-witted elders."* Frank Furedi[346]

There has been a trend for decreasing respect for age and authority for the past one hundred and fifty years. It was given a boost in the sixties when all authority was called into question. Along with this has been a celebration of youth which started in the fifties when the media discovered teenagers and marketers discovered their money. Youth is worshipped and age derided by the mass media. Our culture is now largely shaped by commercial forces happy to corrupt the young in any way that sells products. One aspect of this is that adults, and authority in general, are portrayed as silly, repressive or both while children are shown as bright, smart (but more smart-Alec) and independent. Bart Simpson is the role model for today's children. We as parents are *partly* responsible for our disrespectful children (though we meant well) but a *larger* part of the blame goes to the wider society, (mostly the media) and from the children's own culture. We discussed this earlier in the chapter on our toxic culture, page 99.

Disrespect

'Violence', 'aggression' and 'abuse' are all hard to define. 'Disrespect' is even harder! What is considered disrespect to a traditional parent in Asia is quite different to disrespect to a bohemian New York parent. Disrespect can be rolling their eyes at the dinner table or rolling a joint at the dinner table. Disrespect can be ignoring you or spitting in your face. It can be saying 'Whatever…' or saying "What sort of a f**king slag are you?" There is no clear line between disrespect and abuse. As we've said earlier there is no scientific definition of 'abuse'.

Thinking about the disrespect you experience can help you decide what should be ignored, what should be named as unacceptable, and what is actually intolerable. Different people have differing ideas, but if you find all disrespect intolerable you are likely to find yourself embroiled in almost constant conflict with the youth of today.

Respect for children and children's rights

"When we move into relationships based upon equality and mutual respect, we reduce the major source of misbehaviour…" Balson [347]

The above optimistic quote is typical of many parenting advice books which encourage equality between parent and child (and by most people's standards, permissive parenting). Parent child relationships have certainly moved far closer to equality but I don't hear anyone claiming this has produced a reduction in children's misbehaviour! The above quote is true in that *mutual* respect does mean less behavioural problems, but only when the respect is mutual. As parents you can't simply decide that your children will respect you when there are so many forces acting against this. Lack of respect for children is still a real issue in many families but lack of respect for parents has become more common and more damaging.

The idea of mutual respect, however, is still a valid one. You owe your children respect in the second meaning of the word: consideration of them as people. *Ideally* they should have a different form of respect for you and the relationship should definitely **not** be one of **equality**. If you are your child's equal (unless they are a mature adult and independent), then there is something decidedly wrong.

You certainly do not need to regard your child as an equal to show them respect. You show respect for your children by honouring their individuality, opinions, privacy and basic human rights, by not humiliating them or abusing them. However none of these things are absolute or clear-cut. Here are some examples:

Does a parent have a right to tell a child which religion they should follow? At what age can they decide this for themselves? Most people assume that parents have this right and most Western Governments back this up with tax payers' dollars in supporting segregated schooling and compulsory religious education. Families are allowed to force teens to attend religious schools even if they are atheists (this is becoming far more common – I see children of twelve or thirteen from highly religious families and attending religious schools telling me they are unbelievers). It could be argued that this is disrespectful, yet most people accept this.

If a fourteen-year-old decides they don't want anyone entering their bedroom, is this reasonable? What about an eighteen-year-old? What if you suspect that the eighteen-year-old is taking drugs? Should doctors prescribe the contraceptive pill to thirteen-year-olds without their parents' knowledge or permission? Should a counselling agency or a school counsellor work with a twelve-year-old without their parent's knowledge or involvement (as some do)? Does a parent have a right to read their adolescent's diary if they suspect she is planning suicide, joining a cult, or selling drugs? Is it acceptable to use Facebook to spy on an adolescent if you suspect they are putting themselves at risk? At what age should a child be allowed to decide which parent they live with? What if a child wants to live with over-indulgent grandparents, or a disreputable uncle, rather than with either parent?

Those who fight for children's rights sometimes imply that children have the same rights as adults. This is patently absurd when applied to babies and only a few argue that pre-teens have the right to smoke, get drunk, drop out of school, gamble or consent to sex with adults[348]. Clearly they don't have the same rights to self-abuse that we adults enjoy, and there are lots of grey areas. Where we draw any line will depend on moral judgments and ideally should take individual maturity and circumstances into account. Should we give a highly mature and responsible thirteen-year-old with an IQ of one hundred and fifty the same rights as a wild and disturbed thirteen-year-old with an IQ of seventy-five?

Some parents are treating children not just as equals, but as superiors. They are obeying their children or deferring to them rather than the other way round. I am bemused by parents who let children share their bed, for example, although the parent clearly does not want this arrangement (of course, some parents allow it for their own comfort). These parents often talk as if they have no right to make the child sleep alone. I ask them if any visitor can choose to sleep with them without their permission!

Patrick

The first few times I met Patrick he said, consistently and unequivocally, that he hated his mother. He was only twelve, an odd kid but without any diagnoses or disability and he seemed to come from a fairly normal family. At first I wondered if there is something going on behind closed doors. Was his mother secretly an abuser, a drinker or emotionally unstable? She admitted having got so angry with him that she'd yelled at him, said unpleasant things and once slapped his face. Patrick swore at her on a daily basis, had pushed and slapped her quite a number of times, though he wasn't generally a very violent kid, more a timid victim at school (the introverted nervous type).

223

Both parents seemed to be of above average intelligence and above average niceness. I never did find any reason why Patrick hated her other than her being 'annoying'. Being annoying seemed to mean reminding him of chores (minimal), school uniform, homework and when he should get off the computer. On one session I got him to list the emotions he felt towards both parents. What was striking was that, although he started with nine out of ten hate for Mum, the next emotion was eight out of ten love. Next session he seemed quite cheerful but admitted that he had told Mum he hated her six times that morning (it was 10 a.m.). I mentioned that he seemed to love and hate her equally. He didn't contradict this, though there had been a one-point difference on the previous session. I asked if he ever told her he loved her and to my surprise he said he did, but at about one-tenth of the rate of 'I hate you' (probably in reality a lot less than one-tenth). I asked which was most likely to get him his own way. He said "I love you" was, but it wasn't nearly so satisfying!

When children (especially pre-adolescents) say "I hate you" I generally advise parents not to take it seriously and suitable replies are, "That's sad because I love you," or "That's OK, that means I must be doing my job properly," (my son hated this one). However, when, like Patrick, they are using 'I hate you' as a regular put-down it's reasonable to consider it as verbal abuse and have a small consequence. We decided that Patrick would lose ten minutes of computer time for each insult, swear word or 'I hate you'.

Patrick was certainly not unique in saying he hated a parent. Yet far more parent-abusing young people tell me that they love the parent they are abusing. Statements such as, "I love her but she gets me so mad," are very common.

The sad fact is, and many abusers will agree with this, that we tend to reserve our worst behaviour for the ones we love most. Men who abuse their wives usually claim to love them. I used to think that they didn't really love them as they were acting in such an un-loving way. I no longer see it that way. Certainly they don't love them *enough* but they often do love them, they just don't respect them.

"When I was a boy of fourteen, my father was so ignorant I could hardly stand to have the old man around. But when I got to be twenty-one, I was astonished at how much the old man had learned in seven years." Mark Twain

Regaining Respect

Turning things around and regaining respect can take a long time. Being more assertive and clear about your own rights is a start but things may get worse before they get better. Clear boundaries, rules and consequences can make an enormous difference over time and so can being less exclusively child-focused. So self-care can help. There are other ideas for regaining respect in the books and articles by Haim Omer.

A Sense of Entitlement

"He was raised like a prince but, to his parents' grief, grew up to be a tyrant."
Omer[349]

"When girls [or boys] get everything they want, they grow up to assume life is about instant gratification – instant purchases, instant relationships, instant fun, instant sex – until nothing delights them, or is special anymore." Hamilton[350]

An 'entitlement' literally means a right. Rights are good things! However, we all know people whose belief in their own rights far outweighs their respect for others' rights. This may go with an inflated sense of their own importance, with arrogance, pride and egocentrism. Over-high self-esteem leads to over-entitlement, but it's possible to be over-entitled in some relationships with low self-esteem.

We talked a little about children's rights in the last chapter. Children generally didn't have rights in the past; a father could pretty much do what he liked with his children. Infanticide has been common in many societies. The bible mentions (without condemnation) selling daughters into slavery[351]. Roman law not only allowed fathers to sell children into slavery but they could put them to death if they wished. Beating children was the norm in Western society in the nineteenth century. By our standards, Western society was horribly cruel to children until quite recently and such conditions still apply in some non-Western countries.

So the fact that children have rights, and are now aware that they have rights, is A GOOD THING! What **is** a problem is that young children tend to hear what they want to hear. If a teacher says that no one has the right to physically abuse them, half of the children hear that their parents are no longer allowed to use physical punishment at all, and another quarter believe that parents are not allowed to punish them in any way. I've heard of primary school children going home after a talk on their rights and telling Mum that she can't make them wash the dishes anymore.

Everyone is entitled to basic human rights but when one person's sense of entitlement outweighs their respect for other's rights they may become abusive. Another way of putting this is that abuse occurs when someone's sense of **entitlement** outweighs their sense of **responsibility**. This idea originated with a South Australian family therapist called Alan Jenkins[352].

"The context for most violent behaviour is one in which the initiator experiences a sense of entitlement which exceeds his or her sense of responsibility for the welfare of the other." Jenkins[353]

This diagram is my way of illustrating it.

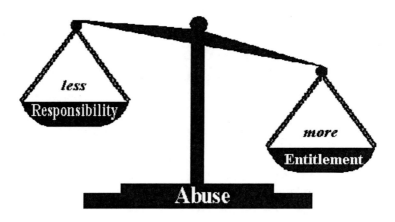

Jenkins applied it originally to men who abuse their partners or children (he acknowledged that it applied to sex abusers also). When I started working with young people who abused their parents, I quickly realised that it applies *even more clearly* to them.

Traditionally, parents felt **entitled** to have their children obey them and treat them with deference and respect. Fathers felt entitled to even more obedience and respect, not only from children but also from their wives. When parents and husbands acted responsibly, this entitlement did not necessarily lead to abuse, even with high entitlement - the scales balanced.

In recent years, with the democratisation of the family, a parent's sense of entitlement has *decreased* dramatically. They have less authority and, as we've seen, there is less respect for age generally. The mass media encourages children to be demanding and materialistic and portrays parents as idiots. Children are more confident and capable in many ways because of child-centred parenting. However, some children develop quite excessive expectations of their parents.

Surveys have found that children in recent years think their parents work too much and don't spend enough time with them. A number of writers have assumed that this means that parents are actually less involved in their children's lives than in the past. Not true! The evidence is that parents are spending more time with children overall and since families are smaller, each child is getting far more attention. Parents are doing more with their children than in the past but children's expectations of their parents, and societies expectations of parents, have increased a lot more. When I was a child I would never have thought of asking my father for a lift if it were possible to catch a bus, walk, or cycle. Now children routinely expect, or demand, that their parents act as a taxi service. Fathers seldom played with children when I was a child, and not all mothers did so. Now children expect to be entertained, either by an adult or (increasingly) by an electronic gadget; those fathers who don't do as much as others are criticised and often feel guilty. The idea of a father feeling guilty for not playing with his children would have been laughable when I was a boy. This is progress, but with most kinds of progress it has a downside to it.

Children want ever more attention. They feel entitled to it. Children given a lot of attention are not necessarily 'spoiled' in the traditional sense of being bought everything they desire (though some are), but they have a high sense of being entitled to their parent's attention and services. Over-entitled, demanding children may expect that their parents will serve them the food they like, chauffeur them around, help with homework, play games on demand, give them their undivided attention and provide the latest consumer goods and gadgets. They believe they have a fundamental right to a life that is easy, comfortable and exciting and often completely disregard parent's rights. Parents who are highly child-focused produce *some* children who are totally self-focused. As children and teenagers often have low responsibility in the Western world, it's possible that they will become abusive towards parents in their attempts to control them or, out of their frustration when their demands are not met.

"We find ourselves slaving after children who laugh in the face of our weak attempts at discipline, demand to be amused all day, and stay up late because we're too exhausted to put up the struggle it takes to get them to bed. These kids are fully in charge" Shaw[354]

"An abuser can seem emotionally needy. You can get caught in a trap of catering to him, trying to fill a bottomless pit. But he's not so much needy as entitled, so no matter how much you give him, it will never be enough. He will just keep coming up with more demands because he believes his needs are your responsibility, until you feel drained down to nothing." Bancroft[355]

It's not just our child- rearing practices that are contributing to a sense of entitlement, our Western culture focuses far more on individualism than other cultures. Individual rights have become an increasing focus in democratic societies, including the perceived right to compensation when anything goes wrong and the right to have someone to blame, or sue. This focus on individuals striving for success and for material goods fosters a sense of entitlement in some people. Commercialism and the consumer focus of our society deliberately (through advertising) try to make us all feel entitled. Even the philosophy of "positive thinking" espoused by pop psychology can create a sense of entitlement. In the hugely popular, though hugely silly, book "The Secret", people were encouraged to believe that they just had to want something hard enough and believe in themselves enough and they would get it. Barbara Ehrenreich in her book "*Smile or Die: how positive thinking fooled America and the world*" attacks the excesses of positive thinking and links it to victim-blaming, greed and to a sense of entitlement[356].

The notion of entitlement has become a common theme in the literature on adult abusers in recent years. Beck wrote that people who are prone to anger "place great emphasis on the protection of their rights... Among the rights asserted are:

- I have a right to do what I want to do.
- I have the right to express my anger if I feel annoyed.
- I have the right to criticize other people if I think they are wrong.
- I expect people to do what I consider reasonable.

- People do not have the right to tell me what to do."[357]

These over-entitled 'rights' will sound familiar to the majority of abused parents. One 13-year-old girl said to her mother, *"You had me. You owe me!"* I've heard similar sentiments, though not as succinctly put, from other young people in recent years.

The converse of high entitlement leading to abuse is that when one's sense of responsibility outweighs our entitlement, we get respect (Alan Jenkins said 'Care' but being responsible makes you respectful not necessarily caring).

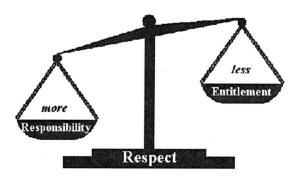

We all try to make our children responsible but many of us fail, sometimes miserably. As we've discussed, this is because our input is just one factor and can be overwhelmed by other influences. In the short term you may find it somewhat easier to reduce your child's sense of entitlement rather than improve their sense of responsibility. In the long run maturity does bring increased responsibility for some individuals – but not for all.

Some authors in recent years have suggested that affluent children in Western countries actually have more problems than do less affluent children. I don't believe this is true, but it's definitely true that they have almost as many emotional and behavioural issues as less affluent children and a sense of entitlement appears to be a crucial factor in this.

"The disturbing sense of entitlement so often observed in affluent kids is partly an outgrowth of parents' efforts to elevate their child's sense of self with persistent praise. The difference between high self-esteem and narcissism can be hard to distinguish in privileged kids who have been repeatedly told that they are special. As one of my [teen] patients said, 'If I'm so special, then why do I have to set the table or take out the garbage?'" Levine[358]

Responsibility in childhood and adolescence

Part of the problem is that our children today are not only *far* more entitled than were previous generations but they are also often lower in responsibility. Let's think about how most children throughout history have been expected to behave:

Adolescence is a historically new stage. In many earlier societies children went from being child to adult almost overnight. This was often marked by an initiation ceremony around the time of puberty. Many boys' initiation ceremonies were brutal and cruel, designed as a test of manhood. Boys were beaten, tortured, tattooed, circumcised without anaesthetic, or even raped by the men of the tribe. At the end of this ordeal they were often considered children no more but men, expected to take responsibility as part of a community.

For girls in many societies, first menstruation was the marker that they were now women and they were then often married off. Their ceremonies often involved them being isolated and enduring hardship while menstruating. By our standards many of the initiation ceremonies for both sexes were brutal and cruel and showed sexist attitudes that we would not want to encourage.

The idea that there should be a long period of semi-childhood stretching into, and even beyond, puberty is a new one. The idea started with universal education and the encouragement of young people to stay at school for longer and longer periods. There was no word in European languages for this stage of development as it wasn't regarded as an important stage of development. Adolescence, as an in-between stage, is getting longer and longer. I joke in my lectures that adolescence now lasts from eight to twenty-eight. In most societies children are given responsibilities from a very early age, long before puberty. Children as young as five are expected to help with animals, fetch firewood, run errands, etc. From around age eight, children are often given responsibility for looking after younger brothers and sisters, or cousins. It's still quite common in some parts of the world to see a ten-year-old carrying a baby on her (occasionally his) hip. They are often not just helping for the odd hour but may be the main carers for much of the day. In many societies such arrangements were the norm and older siblings or cousins often did more caring of toddlers than did parents. Ten-year-olds were also herding animals too (probably considered a bigger responsibility than minding the baby). I'm certainly not suggesting that we should give our ten-year-olds such responsibility (or send them down the mines) but the fact is that they are capable of taking responsibility when it's expected of them.

I don't wish to give the impression that children and young people in earlier times were overall well behaved. There are accounts of youth riots, high youth crime and even gin drinking among young children in historical times. They weren't angels and if they obeyed their parents it was often out of fear. Now we expect far less, in many ways, of our young people and as a result they are low in responsibility.

It has been argued that we infantilise adolescents and that this may be the reason for behavioural and emotional problems being common in this stage of life in Western societies[359]. I think there is a lot of truth in this and the fact that the in-between stage is getting longer and longer may be why some adolescent problems are getting worse.

Girl told to wash up set house on fire: A fifteen-year-old girl was so incensed at being told to wash up she burnt her house down. After finishing the chore she set fire to the sofa, causing £63,500 of damage and endangering the life of neighbours, who had to be rescued.[360]

Box

Dear Eddie,

I teach in a University, as does my wonderful husband. I have three children, two younger girls and a boy of sixteen. My son is abusive and will push or punch me if his dinner is not served when he demands it. He has threatened me with a cricket bat. When his father tried to intervene he punched him. He is much taller than either of us.

He gets angry whenever he doesn't get it his way. He is abusive to his sisters when we are not close by. He annoys them and makes them work for him. He threatens them if they tell on him.

All he sees is that we are bad parents, because we don't always do what he asks and he actually says that it's our duty to serve him. I do give in to him, but it's only to avoid more holes in doors, broken pictures, glass, light fixtures, etc. He is a classic example of what you describe as an 'over-entitled' child who bullies family members to get his own way.

When he is his normal self, he is a bright, athletic and an extremely funny young man.

Thank you for your website.

Lauren

End Box

© Mike Baldwin / Cornered

"Just give me your wallet. Trust me, you do not want to deal with my misplaced sense of entitlement."

CartoonStock.com

Exercise: Parental Influences

This is an exercise I developed to help parents get a sense of proportion about how much responsibility they should take for their child's behaviour. It's an important part of the *Who's in Charge?* group programme. If you have a partner, you may want to both do it separately, writing your scores down on a piece of paper, then compare notes. If you are going to write on this book, use a pencil. I've bought a lot of second hand books and curse those who deface them in ink or highlighter. Pencil marks in the margin are fine.

Some people find this exercise confusing and a few professionals find it challenging. Many parents have found it liberating.

Consider one of your children as they are now: their personality, behaviour, abilities and attitudes. If you have more than one child, choose the one you are most worried about. If you are not worried about any of them (you lucky person), then choose the one nearest to mid-teens. Your influence on this child, past and present, good and bad is a fixed ten points. This is an arbitrary number. It should really be one unit of influence but then we would have to work in fractions. It's NOT ten out of ten (no parent gets ten out of ten) and it's not 10% of anything. You can't give yourself more or less than ten points, this is fixed.

1. Your influence: ten points
We now compare other influences against this. Skip any influences that don't apply to your child or give them a score of zero. If trying to decide between two scores for a particular influence, go for the lower one.

2. Other birth parent: __ points
If your child's other parent has more influence than you, give them a score above ten; if double your influence give them twenty points. There is no upper limit but think carefully before going above 20 for anything. If they have had half of your influence, you give them five points. We are not differentiating between good and bad influences and sadly, when the other parent gets a very high score it's usually because they are a bad influence, i.e. abusive or irresponsible. It's much easier to be a bad influence than a good one. An uninvolved, neglectful parent may have a big influence. If the other parent is unknown, dead or absent you can decide is this is an influence on your child. Some completely absent parents are a big influence and some who come and go from their child's life (usually fathers) have a huge influence.

231

3. Relationship between parents: __ points

Although you and the other parent both have an influence directly there are times when your relationship to each other seems to have an influence all of its own. Usually this is only noticeable when there is high conflict between parents (especially separated parents) or when you are undermining each other. If you don't feel that your relationship with the other parent is significant, give it zero. It's included in the exercise partly to make people consider the fact that all of our influences are in relationship to other people. Children are particularly sensitive to perceived differences in how you treat them compared to their brothers and sisters. This gets too complicated to include in the exercise but it's worth bearing in mind.

4. Step-parent: __ points

Score the step-parent (current or past, or each of them if there have been more than one) in comparison to your ten points of influence. Don't compare them with the other parent; compare them all with your influence.

5. Brothers & Sisters__ points

Brothers and sisters are often a huge influence on each other in subtle, or not so subtle, ways. You can score each brother and sister separately or lump them together and give them one score.

6. Other relatives __ points

In the past extended families had much greater impact on children than they do now, but grandparents or uncles and aunts can be a big influence, good or bad. If there is a relative who has been particularly influential on your child, you can score them separately if you like.

Isolation can be both cause and effect of having a difficult child. Parents who don't have support are slightly more likely to have difficult children and difficult children often further isolate parents.

7. School __ points

School can be an enormous influence on children. The most supportive and encouraging parents will not be able to produce a confident child if he or she does not fit in socially or academically at school. I have often seen children develop behavioural problems at school then bring them home to share with the family. Schools, of course, assume that all bad influences come from home to school.

Some children develop a social role, such as class clown, teacher's pet, schoolyard bully, jock, flirt, outcast, rebel, etc. at school which then affects their behaviour in other settings and perhaps for many years to come. Bullying and ostracism in High School can have a lifelong effect on some people

8. Friends and peer group __ points

Everyone is aware of how influential peers can be for adolescents (both their friends and the wider peer group). However, this peer group influence doesn't suddenly start at high school. It doesn't even start at Kinder but usually before this[361]. Children look to other children for how to behave just as much as they look up to adults. This explains the curious fact that parents who are determined not to indoctrinate their children into sexual stereotypes nonetheless can have little ones who adopt these male-female stereotypes from a *very* early age. Little boys generally look to other little boys (and older boys) in order to learn how to be a boy. They also look to little girls to learn how **not** to be a girl. Girls do the same and children from age four to fourteen will usually sort themselves into single sex groups and may treat the other sex as inferior outsiders.

9. Anyone else __ points

Is there anyone else, not included in the above categories, who has had a significant influence on your child? This could be a neighbour, a friend of yours, a mentor or a role model. Or it could be someone who bullied, abused or assaulted your child or another family member. It's sad how few positive mentors or role models are mentioned when I do this exercise with parents.

10. TV, other media __ points

Children have always had their own culture. What is radically different nowadays is that their culture is transmitted at the speed of light through electronic media. More importantly, and far more worryingly, their culture is filtered and shaped by people who exploit them as consumers, not just advertisers but also many entertainers.

You will probably underestimate this since it's all around and influences you too.

11. Temperament __ points

Temperament is that part of their personality they were born with. See chapter on personality.

12. Physical: appearance, size, etc.__ points

If a child is unusually tall, short, fat, spotty, cute or odd looking, this can have an influence on their development. Having asthma, epilepsy, incontinence or reaching puberty early or late can be a big influence. None of these may apply to your child.

13. Free will and child's own choices__ points

It's not really possible to give a numerical value to your child's free will and the decisions they have made over time. Include it if you feel so inclined. There is no doubt that it's an important factor, especially as they get older, and it's here to remind you that they are not robots being programmed by their genetics and environment any more than you are.

Many years ago I met a charming fifteen-year-old girl who had been beating up her mother (I mentioned her in passing in relation to the MAAD group in the introduction). She was the first girl I had come across who was physically abusing a parent, we'll call her Maddy. She once accompanied her mother to a meeting at a child psychiatry centre and came away very angry. Maddy got angry because the assembled professionals appeared to be blaming her long-suffering mother for Maddy's behaviour. Not only was she feeling protective towards her mother, and vaguely aware of the injustice of her mother being blamed, but she also felt they were not treating Maddy herself with respect by assuming she had no will of her own. She said, "What do they think I am, a puppet?"

The decisions that children make, especially when travelling through the mine-fields of adolescence, can have profound and sometimes lasting effects on their lives.eg whether to smoke, try drugs, have unprotected sex, etc.

14. Any specific events or other influences __ points

There may have been specific events, often traumatic, that you feel have influenced how your child has developed. E.g. a death in the family, an accident, a long illness can all have profound effects and the timing may be very important. An uncle's death may not affect one child in a family yet be huge for a child just starting High School. When stress factors co-occur they can have greatly amplified effects (they don't add but multiply).

Finally, add anything else not already covered. A woman whose son was heavily into drugs said "The chemicals"; once he started putting psychoactive chemicals into his bloodstream this had a bigger influence than anything else and she gave it thirty points.

Now add up all the scores for the influences that you felt were relevant for your child. Remember to include your own ten points.

TOTAL:

To work out your influence as a percentage of the total, divide your ten points by the Total Influences and multiply this by one hundred. If the total is one hundred, then you have 10% influence. If the total is over one hundred (very common), you have less than 10% influence and if the total is under one hundred you have more than 10%. I've only once seen a mother get as much as 25% and this was for a very young child. This table will save you having to do the maths:

Total	%		Total	%		Total	%
40	25%		75	13%		110	9%
45	22%		80	12.5%		120	8%
50	20%		85	12%		130	7%
55	18%		90	11%		140	6.5%
60	16%		95	11.5%		150	6%
65	15%		100	10%		200	5%
70	14%		105	9.5%		200+	under 5%

This is **not** a scientific or precise measure, just a rough indicator. In reality, influences, like stress factors, interact with each other rather than just add or subtract and influences may also cancel out (as happens when parents are pulling in different directions). One major factor not taken into account is random chance, and there are undoubtedly other influences not included.

I believe this exercise does underestimate the importance of parents; but not by very much. The most common situation when parents have a really big influence on the child is when they are abusive or neglectful. Sadly, it's far easier to be a bad influence than a good one.

I've done this exercise with over one thousand parents; both parents with violent or beyond control children and others, mostly professionals who attended one of my workshops. A typical score is around 10%.

This is **definitely not** a measure of good or bad parenting! Extreme scores are not good or bad in themselves; it all depends on why they were high or low. A low score (under 8%) may mean that your child lives an active, interesting life, has lots of supports and has a strong personality. In this case it certainly does not indicate that you are unimportant or shirking your duties. For a few parents, though, a low score is a sign that their child is disengaged from the family and is not letting them **be** a parent.

A high score may mean you are very close and important to each other, but more often than not it means that your child has few contacts or interests. A score over twenty for a teenager is usually not healthy, indicating a socially isolated child with few outside interests.

So, are parents unimportant?

I am certainly NOT claiming that parents are unimportant! If I thought that, I'd be wasting my time writing this book, wouldn't I? But the myth of the super-powerful parent is just a myth.

"Many continue to assume that the most important environmental factors in psychological development derive from experiences in the nuclear family. Behaviour genetics has challenged this belief. Peers, teachers, role models, and the broader influence of the social environment can be as important, and sometimes even more important, than parents." Paris[362]

Most psychologists, social workers, parenting writers, and journalists still believe that the environmental influence of the immediate family, and in particular of the mother at an early age, is greater than all the other influences. The evidence does not support this idea.[363] If the mother's behaviour is within the normal range, i.e. she isn't unusually mad or bad, then she is probably, but not necessarily, the biggest influence pre-teen. But being the strongest player on the team does not mean that you are more important than the rest of the team. After infancy, mother is one of a great many influences, as the above exercise attempts to illustrate, and by the teenage years, she may not the biggest single influence.

Parents are like air or water. They are **essential** even when other influences appear to be greater. Since you are **one of** the biggest influences on your child you have a huge responsibility to do your best and even small influences can make a profound difference at the right time, or in the long term. However, is it realistic for you to either take full responsibility for your child's achievements or to take all the blame for their problems? If you are taking all the responsibility, you are probably feeling a whole heap of undeserved guilt.

Hopefully, by this stage in the book, you are ready to throw out most of your unhelpful guilt and learn to be more assertive and consistent in how you deal with your difficult child. This can make a huge difference in helping you be the Solution to your child's problems.

How much influence do you currently have?

We need to be realistic about what we can and can't *control* (very little except where the child lets us have control) and what we can and can't *influence*. We have a responsibility to be the best influence we know, but taking too much responsibility for our child's behaviour often means them taking less responsibility. Even if you are a strong-minded, confident individual and don't feel much guilt, other people, including professionals, will be keen to put responsibility for your child's bad behaviour on to you. You need to be very clear in your own mind to resist being disempowered by this.

Ask yourself what would happen if you stopped accepting the blame?

Who Has the Power, Child or Parent?

*"I think it's more about what he had, or how he could have the power. And he did,
he was more powerful. And I know that sounds silly because he was a kid and I
was the adult. I know it's all about who's the adult and parents being in charge.
But honestly it can happen so quickly. You can be in charge or be able to control
things one minute and then..., you know, everything is a battle."[364]*

*"Workers told me I did have power. They were wrong. By that stage I had no
power at all over my son. They meant well but they weren't making me feel any
better."* Mother of sixteen-year-old.
"You're not the boss of me!" Many million modern children.

When I start my parent groups, I usually have nicely printed name badges ready for
people on the first session with *"Who's in Charge?"* at the top and the person's
first name below: *"Who's in Charge? ANNIE."* This is both wish-fulfilment and
irony. The truth is that at this point, they are seldom in charge; the teen terrorist is
in charge of their home. What makes them so powerful? Surely parents have far
more power than their children?

Power, Abuse and Bullying

Many writers see an imbalance of power as being *central* to abuse. I used to
define Abuse as 'Power + Violent (or Coercive) behaviour'. This seemed to make
the necessary distinction between violence between equals or, defensive violence,
versus abusive violence. Feminists stress the patriarchal power of men and thus
women's violence is not seen as being abusive *in the same way* that men's violence
is (there is some logic to this but it does not always apply). In many books or
articles on family violence, the fact that more powerful family members (men or
adults) abuse the less powerful (women or children) is sometimes stressed but
often it's just taken for granted as self-evident. This may be one reason that
violence to parents remains a neglected and hidden issue in academic circles; it
awkwardly refuses to fit popular theories.

Even in discussions of school bullying, it's often stressed that this is different
to other playground violence because the bully has more power than the victim.
Most definitions of bullying state that there is a power imbalance even though
children may be the same age and differ only slightly in physical strength[365]. What
is missing from most discussions is that it's the fact that the bully is willing to use
violence which gives him power over more passive children. He, or she, gets
power by being a bully. Incidentally, although there are many books, articles and
conferences on bullying, I've not so far seen bullying *of parents* mentioned in **any**

of them. I wanted to go to a bullying conference to talk about the similarities and differences but they offered me only thirty minutes so I declined.

When I started working with families where children were hitting and bullying their parents, it took me a while to accept just how similar this behaviour was to the men I worked with who abused their wives. I didn't think of it as abuse at first and resisted using the word 'abuse' in this context for years. If Abuse = Power + Violence then how can a child *abuse* his or her parents?

What is Power?

Power (noun) can be defined as:

1. The capacity to influence the behaviour of others, the emotions, or the course of events;
2. A right or authority given or delegated to a person or body;
3. Physical strength or force.[366]

There are many types of power and some are so taken for granted that they are all but invisible in everyday life. Power can be exerted by physical force, financial control, environmental control, withholding or controlling resources, threats, psychological bullying or manipulation, persuasion, role modelling, etc. We tend to use 'power' as a dirty word and so the types of power we notice most are coercive: the bullying, exploitative power that bosses, politicians and violent individuals have over others. We don't notice the fact that we have non-coercive, or minimally coercive, power over others when they cooperate, when they want to please us, when they feel responsible for us, when they love us, copy us, or follow us around. Love is very powerful.

When sociologists have looked at different types of power they come up with a number of different types. They aren't thinking about parents, but it's useful to see how they apply:

1) **reward** power – giving or withholding payment, privileges, etc. (your boss).
2) **coercive** power – forcing someone to do something (the police).
3) **expert** power –comes from superior knowledge (your gynaecologist).
4) **referent** power – when we influence someone because they identify with us or look up to us, i.e. they use us as a role model in some way (your children's heroes, or anti-heroes).
5) **legitimate** power – when the other person *lets you* influence or control them because of a role you play (referee, usher).
6) **informational** power – having knowledge that the other person needs (big overlap with expert power, but it could be someone withholding information, your son hiding letters from school).

Parents start out with **all** of these types of power over a young child. In traditional societies the legitimate and referent power of a parent lasts into old age, even when children are independent adults. In our society many children have been granting less and less legitimacy to authority, whether parents, teachers or police.

A study in the UK found that fifteen-year-olds were twice as likely to lie to, steal from or disobey authority figures as were children thirty years earlier[367].

There has been a recent and dramatic change in children's perceptions of parents' *expert* power and *informational* power. Many children now reach automatically to the internet for information rather than look to a parent. Why ask an adult when you can Google? Furthermore the fact that they can manage gadgets better than their parents (and their world revolves around their gadgets) means that the child may think that he or she is the expert and the parent a dunce. They are Digital Natives while we are Digital Immigrants.

'Power' is not a dirty word

"The empowerment of the powerless is a beautiful thing."

Maggie Kuhn, founder of the Grey Panthers.

The reality in current society is that men have more power than women (in society generally and still within many families), the rich have **far** more power than the poor, whites have more power than blacks, and adults have power over children. The first three, you'll probably agree, we should try to reduce but the last is healthy and normal and you are probably reading this book because you don't have an appropriate amount of power over your child.

In the context of the modern family, 'power' has become a dirty word for many parents and professionals. It's associated with *abuses* of power and with old-fashioned tyrannical parents and abusive, patriarchal husbands. But it's undeniable that in a well-functioning family, parents have a great deal of power over their children, especially when they are young. We have the power to make major decisions, choose where we live, to set the rules of the household, to set the general culture of the home, to insist on certain behaviours, to send them to school, to buy vegetables rather than chocolate, etc. With very young children there are many situations when it's highly neglectful, and downright dangerous, not to wield power. If a young child is putting him or herself, or others, at risk then we will use as much power as is necessary to protect them. We do not allow toddlers to stay up all night or to eat ice-cream until they are sick; we carry them away from danger or physically stop them hitting other children. We have enormous power over small babies and no moral qualms about using physical restraint and blatant coercion to keep them safe and well. If we did not restrain and coerce babies, they would be unlikely to survive!

Though we may feel uncomfortable about exerting power with older children, no parent wants to feel power*less. Em*powerment is positive. When the balance of power is held by a child, the consequences can be dire for the whole family. If no one has power over younger teens, many of them will drink, skip school, have sex and spend most of their time playing computer games or skateboarding.

Coerce (verb): Persuade (an unwilling person) to do something by using force or threats.

Exerting power can be by a variety of means, good and bad, subtle or unsubtle, obvious or hidden, and with varying degrees of cooperation or resistance. Good parents only coerce children when other approaches have failed. But we frequently do coerce children into going to bed at night, into visiting boring relatives, into going to school, or to stop them destroying the home or harming themselves or others. If you never use coercion as a parent, you either have an amazingly compliant child or you are neglectful.

As children grow, wielding power over them, even for their own good, becomes more complicated and difficult. Coercing teenage children is often a sign that things are going wrong. When it comes to questions of safety, however, few parents will hesitate if using some coercion keeps their teenager safe. Preventing a thirteen-year-old from staying up all night, making it difficult for a fourteen-year-old to drink alcohol, removing spray-cans from a fifteen-year-old graffitist; not letting your sixteen-year-old daughter sleep with a forty-year-old boyfriend, not letting your seventeen-year-old grow marijuana in your garden, removing car keys from a drunken eighteen-year-old are all appropriate uses of coercion.

Control (noun): *The power to influence people's behaviour or the course of events – the restriction of an activity, tendency, or phenomenon.*

'Control' is acceptable to more parents than 'power' but some people are also uncomfortable with this term. It's anathema to some liberal professionals, who are far more concerned about over-controlling parents than about non-controlling parents. I hear parents say things like: "*I don't want to control my children, I just want a normal family.*" But having control over children and adolescents is normal and necessary.

In a well-functioning family with averagely cooperative kids, the exercise of parental control is subtle and covert and relies mainly on the children wanting parental approval and a happy home. Obvious, overt control becomes *essential* when children are uncooperative, defiant or difficult.

This can lead to the naïve assumption that parents of difficult children are really authoritarian control freaks who have caused their children to rebel (this does occasionally happen but it's certainly not the norm). In fact parents often appear unduly concerned about controlling their child precisely because they have so little control over them (which may be because they were too easy-going in the past). The idea that these parents are over-controlling is of course supported enthusiastically by the difficult children themselves. It's the wild children who are the most vocal about being controlled; they are also usually keen to blame their parents for everything and to excuse their own behaviour. Sadly, some youth workers and other professionals take what these kids say at face value!

Objections to controlling children are influenced by the idealistic myth that a family can function as a democracy. Families are **not** democracies and even those parents who consult their children and give them a lot of say don't actually let children make the big decisions. Attempts to run a family as a democracy are doomed to failure and lead to confusion of generational boundaries. The attempt at family democracy leads to either anarchy or the ascent to power of a teen tyrant.

Consulting children about decisions that affect them is fine. Just don't overdo it and never give them the impression that they have a right to decide as this increases Entitlement. Parents should be benevolent despots. The benevolent bit is crucially important of course (unfortunately almost everyone thinks that *they* are benevolent).

Influence (noun): *The capacity to have an effect on the character or behaviour of someone or something, or the effect itself;*

No one has a problem with the term 'influence' when applied to parents. We **all** want to be a good influence on our children. For many children, much of the time, influence is sufficient to preserve a modicum of civilised living. How much influence a parent has on a child depends *at least* as much on the child as it does on the parent. Some children are constantly looking to others and soaking up influence, while others are relatively immune to social influence. Some children appear to soak up all the bad influences and ignore the good, while other children ignore bad influences and are easily influenced for the good.

Influencing, coercing and wielding power are on a continuum and are all forms of control. The huge power we have over babies steadily shrinks. As they grow we find that they either co-operate, let us influence them (in which case we don't think about it) or, they are unco-operative and we find we need to use more controlling techniques, such as giving consequences.

Most children cooperate most of the time. A few children hardly ever need any form of coercion as they are eager to please the adults in their lives, or they may be too timid to get into much trouble. It's easy for parents with one or more such children to be liberal and enlightened in their parenting methods and the enormous control they actually exert over their children can be almost invisible. Those with compliant kids often fool themselves that they are not exerting control.

Some kids are just wild from the word go! Parents may find themselves in a constant battle to control them, to stop them a) putting their lives at risk; b) hurting other people; c) wrecking the house. Often the parents win enough battles for the child to settle down and decide to act civilised; for others, the battles become an exhausting and stressful way of life and harder and harder as the child ages.

A few ways we influence, control, or coerce our children:

- Physical control (holding, moving, restraining, intimidating, hitting).
- Making decisions about home, school, work, holidays.
- Guidance (advice, discussion, counselling).
- Persuasion (by argument or with implied consequences).
- Encouragement.
- Social rewards and punishments (e.g. we smile when children co-operate and frown or growl when they don't).
- Psychological manipulation (e.g. distraction, selective giving of information).
- Deliberate rewards.
- Deliberate punishments.
- Nagging, harassing, verbally intimidating, threatening.
- By our example (i.e. role modelling).
- Routines and rituals (e.g. eating together, bedtimes).

- Play and entertainments.
- Influencing media access and content (do we let them watch unlimited T.V., surf the net, watch violent videos?).
- Arranging the physical environment of the home (we don't put up a basketball hoop in the lounge room; we can choose where the T.V.s go in the home; we move breakables out of the reach of small children; put locks on bathrooms).
- Purchases for the home (do we buy chocolates or carrots, DVDs or books?).
- Controlling cash flow.
- Purchases for the child (clothes, recreational items, subscriptions, sports fees).
- Educating them, both at home (reading, instructing) and sending them to a particular school or to out-of-school instruction.
- Working for them: cooking, cleaning, driving, repairing, etc.
- Influencing friendships (e.g. encouraging some friends to visit and discouraging others, transporting, arranging play dates and sleep-overs).
- Influencing which other people they are exposed to (e.g. not inviting our more disreputable friends or relatives round, taking them to church or to the pool hall).
- Involving other people or agencies to help control them (relatives, teachers, priest, welfare, doctor, police).
- Choosing or influencing their diet (e.g. providing healthy or unhealthy food, avoiding stimulants such as coffee or red cordial, not giving alcohol to young children).
- Giving medications (Ritalin, natural remedies).

This list (and it's not exhaustive by any means) reflects just how much *potential* power and influence parents can have over their children. However, they do not have the power to mould children into the type of person they wish. When parents' views are in line with their surrounding culture (as in traditional societies or some sects) then children will tend to absorb their parents' views and behaviours. However, when parents are out of step with the wider society, their influence is far less and is more dependent on the child choosing to co-operate. Unfortunately, many parents (probably most) today feel that the wider culture that their children are exposed to (including the media and other young people) is **not** reinforcing values such as being polite, respectful, non-violent or responsible. Thus many parents feel they have less power than did parents in previous generations as they are being undermined in their attempts to influence and control their children. It's quite possible, though impossible to prove, that modern parents do overall have less influence on their children than in previous generations. The maximum influence by parents may well have been in the 1950s when community and extended family influence had waned but before youth 'culture' and media took over. But even then, as a child of the '50s myself, I don't think most parents had more influence than peers, school or wider culture.

I am constantly dealing with families where the most powerful individual appears to be a diminutive tyrant, and they seem to be getting a little younger as time passes. Occasionally there is a sole parent lacking in self-worth and almost incapable of being assertive with anyone (often a past victim of abuse), but a good number of parents are intelligent, reasonably assertive, people with a supportive partner. How can a teenager, or even a pre-teen, become more powerful than they are?

The answer is pretty simple, and very unfair.

Power in being dependent

"Tantrums are so common precisely because they have had great survival value – natural selection favours the squeaky wheel, providing it with extra grease. Baby chimps dominate their parents just the same way." Frances[368]

Does a small baby have power over us? The baby would die quite quickly without adult help. We could, in theory, walk away from it or drown it in the bath with very little physical effort (exposing and abandoning unwanted babies used to be common). Even thinking about this probably makes you feel queasy. *Potentially*, we have all the power and a baby none. So why does the baby increasingly set your routine for you, determining if you get sleep, when you eat and pretty much controlling your life for the first year? Does this fit with any of the types of power listed above?

A baby has considerable reward power when it starts smiling at you but it doesn't even do this for the first few weeks. And disabled children, for example a socially unresponsive autistic baby, may exert even *more* control over the life of a responsible parent without giving many rewards. Crying is certainly coercive, but there are ear plugs, headphones and alcohol to reduce its impact. Babies do have reward and coercive power but this does not appear to explain their huge influence on us and they have almost no power over an irresponsible, neglectful or abusive parent.

Start Box

The Power in Unrequited Love

Cindy and Mark were initially very much in love. Mark is quiet, introvert and rather passive. Although handsome, tall and quite strong, he is awkward and clumsy and was bullied throughout school. Cindy was a wild child, petite, very bubbly and pretty, she had broken many hearts before meeting Mark. She thought of Mark as the strong, silent type and was attracted, at first, to his stability and responsibility. For a few months, they wanted to be with each other all the time and bent over backwards to please each other. Mark had more money and a car but he always let Cindy have her own way. He was totally besotted by her. It seemed too good to be true, and was never going to last. Cindy was already bored by Mark when she found out she was pregnant. She had already slept with his best friend.

Over the next two years they lived together. Cindy began drinking heavily and taking drugs. She left Mark to look after their baby boy while she went out on the town, getting wasted and getting laid. She soon stopped bothering to hide the many affairs she was having and taunted him with it. Mark was distraught and depressed but was terrified she was going to leave and take the baby. She didn't, she left him and baby and moved interstate. After a few months she contacted him and said she would come home if he paid off her gambling debts of $10,000. He sent her the money, after taking out a bank loan, and then never heard from her again. It's pretty clear who had all the power in this situation, but what type of power did Cindy have? She initially had lots of reward power by giving Mark sexual favours or affection, but this was gone by the time she was pregnant.

There is power in indifference! Unrequited love gives tremendous power to the one who isn't in love. There is also power in being irresponsible, but only if the other person is responsible. If Mark was a shiftless alcoholic who didn't care about the baby, Cindy might have found herself forced to look after it. A less responsible man might have hit Cindy (especially when she kicked him in the nuts) or used her behaviour as an excuse for him to have affairs.

This is fiction, and a bit extreme, but I've known a number of situations like this, where a responsible man is left pining for a beautiful (they always describe them as beautiful) but wayward ex. The book and film "The Shipping News" depicts such a relationship rather poignantly. I've known several 'Marks' who had Asperger's Syndrome and had been abused by previous wives. This is definitely a form of emotional abuse (occasionally with some physical abuse thrown in) but the man potentially has more physical power and often more financial power. Where is his Patriarchal Power as a male in these relationships? He has lots of potential power but is constrained from using it. Sound familiar?

By the way, I'm not for a moment suggesting that men are abused by women in relationships as often as the reverse. I'd say it was about 10 to 1 in favour of males abusing females, but the ratio may be changing over time as men's abuse of women becomes less acceptable in society and for similar reasons that I see many men abused by their daughters.

End Box

Irresponsibility, indifference and power

"The saddest thing in the world is loving someone who used to love you."
Anonymous

In the 1990s I ran a series of groups for separated parents. Both the men and the women who came to these groups often felt disempowered by the process of separation and they almost all felt that their ex had more power than they did. At first I assumed that everyone felt that way, but it was not so simple.

The women who came to the separated parent's groups often had irresponsible, difficult or abusive ex-husbands. Women separating from a cooperative, reasonable man were far less likely to need such a group. The female group members felt that their husbands had more power than themselves and were resentful and afraid. Their irresponsible ex's could harass them, undermine them, mess up access visits, manipulate the children, and often denied or delayed child support payments (this will be sounding sadly familiar to some of the sole mothers reading this).

The men who came to the Separated Parents groups also felt powerless. Only a few of them had irresponsible ex-wives, who played psychological games and abused or exploited their good natures, but almost all felt powerless. Men who came to a Separated Parent's group were almost invariably well-meaning fathers (the irresponsible ones wouldn't come near such a group). They generally didn't dare mess up access, upset their ex-wives, refuse child support payments or have court battles because they did not want to hurt their children in any way (at least that was the aim, but not always achieved). They realised that they could not get any kind of revenge on their ex without hurting their children.

The irresponsible partner in separations has the most power, at least in the short term (in the long run some lose all contact with their kids). The greater the disparity in responsibility the more powerful is the irresponsible partner. This realisation was a bit of a shock. It's just so unfair! However, recognising this was often reassuring for those involved. If you are feeling powerless, it's better to know that it's caused by your *good* qualities rather than by weakness or stupidity. I tell parents that if the other parent is being irresponsible then for the sake of their children they need to be *more* responsible, not less. The men attending the Separated Parent's groups were sometimes even *less* powerful by the end of the group because they were *more* attuned to how easily children can be hurt in these situations. However they often felt a lot better about their powerlessness (less emasculated or pathetic), and found it easier to accept when they saw that it was due to their taking responsibility.

Literature has long recognised the power involved in unrequited love but this is missing from academic discussions on power. Here's an example from a movie:

"Someone once told me that the power in all relationships lies with whoever cares less, and he was right. But power isn't happiness, and I think that maybe happiness comes from caring more about people rather than less..." From Ghosts of Girlfriends Past.

The child who disrupts the game or the classroom has a bigger influence in what happens than the well-behaved child (until they are excluded). The drunk or lunatic in the shopping centre who screams at passers-by exerts more influence, at that point in time, than any of the many hundreds of sensible shoppers going about their business. The terrorist, suicide-bomber or gunman can have an influence on millions of people by not caring about human life. Even in international politics, rogue states exert far more influence than peaceful, responsible ones. In a workplace the uncooperative individual or abusive boss exerts **far** more influence in the short term than the mass of well-behaved individuals.

There is a great deal of power in being irresponsible! This is not something people wish to acknowledge and it's missing from the literature on family violence, though very relevant. Men's power in modern families often depends on them being irresponsible. Sensitive New Age guys don't have much power but old-fashioned chauvinists do (until their wife has had enough and walks out). We've mentioned the common desire to see the world as a fair place. It's *not* fair that the irresponsible can wield power over the responsible! However, when we are willing to accept this fact the evidence is glaringly obvious.

We mentioned that most definitions of bullying stipulate that there must be an imbalance of power. One of the characteristics of many of the victims I meet is that they are non-violent. If one child is willing to use violence (or other dirty tactics) and doesn't care about the rules, while the other child is far more reluctant to use violence or break rules then the aggressor has power for these reasons alone, even if he is no stronger, smarter or popular. I've seen an increase in younger children bullying their older siblings in recent years. There **is** a power difference in these types of abuse or bullying but it comes from the bullying behaviour, from being irresponsible, and from not caring.

Being disruptive and uncaring can make individuals powerful (at least in the short term). If you have a child who is making you feel powerless, they are almost always exerting **coercive power**. Not only do they manage to get their own way some of the time, but feeling powerful can be *very* rewarding for some individuals and controlling others by coercion can be habit forming.

When men come to the Men's Responsibility Group I facilitate we warn them that giving up abuse means giving up some power. They have usually had disproportionate influence in their families, disempowering their wives and controlling their children by might and fear. As long as their families remained afraid or subdued, they ruled the roost. *Their* children are almost never abusive towards them. It's important to emphasise that they don't usually *feel* powerful. This is because their desire to control is higher than usual and often they are defensive and hypersensitive to any slight to their excessive pride (see section on self-esteem). Thus they may feel stressed by their *lack of control* over those around them *more* than the easy-going man next door who accepts things as they are. Because of excessive pride and entitlement they often feel that they are being attacked, controlled or undermined by others.

We have mentioned there is a popular idea that violence comes from powerlessness. So men who abuse their wives and children are often thought to be responding to feelings of powerlessness, possibly being downtrodden at work or in society in general. Lundy Bancroft, in the best book I've found about abusive men, lists this as one of the many *myths* about abusive men. He writes: "*I call this myth 'boss abuses man, man abuses women, woman abuses children, children hit dog, dog bites cat.' The image it creates seems plausible, but too many pieces fail to fit. Hundreds of my clients have been popular, successful, good-looking men, not the downtrodden looking for a scapegoat...*"[369] This fits with my experience of abusive men (I've met hundreds), who are a very mixed bag, and this description is also very relevant to abusive young people.

In a similar way people 'explain' female violence in terms of their being powerless and downtrodden. However, as I've pointed out, girls who abuse their parents are slightly more likely to be affluent than poor and often attractive and popular. Also the genuinely powerless young people of a generation or two ago were not violent to parents, nor are the powerless youngsters in non-Western cultures. Such explanations of youth violence in terms of their powerlessness remain popular but fall apart on any kind of close examination.

Young people who abuse their parents are *occasionally* downtrodden, powerless individuals but they are just as often confident, socially successful, good looking kids from comfortable homes. Bancroft goes on to say that some men use the excuse that they order people about at work and hence find it hard to stop when they get home, the exact opposite of the downtrodden masses idea. Certainly there is no evidence that having a position of power in society makes abuse of others any less likely: bosses, politicians, professionals, priests or police are *no less* likely to abuse others than those of similar education who don't have power, possibly the opposite is true. Poverty is sometimes linked to increased violence not because they are powerless but for complex cultural reasons.

The other side of the coin to blaming victims is that abusers are given excuses and turned into victims. Much of the literature on children's violence to parents has assumed that the violent children are victims. *Some* have been victims, but there is no contradiction in being both a victim and a victimiser. These are roles we play, not our identity.

Children Controlling Parents

"Adolescents use violence and abuse to take power away from their parents and to control decision making in their families." Routt & Anderson[370]

"If you don't let my friend stay over, I'm going to smash this vase over your f**king head!" fourteen-year-old-girl to mother.

"As a way of making people suffer, violence is thus a useful and effective way to establish dominance over another person or to defeat the other person's dominance over you. In simple terms, violence is a tool for taking power." Crichton-Hall et al[371]

Often, children's control of parents is possible because the parents initially take the easy way out. They are not doing anything abnormal or stupid in this, it's fairly common behaviour. When a parent gives in to nagging or emotional blackmail they are allowing the child to control them. This may be quite subtle initially and the parent is not necessarily being unusually soft by contemporary standards. It's certainly not always as simple as parents giving in to tantrums or threats, but if a child manages to use fear of their bad behaviour to unduly influence the family, then the child can slowly seize control.

Many people just can't imagine how such a state of affairs can come about. 'How weak must these parents be?' is a common thought. The widespread attitude towards parents who have a beyond-control or abusive child is that if they aren't over-controlling, violent monsters then they surely must be weak, soft, pathetic and lacking in assertiveness and common sense. This is true of a very few but certainly **not** the majority of the hundreds of parents I've met.

Almost anyone can be slowly sucked into an unhealthy relationship. I've met marriage guidance counsellors who had found themselves in relationships which have slowly soured over time. I've known psychologists who counsel others on stress but have burnt out and ceased functioning due to their own stress. I've known several youth workers with beyond control teenagers. These people could advise others but when in the thick of it couldn't see the wood for the trees. Almost imperceptibly we can find ourselves compromising and adapting in unhealthy ways. You may have heard of the 'boiling a frog' phenomenon. Frogs cannot detect slow changes in temperature, so if you increase the heat slowly enough it will die without realising how hot the water has become (don't try this at home)[372].

In a bizarre role reversal, I have come across teenagers using consequences against their parents, punishing the parents if they did something they didn't like, e.g. hiding car keys and disconnecting the internet when a parent wanted to work from home. Less subtly, children threaten to smash up the house, if parents don't obey them. One mother of a twelve-year-old boy realised how big her problems were when the little prince said angrily to her "How **dare** you not do as I say!" A girl the same age demanded that her mother make her waffles while friends were visiting. When the mother said she'd do it later the girl screamed, in front of her friends, "Do it now, shit-face!" Another girl would stand in the kitchen and calmly pour orange juice all over the floor if she didn't get her own way. Such clearly deliberate, cold blooded attempts to control parents are not the norm. Most children use emotional outbursts and tantrums to manipulate parents. This causes confusion as they may be seen to be 'out of control' or to be 'expressing themselves' or 'letting off steam' and some professionals even encourage parents to tolerate what is seen as *expressive* violence.

Defiance and disempowering parents

Violent youth are not necessarily trying to control their parents. They may simply not want to let their parents have any control over them. This applies particularly to teenagers who are using the home as a hotel and a base for their delinquent adventures. This is an important difference between violence to parents and men's violence to their partners. In Intimate Partner Violence the man is almost always intent on controlling his partner, not just disempowering her.

Conflict can be about power in that children resent their parents, or any adult, exerting authority over them. They see this as a blow to their pride and a loss of 'face'.

"Sometimes a person simply makes a request, politely or not, and the respondent perceives that to comply would be to show deference, which they are not willing to give; then the defiance escalates to violence." Fisk & Tage[373]

Destroying property as a form of manipulation

Four out of five of the parentally-abusive children in my sample deliberately destroy property: punching holes in walls, smashing things, throwing things, breaking windows, scratching and denting cars, etc. Like threats of violence, threats to destroy property are also very common and occasionally include the extreme threat of burning the house to the ground.

Punching holes in walls and tossing objects around may seem like 'expressive violence' but it's only marginally about 'letting off steam'. Take punching holes in walls for example, this may seem like an outburst of angry energy and those who do this (children and adults) are often keen to point out that it's better than punching a person. Usually it's done in front of the person that they are angry with, or trying to control. I've encouraged parents to let kids go punch a hole in an old door at the bottom of the garden or punch a punch-bag (not good ideas except as a transition to stopping the habit). They hardly ever take up such offers, because it isn't as satisfying and they are no longer intimidating those around them. I've had a teenager tell me "It's just not satisfying breaking something that isn't valuable". There is usually a pattern to what is broken and to which walls are punched; flimsy internal walls are favoured. Some children only punch holes in their own bedroom wall, others never in their own room. Hardly anyone ever punches walls anywhere but their own home. Punching walls is usually about showing what they are capable of. Some wall punchers have even said 'This could be you!' but usually this is just implied. Punching holes in walls and kicking doors is usually a deliberate act of intimidation, not just letting off steam. It looks like *expressive* violence but it's *instrumental*.

How does this atrocious behaviour give them such power? How can wrecking their own house, even their own bedrooms, give them power? It's quite hard to imagine a mother smashing up the house or punching a hole in the wall (I've only come across one or two over the years). Some male partners do this to gain power over their wives but it's far less common behaviour in abusive men than it is in abusive teens.

The reason that beyond-control children often have so much power is quite simple but seldom acknowledged - they don't care as much as their parents! If they cared about the house as much as Mum does, then obviously they would not damage property to gain leverage. If they cared about their own safety as much as their parents do, they would not stay out late or wander the streets. The less they care the more power they have over those who do care.

I've heard the suggestion, and my experience would appear to support this, that abusive fathers often get better access deals than more responsible fathers do. They are quite happy to fight through the courts, lie (or hire expensive lie-yers) and often ignore the wishes of the children. The most responsible fathers don't see it as a battle and don't use their children as pawns. The competitive legal system often favours the more aggressive, competitive and dishonest parent and colludes with further abuse of victims. Here again there can be power in being aggressive, pushy and irresponsible. Naturally I'm not suggesting that you adopt these tactics!

What gives children power?

"I'm not properly dressed and I'll sleep in the road if you don't come pick me up!"
Thirteen-year-old girl demanding a lift home after she'd sneaked out at night.

"When it comes to naked force, the aggressive child is far less inhibited than they are. [T]he aggressive child develops systematic behaviours whose apparent purpose is to preserve her total freedom of action, attain benefits, minimize competition, and frighten the parents into helplessness." Omer[374]

Look at the list of ways that we influence children and consider how few of these sources of power and influence are available to most children. They do undoubtedly have a huge influence over us but this is mainly by our taking responsibility for meeting their needs (being there for them, working for them, providing for them). They do not feel that they have much control over this, as they usually take it entirely for granted. They can also influence us legitimately by persuasion, encouragement and social rewards (in so far as we try to make them happy or seek their approval).

Well-behaved, obedient, co-operative children are pretty powerless - they let the parents have power over their lives (and are usually quite happy with this arrangement). However, badly behaved, disobedient and uncooperative children can be terribly powerful!

The main power that disruptive children have comes from not caring. In terms of the six types of power, it's mainly a form of coercive power based on an imbalance of responsibility. If your child is willing to scream and pretend he is being abused in the street, he can exert coercive power over you. If he is willing to embarrass you in front of others (while you cover up for him), he is in a very powerful position. If a young person really doesn't care if he or she lives at home or not, while his parents desperately desire for him to be safe at home, he holds all the aces. The most powerful individuals in families are those who are actively self-destructive or at least unconcerned even about their own well-being. Not caring if you live or die can make you virtually invulnerable to the influence of others. This is, of course, assuming that others care; if nobody cares then no-one has this form of power.

I've mentioned that I've been giving parents and children in these families a personality test recently. Parents, mothers especially, score above average on Conscientiousness and way above average on Agreeableness. The young people who abuse their parents mostly score below average on both of these. The difference in being conscientious and caring between the young person and the parent is one of the main things that gives potential power.

As it's all so unfair, we don't like to admit that not caring gives (temporary) power while being responsible or caring makes us susceptible to exploitation. To love anyone is to give them power over us and love makes us vulnerable if they act disrespectfully or irresponsibly. I am definitely NOT suggesting that you should stop caring about your child. The answer is not to stop loving but to not make our happiness totally dependent on other people and to not take more responsibility for other people than is necessary. You may have to stop caring about some of the trivialities, or stop caring about things that should be their responsibility. For example, if your son doesn't care much about having clean and ironed shirts and treats you rudely then should you care that he looks a mess? If he does care about his appearance, this is a potential source of influence for you.

Sometimes creating some emotional, social or physical distance is required to prevent others controlling or abusing us.

Neil: "one thing that I really held onto was the session [of the Who's in Charge? group] where you were talking about power. The kids do what they do because they've got the power, because they don't care, and I don't have the power because I do care; and that left me in a position of weakness and my daughter in a position of strength, and that was the problem.

Eddie: Was that a surprise to you, that idea?

Neil: "Well yes, it was! You never think that caring about somebody is going to have an adverse effect, and surely the opposite should apply."

-from a recorded interview with ex-*WIC?* group member

The rewarding power of power

The abuser "gains power through his coercive and intimidating behaviours – a sensation that can create a potent, thrilling rush. The wielder of power feels important and effective and finds a momentary relief from life's normal distresses. It isn't the woman's pain that appeals to him; most abusers are not sadists. In fact, he has to go to some lengths to shield himself from his own natural tendency to empathise with her. The feeling that he rules is where the pleasure lies."
Bancroft[375]

Bancroft wasn't talking about adolescents abusing their mothers but about men abusing their partners. However, it applies 100% to most child-to-parent violence. Actually, it's disconcerting how much of his excellent book *"Why Does He Do That?"* applies to adolescent parent abusers (girls as well as boys).

The cheap thrill of feeling powerful, of manipulating adults, is a reward to a great many children when they defy or abuse adults. The thrill, like most thrills, may lose its kick after a while which may be one of the reasons why such behaviour escalates over time.

Much has been written about children misbehaving to get attention but power as a motivator for misbehaviour is seldom mentioned. This fits with the parent-blaming, children-as-victims, world-view held by most people who have written on parenting over the past half century; it's often assumed that parents have been neglectful and stingy with their attention. This is rubbish as the most demanding children are often those who have had the most attention. Certainly, children often do misbehave to get attention, but a feeling of power can be more rewarding than simple attention.

Some parents I talk to have difficulty understanding that being able to exert power can be such a reward. I often use the example of swearing at adults. I ask them to recall a disliked teacher and imagine how good it would have felt if they could have told the teacher where to go in colourful language without repercussions. Most can identify that this would not only have been empowering but would have felt great; children who get away with swearing at, or abusing parents in other ways, get a rush of power (and a surge of dopamine in their brains).

The rewarding power of power means it seldom works to simply ignore abusive behaviours towards parents, even fairly trivial ones. Not giving them attention makes sense in some situations (e.g. young children's tantrums) but if they are willing to escalate the behaviour, it will quickly reach a point where you can't ignore it without appearing submissive. The only exception is if you can ignore something in an assertive, rather than passive manner. You would have to be able to ignore it while fully maintaining your dignity, without danger to you or others, and without your children losing respect for you. This is more likely to apply to attention-seeking behaviour rather than full-on abuse, which usually can't be ignored without loss of respect.

Power corrupts

"Power increases testosterone levels, which in turn increases the uptake of dopamine in the brain's reward network. The results are an increase in egocentricity and a reduction in empathy." Robertson[376]

It's widely recognised that people with a lot of power: politicians, managers, generals, etc. can become egotistical and lack empathy for others. However, even a small amount of power can corrupt. It has been demonstrated in social psychology experiments that those made to feel powerful in some way become more self-focused and have more difficulty in empathising with others[377].

Thus the bully becomes less able to understand or feel empathy for other people's feelings. This can be situational and I have often noticed that a violent child, or adult, who shows little empathy within the home, may be empathetic and caring with friends or others. They are capable of empathy but this all but vanishes when they have inappropriate power. There are psychological mechanisms that make us not want to empathise with our victims. This is usually unconscious but some abusers have talked to me about deliberately trying not to think about how they have hurt others.

Power is like a drug, it may be rewarding at the time but it isn't making these children happy. You need to find a way to reclaim the power in your family, for their sake as much as yours.

What's It Like for Abused Parents?

"To say that we are not coping, would not even begin to describe our lack of emotional stability. I cry as I write this. I am devastated that I have to write this about my own child. I, who am so strong and usually in control, must ask for help. We are desperate. Please help." E-mail correspondent.

"I am terrified of the day he is stronger than I am. Since he was four, I have been pleading for help from any source I can locate, to no avail. I am raising a child that I know will cause harm to someone, but until he does, there is no help. Instead of marrying an abuser I gave birth to one, and it is much harder to escape than an abusive relationship, there are no centres where I can escape, I can't leave him alone." E-mail correspondent.

"I don't know that there can be any parent more devastated than a parent who's been subjected to this sort of behaviour; abused not only by the child but also by the community, by the school community, by everybody". From taped interview with abused mother.

Parenting a delinquent or criminal is in itself devastating for many parents. There have been very few studies of the effect of crime on other family members[378]. There is a trend in some countries to hold parents accountable for their children's wrongdoing. In the UK this has been taken to the extreme and parents are often fined for their children's crimes, including on occasions even being fined for having been assaulted by their own child! Blaming parents obscures the fact that a great many parents of delinquent children are suffering greatly, even those who are not being directly abused. One researcher interviewed parents of difficult adolescents who were not necessarily violent or abusive within the home, and wrote *"the outpouring of parental suffering was simply overwhelming, both in the interviews and in the observation part of the study. The results indicated that the 'effect' of delinquency on parents is a deceptively mild term: parents were actually devastated. Many cried repeatedly during the interviews as well as over the phone.*[379]"

If being the parent of a difficult or delinquent child can be traumatic in itself, how much worse will it be when the parent is the victim of the violence? It's not easy to get across how truly awful this experience can be. Even the parents themselves find it hard to express how bad it can be to have one's own child turn against them, to be repeatedly abused in their own home and to feel even more trapped than an abused wife. When I give workshops interstate or abroad I show videos of interviews with abused parents. Close to home, I get a parent or two to come along and tell their own story. This is powerful for the workers and empowering for the parents.

Words used by many parents I have worked with are:

crushing   *heart-breaking*
                    devastating
like a bereavement   *shameful*   *incredibly stressful*
overwhelming   *tragic*
                    traumatic

Body language and tears often speak louder than words about the emotional effect of parent abuse. Many parents I deal with need anti-depressants and have stress levels that impair their health. They may suffer from insomnia, have frequent minor illnesses, lose or gain weight, and find it hard to concentrate. Some can't work and a few even withdraw from the world. Being fairly responsible child-centred parents makes them more likely to be in this predicament but less likely to carry out a suicide attempt. However, a number of mothers have confessed, usually with a lot of guilt and shame that they've wanted to end their lives. So far I haven't heard of a completed suicide but it remains a possibility

One woman found her beyond control, abusive daughter unconscious after she had taken an overdose. The woman confessed tearfully that she was tempted to take the remainder of pills and lie down beside her. She couldn't do so because she could not let her daughter die, though she could have willingly ended her own life at that point. This is an intelligent woman who in the past had been cheerful and well-adjusted.

Another woman recently was sobbing, shaking and very close to having a panic attack when she described to me how her petite and pretty twelve-year-old daughter bullied her. She talked of running off (the mother, not the daughter) or of the attraction of killing herself. I tried to arrange for her to have a week off while her daughter stayed with relatives but she felt too guilty to follow through with this plan.

The experience of being abused by a child has both similarities and differences to the experience of being an abused wife. I've spoken to a great many women who have experienced both. Parents are not usually **as** afraid of children as they are of violent husbands but they are **far** more worried for the abuser's sake and generally feel more guilt. For most parents, the love they feel for their child is not optional and they feel totally trapped. The sense of betrayal is enormous when a husband abuses a wife but can sometimes be even greater when a beloved child turns on a parent.

Sadness, depression and grief

In the first few *Who's in Charge?* groups I gave participant parents a depression scale. About a half could have been classed as clinically depressed. This was too time consuming and we now just ask a few relevant questions. When starting *Who's in Charge?* Groups, 68% of parents agree with the statement "*I feel depressed or very unhappy*", 22% are neutral and only 10% disagree. Some parents are on anti-depressants, understandable and possibly necessary, but this can be unhelpful if it helps someone tolerate the intolerable.

Unfortunately, depressed parents of difficult children may find that cause and effect are reversed:

"My therapist kept steering the conversation to my childhood 'issues' and tried to connect them to my current unhappiness. She seemed to believe that depression was the root of my troubles as a mother. But what if my troubles as a mother were themselves causing my depression? Incredibly, we never addressed this possibility." Shannon[380]

Some parents feel very real grief. It's as if the child they knew and loved has gone and been replaced by someone (or something) else (Jekyll & Hyde is a frequent comparison but I've heard the Exorcist and zombie movies mentioned too). They truly grieve the loss of the relationship they had and the child they knew. Many parents had close and affectionate relationships with their child but may have seen this dissolve within a few months or over a couple of years.

Depression can make parents less confident and more negative generally, which can add to their difficulties in being an assertive parent to a difficult child.

Your child may be very distant from you at this point in time but he or she is not actually dead (or undead) and they **can** return to the land of the living. You probably feel intensely guilty because you sometimes feel as if you hate your own child, yet hating someone who is abusing you is pretty normal. Almost always, the love is still there and returns if the behaviour changes. Don't give up hope.

Stress

A New Zealand study of abused parents found that they *"described reactions that have been commonly reported as post-trauma symptoms in the literature, including emotional numbing, avoidance, hypervigilance and threat appraisals, intense fear, and a range of other distressing emotions.[381]"* 91% of parents in the Who's in Charge group agreed with the statement, *"I feel stressed or anxious"*, at the start of the group. Many have symptoms of Post-Traumatic Stress Disorder, but the trauma is current, not in the past, so 'post' is not appropriate, they are living the trauma.

The level of stress that some parents are living under is difficult to imagine. They are constantly on edge waiting for the next explosion when their child is at home or waiting to hear some bad news when they are not; tiptoeing around someone while walking on eggshells is a huge drain on their mental energy! Parents are often exposed to high levels of aggression, verbal abuse and threats on a daily, even an hourly, basis. This may continue for years! Sleep patterns are affected and general health suffers. It's surprising really that few parents in these situations have what we used to call a 'nervous breakdown' but mothers especially tend to soldier on regardless. Living with such stress puts enormous pressure on other relationships.

Anger

When someone spits in your face, pushes you over or calls you an 'effin' whore', anger is an understandable, perfectly natural, reaction. Sometimes parents have become so angry at such treatment that they will appear to be angry people, even if they were calm or passive prior to the abuse. From a parent-blaming perspective, of course, this is viewed as the cause of the young person's problem behaviour, rather than a reaction to it.

Anger may occasionally be a healthy response for a victim. Sometimes getting angry about abuse is a precursor to taking action and it may be associated with an improvement in the victim's self-respect. However, a parent's anger is often impotent rage and it can contribute to the vicious cycle maintaining the child's bad behaviour. It can make the child feel justified or make them lose more respect for the parent. There's a whole chapter on Anger coming up.

Isolation

Shame and embarrassment often lead to parents withdrawing from contact with friends, neighbours and family. This is an obvious and quite quick reaction in some families but a slower and more subtle process in others. Parents may be too uncomfortable to have other people around as their child's behaviour shames them. Some friends and relatives stop inviting the family because they don't want the embarrassing scenes or nastiness caused by aggro children.

Some abusive young people use this isolation and their parents' embarrassment as a power play and will deliberately shame their parents in front of others. Other young people simply don't care who is watching and behave abusively or disrespectfully as long as the observer is not actually a threat to them. Others are careful not to let outsiders see their aggressive behaviour.

A few young people are possessive of and dependent on their parents in a similar way to possessive, abusive men. I've heard of young people grilling their mothers about where they have been and who they have seen in almost exactly the same way as abusive men. Making their mothers isolated may be a deliberate strategy by these over-dependent, possessive children, but it isn't usually a conscious strategy. Being isolated makes the problems even more difficult to deal with and a sense of unreality can creep in, making parents begin to doubt their sense of reality and sanity.

Guilt

If you have read the earlier chapters on parent-blaming, you will not be at all surprised to hear that many parents of abusive children feel wracked with guilt. They often blame themselves emotionally even if they consciously know that they have done nothing wrong. There is often the nagging doubt that they must have contributed to their child's behaviour problems. Not all abused parents feel guilty but the vast majority do, especially mothers. Guilt gets in the way of being assertive and being clear about not accepting abuse.

The parents I meet not only feel vague guilt about having somehow caused their child's behavioural problems but are often feeling extremely guilty about their own reactions to their child's abuse. It's not easy to keep calm and logical when you are being terrorised, manipulated, threatened and hurt by someone you love! They know they will be judged, and found wanting, if they have lost their temper, given in or been passive. The professionals who are judging them often react quite similarly when their children have serious behavioural problems, but until you are in that position you can't really predict how you will react.

So don't be too hard on yourself if you have at times reacted in an unhelpful manner. Many abused parents at some point have screamed back, grabbed their child, slapped them or even wrestled or exchanged blows. To the authorities, fighting back may make you an abuser, but it's not *abuse* if you are defending yourself.

Shame

Feelings of shame go hand in hand with guilt, but the two are not the same. If your brother or cousin murdered someone, you may feel shame but probably wouldn't blame yourself, so would not feel guilt. If your child murdered someone, you would almost inevitably feel huge amounts of guilt as well as intense shame. Rachel Condry studied family members of serious offenders and talked about them experiencing a 'web of shame.'[382] Parents abused by their children will seldom admit what is going on to others. They carry guilty secrets and are tangled in a web of shame and guilt. Keeping secrets is in itself stressful and isolates them from others. Shame and guilt interact and reinforce each other.

Levels of shame and embarrassment appear to be highly variable but overall seem comparable to the shame of domestic violence. It's shameful having violence in your family whether you feel guilty or not.

There is a common idea that men are more embarrassed or shamed by being the victims of abuse than are women. This is used to explain why the large numbers of men who claim in surveys (of doubtful validity) to be abused by their wives don't show up in health, legal or welfare samples. I've never seen any evidence that men are any more ashamed of being hit by a family member than are women. Some men undoubtedly feel emasculated if hit by a woman or child, but others take it less personally than women do. I've encountered a number of men over the years who were amused by their partner being violent towards them, or even proud of how tough and tolerant they are. Such a reaction is *extremely* rare in a woman. I've met about a dozen men who were physically abused by female partners but I've met close to a hundred men so abused by children, one third of these being daughters. Men abused by their daughters are no more ashamed of this than are women abused by their children, but they tend to feel less guilty than mothers do. Father's embarrassment is similar to mothers, despite taking less responsibility and feeling less guilt. A few abused fathers do feel that their male pride is hurt, but this is more so if it is a boy who is attacking them, rather than a girl. Though confused, both abused fathers and abused husbands can feel some pride in the fact that they have not fought back when attacked by a female. Chivalry is not dead! This has been called 'benevolent sexism', the idea that women need to be looked after and protected[383]. Some feminists hate this but from my point of view it's helpful in combating family violence.

The effect of being a victim

In almost half of the families in my sample (47%) the abused parent has experienced domestic violence. Having been a victim is often intricately tied up in the whole sorry mess that leads to them being abused by a child (see chapter on DV). The other 53% of parents have not been in a victim relationship before and it's a new and horrible experience. It seems to surprise some professionals that an abused parent can react quite similarly to an abused wife.

Victims of abuse often respond by 'tiptoeing around' the abuser (a phrase regularly heard from both abused parents and abused wives), trying not to cause offence or not to upset the abuser. This may be a simple fear-based reaction or parents may think that their child has problems and needs to be treated delicately, or it may be a combination of the two.

The idea that aggression is primarily caused by frustration, or that anger is a symptom of some mental conditions, can make parents behave passively (some professionals encourage them to 'back-off' rather than take a stand). Such passivity makes things worse. Other parents react to abuse with impotent rage (see section on anger) and many swing between the two.

Being victimized can result in a complex pattern of hopelessness, loss of confidence, disorientation and extreme stress.

A swirling mess of emotions

In four decades of counselling, I have become aware of how often people are reacting to a confused mess of emotions which makes their head reel. People can deal with intense grief, intense fear, or intense anger and these on their own tend to soon fade. When people get stuck, it's often because there is a mix of emotions. I see a lot of children whose parents have separated and I often get them to list all the feelings they have towards each parent; one adolescent girl listed thirteen feelings towards her father (I can't remember what they all were). Here is a typical example: Anger 8/10; Fear 3/10; Guilt 4/10; Loss 7/10; Shame 4/10; Rejection 5/10; Pride 2/10; Hate 4/10; Love 8/10. For these children just listing and talking about each feeling can help them feel less confused and distressed. At one time I was surprised that children could rate 8/10 love along with 8/10 hate. I'm no longer surprised by such displays of extreme ambivalence. It's not usually the parent they are abusing that they feel so ambivalent towards, more often it's an absent, irresponsible or abusive father. They are actually less likely to abuse a parent they are so insecure towards.

Abused parents sometimes wonder why they are in such a distressed and confused state. Yet they are experiencing loss, depression, guilt, shame, fear, anger and stress all at once! What's more, our big, clumsy, human brains are quite capable of having feelings about feelings. So we feel guilty about feeling relief or embarrassed about our guilt and anxious about our depression and depressed about our anxiety. It all swirls round like someone flushed a toilet in your head! Sorting through your emotions on your own (you may want to list them and scale them 1 to 10) or talking them through with someone can be helpful.

Stress factors don't add but multiply in their effects. Thus if you have four sources of stress each with a value of two, this is 2 x 2 x 2 x 2, or 16 rather than 8.

This is just an analogy, it's not scientific so don't worry about the maths. Reducing one stress factor can have a multiplicative, disproportionate effect (besides being motivating and giving hope). In a similar way if your head is reeling from five different emotions about something, reducing or eliminating one (guilt or shame for example) can make the others much easier to deal with.

Past Domestic Violence

"One woman had asked her partner, 'How are you going to feel if [our son] comes to our door twenty years from now and says, 'I beat the **** out of my wife'?"[384]

"I think no one should do domestic violence ever, even in heaven." (Girl aged 7[385]*)*

Some of you will skip this chapter as it doesn't apply to you - be thankful. However, it seems too important an issue to confine it to one of the optional chapters at the end of the book.

Apart from being male, the biggest single factor influencing children's violence to parents is exposure to Domestic Violence. In my sample of four hundred and eighty children who abused parents, almost half (46%) had been exposed to DV. Past DV is even more common for sole mothers (61%).

For a number of years, the proportion of past DV within my sample has hovered around 50% but this is very slowly dropping. The reason for this is simple, the number of indulgent parents is increasing but there has probably been a slight fall in the amount of DV. This is a heretical thing to say in some quarters. Reports of DV have increased dramatically but this is a positive sign that it's being taken more seriously. Twenty or thirty years ago in most countries there was little point in women reporting DV as the authorities did nothing unless it was life-threatening (and not always then). It's odd that some DV workers are claiming there has been an increase despite all the excellent work that has been done over the past thirty years. If it was really increasing then all the work done since the setting up of refuges back in the '60s has been a waste of time.

As explained in the introduction, I'm using the term Domestic Violence, DV, because it's familiar to most people, although *Intimate Partner Violence* is a better term. Both are gender neutral which hides the fact that about 90% of DV is a male abusing a female. In recent years the idea that women abuse men as often as the reverse, or nearly as often, has become quite popular in some circles. It's pushed aggressively by the so-called Men's Movement and supported by a lot of scientific-looking, but highly dodgy, survey research. After forty years working with families, including over a thousand violent families, and reading extensively in other disciplines (such as sociology, anthropology and biology), I find the idea that men and women are equally violent in the family to be absurd! The surveys make gender disappear and often make violence appear to be mutual; this applies to DV and also to abuse of parents[386]. I've been surprised over the past two years by the fact that the majority of workers attending my training sessions initially expect that boys and girls are equally violent to parents.

I have seen a number of families where the man was the victim and his female partner the abuser[387]. Twice I have seen sole fathers abused by their children following DV perpetrated by their mother. It does happen, but it's rare. A bit more common than this role reversal is the situation where both parents are violent or abusive to each other (though this is not especially common in families where there is violence to parents).

It's important to remember that more than half of all families where children are abusing parents have no past family violence. The idea that family violence is almost always intergenerational is a confusing myth. I have known professionals who, on hearing of a young person being violent, ask *"who did he learn it from?"* automatically assuming that there must have been prior violence in the family. Such prejudiced attitudes lead to bad judgements and unhelpful suspiciousness on the part of workers. Children do not need to learn to be violent; very young children discover that hitting people gets results without any need for prior exposure. Of course they are *more likely* to be violent if they have seen others being violent but by the time they start school, even children from non-violent homes will have seen dozens of real life examples of children hitting each other and usually tens of thousands of examples of violence in the media. By the time they reach their teens they may have seen literally millions of examples of violence on various sizes of screen.

"For decades, explanations of partner abuse have generally included a simplistic, deterministic 'violence begets violence' thesis even though most… victims and perpetrators of intimate partner violence did not experience childhood violence, neglect or abuse." Miller & Knudsen[388]

If most victims became abusers, the world would be overrun by abusers in just a few generations. In a few centuries there would be no non-violent people left. Instead *most* forms of abuse are less common now than they were in the past[389].

Although the intergenerational explanation of violence is often wildly exaggerated, it does play a big part in all kinds of family violence. It's a common pattern but certainly not a necessary one. And even when there is exposure to violence within the family this does not have to be inter-generational, as witnessing violence by a sibling can have a huge influence (which is not taken seriously enough).

When I was first working with families, back in the seventies, there was no appreciation of the effect of DV on children. We were only just discovering the effects on women! I knew of families where a child had been abused or put at risk because of DV but our focus was on the mother. I met a few DV perpetrators but don't remember ever trying to do anything constructive about the man's behaviour. We supported women who wished to leave but there were no groups for perpetrators or for victims and little or no useful counselling support. As I mentioned in the introduction, I got interested in DV in the late seventies as a volunteer for a woman's refuge. At that time my day job, doing child protection work, and my evening voluntary work with the children in the refuge, were completely separate. When I was at the Refuge, I never mentioned my day job as it was bad enough being a man, never mind a Child Protection Worker!

At that time, nothing had been published on the effects of DV on children. Nothing! Not a sausage! Awareness started in the late 1980s. Unfortunately, awareness of the effects of DV on children has not always been helpful to victims. Sometimes mothers are blamed for having exposed their children to DV, and they may be re-victimised by the system.

There have been quite a few books and dozens of articles over the past twenty years about the effect of DV on children. Although violence towards mothers is occasionally hinted at or mentioned in passing, it's surprisingly absent as a topic. But violence to parents is similarly missing in the literature on child behavioural problems, delinquency, runaways or drug abuse, although it's common in all of these groups.

One reason it's not picked up in research on DV is that much of the research has focused on younger children and often only follows the family for a year or two after the separation. Parent abuse quite often occurs ten or more years after the mother left the abusive father. By then the mother is also unlikely to be in touch with family violence workers so some DV workers are unaware that it's a common issue. Until recently some family violence agencies turned women away if they were being abused by a son or daughter, even those being abused by an adult son. This is changing and many family violence agencies have become concerned about the amount of abuse towards mothers by children and some have done good work in raising awareness.

The effects of DV on children are not simple or straightforward and the link to violence to parents is complicated. Some of the effects start before birth but are impossible to see in any one child. Research suggests that maternal stress and depression during pregnancy increases children's behavioural problems years later. Women in abusive relationships are highly likely to be both stressed and depressed[390] and they may also be statistically more likely to take drugs, prescription or otherwise, during pregnancy, and more likely to smoke.

It's important to remember that the environment, even an extreme environmental effect such as directly witnessing severe violence, does not have a direct predictable effect on later behaviour. How any child is affected has as much to do with their personality and characteristics so two children with identical experiences can have opposite reactions.

Directly witnessing assaults on their mother

"You know, Mom, I can remember more than you think I can. I can remember the ambulance carrying you away covered in blood."[391]

Witnessing an assault on their mother is obviously a traumatic event for children of any age. An assault by a stranger is frightening and disturbing, but where the attack is carried out by the second most important person in their lives the psychological impact is far greater. It's now generally recognised that this is a form of emotional abuse. Younger children appear to be more affected in the short term but the psychological effects on older children may be more complex and just as serious. Where violence and abuse are happening over a period of time, the majority of children do actually witness the violence. Some parents even report that abuse is **more** likely to occur in front of the children or always occurs in front of the children. Some men use the children's presence as an added humiliation or threat to their partners. This may make more sense if you have read the chapter on power, the woman's concern for her children can disempower her and some men deliberately use this to their advantage.

Parents, both the abusive and victimised parent, often underestimate how much exposure there has been. One study found that 21% of children said they had seen the violence even when *both* parents said they had not witnessed it.[392]

We talk of 'exposure' rather than 'witnessing' because the effect is far more than just seeing the abuse. Sounds of violence can be traumatic and the knowledge of one parent hitting another can be devastating even if the violence isn't witnessed. There is far more going on than can be summed up in a few traumatic incidents and children don't just 'witness' DV but are actively involved in the long, drawn-out, horrible process.

In my work with children who are abusing parents after DV, I have come upon many who never actually saw the violence. In a few cases the actual violence took place before the child was born or when they were very young and not physically present. These children are still often affected by other aspects of the process. Some mothers have assumed that their past DV can't be relevant because the child was not a direct witness. Professionals and researchers also often focus on trauma. Trauma has become a bit of a buzzword. Another focus is on the role-modelling aspect and the expectation is that the child will copy the behaviour of the abusive parent, and especially of the same sex parent. It's a lot more complicated than simple 'monkey see, monkey do' modelling. Modelling is just a part of the picture and may not be the most important part.

The influence of DV can be enormous without any direct exposure. The extent and seriousness of physical violence are only slightly related to violence to parents. A few of the children who are abusing mothers come from families where there was horrific violence involving hospitalisations and lots of police involvement. Far more are from families where there was no serious threat to life and limb and far less obvious trauma. The extent and severity of past DV doesn't appear to make a great deal of difference to which children become violent towards mothers and doesn't necessarily relate to how severe their violence becomes.

Despite the common emphasis on modelling, children don't usually use the same methods of violence towards their mother as their father did. Acts of violence are often complex and confused. Imagine a scene where a father has grabbed and shaken his wife, then thrown her to the floor and kicked her, while watched by a traumatised four-year-old. The trauma is confounded by the police dragging his father off and by his parents separating soon after this incident. A few years later, when the child becomes violent to the mother, copying the father's actual behaviours is not possible since he isn't big or strong enough. The child's memory of the violent incident is confused and he may well remember it incorrectly, incorporating bits from imagination or even from movies. He may have never talked to anyone about it. He may be convinced that his father punched his mother when she fell to the floor. It's the attempt to hurt and control that is copied, rather than the means of hurting. This child when eight may slap, pinch and scratch his mother, none of which he ever saw his father doing. When he is older he may, or may not, punch her, as he thinks he remembers his father doing. He may object strongly to the idea that he is copying his father. He may feel he is not copying his father because he would never actually punch his mother. Or he may have no conscious memory of the incident and deny that his father would be violent.

Even when they do not directly witness the violence, children are usually aware of it. They may hear fights, see bruises or black eyes, see smashed furniture and holes in the wall, or may be told about it by older children or relatives. Both parents, the abuser and the victim, often underestimate and play down the extent to which children are aware of the violence. The knowledge that raised voices or angry looks may lead to violence is highly stressful. Children may even imagine worse things than what actually happens and may fear that Dad will kill Mum. The fact that no one talks about it adds to confusion, fear and insecurity. Children living in such homes learn secrecy and lose trust in adults. If they lose respect for *both* parents, this can put them in a lonely and dangerous place.

Exposure to other forms of abuse

Although exposure to other forms of abuse of their mother (threats, verbal abuse, emotional abuse etc.) may not be *quite* as obviously traumatic as witnessing physical assaults, this is also stressful and can be psychologically damaging. Children as young as six months show distressed reactions to parents' anger. Almost all women who are physically abused are also insulted, threatened or ridiculed (one study found this applies to 95%) and children are highly likely to witness this even if they never witness, or know about, the physical abuse. These other forms of abuse are usually far more frequent than the physical abuse and can be a daily occurrence in some homes. They have a huge impact. Sometimes it isn't taken seriously enough because the physical abuse is so much more dramatic. Abused women do often say that the verbal or emotional abuse is worse than the physical, yet it's often so insidious and constant that they shut out much of it and may not recognise the effects.

Non-physical abuse of mothers (verbal abuse, threats, throwing things) affects children's behavioural problems with or without physical violence.

This is a crucial part of the reason why past DV is associated with abuse of their mother. The verbal abuse has often been an insidious form of brainwashing over many years. What's more it usually continues after the separation in one form or another. Children lose respect for mothers even though they love them and sometimes even though they consciously reject their fathers' propaganda. Advertising can make you feel favourable towards a product even when you know all the ads are rubbish! Abusive fathers put Mum down thousands of times and the child unconsciously absorbs this disrespect. If they are on Dad's side, this will obviously be worse, but I've seen quite a few young people who have rejected Dad and feel they are 100% on Mum's side, yet they have still lost respect and become abusive towards her.

"The superiority, contempt or depersonalisation that children may observe in a batterer's day-to-day treatment of their mother can shape their views of both parents. Children tend to absorb the batterer's view of their mother over time…"
Bancroft & Silverman[393]

Children may have been victims themselves

Children whose mothers are abused are more likely than other children to have been physically and emotionally abused themselves: an estimated third to a half of all those living with domestic violence. Sometimes this is the result of children getting in the way or trying to protect their mother. In other cases, the attitudes and behaviours that led to spouse abuse also led to abuse of the children. In a few cases mothers are so stressed and traumatised that they have become abusive, or at least overly harsh in their discipline, towards the child. Some mothers have said that they have physically punished a child to prevent the father from giving a worse punishment. Then there is the awkward fact that assortative mating means that statistically, aggressive and violent women are *a bit* more likely to have an aggressive or violent partner and there are some families where both parents are abusive.

Given that child abuse often goes with DV, I've been surprised that there aren't **more** direct victims of child abuse amongst the children I work with who are abusing mothers following DV. They have been emotionally abused by exposure to DV and a few have been abused by their fathers, but not as many as I would expect. Having been a direct victim of abuse plays a part for a small number of these children but it's not particularly a risk factor *in itself*. If you haven't read the rest of this book, this probably seems very surprising. It may even be that children exposed to DV who have **not** been abused themselves are somewhat more likely to abuse mothers than those children whose fathers have also abused them. One study found that children exposed to DV who were **not** themselves abused were more negative about their mothers[394]. Children who have not been abused by their father may be more likely to internalise his attitude to their mother, hence more likely to abuse her. This is the opposite to the conclusion of many people who write about violence to parents, they assume that violent children have been victimised and quote the few studies who have mentioned this. I'm certainly not saying it doesn't happen but it's a risk factor because it's associated with DV, not a risk factor in itself. There is also a tendency for difficult children to be more likely to be abused than those with an easier temperament and studies almost never take this into account, probably because it seems to be blaming the child victim of abuse.

Poor parenting and parent-child relationships

Children in families where there has been DV are likely to experience (at least for a time) poor parenting. The characteristics which led their father to abuse their mother are unlikely to lend themselves to him being an involved, caring parent (though some are). Unsurprisingly, it has been found that spouse-abusers tend to be distant from children, less physically affectionate and more likely to use physical punishment to control them[395].

Fairly obviously in families where there is DV, it's likely that the two parents don't work together very well, or communicate well, and inconsistency is a particular problem[396]. Parents may disagree about child-rearing and some mothers treat their children differently when their father is around.

In addition to this, a mother who is severely stressed, depressed and has low self-esteem is not going to be parenting at her best. Many abused mothers are depressed; others become withdrawn and passive which means they are less able to be assertive with their children when necessary.

However, having met a great many mothers who had been abused, I am more often impressed by how well they are doing. Even those mothers who are suffering from abuse at the hands of one child may have others who are doing well and have clearly been well parented. Many women have continued to parent well, despite suffering greatly from bullying men and they often bend over backwards trying to maintain a relationship between their children and irresponsible fathers. I see this far more often than I see women who are trying to alienate their children from their fathers. But this could be because conscientious, caring mothers are more likely to be abused by their children following DV than are irresponsible, aggressive women.

Mothers over-compensating

A common pattern that I see is women trying to compensate for all that the child has gone through:

"I wanted to make it up to them for what their father put them through. I was determined to always be there for them and to be the best mother in the world."

As we have seen, such Indulgent, excessively child-focused parenting can be an additional risk factor for parent abuse. Also some mothers have seen how detrimental authoritarian, harsh parenting can be, so some tend to go to the opposite extreme, avoiding all punishment and minimising control. In addition some women say they either over or underreact when their child becomes abusive towards them. I've had a number of women talk of having 'flashbacks' or being 'stunned' and 'devastated' when their child's behaviour reminded them of the abuse they'd suffered at the hands of the child's father. Sometimes, especially at adolescence, there are upsetting similarities in voice, demeanour or posture that take the woman back to previous abuse. Therefore mothers having experienced DV, may back down from confrontations with their aggressive children, thus unwittingly rewarding the child's aggressive behaviour.[397]

Mothers who have been in DV relationships often feel terribly guilty. They are guilty about having made a poor choice of father and blame themselves to some extent for all that the children have gone through. Often they stayed for the sake of the children, to give them 'stability' or 'security'; with hindsight they often see the bitter irony of this. They often feel just as guilty for having left, which may not have been the easy solution others think it should be, and children seldom thank their mothers for ending the relationship.

I've often told women that it's illogical to feel guilty about both being with the man and leaving him. I say to them, "Choose which one you want to feel guilty about." The usual reaction is to laugh and many say, "What if I don't want to feel guilty about either?" I ask if they could have known what they were getting into and did they really choose to expose their children to the abuse. There may be some genuine cause for guilt but most of their guilt is unwarranted, unhealthy and definitely unhelpful. Guilt, it's worth repeating, gets in the way of good parenting and makes it far harder to be assertive or authoritative.

Family disruption

Children in families where there has been violence are highly likely to experience other forms of family disruption. Parents are far more likely to separate, either permanently or temporarily. Separations are far more likely to be messy and nasty, may lead to restricted or no access to the absent parent and often there continues to be ongoing conflict between parents, sometimes for many years.

There is evidence that the long-term damage to children caused by parent's separation is largely caused by parental conflict (before, during and after the separation) rather than the separation itself. However, it should be noted that the adverse effect of continuing to live in a violent home (or even one with a great deal of conflict) appears to be worse than the effect of parental separation on children. Other forms of family disruption may be associated with DV, such as hospital admissions, stays in a refuge, frequent changes of school, losing contact with other relatives, having alcoholic or drug-dependent parents etc.

We are so shocked by domestic violence that we often fail to see the effects of other traumas. Many children who have been traumatised by having an abusive father still love him and in the short term, may be more upset by the separation and not having contact with him than by the abuse of their mother. It's hard for us to acknowledge or recognise this if we know that the separation is ultimately the best thing for the child. We also frequently underestimate how upsetting moving house or changing school can be for a child. When all these stressful changes happen at once it can be devastating. As we've mentioned, stress factors don't add together, they multiply their harmful effects.

What is it like for children?

Living with the abuse of their mothers has been compared to life in a war zone or experiencing natural disasters such as cyclones, earthquakes etc. Children exposed to violence towards their mothers tend to have fairly similar emotional problems to children who have been directly abused themselves.

These children are likely to be insecure. "*Many children live with fear and anxiety, waiting for the next violent episode. They feel no safety in their own home yet are too young to seek out or even want an alternative...*"[398]

Children find the abuse of their mothers very difficult to talk about for a variety of reasons. Secrecy may have been forced upon them in the past; they often feel shame and guilt; they may be struggling to be loyal to both parents. Loyalty conflicts can be a major stress factor and some children describe a feeling of being 'torn apart' or feel that they are being used as pawns in an adult's game. A twelve-year-old told me recently, "*I feel I'm in a game but I don't know any of the rules or how anyone can win.*"

They are often very mixed up and confused emotionally. They may feel guilty: younger children often believe that their bad behaviour caused the arguments and violence and may blame themselves for their parent's separation. At any age they often feel guilty because they could not stop the violence or protect their mother. They may feel guilty for rejecting their father or for being on Mum's side. They may worry that they are like their father (especially if they are feeling a lot of

267

anger). They may blame their mother for leaving or blame her for the violence. They may just want to escape (e.g. by running away or using drugs or alcohol).

Loyalty conflicts can be confusing for adults as well as the young person. Some people assume that the child will not miss a violent father but their feelings of loss may be every bit as intense as that of a child who loses a loving father. A child seen in the year after a separation may be more upset about the separation than about the violence that led to it – this confuses some adults, including professionals, who may not want to believe that the child genuinely loves an abuser. Sometimes over-zealous attempts to protect the child causes more emotional pain and can even strengthen the child's loyalty to their father (who is often good at portraying himself as the victim). A fair number of fathers who have been abusive to the child's mother and are irresponsible are nevertheless affectionate with the child and may be a lot of fun to be around, especially after separation when they often give the child far more attention.

I have come to see loyalty conflicts as an enormous influence on children in separated families, especially where there has been DV.

Some children are desperate for acceptance by their fathers and loyalty conflicts are often more intense the more insecure they feel. For example, a child who has an absent father who they know loves them and who has always been reliable may find it easy to accept a step-dad, while children with irresponsible, largely-absent fathers are often the ones who find it hardest to accept a step-father. This is especially so around ages ten to fourteen when loyalty conflicts tend to be at their peak.

Behavioural problems and violence to parents

There is lots of evidence that children exposed to family violence show increased levels of aggression, both inside and outside the home[399]. There are higher rates of violence, defiance, truanting, criminal activity, alcohol and drug use. Although it may not be possible to say for sure that such problems in a particular child are a direct result of witnessing abuse (as siblings often have different problems), it's often a large contributing factor.

These kids are often very angry. They may have many genuine reasons to feel angry: life's been unfair to them. They may be angry at life in general or angry at one, or both, parents. Quite often they are angry at their father, but he is too scary for them to confront so they take it out on a safe target, Mum or younger brothers and sisters. For some children, their aggression is shown in class and the playground as well as at home. More anxious children often control themselves in other situations but let rip at home.

It's important to realise that there is nothing inevitable about violence following DV. I saw a family recently where there were three children who had all been exposed to violence from father to their mother. The oldest brother (with longest exposure to DV) was a caring, mature, very protective boy with no behavioural problems and emotionally pretty stable. The second son was aggressive, in trouble at school and being abusive towards Mum. He was only eleven so hopefully we intervened before it could escalate. The third boy wasn't showing any anger or aggression but was anxious and withdrawn. This shows that similar experiences with three different temperaments can lead to three very different reactions. I've seen a great many families where different children have reacted in opposite ways. A few seem to be extremely resilient and show no obvious effects.

Being exposed to DV is a horrible experience for children and it shouldn't be necessary to pretend they are all *scarred for life* to get people to take it seriously. Children can survive terrible experiences and even grow from them. Some children emerge from terrible experiences stronger, kinder, better people, but many are harmed, and some permanently.

Although the literature on DV and children has little to say about violence to parents there are occasional mentions that show clearly it's not rare:

"Children in middle childhood appear to be beginning to identify with the aggressor and act in hostile and emotionally aggressive ways towards their mothers."[400]

"Two-thirds (66%) of the mothers reported that they felt their child copied their partners' aggressive behaviour in some way. 15 (27.8%) mothers reported that their child was verbally aggressive to them and/or their siblings and 21 (39%) reported that their child was physically aggressive to them and/or their siblings, peers or property."[401]

This last is the only study I've come across which attempts to give any indication of how often violence to parents occurs after DV. Unfortunately, it lumps violence to mothers in with violence to brothers and sisters (which is far more common), violence to other children, and to property, so doesn't tell us much. We might guess that about 10 to 15% of these children were physically violent to their mothers, but others may develop such behaviour in their teens. It's interesting that only one-third were not at all aggressive according to mothers, though some of the two-thirds may have been showing fairly normal sibling fighting.

"Beaten wives we interviewed told us that their children began threatening them after seeing their fathers become violent. A child who sees his mother hit by his father comes to view hitting as the thing to do - a means of getting what he wants."
(Straus et. al., 1980, p 104)

Lack of trust and respect for adults

"...they may admire a powerful father but also fear him, or love and worry about a victimised mother but feel angry at her for appearing weak."[402]

Where abuse is prolonged, children often lose respect for both parents. Having no respect for either parent can make children very vulnerable and at risk. This leaves them feeling alone and unsupported and as teens they may be far more vulnerable to influences from their peer group.

"I love my father but I can't ever respect him after what he did to Mum." thirteen-year-old boy.

269

A key element in parent abuse which follows DV is the loss of respect for mother. We lose respect for victims as we have discussed earlier (page 47). These children have seen or heard Mum being abused, perhaps a great many times, and lost respect for her. Then if they begin abusing her they lose more respect which becomes a vicious circle (or slippery slope). A few children have been exposed to their mother being abused by more than one person, which may have included an older brother or sister, which has a double or triple whammy effect. Being exposed to a sibling's abuse of Mum can have just as big an effect as being exposed to a step-dad abusing her. So take abuse very seriously, no matter who it's from. Don't give opportunities for their father to continue abusing you if you can possibly avoid it – if he sometimes abuses you in front of the kids then try to arrange so that you are never together around them.

"Battering is, by its nature, undermining of a mother's authority, and it can have far-reaching effects on her ability to parent her children. Even if the batterer does not overtly undermine the mother, children absorb messages from the batterer's behaviour that can shape their responses to their mother's parenting. The contemptuousness that batterers typically use in arguing with their partners, for example, can indicate to the children that their mother deserves to be insulted and that it's not necessary to speak respectfully to her. Children may learn from the batterer's verbal abusiveness that it's appropriate to yell at their mother or to call her names, and they may absorb specific approaches to deriding or degrading her... The children may also absorb from the batterer the message that physical violence toward the mother is acceptable, as long as the provocation is deemed adequate. Many teenage and pre-teen children of battered women assault them physically..." Bancroft & Silverman[403]

I think undermining of the mother's authority as a parent is a key, central issue connecting past DV and children's abuse of parents (step-dads get caught up in this as well as mothers). Undermining the mother's authority often continues for years after the separation[404]. Unfortunately, there may be nothing that you can do about this. You still need to be assertive in your home and have clear boundaries, rules and consequences under your roof.

Pseudo-maturity (and genuine maturity)

False maturity is where children are forced to take on responsibilities they are not ready for. They may seem to be well adjusted but can be under a lot of strain. On the other hand some children who have been exposed to DV are genuinely mature, responsible and caring. I've made it clear in previous chapters that I think our children generally are not given enough responsibility and not encouraged to be mature, so sometimes what is seen as *pseudo*-maturity by some professionals looks like healthy maturity to me! There is no trauma that can't lead to some growth and a few children are stronger and more caring because they have been through a lot and survived. The concept of Post-traumatic Growth[405] is neglected with adults but is almost taboo when applied to children – it can sound like we are minimising the trauma or abuse.

Most of the early research on the effects of DV looked at children in Women's Refuges. These are often the more extreme cases of DV, the families are more likely to be poor and without other supports, and the upheaval for children is huge. Yet even studies of children in refuges "*have found that some have no identifiable problems and some are even above average in social competence and adjustment.*"[406]

Some children are remarkably resilient and we often underestimate them.

Lowered self-esteem

This is a very common effect of exposure to DV[407]. It can have serious long term effects on social and academic development and has been found to last into adulthood. This is not *in itself* a risk factor for violence towards parents (see chapter on Self Esteem) but it's a risk factor for many other problems, such as depression, drug use, etc., and can complicate all sorts of problems, including violence to parents.

Poor academic performance

Stress can make it hard to concentrate. I've seen adults who have been unable to read a book for several years due to extreme stress (such as DV) but once they recover they can concentrate again. Extreme stress can even lower IQs. Even without the stress of DV, parental separation often results in a drop-off in school performance for a year or two; with DV, ability to concentrate and learn may be affected for many years. Children exposed to DV are more likely to be assessed as having ADHD. Poor school performance can be a result of difficulty in concentrating, lower self-esteem and a loss of confidence, disruption due to moves and changing family situation, disruption due to behavioural problems, depression and losing trust and respect for adults (which means paying less attention to teachers).

One eight-year-old commented, "*My school work has suffered because sometimes I am thinking too much about Mum and worrying about her.*" [408] But many children tell me they are not aware of consciously thinking about family issues in school – it can still affect them.

'Internalising' issues

The traumatic experience of seeing their mother abused can contribute to bed-wetting, insomnia, nightmares, fears, phobias, eating problems, stuttering, depression (even young children can become depressed), self-harm, headaches, gastro-intestinal problems and many other stress related medical conditions (asthma, eczema, ulcers, etc.). Less extreme reactions are feelings of insecurity and unhappiness. Younger children may regress in some ways: stop feeding themselves or start soiling or wetting again.

These are what are often called *internalising* problems: anxiety, depression, self-harm, withdrawal, etc. *Externalising* problems are things like aggression, defiance, stealing, running away, delinquency, drugs, etc. Some children respond to DV with the former, others with the latter and some manage both at the same time, or have first one then the other. Whether a child predominantly shows internalising or externalising issues is mostly determined by their personality: for example a nervous introvert is more likely to internalise and a fearless extrovert to externalise (especially if low on Agreeableness).

It used to be expected that girls will show primarily internalising problems in response to DV, some do but I also see many 'acting out' with aggression, drug taking and promiscuity.

It's not at all uncommon for the same child to have both internalising and externalising problems. Having a child who is aggressive (probably why you are reading this) is complicated if they are also depressed or anxious. This can make it more difficult to be assertive in your parenting and if the reason for their problems is a reaction to DV or parental separation, you will probably feel even more sympathetic. Sympathy is fine as long as it doesn't make you passive about unacceptable behaviour.

Adopting abusive attitudes and identifying with the aggressor

Children absorb many of the attitudes and opinions of their parents. I have stressed that we as parents don't shape our children's personalities to any great extent and we are just one influence on their behaviour and attitudes. However, specific attitudes and sets of beliefs can be picked up directly from parents. Most children adopt their parents' religious beliefs (though this is changing) and many have similar political beliefs to their parents. If parents are criminals or drug abusers, a fair number of children but certainly not all, will adopt favourable attitudes to breaking the law or using illegal drugs.

Unfortunately children often adopt negative, unhelpful and anti-social attitudes more readily than pro-social or moral attitudes. As we've said, it's easier to be a bad influence than a good influence.

Adopting attitudes which support violence and abuse of women appears to be of crucial importance in the intergenerational 'cycle of violence'. Your child may have adopted some of his or her father's attitudes towards violence, towards women and towards you. All of this applies to girls almost as much as to boys. We still live in a sexist society where women are often seen as second-class citizens.

A few children clearly 'identify with the aggressor' and take the side of the most powerful parent. These children (usually boys) are obviously at high risk of adopting abusive attitudes and repeating the pattern of abuse. Many of these children go to live with their father at some point and a few lose touch with their mothers. I have seen some very tragic situations of this type. If they are repeatedly abusing their mother and not letting her have any control over them, they may actually be better off living with the abusive, irresponsible father. It took me quite a while to admit that this is sometimes a better option than having a child actively practice being an abuser. Counselling such children may help them emotionally but it seldom changes their allegiance to the abuser, at least in the short term, and may have little effect on their behaviour since they are not motivated to make life easier for their mother (or themselves when living with their mothers).

It's certainly not necessary for a child to identify with the abusive father to soak up some of his attitudes. Some children are definitely on Mum's side, and may say they don't want to be like their father, yet copy some of his behaviour. In counselling, their desire not to be like Dad can sometimes be used to help them change, but just saying "You're just like your father!" is unhelpful, particularly when said angrily by their mother during a crisis.

Modelling

It tends to be assumed that boys model their father's behaviour and girls model their mothers. Thus many people expect that boys in families where there is DV are going to be aggressive, with externalising problems, and girls passive with internalising problems. However, although many studies report that boys have more externalising issues after DV, this is not surprising since they do so without DV. In my sample of children who are violent to parents, there are twice as many boys as girls but the girls are *just as likely* to have been exposed to DV as the boys.

Children don't just model the same sex parent. They also copy some things from the opposite sex parent, from children and adults in the extended family and outside the family, from real life and from the media. Older siblings can be a huge influence.

I feel that many professionals and researchers focus too much on the traumatic incidents and not enough on the ongoing psychological influences (including psychological abuse). There has been a push to identify children exposed to DV as having Post Traumatic Stress Disorder. There are a number of problems with this[409]. One is that the long-term damage done by DV can be unrelated to symptoms of trauma. A boy who identifies with his father, makes light of the violence and has no obvious symptoms may be more likely to grow up to be an abuser, and to abuse his mother, than the one who is having nightmares about it.

The cycle of violence - males

A great deal has been written about the extent to which violence runs in families. This is often exaggerated and the idea that the process is in any way *inevitable* is both wrong and dangerous. This myth not only leads to faulty assumptions but it could even lead to self-fulfilling prophecies. I've seen teenage boys who are very worried that they are inevitably going to grow up like their abusive fathers. Being determined not to do so is great, but fearing some inescapable fate is not helpful.

There are two related myths. One is that all abusers have been victims in the past. Another is that all victims will go on to become abusers. These are not the same thing though they are often confused. Consider serial killers. Let's pretend that all serial killers were abused as children (many were, but not all). Does this mean that every abused child is going to grow up to be a serial killer? Of course not!

This myth may sound ridiculous to you when baldly stated, yet I have heard many professionals talk as if the intergenerational transmission of abuse was inevitable.

It's certainly a myth that all boys from violent families will become abusive but there is also no doubt that the risks are far higher for them than for boys from non-violent homes. This is partly genetics and partly environment. Sons who are exposed to their father's violence are several times more likely to be violent towards their own partners than those who do not witness violence. However, even if the majority of violent men come from violent homes (my guess is that it's about 50%), it's still a mistake to assume that a majority of children in violent homes will become violent. Some children become violent, some become nervous and some become stronger and more caring.

There are many examples of people who grew up in violent, multi-problem families who are decent caring adults.

The cycle of violence - females

Another aspect of the Cycle of Violence myth is that girls from abusive homes will choose partners who are themselves abusive. It used to be believed (and sometimes still is) that such girls are masochists and deliberately, though unconsciously of course, choose men who are going to abuse them. This is a subtle form of victim-blaming not based on any evidence. If this happens, it's extremely rare. There is, however, a tendency for women who grew up in violent homes to be *more likely* to find themselves in abusive relationships as adults. Best guess is that about one third of women in abusive relationships as adults were exposed to childhood DV[410], so two thirds were not. These numbers are dubious but it's definitely not the majority and is far from being inevitable. Domestic violence can happen to *any* woman (though some will get out very quickly) and even girls from the worst multi-problem homes can have settled relationships if they strike lucky in their choice of mate.

The fact that a girl accepts being abused as normal or inevitable will increase the chance that she is abused by her partner. One pattern may be that women from abusive homes accept verbal abuse and controlling tactics from their boyfriends and partners whereas women without such a background would be more likely to "put their foot down" early in the relationship, either getting out or stopping an escalation of abusive behaviour (this only works with some abusers, not with the worst offenders). I'm not implying that women can usually stop abuse just by being assertive. This is unlikely to work once a pattern of abuse has been established, but occasionally it prevents an escalation early in the relationship. This is a major difference between DV and violence to parents. Being assertive often does stop violence to parents but with DV it's as likely to make things worse!

Some girls from abusive homes adopt ideas of masculinity and femininity which make them attracted to tough, macho males. Macho, aggressive males are not *necessarily* abusive, but they do have a greater probability of being violent and abusive. But I'll repeat, for emphasis, that these women do *not* want to be abused. The idea that women are masochistic and actually *seek out* abusive males is not supported by any research that I am aware of and goes against all my experience. Some theories of mate selection (especially psychoanalytic theories) would have us believe that people subconsciously seek out partners with some of their opposite sex parents' characteristics. However, the evidence on mate choice suggests that we tend to pair up based on height, wealth, social class, ethnic group, and relative attractiveness and then choose from a small number of associates of the right age. This doesn't leave much leeway for subconsciously assessing who is going to turn out like their Dad!

There is also some evidence that girls from abusive homes, being more likely to be themselves aggressive or delinquent, selectively mate with more aggressive men[411]. Also girls who leave home at a young age, for whatever reason, are at increased risk of partnering men who are criminal, substance-abusing or otherwise deviant and are thus at greater risk of DV. So girls escaping abusive homes can have an increased chance of ending up with a violent partner for a number of reasons.

Sadly, DV is not rare and some women get two abusive partners from pure bad luck. I've met a few women who had two partners who were apparently completely different (one a motor-bike riding young thug, the second a shy bookworm, for example) but eventually both became abusive. Naturally women in such circumstances feel it must be their fault and some therapists seem happy to blame them, though no one could have foreseen the bookworm becoming abusive.

Ongoing contact with abusive fathers

Since I've stressed the importance of the post-separation influence on children, you may be thinking that stopping your child seeing their father would solve the problems. It probably won't, even if it's possible. If you are talking about an older child or adolescent, these are some of the possible consequences of stopping all access:

- Child chooses to live with Dad. I'm seeing this happening in younger and younger children. It used to be that up to age fourteen children would live where the Court, or their mother, told them to live. Now I see eleven-year-olds who are voting with their feet. Even when the Family Court has ordered the child to live with their mother, a child who is determined enough may run off or put themselves in danger until they end up with Dad. Others just make life totally intolerable for Mum and some of these end up with Dad.
- Stopping contact can intensify some children's loyalty to the absent parent.
- Some children become angrier and behavioural problems increase because of this.
- They often blame mother for stopping them seeing Dad (even if it was Court ordered) and this clearly can increase the risk of abuse towards mother.
- Influence need not be by face-to-face contact. Thus some fathers who have primarily telephone or internet contact can be a big (bad) influence on their children.

I'm **certainly** not saying that all abusive men should have access to their children. Each case needs to be judged on its merits. Here in Australia I've been shocked over the past ten years to see abusive men getting more and more contact, sometimes 50-50 care, with the mother, and in a few cases they have been granted custody instead of the victimised mother. I think the myths that women are secretly as abusive as men and that most violence is mutual is behind such unjust and dangerous decisions. Court systems can appear to favour good liars and the most irresponsible. Some men use the court system as a means to continue to harass their ex year after year.

275

What can you do about past DV?

You may have become frustrated with this long chapter. You may be wondering when I'm going to tell you how to undo the effects of past DV. There may be little or nothing you can do about it. It happened and some children are going to show long-term effects. You can't change the past and you may not be able to influence your ex in the present. But you can chuck out any unwarranted guilt you are carrying around, get a sense of proportion and get on with being the best influence you can be.

Healing

Although it's safe to say that most children will be adversely affected in some way by their mother being abused by her partner, not every child develops emotional or behavioural problems. Studies of children in refuges (who tend to be those in the worst situations) have found that some have no identifiable problems and some are even above average in social competence. Some children are very resilient.

Fairly obviously, the longer the abuse continues, the greater the effect will be. Good parenting (solo or as a couple) may undo some or all of the damage once the abuse stops. A particularly warm relationship with one parent can help counter (but not eliminate) the negative effects of marital conflict. Support from other adults can also help counter the effects of stress on children.

Getting a step-dad is not a solution. Re-partner for your sake, not for the children's. The rate of past DV in the many step-parent families in my sample is the same as the rate in sole mother families. So adding a step-dad helps in some cases but makes things worse in others, overall balancing out.

Counselling or group programmes for children can be helpful (assuming that the abuse has stopped). Some of the damage can be healed by the abuser admitting his past abuse and making amends. It's important that the fact that abuse is wrong is acknowledged. There's an optional chapter later in the book about relating to an abusive ex.

If children accept abuse as normal, they are more likely to grow up to be abusers themselves (or accept it from a partner). Where a marital separation occurs, men can do a great deal of good if they are able to become reliable, responsible access parents or they can continue to do a lot of harm if they are unreliable, irresponsible parents!

Children are often remarkably forgiving!

Box

Isaiah

Dear Eddie,

I sit here at the moment waiting for the police to arrive in order to get some help with my nine-year-old son, Isaiah, who has been having a violent out-of-control episode for the past five and a half hours. This is one of many episodes that have escalated over the past few weeks and I am at my wits end.

My son has been very difficult to deal with pretty much since birth. He was my second child and I considered myself a very 'switched on' mother, who was not over sensitive to difficult babies, but I just felt there was something different about him.

I was in a relationship with Isaiah's father for eighteen years and was subjected to family violence. I now have four children, all to my ex, who have experienced a lot over the years. I live with this guilt every day. Two years ago I eventually made the final break after many unsuccessful tries, and myself and the children are now in transitional housing.

Isaiah is becoming worse and worse with every incident that occurs and I have had a lot of trouble receiving the right help for him or having him assessed. I had a family doctor of ten years tell me that it's no wonder my son acts the way he does after what I had subjected him to with his father for so many years. I accept responsibility for staying in the relationship for too long, yet at the same time I do not feel that those types of judgmental opinions are helpful or productive to my son or me, and how we can move forward from here?

My son's behaviour has included violence towards me, throwing things at me, hitting and kicking me, even while I am driving a car, smashing property, kicking holes in walls, smashing windows, threatening self-harm, threatening to kill me when he is older, his bedroom door is completely off its hinges from his kicking it in, foul language… He also has issues with anxiety which I have learnt to deal with and I accommodate him to the point it just feels natural to me, for example, no food on his plate can be touching, he won't wear certain clothes because of the way they irritate him. I have had refusals to go to school on so many occasions. He is controlling of me and constantly tries to engage with me while I am having adult conversations. I have to stop while talking to others and explain to him what we are discussing, and if I ask him to go play with the other kids he becomes annoyed and can start an episode which can last for two to six hours. He blows things completely out of proportion. He constantly blames me for how he has reacted to a situation and why he has become angry. He shows signs of anxiety. For example, if he knows the school schedule will change on a particular day then he will refuse to go to school for that day. Yet when he is at school there are absolutely NO behavioural problems or learning difficulties and he has been described as a model student who upholds the school values. When I let the teacher know the problems I was having at home with him, he tried to suggest that I provide a more stable consistent environment at home for my son and punish him by withdrawing his favourite things. I believe I do provide the most stable environment I can, considering I have six children, and my son does not care if I deprive him of the things he values. The other children also have experienced the same things as this child yet I do not have the same severe behavioural problems that I do with my son. Yet they are sometimes starting to mirror his behaviour, as they see him get away with so much and also see me walking on egg shells around him and accommodating him however I can in order to avoid an outburst. The more I accommodate him, the more he pushes the limits.

277

I guess I am at my wits end. I love my son very much. It's so hard to admit this but his behaviour makes it very hard to like him sometimes and is also impacting my ability to be able to parent and enjoy my other children. Whenever we go out for the day for family events, he will upset the day with one of his outbursts and the other children are starting to resent him as well. I know he is a child and I see his pain and how he is suffering through all this and I just do not know how to help him?

Thank you for your time and patience.

Yours Sincerely Sally

End Box

Why Does He (Or She) Do That?

We've discussed some society-wide changes that are making children less respectful to adults and more entitled and demanding. We've shown that modern parenting methods can backfire and greatly increase the chances of a young person abusing their parent. We've seen that children who abuse or defy their parents often have certain personality characteristics. For almost half of the young people who abuse parents, there is past Domestic Violence to add fuel to these fires. These are all influences, but many parents still want an answer to the apparently simple question: *"Why does he do it?"*

We will first look at why children misbehave generally, then at why they may act abusively or violently towards family members.

Four main reasons for children's misbehaviour are often given: attention, power, revenge and withdrawal. Most misbehaviour can be seen as motivated by some combination of these four desires plus there are natural rewarding consequences for some misbehaviour that have nothing to do with relationships, or parents.

Attention

You can't ignore me!

Some children will misbehave in order to get noticed or become the centre of attention. This factor is often exaggerated and seems to be the favoured explanation of some professionals for children's misbehaviour. This can lead to parents being told to 'just ignore it' on the assumption that the behaviour will stop without the fuel of attention. Sometimes you just can't ignore it and sometimes you definitely *should not* ignore it.

Attention is a more common motivator of misbehaviour in early childhood and is of less importance for most teens. This is not because many of them are not craving attention, but parents are no longer their target audience. Not all badly behaved children crave attention and some teenagers are trying hard not to get attention from adults. There is often also an assumption, usually completely unfounded, that if a child is hungry for attention they must be neglected to some extent. This is like assuming that any child who raids the fridge must be underfed; it's just as likely to be the opposite. Parents have told me that they were instructed to give more attention and that this made the child's behaviour towards them worse. More of the children I deal with have had too much attention rather than too little.

Extroverts tend to crave attention more than introverts. Children who are conscientious and agreeable are likely to have better ways of getting attention than those who are lower on these traits, and so have less desire to misbehave. Some children have virtually unlimited appetites for attention.

Attention seeking can be the result of jealousy, for example distracting parents' attention from a rival child. In blended families there may be attention-seeking due to jealousy of Mum's interest in her new partner, or in her new partner's children.

Power

I'm in control

Children may misbehave because defying adults makes them feel powerful, as can having the adults running around like headless chooks! They also may wish to *disempower* you to gain more freedom. As with attention it would be naïve to assume that they are lacking power because they want more. The opposite may be the case.

I'll teach you!

Revenge

Children who feel angry or wronged, for whatever reason, may deliberately try to upset other family members. Sometimes they feel that everyone is against them and annoying everyone in the family gives them some satisfaction. Some children who are swearing at their parents are quite deliberately trying to hurt them for some real or imagined resentment. It's sad but amusing, that some parents when I ask about consequences say that they explained to the child that it really hurt their feelings when they were called a "f**ing whore!" An honest child would probably reply: "Mum, that's the point! It's meant to hurt you."

I've seen children for whom the idea of revenge was conscious. They may blame Mum for making Dad leave (even if Dad was a violent alcoholic) or blame their carer for the fact that they don't live with their birth mother. They may even be furiously angry that parents failed to protect them from abuse in the past. These are difficult and disturbing situations. More often revenge is a short-term thing often linked to feelings of entitlement.

If you make me, you'll be

Withdrawal

Some children, and a few adults, avoid taking responsibility and avoid being asked to do anything by playing dumb or difficult. If you make enough of a song and dance about doing the dishes they might stop asking you; if you break a plate every now and again this also helps. Many parents do report giving up trying to get children to do any chores, or that they tiptoe round them to avoid unpleasantness. The extreme of withdrawal is a child who spends all his time in his room (or out of the home) and abuses other family members whenever they try to communicate. Withdrawal into cyberspace is becoming more common.

Another form of withdrawal is when the child is trying to push someone away, for example being mean to a step-parent in the hope that they'll leave or making life unbearable for Mum because they hope to go and live with Dad.

You're in my way!

They just want to...

Besides the four reasons above there is a simpler one which is often ignored. It isn't popular with those who like to psychologise and make things complicated. A basic rule of science is that we should look for the simplest explanations first and only get complicated when the simple explanations don't fit. Stealing chocolate may be motivated by a desire for attention or revenge or a power struggle but it

280

may just be that chocolate tastes nice. Besides obvious **material rewards** there may be the rewards of **excitement** or other **pleasure** from the misbehaviour. The act of stealing is exciting for some children, as is fighting. A few children will create a scene or conflict because they are bored. Climbing over the fence, or climbing on the roof, may be defiant but may also just be natural exploration. I used to climb on the roof of our two storey house when I was about eight years old just because it was fun. That sort of behaviour is often seen as deviant nowadays but is really quite normal. As our children are over-protected and kept captive, they may well want to break free because exploring and having adventures is natural.

This actually applies to some of the most serious misbehaviour and problems. There are lots of psychological reasons why kids might initially try drugs but the reason most people take them is because they make you feel good. The same applies to alcohol and sex, and some people really enjoy fighting.

Sometimes it's an image thing

An additional reason some children misbehave, or act aggressively or abusively, is to portray a particular image. They often start smoking because they think it's tough, grown-up and cool. Some see drugs, drinking and sex in a similar way. Some children get into fights to prove how tough they are. Risk-taking and showing disrespect for authority, which can include vandalism, stealing and verbal abuse, can be making a statement to their peers that they are a rebel. I've seen disabled children who would rather be feared than pitied. In our modern world *image* seems to have become more important for many young people and some have a fear of being seen as ordinary. Being 'bad' for some is better than boring.

What makes a child use violence or abuse in their family?

There is a modern liberal notion that people, especially children, are basically good and that violence and abuse must be aberrations. Most professionals talk about children learning to be violent. However, the evidence suggests that young children are often violent without prior exposure. Children do **not** have to learn to be violent; they need to learn **not** to be violent.

Roy Baumeister talks about the 'myth of pure evil' in that people who are seriously violent or abusive are seen as being different to the rest of us. We are all, to greater or lesser extents, capable of being violent or abusive and people who abuse others don't see themselves as doing evil. A great many acts of violence are viewed as moral, or at least as excusable, by their perpetrators[412]. In fact they quite often see themselves as being the victim. There is a general tendency for us to see our own behaviour as being a response to the environment but to see other people's behaviour as being due to them: their personality and attitudes. So you see someone else as being violent because they are a nasty, violent individual, or perhaps a troubled, ill person, whereas *they* think they are being violent because people won't leave them alone. They minimise and excuse their own behaviour. They remember wrongs done to them and tend to forget the wrongs they commit.

"The abuser's behaviour is primarily conscious – he acts deliberately rather than by accident or by losing control of himself – but the underlying thinking that drives his behaviour is largely not conscious." Bancroft[413]

I've borrowed the title of this chapter from Lundy Bancroft's book about abusive men. Here's a long quote where he is talking about men abusing their partners but it applies totally to children (boys or girls) who abuse parents.

"The abuser's mood changes are especially perplexing. He can be a different person from day to day, or even from hour to hour. At times he is aggressive and intimidating, his tone harsh, insults spewing from his mouth, ridicule dripping from him like oil from a drum. When he's in this mode nothing she says seems to have any impact on him, except to make him even angrier. Her side of the argument counts for nothing in his eyes, and everything is her fault. He twists her words around so that she always ends up on the defensive. At other moments he sounds wounded and lost, hungering for love and for someone to take care of him. When this side of him emerges, he appears open and ready to heal. He seems to let down his guard, his hard exterior softens, and he may take on the quality of a hurt child, difficult and frustrating but lovable… The beast that takes him over at other times looks completely unrelated to the tender person she now sees." Bancroft[414]

The simplest answer to *'why do they do it?'*
They do it because they can.
But, luckily, not all children who can do it want to do it.
Any form of abuse can be looked at in terms of several levels of cause and effect[415].

Firstly there has to be **some desire** to do the behaviour. Some people hate violence and even find arguments or any conflict disagreeable. They are unlikely to abuse anyone. Some people are meek, passive or fearful and are hence unlikely to be abusive. On the other hand, there are those who greatly enjoy the excitement of a good argument and some who get a thrill from violence, conflict and risk taking. There is a continuum from those who are highly averse to violence or conflict through to those who will fight or abuse others at the drop of a hat. The bulk of the population probably falls in the middle and will only resort to violence or abuse reluctantly. Besides willingness to act aggressively there are major differences in how much some people want to control others. Those with a high desire to control other people are far more likely to abuse them; this is a bigger factor than levels of anger.

Secondly, many people may feel some urge to be violent, abusive or controlling but they either have empathy for others or have been well socialised not to act that way. Clearly this is not only different for different individuals but varies greatly by culture, age group, peer group, maturity level, etc. They need to overcome internal restraints to act abusively. If we are speaking of murder and rape then (hopefully) the internal restraints will be pretty strong, but if we are talking about pushing someone aside or calling them an imbecile, the restraints may be small to non-existent. Most children used to hesitate before swearing in the presence of adults but many no longer feel such inhibition. It thus becomes easier for them to swear *at* an adult. Some early adolescent girls appear to have recently become far less troubled by the 'unfeminine' nature of violence than their predecessors where. The chivalrous idea that boys and men should not hit girls or women is weaker in some quarters and in recent years I've had a few adolescent boys argue that the idea that they should not hit girls is sexist.

Thirdly there are social, legal and practical restraints on violence and abuse. You may not have a conscience about breaking the speed limit (few people do) but if there are speed cameras and fines, these consequences will probably control your speeding. You may really want to slap your boss's face, but losing your job and being charged with assault are good disincentives for most people. Some children would never abuse a teacher because they don't want to be suspended or expelled (for others being suspended is a reward). However, they know Mum won't expel them so can use this behaviour at home to get their own way with minor or no consequences.

Sometimes the process of overcoming internal inhibition to violence is a deliberate one. Some men get drunk so they can act violently. People psych themselves up to be violent by denigrating their victim. Once someone has acted abusively, especially if there are no meaningful consequences, it becomes increasingly easy for them to overcome their inhibitions in the future. People often stop feeling empathy for their regular victims.

Someone may want to act abusively, not have sufficient internal inhibitions to stop them yet they still don't act abusively because the other person is likely to fight back, impose meaningful consequences, or there is some other form of social control. Children seldom fight each other in front of teachers (though this is becoming more common). Some children will abuse their mothers only when dad or step-dad is not at home. Very few children will abuse their parents in front of grandparents (though this is also becoming more common). Being bigger and stronger than the other person obviously makes acting aggressively much easier. This is partly why violence to parents gets worse with puberty. However, physical size is only important if there is some risk of retaliation. If a child knows that a parent will never be violent, even in self-defence, then size doesn't really matter very much, which is why some girls attack fathers who are far bigger and stronger than them.

So to summarise: how often someone feels like being violent or abusive varies greatly with personality and environmental factors. Anger, or a desire to control others, does not necessarily lead to violence. The angry person must also overcome his empathy for the other person. Rage can act to lessen empathy and someone may feel normal empathy, except when in a rage. Finally, and very importantly, there is a judgment made about whether or not they can get away with it – is the other person going to retaliate or impose meaningful consequences?

This way of looking at violence sees violence as a semi-rational (though misguided and/or immoral) act rather than as crazy behaviour. The assumption that the behaviour is a symptom of some kind of pathology is seldom helpful. It confuses parents and leads to pessimism and moral confusion. The pathology approach lends itself to excuses. There are no excuses for violence or abuse!

Pathology View of Violence	Responsibility View of Violence
Violence is a symptom	Violence **is** the problem
Violent person is really a victim	Violent person is acting as an abuser (but often sees himself as being a victim)
They are out of control	They are trying to control others
It stems from irrational, uncontrollable anger	Anger is only a small part of the problem and it stems from attitudes and habits
Violent person has low self-esteem	Violent people are often arrogant, though they may also be insecure
Expectation that the violent person has been exposed to violence	Everyone is exposed to some violence, greater exposure increases risk, but is not an essential condition
Violence is a response to being powerless	Violence is a desire for *more* power (so abusers often feel powerless)
Violence is caused by stress, substance use, lack of assertiveness, poor communication	Stress never *causes* violence, substance use exacerbates existing problems; aggressors are often highly assertive and good communicators.
Anger management or supportive therapy needed	Change the consequences of violence, and/or encourage them to take responsibility
This view increases sympathy for aggressor and may disempower others	This view increases the assertiveness of those dealing with aggressor
Aggressor can use lots of excuses	There is **no** excuse for violence
Victim assumed to play a part in the violence and is often blamed (especially parents)	Strongly opposed to blaming victims
Popular approach for psychiatry and child welfare	Pro-feminists take this approach to DV, but it's rarely taken when a young person is the aggressor
Parents are the problem (even when the aggressor is an adult)	Parents are often the solution when the aggressor is a child

The table above compares the Pathology view of violence with the Individual responsibility view. This may help you make sense of what some professionals are saying about your child's violence and clarify how you are thinking about it. I'm not saying that the first approach is always wrong or never helpful, but it needs to be balanced with a responsibility view.

Start Box

Cale

Hi Eddie,

My son's psychologist has just emailed me the link for your site and I am so glad he did. I am a single parent with five young sons and am at my wits end with one of my sons, the eldest. Life is very difficult; I am exhausted both mentally and emotionally and to the point where I feel like a failure. I am very tolerant and have a lot of patience but I do not know how much longer that will last, the bouts of abuse towards me is absolutely breaking my heart.

So much of what you said made sense and I was somewhat relieved to know that I'm not alone in this. I suppose I should give you a brief outline about Cale, I say brief because in his eleven short years of life he has a massive history. To include everything would mean I would sit for the next year writing a novel for you to read, quite literally.

Cale was born with a severe congenital heart condition requiring immediate medical intervention and open heart surgery. Over the next nine years he had five more open heart surgeries, many tests and invasive procedures as well as medications. As he got older, there was a short period after each surgery or procedure where he would display some anger, however it wouldn't last long.

Skipping forward to 2011.... A series of traumatic events occurred in a very short period of time for Cale. His great grandparents live with us and in 2011 his beloved Poppy passed away (this was also my birthday and for about two weeks I hit a point where I couldn't cope). Then Cale was admitted to hospital due to an infection causing his body to kill his red blood cells. From then until early 2012 his life was a series of hospital admissions and pain. Two days before Easter we were sent to Perth for him to have another cardiac catheterisation. Cale was very upset at this time because it was the first Easter without Pop and we were 1000km from home. The results we were given were heart breaking, Cale was dying. We could take him home and enjoy the time we had left or perform a surgery that he probably wouldn't survive. He did survive. It was a success.

It was November 2012 when Cale started terrible screaming episodes. Then it escalated to breaking things/kicking and hitting walls and finally has escalated to the point that we are at now, when he can't get his own way he physically and verbally targets me. He does it to his brothers a lot also but I'm the prime focus.

Whenever he doesn't want to do what he's told to, it erupts in a massive yelling episode and within minutes he lays into me. This goes from slapping, pinching, punching and kicking me to biting and using objects to hit me. I have to keep the other boys safe, but due to doctors concerns (he is on warfarin to thin the blood) I cannot simply lock him in his bedroom; this means I am the barricade between him and the rest of the house. I can sit for up to four hours in his doorway while he slaps, pinches, punches, kicks and bites me, if there is anything in his room that he can lift, he will use it as a weapon on me. If I move, allowing him into the rest of the house he will get anything he can (including knives) to use on me or his brothers. He has picked up his two-yr-old brother and thrown him against a wall. He pinches and bites my two-yr-old and hits him if I do not barricade him in his room, he also lays into his five yr-old brother in much the same manner. With his nine year-old brother, Cale waits until he is asleep then lays into him also. He eventually gets to a point where he does a total flip and then gets overly affectionate. He clings to me cuddling me, kissing me and telling me how much he loves me and how sorry he is and he will never do it again, by this point I'm so totally exhausted from him that I just want to be away from him for a few minutes (yes as a mother it's terrible to say). He, at that point, insists that I make him do it, it's my own fault and I cause him to hit and hurt me. Two questions I'm sure you'd be thinking, first, what makes him do it? It's simple, I tell him to go to bed. 8:30pm is bedtime for all of them, Cale believes that it's an inappropriate bedtime and I'm being unfair. After insisting he go to bed he gets angry and violent. School is the other set-off, if I insist he is to go to school then I cop it again. I've dropped back on the school bit, after speaking with his psychologist and school it's not a fight worth having. If he chooses to go to school, he goes, if he chooses to stay home, then I don't reorganise my day around him. If he stays home then he is packed a lunch like the other boys, he is only allowed to eat whatever is in that lunchbox for the entire day. I remove the aerial from the TV and turn off the Internet, the idea in this is to make it as boring as possible so that school seems fun. It's worked so far. Three times now he has given in by 9:30am and walked himself off to school. (I leave at 8:30am, if he is not ready to go by then, then I refuse to make a special trip for him plus it's only around the corner, five minute walk), this has also come about because the school have said that they can't stop him running away, which he does quite often. If you pursue him he seems to panic and loses all road sense, just last week he was nearly hit by two cars as he ran randomly across four lanes of traffic. I cannot use the same method at bed time, I have four other little lemmings that follow suit, if I say 'ok I'm not fighting you on this' he sits on the couch on the lounge room, his four brothers then do the same because 'Cale does it and you don't make him go to bed'. My children all get irritable and oversensitive with lack of sleep.

The second question you probably have is how do I react to his violence against me? Easy, I don't. I just sit and defend myself by either crossing my arms in front of my face or gently push him off me. I will sometimes lead or carry him back to his bed, but I do not hit him back. I do not yell at him, it exhausts me faster and my tolerance drops. Last week was the first time I reacted, he was pinning me to a chair and pinching the inside of my arm between my wrist and elbow. I twisted my arm and pinched him back, in the same place, quickly. I didn't hold on as long as him and pinched him quickly two more times. He is unlike normal children. A slight pinch leaves a big bruise due to how thin his blood is. After a painful slap across my face and him saying 'see what you make me do', I went back to my barricade stance of ignoring mostly all the blows for another three and a half hours until I rang my mum's husband to pick him up, by then it was 1a.m. After that it was advised that I arrange for him to stay elsewhere for a week to give both him and I a break. This isn't an ideal arrangement to use a lot because there he has three adults and is the centre of attention; it always leads to an even bigger explosion when he comes home because all of a sudden he has to share adult attention again. Out of all my boys, Cale gets the most attention from me, both positive and negative. Cale and I both share a love of ancient civilisations, we spend a lot of time together reading or Googling this. However the minute I try to do anything at all with the other boys, Cale demands more time with me.

Cale's mind frame is 'I'm going to die anyway so why waste my time on school work and following rules', which is mostly true however no one can say how long he will live. There is a very real chance that he will in fact live to early adulthood.

I'm losing hope that this is ever going to turn around and I am going to be in an abusive relationship with my son until he eventually moves out. This is affecting my family badly, Nan says she is moving out, she can't take any more, my younger three sons' father is demanding I send the boys to live with him safe from the violence and I'm stuck trying my best but failing miserably.

I'm a private person, I don't ask for help, I don't like to and now I'm to the point where I have had to ask for help, before I crash and burn

I'm sorry that this email is so long, I didn't see the sense of telling half the story.

Thank you for your website and making me feel normal instead of a failure of a mother.

Follow-up e-mail, 2 months later:
I'm happy to update that we have virtually eliminated the violence and damage he was doing to both our home and siblings' belongings. In the last month we have had only one episode that I would class as extreme.

On the other hand, the decision was made to remove him from school and begin home schooling from next term with the aim of re-enrolling Cale into mainstream school in term four or at latest the beginning of next year.

The pocket money system I've been working on has worked wonders. Out of twenty days this month he has managed to achieve $16. I'm finally feeling in control, still a long way to go, many other things to tackle but so far so good.

Comment:
To me this shows that big problems don't necessarily have to have big solutions. I would never have expected that a child with Cale's huge burden of issues would respond so well and so quickly to more predictable consequences. Some workers would (understandably) feel overwhelmed by such a case and since we feel such sympathy for Cale, some would be loath to suggest consequences.

End Box

Acceptable and Unacceptable Behaviours

Exercise: List your child's behaviour under the following headings

We start with the positives. Hopefully you can find some!

Positive, co-operative, considerate or sensible behaviour:
What does your child do that is worth encouraging?

Intolerable behaviour
What does your child do that is abusive, seriously destructive or self-destructive?
*Needs immediate action and should have **some** consequence for your child.*

Other highly undesirable behaviour
What does your child do that affects other family members but is not actually abusive? Includes longer term self-destructive behaviour or behaviour affecting their future (e.g. not attending school)

Irritating or undesirable behaviour that could be ignored for now
What does your child do that can be ignored for now? E.g. doesn't complete homework; uses an annoying tone of voice; generally impolite; doesn't care about appearance or cleanliness. Although you may want to influence these behaviours you could let the child take responsibility for them or ignore them until more serious behaviour is under control.

If your child is often behaving in an "Intolerable" way you may have to prioritise and ignore some of the other undesirable behaviours, at least for a while. Choose your battles.

Swearing

My son picked up the word 'smeg' as a swear word from a T.V. comedy show ("Red Dwarf"). Although it may be derived from 'smegma' (an oily secretion in the folds of the skin, especially under the foreskin) it doesn't actually mean anything (and there is an Italian company making fridges etc. under this name). I thought this was harmless and ignored it until one day he told me to 'smeg-off'. Technically 'smeg-off' doesn't mean anything, as he tried to argue, but the intention was abundantly clear. What is often important with any form of abusive behaviour is not the result but the intention. Bright kids will argue that swear words themselves are meaningless and some parents are confused by this argument. However, the intention of swearing **at** someone (and sometimes even of swearing in front of someone) is often to display contempt, derision and a lack of respect. Even if there is an element of humour, there can still be an important element of disrespect, which as parents we ignore at our peril.

What counts as swearing in your home is up to you. When I moved to Australia from the UK I used the word 'bullshit' in meetings (to mean 'rubbish' not as an insult to anyone). This was not considered swearing back in Britain but it was in Australia. Working in a bureaucratic organization and not using the word 'bullshit' was difficult. I was told off recently by a twelve-year-old for saying that it was 'bloody cold' in Scotland. On the other hand Aussies use the words 'bugger' and 'bastard' as terms of endearment! They certainly don't think of the dictionary meaning of 'bugger' when they affectionately call someone 'you old bugger' (at least I hope they don't!). If you find something offensive in your home then you have a perfect right to ban your kids from using it. On the other hand if you go overboard and ban slang or *all* insults, you are unlikely to win the battle as your kids will be convinced that you are overly idealistic and out of touch with reality (and they may have a point). This is like schools who claim they have zero tolerance for teasing: it's just not possible in the real world to have zero tolerance for disrespect or bad language.

If you have a partner, try to agree between yourselves what is acceptable and what is not acceptable. It's highly unlikely that you will both have exactly the same standards (males and females often have different views on swearing, though the gap is narrowing) so be tolerant of the other parent's viewpoint and try to back each other up. If either parent finds something offensive then that word may be considered swearing. If you are a sole parent it may be useful to discuss this with someone else. You don't want to seem out-of-touch but you also don't want your children feeling able to swear at you without you knowing what it means (this can sometimes be tricky for immigrant parents whose children speak better English than they do). Calling someone an 'evodobe' or a 'spronklet' is still rude if the other person doesn't know what these words mean, so don't let your kids swear at you even if they do it in Swahili or Klingon.

Once you are reasonably clear about which words are acceptable to you, and which are not, you need also to be clear about whether the problem behaviour is merely swearing or whether it's swearing **at** someone, which is a form of verbal abuse. You may choose to ignore your children swearing among themselves, or to themselves, but I **strongly** advise you not to ignore them swearing at you! Most people nowadays would agree that "Oh f**k!" when you hit your thumb with a hammer is not such a big deal. "Effin' bitch!" said to a mother **is** a big deal, a very big deal! If children get away with swearing at you, or putting you down, they will lose more and more respect hence disrespect escalates over time. The same applies if your children are hearing you treated in such a way by a partner or an older brother or sister (or even by your parents). If you put up with abuse you will lose their respect.

If you are trying to parent a beyond control child, your reaction may be "Of course I don't like him swearing at me, but I'm powerless to stop it!" Your attitude to your child's behaviour is important even if you can't, in the short term, make them behave as you would like. It's **very** important that you are clear about your rights and about what you are willing to tolerate. Ignoring *any* form of abuse is not a good idea.

Unfortunately I sometimes hear parents say that workers have advised them to ignore their child swearing. If this is swearing among themselves or at the computer, then it *may* occasionally be sensible to prioritise in this way, especially if parents swear. However, if they are swearing *at* you then this is very dangerous advice which you should either ignore or challenge.

Even some well-meaning parenting books show confusion about letting children express their feelings and letting them show disrespect. For example, from a book rather ironically called *'Who's the Boss?'*: *"If he says, 'You're a dope,' avoid taking this 'insult' personally; instead, help him understand the situation... help him express his feelings clearly..."*[416] You don't have to take it 'personally' in terms of being upset by it, but it *is* an insult and you should nip such disrespect in the bud. He is expressing his feelings pretty clearly, it just isn't acceptable. It's probably not a problem with communication (it's quite often bright, articulate children who talk like this) but a problem with respect.

A note on lying, stealing and denying

Some (certainly not all) of these beyond control kids are rather devious, manipulative and street-smart. Some would make great lawyers and can argue their way out of anything. Parents are sometimes rendered powerless by not being able to prove things.

Typical examples:
- There's $20 missing from Mum's purse but no proof who took it.
- A hole has appeared in the lounge room wall but no one admits to kicking it.
- You are 90% sure that your son is lying but there is a tiny element of doubt.

Many of the parents who are abused by their children are very fair and honourable. They feel it would be unfair to accuse their prodigal son if there is a tiny chance that he is innocent. They may, at the same time, be afraid to challenge him as there is a risk of an explosion and you know he'll accuse you of bias and will play the victim.

Here's how I suggest you think about this issue:

In a criminal court, guilt has to be established *"beyond reasonable doubt"*. If there is reasonable doubt about the charges then the court is supposed to find the accused 'not guilty' (in Scotland they sensibly have a 'not proven' verdict). The principle is that it's better for several guilty men to walk free than for one innocent man to be convicted, very admirable (in theory). However, unlike Criminal Courts,

Children's Courts and Family Courts make decisions *'on the balance of probability'*. If there is a greater than fifty percent chance that a child might be harmed then they can take action. In reality we can't calculate the odds so it's all rather vague, but the principle makes sense.

You are a family, dealing with children (of any age) so you should use the standard of proof of the Family and Children's court, not the criminal court. Let the **balance of probabilities** be your guide. You do **not** have to prove things "*beyond reasonable doubt*", which is often impossible. Also in criminal court the fact that someone has been accused, or charged before, may not be admissible evidence; in a family it's admissible. So if your son or daughter has stolen or lied a number of times in the past and you are 60% sure they are guilty this time, you should take action, despite their protests of innocence; if your son has been caught lying to you a number of times then it's up to him to prove he is telling the truth. If your daughter has stolen within the home on several occasions, and (as far as you know) your other children haven't, then tell her that you are going to *assume* that anything that goes missing has been taken by her. She will protest that this is unfair. Don't disagree. Admit that at times it will be unfair and any child with a bad reputation occasionally gets wrongly accused. However, it's even *more* unfair that they can steal from the family without any consequences. If they give up stealing then they can get rid of the reputation and regain trust over a period of time.

Teenagers regularly bemoan the fact that their parents don't trust them. You might want to tell them that trust has to be earned, or even, 'Of course not, you're a teenager.'

Stealing

Stealing is an example of an unacceptable behaviour that can be considered abusive but is not violent. It's not uncommon for children who are abusive to parents to also steal from them and other people.

Stealing can be a semi-compulsive behaviour that may or may not go with other forms of abuse. There are a number of common characteristics in a child who abuses their parents and one who steals: -

- high sense of entitlement,
- low responsibility,
- lack of respect for adults,
- impulsive or craving excitement,
- relatively fearless.

A very different category of children are those who have been abused or neglected who may steal for more complex reasons. Certainly not all children who steal are abusive to parents and not all children who abuse parents steal from them.

When I work with children who steal (especially if it's not part of a pattern of abusing a parent) I treat it as if it's a bad habit. I may talk to kids about the efforts they've made to break the habit, about how easy or difficult it will be to break the habit, and we discuss the pros and cons of stealing. I start with a brainstorm of the 'pros'. Talking openly about the advantages of stealing seems pretty weird to many adults and some kids.

Many adults react to children stealing with shock and horror and may say things like, "You don't need to steal!" "That's crazy behaviour!" "You'll end up in prison!" "You'll ruin your life!" "How could you be so immoral?" Children may react to such an approach by shutting off and not listening. Others begin to believe that it's 'crazy' behaviour and that they therefore can't help it and aren't morally responsible. Emphasising the craziness of any behaviour can encourage them to take less personal responsibility for it (this is also true of violence, drug taking, cutting, etc.).

Here's a typical list by a twelve-year-old boy of his reasons for stealing [with my notes in brackets]:

1. *I get stuff* [often they'll admit that they have taken far more than their parents realise, other times they hardly ever, or never, get to keep the things they steal but possessing them temporarily can still be rewarding]
2. *I enjoy the excitement of sneaking about and taking things* [it's a bit of a game for some thrill-seeking kids, and if it's within the family it's fairly safe for them]
3. *I feel like I'm outsmarting the adults* [again it's a sort of a game, but it's also about feeling powerful]
4. *I get revenge* [the motivation to hurt the victim can be quite similar to their desire to verbally or physically abuse]

Once it becomes an established habit it becomes easier for them to steal things than to resist the temptation. If the first of the above is the main motivator (as it is with some young people), they may not really have a stealing habit, they are just mercenary and opportunistic. The lack of consequences is crucial to these children. If it's more of a compulsive habit then consequences alone may not stop the behaviour *quickly* for the simple reason that the reward is immediate and definite but the punishment is delayed and inconsistent (because they don't get caught every time). This is why it's so important that there are some consequences even when you don't have proof. The *severity* of the punishment matters little but the *likelihood* of punishment is very important. So you need to start catching them as often, and as quickly, as possible, but consequences must be small enough to be meaningfully applied each time. If you remove all privileges they have no incentive not to steal.

Why the child started the habit may not be of any importance in curing it. Habits have a way of self-perpetuating themselves once established and the initial cause may become irrelevant. So if a child started stealing at a time when they were feeling insecure, upset and unloved, but is still stealing a few years later, discussing the feelings that led to the initial behaviour may be worthwhile but is not likely to have any effect on the habit. It's possible that stealing is a symptom of a deeper psychological disturbance, but usually it's not. Lots of children steal at some point while growing up and whether it becomes an entrenched behaviour or gets stamped out quickly may be just luck. If the child is lucky enough to get caught soon, and it's taken seriously, the behaviour may stop abruptly.

When I get these children to list the bad things about stealing they often come up with quite dramatic lists. Here's the same twelve-year-old:

1. *I feel sort of bad about myself*
2. *People don't trust me*
3. *I don't like being seen as a thief*
4. *My parents are angry*
5. *I get punished*
6. *I think I will end up in jail*

Children often think that the long-term consequences of their stealing are far worse than the reality; children who shoplift or steal small amounts from home or school do not go to jail. This demonstrates that making dire threats about them being doomed in the future is seldom helpful.

On occasions, just one or two counselling sessions have made a big difference. By acknowledging the positives of stealing they are able to balance the pros and cons and this helps motivate many children. It's a good thing that adolescents are changing anyway and changes in behaviour are more likely to be permanent than they are for an adult with a problem behaviour.

Take stealing seriously. If your child has a stealing habit you need to be firm about it even if the amounts are trivial. It's irrelevant whether you can afford to lose your small change or not. A child who is stealing cents is still reinforcing the habit even though you may feel that it could be a lot worse. It might get a lot worse if you ignore it.

Rewards for stopping

It would be wrong to pay, or regularly reward, someone for doing what is a normal expectation. However, an exceptional reward can act as an incentive to help break a habit. For example, especially for a younger adolescent, something like: "If you can go a whole week without taking anything at all that doesn't belong to you we will go to the pictures together." Actually paying money as a reward to not steal is probably not a good idea and it's very important that this is clearly not something they can expect in the future. Strange as it sounds, sometimes receiving a reward for changing behaviour is a face-saving device for the young person. The reward gives them a justification for changing.

Tests

If a child appears to have some motivation to stop stealing I sometimes get parents to agree to set 'traps' for him over the next month or so (by leaving small amounts of money lying around, recording serial numbers or marking notes). Parents sometimes don't get round to actually doing this but their child's belief that it will happen can help break the habit.

Locking things up

In an ideal world we would be able to control our children without having to put locks on doors, hide our wallets, or buy a safe. Although it's definitely better to use consequences, and they should be tried first, in reality there are parents who have been forced to lock up their home from their own child. Though second best this is better than letting the child continue to practice their stealing habit (quite apart from the financial and emotional cost for you).

What behaviours to attempt to change?

"I wasn't asking for anything more than common courtesy. Or should I say, demanding it." Rubin[417]

Don't try to change everything: this will be too confusing, too difficult and much too negative.

There is a danger that, having decided to make changes (and perhaps being motivated by the previous chapters) you are going to be too gung-ho in your approach. Some children have a spectacular array of unacceptable behaviours. He may regularly treat you and other adults with disrespect, he may take things without asking, expect you to act like a servant, refuse to do any chores, speak in a horrible condescending tone of voice, not bother making eye contact or looking up from the T.V., leave his room in a mess, beat up his little brother, smoke and drink and swear continually. None of these would be *acceptable* in an ideal world but if you decide to change **all** of them at once you are declaring war. Don't declare war unless you are really willing for him or her to leave home. If that is an acceptable outcome then you may be justified in provoking a crisis (see chapter on Leaving Home). However, generally speaking, war within a family is a civil war; no one wins and they are not very 'civil'!

Prioritise – which behaviours to concentrate on first?

When trying to regain control it's important to **prioritise** and aim at a small number of goals at a time. If he is swearing *and* using an irritating tone of voice it's usually better to concentrate on the swearing and ignore the tone of voice for now. Sometimes the tone of voice will sort itself out. The chances are he is unaware of his tone of voice and probably feels 'got-at' when you go on about his disrespectful attitude.

Forget about "attitude" and concentrate on behaviour.

Try to distinguish between what is **desirable** and what is an **essential** requirement.

A violence free home is an **essential** demand. A loving home is certainly desirable but you can't demand it.

It would be nice if your child showed some appreciation but that is *desirable* not *essential* (it may be a pipe dream till they are a lot older). Not being abusive **is** essential. The following table gives some more examples (though age will affect some of them).

Essential demands	Desirable
Non-violence	Affection
Not swearing at you	Using a civil tone of voice
Basic respect for your human dignity	Respect for you as a superior
Respecting your privacy	Showing appreciation
Not having drugs in the home	Not using drugs at all
Going to school (up to leaving age)	Doing schoolwork or homework
Not stealing from you	Not wasting their own money
Not destroying property	Taking good care of property
Minimum standards of hygiene	Taking a pride in their appearance
Answering when spoken to	Talking to you
Not letting friends abuse your home	Having decent friends
Not hurting brothers and sisters	Playing with brothers and sisters
Coming home at night unless permission given to stay out	Keeping you informed of their whereabouts when they are out

Things in the essential column *should have* some consequences (even if there are no *logical* consequences). Breaking these social rules is **intolerable**. Generally when dealing with a very difficult or beyond-control young person, those things which are merely desirable, even if quite serious and highly desirable, should not be subject to consequences unless these are 'natural consequences'.

With some beyond-control older youth, parents at times have to make some sad choices. If you have a seventeen-year-old child who is using drugs there may be little you can do about it no matter how much you detest the idea or how worried you are about them. However, if they are becoming abusive, bringing illegal drugs into your home, dealing from your home, involving younger children in their drug use in any way, or stealing money to feed their habit, then they have clearly begun to seriously infringe on others' rights and this is *intolerable* and not just very, very undesirable [see section on drugs].

As parents our gut reaction is that a teenager using illegal drugs is intolerable. But many parents find that the reality is that they cannot control this and ultimately their love and responsibility force them to tolerate it rather than abandon their child. More than two thirds of young people nowadays will try some illegal drug during their teenage years. For the majority, this does not become a habit or interfere with their lives in any major way.

It's not always the most serious behaviours that we need to concentrate on first.

There are a number of things to take into account when deciding what to change first:

o   Level of danger
o   Effect on other children
o   Parental stress levels
o   Child's social and emotional wellbeing,
o   How united are parents in wanting to change this behaviour?

o How easy or difficult might it be to change?

o Is it *really* important to you or is it really their business?

Try to clearly define the unacceptable behaviours

Behaviours need to be clearly defined if you are going to impose consequences in a consistent manner and if parents are going to be working as a team. Using swearing again as an example, parents need to clearly agree what *they* mean by swearing and make this clear to the child. If you decide to only concentrate on the 'f' word this is fine but damns and bloodies may increase. This is not necessarily a problem if you have the patience to work through the list one word at a time. It's a problem if they move up the list and begin calling you a c**t instead of a f**kwit. It will usually be more efficient to work on a short list of clearly defined swearwords. If a child decides to say an alternative 'f' word such as "fish" or "ferrets" instead, then this is progress and is weakening the habit, even though they may feel they are outsmarting you. If they are saying "oh fish" under their breath you can probably continue to ignore this but if they are angrily telling you to "fish off!" this quite is a different matter.

Often what really annoys adults is the child's 'attitude', which may be shown by his tone of voice, sneering expression, turning his back on you while you are talking to him, etc. Children are often unaware of their tone of voice and a punishment based on this is likely to be seen as grossly unfair.

It's *usually* wrong to punish a child for his tone of voice but it may be possible to have logical consequences such as: "I choose not to be helpful to anyone who is speaking to me in such an unpleasant way." You may have to tape record your child and point out what you mean. Unfortunately, many parents have tried aping their child's behaviour to show how they are talking to them. This is unlikely to work unless you are a brilliant mimic as they don't identify the way you will sound with the way they sound to themselves. It's not just young people who are often unaware of their manner and tone of voice. We as adults can sound irritated or aggressive without always being aware of it.

Drawing a line

By coincidence both of these families first visited me on the same morning. I'd met one of the mothers before but neither of the teenage boys.

John is a large, stocky 17-year-old lad with a mild to moderate intellectual disability. He is quite definitely disabled and very difficult to manage for his parents or for the teachers in the special school he attends. He frequently punches both his mother and father. His mother is herself a welfare worker and clearly an unusually patient and caring individual. His father is strong enough to restrain him but there is no way his mother could do so. John has also been violent at school on occasions to both staff and pupils. Despite his clear disability and strength, he has never badly injured anyone. When I asked about this his mother said she was good at dodging. I told her I did not believe that there were no opportunities for John to do her real harm if he wanted to. This showed that he had some self-control. What was still more interesting was that he had never once hit his younger sister (aged nine). His mother's response when I expressed my surprise was, "He knows I wouldn't let him get away with that. That's just not acceptable!" I asked when hitting your mother had become acceptable.

An hour later the same day I met Shawn, only thirteen but built like a rugby player and not only taller but twice the width of his petite mother. Shawn is average intelligence and definitely not disabled. He is violent to classmates, verbally abuses teachers, and is violent to his brother and sister. His mother is distressed by his constant bullying of his brother and sister, and doesn't know how to control this. Shawn seemed a likable lad and admitted, a little sheepishly, that he was "a bit of a bully'. His mother seemed surprised that I asked if he had ever hit or sworn at her. "No way!" she said. "That's not acceptable!"

These aren't isolated cases but it was weird that they arrived only hours apart. The first mother tolerated violence towards herself but drew a definite line at violence towards her daughter. The second mother felt powerless to stop violence between siblings but she firmly drew a line about violence or verbal abuse towards her.

Another troubled woman (not the same day, or even same year) was highly neurotic, had low self-esteem, was generally lacking in assertiveness and claimed she had no control at all over her fifteen-year-old son. He had wild tantrums, had pushed and jostled her, destroyed property on a fairly regular basis and was completely refusing to attend school. Yet, though he physically intimidated her, she was adamant that he would never swear at her, and he never had.

It's quite remarkable how these children have responded to parents being clear about what they will and will not accept, apparently without conscious thought or having clearly tested the limits. These mothers could not say how they had somehow conveyed what was not tolerated in their home.

Although some children respond to such limits, others don't and once a line is crossed it's not often easy redrawing it. Deciding you will not tolerate abuse is an important first step but doesn't usually produce a quick fix. Just occasionally, however, it does.

Change can sometimes be fast

The following is an extract from an e-mail I received a week after just one counselling session (plus handouts) with Peta, the mother of fifteen-year-old Sally. Peta had presented with both arms covered with scars from scratch marks inflicted by her daughter in a number of recent attacks by her daughter. Scratching was her response to not getting her own way. Peta, when I first met her, was concerned that there was some form of underlying mental illness causing her daughter to behave violently.

"All is good!!! This standing firm is GREAT!!!! I wanted tonight to just talk with her so asked her if she wanted to and she said yes. She apologised for her language voluntarily this morning and last night so I could see somewhat of a change. Also, I reassured her that I loved her but drew a clear line between what is her responsibility and what is mine i.e. making her lunch and she accepted it. Early days yet, but much better than I have ever felt. I didn't have that scared, powerless feeling that I have lived with for years. Sally also informed me that she is not moving out and is quite happy to see you and wants to move forward. Boy, I can't

believe that this is so simple. Fear is such a liar! After so many years of dysfunction to feel this way is wonderful."

Although many difficult kids will escalate or dig their heels in when parents try to regain control, a few respond positively to their parents being more assertive. As the above shows, sometimes even long-standing problems can be resolved fairly quickly.

This also illustrates how dangerous a pathology model can be, where the child's behaviour is seen as evidence of some kind of mental condition. If Sally had been assessed and labelled with some condition such as "Oppositional Defiant Disorder", "Intermittent explosive disorder", "Bi-polar" (quite likely in some parts of the USA) or even some form of personality disorder, no one would expect a speedy outcome and it's even possible that Sally's mother would become less assertive and assume that Sally couldn't help it.

In fact Sally didn't keep it up, and a few months later was again violent towards her mother. Since her mother was now quite clear that Sally *could* control her behaviour if she chose to, and wasn't suffering from some form of mental disorder, she now took out a legal restraining order. Sally continued to improve despite a few minor relapses and a year later there is no abuse and an excellent relationship between mother and daughter.

In my experience even children who do have a real condition, such as definite ADHD, Asperger's Syndrome or a mild Intellectual Disability can also sometimes respond just as quickly as Sally, yet the common, and dangerous, assumption is that they can't help it!

With adults who are violent or abusive, change is less likely to be speedy than with adolescents. In addition, with adult abusers when change does happen quickly, they relapse more often. I have many times seen teenagers change dramatically and maintain the changes. Adolescents, and their brains, are maturing quickly and can change overnight. This can be for good or ill. On average, in the long term, more of the changes of adolescence are positive than negative. This may seem a surprising idea given how obnoxious some adolescents can be and how much we hear about their violence, sexual promiscuity, drug-taking, and irresponsibility in general. However, by the end of the teenage years there has been a marked reduction in violence, crime, bullying, etc. and a big improvement in empathy and responsibility. By late adolescence we see more serious mental health problems because these are more common among adults than among children or adolescents. Problems like sexual promiscuity and drink and drug-taking are also moving towards adult patterns of behaviour and, for good or ill.

It makes sense to err on the side of optimism even though **too much** optimism can be dangerous.

Start Box

Bill

George and Hazel were caring parents who would stand by their children regardless. Their son, Bill, fifteen, suffered from a potentially fatal condition which required frequent medical treatment. He was generally brave and seemed philosophical about this and had some good friends with the same condition. Unfortunately he had watched several of these friends die over the past few years. In his teens he became self-destructive and began flirting with crime and drugs. He had actually said to his mother recently, "I'm not going to kill myself but if someone else does it for me, then so be it!" He had given up caring if he lived or died and didn't imagine he had a future. In such a situation parents have virtually no power of any kind and the sense of sadness and frustration hang heavily on both parents. They had been willing to stand by their son despite the fact that he had assaulted both of them a number of times. They were far more focused on their son's welfare than their own. However, they had been coming to the obvious conclusion that Bill was putting himself at great risk by his behaviour and letting him use them as a punching bag – literally – was increasing the risk rather than reducing it.

After a few sessions of the *Who's in Charge?* group, they decided to start imposing some consequences for his outrageous behaviour. Rather than accept these (quite reasonable) punishments Bill attacked his father, punching and kicking him. In the past George had taken it and had never retaliated, showing an unusual (possibly unhealthy) amount of patience fuelled by illogical guilt over Bill's genetic condition. This time George sat on his son and Bill then bit George numerous times on his arm. George was covered with bruises and in the course of the struggle Bill sustained a bruise to his cheek. Rather than praising the courage and patience of this loving father, Protective services said that Bill could no longer live at home as his parents could not protect him. This greatly at risk young boy was put at **far** greater risk by being separated for several months from his devoted, long suffering, family. In the hostel where he was placed he met a boy with worse criminal behaviour and they stole several cars, putting their lives (and others) in danger. Bill was also introduced to sniffing glue. George and Hazel were devastated and felt that they were being further undermined by the legal and welfare system. Luckily, the courts overruled Protective services and Bill returned home. There were many more dramas but George and Hazel stuck to their position and refused to be abused. Next time Bill was violent to George they charged him with assault. Things slowly improved and Bill stopped being violent, started an apprenticeship and fell in love. He now deeply regrets abusing the parents who love him so much. Bill is almost as angry towards Protective Services as his parents are. His life still hangs in the balance but he is now determined to make the most of it and has nothing but praise for his long-suffering parents.

End Box
Abusive Behaviour Questionnaire

The following questions are about abusive behaviour that you, or your partner, have experienced from your child or young person.

You may want to answer each question by marking a number 0 to 5 to indicate how frequently they did these things in the last **three months** (or the last three months that you were together if they are not at home). But there is really little point in then adding up the scores and I'm not going to give averages or grades of awfulness based on them. This is because even one of these can be enough to make life highly stressful and may indicate a child who is already beyond your control or at risk of becoming so. If you have a partner or a close support in your parenting, you might want to compare notes. Sometimes two parents living in the same home see things quite differently.

0 **Never**
1 **Once or twice**
2 **Occasionally**
3 **Often**
4 **Very often**

Physical violence
Child used a weapon against parent 0 1 2 3 4
Child has punched or kicked parent 0 1 2 3 4
Child has slapped parent 0 1 2 3 4
Child pushed or grabbed parent 0 1 2 3 4
Child threw things at parent 0 1 2 3 4
Child used other force against parent 0 1 2 3 4

Threats
Child verbally threatened violence 0 1 2 3 4
Threatened with fist or hand 0 1 2 3 4
Stood menacingly close 0 1 2 3 4
Threatened parent with some kind of weapon 0 1 2 3 4
Child threatened self harm or suicide 0 1 2 3 4
Child threatened to call police or Child Protection 0 1 2 3 4

Destruction
Child destroyed or damaged property 0 1 2 3 4
Child stole from parent 0 1 2 3 4
Child incurred debts that parent had to pay 0 1 2 3 4
Child abuses home in other ways 0 1 2 3 4

Verbal & emotional abuse
Child swore at parent 0 1 2 3 4
Calls parent names 0 1 2 3 4
Put parent down in other ways 0 1 2 3 4

Used sexual language to humiliate or taunt 0 1 2 3 4
Insulted or shamed parent in front of others 0 1 2 3 4
Child told lies about parent 0 1 2 3 4
Child ordered parent around 0 1 2 3 4
Child nasty to parent's friends or family 0 1 2 3 4
Shows contempt in other ways 0 1 2 3 4

List other abusive behaviour not covered by the above:
You may want to revisit this in a few months' time to see how things have changed. Sometimes it's very hard to see progress when you are in the thick of it.

Consequences

Rewards and Punishments

As we saw in the section on the history of parenting advice, some writers of advice books suggest that giving children punishments, not just physical punishment but **any** punishment whatsoever, is fundamentally wrong[418]. Some argue it's both negative and unnecessary, others that it's unethical as we should be treating children as equals. Penelope Leach suggests that: '*a gradual and gentle exposing of the child to the results of his own ill-advised actions is the only ultimate sanction you need. Any other kind of punishment is revenge and power-mongering.*'[419] By now you should realise that I think this is poppycock! Most people would agree with me, yet such extreme views (and she is one of the most popular parenting gurus) have sowed the seeds of confusion among a generation of parents.

You may not be surprised by the idea that all punishment is wrong, as you may well have internalised some of this yourself and may feel confused about whether you should be punishing your children at all.

It probably *will* surprise you that some parent educators also tell parents not to use rewards either, even suggesting they are just as bad as punishments.

"Rewarding children for acceptable behaviour is just as detrimental as punishing them. Like punishment, reward is a product of a system which assumes that others know what is best for individuals and rewards them when they conform." Balson
[420]

If we as parents don't know what is best for children about some issues then there is something seriously wrong. Some children would stay up all night if they were allowed to (I know quite a few who do) and nowadays a fair number of thirteen-year-olds believe they should be allowed to drink, come and go as they please, swear at anyone, and experiment sexually.

This rejection of rewards is unrealistically idealistic. You may think that no one, except the highly neglectful, could actually bring up a child without rewards and punishments. You'd be right. We all use rewards and punishments but there are those who twist language so that they believe they are not doing so.

Everyone uses both rewards and punishments of some kind in raising children. Praise, after all, is a form of reward and overall it's the most important one for many children. Parental praise is an extremely powerful reward for some children but unfortunately of little interest to others (especially in adolescence). A frown can be a potent punishment to some sensitive young souls who crave adult approval. But for a child who is currently intent on annoying you, your frown may be rewarding. For an easy, eager-to-please, child, praise and the occasional dirty look might be all you will ever need in the way of consequences (which means that you need never think about it). For average (neither easy nor difficult) children, you should be able to get by with some rewards and only occasional punishments, or even just the implied threat of punishment. You may be able to fool yourself that you are not using punishments at all.

Attempting to do without rewards or punishments with difficult children, leads to powerless parents. Pretending not to use rewards and punishments with these children causes much confusion, which they may use to their advantage.

As we've mentioned elsewhere it's the parent of an easy, eager-to-please child who has the most power, but who thinks about it least. Those parents with difficult children have the least power but think about it most. There is no paradox in this, the starving man thinks about food a lot more than the well-fed. Sadly, however, there are professionals who take the parent of a difficult child's obsession with control at face value, believe the parent is a control-freak and assume that this is the cause of the bad behaviour rather than a response to it.

There certainly are problems with punishment. At times punishments are more about the parent's power, pride and privilege than about the child's behaviour.

Movement against punishment

The move against punishment as the main way of bringing up children has been going on for well over a century and the idea of using natural consequences instead of arbitrary punishment is far from new. Here's a quote from 1927: *"Punishments in the usual sense are not necessary. It will always be sufficient to take care that the actions of a child have their natural and necessary consequences. These consequences should result from the nature of the deed, and not seem to come from the educator, and will fulfil the purpose of punishment but without having the evil effects."* Wexberg, 1927

This sounds modern and sensible. In stating that consequences "fulfil the purpose of punishment", he is being more honest than many later writers.

Gordon, writing in the *1970s says, "Ask one hundred parents, "Should children be disciplined?" and ninety-nine unhesitatingly will answer "Of course". That parents should discipline their offspring has been so commonly believed (and strongly defended) that to question the validity of the idea may seem like heresy or foolishness."* [421]

Thankfully the vast majority of parents would reject his heresy and believe that some kind of discipline is necessary. He rejects all discipline because he rejects the idea that parents should have power or authority over children [422].

However, ideas such as his have percolated down from the lofty heights inhabited by male professional advise-givers to cause widespread confusion and parental guilt.

Some parenting gurus (I'm only using quotes from well-respected writers) thus argue against both rewards and punishments and maintain that consequences are something quite different that does away with the need for old-fashioned methods of control. If you have a child with serious problems or a difficult temperament then such indulgent idealism can land you in very hot water. I find much that is written about parenting without either rewards or punishments dishonest. Here's just one example, from Balson, a well-respected Australian parent educator:

"I see that you didn't clean up after your snack. You may not use the kitchen. Ask again in a few days' time."[423]

This is a good example of a logical consequence but surely it's also a good example of an appropriate punishment? To the young person, the claim that this is **not** a punishment may seem at best comical or at worst as manipulative mind games! Imagine your boss at work telling you that you are suspended without pay for a week because you made a mistake and him adding, "This isn't a punishment but a simple safety precaution". You'd probably feel he was clearly displaying his power by defining what the suspension will be called and adding insult to injury. The simple fact is that the parent has the power to ban the young person from the kitchen but **not** vice versa (hopefully). As we've seen, parents do actually have far more power than children *unless* children use extremes of defiance and abuse. This is as it should be and the pretence that we share power equally with our kids is just that, a pretence... and a dangerous one!

Like most parent educators, I encourage parents to use the term 'consequences' rather than rewards and punishments, but it seems to me hypocritical to deny that consequences in reality are often rewards or punishments by another name.

Why punish?

"The prudent use of punishment within the context of a responsive, supportive parent-child relationship is a necessary tool in the disciplinary encounter with young children.[424]" Baumrind

There are a number of reasons why we punish people. There has been a historical move away from the idea of punishment as vengeance or retribution to one of deterrence or rehabilitation.

Using the word 'vengeance' makes it sound primitive, emotional and irrational, and often that is precisely what it is. When there is a public outcry about a crime there will always be people baying for blood in a way that has nothing whatsoever to do with deterring but is all about retribution. We often feel that someone should suffer if they have done something wrong. For them to suffer feels just and righteous! This may be primitive and somewhat illogical (and another example of us wanting to see the world as a fair place) but it's all too human and few people are immune to such feelings.

Meting out punishments is also often about power and privilege. If you upset your employer and they then give you an unpleasant task to do they are probably showing you just who is boss! They are demonstrating power. Omer talks about *'Who's the Boss?* thinking' to mean parents to whom exercising power is overly important. In a family, demonstrating that you are the boss is *occasionally* appropriate but often it's not very helpful. Think of a step-father who insists that *he* will give a punishment to his partner's child. Though he may argue that his wife is too soft, in reality this is often about personal power and excessive pride. Imposing harsh or arbitrary punishments is often part of an unhelpful power play.

If reasons for imposing a punishment resemble any of the following, then it's about retribution not deterrence:

👎 "What you did is horrible. It's only right that you are made to pay in some way."

👎 "You've displeased me, so I'm going to make you suffer!"

👎 "You've broken the unwritten law. There will be righteous retribution!"

👎 "I'm going to show my superiority to you by enforcing arbitrary rules and applying arbitrary punishments (or rewards) to enforce them!"

Punishments can actively discourage children from taking responsibility if they then simply obey orders out of fear, rather than feeling they are making real choices. This is the aspect of both rewards and punishments that idealistic parent educators object to, though they tend to deny that children ever learn morality in this way, which is not true. It works with some children some of the time, especially if it's started at an early age and is supported by cultural norms.

The reason we punish children is usually because there are no natural or logical consequences available that they care about. Sensible and caring use of punishment is much better for a child than letting them grow up with habits such as violence or abusing others. Punishment has been part of the socialisation process for children in all cultures, though the amount of punishment meted out by parents varies tremendously. The ideological stance that all punishment is bad has caused parents to become confused and less assertive and consistent with children.

I hear people complain that using any form of punishment is 'too negative'. Parents are sometimes urged by professionals to focus on positives and only reward good behaviour. This is good advice for easy children, dubious advice for average children, and very bad advice for really difficult children. Punishment, or negative consequences if you prefer, are *negative*. They are *meant* to be *negative*. The idea that any child exposed to negatives is going to be damaged or harmed by this is nonsense. The idea that children should never experience criticism, failure or negativity is partly responsible for the rise in narcissism that we are experiencing[425]. Some criticism, failure, negativity and stress are necessary for normal development and any child who managed to avoid all of these is likely to be an obnoxious, self-centred, little emperor who can't cope with the real world.

There is often a fine line between regarding something as a reward or as a punishment; they can be two sides of the same coin. If pocket money (or any other privilege) is linked to good behaviour (or doing chores) and a child earns half of the possible total for the week, is he being rewarded or punished? If you take two children swimming and leave the third at home are you punishing one or rewarding the other two? This is another reason that it's impossible to have punishment-free parenting, except by fudging the meaning of words. This is one reason for using the term consequences, rather than rewards and punishments, since it covers those grey areas that can be regarded as both depending on how we choose to look at them: as a glass half full or a glass half empty.

Problems with rewards

There are problems with rewards, particularly with regular rewards. If you are *always* paid for an activity you are likely to stop doing it immediately the payment stops. There are many people who enjoy their paid work but few choose to do the same work voluntarily when they are no longer being paid. Studies have found that when children were directly rewarded for an activity, even one that they enjoyed, they do less of it when the reward stops. When we discuss using pocket money we will talk about the problem of paying kids for making their own bed, etc.

Rewards can mean that the child is not taking responsibility. If I only ever do something because I am immediately rewarded for doing it then I don't *own* the behaviour and won't see it as my responsibility. This is especially true if the reward is consistent and immediate. If a child is paid for doing his homework he isn't taking responsibility for it and may be less likely to do academic work in the future. If he is given an occasional reward in recognition of effort or achievement this is not likely to have such a negative effect. If the 'reward' is in the form of a logical consequence this is less likely to be seen as payment. For example, "You can watch T.V. after you finish your homework" can logically be seen as a reward (or not watching T.V. can be seen as a punishment) but it looks quite different to the child. They don't feel as if they are being *paid* to do their homework and the influence you are having over them is more rational and less confrontational.

Some people are enthusiastic about star charts and other forms of reward. If the child is motivated to get stars for their own sake then this is great, but rare. If the stars are translated into rewards they can become a form of currency. Using currency (whether money or stars) is not a good thing *in itself* as it usually means children being rewarded for behaving as they should be behaving. If children are behaving reasonably well, then there is no need to use such complicated and artificial methods. If you have problems with younger children then star charts can help to break a pattern but their effect seldom lasts long.

Praise

The most important and most commonly used reward is praise. It serves as a reward, more or less effectively depending on the child's personality. It also serves purposes of raising self-esteem, providing motivation and reinforcing relationships. Praise is a good thing! This may seem an inanely obvious statement but it's actually not simple (what is in parenting?). For a start, there are those who are opposed to praise and tell parents they shouldn't do it. They say that 'praise' is about the child's characteristics or abilities and that *encouragement* should be about effort and improvement. Thus telling a little girl that she has pretty hair is irrelevant to her behaviour but telling her that she did a good job of brushing it motivates improvement. They make a good point but often are being too ideological and hence confusing some parents. For one thing, there are plenty of children who don't get enough praise and have low self-esteem. Some praise from their parents would be a *good thing* and anything that discourages or confuses these parents from giving praise is dangerous. Even if a child doesn't have low self-esteem and gets praise from one parent they may crave praise from the other parent (and extra praise from the first parent will not compensate).

Though a moderate amount of praise is good for children, encouragement is usually more useful. However, like anything, you can have too much of a good thing. Past a certain level, praise or encouragement from parents becomes meaningless and for some children it becomes harmful. You cannot create a confident self-assured child simply by continually telling them that they are wonderful or special. If the praise is genuine it does not need to be applied with a trowel and if it's not genuine you are teaching them a strange lesson (including not trusting what you say) by laying it on thick. Some children who are repeatedly told they are wonderful become egotistical, arrogant and prideful. As we discussed in the chapter on Self Esteem, excessively high self-esteem has probably become as common a problem as low self-esteem. Children who have been praised excessively in their childhood often can't cope with anything less than adulation and can easily give up when the wider world doesn't appreciate just how wonderful they are.

The principle of minimal coercion

Generally speaking we would like our children to behave well because they want to behave well and we shouldn't use **any** form of coercion, rewards or punishments, unless *we need to*. As with payment, whenever someone feels forced to do something they tend to stop doing it as soon as the compulsion is removed (this doesn't apply so much to habits established in early childhood). If you were forced to do something at gun point you would become less likely to do it in the future. If you are persuaded or paid to do something the less influence you perceive the other person having on you, the more you are likely to identify with the behaviour as your own and hence are more likely to repeat it.

If you are trying to get a child to do something then a general principle is to use the minimum force necessary, which includes the force of rewards. People are generally more likely to internalise things they do freely. There is an important psychological phenomenon with the fancy name of 'cognitive dissonance'. If you pay a lot of money for something, or go to a lot of effort, you will usually value it more. If you are paid a lot to do something, or forced to do it, you will value the activity less and stop doing as soon as the payment or force stops. In a classic experiment in the 1950s, Leon Festinger[426] paid students to do boring menial tasks. Some were paid well ($20 was a lot back then) and others were paid a measly dollar. Afterwards those paid well said they were bored but those paid poorly said they enjoyed the task more. If you want your child to continue brushing his teeth or cleaning his room for the rest of his life then it's best that he does it with the minimum of rewards or punishments.

This certainly does **not** mean that all compulsion is wrong. Many children will learn to read very happily and read for fun from an early age. Any attempt to force them to read would get in the way of this and actually reduce the chances of them reading for pleasure. For some children, however, reading does not come at all naturally and they will need a lot of practice before reading becomes easy enough for it to stop being a chore. Encouraging these children to spend time reading, for example by turning off the T.V. for an hour before they go to sleep or giving *occasional* rewards for reading, may in the long run make them better readers. Left to themselves a few children would give up on reading and *never* learn. Large or regular rewards will reinforce the idea that reading is a chore. Giving intermittent rewards, however, can be useful. On the other hand, punishing a child for not reading is very likely to increase resistance and anxiety about reading and may discourage reading for pleasure for life.

Sometimes skills, such as reading, **can** be improved through enforced practice and occasionally this can lead to increased motivation (as when someone forced to take piano lessons discovers they have a great talent for it). But otherwise compulsion is more likely to reduce motivation than increase it. We were forced to do many things at school that we would not have chosen to do and we stopped doing most of them the moment we left. Reading is a special case as it's such a useful skill and can give pleasure in different ways. But there a quite a few people, and probably the number is currently increasing, who never read another book once they leave school.

So, as a general principle, if we want our children to internalise and identify with good and helpful behaviour then minimum coercion or influence is almost always the best approach. This is one reason that natural consequences are better teachers than those we impose.

"There is convincing evidence that children who are induced not to misbehave under mild threat are much less likely to do the naughty deed when the threat is removed than are children who are threatened with severe punishment. Several studies have examined children' responses to being forbidden to play with a particular toy: some were threatened with mild punishment, some with more severe. In all cases the toy was liked more by those threatened with strong punishment. Moreover, when the threat of punishment was removed, they played with the toy more than did those who were only under mild threat." Sutherland[427]

Bribery has its place... but use it with care.

Rewards can discourage a child from taking responsibility when they feel they are being paid or bribed, to behave. However, a reward to break a bad habit, help establish a new habit, encourage a child to try something new, or occasionally to ward off disaster, can be beneficial. The basic principle is this: if the issue should be their responsibility (which includes the responsibility not to abuse others) then rewards should be avoided and should *always* be a short term, stop-gap measure. Bribery can help change a pattern of behaviour and can indicate that choices are possible. They can also help a stubborn young person save face. But they are a stop-gap not a long-term solution.

Are consequences different from rewards and punishments?

Although 'consequences' are often really a form of reward or punishment, it's useful to use this term as it can help us change our focus to a more cooperative and logical way of influencing children's behaviour. Consequences are not entirely different to rewards and punishments but are a wider term with slightly different emphasis.

There is a continuum with *natural consequences* at one end; more or less logical consequences in the middle and unrelated consequences at the other end, (which are not logically related to the behaviour and really are nothing more than rewards or punishments with a different name).

The continuum of consequences

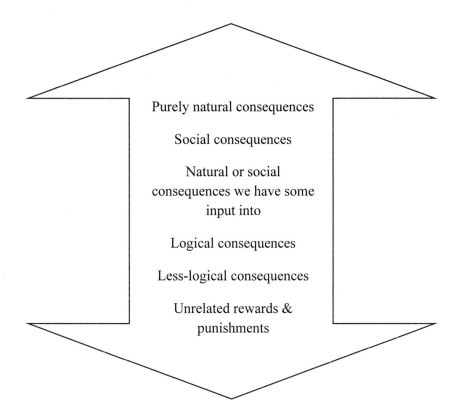

Purely natural consequences

Social consequences

Natural or social consequences we have some input into

Logical consequences

Less-logical consequences

Unrelated rewards & punishments

Natural Consequences

The classic example of a natural consequence is the child who wants to go out in the rain without a coat. The natural consequence is that they get wet. Assuming they don't die of pneumonia, children learn efficiently by being allowed to make such mistakes and suffer the consequences. People learn best from such natural consequences rather than from more arbitrary punishments (or rewards) for the following reasons:

- It's much easier to understand and easier to remember the connection between a natural consequence and the behaviour that led to it.
- When a punishment is imposed by someone else there are emotional complications which can impair learning. If a child focuses more on your unfairness, gets angry or feels unloved, these emotions can overshadow

309

the lesson they were meant to learn. Obviously this is a much bigger problem with oppositional children.

- By imposing a punishment (or giving a reward) we are taking some of the responsibility on ourselves and hence giving the child less responsibility. When someone forces you to do something, you don't see it as your responsibility or your choice.
- The principle of minimal force suggests that the less we have to intervene the more likely that learning is internalized.

Children in the recent past used to learn a lot more than they do now by natural consequences since they were allowed to interact with nature and were not over-protected in the way children are today. There is very little that is 'natural' about our children's lives and we don't let them take risks in order to learn. Many of today's children have never been out in the rain, with or without a coat, for more than the time taken to walk between a car and a building.

However, there is a **major** problem with natural consequences, especially with younger children, which is frequently glossed over or played down. Children tend to have a poor concept of time and many have little or no future orientation. Hence an outcome that is not immediate, or at least follows very quickly after the behaviour, may *never* produce learning. Immediate gratification often tends to outweigh long-term consequences. Many adults are exactly the same and the horrible hangover that follows a night on the grog may **never** produce learning in some adults. Millions of people (even a few intelligent ones) ruin their health, wrinkle their faces, smell bad and ultimately kill themselves with nicotine for what is a very mild immediate reward.

Long-term consequences, such as future educational and career success or failure, are unlikely to motivate many children. Most children, and many adults, are motivated by short term successes or the desire for an easy life, not by something which may be over ten years ahead. I mentioned that children who steal may believe that they will end up in prison or in a children's home in a few years' time. Their estimations of negative long-term consequences are greatly exaggerated but this has not had any effect on their behaviour because it's outweighed by immediate rewards. Generally punishments that are more than a week away are likely to be ineffectual in changing the behaviour of most pre-teen children and many adolescents.

Obviously children's mental timeframes set severe limits on the effectiveness of many natural consequences. Few pre-teen children will brush their teeth because of the long-term benefits (they brush their teeth because it tastes good, it keeps parents happy, they are proud of their skill or it's just a habit). So letting such behaviours be *solely* determined by natural consequences is not practical. Most children will eat unhealthy diets if we don't exercise some control (as will a great many adults). This is made far worse by the unnatural foods that commercial forces have made available, foods designed to be attractive to kids but loaded with excess sugar, salt, fat, colourings and even caffeine. It appals me that we allow big business to exploit our children in this way! This is an example of how our modern, commercial culture makes parenting more difficult. Similarly the exciting electronic media is addictive to many children and can make our jobs as parents much harder. I regularly see young people who are up till dawn playing computer games (they are usually too old for their parents to control, or parents think they have no right to control this).

Children also differ dramatically in how they respond to natural consequences. One child may get such a fright when they almost fall from a climbing frame that they become excessively afraid of heights. Most children will be more wary but not develop a phobia. Some fearless little bruisers can have a number of falls and even some serious accidents but still persist in climbing trees, garages, roofs and anything else they can clamber up.

It may seem that natural consequences are very simple. As a parent one does nothing but let the environment teach the child its own lessons. However, with parenting nothing is simple! There are complex judgments to be made about when to let natural consequences occur, when to protect the child from those consequences and when to reinforce, or replace natural consequences with logical or artificial consequences.

There are many situations when protecting children from natural consequences is the right thing to do. We don't let toddlers taste bleach or try driving the family car. The natural consequences might teach them a valuable lesson but the risk is far too great. Whenever we attempt to control young children's diet, sleeping, school attendance, etc. we are protecting them from natural consequences. The necessity of protecting young children from themselves is obvious but this becomes less and less clear as they mature. To what extent should parents protect older, but still immature children from themselves? Most people would not approve of letting a thirteen-year-old get wasted on whiskey in order to teach him about hangovers. Even letting teenagers try the odd glass of wine is controversial.

The *natural* consequences of not working are poverty and starvation. Thankfully even if parents don't protect their children from these natural consequences, the modern welfare state usually does. But if a sixteen-year-old stops attending school and doesn't look for work, should parents give him or her any money or just the bare essentials to stay alive? The extreme position would be to stop feeding him but few would consider that good parenting. However, I've known parents who give such children the ultimatum, "School, work, or leave home". Not many parents are tough enough to enforce this (and I'm not suggesting you should). However, if youth allowances are generous or if a child has friends (or friend's parents) who are willing to take him in, being thrown out may not even be a consequence he cares about.

What we feel able to leave to natural consequences must be guided by our values, our assessment of risk factors, and very importantly, by what we know about our own child. There are no hard and fast rules and ultimately the value judgments involved must be made by the parents. We cannot logically and mathematically work out how much risk is appropriate; we must use our intuition and common sense

Natural-Social consequences

The word 'natural' has two meanings:

1 Existing in or derived from nature; not made, caused by, or processed by humankind.

2 Normal, inevitable.

Humans are a social animal and in our complex modern society most of the time social consequences are more important than ones that are natural in the first sense of the word. The natural consequence of you running nude through a shopping centre is not just that you might catch cold but that you will be laughed at or ogled (maybe both) and probably arrested. The cold is natural in both senses of the word but the laughter, lechery and legal consequences are all social. They are manmade but are natural in the sense of being expected, ordinary and inevitable.

The natural-social consequence of a child being belligerent or aggressive with peers is a certain amount of rejection and aggression (even violence) in return. Among children, the natural-social consequence of hitting someone is often to be hit back. Nowadays most of us try hard to inhibit this natural-social consequence among children and there are usually adults around to protect the aggressor. Although I strongly disagree with parents who tell a child they should always hit back, I also worry that we are making childhood too safe and that some children may need to learn the lessons of the pack. A pure pacifist approach is so alien to some children that it goes completely over their heads. If all hitting is equally evil, then hitting girls and grandmothers is equated with punching peers in the playground.

If you were to walk up to a stranger and make nasty faces at them, you would find that they will do one of several things: a) abuse you, b) ignore you, c) leave, or d) call the authorities (police or mental health). This is the same when one child in a playground abuses another (the authorities in this case being teachers or parents). These are natural reactions for people in our society, social, learned behaviours.

A major reason why natural-social consequences may not work within families is that family members are stuck with each other. The most consistent natural (social) consequence of being obnoxious to others is withdrawal. If a child at school hits other children they may find themselves socially isolated but within a family our means of escape from one another is severely curtailed. If you had a friend who called you a 'useless shit-head' you would probably stop seeing them and avoid them in the future. This option is not open to your children when their sister says this or to you when your daughter is similarly verbally abusing you. She knows that you will come back for more – as will her brothers and sisters.

When I talk to children about their violence, they are often quite clear about this. They don't abuse their friends in the same way they abuse family members because they would lose their friends. Family members are stuck with them. Even when they visit an access parent they are often aware that they might not be invited back if they are abusive.

Natural consequences don't always work as they ought to in schools. The school bully is not always a hated outcast and a pathetic figure (as many adults like to pretend). Some violent children are quite popular, quite happy and have high self-esteem. Sad but true.

Though we shouldn't ignore bullying and teasing among children, it's generally a mistake to try *too* hard to protect children from these social consequences. One way of protecting them would be to never leave them alone with other children. Unfortunately in our modern society this totally unnatural state of continuous supervision has become quite common for some pre-teens. Many children are *never* left to their own devices and hence this kind of social learning is greatly inhibited. Thus protectiveness may even be one reason why the number of younger aggressive children appears to be increasing. The 'natural' pecking order, or dominance hierarchy, that groups of children develop is not allowed to come into play which can mean persistent conflict rather than a few sort-out-the-pecking-order fights.

Parents are increasingly expecting, or demanding, that schools should be responsible for children's interactions and should put a stop to all teasing, social exclusion and bullying. While anti-bullying policies are *a good thing,* and I strongly approve of schools taking bullying more seriously than they did in the past, this can sometimes go too far. Policing children closely to protect them from all teasing is counterproductive. If children are never exposed to *any* teasing, they become hypersensitive and milder teasing then hurts them more.

"In the current, sometimes alarmist, discussions of bullying, there is a tendency to define as bullying everything from rolling your eyes once at someone to blatant sexual abuse." Heinrichs [428]

Many parents are confused about how far to protect siblings from each other. With children spending more time indoors being over-supervised by parents, younger siblings can often rely on their parents' protection and annoy their older siblings with relative impunity. If an older brother or sister is a bully, the younger child does need parental protection but if the younger child is terrorising the older (an increasingly common occurrence as age is no longer given respect) parents become part of the problem by protecting children from natural-social consequences. It's extremely common for brothers and sisters to actually fight and argue more when parents are around than when they are not. The younger child uses the actual or potential protection of the parent to even the odds. This can help create a situation where the war is interminable and *sometimes* parents backing-off can improve things (though perhaps after an initial increase in conflict).

It gets even more complex when we think about the parent's own reactions to obnoxious behaviour. The acceptable natural-social consequence of you being disrespected or abused is for you to avoid the other person. Within families this is seldom practical (though some teens withdraw to their rooms and some fathers to the shed). An even more natural social consequence of being treated badly is to show disapproval and anger, but if parents do this towards their children it's seen as bad parenting. The view of the ideal parent is often one who is calm and projects 'unconditional love'[429]. Parents are frequently told just to ignore bad behaviour. Thus many parents are trying to inhibit their natural reactions to being abused. This is sometimes appropriate but often leads to greater problems.

Parents who are *too* tolerant and understanding may not be teaching children what reactions they can expect from such behaviour in the real world. If parents don't take their own rights seriously by being too child focused, they will not be giving natural social consequences. Even if the parent doesn't give in to the child's demands, they may still be inadvertently reinforcing the bad behaviour as the child gets attention and a feeling of power from disrespecting adults. The child perceives that the parent doesn't have much self-respect, so why should the child respect the parent?

Furthermore, a parent who tries too hard to ignore obnoxious behaviour usually finds that this unrealistic stance is impossible to maintain. The parent goes from being passive to aggressive, often with occasional outbursts of impotent rage. Thus a parent trying to ignore the un-ignorable behaves inconsistently, and the child associates the parent's occasional tantrum with the parent's emotions rather than the child's behaviour.

Particularly with older children I often see parents who are in some way protecting their child from the natural (social) consequences of their actions. This can take a number of forms, for example:

- Negotiating with schools to reduce punishments or excuse misdemeanours.
- Paying fines, or bailing them out financially in other ways.
- Replacing things they have damaged.
- Covering up for them so they are not shamed socially.
- Continually going out of your way to help them out of a crisis.
- Not protecting them from natural consequences can sometimes be a real challenge.

Logical consequences, related and relevant

Not only is the term 'natural consequences' a bit confusing but the term 'logical consequences' is also not all that logical. Firstly, natural consequences are usually far more logical than parent-imposed 'logical consequences'. Then there is the question of whose logic? What appears logical to one person can appear quite illogical to another. Logic is not absolute and hitting someone back is certainly logical, but not helpful or advisable. Children often have quite a different view of logic than do adults. Also, people from different cultural backgrounds, including different generations in a time of roller-coaster change, may disagree about what is logical.

A good example of this is the old-fashioned idea of washing a child's mouth out with soap when he says *dirty* words. This appeals to a childish form of logic (shared by some adults) but isn't *really* logical at all, it's really just a quick, partly symbolic but also unpleasant, punishment.

So in the context of consequences, 'logical' really means ***related and relevant***. With really difficult teens it's often simply not possible to find practical consequences that are both related and relevant. We'll be arguing below that it's necessary and sensible (hence logical) to sometimes use unrelated rewards and punishments, which are therefore logical in one sense of the word but not what is meant by 'logical consequences'. Though 'logical' is not the ideal word in this context, it's become well known so we'll stick with it. Many parenting writers use terms such as 'logical' to hide value judgments and pretend that what they are proposing is scientific and not based on their own ethical values.

Advantages of Logical consequences

If we create consequences that reinforce natural consequences, are similar to natural consequences, or at least appear to make sense to a child's logic, we gain some of the benefits of natural consequences along with other important benefits.

- As with natural consequences, logical consequences are easier to understand and remember than unconnected punishments or rewards.
- As with natural consequences, but to a slightly lesser extent, the child is more likely to focus on his own behaviour rather than be distracted by considerations of injustice or anger at the adult.
- In addition, with logical consequences we as adults have much more control over the situation and can ensure that the consequence follows the behaviour far more quickly and far more consistently than with most natural consequences.
- If we are very clear about the rules and consequences it does not matter so much *which* adult imposes the consequence. If it's a *house rule* and the consequence becomes automatic and expected then a step-parent, for example, can calmly remind the child of it without their relationship becoming the issue. This can take some of the heat out of conflict situations and power struggles are reduced. An adult can warn a child of a possible consequence in a caring tone of concern rather than in an angry tone of command, which is far less likely to get a stubborn kid's back up.

Some examples of logical consequences:

- *"Despite my warning, you've run up another large phone bill. I'm going to deduct $10 a week from your allowance towards the phone until you get it under control."*
- *"I'm tired of finding half-empty mugs of coffee all over the place. As you and your father are the only ones who drink coffee we will start keeping his coffee separate and you'll have to buy your own unless you show some effort to tidy up after yourself."*
- *"You and your friends woke us up several times last night. We're going to have a two week break from having your friends over."*
- *"You made a dent in the wall when you kicked it during your last temper tantrum. Your father has agreed to fix it this time and we will only charge you for the materials, not for his labour. You may want to thank him for that. Next time this happens you will have to pay for a plasterer to come out, even if this means selling some of your electronic equipment."*
- *"We know you have been smoking in your bedroom again. This time we are deducting the cost of a smoke alarm from your allowance. If you tamper with the alarm or we catch you smoking again, we will remove your bedroom door for one month."*

- *"You have been playing your music too loud again. I've put a mark on the dial at what I find a tolerable volume. If you exceed that volume again you will lose your stereo for one week to give my ears a chance to recover."*
- *"You really hurt your little brother when you kicked him. To compensate him you are going to pay for him to go to the cinema from your pocket money."*
- *"You've eaten all the ice cream again despite my warning. It isn't fair that your brother and sister should have to go without, so for the next two weeks I'm not buying any ice cream but will give your brother and sister extra pocket money to buy their own."*

The last two examples involve relationships between brothers and sisters and could conceivably create more problems in some families. You need to use your judgment as such consequences could put brothers and sisters at risk for more abuse in some cases. With all examples you need to think about how they are likely to work for your own child and family.

As we've said natural consequences are best, but they don't always work. So whenever possible use logical consequences that reinforce or resemble natural ones. For example, leaving things lying around can lead to the natural consequence of them getting lost or broken. But this does not happen often enough or consistently enough for most children (and many adults) to learn from this (my untidy study is a reflection of this). As a parent we can reinforce the effect of natural consequences if we adopt a policy of removing toys that are left lying around for a period of time. We are applying a consequence that is related and relevant to greatly reinforce the natural consequences.

How you present the consequence is important:

When you are presenting the consequence try to keep it simple and straightforward. It's better if it's not part of a lecture, discussion or argument. Avoid negotiating; though don't rule this out completely either. You can choose to negotiate if you wish, but it's important to realise that you don't have to.

Be as clear as possible. Try to avoid any vague statements such as 'we don't like your attitude' while you are giving a consequence. It's far better to say 'no yelling or swearing' than to say 'treat me with respect'. Vague statements allow the young person to argue or dismiss what you are saying, so they make behavioural change less likely.

Present consequences in as calm a manner as possible. Aim at assertive not aggressive. You are solving a problem not trying to make your child suffer. You are showing that you are not powerless but not exerting power for the sake of it. Anger is not always a bad thing if the behaviour is extreme (if they'd done serious damage to a sibling or the home it would be natural for you to be angry) but most of the time, the more calmly you can present consequences the better.

Keep to the point at hand. Don't toss other complaints into the pot. If you want to talk to your child about them not coming home till three a.m. don't add your complaints and opinions about the friends they were out with or what they might have been doing (these just give them scope to argue). If it's going to be useful to have this discussion (though it's probably a waste of time) don't combine it with telling them what the consequence of not coming home on time will be.

Concentrate on the things that are your business and avoid arguable value judgments. For example, if they are playing their music too loud, try to resist the understandable temptation to mention the fact that their music is crap (or rap)! If they are leaving their clothes lying around the floor don't choose this time to point out that they dress like a whore, or mention that they should try a colour other than black. Such personal digs distract from the real message and give them the chance to feel victimised and misunderstood.

Focus on the future not the past whenever possible. Even if they have done something wrong it's not always essential they are punished for this (unless it's really serious) but *far more* important is that there is a consequence in place for the next time it happens. "Swearing at your sister was wrong and we would be pleased if you choose to apologise. If it happens again, you will have to do her chores for a week."

Keep consequences as closely related to the crime as is feasible. If not related, try to make it *seem* more related. *"When you yell at me I feel intimidated and it makes me worried you could become violent. I'd rather not be in the car alone with someone who intimidates me so I'm not driving you anywhere for the next four days."*

Try to make it sound more like a natural consequence than a punishment.

A rule involving logical consequences can be explained to the child as if it were a natural consequence, and if house rules are clear, it can seem just like a natural consequence to the child. In contrast some parents go to the other extreme and talk about such consequences as if they are a punishment, emphasising power and coercion. They may even add unnecessary threats, such as threatening to give away or destroy the toys. This makes children more resentful and less likely to cooperate. Creating consequences that seem logical and more like natural consequences, is far more likely to produce cooperation in a defiant child than giving threats of punishment.

We will reinforce some of these ideas later in the Seven Cs chapter.

'Logical' consequences are not always possible

Logical consequences are desirable but they are **not** always possible and it's not essential that all consequences are logical. We won't call them 'illogical consequences' because there is a sensible, logical reason why they are necessary. We'll call them unrelated, because they are a consequence unrelated to the offensive behaviour. They are usually really rewards and punishments but we can still call them 'consequences'.

Use an unrelated consequence when the behaviour is serious, usually *intolerable*, and you can't find a logical consequence that the child cares about and that you can control.

Try to make it appear logical if you possibly can, even if the logic is pretty tenuous. When we discuss using pocket money it will be obvious that often there is no real logical connection between the consequence and the behaviour. An example is having a small fine for swearing. This often works very well but it's *not* a logical consequence. We can, however, explain to the child that we give them pocket money in proportion to how cooperative, or mature, they are. Since older children get more pocket money, immature behaviour, such as tantrums or swearing, reduces their allowance. And a child who is blowing their money on drink, drugs or gambling should get less money as they are not showing the maturity to make sensible choices. Early bedtimes, or restrictions on freedom, can be explained in similar terms.

Most recent parenting advice stops at logical consequences, implying that it's always possible to find one and that we should never give rewards and punishments. The writers probably don't have much experience with a violent or out of control adolescent and they seldom or never hint that children might be violent to adults or that adults can be afraid to impose consequences. Imagine how our society would function if the legal system only used logical consequences! If you are caught speeding they would have to either somehow slow your car down or else take it away for a while. It's difficult to imagine how logical consequences could work for assaults and robbery!

Possible problems with Consequences

There is never one perfect consequence and what works well with one child may be a waste of time, or even harmful, for another. This is why we are trying to help you create your own solutions rather than telling you what to do. It's not simple creating consequences for an uncooperative or violent child. Here are a few things that can make consequences unhelpful, even when they are logical:

- Too far in the future for the child to relate to.
- They don't believe it will happen (usually goes with previous).
- Not relevant to the child because they don't care about it.
- Makes the child feel powerful, e.g. hurts other family members as much as the target child.
- Gives the child too much attention.
- Is more about your emotions than about the child's behaviour.
- Puts brothers and sisters at risk of retaliation.
- Is over-the-top or too strict so that the child will focus far more on you being unfair than on their own behaviour.
- Makes the child give up trying in an important area (e.g. stops going to sport).
- Child will choose to leave home rather than accept consequences (occasionally this is not a bad outcome).

When to apply consequences

Any technique can be abused. If we try to control every aspect of a child's behaviour using consequences, we create a stressful, artificial environment in which some children are likely to rebel. It's very important that we are clear about what we are trying to influence and why. You may need to consider your own need to control others. Some behaviours (dangerous or abusive) are clearly unacceptable and some kind of consequence should be applied by responsible parents. Some things are clearly the kid's business and we should not interfere. In between are a lot of behaviours that are undesirable, annoying, inconvenient, or inefficient but whether or not a consequence should be applied is debatable. In two parent families it's crucially important that both parents are working together and it's often a good idea to write down together what are the rules and what behaviours are to be discouraged or encouraged. Children can be involved in this process but listening to them and respecting them does not mean that they have an equal say to the adults. Be clear that it's not a democracy.

If a child is showing a lot of behavioural problems or openly rebelling, it's important not to try to change too much at once. Decide on your priorities and focus on behaviour that is clearly unacceptable and can be clearly defined.

Avoid having consequences that are all negative, i.e. punishments. It's really important to find positives and include positive consequences, i.e. rewards.

Being clear about what behaviour is unacceptable is often very important. If you decide to give a consequence for a child being 'cheeky', you will find that adults seldom agree on what exactly is 'cheeky' (one person's cheek may be another's cute) and the child will no doubt disagree. Thus the child may spend a lot of time feeling 'got at' and angry, or may learn to avoid talking to adults. Children's 'bad attitude' is often shown by their intensely annoying tone of voice to adults. However, they are often quite unaware of their tone of voice and would find being punished for this totally unfair, probably making them angrier (and more annoying). However, pointing out that they sound angry and stating how it affects you may be a reasonable natural consequence.

The flowchart below illustrates our philosophy. What you can, or should, ignore and what is truly intolerable will be judgments you will need to make given all the relevant circumstances.

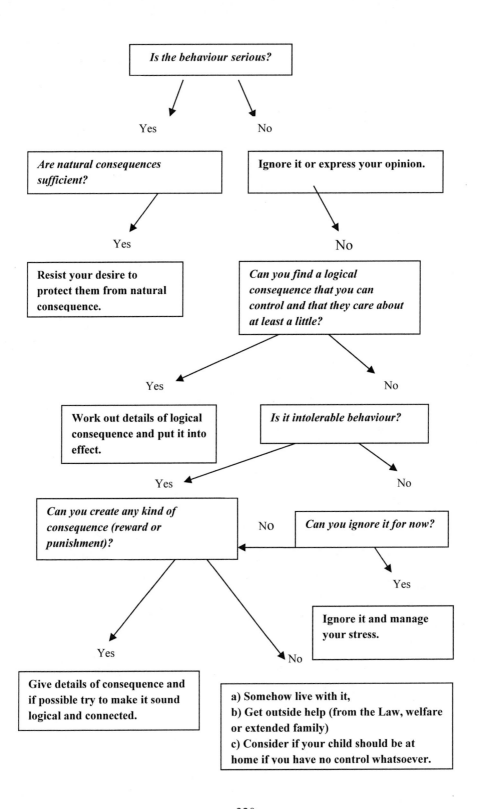

Is the behaviour serious?

Yes — Are natural consequences sufficient?

No — Ignore it or express your opinion.

Yes — Resist your desire to protect them from natural consequence.

No — Can you find a logical consequence that you can control and that they care about at least a little?

Yes — Work out details of logical consequence and put it into effect.

No — Is it intolerable behaviour?

Yes — Can you create any kind of consequence (reward or punishment)?

No — Can you ignore it for now?

Yes — Ignore it and manage your stress.

No — Can you create any kind of consequence (reward or punishment)?

Yes — Give details of consequence and if possible try to make it sound logical and connected.

No —
a) Somehow live with it,
b) Get outside help (from the Law, welfare or extended family)
c) Consider if your child should be at home if you have no control whatsoever.

Be Firm, not Strict

Being firm means being clear and consistent; you can be firm even if you are easy-going with few rules. It's easier to be firm with fewer rules. Strict parents, who have lots of rules or harsh punishments, are often inconsistent. Harsh punishments often lead to parents disagreeing with each other or to one or both parents ignoring misbehaviour for an easy life. Parents using harsh punishments, such as spanking, are especially likely to go from passive to aggressive. They passively ignore misbehaviour although it's stressing them, or escalating, until they explode; since anger breeds anger, their children are more likely to be difficult and aggressive.

Some parents I meet are fairly easy-going, or permissive, until a child becomes abusive or beyond-control. They then try to 'come down hard' by imposing extreme or long-lasting punishments. If this was going to work it would probably have worked quite quickly but it more often widens the gulf between parent and child.

Consistency

Although it's always a good idea to be clear and consistent, parents are not perfect and most kids cope with a certain amount of inconsistency. However, with some difficult children – because of their personality, problems or past experiences – it's crucially important that we are clear and consistent. Normal parents with normal children are probably around 80% consistent. This is good enough for most kids.

For difficult children, such as some children with ADHD, being 80% consistent is not good enough. Many parents of such children try harder and may be 90% consistent. This will work with some kids but for the most difficult, this is still not good enough. The sad irony is that some professionals look at such families and see a parent who is not being consistent enough, though that parent may be inconsistent only half as often as the average parent (and more consistent than the professional is with their children). They partly, sometimes completely, blame the parent for the child's behavioural problems. Not only is this unfair, it's unhelpful for several reasons. If workers imagine that parents are, or should be, 100% consistent they underestimate how difficult this is to achieve in the real world and may give unrealistic advice. The parent often senses the worker's judgment (even if the worker thinks they are hiding it) and becomes defensive and/or feels guiltier. If the child senses the worker's condemnation of the parents (and I've had a number of children tell me that workers openly blamed their mothers for their bad behaviour) they feel justified and are less likely to be motivated to change. We've mentioned several times that guilt gets in the way of assertive parenting.

Even when parents follow through and are consistent 90% of the time, some kids (very stubborn and determined ones) will gamble on the other 10% and for them such inconsistency means that they will pretty much ignore you! This does not mean that you are being a bad parent but for such children you need to be much better than average. Achieving 100% consistency is extremely difficult and probably impossible but you may need to get very close if you have a particularly difficult child.

What we have said about consistency applies equally to one parent being consistent over time or to two parents being consistent and supportive of each other.

In many homes the two parents do not have the same rules and expectations or impose the same consequences. Thus many children know that Dad will let them stay up later than Mum will, and they can use rude language in front of Mum that Dad will object to, etc. For easy children this doesn't matter much. Most children learn early on that there are different expectations in different places. A three-year-old may understand that they can eat as much ice cream as they like and bounce on the settee at Gran's but not at home, although they need to talk more politely at Gran's house. At Kinder the rules and expectation are quite different to either home or Gran's place. Learning this flexibility is not a bad thing in most cases. However, if a child is spending a lot of time at Gran's and she has no rules at all, this may be a problem, especially if she undermines Mum in other ways.

Evidence from crime deterrence, violence, murder, theft, drugs, speeding, etc., all show that it's not the severity of punishment that matters but the likelihood. If you think you can get away with a crime, it may not matter much if the sentence is death or a jail term (regardless of what you think about the death sentence for murder, it's clear that it makes little difference to rates of murder in different areas). If there were enough speed cameras around so that every incident of speeding was recorded and punished, quite small fines would be sufficient to deter most people. If hardly anyone gets caught even severe punishments won't deter many people[430].

Don't make threats you may not be able to carry out

Hitting parents is extremely serious but, thankfully, no longer an offence that merits stoning to death. So don't get carried away and threaten serious consequences if you aren't going to follow through.

Many parents make threats that they are not at all likely to follow through with (though not usually stoning to death). This is everyday bad parenting that won't be the end of the world if you are dealing with easy or normal children. However, most of you reading this book have difficult children who won't let you get away with anything. Making meaningless threats teaches children to ignore you. Your words lose their impact and they may lose trust in what you say. They may lose respect for you as they see you as weak because you don't follow through. When you wriggle out of a threatened consequence they may feel powerful, sensing that you are afraid to upset them or stand your ground.

If you **always** follow through, then your words become an immediate consequence. Imagine the situation where you receive a phone call from the bank manager telling you that you have less money in your account than you thought, or perhaps a message that you are going to lose your job or be demoted in the near future. The impact on you will be immediate although nothing concrete has changed. The words are just vibrations in the air but you are not likely to disbelieve them and so they have an immediate impact. If it was merely a rumour, which may or may not happen, you may decide to worry about it later. This is the same for a child whose parent makes a threat. If they are virtually certain that the threat will be carried out, the impact may be immediate but for some kids any doubt means that they will ignore it for the time being.

Thus it's very important that you don't let yourself blurt out punishments when you are angry. You will either have to go back on your word (occasionally the sensible thing to do, e.g. if you threatened to cancel Christmas) or your partner may feel forced to undermine you.

This applies even to asking your child to leave home, as we'll discuss later.

Keep it simple, keep it short

Good consequences should not be complicated or people forget the rules and some kids are great barrack-room lawyers.

Whenever possible make the consequence short term. Generally stopping a privilege for a week will have exactly the same effect on a child's behaviour as stopping it for a month. Stopping the privilege for a day or two may be just as effective as for a week.

However, stopping a privilege for a long period of time creates several problems:

- More likely to lead to rebellion and escalation.
- Far more likely not to be followed as you lose your determination to make it stick, they wriggle out of it or you forget about it.
- You've lost that ammunition should the same thing happen again soon. If you ever start making such consequences overlap it will probably have lost its impact. In counselling, children say to me with resignation, "I don't get pocket money" or "I'm not allowed out". The parent may think the punishment is for a period of time or until something changes but to the child it's an indefinite sentence. In these situations the punishment is usually having no positive effect on the child's behaviour.

You **don't** have to decide on the spot how long a consequence will last. If it's logical for a child to lose the use of a bike then tell him this immediately but wait till you talk to the other parent, or till you calm down, before telling him how long for. However, do give a definite time as soon as possible. Don't give indefinite sentences; these invite children to give up trying to behave.

Most of the time the principle of "Keep it simple, keep it short" also applies to what you need to say to the child. Long explanations about what the child has done wrong can delay the consequence and lead to arguments that confuse things. Lectures are usually a waste of time. Your kids probably look on them as an additional punishment (by boredom) and tune-out.

"We've already taken away all his privileges!"

Some parents say, usually in exasperation, but occasionally with pride, that they've removed all privileges already and there is nothing left to use as consequences. In these situations I usually advise them to give them all back and start afresh. Some parents say that privileges have to be earned and the child will get them back when they behave. Such an approach seldom works as they are usually battling a highly stubborn child who becomes more and more determined not to give in. Such children may leave home rather than tidy their rooms!

Such a state of affairs has usually come about because parents are giving consequences that are too long-term, so they start to overlap, or are indefinite so that the child loses hope. If you say "You can have your privilege(s) back when you are cooperative and polite" your child may hear "You've lost your privilege(s) forever because you'll never be cooperative and polite by my standards." So why would they try? If you have nothing else to take away then they can misbehave for free.

As I'll suggest in the chapter on 'Using Pocket Money', giving some money or some of a privilege (such as computer time, etc.) is usually more motivating than giving nothing. It's sometimes amazing that a child who seemed to live for an X-box or such will resign themselves to doing without it. Allowing an hour or two of X-box a week may be far more motivating than none.

Of course if you have removed something that you don't really want them to have, the balance of factors may be a bit different. You may have stopped them watching wrestling videos until they can control their temper. This is a more logical consequence and, if you believe that the violent videos were feeding their aggression, you may choose to follow through with this.

I've heard from more than one parent that they'd heard from a TV pop psychologist the idea of removing everything, except a mattress on the floor, from a difficult child's bedroom. Some of the children I know would feel they had nothing more to lose so may well tear up the mattress or smash the walls. Such an approach may work occasionally (any crisis can lead to change in some situations) but I do not advise such outright confrontation.

Working out clear consequences

If a child is highly uncooperative or beyond control it can be very hard finding useable consequences. Any privilege and almost anything that you do for a child can *potentially* be used as a consequence. It may be useful to make a list of these.

There are several important things to bear in mind:

- How comfortable are you, and your partner, about using such a consequence? If you are going to be wracked with guilt or more inconvenienced than the child then it's not likely to work.
- Does the child care about it? Not giving them a lift to school is a sensible logical consequence for them not getting ready in the morning or abusing you before breakfast. But if they really don't care if they go to school or not then it's not going to work.
- Does it need cooperation from the child? If so, do you have enough cooperation to make it work? If not, find a secondary consequence that doesn't need co-operation and either use that instead on its own or make loss of this privilege dependent on non-cooperation with the first one.

- Sometimes you need to give first, in order to have the possibility of taking away. See chapter on using pocket money. If you have already removed all privileges on an indefinite basis then give them back and start from scratch.
- Although it's not possible to work out clear consequences for every possible misbehaviour, the behaviours we are most concerned about are usually repeated ones.
- When you are caught off guard by some new misbehaviour, it's often better to delay giving a consequence until you can talk to the other parent, consult with someone else if you are a sole parent, or at least think about it calmly for a while. It's important that the child knows that there will be a consequence, it's not essential that he knows what it is immediately. After all, **consequences are about preventing the next time not about punishing the last time.**

Give Choices, not orders

If you can clearly define a child's behaviour and clearly define the consequence, it becomes possible to give the child a choice rather than an order. With stubborn individuals, any demand or command may automatically produce determined resistance. Giving them a choice is less likely to produce resistance and anger.

With a younger child, instead of a command: "Put your toys away!" you can say (preferably calmly, even cheerfully), "You've only got 15 minutes till bed time, shouldn't you be putting those toys away? Otherwise they'll disappear for a week."

Instead of "Don't you dare throw that!" (which to some kids is a challenge they can hardly resist) you can say, "Are you sure you want to throw that, you know it means no Simpsons if you do?"

Instead of ordering "Get on with your homework!" you can say, "It's your choice, if you do your homework for twenty minutes you'll be able to use the computer. It's up to you."

Instead of "You'd better be back by ten p.m. or I'll be mad!" you can say, "Don't forget to check your watch; I'm sure you don't want to be late for curfew and lose electronic privileges again."

Instead of "Don't you dare speak to me like that!" you can say, "I can see you're getting angry; you should try to calm down or you'll end up walking home again." Don't say "You had better..." as such commands are like a red rag to a bull to many stubborn children. The less you make it sound like a threat and a power struggle the better. It's a threat and it really **is** a power struggle but the more cards you hold the cooler you can be about it.

There is no guarantee that this approach will stop your child being defiant and aggressive but it does reduce the chances of this over time. Giving choices has an effect on the young person and an important psychological effect on the parent. It's much easier for parents to remain calm when they can give a clear consequence and a choice rather than a command. Commands are inherently more aggressive and more likely to trigger power struggles whereas a choice is more assertive and downplays the power difference.

Much parental anger comes from the frustration of feeling powerless. If you can give a definite consequence you are less likely to become angry, sad or stressed. You can be more businesslike, take it less personally and remain less emotional. You can also sometimes use reverse psychology. Instead of saying "stop your swearing!" you may be able to cheerfully say "you're saving me a lot of money this week". You will find that children's hearing is much better when the consequences are clear. When there are no consequences there is little motivation and both requests and orders seem to make them go deaf, which often results in parents yelling. When your yelling becomes a habit, they learn to ignore you until you yell (as well as learning to yell at people themselves). With consequences, their hearing improves over time because their motivation goes up.

So consequences are about changing parental behaviour as well as changing child behaviour.

House rules

If consequences are well established they become house rules rather than an arbitrary punishment imposed by a particular adult.

If there are two parents in the house, a fairly simple guideline or agreement that has been very useful to a lot of families is that any consequence that lasts more than that day should have the agreement of both parents. You don't have to tell the child immediately after the bad behaviour, or during the behavioural crisis, how long the consequence lasts for, wait until you can consult with the other parent, which also means waiting till you and the child have cooled down a bit. This rule has a number of advantages:

1. Parents appear united.
2. Parents are less likely to undermine each other.
3. More likely to get sensible decisions and workable consequences (two heads being generally better than one).
4. You are less likely to come out with over-the-top or purely emotional consequences.
5. The weaker or more disliked parent borrows authority from the other parent.

On several occasions I've seen application of this simple rule turn a dangerous situation around and let parents regain control of their child.

Step-parents in particular should never unilaterally dish out long punishments. This will not only create resentment, but it undermines the birth parent's authority and hence their ability to control the child.

Don't expect a miracle – stick with it

Consequences will not solve all your problems. Some older kids are too set in their ways and nothing that you or your home has to offer is going to make much difference in the short term. Some children are so incredibly stubborn that they will ignore short-term rewards and punishments in order to prove their point. Quite often really stubborn, rebellious kids will fight back, or undermine any attempt on your part to take control, so they can get worse for a while before they get better. Consequences can have enormous importance in the long run even if they don't appear to be working in the short term.

It's important for you to realise that regaining control may mean more conflict for a while and sometimes temporarily more abuse. It's worth repeating that it may have to get worse before it gets better. This is possibly why you are stuck and have sunk into such a horrible situation. You have tried various things but been defeated by the short-term resistance of a strong-willed child.

He only cares about one thing!

It can be very difficult finding consequences for uncooperative teens who don't seem to care about anything much. If your child has a special interest such as a particular sport, hobby or pastime (soccer, kung-fu, dancing, drama, etc.) it will be tempting to use this as a consequence. Be very careful!

Let's say it's basketball, (but it could be ballet or chess club) which is the only regular, constructive pursuit that your son or daughter enjoys. There are several problems with using this as a consequence:

1. Are you really willing to follow through?
2. Some young people are stubborn enough, or uncaring enough, to be willing to give up the thing they apparently care about most. I've seen a young man, apparently football-mad, drop out of the team just because his parents stopped him going twice.
3. Do you want him to do it *more* than he wants to do it? You may be very proud of your child's sporting prowess or you may get a lot out of attending the matches and helping to coach the team. If this is the case then you will be punishing yourself more than him. He will probably know, or sense, this and call your bluff. Find something else unless you are really at your wits end and willing to risk a major crisis.
4. Do you want him to do it about as much as he wants to do it (or even close to as much)? If so then he will still have the power if he is more determined than you are and you are going to find it difficult to be assertive about using this as a consequence.
5. Are you prepared to inconvenience other team members, or waste money?
6. Is this his major source of self-esteem? If so then it may be dangerous to meddle with this.
7. Are you prepared for a major crisis if he feels he has nothing more to lose? Losing the thing they care about most can send a young person into a spiral of defiance, destructiveness and self-destructiveness.

My suggestion is this:

Don't stop basketball just because he is behaving badly. Keep it in reserve as a last ditch consequence only if he won't cooperate with other consequences. Thus you may say, "Because you did X you are grounded for three days. If you chose not to cooperate with this grounding then you will not be going to basketball this week and will lose all privileges until you accept your grounding. I want you to go to basketball and you won't lose this privilege if you cooperate with the consequences I set." Note that you are only stopping basketball this week. Even if he does not cooperate with being grounded, you can decide whether or not to let him go next week and stop other privileges. You don't want to lose all your ammunition.

Activities you don't want to encourage

If the one thing he cares about is an activity you **don't** want to encourage, you will obviously be keener to use it as a consequence. A typical example is a child who is addicted to the computer (or any electronic entertainment device). If you worry about how much time he spends on the computer then restricting his time as a punishment kills two birds with one stone. However, this may be a dangerous temptation as you may then be too keen to impose such a punishment and if you give in to the temptation to lecture him about what a waste of time it is, you muddy the waters and create resentment. If you are seriously concerned about how long he spends on the computer then restrict it to some extent regardless of how he behaves and beware of deliberately finding fault because you want to restrict it more.

Resist the temptation to stop the activity completely except as a last resort. Banning a child from something he is addicted to can have unforeseen consequences, such as violence escalation or even him leaving home. Most computer games and social websites are no worse than watching most of the drivel that is on TV. People have become complacent about TV addiction. Is it any worse for a child to spend five hours every evening on the computer than spending that time watching commercial TV? If they are surfing the web and 'talking' to people, they are probably learning more than if they are watching "Bloody Boston Crimes" or "So you think you can yodel" or "Harsh Reality Gardening".

Using friends and boy/girlfriends as consequences

Stopping contact with friends, and especially a girlfriend or boyfriend, can be an *extremely* dangerous strategy which I would nearly always discourage. Some young people are intensely loyal to their friends and if it comes to a choice between them and you – forget it, you don't stand a chance! I've seen teenagers who were not at all extreme in their behaviour leave home rather than give up friends. Who they are friends with is their business; who you have in your home is your business.

If your child believes they are in love (and they may really be in love, even if you think they are too young or they don't really know each other) they may feel fully justified in defying you and in doing whatever it takes to keep in contact.

Another problem with trying to forbid them to associate with friends is that you will often increase your child's loyalty to the friend or friends. This is especially true for boy or girlfriends. I've seen boyfriend and girlfriend become firmly attached because their romance is opposed by one or both families. Seeing themselves as tragic lovers fighting cruel fate is a romantic story likely to turn what might have been a quick dalliance into a passionate affair or even an elopement. Thankfully the majority of teen romances tend not to last very long if left to their own devices (there's no guarantees, though, and sometimes the most unlikely affairs last a number of years, a tiny minority actually last a lifetime). The chances may be small but the sixteen-year-old weirdo your son or daughter is going out with just might be your future daughter or son-in-law.

None of this is to say that you can't have opinions about who your child associates with and of course you have the right to say who comes to your home, but your influence should be subtle or they will resist it strongly. Telling young people how terrible their friends are is not only a waste of your breath and time but is more likely to make them dislike you than dislike their friends. Resist the temptation.

A hint for controlling electronic devices

If you are giving your children a fixed time on computer, TV or other device, it may be easier to delay them starting than getting them to stop early. It's a common time for blow-ups and violence when parents try to prise children and their addictive gadgets apart. So if they are allowed computer time between seven pm and nine pm but have lost twenty minutes time, it may be better that they start at 7.20p.m. rather than finishing twenty minutes earlier. If they choose not to cooperate with starting late, they lose the privilege for the entire evening. If you are going to have a confrontation it's better not to have it at bedtime.

Best of all is if you can set the device to switch off automatically at the appointed time. In some versions of Windows it's possible to have different users with time restrictions on computer use, on specific programs or on the internet. Since many young people are using their computers on the internet you may be able to have the modem switch off automatically at a certain time. You certainly should have the modem in a place where you can control it.

Gadgets and internet connectivity are becoming more and more important to young people (and society generally) and they are more and more often a source of conflict.

I could write a lot more about electronic gadgets, social media, etc., but the rate of change is so fast that it will be out of date by the time you read this!

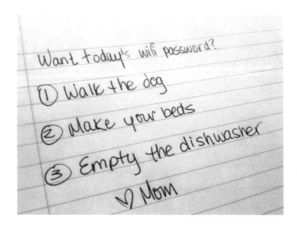

Box

Rick

Rick left home after repeated violence towards his mother and younger brother and was admitted to a youth refuge. Rick felt angry and even rejected by his mother, Rachel, (even though it was **his** choice to leave after he smashed up their kitchen in a drunken rage) but he also felt ashamed of his violent and cowardly behaviour. He told his story to several workers but, naturally enough, played down his own violence to his mother and made many excuses. Most of these workers were young and inexperienced (inevitable as badly underpaid but highly stressful jobs have a high staff turnover). Most of them had been trained or acculturated into the belief that young people with problems are victims and that parents are largely to blame when children go bad. A few youth workers or agencies even have explicit policies of believing what the young person says and of acting as their advocate regardless of how bad their behaviour has been. Rick found that complaints about his mother were not just readily accepted but subtly, and sometimes not so subtly, encouraged. The workers felt that he was "opening up" to them when he talked about his terrible home life. They aren't trained counsellors but they feel as if getting the young people in their care to talk about abuse, neglect and their anger towards their parents is *therapeutic*.

Rick portrays his mother as over-controlling and smothering (not true by most standards). He partly believes this as she was certainly trying hard to control him as his behaviour deteriorated and *any* amount of control was more than he was prepared to accept. The smothering part is pure projection as he himself was until recently very clingy and possessive of his mother, a problem she was well aware of. He finds that viewing her negatively reduces his guilt and he soon begins to really believe that his own behaviour wasn't so bad. Rick is a very adept liar and, like the best liars, he is most convincing when he manages to believe his own stories. He casually mentions to the workers that his mother has hit him, looking upset and choosing not to elaborate. The workers nod knowingly as this fits with their firm preconceptions about the cycle of violence. While technically not a lie, his mother hit him only once in recent years, rather feebly and in pure self-defence as he was physically attacking her at the time. Before that she had slapped his bottom when he was five years old as he had been hitting his little brother with a stick. Before that she slapped him on the hand when he was two. There are those who believe that all hitting of a child is abuse. They may choose to see the abuse as mutual. In some research studies, Rick's violence would be classified as 'mutual violence', as his mother once retaliated, showing what a nonsense some surveys of family violence are.

Like many of the parent-abusing children I see, Rick is bright and articulate and seems such a likeable rogue that the workers really want to believe that he is the victim. This despite the fact that those who have met his mother found her to be clearly intelligent and sensitive. She is an unusually compassionate and kind person, even though currently she is so stressed that she is not at her best. She even looks a bit rough and dishevelled, instead of the elegant and sophisticated woman she once was (she was once an actress). Rick also angrily claims that his little brother is her favourite and that Rick is always seen as the bad one. In actual fact, even though Rick has always been more difficult than his brother, Paul, his mother until recently *slightly* favoured her cheeky older son rather than the quiet and marginalized younger son. It is, of course, inevitable that Rick was seen as the bad one as he has been defiant and difficult for many years while his little brother is timid and well behaved. Paul has become *more* timid because he has been bullied all his life by Rick and his good behaviour is possibly exaggerated because he does not want to be anything like Rick, and does not want to stress their mother even more. The workers conclude that Rick was being 'scapegoated' within the family and they note disparagingly that his mother is quite negative about him and cynical and dismissive about his current good behaviour and the progress they feel he is making in their care. Rachel has been though emotional hell and cannot simply forgive and forget the pain Rick has caused her and Paul. In a very real way she is grieving for the loss of the boy she loved so much, and felt so close to. She is also intelligent enough to know that Rick's behaviour changes with circumstances and she knows her son well enough to realise that he has not made any real attitude changes since leaving home. She feels insulted by the workers implication that he is improving because he is no longer at home. When she tries to warn the residential workers of what probably lies ahead, she meets with icy disapproval of her negativity. It's possible that she is treated even worse because she is beautiful, well-educated and well-connected. The workers actually have more sympathy for mothers who are poor and uneducated and, though they may be somewhat neglectful, such mothers can be seen as victims themselves.

In a joint counselling session at the local child psychiatry service, Rachel was told by a therapist (she said it felt like an order) to tell Rick what his strengths and positives are, without any negativity or blame. She felt humiliated and angry at this and saw Rick smirk behind the therapist's back. She felt that Rick's abusive behaviour was not being taken at all seriously and she felt undermined by the psychologist's approach. She refused to attend another such session and was of course then seen as uncooperative and unmotivated.

Despite their good intentions, workers were helping Rick distance himself from his family and colluding with him in blaming the victim and making excuses. They were thus making it less likely that Rick will deal with his aggression and his desire to control others, and were thus increasing the chances that he will abuse his girlfriends, future wife, and possibly his children in the future. In the short term they are putting him at greater risk since they can't control him either. When he started hanging out with drug takers they were powerless to influence him. After the first two months the residential workers begin to catch glimpses of the kind of abuse that his mother put up with for so long, and they promptly phoned the police when he began smashing furniture. Before it had escalated much more Rick moved on and the workers quickly lost touch with him. The residential workers knew that he had moved in with another former resident who was dealing drugs. They said they couldn't tell Rick's mother where he had gone as that would be breaching

Rick's confidence. Nor did they tell her about his new friend's drug dealing as this was also confidential. It was almost six months before Rachel heard from Rick again. By now he had a drug habit and when she refused to give him any money, he verbally abused her and disappeared for another few months. Devastated, Rachel sank into a deep depression.

Several years later Rick is unemployed and a regular drug user. He has occasional contact with this mother and eventually accepted that she won't let him stay over or give him any money while he is abusing drugs. He's now quite polite to her and has even apologized for past behaviour. He says he's going to go into detox soon. Rachel isn't holding her breath but she is getting on with her life and studying to be a nurse. Without the constant bullying from Rick, Paul is much happier. He's still shy but is a responsible, hard-working A-student.

End Box

Using Pocket Money or Other Quantifiable Privileges

If you have an awkward, uncooperative youngster who doesn't care about your approval or your rules, you may find it difficult to find something he does care about that you can control. Money is one thing that almost all teenagers care about. However, it may not be the best currency to use.

Creating a currency

This chapter discusses using pocket money as a simple and easy to understand *currency*. However, much of what follows applies to using any privilege that you can both quantify and control. For example, if your child has a fixed amount of time on the computer, or on the internet, this can be used as currency. Minutes of computer time are then equivalent to cash. It may be worth changing the rules so that there is a fixed amount of time on a computer, electronic games or TV so that you can then use it as a reward. It **has** to be fixed. If your child is allowed two hours some nights and four on others, then knocking off half an hour is totally meaningless to them. Similarly, if you sometimes give $10 and other weeks give $20 deducting a dollar is too vague to be of interest. You must be very clear about their allowance, whether this is money, time or some other form of credit. If you are on a tight budget, or a bit disorganized, you will need to make giving pocket money a high priority to keep it predictable and regular.

A family I worked with was using bedtime as a quantifiable consequence. Their thirteen-year-old son responded extremely well to this. He was initially given a thirty minute later bedtime (nine p.m. instead of eight thirty p.m.) but could then lose five or ten minutes for swearing or disobedience. For him, this was a meaningful consequence and his behaviour improved quite rapidly. When the couple talked about this in a *Who's in Charge?* group they met with amazement from other parents who asked, 'How do you make him go to bed?' As we've said, consequences have to be of some interest to your child and they must be controllable by you. For the purposes of this chapter, they also have to be controllable in measurable units. Money is easy to understand and so we will use it as an example. It works well for many uncooperative teens who don't care about very much; though computer time works better for some youngsters, it's far harder to control. One advantage is that limiting time playing electronic games is often a desirable goal in itself.

Some possible currencies:

1. Pocket money.
2. Collectables (comics, cards, toys, music).
3. TV time (not really feasible in homes with multiple screens).
4. Computer time.
5. Electronic games (purchase of).
6. Internet access.
7. Access to a prized privilege, such as a motorbike.
8. Bedtime.

In many households (especially if there are more than two children) keeping computers or TV to an exact time takes an awful lot of effort on the part of a parent.

Advantages of giving pocket money

I'm a fan of regular pocket money. My son had $5 pocket money a week at age five, $6 at age six, etc. To our surprise, even at age five he routinely saved it to buy toys. Yet I hear parents of normal twelve-year-olds doubting if their child can handle money. I think this shows how much we infantilize and underestimate our children in some ways.

- Although some children may take a long time to learn the lesson, there is no doubt that having some money of their own can teach children budgeting and the value of money.
- Some children do eventually learn to save and can then buy themselves larger items.
- Children take more responsibility for holidays, pets, hobbies, etc. if they contribute even a very small part of the cost from their own money.
- Children who receive pocket money rather than intermittent treats are less likely to nag parents and may become (somewhat) less demanding. If you give money on demand you are increasing demandingness.
- Should children deliberately damage property or steal they can be made to repay part or all of the cost, making them take responsibility for their actions in a way that arbitrary punishments don't. This very logical consequence won't be available if they don't have any money.
- Parents can use fines as consequences to modify behaviour.
- Children can buy presents for other family members, or friends, on special occasions.

"I can't afford to give pocket money…"

Parents on low incomes often claim they cannot afford to give their children any pocket money. I sometimes get parents to keep a record of all the non-essentials they buy for their children and any money they give them. Often they are giving children **far more** money than those parents who give regular pocket money! Rather than buying sweets and ice creams and occasionally paying for treats such as small toys or cinema tickets, you can give regular pocket money instead. In addition the amount of money we are usually talking about is pretty small when compared to household spending even on non-essential items.

If you are genuinely poor then give them a small allowance.

For older children, some of the money being spent on clothes, phones, transport, holidays, hobbies, etc., can be given as an allowance.

"I can't trust my child with cash..."

If a child is spending most of their money on drugs, alcohol or gambling it may actually be irresponsible to give them cash. If you are unfortunate enough to have a child who is an addict don't give them **any** money if you can possibly help it! An allowance does not have to be in cash.

Some parents of children with an intellectual disability claim that their child is not mature enough to handle money yet such children are often similar to eight to ten-year-olds in maturity and intellect and they are quite capable of handling small amounts of money. If your child is irresponsible and immature then consider giving a smaller amount twice a week, paying them daily, or setting clear rules about how many sweets they can buy.

If necessary you can make rules about how money is spent. Don't listen to arguments that the child has a right to make their own decisions – if they choose to live with you they don't have a *right* to be self-destructive. A common example of parents keeping some control over an allowance is that some of a child's allowance is banked for the child to use for major purchases or holidays. Parents may also pay for club memberships, transport costs, clothes, phones, internet use, hobby materials, books, music, DVDs, etc. directly. You can give vouchers for clothing, petrol, buy tickets for public transport. Any of these can be allocated as a regular allowance with requirements for how the child earns **and** uses the money. But don't make life more complicated than it needs to be. Unless there is a really good reason (such as drug addiction or a disability), it is better that they make their own decisions about spending.

"She doesn't deserve any pocket money!"

Some parents are too angry at their child to consider giving them pocket money. You may have to swallow your pride. If you have *really* given up **all** hope of influencing your child's behaviour you should seriously ask yourself why they are still living at home. If you **are** trying to have some influence over behavioural problems then you may have to give to be able to take away.

Some parents say children have to earn their pocket money by doing chores but since they don't cooperate they don't get any. I hear often that difficult children refuse to do any chores and seem willing to do without any pocket money. If you are trying to change serious behavioural problems then doing chores falls into the 'desirable' category and can wait until the really unacceptable behaviours are under control. If you can improve their beyond-control and abusive behaviour the chances of getting other forms of cooperation become far greater, though still not certain. If you feel strongly that you want to use pocket money to encourage chores my suggestion is that half of their pocket money is unearned and half depends on chores.

The argument that children shouldn't be given money for doing nothing is a bit lame given all the other services parents provide and, that almost all parents are giving children some money on an ad hoc basis.

Pocket money as payment for chores

There is a serious problem with giving pocket money as payment for chores. At the extreme consider a child who is paid for doing his homework and for making his bed. What is likely to happen when the payment stops? He stops. Studies have found that children directly rewarded for doing something, even something they enjoy, will do it less than they otherwise would have when rewards are stopped. If a child is always paid for his contribution to the housework then he will probably never see this as his responsibility. Getting children to eventually take responsibility for their homework, belongings, hygiene, room, etc. is a crucially important part of maturation... and sometimes quite a struggle.

It's interesting that studies in the UK and Australia find that boys are given more pocket money than girls even though girls do far more chores than boys[431]. Obviously people expect girls to help out and are more surprised, and more thankful, when boys do so. Income inequality starts young!

Paying children for doing jobs that are not their responsibility is quite different. Thus many children earn extra pocket money washing cars or mowing the lawn. If these are clearly not **their** responsibility this is fine and quite different to giving pocket money for doing **their** chores. If you think they should be making a contribution to housework then don't pay them for doing so.

If you want them to take the responsibility for cleaning their own room, for example, then paying them for doing so may get the job done but is going to make them less likely to take responsibility for this. This is tantamount to saying that they are doing it for you rather than for themselves. You can turn this on its head by **charging them** for your services. If they don't keep their room to a reasonable standard (and to my mind this should mean dirt and poor hygiene, not just untidiness) then you will be forced to clean it out once a month. The cost of your labour is deducted from their allowance (it will not be good rate of pay, but it makes the point). This reinforces that it's their responsibility, not yours. This reduces their sense of entitlement and over time means they are less likely to take you for granted. You could apply the same reasoning to picking up after them. You could charge them a very small amount, e.g. ten cents per item, if they regularly leave things lying around the house that you have to pick up.

If you want to use pocket money as a consequence for behaviour change then it's confusing to also use it as a payment for doing chores. If a child feels they have earned their pocket money they may be very resentful at it then being taken away because of misdemeanours; if their behaviour is currently very bad then getting them to do chores should be less of a priority (desirable but not essential).

He (or she) works and earns his own money

For some parents, having a teenager who is working complicates things and makes them feel even more powerless. Whether they are working full-time or just a few hours a week it should be easier to make them pay for anything broken or stolen. If you are not charging them any board then I think you should think about why not? If you charge them board you could have different rates depending on whether they are cooperative or not or abusive or not. If they are treating you like shit and the house like a hotel then charge them the going rate for board. If they treat you like a parent then you can be more generous and charge them the family rate. If they refuse to treat you like a parent then why should they get a family rate?

Your response may be that they won't give you any board. If they are working full time then why are you allowing them to remain at home if they are choosing to be independent? In most cases it costs a great deal more to live away from home (see section on Leaving home). If they are still at school and working part time chances are they need your permission to work so ultimately you have the power to enforce compliance. If they persist in refusing to pay any board you should consider strike action.

If they have a poorly paid part-time job you could agree to waive their board as long as they are cooperating and not abusing anyone in the home, or you could take part of their pay as board but return most of this to them minus fines or the cost of any damage.

Never stop <u>all</u> pocket money or give impulsive fines

In counselling young people I've found they will sometimes deny getting any pocket money when, from the parent's point of view, it has been temporarily suspended either as a punishment or to pay damages. The child has quickly forgotten about it and it's usually having **no** influence whatsoever on their behaviour. It seems to have far more impact to receive a part, even a small part, of their pocket money allowance rather than zero. Children who have lost all privileges sometimes just give up. Their attitude is similar to a prisoner on a life sentence who feels he has nothing left to lose. If they are promised that they will get back pocket money, or other privileges, when they 'behave' they often don't believe this will ever happen.

Strongly resist the urge to say "no pocket money for you" and the urge to impose arbitrary fines. Use fines only as planned or it may backfire and you will have an even more angry and defiant youngster. If you are using access to a computer (or such) as currency then taking the computer away completely means that you've lost your ammunition.

You can make a cut-off point where no more fines are imposed but some other consequence comes into play. E.g. it may be that when pocket money reaches $2 in any week you stop imposing further fines but instead suspend certain privileges.

Using fines

I'll use the word 'fines' but this includes time deducted if the currency is computer or internet use.

A common use of fines in the families I have worked with has been to stamp out swearing. This has often been very effective, though it does not work for all children (nothing does). Although some people think swearing is trivial, it's often linked to verbal abuse and it feeds anger. Getting control over this can be a very important step to regaining control and creating a more peaceful home.

I'll give some points about using fines for swearing but they virtually all apply to any other clearly definable behaviour.

Define the behaviour

Swearing is what you decide it is. It's your home, your child, and your money that you are choosing to give or not to give. You need to clearly define what you mean by swearing. Simplest is to ban a few serious swear words. You may even start with just the worst, usually the eff word (though sadly the 'C' word is becoming more common). You may choose to include rude gestures or certain insults, e.g. banning calling people 'retard' or 'gay'. Don't be too strict! You may wish that your children did not use slang, mild profanities, or say 'whatever' in a sneering manner, but if they are also using heavy duty swear words or being verbally abusive to you then ignore the slang and minor profanities for now.

Make a clear contract

Be really clear and precise about what is being fined and how much the fine will be. If you have a partner then make sure they are 100% behind you and compromise about any details necessary to get their cooperation. If you don't have a partner, find someone else to discuss the details with. You might consult your children and you may be influenced by their ideas but you don't have to negotiate and they definitely don't have a veto; they don't have to like it. Don't make it too complicated for your child to understand or so complicated that they can play barrack-room lawyer and argue about interpretations of the rules. It's best if the rules are written down. However, do not get caught in an unchangeable contract. Try out any new rules for a week or two then change them if necessary. If you are making progress and a child is swearing much less then you can increase the size of the fine or even include less serious swear words or insults.

Keep it fair

Fines for swearing should apply to everyone in the family. If parents are not willing to give up or reduce their own swearing then they are unlikely to ever get their children to stop. It can actually be an advantage if one or both parents occasionally swear if they are willing to be fined. My suggestion is that the fine for an adult is far bigger than the fine for a child.

Keep fines small

Any regular fines need to be small fines.

Some parents find small fines distasteful because the punishment does not fit the crime, particularly if they are swearing at you. In families, especially if you are trying to gain control of a badly behaved or disturbed child, the punishment does **not** have to fit the crime and seldom does. If you catch your child the first time they **ever** swear at or abuse a parent, you may be able to impose a memorable punishment and clearly demonstrate that you are not going to take it. I clearly remember the worst punishment of my childhood. When I was about eight-years-old I called my mother 'A big ape' under my breath but a friend told her what I'd said. I was sent to my room for the remainder of the day, which seemed like a long prison term to me. I never did that again!

However, once a child is openly defying authority, in a state of near constant anger or feels unloved and rejected (whether this is realistic or not), imposing harsh punishments will usually make things worse, not better. If behaviour has been allowed to become a habit you need to impose small, manageable consequences. Trying to be **strict** gets in the way of being **firm** and consistent.

Deciding the size of the fine

Work out what you would give them if they had a perfect week, i.e. no swearing (or whatever behaviour we are trying to eliminate or encourage). This should be more than they are getting at present.

The idea is that if they have an average week (given their current behaviour) then they will end up with half of their maximum pocket money. I would advise to aim at more than half rather than less. Some parents think that 'if they continue being so horrible they should end up with nothing or next to nothing.' But the intention is to encourage improvement not to make them suffer. If you make them suffer they may well become more determined not to change. The principle of minimum coercion applies here (see page 307).

Either estimate how often they swear in a week or, better still, keep a record for a week. Divide the Maximum Pocket Money by the Swears-Per-Week and then halve this. This would mean on a typical week they will get half of their Maximum. If this means that they are only being fined ten cents for telling their mother to f**k off you may feel tempted to make it bigger. But if they then end up with next to nothing they are liable to give up, or swear more.

Our hope is that they will improve their behaviour and move towards Maximum Pocket Money.

Let's look at an example. Saul is a twelve-year-old who has taken to swearing at Belinda, his (sole-parent) mother and his brother on a fairly regular basis. She keeps a count for a week and finds that he swears a total of fifty times in a week. He was getting $10 pocket money but she would be happy to give him double this if he behaved well. So Maximum Pocket Money = $20. Dividing fifty into $20 gives 40 cents and halving this gives us a fine of only 20 cents. Belinda, however, finds the idea of such a low fine for such significant disrespect repugnant and first tries a 40 cent fine. Saul, being a stubborn lad who doesn't want his mother to regain control, swears fifty times in the first four days. Since he is now not getting any money he thinks, 'Might as well be hung for a sheep as a lamb!' and swears at twice his normal rate for the rest of the week. The system comes crashing down as Saul doesn't care about next week enough to improve his behaviour. So after a week's break they start all over again with a 20 cent fine. The next week Saul swears slightly above average, sixty times in all, and gets $8 pocket money. Next week he decides to 'fool' his mother by not swearing at all. He doesn't quite manage it but gets $19 pocket money. Belinda pretends to be annoyed at having to hand over so much money but is really delighted. It takes a long time but over the next six months his swearing becomes fairly rare and his mother decides to keep the pocket money at $20 provided he does the lawn once a week and she now removes internet privileges for a day when he swears at her. If she has to cut the lawn he pays her $10 for doing his job (not voluntarily of course, she stops it from his next allowance).

This is not a *logical* consequence but a combination of rewards and punishments. When it works well the child will be getting more pocket money than previously so it's more reward than punishment, as in the example of Saul. Since they can earn extra money, some stubborn difficult young people actually welcome this instead of being determined to undermine it as they are with most disciplinary changes. If you are worried about it being a 'punishment', or anyone suggests that this is too negative, just regard it as a 'reward' for good behaviour (it's both). But don't talk of them being paid for normal, responsible behaviour. That would be counterproductive.

Bonuses

Particularly early on in applying quantifiable consequences you can give one-off bonuses to encourage the child's cooperation and speed up change. For example, Saul could have been offered a five dollar bonus for a perfect week for the first month. Such bribes are sometimes useful in breaking patterns of behaviour and for demonstrating control, but use them cautiously. Be careful what you promise. If Belinda was not prepared to give $30 pocket money on a regular basis she needs to be careful to keep this special offer strictly time limited. Double pocket money only for the first 'perfect' week is reasonable.

Let the consequences speak for you

One of the advantages of using a small fine is that parents can step back and be less emotionally involved. Many parents have found that either getting upset or getting angry can add fuel to the fire with some children, and either can lead to a loss of respect for the parent.

Before starting the system of fines, Belinda was getting either angry or upset, or often both, when Saul swore at her. Since he was doing it in order to feel powerful and to annoy her and his brother, this was positively reinforcing for him. Once starting the fines she reported feeling much less upset. In fact she would sometimes use reverse psychology and said things like, "Can you swear more, I'm a bit short of money this week." Saul no longer felt powerful as he wasn't getting the reaction he wanted. So this is not just about training the young person but it is about changing the dynamics of the interaction and changing the parent's behaviour.

Changing your attitude can sometimes work wonders. Some parents have adopted a calm, "Oh well, I'd rather you didn't swear but at least you are saving me money," attitude rather than lecturing or getting upset. Using humour can also help.

Clear fines, as with other clearly defined consequences, can make punishments less personal and can be especially helpful if parents have been undermining one another, if one parent has a poor relationship with the child, or for step-parents (even those with a good relationship with the child). Instead of "I am going to impose my will on you and punish you," it becomes "You know the rule, you've just lost 20 cents."

Keep track of fines

It's crucially important that you don't get confused and forget about fines. There are a great number of ways of keeping track.

- Keep a notebook where you record each fine.
- Write on a poster or whiteboard (only if you can trust the children not to tamper or destroy these).
- Have a swear box in which cash is put each time someone swears (only if no-one is going to steal or smash it).
- Use tokens, buttons, toy money (coins or notes) to represent the pocket money. These can be added to a swear box or removed from a jar representing next week's pocket money for each child. This visual reminder is very effective for some children (especially disabled children).
- Write or print out dozens of IOUs to represent next week's pocket money.
- Keep an electronic record on a handheld computer or mobile phone.
- If you are a sole parent with a really good memory, you can simply announce the new amount of pocket money when each fine is imposed.

It's also extremely important that you pay them the agreed pocket money. I'm sometimes a bit shocked that parents say they can't afford to give pocket money when this is a tiny part of their budget. If you are using it to regain control of a defiant, abusive child, it's an *essential* that you must put it aside no matter what.

What to do with fines collected

Especially if adults are also paying fines you need to decide what to do with the money. This could be used for something, such as an outing, for the whole family or could be given to charity.

Paying for damage or theft

A major advantage of giving pocket money for those with very badly behaved children is that they can pay something towards deliberate breakages, wastage or theft. It's an important principle that young people be made to pay for damage to the home or property. Thus if a child kicks a hole in the door he should always pay something towards repair. Parents sometimes will say that the child could not possibly pay for the damage done as their pocket money is insignificant compared to hundreds, or even thousands, of dollars' worth of damage. I believe children should always pay *something*, even if this is a tiny fraction of the cost. I once met a mother and ten-year-old son shortly after he had smashed every window in the house. As the cost was about two hundred times his weekly pocket money the mother had not considered making him pay anything towards repair costs. After discussion she decided to make him pay a total of $25 over a ten week period. This was a meaningful consequence for the boy and helped discourage such behaviour.

If a child steals from other family members he can be made to repay the amount from his pocket money or allowances, or by selling his belongings if necessary.

Paying for damage done or for theft should be seen as a responsibility not as a punishment. Parents may want to impose some form of punishment as well as the child making recompense. If the child just pays for things they steal, there is no real economic disincentive. Imagine if you could go to a store and attempt to steal whatever you wanted. If caught you just have to pay for the item. Where's the disincentive?

If it's potentially a large amount (compared to the child's weekly pocket money) then before deciding how much recompense should be paid or what the rate of repayment will be, you should carefully think about it and preferably talk through the details with your partner or someone else. Although you can tell a child that they will be paying for the damage, you don't tell them immediately (when you are still angry) what the details are.

As with fines it's important not to stop **all** pocket money. It's easier for children to forget about it if they simply receive no pocket money for a period of time and there is little incentive for them not to repeat the behaviour. Many children do not look further into the future more than a few weeks (or days for some), and losing pocket money for two months is exactly the same to them as losing pocket money for one month. It's generally not worth continuing with a repayment for more than two or three months.

If you feel that your child is making genuine attempts to change his behaviour you may decide to call an amnesty and cancel all fines and repayments after a couple of months. Don't do this so quickly that they think you are soft or not going to follow through with your threats in future.

The 7 Cs

This is a short summary chapter of points collected together for easy reference.
Most of these points are elaborated in other chapters.

Clarity, Consistency, Consequences, Choices, Cool, Calm & Concise
If you are feeling all at sea dealing with an abusive or beyond control child (or one heading in that direction) the following simple ideas have been found helpful by many parents in your situation. Sadly, there are probably a lot more parents in your situation than you think!

Clarity

Be clear about what behaviours you find *unacceptable*, as opposed to just annoying, disappointing or undesirable. Prioritise. Don't try to change everything or control everything (you can't, and the attempt can lead to civil war).

Be as clear as possible about your rules and expectations. Before you impose consequences, clearly define the behaviour you want to change. Talking about their 'bad attitude' or 'insolence' is too vague.

Consistency

Consistency is crucially important with difficult, stubborn children. This means both your own consistency and consistency between those in a parental role.

Aim for *Firm* not *Strict*. Firm means being consistent and assertive. Being strict means having harsh punishments or lots of inflexible rules. It's easier to be consistent if you have *less* rules and *less* severe consequences.

The punishment does NOT need to fit the crime. With a lot of parental abuse it's impossible to have a consequence which reflects the seriousness of the behaviour that you can apply often enough. If they lose all their privileges, many children will escalate their behaviour since they feel they have no reason to try anymore (and they believe that they are being victimised). For some of these kids, next week is a long time away and next month might as well not exist.

Avoid giving consequences *during* the crisis. You may be too emotional to have good judgment, and when they are in a rage they don't care about consequences and are more likely to escalate than back down. If you do give a consequence while they are still angry just state what the consequence will be but not for how long or how much (i.e. quality but not quantity of consequence).

If you have a partner, don't give *any* consequence that lasts beyond that day without consultation (this goes well with the last rule and has made a big difference in some families).

If you and your partner have different views you need to compromise and back each other up as far as possible. Try to present a united front – this is more important than the exact details of rules or consequences. It's unlikely that you and your partner will have identical ideas about dealing with a difficult child (even if you agreed when things were going well), so compromises will be needed. There is no one right answer to these problems, so don't get stuck in *your* way of doing it. In blended families the step-parent can be consulted though the main decision-maker about consequences should be the birth parent.

Don't try things unless you are willing to follow through. Trying something half-heartedly is not only unlikely to work but it makes you look wishy-washy.

Consequences

They need to care about the consequence, but they don't have to care *a lot* about it (they may not care a lot about anything).

Do *you* care about the consequence as much, or more, than they do? If so, it probably won't work. If you really want them to do a sport or activity then threatening to stop this is usually a waste of time (they will sense your indecision or may just give it up).

It's really important to find consequences that you are able to control, with or without their co-operation. If you use a consequence that does require some co-operation, have a slightly more serious *back-up consequence* that doesn't need their co-operation.

If your child is doing something unacceptable with high frequency, the consequence will need to be both small and measurable (e.g. pocket money, time on computer, bedtime).

Choices

If the rules and consequences are very clear you can avoid giving stubborn, oppositional children orders. You can give them a choice instead, which is less likely to make them dig their heels in and is harder to argue about. "You can go to bed now or you can lose a half-hour of X-box tomorrow. It's up to you?" "I can see you are getting angry. If you choose to have another tantrum, you'll have to pay for any damage and lose electronic privileges for one or two days."

Orders trigger defiance and arguments in oppositional youngsters, choices are less likely to do so. Choices also reinforce the fact that aggression and bad behaviour is chosen behaviour and they can choose to change.

Cool and calm

Take emotional or verbal abuse *seriously*, but don't take it *personally*. They don't usually mean what they say. Don't let them wind you up or make you feel guilty, but don't ignore verbal abuse either. Try not to be either passive or aggressive but aim for assertive. Try hard to keep calm and in command (or fake it till you make it).

If you are either getting angry regularly or becoming distressed and despairing these can both lead to loss of respect. In a crisis, try to act more like a professional than a parent and keep your own emotions in check to some extent (but this is hard, so don't feel guilty about only being human).

Concise

Don't give lectures or sermons when giving consequences. Keep it as simple and straightforward as possible. Don't mix up consequences for serious misbehaviour with comments about other things you disapprove of. If the consequence is for staying out past curfew, don't use that as an excuse to have a go at the child's friends, this will lead to an argument where the child will probably end up feeling that you are in the wrong, not them.

A few other points

Don't excuse abuse. Be very aware of your rights as a human being and as a parent. Part of looking after them is looking after you.

Take it very seriously if other children witness you being abused. They are likely to lose respect for you, even if they are on your side. This can create serious problems at a later date. They will lose even more respect for you if there are no obvious consequences for the abusive behaviour or if the behaviour is rewarded. So consequences give an important message to your other children even if they don't appear to be affecting the difficult child.

The Principle of Least Force: if you want someone to change their attitudes, it works better if they feel it's their decision. The more force you apply the less they see it as chosen behaviour and the more likely they will revert to their old behaviour as soon as the pressure lets up. So don't make rewards or punishments larger than necessary and don't monitor them closer than is necessary if you want them to develop self-control and responsibility.

Don't negotiate with terrorists! If they are using bullying tactics, including threats to get their own way, you need to stubbornly refuse to budge, even when it's easier to give in. If you pay off blackmailers they just come back for more.

In the long run one of the worst things you can possibly do for your child is to let them practise being an abuser. This can not only ruin *their* lives but potentially also the lives of your future daughter-in-law or son-in-law and your future grandchildren.

Plans and Contracts

The following is a contract worked out by a single-Mum and her twelve-year-old son. I had been counselling them both for a month but they worked this out between them. It isn't necessarily perfect and in most cases I would not advise having so many consequences applied at once. If he was being violent more often than weekly, then removing privileges for as long as forty-eight hours wouldn't work. But it worked and has inspired other parents in the *Who's in Charge?* groups. Don't include a sentence like the first one if it isn't true. Not all young people are motivated to stop.

Agreement between Harley & Rose

Harley does not like how he behaves when in a rage and is determined to give up being violent and abusive towards his mother. The following behaviours of Harley's are agreed to be unacceptable:

1. Any violence, including grabbing or pushing.
2. Throwing things at Rose.
3. Deliberately damaging property.
4. Swearing at Rose.
5. Calling Rose names.

Any time Harley does 1, 2 or 3 he will lose privileges immediately for forty-eight hours (two full days). If he does four or five he will lose privileges for twenty-four hours.

Loss of Privileges means:

- Grounded (except for school, appointments, basketball or other things which Rose thinks are important).
- No T.V. or electronic games.
- Loss of pocket money for that day, i.e. 50c per day.
- No special treats.

Harley is expected to cooperate with Loss of Privileges. If he refuses to stay grounded or watches T.V. he will lose the T.V. from his room for a week, miss basketball and be fined an extra 50c each day he does not cooperate.

If violence or abuse is particularly serious Rose may also call the police or impose other punishments. She should not impose other punishments until the following day or once she has had time to talk to someone about the situation.

Time Out

Time Out is not a punishment but a way of cooling down the situation to stop fights. Rose may send Harley to his room if she is getting angry too. This is fair because Harley is the one who has been violent and abusive and Rose has to do things to take care of Harley.

If Rose sees that Harley is working himself up into a rage she will immediately ask him to *take five* minutes time out. This is half the normal time and only applies if Harley goes to his room quickly and reasonably quietly without argument, further abuse of Rose or property (furniture, walls or doors). If Harley does not go immediately to his room then the usual time of ten minutes will apply.

If Harley makes any loud noises or opens the door for any reason then Time Out starts again (a timer will be used).

Time Out does not affect the punishments set out above.

Time Out for Rose

If Rose fears that a serious situation is developing she can take a Time Out in her room or out of the house. She promises that this will be for no more than thirty minutes.

Signed: Harley Rose

When is a contract not a contract?

Fourteen-year-old Toby crumpled up the paper and declared, "I'm not signing that! It just gives you more power!"

"I'm not asking you to sign it. It's what we're going to do. You don't have to like it."

Molly had worked out a plan of action with consequences (and back-up consequences) based partly on the above contract between Harley and Rose. But her son wasn't showing signs of wanting to change and she didn't expect him to sign it. He had signed contracts before when they'd attempted mediation but he had not followed through with his part of the deal. He uncrumpled the plan and tore it up into small pieces, which he let flutter to the floor. Molly was prepared for this and, with a sardonic smile, pulled out another copy. He tore that up too. Next morning he woke to find a third copy stuck to the fridge. It lasted a week before he got into another rage and tore it up too. By then he knew what it said so she didn't bother replacing the paper, but stuck to the plan.

"How can you we have a contract if I don't agree to it and won't sign it?" he asked one day.

"You don't have to agree to the laws of the country. You still suffer the consequences if you break the rules, same here. This is the law of our home."

"What if I don't want to live here anymore?"

"The door isn't locked. The door has never been locked."

"Fine I'll go to Dad's."

"That's always been an option but you know Dad is stricter than me and you don't like his girlfriend. If you think you'd be happier there you can go at the end of term. But you can't return here during term time. I'm sorry if you don't feel happy here. But you were even more unhappy when we were fighting all the time."

Negotiation is nice, but not essential

There's a book I recommend called, "Stop Negotiating with your teen[432]." I've had a couple of parents say that just the title was liberating. The idea that they don't have to negotiate everything was a great relief, and often went against the advice they were being given by other professionals. Negotiating can be a farce if you are dealing with someone who doesn't want to play the game or who has no qualms about lying.

If we are dealing with an uncooperative young person, it makes no sense to think that we have to negotiate or have an agreed contract. You need consequences that you can enforce with or without cooperation and the important thing is that you are firm and clear enough to stick to it. If there are others involved in parenting your child it's important you have their agreement. The next example shows separated parents working together.

Instead of a contract you may want to present your plan of action in the form of a letter (probably an e-mail nowadays).

Dear Bailey,

It's totally unacceptable that you are being violent to me and your brother, damaging property, and staying out all night. I understand that you are going through a bad patch since your father and I separated but this is no excuse for such behaviour. Your father and I both still love you and, although we disagree on lots of things we agree that we do not want you going down the path you have been taking. He has agreed that any consequences I impose, such as no internet or reductions in pocket money, will apply when you go there too. We may not be a couple but are still parents and have agreed to work together. He will no longer be giving you money when I don't. From now on you can get a maximum of $42 pocket money (half from each of us) but this is dependent on your behaviour at either home.

Swearing at any of us, or aggressively swearing in front of your father or me, is not acceptable, nor is verbal abuse or insults. There will be a 40 cent fine for each incident.

Any day in which you are physically abusive to myself, your brother or to property you will lose from $3 to $6 (this will be decided by either or both of us the following day). You will also lose internet access for twenty-four hours.

Any day on which you stay out all night without permission you do not get pocket money so $7 will be deducted. In addition you will have no internet access for the next twenty-four hours.

Not attending school without a valid reason means you lose $5 from your pocket money and no internet for the remainder of that day.

I know you will be angry and resentful about these rules. That is unavoidable. Eventually you will realise that we are doing this as much for your good as for ours.

With love,

Legal Last Resorts

"Calling the police on your own child is a nightmare no parent likes to consider, but the willingness to do so, stated clearly to the teen, can mean the difference between parenting firmly and with impact and watching one's child destroy lives, including his own." Edgette[433]

Calling the police, charging an abusive teen, taking out a legal restraining/intervention order or making them leave home are the desperate last resorts for some parents.

Parents, including some of those struggling with very difficult children, sometimes say to me: "I could *never* kick my own child out of the home," or "I could *never* call the cops on my own flesh and blood." They are almost always deluding themselves. There are situations so extreme that it would be foolish and negligent not to make them leave home or charge them. They may be putting your life in danger, beating up a younger brother or sister, bringing heavy drugs and dealers into your home, destroying your property, pawning your property, stealing from you on a regular basis, etc. Such extremes are thankfully rare and hopefully it will never come to that. But the reality is that there are situations when almost any parent will be *forced* to either make them leave home or use legal remedies. Don't underestimate how subtle bullying and undermining can eventually wear down the strongest parent, so don't be critical of parents who have found it necessary to do the unthinkable.

On the other hand there are people, including some professionals, who make blanket statements such as, "You should always charge them if they are violent" or "Any sane parent will kick out a violent child who is over sixteen." They themselves may or may not be that tough (no one knows until they are in that position) but the majority of people are extremely reluctant to charge their own child with assault or make them leave home. For some ethnic groups, the stigma attached to such actions is even greater than for Anglo families, and it may be enormous for parents who are themselves professionals, such as teachers and welfare workers. There are, of course, a few neglectful, uncaring parents who don't find it difficult to kick their child out once they reach their mid-teens, but they are not likely to be reading this.

Using the threat

Generally speaking I discourage parents from making threats, but threats can be useful at times. While it's really important that you don't make threats that you would be unwilling to carry out, once you are really willing to follow through, then the threat can become a useful tool. But bluffing hardly ever works out well.

Desperate parents sometimes talk about 'giving their child a scare' by calling the police or taking out a legal order. This can be valid in some extreme circumstances. However, this does **not** mean that you need to maximise the scare by springing it on them. In the majority of cases it's better to forewarn the child that you intend to call the police, charge them, or make them leave home if they are violent or destructive again. Don't make such threats idly. You have to mean it or you are likely to lose more respect. Don't be vague: Comments such as 'If you disrespect me again I'm going to call the police' or 'If you break anything else I'm charging you' are too imprecise. This may even increase their low-level disrespect, 'Yeah, whatever, loser!' or they break something of little value by 'accident' to see if you are going to follow through. (If you do follow through they will play the victim and the police may be quite unimpressed and unhelpful).

Make serious threats when you are calm, not in the middle of a crisis. If you have already said it during a crisis, repeat it calmly. You may want to sit down with your child along with your partner, or with someone else as witness, and tell your child what you are planning to do next time they are violent. State it as a promise and try to ensure that they know you mean business. You may want to put it in writing, along the lines of:

"It's not acceptable that you get yourself into a rage and become physically violent or destroy property. If you let this happen again we will phone the police and have you charged. We do not wish to do this but we would be failing in our duty as parents if we let you continue with such behaviour. In the long run this is for your own good but we realise you probably won't appreciate this in the near future."

Legal remedies

Calling the police. At present there are very few places in the world where there are clear police guidelines telling them how to deal with violence to parents. In Melbourne, I hear extremes of both police inaction (more common) and overreaction (rare). Different police stations have different approaches and individual officers may vary greatly in attitude and behaviour, which means a parent cannot predict what sort of response they will get. This is certainly not unique to Melbourne. In Seattle the Step-up program has been running for fifteen years and they have a possibly unique system whereby young people are mandated by the Courts to attend a group program designed specifically for violence to parents so possibly the place in the world where police should be most familiar with violence to parents. Yet this description, from the developers of the Step-up program, sounds all too familiar:

"Unfortunately, because this problem is often misunderstood, and the violence not regarded seriously, some officers respond by reprimanding parents for calling the police about a 'parenting matter.' Parents may be blamed by officers, empowering the teens to continue, and possibly escalate, the violence." Routt & Anderson[434]

The situation is similar in the UK with the added affront that parents can be fined for their children's crime, even if the crime is directed towards the parent!

Calling the police is not an easy or simple solution for parents. I've heard a number of parents say it was the hardest thing they have ever done but it can be a major turning point in letting your child know that you are not going to put up with abuse (of you, other children, or of property). Calling the police is sometimes very helpful but quite often it's not taken seriously[435] particularly by younger children. In recent years I have heard of eleven to thirteen years-olds, boys and girls, being rude to the police or afterwards saying, "Well they didn't do anything, did they?" or even "They can't tell me what to do either!"

So it can be empowering for parents, but sometimes it's more humiliating. Occasionally it's more empowering for the violent young person.

Many parents just want some authority figure to give the child a talking to. Some police officers are happy to do this, and a few do it well, but others see it as a complete waste of their time if the parent is not willing to prosecute. With more children nowadays unafraid of the police and, if you are not going to follow through (either by laying criminal charges or taking out a legal order), then calling the police may be an anticlimax. A few police are too sympathetic and let the child air their grievances rather than lay down the law. Other police make over-the-top threats that may scare the child at the time but might seem empty, even funny, the next day and a minority of police clearly blame the parents and a few convey this to the child.

A sole mother of a violent boy rang the police to say that he was threatening to stab her with a kitchen knife. The policeman at the other end of the phone took it seriously until he asked how old the boy was. On being told he was eleven the distraught mother was told, "For goodness sake, get the knife off of him, kick him up the bum, and get yourself some parenting lessons." That's one extreme.

"For parents, the experience of having police minimize their victimisation contributed to their sense of hopelessness and discouraged them from seeking assistance in the future." Cottrell[436]

The other extreme was shown to the mother of a thirteen-year-old girl who was pushing and verbally abusing her. An over-helpful policeman decided that this mother needed to be protected and coerced her to take out an 'Intervention Order' against her daughter (see next section). The mother was not afraid of the girl and did not need or want such an order.

Occasionally the police action of giving your child a stern warning, or just turning up, makes a child realise that their behaviour is serious and that you can call for help.

There are a few things you can do to increase the odds of a positive response when calling the police.

1. Forewarn the police. If you have a child who is becoming violent or destructive consult the local police prior to the next blow-up.
2. Find out if there is a specialist youth or family violence police officer in your area and talk to them. This can sometimes make an enormous difference.

3. Be clear what you are willing to do and what you are hoping to achieve. If you have a partner, discuss your options before the next crisis and agree on a course of action you can both live with. Being clear in your own mind is important to prevent a) things spiralling out of your control, b) appearing indecisive and wishy-washy to the police and, more importantly, to your child.

4. Don't give your child ammunition to use against you. If your child assaulted you after you slapped them, the police will often be less sympathetic and may even report you as an abuser. If you and your child had a wrestling match and were both being violent, it may not be worth calling the police even if you have bruises and they don't (especially if it's a younger teen or pre-teen). If the police view you as an abuser, the child may feel vindicated, powerful and even less respectful of you. Be aware that for younger children in many places calling the police is likely to result in a notification to Child Protection services. Are you prepared for this?

An investigation by Child Protection can make matters worse even if they then drop the case. I've had several parents say that their child was more cocky and arrogant after being interviewed by protective workers.

5. Investigate your legal options so you can be clear about what you are asking for, e.g. knowing what can and can't be done with a 'Restraining' or 'Intervention Order' in your area.

6. You may want to take a support person with you when you go to talk to the police or have a friend or relative come round when you do phone the police.

Legal Restraining Orders

As the law varies between countries and States, I can't give any detailed information about what legal remedies are available. Besides which, I'm not a legal expert so consult someone who knows your local system. The most commonly used legal remedy here in Victoria is called an 'Intervention Order' but I'll use the term 'Restraining Order' as this is a more common name and makes more sense. It may well be called something different in your locale.

Restraining Orders were designed primarily for the safety of women being abused by their male partners. In Victoria there has been a steady increase in the number being taken out by parents against their children. They can work wonderfully... but they can also be a complete waste of time or even harmful.

A Restraining Order is simply a legal order saying that the person they are served on may not assault, abuse or harass another person or persons. Sometimes there is an element of farce due to the fact that assaulting someone is illegal already so why should we need an order saying they are not allowed to do this? However, the reality is that police are often reluctant to follow through on domestic assaults unless there is an order, and verbal abuse and property damage within the home are easier for them to deal with if there is an order prohibiting it. The order usually (but not always) makes the offender take it more seriously. However, even with an order forbidding verbal abuse or harassment, this can be almost impossible to prove and the line between disrespect and abuse is very blurry.

There are several things that affect whether these orders are useful or not.

1. You **must** be willing to follow through. I meet parents who have been encouraged, or even forced, to take out an Order but were not willing to either have

their child charged or make them leave home. So when the child breaches the conditions of the order and the parent fails to phone the police, the child can end up feeling more powerful. I caution parents not to take out such an order until they feel ready to take decisive action if it's breached. Children usually sense if their parent is serious or not.

2. Your child must be old enough and mature enough to understand the order. I've seen Restraining Orders taken out on twelve-year-olds who didn't really understand the implications and the parents were definitely not going to make them leave home. Even if the parent is willing to charge the child with a breach, there may be little the courts can do and the child may not care. This is not just a waste of time and resources (Courts cost a lot of money) but the parent has fired off their guns and is less likely to use an order in the future, even when the child is old enough to understand it. Beware of premature adjudication! It's not really chronological age that matters, if you have a sixteen-year-old with an intellectual disability, the same thing may apply. But I've seen legal orders be very effective with older teens with intellectual disabilities.

3. How flexible are the equivalent legal orders where you live? Many parents don't consider taking out a Restraining Order as they think this will automatically mean that their child is made to leave home. In most jurisdictions this is **not** the case and the majority of such orders are for the child to stop abusing, not to make them leave home.

4. Does your child care about the law? There are a few individuals who have such contempt for the law that a Restraining Order can actually make them more dangerous, not less.

5. How much does your child have to lose? A child who cares about authority in general (not necessarily your authority) or who cares about being embarrassed is more likely to respond to a legal order. An older child who is working can be fined by the courts if they breach an order and this may be a very good incentive. Would they care if they were made to leave home if they breach the order?

6. A restraining order does not show up in police checks for a criminal record, however breaching such an order does, as this constitutes an offence. Would your child care about having a criminal record (assuming they don't already have one)? I've known children boast about having a legal order on them.

The Juvenile Justice System and residential care

Every treatment has some costs. Taking a child for counselling often helps but it can also reinforce the child's (or others') belief that he or she is different and problematic. Getting parents together (as in my *Who's in Charge?* groups) has very little apparent cost but getting groups of problem children together is a different matter. This has obvious and proven costs. If you have been desperate enough to talk to professionals about your child going into residential care, they probably warned you that many children get worse by mixing with other problem children. I have seen children who have gone into residential care quite quickly take up new vices, sniffing glue, taking drugs, drinking, stealing cars, burglary and even prostitution (boys too). This is well known and there is plenty of evidence that when a young person goes into juvenile prison the chances of reoffending increase dramatically.

Residential care should be a last resort and we need programs that help these families before they get so desperate that the law becomes involved. Abuse has often been going on for a number of years by then and the young person's habits have become entrenched, they may have dropped out of school, began taking drugs or become involved in violence and delinquency outside of the home.

Some situations are so dire that it's justified despite the risks. Here in Melbourne it's very rare for young people who are abusing parents to be taken into residential care of any kind. Ironically, foster care is often ruled out because the young person is violent. Since many of them are only violent towards a parent, or parents, this is usually over-cautious. I've heard of the non-violent children being removed from the home because there were placements available for them, but no suitable placement available for the violent child. This is the systems' abuse of the other children. Residential options appear to be more common in America and more common still in Spain. Spain has some specialist residential services which cater for youth who are violent within the home, something completely lacking in other countries.

She's Leaving Home

Reading about the history of families and childhood, it's striking how the age at which children are considered able to leave home has risen and risen. In the Nineteenth century it was common for twelve-year-olds to leave home. Apprentices often lived with their master from this age. Children often lived with relatives or worked on another farm or in 'service' as a servant. No, we don't want to go back to those days! When I was a boy my brother left home at sixteen and went to work in England (from Scotland). Looking back what is interesting to me is that no one thought this was a problem or looked askance at my parents. Now I find parents are sometimes upset, and feel guilty, about eighteen to twenty-year-old flying the coop. Many young people are staying at home well into their twenties (only partly for economic reasons). Parents who are forced to make a sixteen-year-old leave home nowadays are often heartbroken and guilt-wracked, and seen as failures.

I have seen many situations where a child leaving home for a few weeks or a month or two has created a turning point and greatly reduced, sometimes completely eliminated, abusive behaviour. But it has to be on the parents' terms. It doesn't have to be a punishment and it can work even if the parents take responsibility for finding the alternative accommodation and it's somewhere the young person likes. The young person doesn't have to suffer for change to take place! Aunts and uncles are often the best alternatives. Grandparents are sometimes great but may be more likely to spoil the child than aunts and uncles or parents' friends, and a few grandparents even collude with the child against the parents. Parents of the child's friends are often risky, especially if their own child is out-of-control or, worst of all, if the friend's parent keeps open house for beer-swilling, drug-taking youth.

I've often heard of other people, professionals, police or relatives, telling parents that they *should* make the young person leave home. Here's an example of such advice from the web:

"If none of this works, [speak up and take back control; confront the teen; get therapy] cut your troubled teenager from the family as soon as he/she turns sixteen. Change all the locks and exclude them from your life."[437] The 'exclude them from your life' is not advice that many parents could even consider, especially if your child is one of the many who have other problems.

Generally speaking, although I often explore such options with parents, I don't actively *encourage* anyone to make their child leave home unless there is *serious* physical risk, especially risk to younger siblings. In the same way I don't *encourage* women to leave abusive husbands. This is not because I don't want them to do so, but because such decisions have to be theirs. If it isn't their decision, it won't work. Some professionals appear to believe that separation is always the best option when there is violence in the family[438].

I see many situations where a teenager leaving home is more by their choice than the parents. The parents may have said to him, "*either you stop abusing us and damaging property or you leave.*" He leaves but the parents are confused and worried as they had hoped he'd choose to stop being abusive. They are still feeling very protective towards him and this can give him power. If he asks to return it's important that they are not too eager to have him back. If they immediately accept him back, it's likely that the abusive behaviour will continue where it left off. If parents insist on a delay, and perhaps a written contract or some mediation, the chances are far better that he will change his ways. Mediation can work in such a situation if the abusive young person is no longer in a position of power over the parents.

If you are scared about him leaving and he doesn't really care, then he has all the power. To change the balance of power you may need to pretend you aren't desperate to have him home, even if you really are.

Where young people are almost completely beyond their parent's control and may be abusing other family members, the obvious question arises: should they be at home? This is often one of the most difficult decisions a parent ever has to make.

The following questions are aimed more at parents of older teens, but may apply to extreme cases with younger teens.

? Are you really keeping your child safe? If you have no control over him/her then you probably aren't doing more than making sure he/she is fed and clothed. Kids who leave home seldom go hungry.

? Are you slowing down their maturation by sheltering them from the real world? Are you allowing them to stay in a rut?

? At what age do they have to stand on their own two feet? Eighteen, twenty-one, thirty, fifty? Would you allow them to sponge off of you indefinitely?

? If you are providing free board and lodgings, are you effectively letting them have more money for drink and drugs?

? If you are worried about your child leaving home because he is depressed, consider the possibility that the conflict with you (or other family members) may be contributing to the depression.

? If there is a real risk of suicide, this may increase at the point of him/her leaving home, but could become high or higher if they remain living in an unhappy, conflictual home.

? If they are getting away with acting abusively, isn't this harming them and reducing the chance they will have a decent relationship, or be a decent parent, in the future? Does this harm balance out the positives of possibly keeping them a little bit safer in the short term?

? Are you taking the effect on yourself into account? How much stress are you under? Can this go on indefinitely or are you likely to have physical or psychological problems because of it?

? Are other people affected psychologically, especially siblings?

? If you are not yet ready to make your child leave home, can you create consequences for unacceptable behaviour? If you are afraid that they will punish you and the behaviour escalates, can you use the police or Courts for back up?

? Have you considered a Restraining Order as discussed in a previous section? This can be an intermediate stop before making them leave home.

Don't make your child leave home impulsively. This seldom leads to a good outcome. They will feel that they are the victim and they often get sympathy from others. You, or your partner, are highly likely to let them return home too soon or without any real changes having taken place.

Don't threaten to put them out permanently if you are likely to give in a few weeks later. This may make them feel that your threat was not serious or that you can't live without them. When parents suggest that they are going to make a young person leave home, I ask something along these lines:

"If your son returns in a month's time, wet, bedraggled and hungry and promises to behave will you let them move back in?"

If the answer is 'yes' (and it usually is) then I suggest that they tell him at the start that he has to leave home for a certain amount of time - a week minimum, three months maximum, something the parents are sure they can stick to. At the end of this time, they won't automatically allow him to return, but they will discuss the situation and may or may not allow him to move back home. Don't give the impression that you will automatically let them back, just tell them that you will be willing to discuss it *after* that time. Then if you do let them return, it should be on your terms as the power balance can then shift dramatically.

What if the young person refuses to leave?

If you have definitely decided that your child should leave home but they are refusing to go, you are in a difficult situation. Some parents resort to manhandling them out of the door, sometimes with the help of relatives or neighbours (and they then may claim they've been abused). If you could get a large posse of relatives together this would make a clear statement about solidarity.

The power of a young person often depends on how many rules they are willing to break. I've known young people who will not hesitate to break into their home if the locks are changed. Some will defy legal orders but others will reluctantly respect a Restraining Order. You may have to get the police involved if a seriously abusive young person is flatly refusing to leave.

Example 1

"She came home, then left again a few times. Until that point we were paralysed by our parental emotions of care and concern and were too reactionary. We felt at ransom. We would do anything to have her back home and she knew it (even though our other kids were emotionally safer without her there). She would keep us hanging, saying comments like 'I haven't decided whether I want to live at home, I hate living there'. However, she did get some real life boundaries out there. A friend's mother told her she would have to pay rent and see her boyfriend (who is older and a bad influence) only twice a week. Furious, she came home

357

saying maybe it's not so bad here and she could 'put up with it' (probably since at that point we had every boundary shattered and she could almost do as she pleased).

The power shifted at that point. We had been broken and had already started the grieving process so we were not as desperate to have her home anymore under any circumstances. In a sense we'd let go. She wanted to live at home though (even though telling everyone 'it's still shit') so we said, 'you are welcome to live here but not under just any conditions. If you want to live here, these are the conditions and the consequences for choosing not to comply...'

She broke a major rule in forty-eight hours (having friends round) – received a consequence – does not have a set of keys anymore. She started intimidating me in front of the other kids again - this time my husband dealt with it so it's not hidden.

Finally, we are making boundaries about the rest of the family. Our daughter is not the centre of everything. She can't bring this 'Lad' culture into the house. We let her know that we have no interest in controlling her anymore so if she chooses to live with us under our rules she can, otherwise she is choosing to live independently and we will help her pack. I keep conversations light and her father does the boundary setting at this point since we still don't trust her with me yet. Frankly, I need the break. If she becomes abusive I tell her 'I don't speak to you that way so I am choosing to end this here, if you want to fix the problem we can talk later', then I walk away. I also keep a poker face when buttons are pushed or I feel manipulated so I am no longer reactionary. This is progress, small steps."

Example 2

When June came to see me she was terrified that her seventeen-year-old son, Mark, was going to leave home. He was experimenting with drugs, getting into fights, and hanging around with the wrong sort of boys. She was convinced that he'd be at real risk if he left home. Mark was frequently verbally abusive to her and intimidated her and pushed her around. He refused to come to talk to me, saying to his parents, "You've got the problems. I don't have any." I saw June and her husband for a while and they became more determined not to continue living like hostages. When Mark became abusive again, June ordered him out of the house. To our surprise he only managed to couch-surf for a few days then went to live with an aunt; his behaviour there was perfect. I often talk to parents about the fact that teenagers living with extended family members used to be commonplace and accepted. Now many parents feel that it's a sign of failure and are guilty about it. Mark asked to come home after a month and agreed to come for counselling. He told us that it was OK at his aunt's but he felt like a guest and wanted his own home (he didn't mention missing parents or brother). To their credit his parents did not immediately agree but made a list of conditions and we had a couple of mediation sessions before he returned home.

What was interesting about Mark was that he was not only bright and articulate (I see lots of kids like him who are highly intelligent) but that he was quite upfront about the situation. I said to him, "When I first met your mother she desperately wanted to keep you at home and I'm willing to bet you didn't give a damn. So you had all the power." He readily agreed and added, "Now that I know she can kick me out, I have to keep biting my tongue. I can't say what I like any more." I didn't do much counselling with Mark but he continued to be non-abusive and mostly respected his parents' rules. I've seen a number of cases where a brief period out of home has virtually eliminated abusive behaviour from a young person. It certainly doesn't always work but the success rate appears to be good provided parents are able to be firm and allow the child back *on their terms*. It's not likely to work if it happens chaotically and the parents feel so guilty that they encourage the child to return home without any real change in attitude.

This is a good example of weighing short-term and long-term risks. Although there is a very real short-term risk involved in making your child leave home, the long-term risk can be greatly reduced by doing so.

Alternatives to home

Here is Australia there are very few residential options for young people. I've known despairing parents beg the authorities to remove a violent child to no avail, as there is nowhere suitable for them to go. There may be some residential homes with vacancies, but the authorities are concerned about the influence of the other inmates and the potential risk of their child being exposed to substance abuse, burglary and worse persuades some parents to allow their child to remain at home. The situation is different in different areas. American writers talk about detention being used for children who are violent to parents[439] but this is incredibly rare here in Australia. America does lock up more of its population than anywhere else! When I've given workshops in the UK, professionals mention that being taken down to the police cells for a few hours has occasionally had a salutary effect on young people. Even that hardly ever happens here. Children who have assaulted a parent are often interviewed in the comfort of their own bedrooms. The only out-home option here is often a relative.

The best option for many young people is often being placed with a supportive relative for a few weeks or months. This works well if the relative is sensible and supportive but not if they blame the abused parent and allow the child excess freedom. This happens quite often when the alternative is placement with an irresponsible father. Children often behave well for other relatives, at least during a 'honeymoon period', which may be as long as a few months. Although it's frustrating for the parent to see their little monster turn into an angel at someone else's home, this is a good thing for several reasons: 1. their bad habits are no longer being reinforced; 2. They are clearly showing that they can control their behaviour; 3. It allows a period of calm and reduced stress for all concerned (including the young person) during which more rational decisions can be made; 4. It shows that the child's problems are not too deep-seated and they have been taught manners and how to behave.

Some professionals are generally, sometimes forcefully, against children leaving home, even temporarily, as they see this as not dealing with what they regard as the core problems, i.e. the parent(s) or the family system. However the key issue is the young person's behaviour and this can change with a period spent out-of-home.

If you don't have a supportive relative or friend, and there are no residential options, you may be forced to consider your child's friends; clearly this is far more risky. Your child may persuade his friend's parents that you are an ogre and that he needs to be treated as an adult and given unlimited freedom. Even though this is less than ideal, it can still sometimes work out for the best.

Charlie, fifteen, was abusing his sole-parent mother, Susan, on a regular basis as well as abusing teachers and drugs. It wasn't all that clear if Susan made him leave or if he chose to leave. He refused to go to his grandparent's home (they were very strict) but instead moved in with a female friend, Lyn, and her mother. Lyn's mother drank heavily and smoked dope daily and apparently had no problem with her daughter and Charlie doing the same. Charlie and Lyn insisted they were not boyfriend and girlfriend and shared a bedroom. It was no surprise when it emerged that they were having sex (Lyn's mother was the only one who feigned surprise). Charlie appeared to have almost complete freedom with drink, drugs and sex on tap! He came very close to dropping out of school but somehow hung on (he was yet another bright underachiever). For almost two months, Charlie made no contact with his parents. His mother was utterly distraught. Then he started visiting frequently, bringing her his laundry and asking for money and favours. He started appreciating his mother's cooking for the first time. After four months had passed, Charlie was thoroughly sick of his chaotic lifestyle (and probably sick of his demanding and neurotic girlfriend) and asked to return home. When he did return home, his abusive behaviour had greatly reduced and he gave up drugs. The placement with Lyn's family was rather far from being ideal, but so was living at home while Susan had no control and was totally taken for granted.

With children over sixteen, parents should have the right to evict them for serious abuse even if they don't have anywhere to go; I've been surprised how resourceful these young people often are and in Melbourne, they hardly ever sleep on beaches or under bridges but manage to couch-surf or get accommodation with a youth housing organisation. I'll probably get accused of making light of youth homelessness for saying this and there are certainly other young people who are fleeing abuse or chaotic families. I've known children sleep rough in parks but only for a few days and occasionally this appears to be a deliberate ploy to make parents feel guilty. Several have camped on their parent's lawn, which is often successful in getting their embarrassed parents to readmit them to the family home. The situation may be very different in other areas (and in different climates).

Box

Dear Eddie,

Sorry this is so long. I guess having found someone who seems to really 'get' what we have been going through I want to tell you everything!

I realised some months ago, that my husband and I could no longer function the way we had for so very long in relation to our daughter Zoe's behaviour, and her level of disrespect and disregard of the people around her, and of herself. This has also affected the rest of our extended family in ways we could never have conceived. We have all been making excuses and trying so hard to be understanding and in the process we have created a monster.

When Zoe was born, nearly sixteen years ago, I wanted her to grow up being resilient, honest, and proud of who she was. I wanted her to do things that would make her happy; I didn't care whether she was a lawyer or a hairdresser. When my marriage broke down, less than a year after she was born, I figured I had to do the best I could for both of us. She hasn't seen or spoken to her biological father for almost twelve years (his choice) and in fact we don't even know where he lives. I made sure she maintained a relationship with his parents though, even though he doesn't see or speak with them either. I made sure we always lived in nice homes, and that Zoe lacked for nothing that she would have had if we had still been a two parent family (good clothing, swimming lessons, school camps, toys, the latest gadgets). Friends and family have commented in the past that she had more time and attention lavished on her than most kids in two parent families. I always took this as a compliment. Now I see that it wasn't a good thing. My work hours were tailored so that she only had to spend minimal time in childcare, and I seldom went out because I figured she was my priority.

Six years ago I met Rob, a wonderful man (never married before, no other kids). We took the relationship very slowly because I didn't want Zoe to feel squeezed out, and made it clear to him that we were definitely a package deal. The steps we took to blend our relationship into a family were all carefully measured and considered. When I think of the effort and caring Rob put into making Zoe feel like it was always the three of us, instead of him and me in the relationship, I feel incredible sadness that his only experience of parenting has netted him very little joy and a lot of heartache. A year after we started seeing one another we all moved in together; again, all carefully measured. Suddenly she had two adults who adored her. Three years after we moved in Rob and I got married. The wedding was all planned around Zoe, and was a truly beautiful day. She finally had the family she had told me she was waiting for. Meantime she decided long before that to call Rob 'Dad' so it all seemed to be working out for all of us.

About a year ago, six months after the wedding, Zoe started acting out; little things at first, like deliberately doing things she had been asked not to do. Over time things worsened. She was being very defiant, lying, stealing small amounts of cash (despite a generous allowance) and being very rude, using profanity, constantly pressing house rules to the limits, hanging out after school at the shopping centre, hanging out with 'questionable' kids at school, not trying with school work, fighting with everyone, threatening to bash or stab people who angered or annoyed her, and countless other things. We figured it was all 'normal' adolescent testing behaviour to a degree, and varied our approach with being lenient, using natural consequences for things like homework not being done, ignoring some of the negative behaviour and using a load of non-aversive strategies as well as loads of positive reinforcement for things done well. Just over thirteen months ago, we hit our first big wall, and to be quite honest it's been all downhill from there. Since October of last year she has run away from home at least four times, broken back into our house twice, verbally and psychologically abused us, intimidated and threatened us and frankly we are exhausted. She engages in highly risky behaviours such as drug and alcohol taking, unsavoury, inappropriate relationships, highly sexualised behaviour, associates with people who have criminal backgrounds, ditches school, lies, and then blames us when we catch her out. That's usually when she runs away for days at a time, and comes home when it suits her. I've lost count of the number of times we have done missing person reports with the police. I'm tired of the school, police and other authorities blaming us and not helping. This helps her excuse her behaviour in her own mind. To this point the only thing she hasn't done is become physically violent and there have been times when I thought she might do that.

We have been in and out of family counselling (she refused to go with us after two sessions), she has seen a private counsellor (and refused to go after four sessions) and we have been on a merry-go-round of emotions that simply cannot continue. I have wondered if she has a psychiatric disorder, but came to the conclusion that she can control her behaviour when it suits her.

I think we confused 'good' parenting with being open and honest and giving her too much of a say. She has never lacked for material possessions, all our time and attention, and whatever she wants or needs. I see now she is a classic 'over entitled child' who is 'under responsible'. We have never really expected her to take full responsibility for her actions, and have constantly made excuses and bailed her out, each and every time.

Three months ago, we decided that we would no longer do this and took a stand when she calmly announced she was moving out, basically, she said, because we were awful parents (this had followed her being caught out in a lie). She also screamed at me that she hoped I would die. For two weeks, we asked her each day what steps she had taken to make the move out of home. In the end she stayed, after breaking down and saying she only said she was moving out because she thought that was what we wanted. This is another thing she does - tries to make it all about us. She has used this technique in the past to get her own way because honestly I would allow almost anything if it meant my daughter would remain safe within our care. I calmly informed her when it appeared this latest crisis had been averted that we had really had enough of this behaviour, and the next time she announced she was moving out of home we would take her at her word, and that she wouldn't be staying here for two weeks while she made arrangements either.

We found out she skipped eight days of school last term, and have negotiated with the school for her to do a modified curriculum for the rest of the year to catch up on core subjects. Then Zoe decided to start wagging the free lessons she was supposed to be catching up in and two weeks ago, following repeated warnings by the school, she was suspended. When we questioned her about it that night she screamed profanity at us, and told us she was moving out of home to go live with her father (the father she hasn't seen in twelve years). I calmly stated she should go ahead with that plan and went and got some boxes for her to start packing. She left our house the next morning and is currently living with a friend and her mother, and has informed us she does not wish to come home. We have finally decided to get real about what we will accept as OK behaviour in our home. I would dearly like her to come home with us and try to work this out but she is very angry, and is upping the ante in regard to her behaviour because this has worked in the past in getting us to allow her to do what she wants. I have realised I want a relationship with my daughter but not at the cost of my relationship with my husband, or my sanity!

Standing up to my daughter and imposing limits on her behaviour has not come easily to me. For a long time, I blamed it on normal adolescent behaviour, attachment issues stemming from her father abandoning her, hormones, a possible psychiatric disturbance and all sorts of things. Some of this may still be true, but Zoe needs to accept responsibility for treating us with the respect we deserve, and with which we have always treated her. I am prepared for the long haul here, in terms of her not returning home for some time (if ever). Ten months ago when she ran away, I fell to pieces, had three weeks off work and was on medication. I am a wiser woman today, even if the situation hasn't resolved itself in the way I had hoped, at this moment. Zoe knows she can come home anytime if she wants to be an active part of this family, but that we are no longer here to be abused and treated with contempt. Rob and I are moving on with doing everyday things (ten months ago I sat in a chair for three weeks, not eating, not sleeping, waiting for the phone to ring so I could go pick her up). Today, I went about my usual business, have been going to work since all this blew up, we got a message bank so she can call and leave a message and I don't have to sit waiting for that phone call.

I'm not sure our story will have a happy ending. All I know is that I just need to take this one day at a time. Our family and friends who know the situation are 100% behind us, which really helps in terms of giving us the support we need and the resolve not to fall back into old patterns.

Thanks for listening, and thank you for your website. A friend forwarded me the link to your website two days ago. I cannot express to you how glad I am that they did. Reading through everything on your site, I experienced a range of emotions. I felt relief (so we aren't the only one's experiencing this and we aren't alone!), validation, for the responses to the behaviour we have recently implemented, sadness, at our personal situation, and most of all I felt that someone out there understands what we have been going through. Karen

Hi Karen,

You sound similar to many of the very decent parents who have kids who turn against them for no apparent reason. We may never know the reason! Certainly kids with an absent parent are a bit more likely to have such problems but these are not the majority, and your story would not sound unusual if the step-dad was a natural dad. We tend to assume that such things are relevant but they may not be. Your child certainly seems to fit the over-entitled category. One thing I have become clearer about since I wrote the two articles on my website, is that parenting does *not* have to be in any way extreme for children to develop these problems. Although most of the parents with abusive children lean towards an involved and indulgent parenting style, they don't have to be far from the norm given unusual combinations of child temperament and circumstances. These 'circumstances' are not necessarily dramatic as teens sometimes go one way or another on the roll of a metaphorical social dice, i.e. which friends are being bitches and which boys, or girls, fancy them, or even which teachers are being mean or encouraging. Such influences may not be apparent even to highly involved parents, and the young person may not even be consciously aware of them. In other words, there is a lot of luck involved in how things turn out.

You seem to be taking a very sensible stand. Allowing a teen to be irresponsible, and especially to allow them to be abusive, is not doing them any favours at all in the long run. You also can't help them if you go to pieces.

I'd put the chances of a good outcome as pretty high in your case. As a general rule the quicker and more dramatic the onset of problems the better are the chances that they will go away quickly. A child who has always had behavioural problems is far less likely to settle down than one who had many years of reasonable behaviour. There are, needless to say, no guarantees but I've often seen things turn about pretty fast. So never give up hope and keep the door open, but with a clear insistence that you are not going to be abused.

I'm really glad that my website is reassuring to parents – though it's a bit scary that there is so little available. I also got an e-mail today from someone in New York saying that the police believed the violent, substance-abusing, young person who told them that the mother had made the holes in the wall herself!

Best of luck, Eddie

3 months later

Hello Eddie,

I just thought I might give you a bit of an update about our situation.

It has been three months since we corresponded and at that time our daughter had moved out of home. It seemed unlikely that she would be moving back in anytime soon. We had to deal with Centrelink (she applied for an allowance to leave home permanently citing we had thrown her out) and when that was rejected, the mother of the girl she was living with applied for Family Assistance to enable our daughter to remain out of home.

All this aside, my husband and I decided that our rules would remain in place and we would stand firm about being treated with respect. Our daughter would call us every few days at first to pick arguments. I think she was trying to get us to back down and also trying to get me to break down emotionally as I had done in the past. Somehow, I think she thought it would validate in her own mind that we did love her, and that we wanted her to come home. I remained calm at all times and when I felt I could not deal with her verbal tirades we simply did not answer the phone and let it go through to voice mail. If Zoe left a message I would always call her back, but after I had had time to compose myself and plan how I was going to react if things got ugly. I set the ground rules for phone conversations and contact and advised her that if she became abusive I would hang up. Twice I actually did that. I made her be responsible for her own behaviour and to accept the consequences of her actions. One example of this was when she told us to send her the rest of her things (eight packing crates of them!). I calmly stated it was her responsibility to arrange for her things to be collected. We even went so far as to put them under the car port and advise her they were there to be picked up. Of course she never did get around to getting them.

My husband decided we needed to get away. We figured that if Zoe truly wasn't coming home, we needed to spend some time together adjusting to it being the two of us instead of the three of us, and like many parents in this situation after eighteen months of this, we were physically and emotionally exhausted. To be honest I think we also knew there was a storm coming and we didn't want to be too easily accessible. In the past Zoe has manufactured crisis situations to gain our attention and we have always responded immediately. In this way in her own mind the balance of power is restored in her favour.

To cut a long story short, while we were away Zoe made contact and advised us that she wanted to come home. She was told that we would discuss it when we when we returned home from holiday and until that time she was to stay where she was, or to go to her grandparents to stay. She elected to stay where she was. Three days later we got an emergency phone call from her stating she had to leave as the adults in the house where she was staying were taking drugs (see what I mean about manufactured crisis - she had been living there at this point for five weeks and this was the first mention of drugs). She demanded to be allowed to return home in our absence. Not likely! I calmly re-stated she needed to contact her grandparents and ask permission to go stay there for two days until we returned, which she grudgingly did.

She has been home now for ten weeks. We made it very clear before she came home what the rules would be. She hasn't faltered once. I believe she is being open and communicative. She is seeing a private psychologist and working through some of the things that may have led her to engage in self-destructive (and parent destructive!) behaviour. We have our GP on board with a mental health care plan. She has returned to school and she made the decision to repeat Year 10 because she spent most of it wagging last year. We arranged a mentor and school support program for her through a youth-work organisation so she has someone else to help her if she needs it. She was really receptive to this idea and likes the mentor a lot. She is attending school every day and doing required homework. Her grades are actually pretty good! This week she brought home a B for an assignment and was genuinely peeved a couple of weeks ago when she got 1% off a B for Maths ("I should have tried harder mum" was what she said instead of something like "stupid teacher marked me down"). She has made some new friends. I'm not saying she doesn't have her moments ...all teenagers do, but things are so much better than they have been in a long, long time. I am so proud of the gutsy way she has tackled decisions over the past couple of months, I could burst! She helps out around home and is a genuine pleasure to be with. She actually wants to talk to me about things that matter to her and will often creep into my bed for a chat before I go to sleep. I ran for governing council at her school and got elected and she didn't even tell me how embarrassing that would be for her!

Today is her sixteenth birthday. Sixteen years ago tonight I thought I was the luckiest woman alive. A year ago, I despaired that she would even make sixteen and still be living under our roof. I know we have a long way to go but it seems we are on the right track (fingers crossed). There will be more dips before she grows up, but I think I'm prepared for them this time.

I'm happy to share our experience if you think it would be helpful at all.

Kind regards, Karen

One Year Later

Hi Eddie,

As it has been some time since we last communicated, I thought it might be time for an update. It has been a good year! How different things are now compared to when I communicated with you a year ago.

Things at home have been very normal and by normal I mean we occasionally disagree, have slammed doors, swearing, pushing boundaries and rules and all the very typical teen stuff. I have to say that when people grizzle about their normal teen's behaviour I have a chuckle and think "well I actually welcome that level of behaviour in my own child". I know things could be and have been so much worse in the past. On the whole she is a different child. Setting limits really worked for us, and not responding to her behaviour in the sense that we made her responsible for her actions was the best thing we ever did. I'm not saying nor expecting her to be perfect (we had a severe curfew breach a few weeks ago) but everything is really positive. She really is a typical teen.

Zoe landed a dream part time job recently through all her own hard work, and is loving it. Everything she has achieved has come to her through her own motivation and with the support of those around her. She realises now she makes the choices which shape whatever life she chooses to live. And whatever choices she makes she will have to deal with the outcomes (good or bad). I think I am most proud of how she handled adverse events this year, because it isn't always smooth sailing for her. On the whole she is a happy and confident young person, which is all we ever hoped for.

She has now successfully finished Year 10. She is planning to do Year 11 next year and wants to go on to Uni but we are taking it one year at a time.

She is still seeing the psychologist every so often. The school mentor program ended last week because Zoe finished the year and she will not be needing that next year because she is longer deemed at risk of leaving school. My daughter was actually one of eighteen students from two hundred selected by the school to be a Peer Leader for next year, mentoring Year 8 students for the 2008 school year. She nominated herself initially (I was so proud!)

Eddie, I still think that it was your website that gave us the confirmation that we needed to take a stand and try a different approach to responding to our daughter's behaviour. Twelve months on the philosophies and ideas are still working for us. I pass on your website details to other parents that I know could use your help just to realise they aren't alone in this, and that there is a time and place for setting reasonable boundaries and limits, regardless of possible responses by their children. I hope that they are able to take away as much from it as we did. Sadly, I know not everyone will have the outcome we had.

End Box

Anger

"Anger is an acid that can do more harm to the vessel in which it is stored than to anything on which it is poured." Mark Twain

"When people conclude that anger causes abuse, they are confusing cause and effect...He isn't abusive because he is angry; he's angry because he's abusive."
Bancroft[440]

There is a lot of rubbish written about anger. We don't understand emotions very well generally but anger also suffers from being used in ideological battles. One example is whether or not violent men should do 'anger management' courses. Pro-feminists (such as the author) see focusing on their anger as often unhelpful and providing them with convenient excuses. The men are seen as wanting to control those around them and getting angry as a by-product of this desire for control. Following this approach, most men's behaviour change groups nowadays (such as the one I've been involved in for over twenty years) focus on attitudes and behaviour and see emotions as less important. They are definite that they are not 'anger management' groups. However, professionals of a clinical bent, most medics, and many psychologists, focus on the men's emotions and see an inability to regulate emotion as the core problem, perhaps needing medication.

With regard to treating young people who are violent within the home, a similar debate has hardly begun. It's almost always assumed that *anger management* is the best way to deal with these youngsters. It's true that some of these young people have difficulty controlling their emotions, including anger, in a variety of settings, but quite a few only get angry at home and quite a few only get angry when they don't get their own way. It doesn't make much sense to regard this as *primarily* an anger issue. Attitudes are far more important than emotions. However, I do find anger management far more useful for young people than I do for adults, though it's not usually enough on its own.

Although anger is usually associated with violence, it's certainly not necessary for someone to be angry to act violently. Some of the very worst violence is done in 'cold blood' and the most dangerous individuals are emotionless psychopaths. The vast majority of violent acts that I have suffered in my life were at the hands of teachers (with a stiff leather strap on my hands) and most of them were not even slightly angry. When I was bullied or got into fights as a child or teenager, anger played almost no part in this; these incidents were about pride and power. The last two times I hit someone it was done quite calmly to defend a friend (in a Scottish pub) or myself (on the streets of Rio). Throughout history and in most cultures the vast majority of acts of violence were not motivated by anger.[441]

Other emotions often lead to an individual becoming angry and precede the anger. Violence is just as often about Pride, Prejudice, Paranoia, Entitlement and a desire to control as it's about Anger.

In the men's behaviour change group I work with, only one session out of twenty focuses specifically on anger. Nonetheless, those men who do well in the course almost always report that they are getting angry a lot less often. The reason for this is that they have changed the attitudes that led to them becoming angry, such as a sense of entitlement, defensiveness, male pride and a desire to control others. Such changes in attitude don't always last but they are more likely to lead to a long-term reduction in violence and abuse than just learning techniques to control anger. Someone who just learns anger management, but doesn't change their attitudes, will almost certainly slip up at some point.

I see the same with young people who have settled down, they also say they are not getting so angry, though they may have little or no insight into why and sometimes they insist that all the people around them must have changed as other people aren't provoking or annoying them so much.

So, although anger is *the most common* emotion associated with acts of violence, it's *not essential* and is not necessarily the most important emotion. Whether anger (a feeling) leads to violence or abuse (behaviour) is complex with a large number of factors involved. These factors can be at the individual level, the relationship or family level, or societal. In fact all three are almost always involved. Then there are historical influences (e.g. past exposure to violence), recent events (what happened in previous days) and immediate influences (e.g. whether the other person is passive, aggressive or assertive and if an authority figure or witnesses are on hand). The (simplified) decision-making tree below gives some idea of what may be going on and how complicated it may be.

Deciding to act violently

People often talk of violence or aggressive behaviour as if it's one (or more) of the following:

a) Just the result of anger.
b) Uncontrollable.
c) An instinct.
d) Insane or completely illogical behaviour.

Such simplistic ideas can be unhelpful. An act of violence is the outcome of a complicated serious of decisions, not all of which are conscious. The process can take years or may be over in a flash.

There are a number of stages of decision making that take place in an act of violence, from wanting to control or hurt someone to the effect of violence. These stages may overlap and are seldom clear. Stages 2 to 4 may all occur at the same time and interact with each other.

1	• Desire to hurt or control another person
2	• Violence seems possible
3	• Internal inhibitions to violence overcome
4	• Advantages appear to outweigh consequences
5	• Choice of attack
6	• Victim fails to defend or flee
7	• Violent act
8	• Immediate impact on victim

1. Desire to hurt or control

People vary greatly in their desire to hurt or control other people. Passive individuals may have little desire to control others. Some people have a strong urge to control their partners or their children. A desire to hurt another can also be based primarily or partly on pride (saving face), revenge, honour, defensiveness or can be primarily for excitement or entertainment (e.g. some school-yard and pub fights). These factors will obviously depend greatly on personality, social culture (some cultures and subcultures encourage violence while others strongly inhibit it), past experience, attitudes to the other person (e.g. respect and entitlement) and specifics of the situation. The desire with some young people may not be to control others but to disempower them, stopping parents or teachers from exerting legitimate control over them.

2. Violence must be seen as possible

Even if there is a will to be violent, an act of violence may be ruled out by the perception of the other person having more physical strength, authority or protection from others. In the past the vast majority of school children would not have considered violence towards teachers or adults as being within the realm of the possible. Now many children have seen or heard of other children abusing teachers and some see such violence as an option for them. Likewise in the past many adolescent girls did not consider physical violence as an option for them but cultural changes make this a possible behavioural choice.

The perception of the feasibility of violence may depend on proximity and on physical characteristics of the two people, the availability of weapons, etc. Many people can have a desire to hurt distant or powerful individuals but violence is not a realistic option. A young person may never consider assaulting an adult who they know would fight back but may pick on a timid or caring individual. Having seen someone being victimised by someone else, makes them appear a more viable target.

I think that a societal change in this factor is one of the main reasons we have seen an increase in violence to parents. Why this has changed is of course, quite complicated, as discussed in previous chapters.

First hand exposure to violence is obviously a powerful factor in making violence seem a possible choice. But media exposure is more important for types of violence such as the epidemic of mass shootings currently happening in the USA.

3. Overcoming one's own inhibitions

Some people find violence highly distasteful while others can act violently on little provocation and with more pleasure than repulsion. Some people greatly enjoy the excitement of violence and may recall it with pride and amusement, while others find it disgusting and traumatic. Still others may enjoy the excitement and surge of power at the time yet feel guilty and bad about it afterwards. Some people describe violence as being a kind of compulsion (once they are in a rage) but not one that gives them any pleasure. Pride or a sense of honour (legitimate or misguided) may make people feel that they *have* to act violently (they may or may not feel any anger when carrying out such violence). Some people feel such a strong sense of entitlement to punish or control others that they feel no guilt at all. Past exposure to real violence (as a witness, victim or participant) or to media violence may be very important in overcoming inhibitions.

Compassionate people don't want to hurt others. They are less likely to feel intense anger because the possibility of hurting others is not something they consider. The idea that we all have frequent violent urges which need to be repressed is pure nonsense. Even when an empathic, caring individual does get very angry, they generally do not act violently.

Although those with empathy for others will be inhibited generally from being violent, their empathy can vary for different groups of people, e.g. a few adults appear to have little empathy towards children; some men have little empathy towards women; racists, soldiers or gang members may view another group of people as less than human and thus suspend normal empathy. Abusers in general devalue their victims and try not to think about how they are hurting them. Overcoming moral inhibitions against using violence will depend on the individual's personality, maturity, intelligence, culture, upbringing, gender, age and empathy. In terms of personality, low Agreeableness and Conscientiousness usually mean fewer inhibitions about being violent. Overcoming inhibitions can be either a long-term process (taking months or years) or can happen in seconds during a particular incident. This is generally a bigger causal factor in violence than the degree of anger and this is why desensitisation, for example from media exposure, is of concern. Exposure within the home is also a huge factor in desensitising individuals to violence.

4. Advantages seen as outweighing the disadvantages

The advantages of being violent must be seen, *at least at that instant*, as outweighing the negative consequences. Of course rational considerations become quite different when someone is in a rage (or in a state of panic) and the advantages are usually immediate whereas the consequences are delayed and probabilistic. Even those committing serious assaults or murder may be well aware of the possible consequences but either vaguely hope they can get away with it or else *at that point in time* don't care about their future. These perceptions depend greatly on the individual's personality. This is primarily about overcoming caution, and fearless individuals are overall more likely to act violently than anxious ones. More nervous individuals are usually far more selective about where they are violent and are thus more likely to be violent only within the home or to easy targets. Impulsivity, intelligence, maturity and other personality characteristics are all of importance in this decision making. Consequences may not have an immediate effect on impulsive violence yet may be crucial in how such behaviour develops over time. This is not a logical, rational process and may operate on a very short timeframe, especially once the individual is in a heightened emotional state, so that longer-term consequences are more likely to be ignored when in a rage.

5. Choice of attack

Once someone is committed to acting aggressively to hurt or control another person, there is still a decision making process in which the aggressor could choose to use verbal aggression, destroy property or use some form of psychological attack rather than physical violence. Verbal aggression is far more common than physical attacks and overall, only a small minority of aggressive encounters proceed to physical violence. If physical violence is intended a decision is made about methods, i.e. whether to push, slap, punch, kick, bite, scratch, head-butt, throw something, use a blunt instrument, a sharp weapon, or a gun. For each method of attack, there are also choices about how it will be conducted. For example, siblings frequently punch each other but it's surprising that most of them seldom do damage: they usually pull their punches and punch to the face far less often than if they were fighting other children. Thus black eyes, cut lips and bloody noses are all more common in fights outside of the home. The same child may punch his brother, slap his sister, push the toddler out of the way, swear at his mother but merely scowl when angry at his father. The majority of men who abuse their wives do not hit them *in the same way* they would hit another man in a fight. Only the most brutal wife basher hits his partner in the same way he would hit another man.

The consequences, physical, emotional and social, can be very different depending on how a blow is delivered. A blow to the eye or the groin is quite different to a blow to the shoulder or chest. Clearly the fact that there are so many choices available makes claims that someone acted out of 'instinct' or was 'out of control' highly dubious. The comparative rarity of lethal violence (unless there are guns lying around) shows that very little violence can truly be said to be out of control.

6. Defence or avoidance by victim

Attempts at violence may fail if the victim blocks, defends or avoids. Some attacks, e.g. from very small children, may be violently motivated but not perceived as an attack or taken seriously because of size and weakness. Similarly throwing an object that misses, or slapping in a feeble manner, may not be seen as real violence even if the aggressor had serious intent. In families, failure to defend is often about responsibility, respect, or fear. Children traditionally allowed adults to hit them without attempting to defend or retaliate, out of respect or fear. At school we had to stand with our hands outstretched while the teachers hit our open palm with a thick leather belt. The first one hurt but subsequent ones could be agonizing. It would never have entered our minds to fight back and even involuntarily pulling our hands away, which did happen, was seen as both cowardly and defiant.

Nowadays parents often do not defend themselves when attacked by children. I see some hulking men who are hit by petite girls and pre-pubescent boys without defending themselves. On the other hand some women may not defend themselves against violent partners or adolescents out of fear of further violence.

Avoiding the violence may be limited within the home and parents who leave the house to avoid a violent child can find themselves accused of neglect.

7. Actual violent act

The actual act of violence is often a very brief event. It's easy for those who are later feeling guilty, or else being forced to face consequences, to pretend, and probably also to believe, that they did not intend the act of violence to be serious. If they were in a rage at the time, or it was just a chaotic situation, their memory is often unclear or distorted and they may try not to think about it afterwards.

8. Victim and situational characteristics

The effect of any attack may depend greatly on characteristics of the victim, such as their size, strength or infirmity, agility, tolerance for pain as well as on chance factors. Any blow or push which causes someone to topple over or to have a heart attack could be fatal yet on the other hand attempts to kill often fail. Thus random factors mean that there is not necessarily a clear correspondence between the perpetrator's intention and the damage done. The long term psychological and social consequences may be even more complex and unpredictable. Very serious abuse is often trivial to the perpetrator *at the time* but can have life-changing consequences for victims, and sometimes also for the perpetrator. The 'banality of evil' means that some of the worst atrocities are carried out in a casual way by the perpetrator[442].

When all of the above factors are considered, it can be seen that there are a number of choice points and that the majority of potentially aggressive sequences do not end in physical violence. Most of these choices will be dependent on both emotion and conscious thought processes.

With sufficient anger, the various choice points may be tipped towards violence but for some individuals, or in some unusual circumstances, little or no anger may be needed for violence to be chosen. For example, violence on the battlefield, sportsfield or in self-defence may be chosen quite rationally with little or no emotion involved. Anger is just one of many factors in determining whether or not violence is chosen and anger may be just as much *the result of* these choices as it is *the cause of* the choices made.

Anger and violence

A consideration of the above sequence makes it clear that there will be no straightforward correspondence between anger and violence. Some individuals can have very high anger without acting violently and others may have low anger yet act very violently. Intensity of anger will be affected by the decisions made in all of the first five steps above as well as individual personality, current state (stress, tiredness, excitement, inebriation, etc.), cultural norms, relationships and situational factors. In addition it's not always easy to judge another's level of anger as some individuals and some cultures, effectively hide their feelings of anger while others readily display them (or exaggerate them as a form of threat display). Many individuals are poor at judging their own feelings, especially in retrospect, and how angry they remember being will often depend on how they behaved, and on the outcome.

There are people for whom anger is a real problem who are never violent, some of them torture themselves but don't hurt others. Then there are those who are violent without anger or who deliberately make themselves angry. We often talk of someone having 'an anger problem' when really they have a violence problem.

Choice and moral responsibility

When we speak of 'decisions' and 'choice' this does not necessarily imply *conscious* decision making. In complex behaviour such as violence, there are actually too many options in most situations, for each to be considered *consciously*. Our attitudes and beliefs, e.g. believing that the other person is inferior, or that we have a right to hurt or control others, will affect what options we consider and what choices we make even in split-second, unconscious reactions. Although some individuals are aware of their 'self-talk', or 'winding-up' thoughts, others have no conscious awareness of what is going through their heads, even when not acting violently. In other complex behaviours, it's obvious that we make choices without being conscious of these. When we are driving we are constantly making crucial decisions about speed, route, safety, etc. even if we are thinking about what to have for dinner. Most of the time, such decisions are made semi-automatically without conscious thought but they still reflect our personalities, values, habits and beliefs. Some people drive aggressively with a high sense of entitlement and frequent anger, while others are considerate and obey the rules.

We are morally responsible for the choices we make regardless of whether they are made consciously or unconsciously. In states of extreme emotion, e.g. rages or panic attacks, perceptions of time may be distorted and memory may be confused and incomplete. This is sometimes taken as a sign of mental illness, but it's not. Whether an act is remembered or not has no direct bearing on whether or not the behaviour was freely chosen and our responsibility for it. When our choices are distorted by drink or drugs our responsibility is just as great as when we're sober unless we genuinely had no idea how the substance was likely to affect us.

Someone who has a car accident driving while drunk is seen as fully responsible for their actions and so should a husband who goes home drunk and hits his wife. There are degrees of moral responsibility depending on how pre-meditated and deliberate is the violent behaviour, but even purely impulsive behaviour is a chosen act and remains our moral responsibility.

Myths of Anger

There are some common myths about anger which cause confusion, lead to mistakes in thinking and are frequently used to excuse violent or abusive behaviour.

Myth 1: Other people make us angry

We often talk about (and *think* about) other people **causing** us to get angry by their behaviour: "You make me so mad!"; "I couldn't help it, she made me so angry!"

Although we may also speak about people causing other emotions ("my little bundle of joy!"), we are **more** likely to say this when the emotional reaction in question is anger. We clearly can choose whether or not to let someone else's behaviour make us happy or sad yet we frequently talk as if anger is **directly caused** by other people's behaviour. This is probably because we use anger as an excuse for **our** worst behaviour. Also when we are very angry we think less clearly and tend towards simplistic, black and white thinking. Our focus when angry is on the object of our anger not on ourselves, and this natural tendency serves to back up our excuses.

Sometimes it's quite clear that we **can** choose to get angry or not. We **choose** whether or not to get angry about social problems, injustice, politicians, sports commentators, game show hosts etc. Even with provocative, insulting behaviour from strangers most of us know that we can choose how we will react. Picture a drunken teenager trying to provoke a group of older men: although the teenager's behaviour may be totally unacceptable, different men (or groups of men) will react quite differently and they may say things like, "He's not worth bothering about!" or "Don't let him get to you!" They realise they have the choice of getting angry or not depending on how they view the other person.

Now imagine that the provocative teenager is your son. If you react violently you may say afterwards that his behaviour caused you to get angry and that this caused your reaction. However, what if your son's girlfriend had dumped him, his favourite uncle had just died and he had then got drunk for the first time? You may feel sympathy and little or no anger, though the behaviour is the same.

It's especially with regard to close relationships that we assume that others **cause** our anger. However the same behaviour by others will produce markedly different reactions depending on who does it, how we feel, what the circumstances are, etc.

Imagine the worst insult anyone could give you. Is it **inevitable** that you will get angry? What if you and your best friend were taking part in a play, or a game, that involved him or her saying this to you? What if the person you love most said it while delirious from a fever or someone you know had become psychotic? You may or may not get angry depending on your attitudes and beliefs about the other.

I knew a woman, diagnosed with schizophrenia, who would occasionally attack her long-suffering husband when he returned home. He was stronger than her and usually managed to subdue her without any serious harm to either of them but she still managed to hurt him and there was always the danger that she would use a weapon. He had never hit her and appeared to accept that this behaviour was her illness and not her. He felt little or no anger towards her and surprisingly little anger at the unfairness of fate.

These examples should make it clear that it's not the other person's **behaviour** that makes us angry; it's **always** their **intention** that is important. To be precise, it's **our interpretation of their intention**. We can always choose how we interpret someone else's behaviour (although we may not consciously think about the choice). Some individuals are habitually negative in their views of others and have a far higher tendency to interpret the other's behaviour as intentionally hurtful. Proud individuals (with high but unstable self-esteem) may see others as insulting or belittling them on the flimsiest of evidence. Temperament and past experience will have a big influence in how people differ in their interpretations of others' behaviour and this will greatly affect how often they feel angry.

If we are feeling very irritable (perhaps due to lack of sleep, a headache, stress or low self-esteem) we are much more likely to interpret someone else's behaviour negatively or as an attack. Some drugs, including alcohol, can make people hypersensitive to perceived attacks. At the extreme, a truly paranoid individual may challenge complete strangers with "What are you looking at?" interpreting almost any behaviour as a personal attack.

Thus our feelings, including anger, are never **caused** solely by someone else. Their behaviour is a major influence but our habits, attitudes and how we think about things will affect how we interpret their intention and this is always **just as important** as the other person's actual behaviour.

Pride plays a big part in this process for many violent individuals (see chapter on self-esteem).

Myth 2: Feelings cause behaviour

After a violent act, people will often say things like: "I just saw red!", "I was so angry I couldn't control myself!", "When I'm in a rage I can't stop!" I hear things like this all the time, from young and old.

The implication is that strong feelings **force us** to behave in particular ways – that we simply **cannot** control our behaviour in such circumstances. As a young lad said to me recently, "I'm not to blame, my brain made me do it!"

I have had many conversations over the years along the following lines:

"I just see red! I go from naught to one hundred in seconds. I just lose it!"

"Have you ever hit a teacher?"

"I've come close once or twice. I've sworn at my English teacher, she's a real pain!"

"So she gets you angry, does she?"

"Does she ever!"

"So how come you've hit your Mum and your brother but never a teacher?"

"I'd get expelled!"

About 95% of men who are violent towards their partners will stop if the police appear on the scene. If their emotions are in control of their behaviour, what is it about the presence of the police that causes them to stop being angry? Are the police so soothing? In fact the arrival of the police is quite likely to make many men more, not less angry but the consequences of the violent behaviour suddenly become quite different. Of the remaining 5% of men who are not afraid of the police or prison, most would stop abusing their wives if their mother (grandmother, the pope, or someone significant) arrived on the scene.

Another interesting question: if people are really *out of control* why are there not far more murders? We've mentioned that few men assault their wives in the same way they would fight or assault another man, and some are very careful not to leave bruises. Similarly, battling siblings seldom cause real injuries, even with differences in size and strength. Both children and adults may smash things or throw things about in a rage and typically claim to be *out of control*. However, there is always a pattern to what is broken: some individuals smash only their own property, sometimes only their partner's or parents' property, sometimes only things of value, sometimes only things of low value, sometimes things that make a satisfying noise when they smash. In my experience there is **always** some pattern to what they choose to throw or break. These patterns show that their behaviour is never completely uncontrolled even when in a rage. A teenager said to me recently, "Breaking something that isn't worth much just wouldn't be satisfying."

We talk (and think) about anger as being different to other emotions. We do not assume that sadness or happiness will **cause** a particular behaviour. "I couldn't go to work today, I was too happy" does not sound like a reasonable excuse and only extreme sadness or depression might be taken as an excuse for not doing something. Even severe depression does not **inevitably** lead to suicide or **any** other specific behaviour. No sane person would accept strong sexual urges as an excuse for rape[*]! It's **only** with anger that we talk as if our feelings force us to act in particular ways, and especially with our close relationships. This excuse sounds more obviously ridiculous if it's used as an excuse for violent assaults in public or an assault at work.

People get angry all the time without acting violently. In fact for adults, and even for most teenagers, there are far, far more episodes of anger than there are of violence.

Since it's possible to be very angry without being violent and also possible to be very violent without being angry, we clearly cannot use anger as an **explanation** of violence. It's even more important that we do not use anger as an **excuse** for violence.

Anger **never** directly causes violent or abusive behaviour. There is **always** an element of choice. Naturally there are situations where we feel as if our emotions are almost overwhelming and choosing another course of action can seem very difficult. However difficult, there does still exist a choice even when seriously provoked, drunk or drugged. Even with the vast majority of mental illness, people

---

[*] Yes, I know some judges have allowed provocation based on how the woman was dressed to be discussed in court – I did say no 'sane' person!

are responsible for their actions. The example of the woman with schizophrenia who became periodically violent is highly unusual and even if someone has such a diagnosis that does not mean that all their behaviour is a result of the psychosis.

Once in a rage it may be extremely difficult to maintain self-control but in most cases, the rage is the end result of a process of escalating confrontation and of escalating angry 'self-talk'. We work ourselves into a rage by our thoughts and actions. There are many points along the way where self-control is easier than it is once we are in a rage.

Myth 3: Anger is always masking another emotion

Another myth-conception about anger is that all anger is masking, or derived from, some other emotion. This harks back to psychoanalytic ideas about emotions (popularised by Freud) that see emotions transforming into one another in complex ways. In the weird world of psychoanalysis things are almost never what they seem to be. Thus almost any emotion can *really* be its exact opposite or another emotion entirely. This is not helpful in actually understanding anything.

Emotions are complex, frequently multi-layered and changeable and thus the idea that one transforms into another seems to make some intuitive sense (especially since we have all grown up hearing such ideas batted around). In such a complex area we should beware of setting our intuitions up as absolute truth (everyone's intuition said that the world was flat for an awfully long time).

Love can turn to hate and often the more intense the love, the stronger the hate. However, intense love does not inevitably lead to hate or to any other strong feeling. When we feel strongly about something we are *more likely* to feel strongly about it in a different way rather than become indifferent to it. But the situation where intense love, or hate, gives way to indifference is certainly not rare, and is probably more common than love turning to hate (especially if there are no children to complicate the separation). Love can, and often does depart, leaving nothing more than a little sadness, emptiness or numbness. Love and hate can also coexist, sometimes for many years. The idea that one is actually *transformed* into another doesn't really work psychologically, though it does dramatically.

I was recently talking to an abused parent whose son has turned against her dramatically since starting High School. She had no idea why. I found her intelligent, charming, interesting and clearly she was a loving and devoted parent. I guessed that they were unusually close before he turned against her and she confirmed this. This is not inevitable but it's quite common – making nonsense of those who suggest (without a shred of evidence as far as I can see) that such problems are caused by subtle attachment problems early in life. It's not uncommon for teenagers to distance themselves from one or both parents for a while and this distancing may, for a few, be particularly strong when they have been very close. Although they may *act* as if they hate their parents, and use 'I hate you!' as a form of attack, it's unusual for them to say to me that they actually hate the parent they are abusing in counselling. Young people can be in active rebellion against parents and be treating them like *merde* (pardon my French) yet still say they love them. However, one of the sad trends I *may* be seeing in my counselling, is more children telling me that they hate their parents, often for trivial reasons. Abused or neglected children very seldom say this.

A popular idea involving transforming emotions is that depression is anger turned inwards. This is another psychoanalytic idea, with no scientific basis that I can find, and it doesn't seem to make much practical sense. Does it mean that depressed people are going to be more or less angry than non-depressed people? If someone stops being depressed, do we expect their level of anger to increase or decrease? Since the theory (if you can call it that) doesn't give answers to such simple questions and makes no useful predictions whatsoever, it's neither testable or useful. It does however serve to confuse parents who have depressed teenagers who are also aggressive. Most of the young people abusing parents are not depressed (remarkably few in my sample had been diagnosed with depression, only 2.5%) and of these, some have made themselves depressed by alienating everyone around them and by a generally negative view of the world. Far more of the parents are depressed. There is an optional chapter on depression later in the book.

I'm puzzled why the idea of anger always being a mask for other emotions is so popular given that anger is undoubtedly one of *the* most basic emotions, clearly seen in animals and in early infancy. I suspect that it's yet another aspect of viewing the world as a nice and fair place, and gives scope to view victimisers as victims. For example, we can assume that the arrogant, socially successful bully is secretly suffering rather than enjoying life; he's not really angry but instead is feeling insecure and unhappy. The research on bullies contradicts these ideas, as we have mentioned. If an aggressive young person does feel insecure, and of course many do, it's often because he won't let his parents be parents; he has made himself unhappy by rejecting the people who love him, and he may also realise on some level that he's acting appallingly.

A mother I spoke to recently said that a child psychiatrist had urged her to 'identify with his pain' when her fourteen-year-old son was running amok. 'What about *our* pain when he hits us?' she asked indignantly.

Since anger is a **very** basic emotion it does not need to be hiding another emotion. However, for humans past infancy, there is probably no such thing as a pure emotion as we humans are too complex for our own good. This applies to anger just as much as it does to any other emotion. It's common for us to have a mix of feelings, including feelings about feelings (and probably feelings about feelings about feelings). Thus someone who is acting violently may be feeling rage but *at the same time* hurt, shame, guilt, embarrassment and fear. That doesn't mean that the anger is caused by the other emotions, or that the anger isn't real.

Anger, on the other hand, is usually derived from the *attitudes* of the angry person (such as a sense of entitlement) and these attitudes fuel the anger while the anger in turn feeds these attitudes.

Myth 4: Anger builds up inside and has to be released

"My younger brother used to kick the furniture when he got mad. Mother called it 'Letting off steam.' Well, he's thirty-two years-old now and still kicking the furniture – what's left of it, that is. He is also kicking his wife, the cat, the kids and anything else that gets in his way."[443]

There is a common idea that anger is something like a fluid or substance that "builds up" inside us so that we have to 'get it out'. This idea (sometimes called the 'hydraulic theory of anger') was popularised by Freud and his followers.

378

Scientifically the idea has been thoroughly discredited and is really more of an analogy which is still popular for the simple reason that it often matches how we actually feel ('He makes my blood boil!'). We talk about anger (and occasionally other feelings e.g. 'love overflowing') as if it was some kind of substance that increases in pressure within our bodies. This may seem a harmless simplification but it has implications that are often wrong and sometimes dangerous.

Imagine that you are waiting for a lift to an important job interview. Your friend has sometimes been late in the past but knows how important this is to you and has promised to be early. As the time for the interview approaches you feel mounting anger, as your friend hasn't arrived yet. You feel the anger building up like a pressure inside your head. Your blood pressure probably is rising and there is an increase in adrenaline in your bloodstream and generally increased arousal. Then the phone rings and you are told that your friend was in a car crash. Instantly the anger is gone. Anger itself is not a substance or some kind of physical energy but is more like an idea, one which causes physiological changes in your body (your heart races, your palms sweat, the blood pumps in your veins). The physiological arousal does not instantly go away but it isn't anger any longer.

Not only can an external environmental change, some new information, alter our perception but our own thought processes can do the same. We can instantly cease to be angry if we suddenly see the funny side of a situation or find a more helpful way of looking at things; perhaps we suddenly remember why the other person is irritable or immature. This change in our point of view happens less when we are in a rage because we become blinkered and our thoughts tend to become focused on the perceived source of our anger and our own sense of injustice. We become much more rigid in our thinking when really angry and see things in black and white, in a more immature way. When in a rage we do not **want** to calm down or see any other point of view. No matter how wrong we are, we tend to feel *righteous* once in a rage.

One dangerous implication of the idea of anger as a substance is the idea that we can get rid of it by acting angrily (or even by watching violence). This idea is known as '*catharsis*' and some professionals still believe in it despite the abundant evidence against it[444]. It has been suggested, for instance, that watching violent movies or sports somehow gets rid of aggression. The evidence is clear that these activities make people **more** aggressive, not less (see section on Media). There is an increase in murders in America immediately after a major boxing match is shown on TV. People who have plenty of opportunity to act out their aggression (e.g. police, soldiers, boxers, footballers) do not generally become more passive and gentle. During and after wars the rate of crime and domestic violence goes up rather than down.

Punch bags and Pounding Pillows

"We have always taught him it's okay to be angry but it's not okay to be violent. Releasing and recognising the anger is the difficulty. When he was little we taught him to pound his pillow or jump on a bed. Then it was the punching bag and trampoline. Now he bounces his basketball or even gets into bed, or sits in a

wardrobe. Unless I am in hitting distance. Then he punches me. I have to always be on my guard." Parent of eleven-year-old.

I often hear of parents who have been told by professionals to buy a punch bag or encourage their little terror to punch a pillow. Like the parent in the quote above they are misguided. In many cases it probably does no harm and occasionally it can serve as a distraction or a diversion, but by associating anger with punching we are reinforcing part of the problem. It's far better that a less obviously aggressive alternative is used (the trampoline in the example above is reasonable).

Burning up energy in some way is certainly helpful and going off to punch something (a punch bag or a pillow) can *at times* be a useful distraction, but it's **not** the aggressive part that is useful but the distraction and burning off of energy. I've heard a number of men say that punching a punch bag is an opportunity to imagine who they would like to punch, which makes them more, not less, likely to punch someone in the future. For others, a punch bag can help get rid of their energy, but a less aggressive way of burning off energy, e.g. going for a run or a cycle, bouncing on a trampoline or digging the garden would be better.

Aggressive people often use the excuse that 'It's better to punch a wall than to punch you.' This is true in the same way that punching someone is preferable to shooting them. If the wall punching continues, in the long run it *increases* the chances of them also punching people.

If someone who was punching walls is persuaded to go to the bottom of the garden and punch an old door, this means he is no longer either damaging the home or directly intimidating the people within it and this can be a move towards breaking the habit. But those who punch holes in walls often refuse to use such alternatives, showing that it's more about intimidation rather than about releasing energy. Punching walls, throwing things and smashing things has little to do with releasing energy but a lot to do with intimidation and power.

Generally speaking, acting violently or aggressively leads to more aggressive thoughts, more anger and more aggressive behaviour. Aggression becomes a habit and violence can be very habit-forming.

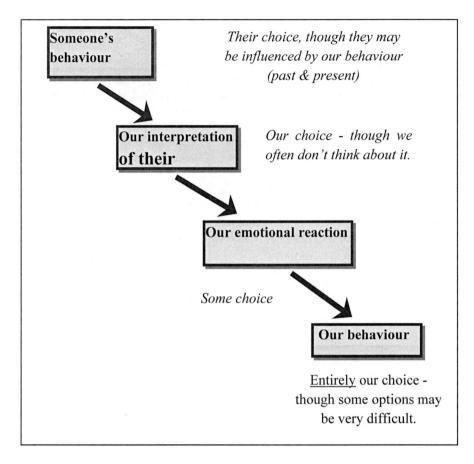

Someone's behaviour

Their choice, though they may be influenced by our behaviour (past & present)

Our interpretation of their

Our choice - though we often don't think about it.

Our emotional reaction

Some choice

Our behaviour

<u>Entirely</u> our choice - though some options may be very difficult.

Martial arts

I am often asked about martial arts for aggressive young people. I've seen plenty of young people who are doing martial arts and also being violent within the home. I believe that when taught well this can *occasionally* help *some* young people by teaching them self-control and positive attitudes. However, I also have no doubt that it's often not taught in this way and it can contribute to aggressiveness. I'm personally disgusted by boxing and kickboxing, to me they are brutal and dangerous, but I've met mature, non-violent young people who were involved in these sports. On balance I haven't seen any clear relationship between learning martial arts and violent behaviour; it's swings and roundabouts. I've seen quite a few young people who were doing very well in their chosen martial art without it making any obvious difference, good or bad, to their aggression and violence at other times. I would not encourage any young person to learn a martial art unless he shows signs of at least trying to control his violence. I've heard adolescents say that they want to learn a martial art so they can 'knock people out' or 'beat people up.' Naturally I wouldn't be advising their parents to spend money on martial arts training if they are likely to use their skills to harm others! If a child shows little control over their violence, it seems crazy to teach them a violent art such as karate or kickboxing – giving a lunatic a loaded gun. Martial arts are not all the same and Tai Quon Do and judo appear far less likely to be abused than karate or kick boxing. Even more ridiculous is the idea that shooting or archery is somehow going to purge them of aggressive impulses. It may be fun but it's not therapy for violence.

In summary it's impossible to predict in most cases if taking up a martial art will be helpful or harmful to an aggressive young person. The idea that they will 'get their anger out' and they will thus be less angry overall is baloney. Whether they develop more self-control or not depends on them, their teacher, and the culture of the club. Even if they learn self-control in a sport they may or may not apply this in other situations. If they increase their self-esteem this may or may not have an effect on their violence (see chapter on Self-Esteem).

My suggestion is: if they are keen to learn martial arts, they have to make an effort to control their temper for a period of time before commencing, showing evidence of self-control and maturity. And stay well clear of boxing and kick-boxing, which can cause brain damage as well as encouraging violent attitudes.

Just to make my prejudices clear: I'm not into competitive sports and have never understood why a boxer who kills another boxer isn't charged with manslaughter, or how people on hockey or football fields are immune to prosecution for assault. Since they are role models their violence is actually more serious than a brawl in the street or bar.

Aggression and violence **can** build-up

Though anger does not itself build-up over time there are certainly things which can build up which often result in increased anger:

1. Thinking angry thoughts and acting abusively can be habit forming hence can build up over time.
2. Resentments can accumulate, especially if they are not discussed or acknowledged.
3. There are downward spirals in relationships where A's negative behaviour produces more negative behaviour in B (not necessarily aggressive, as B may withdraw or be more passive) which produces more negative behaviour in A, etc. Such patterns are more likely where there is poor communication. They can be complex and can span timeframes of minutes, months, years, even decades. The most common vicious cycle I see is where an abusive young person loses more and more respect for their victim and the parents either give up or become rigid and aggressive.
4. Developmental changes associated with puberty, physical growth (which can make them less fearful of adults or better equipped to be a bully) or changes in their friends (as when troubled teens increasingly gravitate to troubled and violent peers and lose touch with their non-deviant companions). These can all result in increased aggression over time.
5. There can be other downward spirals where a young person gets deeper and deeper into trouble, delinquency, drugs, or increasingly sees him or herself as a bad or hopeless person.

So anger itself cannot "build up" over time but resentments, habits (of thought, emotional reactions & behaviour) and deteriorating relationships can **all** build up over time and result in increasing anger.

Is expressing anger a good or bad thing?

There are a number of processes that give the appearance that venting anger reduces it.

Being violent or abusive *may* produce *short term* changes which can result in a decrease in anger. People may simply exhaust themselves. Some individuals feel good after yelling, screaming or hitting walls. Acting aggressively in this way can be very satisfying for some people. The angry individual may feel that they have evened the score, demonstrated their power, or saved face, thus allowing them to relax more. This is all at the expense of the victim, of course. Thus the actions of the abusive person may decrease their own feelings of resentment – while increasing the resentment in the victim.

Many violent individuals *do* feel guilty after acting violently and there may then be a honeymoon period when they are less angry. This cycle of violence is common for men who abuse their partners but less common for young people who abuse their parents.

Deteriorating relationships can be masked if a victim becomes more passive. This happens when a parent gives up trying to control their errant child and effectively stop getting in his or her way. From the aggressor's point of view their angry tirade has got them what they want ('Dad backed off once he realised what I was capable of!' 'My brother doesn't tease me any more since I pulled a knife on him.')

Violence quite often inhibits other people from being violent towards the aggressor. These short term rewards are the reason why they do it.

Expressing anger by talking about it can stop the build-up of resentments. Sometimes this is accompanied by some aggressive behaviour but it's the expression that is important not the acting out. It's good to be assertive and to communicate our hurts but not to be aggressive and blame others, or to use our emotions as a weapon against others.

Thus there are a number of reasons why an aggressive act may decrease anger in the short term, so reinforcing the idea of 'getting one's anger out', but in the long run, anger breeds more anger and violence breeds violence.

Anger is a feeling; violence is a behaviour

Though stating the obvious, this is an important distinction. Controlling your anger is not always possible. Controlling your behaviour is always possible (though it may be very difficult, it's never impossible).

For a particular individual, the amount of anger and the extent of aggressive behaviour are usually closely linked. However, comparing different people there is only a very weak link. Some individuals are intensely angry but never violent. Some individuals can be very violent with little or no anger.

It's very important that children are not punished for getting angry as controlling one's emotions requires a level of maturity that most children are just not capable of. It's not getting angry that is the problem but the behaviours that accompany anger. Try to be clear that being angry is OK but being abusive is *never* OK.

The distinction between anger and abuse is a very important one for a number of reasons, but it isn't **always** a simple distinction. How nasty does a tone of voice have to be to become threatening or hurtful?

Occasional anger **isn't** a problem in itself **but** it's often a sign of other problems, even when it doesn't result in bad behaviour.

Excessive anger is bad for you. Those who are persistently angry are prone to the same health problems as the highly stressed. With either stress or anger, an occasional burst of adrenaline doesn't do much harm but on-going anger or stress increases mortality rates in middle age. The popular idea that anger is only bad for us if we suppress it is pure myth. Those who are persistently angry often express it all over the place and they, along with anyone around them, still suffer. Expressing occasional anger can be useful but persistent anger becomes more and more of a habit. They never 'get it all out.' Our brains can produce an infinite amount of aggro!

Frequent anger which is the result of harmful attitudes **is** a problem. Some people are constantly angry because they have such high feelings of entitlement that things are never going to go the way they think they should and the world always seems unfair to them. If they are angry because they want to control others or have a distrustful, negative view of other people, this *is* a problem. Some youngsters get extremely angry about quite ridiculous things: such as not being able to drive when below the legal age; not having the latest technology; not being allowed to smoke in the home; not being allowed to stay out all night, etc. Such anger is an important sign of someone with too much entitlement and unhealthy egotism.

Anger is abrasive. Someone who is constantly grouchy and irritated is unpleasant to be around, even if they aren't actually being abusive. Although we should not condemn the emotion in the same way we condemn the bad behaviour, we are within our rights to apply *natural* consequences to exceptional signs of irritability or anger. So we should not punish (or apply logical consequences to) a child just for being angry but it's reasonable for us to choose not to spend time with them or do things with them if they are so prickly that they are not nice to be around. This should be used to encourage change, not as an excuse to reject them. Bear in mind that some young people have little conscious awareness of their emotions, tone of voice, mannerisms, etc. It may be useful therefore to give them feedback (in an assertive, not aggressive way) about how they are coming across, but punishing them will produce resentment and feelings of unfairness, and probably more anger.

Although it's wrong to reward children for their violent or abusive behaviour by giving them pleasant distractions, sympathy or undue attention, if a child is getting angry and upset, it's OK to distract, cajole or sympathise, provided they haven't behaved badly yet.

The axe-wielding maniac scale

When I'm working with young people (and some adults) on their violence, I find it helpful to ask them to rate how angry they are generally, or how angry they got at a particular time. I use a zero to ten point scale where zero is perfect peace and ten is where they actually want to kill someone. The ten represents turning into an axe-wielding maniac. This makes it amusing and lightens what can be a very difficult discussion. It also has the advantage that hardly anyone ever says they were a ten. It's useful to emphasise that things could have been worse and since they weren't at the top of the scale they could have been angrier and more violent.

I mentioned above that when we are in a rage we don't want to calm down. I ask where on the scale they stop wanting to calm down. Even younger children seem to understand this and typically they will say at a six or seven on the scale. Note that no amount of anger-management training, relaxation exercises or techniques will work once they pass their personal I-Don't-WANT-To-Cool-Down point [IDWTCDP]. They need to become more aware of the processes that move them up the scale and do something about it before they reach their personal IDWTCD point.

THE AXE WEILDING MANIAC SCALE

- 10 — KILL!
- 9 — RAGING
- 8 — FURIOUS
- 7 — MAD
- 6 — VERY ANGRY
- 5 — PRETTY ANGRY
- 4 — SLIGHTLY ANGRY
- 3 — ANNOYED
- 2 — IRRITATED
- 1 — FAIRLY CALM
- 0 — PERFECT PEACE

When dealing with someone who is in a rage or tantruming, it's as well to be aware of when they have passed their IDWTCD point. You are usually wasting your breath trying to negotiate or reason with someone at that point and threatening them will often make no difference. Beware of getting into a power struggle where you are determined to make them calm down and they are determined not to, this can lead to escalating violence. It's especially futile with many young people in a rage to make any kind of threat that is not 100% certain to happen (they'll gamble on the 5% uncertainty) or is delayed by more than a day or two. While in this primitive, childish emotional state, they really don't care about next week and may not care about tomorrow (but may also pretend not to care). Kids in such an adrenaline-charged state will sometimes taunt parents into giving longer or harsher punishments. An exteme example was a young lad who, rather than let his mother remove his gamebox, went and smashed it himself, even though it was his most treasured possession.

It's very important that your child learns that there will be consequences when they act violently, abusively or destructively, but **while** they are in a rage it's not important that they know exactly what the consequence will be. Don't get into a discussion about how long they are going to lose priviledges for. Once they have calmed down tell them what the consequence is. If they want to apologise let them but this does not mean a lesser punishment (or you will have no way of knowing if it's genuine or not). Don't go into lengthy lectures about what they have done. In most cases they know exactly what they have done wrong. If you wish to express how they have hurt or disapointed you, make it short and factual. There is usually no point in trying to make a young person feel guilty, they either do or they don't.

"The one thing that people spiraling out of control do not need are people around them who are spiraling out of control. They need people with strength and resilience – not physical strength, psychological strength. They need people who can stand by them, stand up for them and stand up to them. They need people with commitment but a degree of distance (this of all things is hardest for families) – people who are there for them but are not going to be overwhelmed and not going to be rushing around doing everything possible to make it all right for them. They need people with cool determination who will not engage in high expressed emotion." Clements[445]

Women and anger

In our society anger and violence are seen as primarily male prerogatives; violence and rage are just not seen as feminine. As there have been more violent females portrayed in the media over the past few decades, this view has been changing and teenage girls do appear to be getting into more fights of late. Despite this undesirable narrowing of gender differences, violence is still far more common for males of all ages than for females.

However, there is actually no evidence to suggest that females are actually less *angry* than males and within the family, wives and mothers probably feel *more* anger overall than do husbands and fathers because they are in the frontline more often than fathers, more involved in nurturing and controlling children, more emotionally involved with everyone.

Women often feel very guilty about being angry and are more likely than men to go from passive to aggressive within the home. Women may inhibit their anger and let their frustration and resentments build until they explode in, usually impotent, anger. They are then more likely to feel guilty about their anger, which may get in the way of taking the other person's bad behaviour seriously enough.

Men are more likely to either be assertive or aggressive early on in an interaction. They may either stop the other person's behaviour or provoke an escalation. There is a popular view that aggression is caused by a lack of skills in assertiveness. There is some truth in this but high assertiveness and aggression can occur together. Many people are good at being assertive in some situations but are aggressive in others. I've met many men who are highly assertive at work but aggressive at home. Many of the young people who are abusive to their parents are also very good at being assertive and many are above average in assertiveness, sometimes way above average.

Can Anger be useful?

Anger is not always a bad thing. Righteous anger against injustice has helped bring about some major reforms (such as ending slavery). In therapy we often see it as positive when an abuse victim gets angry about being abused. But when the victim is a parent and the abuser a child, workers are not at all likely to see parents' anger as useful. Parents' anger is seen as a risk factor for child abuse and there is an assumption that good parents don't get angry at their children – a totally unrealistic myth.

For an abused parent, getting angry can indeed be useful at times, as the following quote suggests:

"Anger can help us to overcome our feelings of powerlessness: When we see that we don't deserve to feel powerless (or humiliated or hurt) and that we have the right to object to such treatment, then showing some anger can be empowering.
Anger can be a way to say, 'I deserve better than this, and I can speak up and defend myself. I don't have to wait quietly, hoping I'll be treated better." Caplan[446]

Getting angry is often a useful part of empowerment. Staying angry, or getting into a state of impotent rage, is not.

Losing control or gaining control?

"My parents were strict with me and way over-protective up until I rebelled. It was a deliberate strategy… and it worked. They're much less strict now… I'm a confident person. In fact some people think that I'm up myself, but I don't care what they think." Fifteen-year-old girl who had become violent to both parents on entering High School.

This quote gives the impression that this girl planned her violence; she didn't. She consciously began rejecting her parent's authority and the rebellion was 'deliberate' but this led to her getting very angry with them and lashing out. The emotion was genuine, and she didn't pre-plan her violent outbursts. Her parents backing-off meant that the aggressive behaviour was rewarded more than it was punished. Violence is often talked about as if it's out-of-control, crazy behaviour. What is referred to as expressive violence is emotional and often irrational. It appears to be an explosion of emotion not aimed at any particular goal. We've all had flashes of such anger that make us want to lash out or smash something. Most of us don't do so but the impulsive and the young more often do. Children's violence is particularly likely to be seen in this way, especially children with disabilities or problems. Temper tantrums are usually expressive violence.

Instrumental violence is used to gain a goal; crime committed in order to steal or extort is clearly of this sort. Some bullies show little emotion when they hurt or intimidate their victims, either for material gain, power, or entertainment.

The distinction between expressive and instrumental violence is a useful one provided we are aware that much violence is a mix of the two. Violence may appear to be the result of overwhelming rage. However, if we look at the process of getting into a rage, it may be clear that the individual works himself up into a rage because he isn't getting his own way and he doesn't expect any serious consequences for acting violently. If such rages are never rewarded they tend to become less frequent and may stop, but if they sometimes result in the person getting their own way they increase in frequency, as can happen with toddler tantrums. So are they purposeful or not? Depends on how you choose to look at it.

Communication

I don't see communication as being of much importance in *causing* violence to parents. Many of the parents involved are excellent communicators (including many professionals) and many of the young people are also highly articulate (though a few are monosyllabic). Naturally, communication is often extremely poor once open hostilities have broken out and a few young people have virtually stopped talking to their parents. In other cases the young person has a good relationship and good, even excellent, communication with his or her parents most of the time despite being intermittently abusive. I also have often seen good communication return to the parent-child relationship once the abusive and defiant behaviour has stopped.

It's not unusual for adolescents nowadays, not just those who are beyond control or aggressive, to go through a protracted period of limited communication with parents; usually this passes. My son, who never stopped talking as a younger child, went through a surly, uncommunicative stage for a year or two in his teens.

It's sometimes a bit insulting to abused parents when workers imply that better communication is going to solve their problems. Without clear rules, boundaries and consequences you can communicate all you like with an abuser but to no avail. It's also assumed by some professionals that children are trying to 'communicate their *needs*' when they are screaming, throwing things about or lashing out (seeing them as victims). Sometimes the young person is communicating their hurt but often the only communication involved is along the lines of 'get out of my way or I'll hurt you!' or 'you can't control me, I can do what I like!' It's not needs, but wants that are being communicated.

Although poor communication has little to do with *causing* the problem of violence to parents, good communication can be a part of the solution. This is largely about communicating assertively rather than either passively or aggressively. Parents often say that they are being less emotional and clearer once they have made some attitude changes – such as tossing the guilt overboard. This is just as relevant to communicating with a partner, or ex-partner as with a teenager.

Passive communication

Some parents have become excessively polite with their children. Treating children with respect is great but parents nowadays often sound unsure of themselves and unassertive when requesting that their children do something. Like most aspects of modern parenting, this approach works OK with many children but not with others.

What you say	What you mean	What it means to the difficult child
Could you please brush your hair, darling?"	Your hair needs brushing.	I could. I do know how, but I'd rather not. Since you asked so nicely it must be a big favour you are asking of me and I don't feel like doing you any favours.
Would you like to empty the garbage?	Empty the garbage, please.	You know I don't 'like' doing the garbage so why do you ask such stupid questions?
Could you please get ready?	I need you to get ready now.	I could, and I will, but I'll put it off as long as I can.
I'd really like your room tidied.	Tidy your room.	That's what you'd like; I'd like to keep watching TV. I don't much care if my room is tidy, so you can do it if you like just don't move any of my stuff.
What would you like for breakfast?	Cereal or toast?	You know I'd like chocolate or ice cream but you won't let me have them, so why do you bother asking when we only have a choice of five cereals or six spreads? I'll ask for waffles and see if I can bully you into making them, or at least make us late for school.
I get annoyed when you leave your dirty dishes on the floor.	Pick up your dishes.	Clearly you are an obsessive-compulsive clean freak and I'm not going to cater to your neurosis without some extra motivational consequence.
It upsets me when you talk like that.	Stop the verbal abuse.	It was meant to upset you! Result!

Imagine a police officer saying, "I'd really like it if you stepped away from the vehicle, Sir" as opposed to "Step away from the vehicle, Sir." The second is still polite but it's clearer and carries more authority.

All the examples on the left are fine with easy children and may only be a problem if delivered in a wishy-washy way.

What is important here is the need for a balance between being wishy-washy and being aggressively tough. It's fine to be polite and invitational with children as long as we don't lose sight of the fact that some things are not negotiable and, especially with younger children, we have to issue commands at times. I'm not suggesting that we issue abrupt commands as a matter of course or that we stop being reasonably polite. I've suggested that giving choices rather than commands is usually more effective with oppositional children. If you have an oppositional teen, then giving choices is going to work better than giving orders, but give limited choices backed by consequences. If there are no consequences they will often choose not to co-operate. Children with autistic traits may be particularly confused by wishy-washy language (see section on Autism and violence).

Listening

Good listening is just as important as good talking in communication. Some adults don't really listen to children generally and a surly bad-tempered adolescent may make listening rather difficult and unrewarding. It's easy for some parents to give up trying to listen.

"We were given two ears but only one mouth, because listening is twice as hard as talking." [447]

Three Types of Listening

1. Competitive or Combat Listening
You are treating the interaction or conversation as an argument, a power struggle or an opportunity to show off or put the other person down. You are pushing your own agenda and looking for rebuttals or openings to shoot them down. You are generally not interested in what they feel but only in dissecting the facts and listening for mistakes. It's not a cooperative exchange of ideas or a genuine attempt to solve problems but a competition. You are seeing it as a win-lose situation not a win-win one. If you have read the chapter on power you should realise that in pure matches of aggression the one who is most aggressive, or willing to use the dirtiest tactics, usually wins. That sort of power struggle is usually a complete waste of time and makes thing worse.

"Two people will often fall into a pattern of discourse that resembles a negotiation, but really has no such purpose whatsoever. They disagree with each other over some issue, and the talk goes back and forth as though they were seeking agreement. In fact, the argument is being carried on as a ritual, or simply a pastime. Each is engaged in scoring points against the other or in gathering evidence to confirm views about the other that have long been held and are not about to be changed." Fisher & Ury[448]

2. Passive Listening
This is one-sided and is appropriate when the other person just wants to tell a story or when the other person has expert knowledge or technical information to impart to you. This is less appropriate if the other person is struggling to explain or to make you understand, or if the subject is very emotional or personal. In passive listening it's easy for misunderstandings to occur as we tend to hear what we expect or want to hear.

3. Active Listening

In active listening we don't just sit back and let the other do all the work but check that we are understanding. We can do this by repeating back what we are hearing in slightly different words, checking our understanding, asking for clarification, or asking about the other person's feelings. In relationships (rather than a work or technical context) it's important to listen for feelings as much as listening for facts. The focus is on the other person and we are cooperating with them not competing with them. There is a feedback process as you are checking what you hear for understanding and emotions and feeding this back into the communication process.

Listening is an **essential** part of all negotiations and its importance cannot be stressed enough! Listen to what the other person has to say (even if you think they are talking rubbish at the time). The cheapest concession you can make in *any* negotiation is to let the other person know that they've been heard. Understanding does not imply agreeing: you can make it clear that you understand the other person's position even if you totally disagree with it. It's good practice to repeat back, in your own words, what you have heard to check that you have got it straight.

"So you're saying that you'd like to go out more, but not to sports, is that right?"

Don't just listen for *facts* listen for feeling too.

"You're saying you don't mind but I get the impression that you really do, is that right?"

To listen actively:

- Focus on them, on their ideas (even if muddled or you don't agree) and on their feelings (even if you think they are irrational).
- Suspend judgment as far as possible, try to keep an open mind and see their point of view – this does **not** mean you have to agree with it.
- Stop what else you are doing. Turn off TV and remove distractions; turn fully away from the computer or switch off the screen.
- Face them; make eye contact; get to their level; not too far or too close.
- Don't raise your voice and be aware of your body language.
- Check that you are understanding: "So is what you are saying…?"
- "Can I check I've understood you correctly…?"
- "It sounds to me like you're upset about…?"
- Try to use your own words. Any new skill may feel awkward at first but after a while such habits become more natural and start to come automatically.

393

Communication difficulties created by the speaker

- Voice volume too low to be easily heard or so loud or forceful that it causes anxiety or fear (which makes it much harder for them to understand you).
- Making it too complicated, adding too many details, throwing in different issues, trying to blind them with science or your brand of logic or too many issues.
- Not sticking to the point, beating around the bush, losing the point of the discussion.
- Body language or non-verbal elements contradicting or interfering with the verbal message, such as smiling when anger or hurt is being expressed.

Communication difficulties created by the Listener

- Not giving the speaker your full attention.
- Interrupting.
- Focusing on what **you** want to say and how you can 'win' the argument or discredit the other.
- Thinking ahead to what you want to say next instead of listening.
- Hearing it only from your point of view and not empathising with the other person.
- Judging the speaker more than the message.
- Not asking for clarification or explanations (perhaps because you are afraid to look stupid or don't really care what they mean).
- Rushing to conclusions or solutions.

"The first duty of love is to listen." Paul Tillich

Guidelines for difficult negotiations

Although we tend to think of negotiations as being formal and about highly conflictual situations (such as employer vs. union), we can regard any situation as a negotiation where two people need to sort out some difference of opinion or different needs. In a well-functioning relationship most compromises and decisions may be made without anyone paying any attention to the process and the more smoothly such negotiations happen the less we are aware of them. Unfortunately things do not always go so smoothly and following the guidelines below can help prevent escalating arguments or situations where the most powerful person's wishes override everyone else's.

Negotiations are seldom just about the issue at hand. Often saving face or scoring points (which can be in an intellectual way or in a bullying, controlling or aggressive way) can be just as important, or more important, to one or both parties. The importance of the relationship should **always** be taken into consideration: winning an argument with an official you will never see again will have very different consequences to winning an argument with your partner or children. Try to become aware of how important winning is to you. An excessive need to win can result in losing respect, friends, love, etc. Allowing the other person to win can be a sign of maturity and strength rather than weakness. Try to develop the habit of thinking of negotiations as mutual problem solving rather than always as a competitive, win or lose situation.

The following guidelines may be easy to apply if the other person also plays fair but they may be **even more important** when the other person is not playing fair! (Though much more difficult to apply). Meeting aggression with aggression leads to escalation and almost never to a satisfactory solution to the problem. These guidelines apply to dealing with anyone where there is some kind of relationship, i.e. it's not a purely practical, contractual matter.

In family situations a general rule is that if the other person is being irresponsible (whether this is a child or your partner or ex-partner) it becomes **more** important that you are acting responsibly.

Be aware of power differences

Equal negotiations are not possible when one party has much more power than the other. If you want negotiations to be fair then you may have to equalise power or resources *to some extent*. Formal mediation sometimes does not work because there is the pretence that everyone is equal. In a parent-child relationship everyone is **not** equal, and **should not** be equal. If there is equal power that is probably why there are serious enough problems to require mediation in the first place. If you have read the chapter on Power you will realise that what power you and your child wield is largely dependent on what you are willing to do.

Choose the right time and place.

Do both parties feel safe? Can other people hear? Do you need a mediator? Don't assume that all negotiations have to be done face to face. For example, after a marital separation it may be easier to contain emotions over the phone. This also has the advantage of removing any (immediate) physical threat and either party can hang up if there is verbal abuse. With some very difficult issues sending an e-mail or writing a letter can be an effective way of stating clearly what you think and feel without an emotional drama. If it's important and sensitive, get someone impartial to read it before sending. Beware of text messages over anything important. It's very easy to fire off an inappropriate text and for it to be misunderstood.

Take emotions into account

Try to understand the emotions involved - yours and theirs. Think about what they may be feeling, ask them about this, and try to be clear in your own mind how you feel and how this is affecting your behaviour and the other person. It's much easier to control your feelings if you are clear about what they are and expressing feelings can often effectively defuse them. Saying "I'm feeling irritated about..." can help prevent the irritation becoming anger and rage.

There is a strong tendency, especially by men, to emphasise rationality and objectivity and to devalue emotionality and feelings. In fact what appear to be objective and rational solutions often *assume* certain emotions as being normal. For example, the desire for power and for money, are often assumed to be rational and objective whereas valuing relationships, empathy and caring are assumed to be irrational. There is nothing inherently *rational* about greed and desire for power and nothing *irrational* about valuing relationships – in terms of human happiness the opposite makes more sense!

"Fears, even if ill-founded, are real fears and need to be dealt with. Hopes, even if unrealistic, may cause a war." Fisher & Ury[449]

Respect the other person

Develop an attitude of respecting the other person. Their ideas, opinions, hopes and fears are as important as yours. Without respect there is little meaningful communication. You don't have to like or agree with someone to respect them.

Be Concise

Keep your statements as **brief and clear** as possible. There is much less risk of misunderstanding and more time to explore the real issues. The other person is less likely to feel bored, bamboozled or bullied if you are crisp, clear and concise.

Stick to the point.

If there is a conflict, it's usually best to tackle one issue at a time. If you agree to discuss a particular issue then respectfully resist attempts to sidetrack the conversation and resist your impulses to score points by reminding them of their past failures or present inadequacies.

- "That's an important issue but right now let's stick to..."
- "I know you feel strongly about that but we agreed to discuss..."
- "I promise we'll discuss that later... what about..."

Look for Alternative Solutions

Don't assume that there is only one possible solution to any problem (which of course happens to be yours). Think of alternatives before you start the discussion. It's often a good idea to brainstorm possible solutions. Brainstorming just means listing all the possibilities you can think of, whether good, bad or ridiculous. During the brainstorming part don't criticise any ideas however outrageous. Sometimes crazy ideas can be adapted into creative solutions.

Avoid the Past - except where there are current emotional effects

If you are trying to solve a problem then it's better to stick to the present and the future. However, there are some situations (such as where there has been abuse or a major loss) where the emotional effects of the past are very much *current* issues and need to be taken into account.

Ask for changes in behaviour not attitude

Requests should be for clearly identifiable changes in behaviour or concrete arrangements rather than changes in attitude, personality, values, or anything at all vague. "Show me more respect!" is not as likely to lead to any change as a request for less swearing. Parents very frequently complain about their teenager's "attitude", but the teenager may be completely unaware of their permanent sneer and just feels unfairly picked on.

It's not a WAR!

Examine your motives. Are you trying to communicate and negotiate or are you trying to get revenge, boost your ego, or put the other person down? Are you going in assuming conflict and aggression? If you are, then that is probably what you will find!

Find something to agree with.

Search for some point that you can both agree on. In conflict situations this is not always easy.

"There frequently exists a psychological reluctance to accord any legitimacy to the views of the other side; it seems disloyal..." (*Getting to Yes*, p 62)

"I think we all agree that there needs to be less shouting."

"I agree it's been difficult for you, however..."

"Yes, your plan would improve *this and that* but what about *the other*?"

What's in it for them?

Don't assume that the logic and justice of your case will sway the other person to your point of view. What are the benefits of your proposal for them? If you are negotiating with an ex-partner or a rebellious teenager, it may go against the grain to even think about making things easier or more pleasant for them. However, it's often essential to think through the benefits of your request or plan for them in order to reach any agreement.

"If you start putting your clothes in the laundry basket we will not have to enter your bedroom except at weekends, so you can be as messy as you like during the week."

Attack the problem not the person

Any kind of personal attack is likely to delay finding a solution. Telling your teenager what a lazy person he is, is not likely to motivate him to cooperate. Try to look on the problem as something you both have to defeat. Even in conflict situations you can think in terms of needing a temporary alliance with the other person against your mutual problem. If it's not obviously a mutual problem, try to think of ways of seeing it as such. In any negotiation try to be aware of what you have in common not just your differences. Even warring ex-partners usually have a common concern for the kids (or the desire to maximise the value of property or minimise court fees).

Be prepared to give some ground.

You should be prepared to compromise in some way if you expect the other person to compromise. It's a common negotiating tactic to start out with higher demands so that you can lower them in the course of bargaining. Beware of overdoing this in any negotiation as it can result in a strong emotional reaction if you are seen as being deliberately obstructive or vindictive. Making unreasonable demands in negotiations with anyone with whom you have an ongoing relationship is obviously not a good idea; which do you value most, the outcome of the negotiation or the relationship?

If the main issue is not one where you can give ground (and it's good to be very clear in your own mind about this) it may be possible to give ground over some less important matter. This keeps the discussion going and, importantly, helps the other person save face.

Helping them save face

Do you have a temptation to gloat if someone gives in to your request or concedes that you are right? If so, then fight this tendency. Gloating over your 'victory' means that they are less likely to keep their side of the deal, that they will be less likely to give ground in future negotiations, and that they will think less of you! If you get concessions try very hard not to follow it with a lecture.

Remember that children, especially teenagers, may have a strong need to save face. Try to let them feel they are getting some concession, however small or symbolic. A stubborn, proud adolescent may be willing to *cut off their nose to spite their face* rather than be seen to be giving in.

"Often in a negotiation people will continue to hold out not because the proposal on the table is inherently unacceptable, but simply because they want to avoid the feeling, or the appearance, of backing down to the other side." (Getting to Yes, p29)

Absolutely avoid absolute terms

Try not to use words such as "always", "never", "totally" as they ~~always~~ often lead to a debate about exceptions. "You're always late!" may produce a defensive angry response even if the culprit is actually late 90% of the time. He or she will recall the 10% that you have forgotten! Statements such as "You **never** think of anyone but yourself!" are almost certainly inaccurate and often more a personal attack than an attempt to negotiate.

No one is ever always anything!

Use "I" statements

Try to speak about yourself, rather than about the other person. Statements that begin with "*You...*" are often aggressive, blaming or controlling. Statements beginning with "*I*" are less threatening and often (but certainly not always) more honest and open.

"*I feel let down*" is better than "*You let me down*".

"*I feel angry...*" is more honest than "*You make me angry!*"

Make it clear that your feelings and opinions belong to you and don't project them on to others. It may seem like a subtle difference but such differences can make the difference between a conflict that escalates and one that is resolved.

Note: "I am wonderful" and "I think you are a complete idiot" are not what we mean by I statements!

Be Prepared - Rehearse

Forewarned is forearmed! With any difficult negotiation think about what you are going to say in advance. What are your arguments? What is the other person likely to say? If it's really important write it down, rehearse and ask someone else how it sounds.

State the problem before the solution

Consider formulating a statement which includes the following, in order:
1. Your view of the problem (*I think...*);
2. How it affects you (*I feel...*);
3. One (or two) possible solution(s) (*I would like it if...*).

I think...	I feel...	I Would Like...
Describe the situation or problem as objectively as you can. Recognise that even concrete "facts" will often be seen differently by others.	State how you feel about the problem without blaming anyone. Stick to feelings of relevance to this problem. Resist the impulse to make the other feel guilty.	State the changes to behaviour or arrangements that you would like without making demands or assumptions. Point out possible advantages for the other person.

The order is important. Always state the problem before your solution.

This simple framework - I think, I feel, I would like - can help you clarify what you are going to say, helps you avoid being sidetracked and should become second nature with a bit of practice.

Self Care

'Time we enjoy wasting is not wasted time.' Anon

Looking after yourself is important for a number of reasons. First, it's a good thing in itself: you deserve to be healthy and happy – everyone does. As the parent of a difficult child you need all the energy and mental strength you can muster. If you can reduce your stress and depression you will cope better with challenges. In addition, though your children are probably not going to like you paying more attention to yourself, in the long run they are going to respect you more and be less entitled if you have more respect for yourself and are less other-focused.

If you don't value yourself, why would anyone else?

"Self-care comprises those activities performed independently by an individual to promote and maintain personal well-being throughout life." Dorothea Orem

Since well-being includes happiness and mental health, self-care can include things that make us happy even if not really healthy (everything in moderation, including moderation).

Self-care can mean finding time for:

relaxation/ running/ socialising/ sport/ meditation/ massage/ prayer/ pampering/ fun/ frivolity/ novels/ nature/ wine/ walks/ sex/ self-indulgence/ spontaneity/ random gaiety/ humour/ hobbies/ baths/ crafts/ down-time/ time-out/ cakes/ camping/ dancing/ romancing / etc.

Self sacrifice

"Don't sacrifice yourself too much, because if you sacrifice too much there's nothing else you can give and nobody will care for you." Karl Lagerfeld

There is a myth in our society that a good mother should be *totally* dedicated to being a mother. This is a strange, illogical and historically new idea. Throughout most of human history, and in most societies today, women do not have the luxury of giving up all their other tasks and responsibilities to concentrate on their latest child. Many women feel guilty when they fail to live up to this ideal of total dedication (see section on Perfect Parents). This causes a lot of totally unnecessary guilt, even though logically most women don't *consciously* aspire to being *just* a parent. A few mothers do try to dedicate themselves utterly to their families and hence do almost nothing for themselves, not taking any time out for themselves, or doing anything for their own pleasure or personal advancement. (If you have read the rest of this book you will not be surprised that I regularly meet mothers like this in *Who's in Charge?* groups and in counselling). Though some children in such families do well, others are harmed by such an unnatural form of parenting. For a child to believe that they are the centre of the universe is unhealthy and they may develop grandiose ideas of entitlement. If they are centre of their parent's universe, they often come to think of themselves as centre of The Universe. An extreme child-focus can lead to an extreme me-focus!

Costs of neglecting your self-care

"I had come to believe that caring for myself was indulgent. Caring for myself is an act of survival" Audre Lorde

Of course, it's not just children's maturity, morality and social skills that can suffer from obsessive child-focus. Neglecting self-care is bad for the parents themselves and for their relationships with other people. Their physical and mental health may suffer, not to mention happiness, especially if they have a difficult child.

If you are constantly flat out and stressed you don't have resources to cope with emergencies and find it difficult to cope with change.

If you act like a servant you will be treated as a servant. It's easy for some people to abuse servants. Children do not respect parents who act like servants. Although your over-entitled children may object to you doing things for yourself, including going out to work, they will not respect you if you act like a servant/slave/doormat. Children respect parents more who have lives of their own there is no evidence that mothers working reasonable hours causes harm to their children.

Looking after your own welfare and mental health is an important part of being a parent. Highly stressed or unhappy parents are not as good at making children feel secure or at setting clear boundaries and giving consistent responses.

Looking after yourself, respecting yourself and taking time to be yourself are an important part of being assertive and non-passive. If you have been passive, lacking in confidence, or a victim, doing things for yourself can be part of breaking free of subservience and becoming a more assertive person.

Self-care is part of showing the children that you value yourself, have rights, demand respect and refuse to be victimised.

Relationships also suffer when one or both parents are too child-focused. This creates a number of stresses on marital relationships. Couples don't leave time for them as a couple. In a healthy family there should still be a couple-relationship in addition to the joint-parent relationship. With over-child-focused parenting this often goes out the window when the first child comes along. This can lead to divorces a few years later. It's healthy if both parents still have some time for themselves as individuals and also some time for them as a couple without the kids. Realistically this may only be once a month but it's worth making the effort to keep this relationship special or it becomes staid and boring.

"I don't have the time, or the money, for self-care"

"Those who think they do not have time for bodily exercise will sooner or later have to find time for illness" Edward Stanley

Some parents (mostly mothers) claim that they have no money to spare and can't spend any money on themselves. The interesting thing is that people nowadays are materially richer than *any* previous generations yet people often claim that they have exactly the amount of money they need to survive (or a little less than they need). It's curious that people with dramatically different amounts of money appear to all have just enough to survive. We expand our 'needs' to take up the available resources. If we had less, we would live off less. So how can it be that we have no flexibility to put just a little aside for self-care?

Do you feel guilty spending money on yourself, if so, why? If this is because you feel that you should spend all your money on the kids, consider how this attitude is making them more entitled. If your partner makes you feel guilty about spending money on yourself, work out how many hours a week you put into child care, housework and cooking and negotiate how you can have some money *of your own* to spend each week.

What applies to money applies just as much to time. One mother has four children and a large house and garden. Another has one child and a small house and simple garden. Both claim that they need all their available hours to keep their home and family running smoothly.

The fact is that most women do far more cleaning and tidying than is necessary for hygiene or comfort and the amount of housework tends to expand to fill the time available. If housework takes up most of your time, you are probably being obsessive; so take some time out and work on being a bit messier (it gets easier with practice).

Think what you would be doing if you didn't have kids: this may involve a hobby, a new work endeavour, study, learning a new skill, socialising more. Now consider how you can make at least a few hours a week available to move towards one or more of these goals.

"If you don't take care of yourself, the undertaker will overtake that responsibility for you." Carrie Latet

Some Reminders

- Families are not democracies.
- A healthy family should be people-focused **not** just child-focused.
- Respect yourself, or they won't respect you.
- Be a parent first, befriending is an optional extra.
- If your kids always like you, you probably aren't doing your job properly.
- Some stress is normal and healthy, as is some conflict.
- Parents don't need to be perfect. You have a right to make mistakes.
- What is good enough parenting for one child may be bad for another.
- To give them responsibility you have to let go of it.
- Cotton wool doesn't prepare them for harsh realities.
- The biggest risk is not taking any risks.
- Be hyper-vigilant about disrespect, it escalates.
- Don't accept abuse from ANYONE.
- Don't excuse abuse (theirs or other peoples).
- If behaviour is really unacceptable there SHOULD be a consequence, even if it's largely symbolic.
- Consequences are about demonstrating displeasure and power, not about inflicting pain.
- Give choices rather than orders.
- You can't make the punishment fit the crime with a really difficult child.
- Be firm not strict.
- Sometimes it has to get worse before it gets better.
- Don't let your happiness be totally dependent on another person. Life goes on.

What Does the Future Hold?

Is violence to parents getting worse?

Though I've had a focus on working with children who abuse parents for over twenty-three years, there are a few things that appear to have become far **more common** just in the past five to ten years:

- Abuse of grandparents.
- Abuse of teachers in primary school.
- Abuse of primary school principals (something I've only come across recently).
- Children admitting violence to family members but expressing no guilt or remorse.
- Children either abusing parents in my office or waiting room, or disrupting the counselling session (usually just by walking out).

Although the trend appears to have been towards more violence to parents over the past quarter century, we cannot assume that this trend will continue. However, I fear that it will.

I think the influence of social media and violent video games are going to increase. I've noticed an increase in rudeness and generally nasty attitudes on the internet over recent years (in social media, YouTube and elsewhere) and children are being exposed to this at earlier ages. As more devices are going on-line it's getting harder for parents to control this. Cyber bullying is dramatic and worrying but low level offensiveness can also have a big effect on attitudes and behaviour over a period of time. New forms of social media appear to be even more prone to rudeness and negativity than Facebook and are anarchistic free-for-alls with no checks and balances on people expressing their aggression and bitchiness. This is inevitably going to spill over into the real world. As children are increasingly wired to a wide world of gratuitous trash and weirdness, they more are likely to distance themselves from family and find support in rejecting parental authority (an extreme form of this may be shown in the radicalization of teenage Muslims). This all means that the influence of parents is decreasing, though I am sure that this won't stop people blaming parents just as much.

Many of the problems we associate with adolescence and youth in Western culture may be due to our infantilising young people[450]. This appears to be getting worse in some ways, with the period of being neither child nor adult lengthening, and with parents attempting to protect children for longer periods. Luckily there are positive trends countering this so there has not been as big an increase in violence, delinquency, suicide and mental health problems as there might have been. No one has a crystal ball and society is too complex for any clear predictions, but I think we should be worried about the direction in which Western society is heading and its effect on our children.

May you live long enough to be appalled by the future!

What about individual children?

I have seen young people turn around dramatically. There is always hope.

No one has done any long-term research on children who abuse parents. There is a general assumption that these young people, at least the boys anyway, are at risk of abusing their partners in the future. I certainly have come across a small number of young men where there have been incidents of violence or other abuse aimed at girlfriends, but how common this is we have no idea. I hope, once this book is out of the way, to follow-up some families who I worked with eight to twelve years ago and if possible interview a parent and the young person in a number of families. So look for a book on that around 2020.

My guess is that not many of the girls who are abusing parents will go on to abuse partners, more of them will probably be abuse victims in future relationships. But I'm guessing.

I've sketched two very different personality 'types' who may be violent to parents: the fearless extroverts versus the neurotic introverts (remember, I'm not for a minute suggesting that all of these children fall into one of these two types). Long-term risks appear to be different with both groups.

The fearless extroverts are more likely to leave home early. Some (maybe half, but I'm guessing) are likely to get into some kind of irresponsible lifestyle, possibly involving substance abuse or petty crime, though they may settle down later in adulthood. Others grow out of their abuse of parents (or stop through some form of legal or clinical intervention) and they may be successful in life (some of these are probably going to be very successful). They are likely to partner and have children, but some may have a number of partners. We fear that a number of the men are going to abuse future wives and girlfriends.

The extremes of the introverted neurotics are far more likely to remain at home into adulthood and may become socially isolated. They are less likely to get into any form of delinquency or substance abuse. In the future more will live their lives largely on the Weird Wired Web. They are less likely to partner and many more will remain living with long-suffering parents who will grow old before their time. When they do partner they may be verbally and emotionally abusive but are probably less likely to be physically abusive to partners (I'm basing this on working with adult men with Asperger's and their partners).

There are some factors that might increase the chances of a young person ceasing to be violent and doing well in adulthood:

- Onset of violence in adolescence rather than starting in the early years.
- The faster the onset of problems the better the chance for a speedy recovery.
- Lack of a disability.
- Intact family.

- No previous violence in family.
- Girls are slightly more likely to mature out of violence than boys.
- Parents who are capable of being assertive and strong-willed.
- No other serious problems in the family.

In giving such a list, and these are all merely probabilities, not set in stone, there is a risk that I'll be reducing the hopefulness of others. If you are a single mother with problems of your own, a boy with a disability who has been exposed to past domestic violence and has been difficult all his life, you might be feeling pretty depressed about his outlook. But there is **always** hope. I've seen such kids mature and become non-abusive.

In saying 'Don't give up hope', this is definitely not to encourage you to live in cloud-cuckoo land. 'Always look on the bright side of life' doesn't apply to putting up with abuse! Long-term hope should not stop you being realistic about the chances of change in the short term.

Fool me once, shame on you. Fool me twice or thrice and you are probably a relative. Fool me four or more times, shame on me.

WHAT FOLLOWS ARE OPTIONAL CHAPTERS. READ THOSE THAT APPLY TO YOU, AND BE THANKFUL FOR THOSE THAT DON'T.

Therapists, Counsellors, Youth Workers, etc.

"My ex was already undermining me with a vengeance. He wasn't trying to be nasty but he just gave in to Julie (fifteen) all the time and let her drink and smoke. At first the therapist, who was in her twenties, said she'd try to get her and me on the same page. She met with Julie a few times then had a meeting with all of us. I felt like I'd been ambushed as the therapist seemed to be backing up Julie's demands that she can drink, smoke, and stay out all night at parties. I was treated as if I was out of touch with modern life. I don't think I'm stricter than most parents."

Mother of rebellious (not abusive) 15-year-old

"'Mother blaming' is the bread and butter of traditional psychotherapy." Caplan

"There is still a widely-held assumption, especially in private practice, that parents' handling of the child cause all emotional disorders. Consequently, parents may feel needlessly guilty and frustrated." Ambert[451]

I'm going to use the term 'therapist' in this chapter, but almost all of it will apply to professions, and semi-professionals (or downright un-professionals), in health, welfare, education or justice roles, who may be involved in your family or in supporting your difficult youngster. Some psychologists and 'therapists' like to make out that what they do is quite different to what youth workers, family support workers, pastoral counsellors, residential workers, etc. do. In reality all these people do some counselling in an informal way and often have absorbed some of the same theories and myths. Psychiatrists are likely to give medication, but many also do some counselling, and they have the same prejudices.

As a counsellor and family therapist, it saddens me how often parents of violent children tell tales of ineffectual practices and unhelpful attitudes from those who are supposed to be helping. Here are some complaints about therapists that I hear from parents:

- Clearly blaming the victimised parent for the child's behaviour.
- Minimising or making excuses for the child's violent behaviour.
- Criticising and undermining parents in front of the child.
- Excluding the parent and not keeping them informed about their child's therapy.

- Telling the parent to give the child more love or more praise (sometimes in front of an aggressive, manipulative, over-entitled child).
- Allowing the child to verbally abuse parents in joint sessions.
- Implying that the parent is weak or stupid for letting it happen.
- Implying that the parent can easily regain control if they want to.
- Threatening to have other children removed from the home.
- Passing the buck from agency to agency.
- Mocking a parent who is being attacked by a much smaller or younger child.

I've heard of all of the above on a number of occasions except the last one (just once about a therapist but also a couple of times about police). The first four are extremely common, though often in a veiled, subtle form. This is definitely not a reflection on the geographical area where I work (Melbourne has higher awareness of CPV than most places). Researchers who have talked to parent victims of CPV tell very similar stories whether the parents are in Australia, USA, UK, Israel or Canada. They generally feel that the health and welfare systems have failed to take the violence seriously or have failed to be helpful:

- *"Parents have horror stories to tell about mental health professionals' unhelpful attitudes"* Cottrell (Canada)[452]
- *"I believe that parents have often been treated unkindly by the helping professions... The upshot of the professional encounter is that the parents are left feeling even more incompetent, weak, and guilty."* Omer (Israel)[453]
- *"Parents tried on average nine different counselors... very few of them believed it had any long-term positive effects on the abusive situations."* Eckstein (USA)[454]
- *"It seems that professionals generally meet reports of parent abuse with condescension and implications of ineffective or bad parenting."* Regaldo, (USA)[455]
- *"...they often find the brutality from their children mirrored by indifference from the courts."* Smart[456]
- *"...there was a sense conveyed by all professionals that in some way these youth were not responsible for their actions."* Frizzell[457]
- *"Therapist and counselors are often at a loss to help parents who are victims, or youth who are assaultive."* Routt & Anderson (USA) [458]

Many parents say that 'the system' adds to their guilt, undermines them as parents, gives the abusive young person more power and generally adds more stress to their lives.

Therapy that excludes parents

I recently heard a mental health therapist who was working with a twelve-year-old make the amazing claim that he only worked on what the child herself brought to the session. He did not want to hear about her phobias from her parents but would only work on what the girl raised. Thus he probably had no idea that she was terrified of monsters under the bed since she was too ashamed to talk about this outside the family. Such a therapist is not at all likely to know about a young person's violence towards parents as they hardly ever volunteer such information. On the rare occasions that they do decide to talk about their violence, it will invariably be couched in a web of excuses and minimisation. Very likely the child will blame the parent (as most abusers try to blame their victims) and many therapists go along with this and even encourage it (since blaming parents is their default mode).

One thing is pretty certain, if your child is having therapy that does not involve *some* communication with you, it's unlikely that they are working on the child's abusive behaviour. If the therapy is helping them develop maturity or solve other problems then there is a *small* chance that it may help over time; but don't hold your breath.

All therapies and intervention have costs (not just financial ones). One cost of all therapy is the stigma of needing help which can reduce children's self-esteem or reinforce their belief that they are damaged goods, disabled, or a victim. Therapy with younger children and adolescents that excludes parents is probably also doing some harm by creating distance between the young person and their family. Reinforcing excuses or endlessly going over their complaints about their family can be very harmful. I've occasionally had young people who were having psychotherapy where the therapist was blatantly blaming the parents (who they had minimal or no contact with) for the young person's problems and was clearly making things worse.

Therapists who take a morally neutral stance may be normalising deviant behaviour. Some therapists think that being neutral about sex, drugs or violence is harmless and necessary to engage the young person. We therapists can't be blatantly moralistic or people with deviant behaviour won't talk to us, but there is a fine line between not condemning and condoning. However, if a child is able to tell an adult that they are sniffing glue, having promiscuous sex, stealing, or beating people up and the adult does NOT condemn this behaviour then to some extent this is minimising the harm they are doing and making the behaviour seem more acceptable. If a thirteen-year-old girl tells her therapist that she had oral sex with ten boys and the therapist's only response is to calmly ask, "How did this make you feel" the child will likely then feel that the behaviour is not so bad after all and may be more likely to repeat it. The reality is that we cannot be neutral about some moral issues because the pretence at neutrality gives the message that you don't disapprove!

Therapists are in a position of power and have a moral responsibility not to implicitly condone harmful behaviour: having said that, a good therapist is not going to lecture them on morality. It's often a difficult balancing act to not alienate the young person while remaining moral, and there are a lot of grey areas. So don't be too hard on a counsellor who occasionally says the wrong thing (especially if you are relying on the biased report of the young person). People often quote me as having said what they wanted to hear. I might list several possibilities, sometimes including outrageous ones to make a point, only to have my client say I suggested just one of these options.

Therapists vary greatly in their attitudes and behaviour. One important example is when they are willing to breach confidentiality and inform parents about a child's behaviour. Research shows that there is little consensus even among the same profession, such as psychologists. All codes of ethics say that we should respect a young person's confidentiality unless they are putting themselves or others at risk so most therapists will breach confidentiality if there is a clear suicide risk, though even this is not always clear cut. Many children nowadays (even pre-teens) might talk vaguely about killing themselves when they are not actually suicidal. In a survey of Australian psychologists[459], half would not tell parents if a fifteen-year-old were breaking into houses or stealing cars. Since stealing cars can be lethal, this surprises me. Yet 40% would breach confidentiality if the fifteen-year-old was smoking marijuana once a week and 22% would tell parents if he was smoking cigarettes. Fifteen percent of psychologists would report a young person for having sex with a steady girlfriend, so clearly their own moral values are more influential than any logical judgment of risk.

Naïve and over-idealistic attitudes

"The parents of an aggressive child who apply for professional help are often told that all they have to do is give their child more love and acceptance. This therapeutic attitude can be doubly harmful, for it increases the parents' sense of guilt and helplessness and fosters a parental attitude that may actually worsen the problem behaviours." Omer[460]

The attitudes of some professionals that lead to rampant parent-blaming are often well-meaning, idealistic liberal ones. Here are a few common examples that can create problems for parents (and indirectly for the children too).

Children are seen as inherently innocent.

It was not very long ago that the opposite assumption was the norm. The idea of 'original sin' was often taken to mean that children were bad until trained. Up until the Second World War, it was a common belief that young children are little savages who need to be tamed. Freud saw young children as inherently violent, lustful primitives. It's curious that some of Freud's successors are now among those who are most likely to see children as inherently good. On balance, I prefer the inherently good to the inherently evil notion but both are a bit silly. The propensity for both nurturing and love and for violence and hate are there from very early on and how these develop, depends a great deal on the entire environment and the wider culture. It makes no sense to say that children, or people, are basically one or the other. We are flexible depending on the social context.

Children's violence is assumed to be expressive not instrumental.

This is shown in the language used: 'letting his anger out', 'expressing his hurt', 'externalising behaviour', 'acting out'. Words such as 'violence' and 'abuse' are avoided. There is much talk of emotions and little or none of children controlling parents. When I first started writing and talking about violence to parents, I avoided the word 'abuse' for a number of years and some professionals still react with shock at the idea of a child *abusing* a parent.

It's assumed that parents need to give more love, attention, praise and be more child-focused

The idea that you can't really have too much love, too much attention and too much praise is common among parent educators and professionals. Yet at the same time individual parents are often blamed for being over-involved and over-protective. Although families have become dramatically more child-focused, we are still being told that we need to be more and more child-centred and increasing problems among the young are often blamed on parents not spending enough quality time, on working mothers, or on uninvolved fathers. Let's face it, you can't win!

If you've followed the argument in the rest of this book it should be obvious that giving more attention and affection can sometimes make over-entitled violent children worse.

Pacifism, love and good communication will conquer all

Parents are expected to never get angry or be aggressive back. It's assumed that if parents are caring and accepting enough, all bad behaviour will eventually stop. Parents are always expected to 'turn the other cheek' and to give *unconditional positive regard*. In short they are expected to be saints. Most saints did not have children, which was probably just as well.

Children never lie about abuse

This strange idea became trendy in the eighties and nineties. It was a reaction to the fact that for many decades children who complained of abuse were not listened to. Children are far more knowledgeable about sex and abuse than in previous decades and they were always capable of making up lies for a variety of reasons. I've come across far more young people in recent years who are either blatantly lying about being abused or else wildly exaggerating. Even when abuse has happened, it's common for children to distort what happened and either exaggerate or minimise. For example, a child may leave out some of the more embarrassing parts or they may exaggerate in an effort to get across how awful the abuse was for them. They can also be easily manipulated by well-meaning but misguided therapists. We should take seriously what they say about abuse, but this is not the same as automatically believing what they say, which is very dangerous (it harms them as well as others). This is even taken a step further by some workers who profess to believe everything that their teenage clients say. I find this scary! Some teenagers lie quite a lot!

Viewing violence as a symptom

Many professionals view acts of violence in children as a symptom of some underlying condition. This means it's not taken sufficiently seriously. Refer back to the table about the Pathology view of violence versus the Responsibility view in the Chapter on 'Why Does He Do That?' It may help you make sense of why different professionals appear to be talking different languages (or living on different planets) from each other or from you.

Mediation and Conflict Resolution

It has been generally accepted in recent years that mediation is not ethical, safe or effective between couples where there is on-going violence or serious abuse. If a man terrorises and dominates his partner she is hardly likely to be able to face him across a table as an equal to work things out rationally.

There are mediators, and mediation agencies, who would never dream of trying mediation with a husband who bashes his wife but they will attempt mediation between a violent teenager and his (or her) victimised parent. Occasionally it's helpful but often it's a farce. I've several times seen young people go through elaborate mediation in order to be allowed to return home or avoid prosecution only to *immediately* afterward disregard the agreement. So tread cautiously if mediation is suggested. At the very least some groundwork should be done first, to assess if it's safe and likely to be at all useful. I think any agreement should make explicit what the consequences are if it's broken. This goes against the non-coercive approach of some mediators. It can also be undermining of parents' authority if there is no recognition that they and their child are not equals.

Group treatment for violent youth

There has been little written about group treatment for children who abuse their parents and very little research as yet on its effectiveness. Group treatment has been used a great deal on delinquents and to a lesser extent on school bullies. I ran groups for delinquent youth in Britain in the 1970s when the government put a lot of money into this. The results were very disappointing. There is one very big problem with getting such kids together: they are a bad influence on each other.

"Group treatment for children who bully: Unfortunately, these groups are often ineffective, even with well-intentioned and skilled adult facilitators, and they may actually make bullying worse, as group members may reinforce each others' bullying behaviours."[461]

In groups for youth with problem behaviours generally, it has been found that *"The presence of many aggressive peers together in a group has been shown to contribute to a shifting of social norms, including a higher level of social acceptability and reinforcement for aggression.*[462]*"*

A study in the U.S. followed up youngsters who had either done a therapeutic group or attended camps. Both of these helped reduce delinquency in the short term (over the next year) but, alarmingly, both increased delinquency in some young people over the next five years. The reason for this was that some young people made new friends – new *delinquent* friends. This certainly does not mean that all group treatment is going to be harmful but it does mean that group leaders have to be able to counteract the potential negative effect of grouping deviant kids together. This is especially so if the participating youngsters are not really motivated to change.

Having put these cautions forward I should stress that I am certainly not ruling out all group treatment for youth who are violent to their parents. Programs where there are simultaneous groups for young people and for their parents are different and appear to have good outcomes. There are some effective group programs (such as the Break-4-change group and Step-Up) and it's possible to overcome the potential pitfalls. What I am saying is that the assumption that getting these kids together is a good thing *in itself* is naïve. Hence I am very sceptical of programs where the aim is general, especially if the aim is primarily to raise self-esteem. If more time and effort isn't put into addressing violence and abusive attitudes, it's better not to introduce these young people to others with problems. Programs are more likely to be useful if they are well structured and thought out and if they keep parents informed and involved. As I read the evidence, 'Boot camps' and most residential programs seldom work and may make things worse.

It can be argued that it's unfair that it's usually the parent-victims who have to attend groups and make the changes rather than the abusive young person. I heartily agree with this, it's unfair. But unfortunately unless there is a legal mandate for young people to get treatment (there are very few places where this happens) the reality is that parents are the ones who are motivated. Waiting until things are bad enough for the legal system to get involved is not a good idea, far better to take action before things get anywhere near this bad. We need more programs that are suitable for families where eight to twelve year-olds are becoming abusive to parents (such as the Who's in Charge? group program).

Anger Management

I use anger management techniques in my work with young people far more than I do with violent or abusive adults, but it's important to be aware of their limitations. Unless there is some attitude change that helps the individual stop getting into a rage, or believing they have a right to control others, such techniques are not likely to help much. I've spoken to many young people, and adult men, who have done 'anger management' and learned various techniques, but don't use them once they are in a rage.

Some problems with Anger Management

- Anger is only a part of the picture, abuse and violence can be related to pride, saving face, a sense of justice, jealousy, fear, anxiety, boredom, and especially the desire to control others.
- Anger is often used as an excuse for abuse – so focusing on anger can reinforce excuses.
- Motivation usually needs to be cultivated but much anger management assumes motivation.
- Even when there is motivation to change, this may vanish when the individual feels justified or enraged.
- Most rage is **Righteous** rage! Once in a rage we don't **want** to calm down, so why would we then use anger management techniques?
- People may make themselves angry in order to achieve a goal (control, power, excitement, attention).

413

- Attitude change is often necessary before any techniques will actually be used.

Motivation and attitude change are far more important than techniques. However, attitude change and techniques can reinforce each other. A simple, structured 'anger management' course (whether in a group or individually) is only going to work for a small number of motivated individuals, but as part of an attitude change course, or wider counselling, it can be very useful.

Child Protection

In recent years I have seen an increase in young people making allegations against parents whom they are abusing. Often these seem to me to be either trivial, gross exaggerations, or downright lies. Sometimes they are vague or contradictory and some children don't seem to be taking them very seriously themselves, just making excuses and sowing confusion. I once watched a twelve-year-old girl kick her father during a counselling session. He was about four times her size but showed remarkable (excessive?) patience. When her father left the room she told me she was afraid of him and that he hit her. When I said I found this hard to believe given what I'd just seen she said indignantly, "But you are supposed to believe me!" Given that her parents were intelligent, well-educated, obviously kind, and very child-focused, and that the girl's accusations were casual and inconsistent, I was horrified to hear that at least one Protective Worker actually believed them. The attitude is sometimes along the lines of, "For such a nice kid to be so violent, there must be *something* going on behind closed doors."

It's in the nature of Child Protection investigations and interventions that parents are undermined. Some really good workers manage to avoid this but often parents lose a little more of their child's respect and some Child Protection workers see their job as empowering children. If you have followed the argument of this book then it will be obvious that the last thing these families need is a more empowered child! I have had several parents tell me that their child's behaviour deteriorated after a Child Protection investigation even though no further action was taken.

Parents whose violent children make allegations of abuse against them can find themselves in a strange topsy-turvy world reminiscent of Camus' *The Trial* or Lewis Carroll's *Through the Looking-glass*.

- If the child is only violent towards the parent this is seen as evidence that the parent is to blame and must be either secretly abusive or mentally ill.
- If the child is violent in other situations, this is seen as evidence that the parent has failed to give a good example and therefore is indirect evidence that the parent is violent or a bad parent.
- If the child presents as articulate and socially appropriate with few problems, this is evidence that the child is telling the truth.
- If the child presents as disturbed with many problems this is seen as evidence for bad parenting and increases the suspicion of parental abuse or neglect.

414

- If the parent presents as calm and business-like this is evidence that they are cold and unfeeling and not taking their child's concerns seriously.
- If the parent is distraught and stressed (most likely) this is seen as evidence that they are mentally unbalanced, and possibly guilty.
- If the parent is angry about the allegations, and especially if they are angry at the Protective Workers, this is seen as evidence of them being unbalanced and dangerous.
- If they are angry at the child who has made the allegations this is seen as evidence that they are both aggressive and rejecting towards the child.
- Although the child is believed even if their story has inconsistencies, if the child withdraws the allegation this is not taken as evidence that the allegation is untrue but may be taken as showing that there is emotional pressure on the child.
- Although children's violence to parents is frequently influenced by someone undermining the parent, that person (usually the father, but can be grandparents or older sibs) is now allowed to give evidence against the parent.
- Fighting for your rights (e.g. by getting solicitors, politicians or support groups involved) is often taken as evidence that you are uncooperative and aggressive.

Keep detailed records.

Don't underestimate the power that the police and Protective Services have. I have seen children removed from obviously caring homes and alienated from their parent for a number of years. Children placed in residential facilities are often greatly at risk (of abuse, crime, substance abuse, sexual promiscuity, school failure and homelessness) so try to find alternatives if they can't remain at home (usually relatives or friends) and work towards making this as short-term as possible.

Try hard to keep your temper. It's understandable that you are angry if you are being wrongly accused but it won't help if you appear aggressive or unstable. You need to be assertive but not aggressive.

Don't blame individual workers. Remember that they may be following orders and may not even agree with the actions they are taking. They may be a very small cog in a large bureaucratic machine with very little individual power.

Try to cooperate but don't admit to anything you haven't done or compromise your principles. Beware of saying things like, *"Take him away then. That's what's obviously going to happen."* Such statements, made in desperation or despair, or just sarcastically, can be used against you at a later date.

E-mail from mother who eventually handed her son over to Child Protection

My ordeal ended up with my eldest son taking my three-week-old daughter hostage. I called the police for help. My son smashed me into a door with my three week old daughter in my arms and her head was pushed into the door as well. I pushed my son off of us with my free hand which led to him being injured by hitting a door frame. He then climbed on the roof of the house and threw tiles at me, he chased me through the street with a tire-iron and yelled abuse that was unspeakable. A neighbour called 999 again while he was choking me and smashing my head into a rock. When police arrived I asked about having him charged but was told I couldn't as he was only nine. The officer told me that he was going to get bigger and stronger and that one day he could kill me, so that handing him to CP was the best choice. I had to be helped to my feet by a neighbour as I was dizzy and upset, surprised that a child could do so much damage.

Since handing my son to CP the blame has been placed firmly on me and my ability to parent. This causes me to second-guess every move I make as CP keep informing me they can investigate my other children whenever they want, even though I'm not doing anything wrong. Once you read the CP stature on raising children it scares you as it seems that even sending your child to their room can be classed as child abuse! My son has made a complaint against me as a result of me having him removed and CP are more than happy to record that he is now happy and in a safe, nurturing environment, which makes me feel unfit to parent. Even though this thought only stays for a minute, it's the reason why many parents don't report parent abuse, because children are seen as innocents.

I admit to my mistakes in life but every parent has made some. Child Protection has told me they are the department of *child* protection not *adult* protection, so where is the department for adult protection?

End Box

416

Some Notes on Substance Abuse and Parent Abuse

"A drug is neither moral nor immoral -- it's a chemical compound. The compound itself is not a menace to society until a human being treats it as if consumption bestowed a temporary license to act like an asshole." Frank Zappa

"Knowing what to call CPV [Child-Parent Violence] and how to conceptualise it was very problematic for parents. Most saw it as an extension of their child's substance use – with the corresponding assumption made that if treatment was found for the substance use it would also resolve the problem of CPV. Because of this very few parents considered what they were experiencing as domestic violence, and the thought of accessing dedicated domestic violence services only crossed the mind of a handful of parents."[463]

I'm often asked if drugs and alcohol play a part in violence to parents. They do, but to a lesser extent than most people expect. I've heard self-appointed experts claim that drugs and alcohol are the **main** reasons for the increase in violence to parents in recent years and a few studies have even suggested that most children who are violent to parents are substance abusers[464]. This is certainly not my experience. I don't have exact figures on the use of drugs in my sample of parent-abusing youngsters but my guess is that about 25 percent of those sixteen and over were either regular drug users or binge drinkers (often both). So three-quarters in the older teens were not substance abusers, and if you include the many younger adolescents and pre-adolescents who abuse parents, it's only a small number where this could possibly be a cause of the initial abuse of parents. Even when it's related it usually is not the original cause of the violence to parents. In *almost all* cases in my sample, abuse of parents preceded the abuse of drugs, often by several years. In my experience it's rare for a young person to have begun abusing their parents after they began abusing substances rather than the other way round. Far more common is that adolescents become increasingly abusive, break free from parental control, and start taking drugs or binge drinking somewhere into this process. However, my sample is not representative of all young people who are abusing parents, and excludes those who start after age eighteen, where drug issues and major psychiatric problems are far more common. Even if substances are part of the picture the other things discussed in this book, such as parenting styles, past domestic violence, entitlement and personality, are likely to be relevant.

There certainly are drug abusers who begin being abusive to their families because of drug or alcohol use. One study of two hundred and fifty adolescent substance abusers found that 20% were known to be abusive of other family members, but it didn't specify whether parents or brothers and sisters were being abused[465]. We don't know how many of these started abusing their parents before abusing drugs.

It's clear that abuse of family members by substance abusers is quite common and it's often not taken seriously enough by drug and alcohol workers (see below). These parent abusers are more likely to be in their late teens, twenties and older. I am less likely to meet them (though I've met quite a few) for several reasons:

- I see more of the younger teens than older.
- There are specialist agencies dealing with drug abusers.
- They are less likely to be living at home (hence abuse of parents is more intermittent).
- Their parents often can't make them come for counselling but when they do the young person almost always prefers to focus on their substance abuse rather than on their violence (and they often use their substance abuse as an excuse for abusing others).

"The playing out of problematic drug-associated behaviours such as stealing, violence, argumentativeness and unpredictability in the home have all been identified as contributing to the enduring difficulties of living with a family member who develops drug problems[466]"

Such mentions of violence from drug abusers to family members are rare in the literature on substance abuse, though any drug and alcohol worker will have come across many examples. There has been some research on child abuse by drug abusing parents and more research on violence to wives by alcohol-abusing men but violence to either parents or siblings by drug abusers is a greatly neglected issue.

"In some cases, youth acknowledged abusing their parents when they were 'high' or 'coming down' but more often, violence was precipitated by an argument between youth and parents over issues related to substance misuse. 'I just wanted to mellow out and sleep before I got high again. And if you're coming down you're really edgy. The slightest thing can set you off just like that'." Cottrell[467]

Are parents to blame for substance abuse?

There are certainly parents who are partly, occasionally even largely, responsible for their children's drug or alcohol use. If you used illegal drugs around your children or abused alcohol then you have increased the risk of them modelling this behaviour. If you didn't do this then you are **not** to blame. As discussed in other chapters, you may have contributed a little by being an indulgent, modern parent with a child whose temperament didn't suit this approach. This does **not** mean you are to blame as you didn't know you were doing any harm at the time and this outcome was **not** predictable.

I recommend *"Don't let your kids kill you"* by Charles Rubin, an excellent book by the parent of two drug-abusing boys. He writes:

"As if this monumental self-blame and self-condemnation aren't enough, the mainstream of society is just as eager to point the finger, placing all responsibility for the child's actions squarely on the parent's shoulders, compounding the problem even further.[468]"

It's a common assumption that parents must somehow be to blame for substance abuse. Movies and books often use this as an "explanation" and alcoholics and drug abusers themselves are often very keen to blame their parents as a convenient excuse. One New Zealand study followed up several hundred children over several decades. Those who later became alcoholics recalled their childhoods as being more abusive and neglectful than others. However, when the researchers looked at the evidence from earlier years, their families did not appear to be significantly different to those whose children turned out fine.

Another research study compared the influence of parental, sibling and peer drug use on an individual's subsequent drug use. They found that peers and older brothers had a larger influence than parents[469]. This certainly fits with my experience and should worry you if you have a drug abusing older child at home along with younger children.

A cautionary tale

Martina was an intelligent, articulate, confident girl who'd just turned sixteen when I met her. She'd been having regular counselling for almost a year from a colleague who was leaving. The previous worker had been counselling her for a variety of issues but mainly for emotional and verbal abuse by her parents. She seemed like an easy and rewarding young person to work with but I had mixed feelings about taking her on because Martina was unusually keen on confidentiality and her parents did not even know that she was seeing a counsellor. I'd never, at that point in my career, counselled a young person living at home without their parent's knowledge. If she'd been under sixteen I could have refused but at this age she had the right to receive counselling from the agency without parental consent. At that time a youth work agency a stone's throw from the one I worked in advertised that children from age twelve could come for counselling without parental knowledge! I only saw Martina a few times as she left home and moved away. She said little about her family to me but mentioned rather vaguely that they abused her emotionally. She never mentioned drug use to myself or, as far as I know, to her previous worker.

Five years later her younger brother, Adam, came for counselling along with his parents. They didn't know I had seen Martina. Adam was a generally well-behaved and likable lad but had been introduced to heroin by his sister, Martina, who he said had been using drugs heavily for some time. Adam was close to his parents and saw them as supportive and caring, which is how they appeared when I met them. He spontaneously talked about his big sister, whom he described as "brilliant, but irresponsible and manipulative." He thought she had rebelled against his parents just because they were too ordinary.

Substance use and substance abuse

It's understandable that you are going to be concerned if your thirteen-year-old is drinking. You may or may not be concerned if your sixteen- or seventeen-year-old is drinking. You are far more likely to be concerned if your child, of any age, is using illegal drugs (though some parents see marijuana as less harmful than alcohol). However, this chapter is aimed at parents of young people who have drink or drug **problems**. Occasional use of alcohol or marijuana is not *necessarily* a serious problem and may be of no relevance to their abusive behaviour towards you. If they are *regular* users of illegal drugs or are coming home drunk then there is definitely a problem. I don't want to sound as if I am excusing illegal drug use or under-age drinking but they are both, unfortunately, quite common activities for young people, so, depending on their age, it is as well not to panic unduly; take it seriously but try not to overreact. I've seen studies suggesting that about three quarters of young people will try marijuana at some point during their teens. **Very few** of these develop drug problems and I believe a lot of harm has been done by the "all-drugs-are-equally-evil" approach. Your kids may know someone who smokes marijuana regularly (it may even be the parents of their friends) yet appears to function well, so scare-mongering will just mean that they disbelieve **anything** you say on the subject.

Moderate marijuana use (NOT every day use, this is always excessive) appears to be fairly safe for **most** people but very dangerous for a few (who may be prone to psychosis). Alcohol is definitely a dangerous drug despite it being legal and ubiquitous in most Western societies. Many other drugs can be extremely dangerous indeed, but the danger from occasional use varies greatly.

A major concern is that some children appear to be turning to drugs and alcohol at younger and younger ages (see sections on mass media and popular culture) and we don't really know what the effect is on rapidly developing brains. However, recent New Zealand research suggests that regular marijuana use during adolescence reduced IQ by eight points on average.

Alcohol and abuse

One of the popular myths about family violence is that most often it's a drunken father beating his wife and/or children under the influence of the demon drink. In fact most wife abusers are not substance abusers and most substance abusers are not (physically at least) abusive to their wives or children. The two behaviours are certainly related but the "drunken bum" idea of family violence has largely been discredited[470].

The assumption is often made that drink directly *causes* violence. This is misleading. There are a few normally placid individuals who turn nasty when drunk but there are also aggressive, nasty individuals who are placid or amiable when drunk. I've met several adults who described childhoods with abusive, alcoholic fathers who were violent when sober and amiable when drunk! Admittedly, this is somewhat unusual and the more common pattern is that alcohol makes someone who is controlling and aggressive *more* volatile and *more* dangerous. But it's rare that someone who is abusive while drunk is not also abusive *to some extent* when sober. Some men are verbally abusive and generally controlling but only physically abusive when drunk. With many other drugs, being more abusive when **not** under the influence is actually more common.

The idea that the addict or alcoholic is "ill" is one which is nowadays often taken for granted. At times this is a useful idea but in other ways it's confusing nonsense[471]. A physical addiction does have *some* of the characteristics of an illness, and substance abusers certainly may make themselves physically or mentally ill. However, the important point is that they *make themselves* ill. Quite unlike most illnesses, alcoholism and drug addiction are chosen behaviours. Not only does the addict choose to take the substance in the first place but even after detoxification, when the *physical* addiction has been removed, they often choose to return to their habit. Physical addictions are seldom as important as psychological addictions. Drugs and alcohol are at the end of the day more of a lifestyle choice than an illness. This is not say that anyone can easily choose to give up an addiction and we can still have sympathy for the addicted.

Very few of the young people I have dealt with who abuse drugs have a physical addiction (though no doubt some are going to develop this in the future). Certainly, psychological addictions can be very strong but *choosing* to stay stoned or *choosing* to stay in front of a computer sixteen hours a day are hardly good reasons to be abusive. The compulsive character of addictive behaviours means that it's very difficult to stop, but it's **not** impossible. Thwarting someone who has addictive behaviours may make them excessively agitated and angry, but this is never a valid excuse for them to be abusive and they are still usually very selective about who they abuse.

The connection between abuse of family members and substance abuse is complex. Most of the next section applies to partner abuse as well as to parent abuse.

Some connections between substance abuse and abuse of family members

The following is not meant to be an exhaustive list of the possible connections between substance abuse and abuse of other family members but serves to illustrate the complexity of the situation and point out some connections you may not have thought of:

- A number of personality traits that make someone likely to abuse others can also make them more likely to abuse drugs or alcohol. On average, introversion, agreeableness and conscientiousness will all *reduce* the risk of both types of abuse. Traits such as impulsiveness, egotism and a desire for instant gratification can all make both problems more likely. It has even been suggested that there is an "anti-social personality type" who is more likely to be violent but also more likely to be criminal, sexually promiscuous and to abuse drugs and alcohol.

- I see responsibility as a key variable. The more irresponsible someone is the greater the chance that they will abuse others and the greater the chance that they will abuse drugs and alcohol (or their own bodies in other ways). This applies both to adults and to young people. This *certainly* does not mean that the two will *always* go together.

- While someone is substance affected, the chance of violence may either increase or decrease. As noted above, for many people being drunk makes aggression or violence far more likely but for a few it makes them less aggressive. Stimulant drugs such as cocaine, speed and Ice can greatly increase the risk of violence for *some* individuals. For many users, being stoned on marijuana or high on heroin makes them *less* likely to be violent *at that time*. Reactions to drugs can vary greatly between individuals and are partly dependent on expectations. In the hippy era people expected marijuana to make them peaceful but the Zulus took it before going into battle. I've spoken to young men who say that they and their friends get aggressive when high, though this is not at all the usual reaction.

- Withdrawal effects, hangovers and cravings can all make people irritable and more aggressive. It seems to be quite a common pattern for daily dope smokers to be irritable when they are not high. Being irritable in itself does not make anyone violent or abusive, but if they have the attitudes and behaviours of abusers then irritability will make matters worse.

- Cravings for drugs can make people want to control or exploit others. Some addicts will steal from those they love to get money for drugs or assault those who get in the way.

- The compulsive nature of addictive behaviours means that they may become very agitated and angry with anyone who gets in the way of their compulsion. This may at times be similar to those whose compulsions stem from OCD or autism. Thus anyone (usually a parent) who tries to control their compulsive behaviours may be abused.

- Although having a drink or drug problem is socially stigmatised it does not carry as much blame, or legal consequences, as family violence. Substance abuse is more often seen as a medical problem which is not the case with family violence. Thus some people use their drink or drug use as an excuse and may even exaggerate substance abuse problems in order to minimise blame for their abusive behaviour. Some people even use drink to desensitise themselves and reduce inhibitions with the intention of being abusive or irresponsible: *"Alcohol provides an abuser with an excuse to freely act on his desires. After a few drinks, he turns himself loose to be as insulting or intimidating as he feels inclined to be.*[472]*"*

- Substance abuse is poison for all sorts of relationships. There are a number of reasons for this: the drugged person being effectively absent, personality changes, lack of communication, disgust, the drugs becoming more important than anything else, etc. Deteriorating relationships can increase the incidence or severity of violence or abuse and the poorer relationship can then feed the substance abuse in a vicious circle.

- For young people who abuse parents, there is not only a general and often dramatic deterioration in relationships, but their behaviour prevents parents having control over the young person. This makes the young person far more vulnerable to a variety of problems. They may be directly exposed to drink and drugs because they are beyond parental control or they may drop out of school, become delinquent or have periods of homelessness and these can reinforce drink or drug use.

- Those young people who have been exposed to violent role models are more likely to have also been exposed to drink and drug abusing role models. This is often, but not necessarily, the same parent (typically their father or step-father). However, there is a somewhat increased risk that a mother who has been abused will become an alcoholic or drug user (especially if we include prescription drugs). A mother's drinking or drug use, even if it's in the past, can result in her children having less respect for her, and/or can increase her feelings of guilt and make her less assertive as a parent. All of these factors can make violence to parents more likely.

- Children with an alcoholic or drug-abusing parent are far more likely to experience other forms of family dysfunction, for example the other parent may be depressed or their parents may go through a messy divorce. Parental neglect related to substance abuse can lead to abuse by others, school failure, health problems and even disability. Thus family influences that increase substance abuse can go together with family influences that increase other problems, including aggression.

- More generally, almost all social, psychological and health problems tend to correlate to some extent (things like social class and poverty are the most obvious links with lots of different problems).

- Sub-cultures based around drugs or alcohol may encourage all sorts of anti-social and irresponsible behaviour as well as weakening ties to family, friends and social organisations such as school, church, etc. Thus once someone is *into* drugs or heavy drinking, they are more likely to have friends who are a bad influence on them in a number of ways. Individuals can sink into a vicious circle of deteriorating behaviour and worsening social situations; all sorts of problems get steadily worse as they lose self-respect and cut themselves off from 'straight' society and from family and 'straight' friends.

So the idea that there is a straightforward relationship between substance abuse and violence is a massive simplification.

Addiction: is it an 'illness'?

"Drug misuse is not a disease; it is a decision, like the decision to step out in front of a moving car. You would call that not a disease but an error of judgment."
Philip K. Dick

"There is little benefit in calling addiction a disease, because 'disease' and 'normality' are vague, overlapping categories..." Lewis[473]

Understandably, many parents who know their children are using drugs worry that they may be, or may become, an 'addict'. However, the majority of young people who are using drugs are either experimenting with multiple drugs or are occasional users and are not addicted to any one drug (this does **not** imply that it's not serious cause for concern). Addiction is not a simple or straightforward thing.

423

Most often psychological addiction is more important than physical addiction. Heavy drug or alcohol use is often tied up with a particular lifestyle and giving up the drug is more about changing lifestyle than about overcoming a physical addiction, which is why so many people relapse after 'drying out' in rehab. Many years ago I worked briefly with homeless alcoholics. These were hardcore addicts by anyone's standards. However, at that time in the UK (early '70s) they would often be arrested for public drunkenness or some other misdemeanour and sent to prison for a few weeks. They coped without alcohol while in prison and dried out, but once back on the streets it took most of them only a few hours to be back on the booze if they were homeless, but days or weeks if they went to a hostel. To give up drink for them meant giving up all their friends and their main, or only, source of pleasure. If they could have been given accommodation, occupation and a new group of friends they could almost all have overcome the addiction, if they chose to.

Heroin use among troops in Vietnam was extremely high but the *vast majority* of them gave it up when they returned to civilian life. The context is more important than the chemical. One researcher got rats addicted to drugs and they would press little levers all day to get a hit. However, like most lab rats they were kept in the equivalent of solitary confinement in bare cells. When the experimenters constructed a luxury 'rat park' they found that hardly any of the rats got addicted when offered drugs[474]. This has obvious relevance to the amount of drug use in urban ghettos or demoralised indigenous communities.

The idea that drug abuse or alcoholism is an 'illness' has become very widely accepted and the concept does have some usefulness; in the welfare field, it's heresy to question it. However, it's a strange idea when you really examine it:

- In a sense a *physical* addiction **is** a type of physical illness, but one that is initially self-inflicted.
- It's a chosen behaviour. I've never met someone who became addicted to a substance which was initially forced on them (except for prescription drugs).
- There are many binge drinkers, and binge drug users, who have a serious problem but are not physically addicted. Overall, only a small proportion of those with substance abuse problems have a serious **physical** addiction.
- A physical addiction is not the same as a psychological addiction. Many people become physically addicted to prescription drugs but are not psychologically addicted and withdrawal symptoms may make them more determined to do without the drug.
- Psychological addictions can be just as hard to break as physical addictions.
- Not everyone with substance abuse problems even has a psychological addiction to a particular substance and some use a variety of different methods to escape reality. Attempting to equate substance *abuse* with *addiction* can be misleading, as they don't always go together. The young people I have met who were abusing substances and abusing parents were typically poly-substance users.
- Whether or not any psychological addiction (to drugs, gambling or the internet) is seen as a mental illness is a matter for debate and usually based on

value judgments. *Compulsion* is the essential element in a psychological addiction but there is no clear cut off between someone who really likes doing something and someone who has a compulsion to do it. A bright young man recently told me that although he was spending over ten hours a day playing a computer game it wasn't an addiction, he just didn't have anything better to do. If he was spending ten hours programming or writing on the computer we would not consider this an addiction because we see it as constructive (and he might even be paid to do it!). A great many people in our society spend many hours a day in front of a TV watching rubbish yet we don't usually consider this an addiction.

- Since there is no clear definition of 'mental illness' it's almost a waste of time to argue whether a compulsion is or isn't a mental illness.
- Lifestyle is not just of *some* importance, as it is in many mental conditions, but is *all important* in substance abuse (even in rats).
- Addictions, physical or psychological, can be overcome with sufficient willpower, responsibility, or common sense – though we should not underestimate that this can take an incredible amount of self will once someone has become sucked into an addictive lifestyle.
- If you can choose to stop having a condition, does it really make sense to consider it an 'illness'?

Those who work with substance abusers often rankle at talk of willpower as this seems far too blaming of their clients. Similarly they avoid talk about personality variables that lead to addiction though these are obviously of crucial importance in determining who does or doesn't develop a substance abuse problem. Willpower, motivation and personality are important in *any* behavioural problem (and in most emotional problems). They affect how people react to, and recover from, almost all mental and also physical conditions. It's almost comical that although most people accept that positivity and attitudes are important in recovering from a physical illness, many avoid the implication that they are important in recovering from a mental condition. Partly, this is because it can sound like the 'just snap out of it' simplistic advice given to people who are depressed or anxious and the simplistic, 'Just say no!' advice about drug use, which is usually a waste of breath (or ink).

None of the above denies the fact that the choice to go 'straight' can be **incredibly** difficult for some people with substance abuse habits. Yet this is not *always* the case. I've spoken to some people over the years who say it was fairly easy, even very easy, to give up regular drug use (especially marijuana), once they'd made the actual decision. In fact I've heard a few regular marijuana smokers say they felt better almost immediately when they gave it up and serious withdrawal effects don't seem to be the norm for this drug (though they sometimes can be serious, and it's not unknown that extreme irritability increases violent behaviour during withdrawal). I've had several people tell me that giving up smoking cigarettes was more difficult than giving up illegal drugs.

The Alcoholics Anonymous idea that you remain an 'alcoholic' forever even if you never ever drink again is useful to some people but not really very logical; if you have an allergy to a particular food, medicine or chemical, but can avoid it for the rest of your life, is this an 'illness' or a health condition that needs to be controlled?

The main problem with the disease analogy of addiction is that it can imply that substance abuse just happens to people and they have no control over it; this is clearly not true. Like controlling one's temper, saying 'no' can be very difficult but is *never* impossible.

The danger *for parents* with adopting the disease analogy is that they stop demanding responsible behaviour and come to believe that their child is *being* controlled rather than being controlling. The idea of addiction as illness is sometimes disempowering to addicts (see Marc Lewis's excellent book, The Biology of Desire[475]) but is more often disempowering to parents of addicts.

If your child is a drug abuser

There is such a variety of drugs out there that I'm not going to say anything very specific. I'm not an expert and names and chemicals change all the time. If you know what drugs your child is taking try to get information from a *reliable* source. If you use the web be wary of sites that are trying to push a political or moral point of view or trying to make money from you by selling (mostly bogus) cures. The internet is full of pro-marijuana propaganda. People on-line talk about it as if it's a magical mystery cure for everything and totally harmless!

Here are some questions to consider:
- Does your child see their drug use as a problem?
- Are they willing to get help?
- Are they harming only themselves or also abusing others?
- Are they physically addicted to one or more substances?
- Are they psychologically addicted to one or more substances?
- Do you have *any* control over your child?

If you don't have any control over them and they are putting others at risk then you need ask yourself if they should remain at home as you can't keep them safe and you may be delaying the day when they will choose to grow up. The decision to put them out of the house can be absolutely heartbreaking but often parents are simply delaying the inevitable, at great cost to themselves and other family members.

Drug screens

The technology to monitor children's behaviour by means such as blood or urine screening is improving all the time, but as I've mentioned elsewhere, some of the parenting strategies I'm suggesting are not good parenting but desperation measures. If your child wants to come home, or remain at home, but being drug free is an essential part of this (e.g. if they have been violent while substance affected or their lifestyle is putting others at serious risk) then regular drug screens make sense. You can't believe what *anyone* with a substance abuse problem says about their substance use! But getting blood or urine tests is only useful if you are prepared to follow through with a meaningful consequence should it come back positive.

Harm minimisation

This is a very emotional issue. There are those who are so anti-drug that the idea of 'harm minimisation' is abhorrent to them. I support needle exchange schemes 100%. However, it's a different matter when a family member facilitates safe drug use for someone in the name of harm minimisation. Most of us would be horrified at a parent who let an adolescent shoot up heroin at home, yet there are lots of parents who buy their children cigarettes or let them smoke dope out in the yard. This is often initially done with the best of intentions.

"If they are smoking dope out in the shed they are a lot safer than if they were out in the park. At least I know where they are."

"If I don't give him smokes he'll steal."

"I'd rather my fifteen-year-old was drinking here than at someone else's home."

"If I don't drive her to the dealers she walks and probably won't come straight home."

"I'd rather my fourteen-year-old daughter was sleeping with her boyfriend (eighteen) here than somewhere else."

These are all real people and all of them cared deeply for their kids. In a sense all of these parents are applying the idea of 'harm minimisation' but in most cases such compromises do **not** help keep children safe. Making it easy for your child to do things you really disapprove of will not foster taking responsibility for themselves or having respect for you. Such compromises really are a 'slippery slope' and I've heard a number of parents say despairingly 'how did I get to this?' or 'How did I let my standards fall so low?'

If you have clear moral objections to certain behaviours then you should be clear about where you draw the line. To take a common example: you can't stop your child smoking, but you can stop them smoking in your home. You can't stop your fifteen-year-old daughter sleeping with her seventeen-year-old boyfriend but if you don't approve then don't let them share a bed at your home. My son used to make pretend guns from Lego, sticks and sandwiches but the argument that I might as well have bought him a toy gun is simply rubbish as I would then be giving guns my seal of approval. You may be powerless to stop them using drugs, alcohol (or sleeping around, shoplifting, or graffitiing) but do you really want to give it your support and approval?

There is a world of difference between being unable to stop a bad habit and actually supporting it.

Your child's drug counsellor

"Drug counselling is a crock! How can someone be helped when the experts are so easily conned and lied to? And they [counsellors] pander and tell the offender it's never their fault. It does not matter that they are putting everyone else through hell! They treat them like they have taken one too many cookies from the jar, big deal!"[476]

"Why would we talk to parents? They caused the problems in the first place." –
Drug & Alcohol worker to family therapist.

Drug counselling is a very difficult role. Taking a non-directive, mostly morally-neutral stance towards drugs and drug-users is pretty much essential or their clients just won't talk to them. They also have to be very careful about confidentiality and respecting their clients. Thus many drug agencies appear to be very individual-focused, rather than family-focused, and the effect of the substance abuser on their family may be very low on their list of priorities. They may try not to have much communication with the parent as they are afraid of losing the cooperation of their client or of inadvertently breaching confidentiality. These are not good reasons to exclude parents and working with the family is usually an effective strategy in helping drug users of any age. Not many drug and alcohol workers are trained in family therapy and if their client is over eighteen they may see involving the parents as being infantilising and disrespectful to the young person – unfortunately I've seen this attitude extended even to underage drug users still living at home. Some researchers in Scotland interviewed family members of drug takers and a number of workers. They concluded that the needs of other family members "tend to go unnoticed in the focus on finding means to assist the person with the drug problem."[477]

You should certainly encourage your substance abusing teen to get drug counselling but don't expect much to come of it if they don't really acknowledge that they have a substance abuse problem, or have no motivation to change. You may also find that the drug counsellor will not pay nearly as much attention to their abuse of other family members as you would like. You also can't assume that their giving up drugs or alcohol will automatically stop them being abusive or beyond your control.

When we discussed what are 'essential demands' and what are merely desirable, I mentioned that not having illegal drugs in your home should be an essential demand. However, the fact that your (older) teenager sometimes uses drugs outside the home, or drinks, may well be something you have no control over. It's thus desirable that they don't use drugs or drink but usually it's not an essential demand. However, coming home drunk or obviously drugged makes it very much your business. Involving other family members, or your home, in drug use or dealing is definitely intolerable. So is all violent or abusive behaviour, whether related to substance abuse directly, indirectly, or not at all.

Partly because the disease model of addiction is so popular, people often assume that someone must have 'treatment' in order to give up drugs or alcohol. I hear of fifteen year-olds who have been smoking dope a few times a week, or binge drinking, being referred to specialist drug counselling, sometimes when they are already working with a counsellor or youth worker, and people even suggest that such kids need to go into detox! Usually they just need to decide to quit. If they don't want to quit then specialist treatment or detox is a waste of time and if they were not taking a drug every day they are unlikely to have any withdrawal effects. Sending a fifteen-year-old into detox is a very dangerous strategy and the biggest worry is the people they are going to mix with. I've twice seen girls of fifteen and sixteen, who were experimenting with drugs but not addicted, get addict boyfriends in their twenties through contact facilitated by a drug and alcohol agency! In addition, a few young people may think that this is all pretty cool and being a drug user could become more central to their self-image. If desiring a self-image as drug abusers seems incredible to you, remember that we are in a society where the term 'junky chic' is not a joke. The media is full of celebrities going into detox, and rock stars who die of overdoses are often seen as tragic heroes, rather than tragic idiots.

Why Children Should Not Have Mobile Phones in Their Bedroom

There are a number of reasons why children should not have mobile phones, or any web-connected devices, in bedrooms at night. This is a bad idea for any child under sixteen and possibly for older children, depending on their maturity and situation. More and more devices have the potential to connect to the web and if they have to have a computer in their bedroom, internet connection should be unavailable after bedtime. If you cannot turn the internet off then they should not have the device in their room.

      Many children stay up late using such devices and lose sleep. Young people are sleeping an hour less on average than they were twenty years ago and this can have serious consequences. For some children becoming semi-nocturnal can be linked to school drop-out and depression.

      If young people get even occasional calls or text-messages during the night they are effectively on-call and may not get into a deep sleep. This can lead to long-term sleep deprivation and may have implications for adolescent brain development.

      Internet games seem to be more addictive than sole player games and, if allowed to, some children would play these all night long.

      Cyber bullying victims may be emotionally more vulnerable late at night or during the night. Depression and anxiety are often at their worst late at night and the victims can feel very alone. You do not know if your child is going to become either a victim or a bully. Some children who would never bully face-to-face become cyber bullies when they can pick on someone in apparent safety.

      Young people who have long periods of unsupervised access to electronic communication, such as social media, are at much greater risk of being groomed by internet stalkers.

      Sexting and sexually explicit calls, pictures and videos are becoming more common among younger children. It's not rare for twelve-year-olds to be sending or receiving sexually explicit material. This can be highly distressing, or it may be titillating – neither of these is desirable in early puberty!

      Young people who are feeling depressed, suicidal or panicky, or who want to discuss issues such as cutting, bulimia or black magic find enthusiastic audiences among many of their friends. Although occasionally young people give each other useful support with such issues, more often they stress and distress each other and a kind of group hysteria spreads through their friends. Sensitive children may become very stressed by feeling they need to support their friends late at night. Often groups of friends discourage anyone from confiding in parents or carers and this secrecy can become a heavy burden on some children.

     Young people are 'going steady' at younger ages and constant communication, e.g. texting every hour and talking into the night makes these relationships more intense and exclusive, which damages other friendships and relationship with family. When they do break up they may stalk each other on social media or continue to text each other, with an enthusiastic electronic audience who make the process of splitting up more dramatic and stressful.

     Some young people are getting involved in on-line gambling or shopping.

     The wonderful world of the World Wide Web is changing faster than any of us can keep track of. As connection speeds improve and video technology improves, young people (and those who exploit them) will find new vices to explore in the privacy of their bedrooms. Even if you think your child would never do any of the above, is it worth the risk?

By the time you read this the above list will be partly out of date. Currently here in Australia there is concern about children as young as twelve being recruited on-line by Islamic fundamentalists.

Children are getting phones younger and younger but many parents don't worry about the above issues until their children are well into their teens. Children may have had electronic devices in their rooms for several years before it becomes an obvious issue and they then resent a change in the rules. Many young people nowadays use their phones as an alarm clock. Don't fall for this! Buy a separate alarm.

Some families establish the rule that all mobiles are put on charge in the kitchen or lounge at night. If you keep your mobile phone by your bed you are setting a bad example and you may be raising your own stress levels and interfering with the quality of your sleep. Unless you need to be on-call don't keep your phone to hand all the time. Since when did we need to be contactable every hour of the day?

Depression

It's a sign of how primitive our understanding of the brain and psychiatry is that we still talk about 'depression' as if it was *itself* an illness. This is like saying that cramps or a cough are an *illness*. It's a symptom of many different things. But really it's not even *a* symptom, but rather a complex of connected symptoms[478].

There is an idea floating around at present, popularized deliberately by the powerful drug companies, that depression is a '*chemical imbalance in the brain*'. This contains a grain of truth, but not much more than a grain. Any change in our emotions will create chemical changes in our brains. Love is a chemical imbalance in the brain but we don't talk about it as if the chemicals *cause* the emotion. There are undoubtedly cases of depression that *are* caused by chemical imbalances, but these appear to be rare (except post-natally and perhaps in the elderly). Many medical conditions (and side-effects of other medications) can result in depression. Ironically, the chemical-imbalance in the brain idea may stop medics properly exploring other physical causes of depression; it certainly leads to them down-playing social and psychological causes.

It's a lot quicker to prescribe a pill than to explore family or personal issues and many doctors also use the chemical-imbalance idea to encourage people to take medications that often have side-effects and can take a while to work (when they do work). We don't understand how anti-depressants actually work in the brain and the fact that they usually take several weeks to have a positive effect (and only work well on a minority of people) should make it pretty clear that they are **not** simply correcting a 'chemical imbalance' in the vast majority of cases. The drug companies talk about particular neurochemicals but there are actually dozens and they can have different effects on different parts of the brain.

The majority of depressed people are depressed for social or behavioural reasons, (poor relationships, abuse, loneliness, grief, unemployment, severe sleep disorders, etc.). Loneliness, unemployment, grief and being victimised are all common causes. I've dealt with many hundreds of depressed people over the past forty years and have only seen a handful where it was not clear why they were depressed. It is possible the hormonal changes in adolescence may contribute in some cases but **far** more common are the feelings of purposelessness, difference, or failure that often accompany adolescence *in our culture*. Depression in adolescence appears to be becoming more common and appears to be more common in adolescents in Western culture, although the hormonal changes are the same the world over. Young people who have been exposed to family problems (such as violence or conflictual separations), who have personal problems (learning difficulties, communication or social difficulties, obesity, even acne) or who are negative and nihilistic (which can be associated with some teen sub-cultures and the media culture generally), are all more likely to become depressed. I've found that problems with boyfriends or girlfriends are often the trigger that starts a depression or even makes a young person suicidal (even though the relationship seemed trivial to the adults in their lives).

Motivation and lifestyle can play a part in depression just as they can in almost any illness. It's weird that people acknowledge the importance of mental factors, such as being positive or motivated, in purely physical illnesses, including cancer, but down play them in mental illness. Professionals sometimes get irritated if I try to talk about the fact that motivation, habits and lifestyle are important in depression as they have a knee-jerk reaction to anything that sounds as if it is blaming the depressed person. But just as positive, motivated, active people are more likely to do well with a physical condition, they are also more likely to shake off depression. That certainly doesn't mean they can't get depressed, they can. I would expect that those who are low on Conscientiousness would be more likely to become depressed, and the research backs this up[479]. We have seen that low Conscientiousness is associated with abuse of parents. Depressives tend to be higher on Neuroticism too.

Depression is almost always clearly a vicious circle. When someone is feeling low they stop doing so much, so life becomes more boring, they feel worse about themselves and may become isolated and lonely. Lack of physical exercise seems to encourage depression and also is part of a vicious circle. The sedentary lives many of our young people live nowadays may be contributing to an increase in depression, as can lack of sleep and being nocturnal.

We really don't know for sure if there has been an increase. Official statistics are no guide to this as diagnoses are not objective and fashions change. It's very common for people to have both anxiety and depression. Twenty to thirty years ago doctors were likely to prescribe a tranquiliser and record the individual as suffering from an anxiety condition. Now they prescribe an anti-depressant (which can also help with anxiety) and record the person as 'depressed'. Teenagers were seldom diagnosed with depression in the past.

Sadly, in our society, being adolescent seems to be a contributing factor for many young people becoming depressed. Perhaps as many as one third of young people will get depressed at some point during their adolescent or teen years (precise figures are pretty meaningless without a precise definition of depression). It appears to me to be increasing somewhat but it's difficult to tell. Young people are more willing to talk about it, which is good. But often they talk endlessly to friends on social media about how bad they feel, which is usually not good. Some young people both normalise and glamourise depression and self-harm (and websites are available that help with this). Acknowledging that adolescent depression is common is helpful as long as it is emphasised that it doesn't last.

When I talk to young people about their moods, the fact that they feel useless and aimless often comes up. Adolescence has lengthened in our society and our young people are given less responsibility (or take less) and may feel that their future careers are uncertain and far off. Schools have become more academic and more focused on those who will go on to further education. It actually surprises me how many young people are willing to work hard towards a vague goal that may be as far as ten years off. Many adults won't do that, so it's not surprising that some of our young people can't see the point of these long years of dependency and (to them) boring graft at school. High youth unemployment can also affect younger children as they see leaving school as scary rather than hopeful.

Depression and Violence to Parents

There is definitely a strong *association* between violence to parents and depression. Abused *parents* are often depressed. The majority of young people who abuse parents are **not** depressed, though many are intermittently unhappy and some may appear depressed to their parents because they are so sullen and withdrawn around them, but not around their friends. A few are depressed to a greater or lesser extent though not often diagnosed. In my sample, only one in forty of the young people who are abusing their parents has *a diagnosis* of depression. If depression is ever a *cause* of parent abuse, and this is doubtful, it's certainly not a common cause.[480]

Some young people clearly make themselves depressed, or at least unhappy, by their behaviour. Children or young people who are at war with their families are emotionally troubled and may be miserable. But often they have caused this unhappiness or depression by alienating the people who love them and causing themselves a great deal of stress. I have seen many unhappy young people become dramatically happier when they stop abusing their parents or once the parents manage to regain control (even though some still complain bitterly about it).

I have heard of parents being told by psychiatrists that in adolescence depression can 'come out' as anger. There is some truth in this but not a lot. If you have read the chapter on anger you will know that I don't believe that emotions can directly transform one into another. However, depressed adolescents are more likely than depressed adults to have *agitated depression* and some are full of nervous energy, jumpy and irritable, rather than withdrawn and passive. This can make violence more likely in a few individuals.

We have already discussed (and dismissed, in the section on Anger) a related, less harmful but also confusing, idea that depression is anger turned inwards.

Parents find all this rather mystifying and often want to believe that their child can't help their behaviour. They obviously sympathise strongly with their child's depression and hence find it more difficult to be assertive when the child behaves abusively. They are also greatly disempowered by fears that being firm, for example removing privileges, will push their child into deeper depression or even suicide. Some parents thus become more indulgent and passive because they are afraid that any pressure on the child will make him or her more depressed.

There are a number of ways that depression can affect violence or abuse.

Overall, the depressed are somewhat *less* likely to be violent than the non-depressed for the simple reason that they have less energy and motivation (similarly I have heard a number of parents say that their children are much better behaved when they are physically ill).

There are a number of ways however that depression may be *associated with* increased violence:

434

- Depressed people can be very irritable. Irritability is *never* enough on its own to cause violence but it can contribute if someone is at all prone to violence or abusive behaviour. Since adolescents are more prone to have *agitated depression* than depressed adults, it is more likely to be linked to aggressiveness than in adults.
- Depression and negative thinking go together and negativity can result in aggression in some situations.
- Those individuals who are negative, egocentric and untrusting of others are more likely to be both depressed and aggressive towards others.
- Depressed people may stop caring about the consequences of their actions (we've talked about your influence being reduced the less the child cares about and this may also affect the timeframe of effective consequences). You can't ground a child who isn't going out, for example.
- People who are acting violently or abusively are often isolated, stressed (by their own behaviour) and may feel guilty and ashamed. They are thus more likely to become depressed.
- Depression can be both cause and effect in drug or alcohol abuse and this can greatly affect violence and abusive behaviour in some young people (see section on substance abuse).
- Children who have been exposed to domestic violence or family disruptions are at increased risk of violence to parents and may also be at increased risk of depression for a number of reasons.
- Depression may be associated with other mental health problems or social problems that can also affect violence. I see a number of children with Asperger's who are violent to parents and such conditions can be associated with depression particularly if they are feeling worthless or rejected by peers and society.
- Depression and anxiety frequently go together and anxiety can *occasionally* increase controlling and abusive behaviour.
- A small, but significant, number of adolescents appear to react to anti-depressant medications with agitation, mania or aggression which can result in violence (as well as suicide)[481].
- Parents who are aware that their child is depressed often give in to them more and are afraid to enforce boundaries or set meaningful consequences. Occasionally it's quite reasonable to not push a depressed, especially a potentially suicidal, young person too far and to turn a blind eye to *some* bad behaviour. Temporarily not pushing them to do homework or keep their room tidy makes sense during an episode of depression. However, putting up with abuse is actually more likely to make the young person worse in the long run (or even in the short term) and other people, including you, have rights regardless of conditions such as depression. As discussed elsewhere it often comes down to balancing short term and long term risks.

I'm certainly not arguing that sadness and depression are incompatible with anger. On the contrary I see many people who are both sad and angry at the same time, and often about the same thing (especially about their parents' separation). Overall, severe or moderate depression makes people less likely to act aggressively but for the above reasons, mild depression and aggression can occasionally be linked.

As a parent you may have to make some very difficult decisions. At the extreme a parent might have to make a violent eighteen-year-old leave home to protect other family members, though this can be terrifying if there is even a small possibility that he could be potentially suicidal? Frequently parents are faced with difficult decisions that are less severe. If your child is depressed, any consequences that result in them having less contact with friends or might make them lose interest in activities should be considered very carefully. I generally discourage parents from using sports, scouts, dance classes, etc. as consequences unless all else has failed, but this is even more important if a child is depressed.

Avoiding conflict about trivia is even more important with a depressed or potentially suicidal young person, but avoiding conflict about the really unacceptable behaviours, such as abuse or substance misuse, may make things worse in the longer term. I've seen many youngsters who have dropped out of school due to depression. If they are allowed to do so, without an alternative, this it often makes the depression deepen.

Helpful and unhelpful attitudes to depression

The following may give you some ideas about how to talk to a young person about depression. Denying their feelings does not help. Adults often wish to play down the depth of despair that young people may feel and tell them "you should be thankful" or "it could be a lot worse". Worst of all is telling them that these are the best years of their life! Think about it. You are saying it's only going to get worse!

UNHELPFUL ATTITUDES THAT FEED DEPRESION ☹	HELPFUL ATTITUDES THAT FIGHT DEPRESSION ☺
Depression is a brain mal-function (such as a chemical imbalance). So it's out of my hands.	My brain and past experiences may be making me vulnerable, but my thoughts and behaviour are keeping me depressed.
It's up to the specialists to cure me.	It's up to me in the end, with or without help, guidance, or medication.
I **can't** just snap out of it!	Of course I can't snap out of it – but I can move in the right direction.
I must find out the cause of my depression.	The past is past and I'll probably never know the combination of causes. The future is what counts.
I'll get better then start living.	Living is how I get better. If I wait until I feel good I'll remain in a boring rut and never do anything.
The mountain is too high to climb. I can't even see the top.	Unless I start moving I'll remain stuck where I am now. Even tiny steps still move me towards my goals.
The future looks bleak and hopeless.	The future looks bleak **because** I'm depressed. No-one knows what is around the corner – good or bad.
I have to hide from the world because I'm depressed.	Depression wants me to curl up and die. I have to fight it.
I can't let anyone know. They'll think I'm crazy.	I'm not ashamed. Depression is common. Most people are sympathetic (but some are just ignorant).
I'll avoid my friends so not to depress them.	I'd want my friends to keep in touch if they were depressed. Being bored and lonely is no way to get better.
The depression makes it impossible to do things.	Depression makes it very difficult to do things so I need to be realistic but try very hard to take small steps.
I don't do things because I don't usually enjoy them anymore.	I'm not happy doing nothing so I should do the things I used to enjoy and I'll learn to enjoy them again.
I'll do the things I need to when I feel up to it.	I'll do what I need to whether I feel like it or not (because I'll never feel like it while I remain depressed).
This is unbearable!	I've borne it so far. This is highly unpleasant but it **will** pass.
I'd be better off dead!	I can get over this and enjoy life in the future. There's plenty of time to be dead but less time to live.

These symptoms show that I'm a failure.	These symptoms could happen to anyone. I'm viewing everything negatively, including myself.
I am weak.	Strength is overcoming obstacles. Right now everything is difficult and even small steps require a lot of real strength.
I must avoid all stress!	I won't take on too much, but some stress in life is healthy and inevitable. I'll cope.
I mustn't get depressed!	Some depression is probably inevitable, I can deal with it.
I must watch constantly for signs that I'm getting depressed or stressed.	The world is an interesting – sometimes scary place. I'll get on with life and think less about myself.
I'll never do all the things I should.	No one ever does! But never mind 'shoulds', what do I really **need** to do and what do I **want** to do?
If I don't try I won't fail.	If I don't try I can never succeed, so I definitely fail. Failure is part of life.
I'm hopeless. Everything is hopeless.	Depression clouds my vision and judgment. I know it's making me negative so I have to try very hard to see through to the positives.
I'll never get better.	This is a bad patch; life is full of ups and downs. Depression passes unless I cling to it.
☹ ☹ ☹ ☹ ☹ ☹ ☹	☺ ☺ ☺ ☺ ☺ ☺ ☺

ADHD

"Too many children of abused women are labelled "ADD' or 'ADHD' and given medication instead of receiving the assistance they need. Children need us to take an interest in their predicament, help them to learn positive values and support their crucial connection to their mothers." Bancroft[482]

Colin, age 16, told me about an angry confrontation between him and a female teacher at his new school. He said he'd 'lost it' and had sworn and shouted at her. I asked if he'd been suspended. "No, I played the ADHD card," he said with a wry smile, both amused and slightly embarrassed. "You mean you used it as an excuse?" I asked. "Yeah, and they fell for it! It's a get-out-of-jail-free card!"

Next time I saw Colin, I asked how ADHD had affected him in the past.

"I used to use it as an excuse a lot. In primary school when I hit another kid they'd get suspended for provoking me. I thought of myself as untouchable."

"Do you think that made your anger better or worse?"

"Definitely worse, and I got worse still at High School. Up until a school counsellor told me that ADHD didn't make me hit people. I realised I was using it as an excuse to take my anger out on people. But by then it was a habit."

Colin is unusually honest and up-front about using a 'disability' as an excuse. He illustrates that the unhelpful justification can act on two levels. He himself believed for years that his ADHD caused his violence; then he stopped believing this but still used it as an excuse. There is an effect on the child himself, on his family and on his teachers and other adults. These effects interact with each other in complex ways.

In my sample of over four hundred children who have been abusive to parents, 20% have been labelled ADHD. In the sample as a whole, half have been exposed to past domestic violence (48%). Guess what percentage of the children labelled with ADHD had been exposed to past domestic violence? Yes, the same proportion, 48%, of those with ADHD and those without ADHD had been exposed to past domestic violence!

Being hyperactive definitely does increase the risk of behaviour problems, including violence towards parents. I don't think that attention deficits have much to do with it on their own. Boys are more likely to abuse parents (and indulge in most bad behaviours) than are girls. Boys with ADHD are more boyish boys than other boys and the risk is further increased. This may sound simplistic but I really don't see any reason to believe that it's much more complicated than this. It's similar to the fact that extrovert children are more likely to have all sorts of behavioural problems (but not emotional problems) than are introvert children. We don't see extraversion as some kind of illness and make excuses for these children, nor should we with kids with ADHD. That is their personality and they have to learn to adjust to society as best they can. They may not adjust very well to formal school but they should certainly be expected to adjust to not hitting or otherwise abusing other people.

So shouldn't children who are hyper show higher rates of violence towards parents whether or not they have been exposed to DV? Perhaps they do but since our assessment techniques are so primitive and our definitions are so vague, whether a child is labelled as having ADHD or not has as much to do with chance and their family situation as it does the child's temperament. Children who have experienced past domestic violence appear to be far more likely to be assessed and labelled as ADHD than those without such experiences. This is unlikely to be a genetic effect. It has become popular to see ADHD as being largely, or entirely, genetic. This is simplistic. At present there is no objective measure of ADHD so the decision to label or not label is based mainly on the reports of teachers and parents. These are inevitably affected by prejudices and random factors. A disturbing study from America shows just how arbitrary it can be.

A large study found that children born in December were significantly more likely to be labelled as ADHD, and given medication, than those born in January. The reason is quite simple. The cut-off for grade assignment was January 1st so the younger children in a class were far more likely to be seen as immature and as having poor attention and behaviour[483]. Children with disturbed home environments or who are stressed, e.g. by parents separation or exposure to DV (usually both), are all more likely to be seen as immature and difficult and are hence more likely to be assessed and labelled.

Given how arbitrary the labelling process is, it scares me that professionals frequently tell parents and young people that conditions such as ADHD, mild intellectual disability or Asperger's are *permanent* disabilities! This is not necessarily the case and such unwarranted predictions are very dangerous. They can easily create self-fulfilling prophecies if believed. One common assumption is that they are going to need medication for ADHD at least till adulthood, if not forever. This is a very dangerous assumption. I have seen a great many youngsters learn how to control themselves better and no longer need meds in High School. Since we know that adolescent brains change dramatically, even if ADHD were a brain disorder (arguable), how can we assume that it will persist despite the huge changes in brains in adolescence?

Effects of the Medication

Any parent with an aggressive child who is on meds for ADHD needs to consider if the pills are helping or harming. Often the answer to this is simple but medications affect everyone differently and may have quite unforeseen effects when combined with other drugs (legal or illegal). I've spoken to quite a few parents who have told me that ADHD meds made their children more aggressive. Usually they took them off quite quickly, but disturbingly, they often did this against the advice of medical professionals, who often wanted them to persist, add another drug, or up the dose.

The only child who has ever physically harmed me during counselling (nothing serious) was showing dramatic and violent tantrums which stopped abruptly when the ADHD medication was stopped. Of course the mother was blamed by a number of professionals and even suspected of abuse without any evidence, just on the basis that her child was acting strangely.

More common, and well established, is the fact that some children get withdrawal effects late in the day when the meds are leaving their system (ADHD meds don't hang around in the body, which is a positive) and some children are better behaved at school only to act out even more at home for their beleaguered parents.

I'm not opposed to medication but there is no doubt that they are over-prescribed and should never be the first response. Counselling for child and family should be tried before putting any child on potentially dangerous drugs. Long term effects of these meds have not been properly studied (the drug companies have no desire to do this research) and one side-effect is to delay puberty. This has only recently been firmly established although I've noticed for years that children on heavy meds are often tiny when fourteen or fifteen, adding to their problems. I've heard this effect dismissed because they catch up with their peers eventually. But it's well established that late puberty makes boys the bottom of the pecking order for a few years. This can have a lasting, effect.

Anxiety Disorders

When we discussed personality and violence to parents we said that both high and low anxiety can be associated with violence to parents. There are actually more young people who are violent to parents who are fearless than there are highly nervous ones. But there are a significant minority of young people who are violent to parents and who do have anxiety conditions. Those with high anxiety are more likely to only be violent to their nearest and dearest and may be victims rather than bullies in other settings.

For children who have an anxiety condition (diagnosed or undiagnosed), there can occasionally be a fairly direct link with abuse of parents. The clearest is in children with Obsessive Compulsive Disorders, OCD. Obsessions and compulsions can give young people a strong desire to control things around them. This can take the form of arranging the environment, e.g. when someone obsessively cleans to remove imagined germs or when someone throws out what he or she imagines are dangerous chemicals or covers everything having sharp corners from fear of accidents. A school phobia makes a child resist going to school and agoraphobia may make them resist leaving the house. This desire to control can include controlling other people if they can get away with it. A simple example might be the obsessive housewife who won't let her husband come inside unless he changes out of his work clothes in the shed or who won't let a newspaper into the house for fear of ink marks. In the past children couldn't exert such control even if they wanted to, but this has changed with more indulgent parenting. One youngster I knew with a variety of food obsessions bullied his mother if she tried to bring the 'wrong' kind of food into the home. He used intimidation, verbal abuse and pushed and shoved her to impose his obsessive wishes on her. However, the same young man would let his friends eat the taboo foods in his car. He later made a lot of progress and agreed that though the OCD had made him *want* to control others, the choice of how to do this was entirely his. I had told his mother in one of my *Who's in Charge?* groups that the OCD made him want to control others but didn't make him abusive. It was good to have it confirmed from the horse's mouth.

There are a tiny number of people with very severe mental illnesses who are out of touch with reality and have no real control over their behaviours. This is *extremely* rare and most mentally ill people choose how to act even though their emotions and perceptions may be distorted somewhat.

OCD cannot *make* someone violent or abusive but can greatly increase their desire to control others. We can have sympathy for their genuine emotional pain but they don't have the right to control or abuse anyone and their condition is never an excuse for abuse.

Although it appears to me that there is a clear link between OCD and abuse of parents in some cases, under 2% of the children in my sample have been diagnosed with this condition, which may not be much higher than we might expect in the general population[484]. So this is not a very common cause of violence to parents.

Other anxiety symptoms or conditions can also make controlling others more appealing. The most common, and somewhat confusing, situation is when a young person's anxiety is reduced by the presence of the parent (this may be termed an "attachment disorder" but this is just a description of the behaviour rather than an explanation). This is, in some ways, just a development from the clingy toddler who won't let his mother leave him. This can be cute with a three-year-old and we may have a lot of sympathy for a nervous, fearful child. However, when the child is thirteen or older, is bigger and stronger than his unfortunate mother and is willing to use force and abuse to keep her close to him, the situation is not at all cute but harrowing in the extreme. The young person may be a clingy child but also closely resembles dependent, possessive, stifling husbands who abuse the wives they claim to love.

Our sympathy for these children and young people should not blind us to their use of abuse and the terrible effect on their parents (almost always mothers). These situations often deteriorate because parents are genuinely sympathetic and concerned for their child (who is suffering too) and thus they don't take their own rights and the stress on themselves, seriously enough. An anxious child can make a caring parent be more child-focused, more protective and more indulgent. This can cause the child to have high entitlement and become ever more demanding. Other people, including professionals, blame these parents for causing dependency, often seeing this as meeting the parents' needs. Even when there is a grain of truth in this it's only a part of the picture. Such a parent-blaming approach may muddy the waters, excuse the child, and make the parent defensive. This can result in the parent being uncooperative with professionals and less assertive with the child. Thus well-meaning professionals can make things worse by seeing the child primarily as a victim.

Ironically, when these children have effectively disempowered their parents this can sometimes contribute to their anxieties and fears getting worse. The main way to conquer fears is to face them (preferably gently and a little at a time). If a child who is becoming anxious about going to school is allowed to drop out they may then develop a full-blown school phobia and agoraphobia, while if they were kindly but firmly made to return to school they usually get over it. If parents have no control over a child, it may take very little anxiety for them to opt out of school. The parent also can't control what they do during the day so they have an easy, pleasant time watching T.V. and playing electronic games.

I have seen school phobias lead directly on to agoraphobia when young people avoid all anxiety by not going outside at all. A moderately controlling parent would make these children face their fears more than a parent who is too sympathetic or who has no control over the child (perhaps because the child is violent or uses major threats). I am not advocating here that parents can cure their children's fears by being authoritarian bullies. Too much pressure or control can lead to worse problems but too little also leads to increased anxiety.

I believe we are going to see an increase in school phobia and agoraphobia over the next decade or two. Children are being overprotected and are spending less and less time alone pre-teen, electronics make staying at home more appealing, and parents have less power to make their children face their fears. In Japan there is a name for the modern phenomena of young people becoming hermits. They are called *hikikomori* and there are estimates that as many as forty thousand young Japanese are full-time hermits (often spending all their time on computers). Interestingly they are generally middle-class kids[485]. I'm beginning to see the start of this in Australia where young people find it easier to avoid the world and get their entertainment, and limited friendship, electronically. A young man told me recently, "I don't need friends, I have the internet."

Helpful and Unhelpful Attitudes to Anxiety

UNHELPFUL ATTITUDES ☹	HELPFUL ATTITUDES ☺
I must avoid panic attacks at all costs.	I've survived panic attacks. It's not the end of the world if I have another.
I must avoid all stress!	Some stress in life is healthy.
I mustn't get anxious!	Some anxiety is inevitable, I can deal with it
I can't let anyone know. They'll think I'm crazy.	I'm not ashamed. Anxiety is common.
These symptoms show that I'm weak.	These symptoms could happen to anyone.
I am a coward.	Bravery is facing fear, not being a robot who can't feel.
This is awful!	This is a normal bodily reaction, unpleasant but not dangerous.
I must watch constantly for signs that I'm getting anxious.	The world is an interesting (sometimes scary) place. I'll pay attention to the world and other people.
I must pass this test.	This is practice. If I never fail then I'm not really living.
I'll never do all the things I should.	Never mind 'shoulds', what do I really need to do and what do I want to do.
I'll never be able to do it well enough.	If a thing's worth doing, it's worth doing badly.
I'll never get better.	This is just a bad patch - life is full of ups and downs.

High Functioning Autism

"Violent behaviour is one of the most difficult issues that some of us [parents of children with AS] must deal with… All my questions were responded to with references to my lack of parenting skills. I found this frustrating and sometimes even amusing since I also had another child who was happy, easy-going, and successful." Quint[486]

If you need general information about these conditions then look elsewhere (Tony Attwood's books are recommended). This is aimed at those whose children already have a diagnosis but much of it is relevant if your child has autistic traits, and some of it is relevant to those with other developmental conditions.

Not long ago many of us regarded young people with high-functioning autism (or Asperger's[*]) as generally mild mannered and much more likely to be passive than aggressive. I'd come across a few who had tantrums but occasional outbursts were not enough to alter my impression that violence was rare. More recently I have developed an interest in violence to parents and find children with autism over-represented among the swelling ranks of youngsters who bully, victimise or assault their parents (I've dealt with thirty-five youngsters, or 9% of my sample). This is not necessarily representative of all children who abuse parents (since both autism and violence to parents are special interests of mine) but it's eight times higher than the local incidence of autism in children locally.

Although I'm writing about violence to parents, most of what follows is relevant to other violence by those with autism, such as violence to brothers and sisters and partner violence in adults (I don't know of any studies of this).

It's important to remember that the majority of children who are violent to parents have **no** diagnosed condition (62% in my sample of four hundred plus). And the majority of children on the autism spectrum are **not** violent to family members. Some are gentle and passive.

Our current definitions are vague and changeable and our assessment methods not very scientific. Although there is controversy about whether there has been a real increase in autism or not (I'm not convinced, but it's possible), there is *no doubt* that we have widened definitions so that many children are being diagnosed who would not have been labelled in the recent past. As 'autism' is used in a much wider way in recent years, autistic traits in diagnosed children are clearly less

---

[*] The DSM 'Bible' of psychiatry recently abandoned the diagnoses of 'Asperger's Syndrome'. This is a shame, and shows how little concern they have for stigma, as 'autism' is a far more stigmatised term than 'Asperger' or 'Aspie'.

severe. Some behavioural problems in children with autism and intellectual disabilities are *more* common in those with *less severe* disabilities (one reason being that they are more aware of being treated differently). However, it could be that children with behavioural problems and very mild autistic traits are now being labelled 'autistic'. Either of these trends could affect the level of behavioural problems in general, and violence in particular, that we see in these children. Understanding changes in children with autism is very tricky as we keep moving the goalposts. My guess is that the factors leading to increased numbers of disabled children being violent to parents are the same as those causing an increase in this behaviour among non-disabled (partly societal changes and partly more indulgent, child-focused, intensive parenting).

Although it's clear that violence by people with autism is **far** from being rare, it's rarely discussed. Even when people write about autism and bullying, they hardly ever mention that autistic children can be bullies as well as victims. Certainly they are more often victims in school (this is very common) but some are bullies when they can get away with it[487]. This silence about violence by children with autism can leave parents feeling isolated and assuming that they must be at fault, especially since blaming parents is almost a knee-jerk reaction in our society. Not so long ago mothers were actually blamed for causing autism (the ridiculous 'refrigerator mother' theory). Although this has almost died out, they are still often blamed for any behavioural problems even when children have a genetic condition.

When aggression is mentioned, it's almost always assumed that it's *expressive* (a purely emotional outburst) rather than *instrumental* (a deliberate strategy) – more on this later. However, both autistic children and adults can be bullies at times and can become very controlling of those around them. There is nothing that says a disabled person cannot be abusive. Being disabled does not make you a saint!

"This topic [the autistic controlling other people] has also been made difficult to discuss because there is a very little mention of it in the contemporary literature and, indeed, there is almost a denial that people with autism could behave in this way. This neglect or denial is particularly obvious in the literature on Asperger's syndrome/ high functioning autism." Clements[488]

Tony Attwood mentioned that there had then been two thousand studies on Asperger's published, yet he says that, "We do not know how common anger management problems are with children and adults with Asperger's syndrome"[489].

Autism & violence
There is nothing about having autism, that *directly* causes aggression and it's certainly not *inevitable* by any means that these children will be violent. There are however, several factors that can make individuals more prone to violence at certain times or in certain circumstances:

1. Emotional immaturity.
Emotional immaturity can lead to extreme mood swings and emotional overreactions in some situations. For children in general, violence decreases from

age four and continues to decrease throughout the lifecycle. The fact that adolescent violence becomes scarier, more noticeable, and more visible in the community obscures the fact that the number of acts of violence actually decreases throughout this period. It's thus understandable that immaturity may be associated with increased violence. Intellectual maturity combined with emotional immaturity can create specific problems, as it does in adolescents generally. Some teenagers with autism have tantrums that resemble those of a young child, though unfortunately with a far bigger, stronger and more intimidating body.

2. Frustration.

Not being able to understand social rules or other people's behaviour can make the world a very frustrating place. It's not easy being autistic in a *neurotypical** world. Feeling as if you don't fit in or being the target of teasing, ostracism or prejudice (all **very** common experiences for people with autism) can cause understandable anger. Frustration and anger are often aimed at the safest targets (usually the mother and siblings) rather than at the source of the frustration. This is particularly true of highly nervous young people, which includes most autistic children. Obsessive traits can add to frustration when things don't go according to plan.

Most autistic people are overly sensitive to some stimuli and this can greatly raise stress levels and make the world confusing and frustrating.

3. Stubbornness, rigidity and obsessions.

Rigidity can make us want to control things, including people around us, which can sometimes lead to aggressive attempts to control others. Extremes of rigidity are sometimes shown in those with Obsessive Compulsive Disorder, severe anxiety, or autism. This never *directly* causes violence or abusive behaviour. These individuals are often very selective about who they attempt to control and who they abuse. Such ways of controlling others can be an attempt to create order from chaos. Stubbornness can also make aggressive outbursts and tantrums last far longer and escalate further regardless of their cause. A parent getting in the way of a young person's obsessions is a common spark for defiance and violence. This is especially true of children, with or without autism, addicted to computer games or the internet.

4. Lack of more appropriate social responses.

Communication problems and a lack of social skills can lead to individuals with autism using less appropriate ways of communicating or solving social problems, which at times may include brute force or sheer aggression. Being assertive is complicated and difficult for those with poor interpersonal skills, and a common pattern is to go from being passive to aggressive as frustration builds. Poor social skills can also increase conflict with others and thus increases the probability of aggression (or withdrawal). However, as with most of these factors,

---

* 'Neurotypical' is anyone without autism.

poor skills in assertive communication do not cause aggression *in itself* but can make it more likely.

5. Reduced empathy.

It's common to read or hear that people with autism 'lack empathy' or don't have any insight into other people's thoughts or feelings. This is regularly overstated and it can sound as if they have **no** empathy for others, which is not true. Though they do generally have restricted or underdeveloped empathy they are not psychopaths! Nor does a lack of empathy automatically mean that someone will be violent or criminal. This is true of actual psychopaths, who are capable of being cruel and violent but don't necessarily choose to be so. Many people lack empathy towards animals, for example, but this does not automatically mean that they are cruel or violent towards them. Some autistic people are less aware of the effect they have on others when they do act violently and they are often insensitive if they say hurtful things to others. Egocentrism is a common trait in adolescents generally and autistic adolescents, slower to mature emotionally, may exaggerate this trait and be unusually self-centred or self-obsessed during their teenage years. Egocentrism can lead to high feelings of entitlement and make the individual very demanding, both of which are common factors in violence to parents.

6. Exaggerating elements of youth culture

Some autistic young people are blissfully unconcerned by social pressures, some are unusually immune to peer pressure, and some take pride in being different. However, this is not always the case and some may exaggerate aspects of their peer culture. Thus for some autistic youth, if they become Goths for example, they are more obsessively Goth than others. I have come across several young people with Asperger's who have American accents derived just from watching TV and movies. There has been a move in children's culture, fed by commercial mass media and the internet, towards glorification of the brat and portrayal of adults as idiots or killjoys. In her book Toxic Childhood, Sue Palmer argues that the media *"panders to children's enthusiasm for backchat, sneakiness and challenging authority, it sends a message of endorsement – even encouragement – for breaking parental rules."* This culture of cool couldn't-care-less defiance affects many children but is sometimes exaggerated by vulnerable children. The effect of this cultural shift may mercifully miss some of our autistic youth (who thumb their noses at 'cool') but can be exaggerated by others. There are several reasons why they may exaggerate disrespect for authority: 1) they obsessively overdo everything; 2) they don't pick up social cues and don't know when to stop; 3) they may be trying extra hard to be accepted by other children.

Children with disabilities live in the same culture as the rest of us and are subject to the same cultural forces. Thus as many more young people are acting abusively towards parents than did in past generations, it's not surprising that this is affecting young people on the autism spectrum too.

There are also some factors that are common to other disabilities as well as autism. But first we'll consider the factors that can act to make children with autism *less* violent.

Some factors common to most childhood disabilities

1.   Children with any kind of disability, real or imagined, may feel stressed by it, may lose self-esteem because of it, and may feel angry about being different. All of these can increase the chances of difficult behaviour, including violence within the family.

"Some will direct their anger and hate at others (for example at their parents for 'making me this way'). Some will direct it at themselves ('I'm no good' 'My brain needs to be fixed'" Clements (p 138)

2.   Indulgent, child-focused parenting is very common among parents abused by their children and is a key risk factor. Parents of children with any kind of disability often have to be more child-focused. Sympathy for the disabled child can lead to more indulgent parenting and they may be less firm and lower their expectations of behaviour. This over-compensating is understandable but can have serious consequences. Parents may try *too* hard to make the child happy, become over-protective, and excuse bad behaviour. Parenting any child who differs greatly from the norm requires a lot of flexibility and adaptation. Some stubborn, difficult children require firmer parenting and greater consistency than do most children. Thus parenting may have been perfectly normal, even better than average, but not be quite 'good enough' for a really difficult child. Thus we should not be too ready to blame parents if they don't appear to have got it just right.

3.   Children themselves may see their condition as an explanation and/or an excuse for their bad behaviour. Some deliberately use their condition as an excuse while others have lowered their own expectations. Spending time with other children with disabilities can mean that they copy bad behaviour.

Factors that can <u>reduce</u> aggression and violence in people with autism

The above traits can all make *some* young people with autism more likely to be violent under certain circumstances. Taking the above factors into account, and especially given the way autistic children are treated by their peers, we might expect most of them to be aggressive in adolescence. However, there are also common Aspie traits that may make violence **less** likely.

1. A tendency to follow rules and routines

Most autistic individuals appear to be basically law-abiding and some are very keen to follow rules. This can help them keep out of trouble and help them learn to control aggressive impulses. It may be very important that rules are spelled out in a straightforward manner. They can also sometimes respond well to ritualistic ways of controlling anger.

2. Anxiety and timidity

Fearfulness and anxiousness generally make individuals *less* likely to confront others or to be aggressive or violent. The most violent children and adults are those who are fearless not fearful. The inhibition of aggression by anxiety is however lower for aggression within the home and so parents, especially mothers, and younger siblings are more likely to be victims of those who are aggressive but also anxious.

3. Logical, rational thinking
Violence and aggression are seldom logical and in the long run are usually counterproductive. Many autistic people learn this lesson as they mature and some can use their logic and common sense to avert or defuse aggressive impulses.

4. Social insensitivity and introversion
Ironically, a lack of social sensitivity can sometimes be an advantage. *Some* youngsters with autism appear to be able to ignore teasing and social ostracism better than neurotypicals. However, we should certainly beware of assuming that this does not hurt them as they may not be showing their true feelings. In addition, autistic individuals are often very introverted and hence have a lower need for social interaction and approval; introverts overall have fewer 'externalising' (acting out) behaviour problems than do extroverts.

Bad behaviour may just be bad behaviour
Once someone has a mental health or disability label, there is a tendency to explain any negative behaviour or personality quirk in terms of this label. Thus if an individual diagnosed with autism (or an intellectual disability or serious mental illness) is violent or otherwise anti-social, we assume that this must be *caused* by their condition. However, there are far more violent people who have no disability or mental health condition than violent people who have one, and some forms of violence are common in children and adolescents generally. They may be aggressive or violent for reasons that have nothing to do with their condition or are only very indirectly related. For example, if a child has been exposed to domestic violence, or abused themselves, this is quite likely to lead to some aggressive behaviour regardless of whether or not they have a condition such as autism. In my sample of four hundred and sixty children who have been abusive towards parents, almost 20% have ADHD and this is often seen as an explanation for this behaviour. However, the biggest single factor in violence towards parents is having been exposed to domestic violence (almost always towards their mother by their father or step-father). The ADHD kids are just as likely to have been exposed to past DV as are the other children, suggesting that exposure to DV is causing the ADHD in some cases. Those with autism are less likely to have been exposed to DV, but some have been and it's a significant factor for them (of thirty-five children with autism who were violent to parents, ten had been exposed to past DV).

Whether any individual is aggressive or violent will *always* depend on a number of factors. It's always a simplification to say that their violence is *caused* by their condition, though sometimes it may be a major contributor.

Especially if they are violent in some circumstances but not in others (e.g. in the home but not in school), or are only violent towards certain individuals (e.g. only their mother or only towards younger children), then it's clearly wrong to say that their condition directly causes the violence. Having a condition such as

450

Asperger's, ADHD or a mild intellectual disability does not turn someone into a mindless robot and self-control is *always* possible – even if it may be far more difficult in some circumstances. It's important that we have sympathy and set realistic expectations but it's *just as important* that we do not excuse or minimise abusive behaviour.

Don't excuse abuse.

Two personality types of young person who are violent to parents

I have found that many children who abuse parents fall into one of two very different personality patterns[*]. Slightly more common, you will be surprised to hear, are extraverted, fearless, confident children. However, the second type, a large minority, are nervous, introverts, often with low self-esteem. Autistic children are often at the extremes of this second personality type, but other neurotic introverts can show similar behaviour without being on the spectrum. Compared to the fearless extraverts they are far less likely to be delinquent or violent outside the home, less likely to leave home or stay out, less likely to take drugs or drink, and are more likely to be victims than bullies in school. However, as they may be socially withdrawn and remain in the family home, their violence towards other family members can continue into adulthood if not treated firmly and taken seriously.

Anger and violence are not the same thing.

It's OK to be angry but never OK to be violent. This is a very important distinction. Adults sometimes tell a child off for feeling angry, especially if the reason for the anger appears irrational to us or if the anger results from attitudes we don't like. Anger **is** a problem when it often results from attitudes of entitlement, arrogance, or defiance of authority, but it's often futile to focus on the anger rather than the behaviour.

We may make too many allowances for bad behaviour because we sympathise with the child's anger. A child who has had a raw deal from life, because of a disability or hurtful experiences such as abuse or rejection, evokes our sympathy and it's certainly helpful to understand why they feel so angry. However, this does **not** make it okay for them to hurt others in any way. Vague ideas that they need to 'get their anger out' can lead to unclear boundaries and a lack of consequences for bad behaviour. *Getting their anger out* by being violent does not make the anger go away but leads to more anger and more acting out. *Expressing anger* in non-destructive ways is useful and burning off adrenaline can help, but acting out aggressively becomes a habit and makes anger more of an automatic response.

Not all violence is motivated by anger. Much violence is associated with pride, a desire to control others, or a sense of justice or fairness (which may be irrational or out of all proportion to the situation). Some individuals have high anger but are

---

[*] I've been giving them personality tests recently, but this is still speculative.

never violent while others can be quite violent with little or no anger (these latter can be the most dangerous).

Expressive violence and instrumental violence

Young children are quite often violent in a way that is (inappropriately) expressing their feelings rather than being a deliberate attempt to control or hurt others. This is called *expressive* violence. This is more common for younger children and the disabled, and women tend to show this form of violence more than men. Sometimes disabled individuals are lashing out blindly from intense emotional upset.

"Behaviour that looks antisocial to an outsider might actually be an expression of fear." Temple Grandin 2013 (p 87)

When one person abuses another they are usually using their aggressive behaviour (more or less deliberately) in order to control the other person and their violence or aggression is purposeful or *instrumental*. With young people who are abusive towards their parents, they may be actively *controlling* them but quite often they are just deliberately *disempowering* them to prevent the parent from having control over the young person.

If violence is infrequent and mainly associated with temper tantrums it might be primarily expressive. If it seems to be an attempt to exert power and is frequent then it's more likely to be instrumental. Threats and verbal abuse may be substitutes for violence as means of controlling others. Unfortunately there is often no clear distinction between expressive and instrumental violence. A toddler starts off having tantrums that are purely expressive but quickly learns that he can use them to get his own way.

If behaviour is unacceptable (for example abusive to others) then there should be some consequence. This is important even if the aggression is primarily expressive with only a small element of the instrumental or controlling.

Explanations are not excuses

We are more sympathetic towards a child who is violent than towards a violent adult, and more sympathetic still towards a child with a disability. However, this sympathy should not prevent us from expecting common decency or make us so tolerant that we forget about our own or other people's rights. People with autism are not robots and they can learn to behave decently towards others. If they don't learn this crucial lesson they are not likely to have a very good life. Some aspects of this learning may be far harder and may take longer but if we never expect maturity and non-violence then we not likely to get it.

Firmness and consistency

"Children who suffer from psychopathology are no less in need of rules and values than are "normal" children. The opposite actually may be true, for the more chaotic the child's inner world, the greater is the need for an orderly, stabilizing framework." Omer 2000 (p 82)

Along with understanding and parental flexibility, children with any form of disability often need **clearer** boundaries and **firmer** handling than other children. 'Firm' does not, and should not, be harsh or strict but needs to be assertive, clear and consistent. Parents with difficult children may have to work far harder to be consistent than do parents of easier children. Consistency between parents may also be more important.

Because of their low tolerance for change and love of routine, it's very important for children on the autism spectrum that rules and boundaries are clear and that parents are consistent and firm. Many parents are unclear about rules and inconsistent in following through. This does not matter so much with an easy child but some stubborn, difficult children need near-one-hundred-percent consistency. This is not easy!

"The younger generation doesn't know how to behave. Maybe the families and facilitators of kids who have received official diagnoses since the addition of ASD to the DSM in 1980 have become so focused on the label – and the deficits – that they think they don't need to attend to the social skills that are necessary to advance in society." Temple Grandin 2013 (p 192)

There is a delicate line between having sympathy and understanding a disabled person's limitations and problems, and excusing them from being decent and responsible. We can have empathy and flexibility while still expecting that they show others due respect. You need to value and respect yourself and not become too child-focused or your child may not treat you with respect.

Parenting style is a factor in violence within the home by Autistic children, though the odds of such violence may be different. Modern, indulgent, child-focused parenting no doubt results in autistic children being better-functioning overall than did the old-fashioned, less involved parenting. However, a sad side-effect is that it may also be increasing the rate at which such children are being violent and abusive towards their parents. One study of violence in autistic children found that, to their surprise, family income was associated with violence within the home for children on the spectrum "Though the current study indicated that level of income was also a significant predictor in ASD, the results were in a direction opposite than expected, with higher income predicting aggression. This result is surprising and not amenable to easy interpretation.[490]" If they had looked at the literature on children's violence to parents then the obvious explanation is that better off parents are more likely to be 'Indulgent' as we described in the chapter on parenting Style.

Consequences

I have heard parents say 'consequences don't work on him' and have even heard professionals make blanket statements that rewards and punishments are not effective on children with autism. If there are no consequences then you have basically given up as a parent, though you are probably are still applying some consequences (such as praise and criticism). When there are no consequences for truly unacceptable behaviour the child tends to lose respect for the parent and things usually get worse over time. Consequences can take a loooong time to work on stubborn children (with or without autism) but in the long term they can be crucially important in determining whether children grow out of problem behaviours or they just get bigger and stronger and more intimidating.

To repeat a few crucial points from previous chapters: Consequences are about rehabilitation not retribution. Consequences do not need to be harsh to be effective. In fact it's easier to be consistent with small, sometimes almost symbolic, consequences. If you can control computer use, for example, timing it exactly can give you flexible, measurable leverage to encourage better behaviour. Don't stop it entirely or you have lost your ammunition.

Have hope

"These days there is much emphasis on intervention in the early years of life. However, it is now clear from basic biological research that the brain remains open to growth and development across most of the life span. This ties-in with clinical impressions that for some people with autism, adolescence and adulthood can be times of positive and explosive growth. This is doubly exciting as adult life is in many ways potentially easier to manage than childhood for people identified as on the autistic spectrum." Clements 2005 (p 150)

Adolescence can be a time of growth and improvement as well as a time of emotional upheaval. As there is nothing inevitable about aggression in people with autism we can hope, expect, and insist that they grow out of it. Most autistic adults are not violent and violence towards partners appears to be fairly rare though some adults are quite controlling if they can get away with it.[491] Violent crime in adults with autism is rare[492].

As we have only been labelling children as 'Asperger's' or 'High functioning autistic' in any numbers over the past ten to fifteen years no one can say what these children will be like as adults. The common idea that they have a life-long disability is not based on any research. Such conditions are only 'disability' if they cause some deficit in functioning. Some children are disabled in school but not later in life. Undoubtedly, some people now being diagnosed as autistic will adapt well enough so that they have no significant deficits once they are fully mature and it's illogical to say they are then 'disabled' just because their brains function a bit differently to *neurotypicals*.

"People with Asperger's Syndrome are like salt-water fish who are forced to live in fresh water. We're fine if you just put us into the right environment. When the person with AS and the environment match, the problems go away and we even thrive. When they don't match, we seem disabled." Quoted in Baron-Cohen 2004 (p 180)

Oppositional Defiant Disorder

"The essential feature of Oppositional Defiant Disorder is a recurrent pattern of negativistic, defiant, disobedient, and hostile behaviour toward authority figures that persists for at least 6 months and is characterised by the frequent occurrence of at least four of the following:"[493]

1. *often loses temper*
2. *often argues with adults*
3. *often actively defies or refuses to comply with adults requests or rules*
4. *often deliberately annoys people*
5. *often blames others for his or her mistakes or misbehaviour*
6. *is often touchy or easily annoyed by others*
7. *is often angry and resentful*
8. *is often spiteful or vindictive"*[494]

Reading the above it probably strikes you that your child has ODD. This may be the case even for those reading this who **don't** have a beyond control adolescent as the above is vague enough to fit a great many children. The *majority* of the children I deal with who are abusive towards parents or are beyond control, fit more than four of the above criteria (sometimes all of them). However, it's somewhat surprising that only a very small number have ever been diagnosed as having ODD. One in thirteen (7.5%) of the four hundred and eighty children in my sample of parent-abusing children have at some point been labelled ODD. *Most* of these have also been labelled ADHD and only three children have the ODD label without another one or two pseudo-psychiatric labels. As I've mentioned, most of these children have been assessed before they get to me but over 60% have no label of any sort. So why so few diagnoses of ODD? I'd like to think that this is because professionals realise that this is an unusually unhelpful diagnoses.

The label 'Oppositional Defiance Disorder' could be translated as 'lack of respect syndrome' but that would be far too obvious.

I've not been able to find any research suggesting that there are any genetic, neurological or even common environmental factors that link together the majority of children given this label. There is no treatment specifically for ODD. These behaviours can change very rapidly. I've many times seen children give up these behaviours over a short period of time (usually, not always, responding to a change in their parents' behaviour). It's a strange sort of 'mental disorder' if you can just decide to give it up! Once a child has decided to stop being oppositional, it may not even be very difficult for them to do so. Some report that it was an easy habit to break, perhaps because a change in their behaviour can lead to positive changes in other's behaviour (a virtuous cycle).

Just how arbitrary the label is can be easily illustrated. Importantly, there is no indication if 'often' means daily or more than once a month. Another point is that only four of the eight criteria must be met. Let's consider two adolescents who have been diagnosed as ODD.

Jessica is a highly intelligent fourteen-year-old girl attending an expensive private school. She often argues with adults. She is witty and wants to be a lawyer and loves out-arguing her teachers and parents, especially her father who is a lawyer and an orthodox Jew. She doesn't often lose her temper, seeing the arguments as more of an intellectual game. She very often actively defies or refuses to comply with adults' requests or rules. She currently claims she is an anarchist and dresses in dramatic Goth garb. She is sent home from school on a regular basis for not having proper school uniform, usually wearing outrageous makeup, huge crucifixes (it's a Jewish school), skull rings, etc. This is affecting her school grades, though no one seriously doubts that she can catch up if she chooses to. It's not clear if she *deliberately* annoys people – that seems to just comes naturally (and how scientific is it to decide if a child's behaviour is 'deliberate' or not). She often blames others for her mistakes or misbehaviour, usually giving the adults involved a verbal tongue-lashing for being small-minded and refusing to treat her as an equal (though she clearly thinks she is their superior). She is often touchy or easily annoyed by others; she claims that this is hormonal and that she can't help it. Jessica has never been violent or done anything illegal except try marijuana and have sex with an eighteen-year-old boyfriend.

Logan is also fourteen and no longer attends school. He is street-smart but academically a dismal failure. He often loses his temper and has been violent to a great many people, including his sole-parent mother, teachers, his older brother and many children his age or older. Surprisingly he has never badly injured anyone and has so far not been charged with assault. Logan doesn't argue with adults but just ignores them and, since dropping out of school, largely avoids them. He doesn't need to defy or refuse to comply with requests or rules, as his mother has completely given up trying to control him. She has begun drinking herself into a stupor every night. He greatly enjoys deliberately annoying others, including his mother, brother and neighbours by playing cruel pranks on them. He doesn't blame others for his mistakes or misbehaviour since he doesn't really acknowledge any mistakes or misbehaviour. He sees himself as tough and independent and clobbers anyone who upsets him. He doesn't appear touchy or easily annoyed though he is certainly often angry. It's hard to say if he is resentful or not as he currently appears to be quite happy with his life, mysteriously having a steady supply of money and lots of friends. He can certainly be spiteful and vindictive, though he sees this behaviour as a matter of pride and he views his violence as pre-emptive defence.

Logan is heading for a life of crime and will very soon be eligible for the label of 'conduct disorder' (which pretty much means ODD + crime) rather than ODD. Jessica is heading for a passionate, turbulent but successful life as a human rights lawyer.

These two, very different, children fit the same 'mental disorder' label although they have quite different behaviours and each fits a different four of the eight criteria! Neither shows any evidence of what most people would call 'mental illness'. Calling Jessica 'mentally ill' because of the choices she is making might remind one of when psychiatry in the USSR regularly labelled political dissidents as 'mentally ill'. Logan's behaviour in an adult would be considered anti-social and criminal but not psychiatric. Neither of them is 'suffering' from their condition. It's usually parents who suffer from ODD, not the child.

These behaviours are often very selective. Some children are defiant only at home, some only at school, some only with some adults but not others. I once had a mother tell me, *"he has Oppositional Defiant Disorder... mind you, he's an angel for anyone but me."* This child certainly should not have been given the ODD label as they should show oppositional behaviour in more than one situation, but in practice this is often ignored.

Since ODD is not associated with any biological condition it's assumed to be environmental, which for many professionals automatically means that it's all the parent's fault. Thus there is usually no reduction in blame for parents when children get this label and there is only a reduction in their guilt when they really don't understand what ODD means.

Removing the *child's* guilt for their bad behaviour is not at all helpful but can be quite harmful.

This label doesn't usually allow parents to access any services or benefits (and it's a big worry when availability of services or benefits is dependent on such arbitrary criteria).

It tells us **absolutely** nothing about the cause of the behaviour.

It gives no indication whatsoever of how it should be dealt with.

It gives no indication whatsoever about what the likely outcome is. However, there is often the assumption that a child given such a label is more likely to continue having problems into the future than one without the label. This is false unless it becomes a self-fulfilling prophesy.

This label causes parents (and some professionals) much confusion. I've heard a few parents say that their child can't help it because they have ODD. By making parents think that there is something *wrong* with the child, rather than them displaying wrong behaviour and attitudes, it makes many parents less assertive and more permissive or indulgent, precisely what these children **don't** need.

Some children quite consciously use the label as an excuse, for others it adds to an expectation that they won't grow out of their childish behaviour and may make them try less hard to control themselves or to change.

Once a child is given such a label they are more likely to be prescribed various psychoactive drugs, many of which have not been properly tested on developing brains.

Schools sometimes use the labels to get funding and are occasionally sympathetic, but at other times are more likely to get rid of children with troublesome behaviour if they are labelled.

I've seen quite a few children benefit from being diagnosed with Asperger's and I've seen a smaller number benefit from the diagnoses of ADHD but as yet I've not seen a single child benefit from being diagnosed as ODD. Three-quarters of the children in my sample diagnosed ODD have other diagnoses (most often ADHD). Parents sometimes are very happy to get any diagnosis, misguidedly thinking that this means better targeted help or that someone finally understands what is going on. They are usually soon disillusioned and since most of these children get other labels (sometimes quite a few), it can contribute to (perhaps realistic) disillusionment with child psychiatric services.

Is the rate of ODD increasing?

This is an interesting question. There does not appear to have been a big increase in the number of children getting this label over the past few decades. Why not? I have absolutely no doubt that there are **far** more defiant and oppositional children around than there were twenty to thirty years ago. The criteria of arguing with adults and defying or refusing to comply would seem to be met by a lot more children nowadays than it was in previous generations. I also strongly suspect that the criteria about temper, annoying people, blaming others, being touchy and angry and resentful are all *somewhat* more common nowadays. So does that mean that there are a lot more children around today with ODD than when the term was dreamed up? Ironically, it does not.

How is a psychiatrist (or paediatrician) to decide if a child fits one of the criteria? A great many adolescents often lose their temper, as do a great many younger children and a great many adults. There is no precise measure and no clear guidelines are given.

Psychiatrists are supposed to consider that one of the eight criteria is "met only if the behaviour occurs more frequently than is *typically* observed in individuals of comparable age and developmental level."[495] There is no hint in the DSM as to how a psychiatrist is supposed to make this assessment. How many normal children do you need to know before you can decide what is *atypical*? In practice a child psychiatrist may know very few 'normal' children to compare them with.

If there is an increase in temper, arguing, or defiance in the population of young people, then only the most extreme should still be diagnosed as having ODD as the rest are 'typical'. The DSM4 says that the rate of ODD may be from 2% to 16% but doesn't indicate which of these is the correct interpretation. Thus even if they took everything into account and had accurate measures of these behaviours in particular children, (which they hardly ever do), and comparison measures about the general population (which they certainly don't), then still one psychiatrist could judge eight times more children to have ODD than another (which certainly happens). However, overall the number of children having ODD shouldn't change even if *all* children got ten times worse than the previous generation; if **every** child was extremely angry and defiant, then **none** should be diagnosed as having ODD since they would not be showing the behaviours "more frequently than is typically observed"!

People often assume that "mental disorders" are illnesses. But what sort of "illness" has:

- no known cause,
- no recommended treatment,

459

- depends on judgment about how certain common behaviours are in the general population (behaviours that are invariably reported by someone else not the patient),
- only needs four out of eight symptoms (so two patients can have no overlap),
- 'sufferers' hardly ever think there is anything wrong with them or want to be 'cured',
- the 'illness' can be given up by a conscious decision?
- It becomes a different 'illness' as they get older, or if they start breaking the law (see section on Conduct Disorder)?

How ODD!

Conduct Disorder

You may think I'm picking on one vague and slightly silly diagnostic category. In fact the psychiatric bible is full of such stuff. ODD often morphs into Conduct Disorder when children are a bit older and especially when their bad behaviour moves more out of the home. This is even more illogical as an 'illness' category than ODD! For CD, there are fifteen behavioural criteria and the young person only needs to have shown three of these in the past year. Thus there could be five young people all with different patterns of behaviour who are all given this grab-bag label! Naturally it tells us absolutely nothing about how the young person should be treated, what the cause is, or what the outcome is likely to be. It includes such things as:

- Often bullies, threatens or intimidates others.
- Has used a weapon that can cause serious physical harm.
- Has been physically cruel to people.
- Has stolen while confronting a victim (e.g. mugging, purse snatching…).
- Has deliberately destroyed others' property.
- Often stays out all night despite parental prohibitions.
- Is often truant from school.

I'm sure you get the picture and it's notable that there is not a single criterion that is about any kind of cause or about how they feel about it all. Thus there is absolutely no requirement that they see any of it as a problem or that they are 'suffering' from their condition. It's clearly a criminal category, or a lifestyle choice, not 'medical' in any meaningful sense of the word. It's hard to avoid the conclusion that this is only included as a 'psychiatric' category because psychiatrists want to be able to continue treating such children, whether or not they have anything to offer (some are good counsellors, but that is not based on their training as psychiatrists). The label wastes clinicians' and courts' time and energy and I've yet to see it being of any use.

Pre-teen children with such a pattern of behaviour will usually be labelled as ODD and once they pass eighteen, the very same pattern of behaviour can be labelled as 'Antisocial personality disorder'. So the same behaviour can officially be three different conditions over a period of years. Parents and the young person themselves, are often confused and regularly will say that they have both ODD and CD, or that they have both CD and Antisocial Personality disorder.

In my sample of over four hundred and eighty young people who are abusing parents, only 2% have been diagnosed with Conduct Disorder and only one young person had this 'diagnosis' without also having other labels. Since over half of them clearly fit the criteria it's hardly being used consistently! It seems to be a lot more popular in the United States and I've heard it said that it's the most common diagnostic label there among teenage girls.

The latest version of the Diagnostic and Statistical Manual (5) has changed the criteria so that children can now have both ODD and CD at the same time. This makes them look worse on paper. Such changes, with no scientific basis whatsoever, highlight how arbitrary the system is.

Advice for Women Who Have an Abusive Ex

As we have discussed, having been exposed to past domestic violence is the biggest single risk factor for children abusing parents. To have left an abusive partner only to have your child later turn on you is devastating. My experience of women who are parenting after domestic violence is that they are often heroic and almost all are doing a good job *in the circumstances*. However, the circumstances can make doing a good job as a parent almost impossible.

For mothers who have left an abusive man, it can be very difficult knowing how best to deal with the children and your ex. There are many dilemmas: what to tell the children, do they need a firm hand or more love and understanding, do you need to be friends with their father, is contact with their father a good or a bad thing? The following guidelines may need to be adapted as every situation is different.

I make no apology for talking only about women as victims and men as the abusers. The reverse does occur and I've dealt with such situations but I am convinced that men abusing women is at least ten times more common. If you are a sole father who has an irresponsible or abusive ex (or a parent who has left an abusive same sex relationship) you will obviously have to adapt the following, but most of it will apply regardless of gender.

Be very clear, to yourself and to others, that exposing children to ongoing violence and abuse of their mothers is also emotional abuse of them. Even if you yourself were willing to put up with being abused, you simply don't have the right to impose this on your children. Of course if you are sensible enough to be reading this and have left your abusive partner, you won't be crazy enough to *let* him be physically violent again. However, some women who have escaped from violent men and are no longer afraid of them think that putting up with some verbal abuse or the odd threat is not of much importance. Don't make light of your ex abusing you in *any* way – swearing at you, shouting, putting you down, being threatening. If the children know that you are putting up with this behaviour, they are likely to lose respect for you. If he starts to be aggressive or abusive in any way, leave the situation or hang up the phone. It's **not** acceptable!

In general try to minimise situations where the children see you and your ex together. With high conflict or continuing threats, no contact at all between parents, or as little as possible, is the best thing for children. Try to arrange access handovers at a neutral place where you can leave the children for him to pick them up when you aren't there. His parents are often a good option. A trustworthy relative or friend (yours or his) may be willing to provide this service.

You **don't** have to be friends with your ex. "Co-operative colleagues" is the ideal, not "perfect pals". Some misguided parents think that they must forget the past and appear to like each other, even trying to celebrate birthdays and holidays together. This often ends in more trauma for the children (and everyone else). Children are quite happy to have two birthday celebrations and Christmas can be shared. In some cultures Christmas Eve or Boxing Day is just as big a deal as Christmas Day so stretch out the period of celebration if necessary. In general you should aim for a formal, working relationship rather than friendship. Abusive men are often possessive (this **doesn't** mean they care) and they may try to remain emotionally involved with their ex, which means that any signs of friendship may be misinterpreted or used against you.

Be **very** clear about boundaries. Don't let him invade your space or your time. Not only can this be dangerous or upsetting for you but it confuses children and creates opportunities for more trauma and stress. Even casual or trivial displays of affection between ex's can be confusing for children and delay them coming to terms with the separation.

'Not in front of the children' applies even more to arguments and conflict than it does to affection. Be **insistent** that you don't argue or have serious discussions when the children are around. This is not the time to discuss arrangements or issues (do this by phone or e-mail). Once there has been violence in a family, raised voices can have a different meaning for children for many years to come. You can't win in this situation as many children are hypersensitive to tone of voice, body language and facial expressions and any negativity between you will be stressful to them. On the other hand if you manage to appear friendly and pleasant, you may either be giving the children the false impression that you are getting back together again, or else appear to be minimising your ex's violence and irresponsible behaviour.

If the other parent is being irresponsible you have to be **more** responsible with regard to the kids. Don't sink to his level!

Avoid criticism of the other parent *as far as possible*. Not only is this upsetting and stressful for children but criticism can also backfire as children often defend, openly or mentally, a parent who is attacked. If the children tell you that he is criticising you, don't believe you can even the score by criticising him. If he is lying to them about anything important then tell the children the truth (but never all the gory or adult details). If it's a matter of opinion then just state that this is just their father's opinion and you don't agree. It may be helpful to find someone neutral, such as a counsellor, for the children to talk to about this. Don't expect the children to be able to stand up to their father even if they know he is lying or they say they hate him criticising you.

Avoid talking to other people about your ex when the kids are around because even if you can resist being critical, your friends and family will often say things that are hurtful to the children.

On the other hand don't lie to the children to minimise their father's faults or to protect their feelings. Though you should *avoid* criticism of their father this does not mean that *all* criticism is forbidden or inevitably harmful. Making excuses for abusive or seriously irresponsible behaviour means that they may grow up thinking that abuse is acceptable or normal, greatly increasing the chances that they will repeat such behaviour in the future. Saying things like "you know your father loves you" is confusing, if he hasn't made contact for six months, as well as being untrue (how would they know this, even if it were true). Saying, "he only acts like that because he's an alcoholic" may contain *some* truth but is suggesting that he does not have responsibility for his abusive behaviour. **Don't excuse abuse!** Don't cover up for him and don't lie to your children to make him appear better than he is. It's important to state that abuse is wrong though you should try to condemn the behaviour not the person as far as is possible.

"Often mental health professionals and members of the clergy have been quick to tell divorced mothers never, under any circumstances, to say anything negative about their children's fathers. They offer this advice as though it were undoubtedly in the children's best interests. As a result, even when a father routinely ignores or mistreats his children, the mother feels she must watch helplessly and in silence as her children decide that it must be their own failings that lead him to behave in that way." Caplan[496]

Not only do children sometimes blame themselves if an absent father is being irresponsible but they even more frequently blame their mother.

Generally, even when there is no contact whatsoever, it's not healthy for children to grow up imagining their father either as a hero or as a devil. If they imagine a hero they may blame you for the separation and are likely to be greatly disillusioned at some point in the future. If they imagine a devil this can affect their self-esteem as they are likely to wonder if they take after him. For these reasons, some contact with an irresponsible father may often be better than no contact whatsoever (providing, of course, that it's safe). Similarly, some knowledge is better than a vacuum which will be filled by their imagination, or by snippets of gossip. Dwelling on past trauma is unhealthy but so is *never,* ever mentioning it. It's very tricky finding the right balance (so be wary of those with easy answers or preset ideas).

There are no easy answers about how much to tell a child about the past if a parent has been abusive. They have a right to know if their father committed *serious* acts of abuse but they don't need to know all the details (or the adult stuff) and you should keep as far as possible to objective (provable) facts. They don't need to know *your* opinion of their father but they should probably know if he was charged with assaulting you or went to prison.

Understand that your children are likely to be very confused about their feelings for their father. It's possible to feel lots of different emotions at the same time and children's feelings can also change quite quickly over time. Pre-teen children are usually concrete thinkers who try to see the world as black and white – good guys and bad guys – rather than in shades of grey. Thus loving a father who has been violent can be bewildering for them.

Children often struggle *very* hard to be loyal to an irresponsible or rejecting parent. Loyalty conflicts can be intense (often worst around ages twelve to fourteen) with children sometimes not only turning against your new partner but against brothers and sisters and even against their mother (often temporarily) as they try to resolve their loyalty conflicts. Some children say they feel as if they are pawns in their parents' games or that they are being torn in two. It can be an extremely hard balancing act trying to protect your children without taking part in a tug-of-war.

Don't expect children to accept your new partner with open arms. Children struggling to be loyal to their father are actually *more* likely to reject a step-father than are children who have a happy, stable relationship with their own father. Never, ever, suggest that a step-father is a substitute for their natural father and don't bother to point out that he is better as this is just as likely to strengthen their loyalty to their natural father.

Don't even think about re-partnering *for the children's sake*! The idea that boys *must* have a father-figure in the home to grow up well is a dangerous myth. The evidence is clear that sole mothers (or lesbian mothers) can bring up boys (or girls) well on their own. Re-partner when you are ready, but don't rush it, and don't expect it to make things any easier with the children.

Loyalty conflicts can also make it very hard for the children to open up to you about their father or about their feelings. Don't push them to tell you everything. Don't interrogate them about what happens with their father or they will learn to lie or clam up. They also may find it hard to talk to you about the situation because they are protective of you and don't want to see you upset.

Don't add extra stress to your children's lives if it can be avoided, especially in the year or two after a separation. Avoid unnecessary moves, changes of school, on-again/off-again relationships (with their father or others) and court cases.

Looking after yourself is very important for your children's well-being. Getting your own life back on track may be the best way to help children. Children often don't have any respect for a parent who lives to serve them. It's definitely possible to be too child-focused. Get a life!

Try not to feel guilty about what the children have gone through in the past – you didn't plan it and you've done your best to stop it. Many women say they feel guilty about having exposed the children to abuse (by choosing the wrong partner and staying with him too long) and also feel guilty for leaving him. Clearly this is illogical so choose one to be guilty about… but better still, why not stop feeling guilty for both?

You can't 'make it up' to your children by being soft or indulgent – they need clear boundaries and firm consequences. Lack of boundaries can make them feel more insecure. If you are too soft they often won't respect you. You need to deal with their behaviour *regardless* of where it's coming from. If there were too many rules or harsh punishments when you were with their father, it may be tempting to now have too few rules and no consequences. Don't fall into this trap.

All children need consequences and for difficult children these will need to include both rewards and punishments. Punishment does *not* need to be physical. Children who have been abused or witnessed abuse don't need more violence so find alternatives to hitting them.

Don't accept abuse from anyone – including your kids. If you do, it's likely to get worse as the abuser loses more respect for you over time. If your children have seen you abused by more than one person (including another child) it will be harder to regain their respect. Avoid, if at all possible, exposing them to you being put-down or abused in *any* way by *any*one. It's important that *all* abuse is taken seriously. If they see an older brother or sister abusing you and there are no consequences, they are more likely to copy this behaviour. It can thus be important to have consequences even if these appear (in the short term) to have no effect whatsoever on the abusive child.

Beware of saying that a child is like his father. You may hope to change his behaviour or attitudes because he doesn't really want to be like his father but not only may he have mixed feelings about being like his father, but such a belief can be a self-fulfilling prophecy and he may come to believe that he is doomed to repeat his father's behaviours.

Dealing with all this can be like walking through an emotional minefield! Don't feel that you are a failure if you need to ask for help for yourself or for your children. A few children may need a lot of help but some benefit from just a few counselling sessions with an independent adult.

For Non-Custodial Parents Whose Ex Is Being Abused by Their Child

This chapter is for parents who have visitation or shared custody where the other parent, your ex, is being abused by your child. By far the most common situation is that the custodial parent is the mother and the access parent is the father, and I've made this assumption in this chapter. If your situation is one of the exceptions you will be able to decide which parts of the following apply to you.

As an access father whose child is acting abusively towards your ex, you may feel quite confused about what to do. There may be a part of you still bitter about the separation (or about being sidelined as a parent). I doubt that you would actually want your ex to be abused (sadly such people do exist but they are unlikely to be reading this and won't pay any attention to anything I write). I'm also sure that you don't want your child behaving like that. You probably realise that the more your child practises this form of abusive behaviour, the greater the chance they are going to screw up future relationships (as partner or as parent) later in life. They are also likely to be putting themselves at risk if they become beyond control. You may be able to control your child in early adolescence but some progress to defying both parents as they get older.

However, you may also have some mixed feelings about it. You may catch yourself thinking: "*She deserves what she gets*" or "*Johnny's reacting to her nagging the way I used to*" or "*She's always been far too soft with them, this is where it's led. If only she'd let me discipline them properly...*" If you have such thoughts keep them to yourself. Ask yourself if there is a chance that your child is picking up on your attitudes? If you are transmitting these ideas to your child, you are part of the problem rather than part of the solution.

"It's her problem... and she deserves it!"

"*I can understand why she hits you.*" said to a mother by her ex in front of the violent fifteen-year-old girl.

If you have read the rest of this book you hopefully have let go of most of the blame you have towards your ex for your child's behaviour. It's more likely that you are just reading this chapter (your ex or a counsellor has probably copied it for you). I'm asking you to put aside blame about what has happened in the past for the sake of your children. Even if your ex dumped you in the most nasty way possible, even if your ex is the worst nag in the world, even if your ex really is a hopeless parent, they STILL don't deserve to be abused. Blaming the victim can be comfortable and easy but in this case it's often disastrous! Sadly, and ironically, it's those men who have most clearly contributed to their children's bad behaviour by their own example, who are the most blaming of the victimized mother. Does this apply to you even a little? You can at least admit it to yourself and try to make amends to some extent.

The effect on a parent of living with an abusive and beyond control young person can be absolutely devastating! They are often depressed, extremely stressed, confused, feeling ashamed and guilty while also very concerned for the young person and their future.

But I'm not even asking you to care about your ex (even though you no doubt loved her once). Even if you do believe that she deserves all she gets, you need to help your child to get over this behaviour. If your child does not get over this behaviour it can wreck their life. This is **not** an exaggeration.

Children who are abusing their mothers are very often miserable. I have often been surprised how much happier such children are once their parents re-establish control. They stress themselves by their behaviour and usually (hopefully) feel some guilt and shame. They feel insecure if no one can control them, even though they fight against that control.

Such children are often at risk. When children break free of parental control, they are at risk of educational failure, homelessness, abuse by others, drink or drug use, criminality and early pregnancy or fatherhood. There are also increasing numbers of young people becoming recluses living only through the internet (often nocturnal).

If there are other children in the home they are often also at risk of abuse or are at least stressed and are having their lives disrupted.

In the longer term, it's likely that a young person who practices abuse within the home will go on to be abusive to partners and children. I'm sure this is not the sort of life you want for your child.

So I am asking you to take it very seriously and do whatever you can to help stop it.

"She's exaggerating"

From your vantage point, looking at the situation from the outside with inevitably prejudiced eyes, you may feel that it's all being exaggerated. After all, your child is never abusive to you (or very rarely). This is perfectly normal. It may even mean that your child is too insecure with you, or afraid of you, to show his or her worst behaviour. Children tend to be far better behaved on access visits or short holidays than they are at home. I've experienced this first hand as a foster parent. We had children coming for respite weekends who were always well behaved on their short stays with us although they were violent and disruptive at home and at school.

Another factor is that mothers in most homes come into more conflict with children because they take more responsibility for things like chores, homework, routines, etc. The other extreme is the parent (usually a father, I'm afraid to say) who doesn't impose any restrictions on the children at all hence doesn't get in their way. Even the most angry and uncooperative adolescent can find little to fight about if they can stay up as long as they like, wear what they like, eat and drink what they like and generally do what they like. Really neglectful parents seldom get abused by their children. The point I'm making is that these children are most abusive to parents who do the most for them and who they then take for granted.

That's usually Mum rather than Dad. They abuse the ones they love most (as do many men). Abuse has to do with lack of respect not with lack of love.

So the fact that your child does not behave abusively when with you does **not** mean that any of the following are true:

1. That you're a better parent.
2. That it must be exaggerated. I meet many charming, intelligent and likeable young people who are violent behind closed doors and typically to the person they feel most secure with.
3. That your ex is provoking them. Some of these young people are awfully good at blaming their victims and can make normal parenting sound like extreme provocation.
4. That they would be better off living with you. They may, or may not, depending on a number of circumstances. If you use this as a threat against your ex or to allow your child to escape the consequences of their actions, you are almost definitely making things worse by undermining your ex and allowing your child to avoid the consequences of their actions. Besides which, if they can run off to your house they can (and probably will) do the same in the opposite direction in the future.

"What can I do? I'm not around when it happens."

The first and most important thing you can do is to *not* undermine your ex. Some of the common ways that custodial parents are undermined by ex's:

1. Verbal abuse: calling her names when picking up the children, dropping them off, or when on the phone (kids are often more aware of phone calls than the adults think).
2. Arguing with her in front of the children. Just don't do it! Even if she starts it leave it for a phone call when little ears aren't flapping.
3. Running her down more subtly. *"You know your mother's mentally unstable you just have to make allowances for her."* or *"You should respect your mother even when she does act like an idiot."*
4. Minimizing and excusing your child's bad behaviour. *"I don't think she realizes how stressed you get. At least you punched the wall and not her this time."*
5. Undoing her attempts to impose consequences. *"If she's stopped your pocket money again I'll make up the difference." "I gave you that TV so she's no right to take it out of your bedroom." "Sure you can come for the weekend; she doesn't have to know that I let you go to the party."*
6. Giving excessive gifts or treats that she can't match. This is particularly underhand when men are not paying maintenance.
7. Not imposing reasonable rules and restrictions. You don't have to go along with all her opinions (though often it's worth compromising), but some irresponsible men let children on visitation watch R-rated movies, drink and smoke under age, stay up as long as they want or binge on chocolate or fizzy drinks. The children return hyped-up and unwilling to cooperate

with normal guidelines – men who do this are harming their education, health and future, as well as their home life.

8. Allowing children to come to stay with you because they have had an argument with their mother or are being punished for something is a major form of undermining. This should always be done in consultation with your ex.

9. Coming in like Rambo to punish the child (see below). Beware of this even if she asks for your help. Even in emergencies you need to back her up not try to replace her.

Why should I put myself out?

Quite simply, because you love your child, even if the other parent is **not** doing the best they could (though they probably are), even if you believe she is unstable, mentally ill, an alcoholic, stupid or just weak and pathetic, you need to do the best you can for your child.

If the other parent is not being responsible, you need to be **more** responsible for the sake of your children, not less responsible (or even equally as irresponsible).

Stop fighting with your ex

Research consistently shows that conflict between parents is the most harmful thing about parental separation. Children are often feeling very angry about parent's separation and if the ex-couple continue to fight, or run each other down, children don't get over it. They never get used to this and it can make them very unhappy and angry. This can lead to behavioural problems, emotional problems and academic problems. Their anger may be shown in various settings or may be saved up for the safest target, usually Mum.

You can't get revenge on your ex without also hurting your children. It's not worth it so just get over it!

Backing her up

A step further than simply not undermining is to actually support her in her parenting and back-up her authority.

First step is being VERY clear to your child that his or her behaviour is not appropriate. If you yourself have behaved similarly in the past, i.e. he or she has seen you punch walls or verbally or physically abuse your ex or someone else, then you should try hard to make it clear that you behaved wrongly and have now changed (if you haven't changed then get help to do so). Have you made a formal apology to those you have harmed or threatened, including your children if they were witnesses?

There is no excuse for abuse.

Establish good communication with your ex if you possibly can. A really important principle is that you two do NOT need to be friends. What you really need at a time like this is a working, collegial, professional-type, relationship. You need to work together at the job of being separated parents. This is nothing like your couple relationship and can work even if you don't like each other at all. In fact, it can confuse things if you are too friendly. Attempting to be friends can either reawaken all the couple crap or else make your child believe that you may get back together again (and this can open old wounds for them as well as you and your ex).

Help your ex find consequences that can be imposed to stop the abuse and encourage your child to control him- or her-self. In normal circumstances, a grounding or loss of privileges would not continue over an access weekend but for serious offences, such as physical violence, running away or stealing, you could make a statement of support and solidarity by negotiating with your ex and continuing the punishment. If your ex is using withdrawal of pocket money, or a privilege such as internet access or phone usage as a consequence, you can help her impose this and show your support of her parenting and condemnation of the bad behaviour. If she is using pocket money as a consequence you need to limit what you give them or you will be undermining her.

If your child is blatantly defying their mother, but you still have some authority over them, you can use this to help her impose sanctions. E.g. if a child is likely to, or threatening to, become violent if his mother removes his phone or turns off the internet, you can agree to be present for an hour to prevent this violence and let her regain some control. These are desperation measures and **must** be done with her full cooperation. Beware of being called in every time there is a crisis as some children actually like getting the attention from you, or they get a kick out of getting their parents together again even for a brief time.

"He just needs a firm hand"

In a sense, this is true, but not literally, i.e. not physical punishment. And he (or she) especially needs firmness from the main carer and this may be a lot easier said than done.

One way to undermine your ex is to come in like Rambo to "sort it out". In a crisis, she may actually be glad to have this happen but it can make things worse. If you charge in like the cavalry you are emphasizing the fact that she can't cope. If you use physical discipline or force that she can't use, you may be making your child less likely to obey her when you are not around. You are also likely to be making your child more angry and may be giving them another example of the philosophy of "might makes right".

It's not up to you to **take over** the disciplining from your ex. This is not your job. Backing them up means just that, that you are behind them, or occasionally alongside, but don't get in the way. So don't assume that you can fix things by brute force or without consultation and a well thought out plan.

If your child needs to come live with you

If violence is severe or a child is dangerously beyond control it may be necessary that they live with you, at least for a time. This should not be seen as a punishment but nor should it be a reward for bad behaviour. Don't go to either extreme. Trying to make them have as tough a time as possible is not likely to work but having a terrific fun time is hardly showing that you take their behaviour seriously. Talk to your ex and work out a reasonable compromise.

It's not up to children to decide where they live but up to the parents. If you let your child decide to come to live with you on a whim they are just as likely to move out again on a whim. Ideally the decision of where they are to live is made by both parents, even when separated, though in consultation with the child. The child's wishes should always be taken into account but it's not their decision but their parents.

A case study

Mike was a serious, intelligent, cute little boy of eleven. You'd think on first meeting him that butter wouldn't melt in his mouth. His behaviour was deteriorating both at home and at school. At this age this is a serious worry as such deterioration can accelerate dramatically during puberty (often when they start High School). His mother, Diane, was a sensible and fairly assertive woman but her attempts to control Mike were failing. She had separated from Mike's father, Colin, five years before. She said there had been some verbal abuse from Mike's father and she considered him controlling and aggressive but not physically violent. She did wonder if Mike was taking after Colin, though. He had been an easy child in his early years but she saw him getting more like his father. Her relationship with Colin had been up and down since their separation but for the past year was definitely deteriorating. This was probably because Colin blamed her for Mike's problems and said, repeatedly, that he had no problems with Mike. This is the kind of vicious circle I see repeatedly. Mike's deteriorating behaviour was giving the parents things to argue about and their arguing was making Mike angry, stressed and making him lose respect for his mother. It's a chicken and egg situation*. Colin thought that Mike should come and live with him, though he would have to first change his working hours and probably his job before this was possible. Mike loved both his parents but at this stage wanted to live with Mum. He was a bit afraid of Dad, but would never admit this to either parent.

Although Diane had not said much about Colin on our first session, what she did say was almost all negative and I wanted to meet Mike before I would meet his father. I find that fathers who have been controlling and aggressive are unlikely to take up the offer to meet me.

To my surprise Colin turned up along with Diane and Mike at the next counselling session. The atmosphere could have been cut with a knife. Colin was angry because he had only found out about the counselling by chance the night before. He initially seemed aggressive and controlling. He felt he was being left out of an important decision about his son's life, as many non-custodial fathers do. Mike slumped down in his chair and looked close to tears as I tried to keep things calm and explained counselling and confidentiality to the three of them. I sent both

---

* The egg came first – the first chicken was hatched from the egg of an egg-laying proto-chicken ancestor of the chicken. Even if you don't believe in evolution but Creationism, then the chicken must have been created before the first egg (or who would have sat on it?).

parents out after ten minutes and talked to Mike alone. He still hadn't relaxed by the end of the first session. Next time I saw him (brought by Dad) he relaxed and was quite talkative and articulate for a boy of his age. It became very clear that he absolutely hated the fact that his parents were enemies and whenever he saw them together it was horribly tense, as I'd experienced. He told me that both parents ran each other down, Dad openly, Mum subtly.

Like many children I see, there was a lot of anger about his parents' separation and the continuing conflict between them. I wrote a short summary of how I saw the situation and got Mike's OK to send this to both parents. I only saw Mike a couple more times over the next few months but he told me that his parents had completely stopped criticising each other and he was feeling much happier. His tantrums and defiance decreased very rapidly and within two months had virtually stopped.

The fact that I'd seen, and felt, the tension between the parents for myself was unusual. In such cases, I rarely see them together. The fact that **both** parents took heed of how upsetting it was for Mike to hear them criticizing each other was even more unusual.

Given how beyond-control adolescents put themselves at risk of school failure, depression, crime, drugs, alcohol and homelessness the possible difference to Mikes's future is enormous. It was very powerful that both parents apparently decided to stop criticizing and undermining the other. However, you can only control **your own** behaviour and hope that this will influence the other parent, but it may not.

If the other parent is being irresponsible then for the sake of your children you need to be more responsible, not less.

Riding Zebras (A Parenting Parable)

In the land of Parentia, there is an unusual horse race. Contestants (and most natives compete at some point in their lives) must cross the land from west to east by a variety of routes. The people take this race very seriously despite the vague nature of the rules and the fact that the finish line is unclear, ill-defined and frequently moved. The land is full of hazards including potholes, chasms, mountains, swamps, quicksand and jungles. Jockeys do not necessarily ride their mounts but can also lead them, walk alongside them, entice them onward with tasty titbits, or herd them with a riding crop (although riding crops are nowadays frowned upon).

As the route taken varies so much, what may be an easy ride for some can be treacherous and difficult for others. Some riders have helpers and supporters; others must face the challenges alone. So complicated is the whole affair that a clear winner is seldom agreed upon and just completing the course is generally acknowledged to be the most important thing. "Experts" do not even agree on what is the most important goal: is it speed, distance covered, endurance, style or even having a happy horse? These experts write hundreds of contradictory guidebooks while the riders constantly complain about the lack of a manual.

Although an obstacle that kills or maims a horse will be acknowledged as being bad luck, hazards such as hills, swamps and deep valleys are not accepted as excuses for poor performance and a rider who complains about these, or asks for help, is seen as lacking in skill. Perhaps the most surprising aspect of the whole thing is that what is called a "horse" varies tremendously. Some riders are given well-behaved mares or stallions while others have plodding carthorses and others bucking broncos. Still others find themselves allocated by chance a stubborn mule or even a virtually unrideable zebra. Despite the diversity of mounts, it's an important part of Parentia mythology that all steeds start equal and that only the skill of the rider is significant.

Obviously it takes tremendous skill to ride a zebra or a bucking bronco and such riders may develop the most skill but gain no recognition. If they do well they complete the course long after others have finished, battered and bruised from having been thrown many times. A few give up, to their eternal shame, but most show heroic persistence and determination. It seems unfair and cruel that the jockeys of mules, broncos and zebras are held entirely accountable for any problems by those who rode horses. Strangely enough, the riders themselves often accept all the blame. The obvious contribution of the nature of the beast, the terrain, supports, luck and even the weather are all disregarded when prizes are being given out. This belief in the all-important, all-powerful jockey is clearly a form of magical thinking. The natives often declare "all animals are equal", though a few have been heard to add under their breath, "although some are a lot more equal than others."

A few recommended books

Cottrell, B. (2005). *When teens abuse their parents.* Halifax, Nova Scotia, Fernwood Publishing.

Doherty, W. (2003). *Confident Parenting.* NSW, Finch Publishing.

Caplan, P. J. (1981). *Don't Blame Mother.* N.Y., Harper & Row.

Edgette, J. (2002). *Stop negotiating with your teen.* N.Y., Perigree.

Omer, H. (2000). *Parental Presence.* Phoenix, Zeig, Tucker & Co.

Rubin, C. (1996). *Don't let your kids kill you*: A guide for parents of drug and alcohol addicted children. Rockport, MA, Element Books.

Samenow, Stanton (2001) *Before It's too late*: *Why some kids get into trouble and what parents can do about it.* Revised edition. New York: Three Rivers press.

Sells, S. (2001). *Parenting Your Out-of-Control Teenager*. N.Y., St. Martin's Griffin.

Taffel, R. 2001. *Getting Through to Difficult Kids and Parents*. N.Y., Guildford Press.

Weinhause, E. and K. Friedman (1991). *Stop struggling with your teenager.* Melbourne, Australia, Penguin. [sadly, out of print]

About Domestic Violence:

Bancroft, L. 2002. *Why does he do that? Inside the minds of angry and controlling men.* N.Y., Berkley Publishing.

On Child Development

Harris, J. R. (1998). *The Nurture Assumption*. NY, Free Press.

Paris, J. (2000). *Myths of Childhood*. NY, Routledge.

Twenge, J. M. and W. K. Campbell (2009). *The narcissism epidemic*. N.Y., Simon & Schuster.

Websites

It's surprising how little there is on the web about violence to parents! If you find sites useful for parents please send me the links and I'll put them on my website.

www.eddiegallagher.com.au (there's a link to e-mail the author on this site)

http://holesinthewall.co.uk/ UK blog on violence to parents. Links to resources and services in the UK especially.

http://break4change.co.uk/ Brighton's Break4Change program.

http://www.kingcounty.gov/courts/clerk/step-up.aspx Info on the USA Step-up program

https://www.law.ox.ac.uk/content/adolescent-parent-violenceOxford University's Rachel Condry project on violence to parents.

References

Abramovich, R., Coret, C., et al. (1986) "Sibling and peer interaction: a final follow-up and a comparison." Child Development 57: 217-229.

Alexander, B. K., Beyerstein, B. L., et al. (1981) "The effects of early and later colony housing on oral ingestion of morphine in rats." Pharmacology, Biochemistry, & Behavior, 15: 571-576.

Ambert, A. (1992) The Effect of Children on Parents. New York, Hayworth Press.

Ambert, A. (2001) The Effect of Children on Parents, 2nd ed. N.Y., Haworth Press.

Anderson, C. A., Berkowitz, L., et al. (2003) "The influence of media violence on youth." Psychological Sci Public Interest 4(3): 81- 110.

Apter, M. J. (1992) The Dangerous Edge. N.Y., Free Press.

Archer, J. and Côté, S. (2005) "Sex differences and evolutionary perspecitive." In. R. E. Tremblay, W. W. Hartup and J. Archer. Developmental origins of aggression N.Y., Guilford Press: 425-443.

Arendell, T. (2000) "Conceiving and investigating motherhood: The decade's scholarship." J. of Marriage & the Family 62: 1192-1207.

Arnett, J. J. (1999) "Adolescent storm and stress reconsidered." American Psychologist 54: 317-326.

Ashton, M. (2014). The other half of Asperger syndrome, 2nd edition. London, Jessica Kingsley.

Attwood, T. (2006) Complete Guide to Asperger's Syndrome. London, Jessica Kingsley.

Baillargeon, R. (2002) Gender differences in physical aggression at 17 months of age. 15th world meeting of the International Society for Research on Aggression, Montreal, Canada.

Balson, M. (1981) Becoming Better Parents. Melbourne, Victoria, ACER.

Bancroft, L. (2002) Why Does He Do That? Inside the minds of angry and controlling men. N.Y., Berkley Publishing.

Bancroft, L. and Silverman, J. G. (2002) The Batterer as Parent: Addressing the impact of domestic violence on family dynamics. Thousand Oaks; London, Sage.

Barnard, M. (2007) Drug Addiction and Families. London, Jessica Kingsley.

Baron-Cohen, S. (2004) The Essential Difference. London, Penguin.

Bateson, G., Jackson, D., et al. (1956) "Towards a theory of schizophrenia." Behavioural Science 1: 251-255.

Baumeister, R. F. (1997) Evil: Inside Human Violence and Cruelty. N.Y., Holt.

Baumeister, R. F., Smart, L., et al. (1996) "Relation of threatened egotism to violence and aggression: the dark side of high self-esteem." Psychological Bulletin 103: 5-33.

Baumrind, D. (1971) "Current patterns of parental authority." Developmental Psychology Monograph 4(1(2)).

Baumrind, D. (1989) "Rearing competent children." In. W. Damon. Child development today and tomorrow San Francisco, Jossey-Bass: 349-378.

Baumrind, D. (1991) "The influence of parenting style on adolescent competence & substance abuse." J. of Early Adolescence 11(1): 56-95.

Baumrind, D. (1996) "The discipline controversy revisited." Family Relations: Journal of Applied Family & Child Studies 45(4): 405-414.

Beekman, D. (1977) The Mechanical Baby. Connecticut, Lawrence Hill & Company.

Bennett, D. and Rowe, L. (2003) What to do when Your Children turn into Teenagers? Doubleday.

Berkowitz, L. (1993) Aggression: Its causes, consequences and control. N.Y., McGraw-Hill.

Berne, S. (1996) Bully-proof Your Child. Port Melbourne, Australia, Lothian.

Bettelheim, B. (1967) The Empty Fortress: Infantile autism and the birth of the self. N.Y., Free Press.

Biddulph, S. (1997) Raising Boys: Why boys are different, and how to help them become happy and well-balanced men. Sydney, Finch Publishing.

Biehal, N. (2012). "Parent Abuse by Young People on the Edge of Care: A Child Welfare Perspective." Social Policy & Society 11(2): 251-263.

Blanchard, A. (1993) "Violence in families: the effect on children." Family Matters 34.

Boehlich, W., Ed. (1990) Letters of Sigmund Freud to Edward Silverstein Boston: , Harvard University Press.

Bongers, I. L., Koot, H. M., Van Der Ende, J., & Verhulst, F. C. (2004). Developmental trajectories of externalizing behaviors in childhood and adolescence. Child Development, 75, 1523–1537.

Brame, B., Nagin, D. S., & Tremblay, R. E. (2001). Developmental trajectories of physical aggression from school entry to late adolescence. J. of Child Psychology, Psychiatry, & Allied Disciplines, 42, 503–512.

Brezina, T. (1999). "Teenage violence toward parents as an adaptation to family strain." Youth & Society 30(4): 416-444.

Brook, J., Whiteman, M., et al. (1989) "Older brother's influence on younger sibling's drug use." J. of Psychology 114(1): 83-90.

Brooks, K. (2008) Consuming Innocence: Popular culture and our children. Queensland, Australia, University of Queensland Press.

Brooks, R. (2011) Sex, Genes and Rock 'n' Roll. Sydney, Australia, New South.

Bruer, J. T. (1999) The Myth of the First Three Years. N.Y., Free Press.

Buffardi, L. E. and Campbell, W. K. (2008) "Narcissism and social networking web sites." Personality & Social Psychology Bulletin 34: 1303-1114.

Cable, M. (1972) The Little Darlings: A history of child rearing in America. N.Y., Charles Scribner's Sons.

Campbell, T. W. (1998) Smoke and Mirrors: The devastating effect of false sexual abuse claims. N.Y., Insight Books.

Caplan, P. J. (1981) Don't Blame Mother. N.Y., Harper & Row.

Caplan, P. J. (1994) You're Smarter Than They Make You Feel: How the experts intimidate us and what we can do about it. N.Y., The Free Press.

Caplan, P. J. and Hall-McCorquodale, I. (1985) "Mother-blaming in major clinical journals." American J. of Orthopsychiatry 55: 345-353.

Christakis, D. A., Zimmerman, F. J., et al. (2004) "Early television exposure and subsequent attentional problems in children." Pediatrics 113: 708-713.

Clements, J. (2005) People with Autism Behaving Badly. London, Jessica Kingsley.

Cloud, H. and Townsend, J. (1996) The Mum Factor. Michigan, Zondervan.

Coleman, J. C. (2011) The Nature of Adolescence, 4th Edition, Taylor & Francis.

Collishaw, S., Maughan, B., et al. (2004) "Time trends in adolescent mental health." J. of Child Psychology & Psychiatry. 45: 1350-1362.

Condrey, R. (2007) Families shamed: The consequences of crime for relatives of serious offenders. Cullompton, UK, Willan Publishing.

Coontz, S. (1992) The Way We Never Were: American families and the nostalgia trap. N.Y., Basic Books.

Cottrell, B. (2001) Parent Abuse: The abuse of parents by their teenage children. Ottawa, Family Violence Prevention Unit, Health Canada.

Cottrell, B. (2004) When Teens Abuse Their Parents. Halifax, Nova Scotia, Fernwood Publishing.

Craig, L., Powell, A., et al. (2013) "Towards intensive parenting? Changes in the composition and determinants of mothers' and fathers' time with children 1992–2006." The British journal of sociology 65.3 (2014): 555-579.

Crews, F. (1995) The Memory Wars: Freud's legacy in dispute. London, Granta.

Crichton-Hill, Y., Evans, N., et al. (2006) "Research Focus: Adolescent violence to parents." Te Awatea Review 4(2): 21-22.

Davis, L. and Carlson, B. (1987) "Observations of spouse abuse: What happens to the children." J. of Interpersonal Violence 2(3): 278-291.

Dawes, R. M. (2001) Everyday Irrationality: How pseudo-scientists, lunatics and the rest of us systematically fail to think rationally. Cambridge, MA, Westview Press.

Dawson, M., Souliéres, I., et al. (2007) "The Level and Nature of Autistic Intelligence." Psychological Science 18: 657-662.

De Lange, N. and Olivier, M. (2004) "Mothers' Experiences of Aggression in Their Tourette's Syndrome Children." International Journal for the Advancement of Counselling 26(1): 65-77.

De Wall, F. (2009) The Age of Empathy. London, Harmony Books.

Diener, M. L. and Kim, D. Y. (2004) "Maternal and child predictors of preschool children's social competence." Applied Developmental Psychology 25: 3-24.

Dill, K. E. (2009) How fantasy becomes reality: Seeing through media influence. N.Y., Oxford University Press.

Dobson, J. (1970) Dare to Discipline, Tyndale House.

Dodge, K. A., Petit, G. S., et al. (1994) "Socialization mediators of the relation between SES and and child conduct problems." Child Development 65: 649-665.

Doherty, W. (2003) Confident Parenting. NSW, Finch Publishing.

Dolnick, E. (1998) Madness on the Couch: Blaming the victim in the heyday of psychoanalysis. N.Y., Simon & Schuster.

Dornbusch, S. M., Ritter, P. L., et al. (1987) "The relation of parenting style to adolescent performance." Child Development 58: 1244-1257.

Douglas, S. J. and Michaels, M. W. (2004) The Mommy Myth: The idealization of motherhood and how it has undermined all women`. N.Y., Free Press.

Dreikurs, R. (1964) Happy Children. Glasgow, Collins.

Duncan, R. E., Williams, B. J., et al. (2013) "Adolescents, risk behaviour and confidentiality." Australian Psychologist 48: 408-419.

Duncan, T., Alpert, A., et al. (1996) "Multilevel covariance structure analysis of sibling substance use and interfamily conflict." J. of Psychopathology & Behavioural Assessment 18(4): 347-369.

Dunn, J. and Plomin, R. (1990) Separate Lives: Why siblings are so different. N.Y., Basic Books.

Eckstein, N. J. (2002) Adolescent-to-parent abuse: A communicative analysis of conflict processes present in the verbal, physical or emotional abuse of parents. Lincoln, University of Nebraska: 285.

Edenborough, M., Jackson, D., et al. (2008) "Living in the red zone: the experience of child-to-mother violence." Child & Family Social Work 13: 464-473.

Edgette, J. (2002) Stop Negotiating with Your Teen. N.Y., Perigee Book.

Ehrenreich, B. (2009) Smile or Die: How positive thinking fooled America and the world. . London, Granta Pubs.

Eller, J. D. (2010) Cruel Creeds: Virtuous Violence. NY, Prometheus.

Epstein, R. (2007) The Case Against Adolescence. Sanger, CA, Quill Driver Books.

Esterson, A. (1993) Seductive mirage. Illinois, Open Court Books.

Evans, E. and Warren-Sohlberg, L. (1988) "A pattern analysis of adolescent abusive behaviour toward parents." J of Adolescent Research 3(2): 201-216.

Evans, P. (1996) The Verbally Abusive Relationship, Adams Media.

Eyer, D. (1996) Motherguilt: How our culture blames mothers for what's wrong with society. N.Y., Times Books.

Farrell, J. (1996) Freud's Paranoid Quest. , New York University Press.

Farrington, D. P. (1988) "Studying changes within individuals: The causes of offending." In. M. Runnter. Studies of psychosocial risk: The power of longitudinal data N.Y., Cambridge University Press: 158-183.

Farrington, D. P. (2000) "Psychosocial predictors of adult antisocial personality and adult convictions." Behavioural Sciences & the Law 18: 605-680.

Felson, R. B. and Russo, N. (1988) "Aggression and violence against siblings." Social Psychology Quarterly 46(4): 271-285.

Festinger, L. and Carlsmith, J. M. (1959) "Cognitive consequences of forced compliance." J. of Personality & Social Psychology 58((2): 203-210.

Fisher, R. and Ury, W. (1981) Getting to Yes. London, Business Books, .

Fiske, A. P. and Tage, S. R. (2015) Virtuous Violence. Cambridge, UK, Cambridge Universtity Press.

Fojtik, K. Wife Beating. (1976) Michigan, Ann Arbor-Washetanaw County NOW Wife Assault Task Force.

Frances, A. (2013) Saving Normal. NY, HarperCollins.

Frizzell, A. W. (1998) "Biting the hand that feeds? The social construction of adolescent violence toward parents as a social problem." Sociology, University of New Brunswick (Canada).

Funk, J. B. e. a. (2004) "Violence exposure in real-life, video games, television, movies and the internet: Is there desensitization?" Journal of Adolescence 27(1): 23.

Gadoros, J. (1990) "The 'abused' parent: Some cases of intrafamilial child to parent aggression." [Hungarian]. Psychiatria Hungarica 5(3): 195-211.

Galinsky, A. D., Magee, J. C., et al. (2006) "Power and perspectives not taken." Psychological Science 17(12): 1068-1074.

Gallagher, E. (2002) "Adult Clients with mild 'Intellectual Disability': Rethinking our assumptions." A. & N.Z. J. of Family Therapy 23(4): 202-210.

Gallagher, E. (2008) Children's violence to parents: A critical literature review. Monash Uni, Melbourne. MSocWk(Research).

Garbarino, J. (2006) See Jane Hit. London, Penguin.

Gelles, R. J. (1974) The Violent Home. California, Sage.

Gelles, R. J. (1980) "Violence in the family: A review of research in the seventies." Journal of Marriage & Family 42: 873-885.

Gelles, R. J. and Straus, M. A. (1988) Intimate Violence. New York, Simon & Schuster.

Gesell, A. and Ilg, F. (1943) Infant and Child in the Culture of Today. N.Y., Harper.

Ghaziuddin, M., Tsai, L., et al. (1991). "Brief report: Violence in Asperger syndrome, a critique." J. of Autism & Developmental Disorders 21: 349-354.

Gill, T. (2007) No Fear: Growing up in a risk averse society. London, Calouste Gulbenkian Foundation.

Glass, D. C. (1964) "Changes in liking as a means of reducing cognitive discrepancies between self-esteem and aggression." J. of Personality, 32: 531-549.

Glick, P. and Fiske, S. T. (2001) " An ambivalent alliance: Hostile and benevolnet sexism as complementary justification for gender inequality." American Psychologist 56(2): 109-118.

Goddard, H. H. (1912) The Kalikak Family: A study in the heredity of feeble-mindedness. N.Y., Macmillan.

Goldstein, J., Freud, A., & Solnit, A. J. (1973) Beyond the best interests of the child. New York: The Free Press.

Golombok, S., Cook, R., et al. (1995) "Families created by the new reproductive technologies: Quality of parenting and social and emotional development of the chidren." Child Development 66: 285-298.

González Álvarez, M. (2010) "Adolescentes que agredenen a sus padres: Caractrización de los menores agresores." Facultad de Psicología. Madrid, Universidad Complutense de Madrid. Doctorado en Psicología Clínica, Legal y Forense.

Gordon, T. (1970) Parent Effectiveness Training. N.Y., Plume.

Gordon, T. (1976) P.E.T. in Action. N.Y., Bantam.

Gosman, F. G. (1990) Spoiled Rotten: Today's children and how to change them. N.Y., Warner books.

Grandin, T. (2013) The Autistic Brain. N.Y., Houghton Mifflin Harcourt.

Greenberg, G. (2010) <u>Manufacturing Depression: The secret history of a modern disease</u>. London, Bloomsbury Pub.

Greenfield, S. (2014) <u>Mind Change</u>, Rider.

Hamilton, M. (2008) <u>What's happening to our girls?</u> London, Penguin.

Hardyment, C. (1995) <u>Perfect Parents</u>. Oxford, Oxford University Press.

Harris, J. R. (1998) <u>The Nurture Assumption: Why children turn out the way they do</u>. N.Y., Free Press.

Harvey, E. (1999) "Short-term and long-term effects of early parental employment on children of the National Longitudinal Survey of Youth." <u>Developmental Psychology</u> 35(2): 445-459.

Haste, H. (2000) <u>Mapping Britain's Moral Values</u> London: , Nestlé Family Monitor/MORI.

Hay, D. F. (2005) The beginnings of aggression in infancy.In. R. E. Tremblay, W. W. Hartup and J. Archer. <u>Developmental origins of aggression</u> N.Y., Guilford Press: 107-132.

Hays, S. (1996) <u>The Cultural Contradictiosn of Motherhood</u>. New Haven, CT, Yale Uni P.

Healy, D. (2004) <u>Let Them Eat Prozac</u>. N.Y., New York University Press.

Heinrichs, R. (2003) <u>Perfect Targets: Asperger's syndrome and bullying. </u>. Kansas, Autism Aperger Pub Co.

Henrich, J., Heine, S., et al. (2010) "The weirdest people in the world?" <u>Behav Brain Science</u> 33: 61-83.

Hershman, D. J. and Lieb, J. (1994) <u>A Brotherhood of Tyrants: Manic depression and absolute power.</u> N.Y., Prometheus Books.

Herzberger, S. D. (1996). <u>Violence within the Family: Social Psychological Perspectives</u>. Boulder, CO., Westview Press.

Hewlett, B. S. (1991) <u>Intimate Fathers: The nature and context of Aka pygmy paternal infant care</u>. Ann Arbor, Uni. of Michigan Press.

Heyman, G. (2009) <u>Addiction: A disorder of choice</u>, Harvard University Press.

Hilton, N. Z. (1992) "Battered women's concerns about their children witnessing wife assault." <u>J. of Interpersonal Violence</u> 7(1): 77-86.

Hinde, R. A. (1998) Through categories toward individuals.In. R. B. Cairns, L. R. Bergman and J. Kagan. <u>Methods and models for studying the indiviudal</u>, Sage: 11-31.

Holden, G. W. and Ritchie, K. L. (1991) "Linking extreme marital discord, child rearing and child behaviour problems: evidence from battered women." <u>Child Development</u> 62: 311-327.

Holt, A. (2011) "'The terrorist in my home': teenagers' violence towards parents – constructions of parent experiences in public online message boards." <u>Child & Family Social Work</u> 16: 454-463. .

Holt, A. (2013) <u>Adolescent-to-parent Abuse</u>. Bristol, UK, Policy Press.

Holt, J. (1974) <u>Escape from Childhood</u>. Boston, E. P. Dutton.

Honoré, C. (2008) <u>Under Pressure: How the epidemic of hyper-parenting is endangering childhood</u>. Australia, Allen & Unwin.

Hotaling, G. T. and Sugarman, D. B. (1986) "An analysis of risk markers in husband to wife violence: The current state of knowledge." <u>Violence and Victims</u> 1(2): 101-124.

Huggins-Cooper, L. (2006) Raising Teenagers. Oxford, Infinite Ideas.

Ibabe, I. and Jaureguizar, J. (2010) "Child-to-parent violence: Profile of abusive adolescents and their families." Journal of Criminal Justice 38(4).

Jaffe, P. G., Wolfe, D. A., et al. (1990) Children of Battered Women. California, Sage.

Jasinski, J. L. and Williams, L. M., Eds. (1998) Partner violence. Thousand Oaks, CA, Sage.

Jeffers, S., J (1999) I'm Okay, You're a Brat. NSW, Hodder.

Jenkins, A. (1990) Invitations to Responsibility. Adelaide, Dulwich Centre Publications.

Jenkins, A. (1991) "Interventions with violence and abuse in families." A&NZ J. of Family Therapy 12(4): 186-195.

Joseph, S. (2013) What Doesn't Kill Us: The new psychology of posttraumatic growth, Basic Books.

Kagan, J. (1998) Three Seductive Ideas. Cambridge, Mass, Harvard University Press.

Kagan, J. (2010) The Temperamental Thread: How genes, culture, time, and luck make us who we are. N.Y., Dana Press.

Kanne, S. M. and Mazurek, M. O. (2010) "Aggression in children and adolescents with ASD: Prevalence and risk factors." J. of Autism & Developmental Disorders 41: 926-937.

Kanwar, M. A. (1971) The Sociology of Family. Connecticut, Linnet Books.

Kaufman Kantor, G. and Straus, M. A. (1987) "The 'drunken bum' theory of wife beating." Social Problems 34: 213-230.

Keller, M. B. and al, e. (2000) New England J. of Medicine 342: 1462-1470.

Kethineni, S. (2004) "Youth-on-Parent Violence in a Central Illinois County." Youth Violence & Juvenile Justice 2(4): 374-394.

Kindlon, D. (2001) Too Much of a Good Thing. N.Y., Hyperion.

Kolvin, I., Miller. J. J., Fleeting, M. & Kolvin, P. A. (1988) "Risk/Protective factors for offending with particular reference to deprivation." In. M. Runnter. Studies of psychosocial risk: The power of longitudinal data N.Y., Cambridge University Press: 77-95.

Koman, A. and Myers, E. (2002) Who's the Boss? N.Y., Perigee.

Konrath, S. H., O'Brien, E. H., et al. (2011) "Changes in Dispositional Empathy in American College Students Over Time: A Meta-Analysis." Personality and Social Psychology Review 15(2): 180-198.

Kowalski, R. M., Limber, S. P., et al. (2008) Cyber Bullying. Malden, MA, Blackwell.

Krienert, J. L. W., J. A. (2011) "My Brother's Keeper: A contemporary examination of reported sibling violence." J. of Family Violence 26: 331-342.

Krista, A. (1988) Victims: surviving the aftermath of violent crime. London, Century Hutchinson.

Krueger, R. F., Johnson, W., et al. (2006) Behavoiur genetics and personality development.In. D. K. Mroczek and T. D. Little. Handbook of Personality Development Mahwah, N.J., Lawrence Erlbaum: 81-108.

Kumagai, F. (1981) "Filial violence - a peculiar parent-child relationship in the Japanese family today." J. of Comparative Family Studies 12(3): 337-349.

Lamborn, S. D., Mounts, N. S., et al. (1991) "Patterns of competence and adjustment among adolescnt from authoritative, authoritarian, indulgent, and neglectful homes." Child Development 62: 1049-1065.

Langhinrichsen-Rohling, J. and Neidig, P. (1995) "Violent backgrounds of economically disadvantaged youth: Risk factors for perpetrating violence?" J. of Family Violence 10(4): 1995.

Leach, P. (1986) Your Growing Child, 2nd ed, Borzon Books.

Lebowitz, E. R., Vitulano, L. A., et al. (2011) "Coercive and Disruptive Behaviors in Pediatric Obsessive Compulsive Disorder: A Qualitative Analysis." Psychiatry 74(4): 362-371.

Leon, I. (2002) "Adoption losses: Naturally occurring or socially constructed?" Child Development 73(2): 652-663.

Lerner, M. J. (1980) The Belief in a Just World. N.Y., Plenum Press.

Levendosky, A. A. and Graham-Bermann, S. A. (2000) "Behavioral observations of parenting in battered women." J. of Family Psychology 14(1): 80-94.

Levendosky, A. A., Lynch, J. M., et al. (1998) "The moderating effects of parenting stress in woman-abusing families." J. of Interpersonal Violence 13: 383-397.

Levine, M. (2006) The Price of Privilege. N.Y., Harper.

Levy, D. (1943) Maternal Overprotection. N.Y., Columbia University Press.

Lewinsohn, P. M. and Rosenbaum, M. (1987) "Recall of parental behaviour by actue depressives, remitted depressives, and nondepressives." J. of Personality & Social Psychology 52: 611-619.

Lewis, C. and O'Brien, M. (1987) Reassessing Fatherhood, . London, Sage Pubs.

Lewis, M. (2015) The Biology of Desire: Why addiction is not a disease. London, Scribe.

Lilienfield, S. O., Fowler, K. A., et al. (2005) "Pseudoscience, nonscience, and nonsense in clinical pscychology." In. R. H. Wright and N. A. Cummings. Destructive trends in mental health N.Y., Routledge: 187-218.

Lindberg , L., Ulfsdotter , M., et al. (2013) "The effects and costs of the universal parent group program - all children in focus: a study protocol for a randomized wait-list controlled trial." BMC Public Health. 13 (July 29): 688-.

Linn, S. (2004) Consuming Kids. N.Y., The New Press. .

Lippa, R. A. (2002) Gender, Nature and Nurture. New Jersey, Lawrence Erlbaum.

Lloyd, A. (1995) Doubly Deviant, Doubly Damned. London, Penguin.

Lomax, E. M. (1978) Science and the Patterns of Child Care. San Fransisco, W.H. Freeman.

Lykken, D. (1999) Happiness. N.Y., St. Martin's Griffin.

Maccoby, E. E. and Martin, J. A. (1983) "Socialization in the context of the family: Parent-child interaction." In. E. Hetherington. Handbook of Child Psychology, Vol 4: 1-102.

Mackay, H. (1997) Generations. Sydney, Macmillan.

Mackay, H. (2007) Advance Australia... Where? Sydney, Hachette.

Magid, K. and McKelvey, C. A. (1987) High Risk: children without a conscience. N.Y., Bantam.

Mahoney, A. R. and Knudson-Martin, C. (2009) "Gender equality in Intimate relationships." In. C. Knudson-Martin and A. R. Mahoney. Couples, Gender and Power N.Y., Springer: 3-16.

Maier, T. (1998) Dr. Spock: An American life. Orlando, Florida, Harcourt Brace.

Marano, H. E. (2008) A Nation of Wimps. N.Y., Doubleday Broadway.

Martin, B. and Hoffman, J. A. (1990) "Conduct disorders." In. M. Lewis and S. M. Miller. Handbook of developmental psychopathology N.Y., Plenum Press: 109-118.

Masson, J. (1984) The Assault on Truth. London, Fontana.

May, J. (1958) A Physician Looks at Psychiatry. N.Y., John Day.

Mayo, E. (2005) Shopping Generation. London, NCC.

McBride Dabbs, J. (2000) Heroes, Rogues and Lovers. N.Y., McGraw-Hill.

McCord, J. (1991) "Questioning the Value of Punishment." Social Problems 38(2): 167-179.

McDonald, P. (1995) Families in Australia. Victoria, Australia, Australian Institute of Family Studies.

McInnes, J. (1995). Violence within families: the challenge of preventing adolescent violence towards parents. Adelaide SA, The Office for Families and Children.

Media Violence Commission (2012) "Report of the Media Violence Commission." Aggressive Behaviour 38: 335-341.

Mednick, S. A., Gabrielli, W. F., et al. (1884) "Genetic influences in criminal convictions:evidence from an adoption cohort." Science 224: 891-894.

Mercer, J., Sarner, L., et al. (2003) Attachment therapy on trial: The torture and death of Candace Nemaker. Westport, CT, Praeger.

Milgram, S. (1974) Obedience to Authority. . New York, Harper & Row.

Miller, J. and Knudsen, D. D. (2007) Family Abuse and Violence Plymouth, UK. , AltaMira Press. .

Mintz, S. (2004) Huck's Raft: A history of American childhood. Harvard, Belknap Harvard.

Molina, S. G., Brooke, S. G., et al. (2009) "The MTA at 8 years: prospective follow-up of children treated for combined-type ADHD in a multisite study." Journal of the American Academy of Child & Adolescent Psychiatry, 48, : 484-500.

Montes, G. and Halterman, J. S. (2007) "Bullying among children with autism and the influence of comorbidity with ADHD: A population-based study." Ambulatory Pediatrics 7: 253-257.

Morgan, P. (1974) Childcare, Ssense and fable. London, Maurice Temple Smith.

Morrow, R. L., Garland, E. J., et al. (2012) "Influence of relative age on diagnosis and treatment of attention-deficit/hyperactivity disorder in children." CMAJ 184(7): 755-762.

Murphy-Edwards, L. J. (2012) Not just another hole in the wall: An investigation into child and youth perpetrated dometic property violence. University of Canterbury. Doctor of Philosophy.

Nagin, D. S., & Tremblay, R. E. (1999). Trajectories of boys' physical aggression, opposition, and hyperactivity on the path to physically violent and nonviolent juvenile delinquency. Child Development, 70, 1181–1196.

Nathan, D. and Snedeker, M. (1995) Satan's Silence: Ritual abuse and the making of a modern American witch hunt. N.Y., Basic Books.

NCA Action for Children. (1995) The Hidden Victims: Children and domestic violence. London, NCH Action for Children.

Nelson, J. (1999) Positive Discipline for Single Parents, 2nd edition. California, Prima Publications.

O'Brien, M., John, R. S., et al. (1994) "Reliability and diagnostic efficacy of parents' reports regarding children's exposure to marital aggression." Violence & Victims 9: 45-62.

O'Guinn, T. and Shrum, L. J. (1997) "The role of television in the construciton of cunsumer reality." J. of Consumer Resaerch 24: 278-294.

O'Keefe, M. (1994) "Adjustment of children from maritally violent homes." Families in Society(Sept): 403-415.

Offer, D., Rostov, E., et al. (1984) Patterns of Adolescent Self Image. San Francisco., Jossey-Bass.

Offer & Schonert-Reichl (1992) "Debunking the myths of adolescences: Findings from recent research". J. of American Academy of Child & Adolescent Psychiatry, 31,1003-14.

Olatunji, B. O., Lohr, J. M., et al. (2007) "The pseudopsychology of venting int eh treatment of anger." In. T. A. Cavell and K. T. Malcom. Anger, aggression, and interentions for interpersonal violence Mahwah, NJ, Lawrence Erlbaum: 119-141.

Olweus, D. (1991) "Bully/victim problems among schoolchildren." In. D. J. Pepler and K. H. Rubin. The Development and treatment of childhood aggression Hillsdale, N.J., L. Erlbaum Associates: xvii, 470.

Olweus, D. (1993) Bullying at School. Oxford, UK, Blackwell.

Omer, H. (2000) Parental Presence. Phoenix, Zeig, Tucker & Co.

Omer, H. (2004) Nonviolent Resistance: A new approach to violent and self-destructive children. Cambridge, UK, Cambridge University Press.

Orme, N. (2001) Medieval Children. New Haven, Yale University Press.

Palmer, S. (2007) Toxic Childhood: How the modern world is damaging our children and what we can do about it. London, Orion.

Paris, J. (2000) Myths of Childhood. NY, Routledge.

Patterson, G. R. (1982) A social learning approach, Vol 3: Coercive Family Process. Eugene, OR, Castalia Press.

Patterson, G. R., DeBaryshe, B. D., et al. (1989) "A developmental perspective on antisocial behavior." American Psychologist 44(2): 329-335.

Patterson, G. R. and Dishion, t. J. (1988) "Multilevel family process models: Traits, interactions, and relationships." In. R. A. Hinde and J. Stevenson-Hinde. Relationships within families: Mutual influences Oxford, Clarendon: 283-310.

Paul, P. (2008) Parenting, Inc. N.Y., Times Books.

Pinker, S. (2002) The Blank Slate. London, Penguin.

Pinker, S. (2011) The Better Angels of our Nature. London, Allen Lane.

Pleck, E. (1987) Domestic Tyranny. N.Y., Oxford Uni Press.

Pollak, R. (1997) The Creation of Dr. B. N.Y., Touchstone.

Potter-Efron, R. T. and Potter-Effron, P. S. (1985) "Family violence as a tratment issue with chemically dependent adolescents." Alcoholism Treatment Quarterly 2: 1-15.

Quint, F. L. (2005) "From despair to hope: A mother's Asperger story." In. K. P. Stoddart. Children, youth and adults with Asperger syndrome. London, Jessica Kingsley.

Raine, A. (2013) The Anatomy of Violence. Toronto, Random House.

Regalado, F. L. (2004) "The problem of child on parent domestic violence: A multi-modal, multi-family intervention model." Florida, Carlos Albizu University: 114 pages; AAT 3150905.

Rheingold, J. C. (1964) The Fear of Being a Woman: A theory of maternal destructiveness. N.Y., Grune & Stratton.

Rhule, D. M. (2005) "Take care to do no harm: Harmful interventions for youth problem behavior." Professional Psychology: Research and Practice 36(6): 618-625.

Rigby, K. (2002) New Perspectives on Bullying. London, Jessica Kingsley.

Rizzo, K. M., Schiffrin, H. H., et al. (2013) "Insight into the Parenthood Paradox: Mental Health Outcomes of Intensive Mothering." J. of Child & Family Studies 22(5): 614-620.

Roazen, P. (1979) Freud and his Followers, Knopf.

Rosemond, J. K. (2005) "The diseasing of America's children: The politics of diagnosis." In. R. H. Wright and N. A. Cummings. Destructive trends in mental health N.Y., Routledge: 219-234.

Rosenthal, P. A. and Doherty, M. B. (1985) "Psychodynamics of delinquent girls rage and violence directed toward mother." Adolescent Psychiatry 12: 281-289.

Rothbart, M. K., Ahadi, S. A., et al. (1994) "Temperament and social behaviour." Merril-Palmer Quarterly 40: 21-39.

Routt, G. and Anderson, L. (2011) "Adolescent violence towards parents." J. of Aggression, Maltreatment & Trauma 20: 1-19.

Routt, G. and Anderson, L. (2015) Adolescent Violence in the Home. NY, Routledge.

Roy, M. (1977) Battered women: A psychosociological study of domestic violence. . N.Y., Van Nostrand Reinhold.

Rubin, C. (1996) Don't Let Your Kids Kill You: A guide for parents of drug and alcohol addicted children. Rockport, MA, Element Books.

Ruskin, G. (1999) "Why they whine?: How corporations prey on our children." Mothering, Nov-Dec,: 41-50.

Rutter, M. (1982) Maternal Deprivation Reassessed, 2nd ed. Londong, Penguin.

Rutter, M. (1993) Developing Minds. London, Penguin.

Rutter, M. (2002) "Nature, nurture and development: From evangelism through science toward policy and practice." Child Development 73: 1-21.

Sapolsky, R. M. (1997) The Trouble with Testosterone. N.Y., Simon & Schuster.

Scarr, S. and Dunn, J. (1987) Mothercare/Othercare. Middlesex, England, Penguin Books.

Schachter, S. and SInger, J. (1962) "Cognitive, social and phsyiological determinants of emotional state." Psychological Review 69: 379-399.

Schaffer, H. R. (2000) "The early experience assumption: Past, present, and future." International Society for the Study of Behavioural Development 24(1): 5-14.

Schlegel, A. and Barry, H. (1991) Adolescence: an anthropological inquiry. NY, Free Press.

Schor, J. B. (2004) Born to Buy: The commercialized child and the new commercial culture. N.Y., Scribners.

Selwyn, J., Wijedasa, D., et al. (2014) Beyond the Adoption Order: challenges, interventions and adoption disruption. England, Department of Education https://www.gov.uk/government/uploads/system/uploads/attachment_data/file/301 889/Final_Report_-_3rd_April_2014v2.pdf.

Shannon, A. (2005) "Beloved stranger: temperament and the elusive concept of normality." Psychotherapy Networker 29(3 (May/June)): 63-69.

Sharma, A., McGue, M., et al. (1998) "The psychological adjustment of US adoptive adolescents and their non-adopted siblings." Child Development 69: 791-802.

Shaw, R. (2003) The Epidemic. . N.Y., Regan Books.

Simmons, R. (2002) Odd girl out: The hidden culture of aggression in girls. Orlando, Fl, Harcourt.

Simons, R. L., Johnson, C., et al. (1993) "Explaining women's double jeopardy: factors that mediate the association between harsh treatment as a child and violence by a husband." J. of Marriage and the Family 55: 713-723.

Singer, M. A., Gatz, M., et al. (1998) "Childhood adoption: Longterm effectws on adulthood." Psychiatry 61: 191-205.

Skenazy, L. (2009) Free-range Kids. San Francisco, CA, Wiley.

Small, L. L. (1999) Maybe Mother Did Know Best. N.Y., Avon.

Smart, E. (1984) "Parents in the closet. (parent abuse by teenagers)" Victimology 9(3/4): 304-307.

Smith, J., O'Connor, I., et al. (1996) "The effects of witnessing domestic violence on young children's psycho-social adjustment." Australian Social Work 49(4): 3-10.

Snyder, H. N. M., C (2008) "Domestic Assaults by Juvenile Offenders." Office of Justice & Delinquency Prevention Nov 2008(www.ojp.usdof.gov): 1-8.

Somerfield, D. P. (1989). "The origins of mother blaming: Historical perspectives on childhood and motherhood." Infant Mental Health Journal 10(1): 14-24.

Sommers, C. H. and Satel, S. (2005). One Nation Under Therapy: How the helping culture is eroding self-reliance. New York, St. Martin's Griffin.

Spaccarelli, S., Sandler, I. N., et al. (1994) "History of spouse violence against mother: correlated risks and unique effects in child mental health." J. of Family Violence 9: 79-98.

Spitz, R. (1965) The First Year of Life, . N.Y., International Universities Press.

Squires, P. and Stephen, D. E. (2005) Rougher Justice. Cullompton, Devon, UK, Willan.

Stattin, H. and Kerrr, M. (2000) "Parental monitoring: A reinterpretation." Child Development 71: 1072-1985.

Steinberg, S. R. and Kincheloe, J. L. (1997) "No more secrets - kinderculture, information saturation and the postmodern childhood." In. S. R. Steinberg and J. L. Kincheloe. Kinder-culture: The corporate construction of childhood Boulder, Lolerado, Westview.

Sternberg, K. J., Lamb, M. E., et al. (1993) "Effects of domestic violence on children's behaviour problems and depression." Developmental Psychology 29: 44-52.

Stith, S. M. and Farley, S. C. (1993) "A predictive model of male spousal violence." J. of Family Violence 8(2): 183-201.

Stoneman, Z., Brody, G. H., et al. (1984) "Naturalistic observations of childrens' activities and roles while playing with their siblings and friends." Child Development 55: 617-627.

Strauch, B. (2010) Secrets of the Grown-up Brain, Black Inc.

Streatfield, D. (2007) Cocaine: An definitive history, London, Virgin Books.

Summers, G. and Feldman, N. S. (1984) "Blaming the victim versus blaming the perpetrator: An attributional analysis of spouse abuse." J. of Social & Clinical Psychology 2(4): 339-347.

Sutherland, S. (1992) Irrationality. London, Penguin.

Symonds, A. (1979) "Violence against women - The myth of masochism." J. of American Psychotherapy 33: 161-173.

Thornton, E. M. (1983) The Freudian fallacy. Dial Press.

Torrey, E. F. (1992) Freudian Fraud. N.Y. HarperCollins.

Travis, C. (1982) Anger: The misunderstood emotion. N.Y., Simon & Schuster.

Twenge, J. M. (2014) Generation Me. N.Y., Atria.

Twenge, J. M. and Campbell, W. K. (2009) The Narcissism Epidemic. N.Y., Simon & Schuster.

Ungar, M. (2008) Too Safe for their Own Good: How risk and rsponsibility help teens thrive. NSW, Allen & Unwin.

Utech, M. R. (1994) Violence, Abuse and Neglect: The American home. N.Y., General Hall.

Vaillancourt, T. (2005) "Indirect aggression among humans." In. R. E. Tremblay, W. W. Hartup and J. Archer. Developmental Origins of Aggression N.Y., Guilford Press: 158-177.

Vaillant, G. E. and Milofsky, E. S. (1982) "The etiologyof alcoholism: A prospective view." American Psychologist 37: 492-503.

Van Goozen, S. H. M. (2005) "Hormones and the developmental orgins of aggression." In. R. E. Tremblay, W. W. Hartup and J. Archer. Developmental Origins of Aggression N.Y., Guilford Press: 281-306.

van Roekel, E., Scholte, R. H., et al. (2010) "Bullying among adolescents with autism spectrum disorders: prevalence and perception." J. of Autism & Developmental Disorders 40: 63-73.

Veenstra-Vanderweele, J., Christian, S. l., et al. (2004) "Autism as a paradigmatic complex genetic disorder." Annual Review of Genomics & Human Genetics 5: 379-405.

Vitaro, F. and Brendgen, M. (2005) "Proactive and reactive aggression." In. R. E. Tremblay, W. W. Hartup and J. Archer. Developmental origins of aggression N.Y., Guilford Press: 178-201.

Volavka, J. (1995) Neurobiology of Violence. Washington, D.C., American Psychiatric Press.

Walker, S. (1996). A Dose of Sanity: Mind, Medicine, and Misdiagnosis. N.Y., John Wiley.

Watson, J. B. (1928) <u>Psychological Care of Infant and Child,</u> . N.Y. , Norton.

Webster, R. (1985) <u>Why Freud was Wrong.</u> London, Fontana.

Weisner, T. S. and Gallimore, R. (1977) "My brother's keeper: Child and sibling caretaking." <u>Current Anthropology</u> 18(2): 169-191.

Wilcox, P. (2006) <u>Surviving Domestic Violence</u>. Hampshire, UK, Palgravce Macmillan.

Wilson, J. (1996). "Physical abuse of parents by adolescent children". In. D. M. Busby. <u>The impact of violence on the family: Treatment approaches for therapists and other professionals</u> Massachusetts, Allyn & Bacon: 101-123.

Wolfe, D., Jaffe, P., et al. (1985) "Children of battered women: The relation of child behavior to family violence and maternal stress." <u>J. of Consulting & Clinical Psychology</u> 53: 657-665.

Yapko, M. D. (1994) <u>Suggestions of Abuse</u>. N.Y., Simon & Schuster.

Zimmerman, F. J., Glew, G. M., et al. (2005) "Early cognitive stimulation, emotional support and TV watching as predictors of subsequent bullying among grade-school children." <u>Archives of Pediatric & Adolescent Medicine</u> 159: 384-388.

Endnotes

[1] Eyer (1996) p102. By a meaningless coincidence I had a Grandma Minnie and an Aunt Ellen.

[2] *"Not to put too fine a point on it, but much of the advice from the parenting experts is flapdoodle."* Pinker (2002) p384.

[3] E.g. see Harris (1998), Amber (1992), Kagan (1998), Rutter (1993).

[4] E.g. Utech (1994) p198.

[5] Langhinrichsen-Rohling (1995).

[6] From "Teen Health" on About.com, emphasis added, http://teenhealth.about.com/od/relationships/a/cycleofabuse.htm accessed Oct 2015.

[7] Holt (2013) p47.

[8] Cable (1972) p182.

[9] My Master's thesis Gallagher (2008) is available on my website if you are interested in the more technical stuff.

[10] Details in my thesis. Studies since then have had similar results. Clinical studies, legal samples and qualitative research studies are all fairly similar and overall now add up to a metasample of several thousand giving an overall figure of around 70% boys. I've found only one non-survey study which found equal numbers of boys and girls, a sample referred to Protective Services in England, Biehal, N. (2012).

[11] E.g. Hays (1996).

[12] 24% in the first two hundred families in my sample, up to 36% in the most recent two families.

[13] Hays (1996).

[14] The Aka pigmies appear to be the most involved fathers of any culture. But even they don't do as much as mothers. And despite their cultural expectations that childcare is men's work as much as women, Aka grandmothers hold babies one hundred times more than do Aka grandfathers (Hewlett, 1991).

[15] Brooks (2011).

[16] For example, Hotaling (1986), 'in reviewing the literature, suggests that over two hundred reports of Intimate Partner Violence have found higher rates associated with lower educational level.' The association is even stronger for child abuse. There's a more detailed discussion of this in my Master's Thesis, Gallagher (2008), on my website.

[17] Gallagher 2008 has a chapter summarizing this evidence.

[18] E.g. Hays (1996) says: "stronger tendency of middle-class mothers to focus on negotiating and reasoning with their children, whereas working-class and poor mothers are somewhat more likely to emphasize the importance of giving their children set rules." p93.

[19] Routt & Anderson (2011) in the USA and González Álvarez (2010) in Spain (also had correspondence with both).

[20] It is a scandal the way the drug companies, aided by some clinicians, have pushed the label of bi-polar onto many children and given them drugs untested on growing brains. More in chapter on Labels.

[21] Details in Gallagher (2008). Most of the studies showing this are surveys, which are admittedly of doubtful validity. However, American crime statistics also back the fact that Anglo kids abuse their parents more than black kids, e.g. Snyder (2008). In Spain immigrant children have higher crime rates overall but lower rates of violence to parents. My own work in a highly multi-ethnic part of Melbourne would also tend to suggest that violence to parents is more common among Anglo families.

[22] I've tested thirty-five child-abused parents recently on the Big 5 personality test. All but one were above average on Agreeableness and a few got the maximum possible score. All but three were also average or above on Conscientiousness.

[23] The British neuroscientist Susan Greenfield thinks children's brains are being altered by electronics, e.g. Greenfield 2014.

[24] "There will never be an accepted or acceptable definition of abuse, because abuse is not a scientific or clinical term. Rather, it is a political concept." Gelles (1988).

[25] I've found a few mentions of violence by toddlers in anthropology books but only one or two mentions of violence by older children, in very different circumstances and by pre-adolescents rather than teens.

[26] E.g. see Hay (2005).

[27] Pinker (2011) p345.

[28] Rosemond (2005) p230.

[29] Summers (1984).

[30] Pleck (1987), Symonds (1979).

[31] "Another theme which women [DV victims] mentioned frequently was their perception that agency workers viewed them with suspicion and/or blamed them in some way for the violence, this was especially the case in relation to their children." Wilcox (2006) p161.

[32] Lerner (1980).

[33] Skenazy (2009) p56.

[34] "The victim of undeserved suffering runs the clear risk of being condemned by those who witness his or her fate" Lerner (1980) p70.

[35] Milgram (1974) p10.

[36] "As a result of repeated attacks and degrading comments, the victim will gradually be perceived as a fairly worthless person who almost 'begs to be beaten up' and who deserves to be harassed. Such changes in perception also combine to a weakening of possible guilt feelings in the bullies." Olweus (1993) p45.

[37] Cognitive dissonance theory says we try to eliminate contradictions. a) I did a bad thing to this person, b) I'm not a bad person. These two ideas are dissonant and we can sort this in our heads by adding c) they must deserve it, they must be a bad person. There is research evidence to support this idea, e.g. Glass (1964).

[38] Krista (1988) p66.

[39] Gelles (1980).

[40] Caplan (1981) p45.

[41] Caplan (1985).

[42] Cloud (1996) p13.

[43] Caplan (1994) p39.

[44] Hart and Teeter/NBC/Wall Street Journal, 6/1999.

[45] in Boehlich (1990) This is not an isolated remark, he also said: *"In the depths of my heart I can't help being convinced that my dear fellow men, with a few exceptions, are worthless."* Roazen (1979) p 163. His negativity flows through his entire theory. It has even been suggested that he was paranoid Farrell (1996).
Some excellent Freud-bashing books: Esterton (1993), Thornton (1983), Torrey (1992), Webster (1985).

[46] 'Hysteria' is an obsolete category which would then have included all sorts of mental and physical ailments (physical ailments that in those days often went undiagnosed and untreated).

[47] The image of Freud as a laid-back therapist listening patiently to his patients outpouring doesn't fit with accounts of his methods. He was directive, forceful and arrogant in pushing his ideas on his patients. *"One only succeeds in awakening the psychical trace of a precocious sexual event under the most energetic pressure"* admitted Freud (cited by Masson (1984) p 91. Freud once complained to a colleague that he was *'almost hoarse'* from pressuring patients to accept his interpretations for ten or eleven hours a day (*Standard edition of the complete psychological works of Sigmund Freud, Vol 3*, London: Hogarth Press, p 153.)

[48] Freud, S 1884 'Über Coca', *Centralblatt für die ges. Therapie*, 2, pp. 289–314. Freud has even been given credit for popularising cocaine as a recreational drug: Streatfield (2007)*: "if there is one person who can be held responsible for the emergence of cocaine as a recreational pharmaceutical, it was Freud."* He did have a big impact on our culture!

[49] Rheingold (1964) p25.

[50] Ibid.

[51] Spitz (1965) p206.

[52] Freud in *The Psychology of Women*. New Introductory Lectures in Psychoanalysis, Ch. 5.

[53] Here's a typical example: *"A child's disappointment in the love object [mother], imagined or real rejection, or possible object loss, leads to insufficient available libidinal energy to neutralize or bind the aggressive impulses."* Rosenthal (1985).

[54] Dolnick (1998) p294.

[55] Levine (2006) p202.

[56] Caplan (1985).

[57] Bruer (1999), Krueger (2006), Snyder (2008).

[58] Lewinshn (1987).

[59] Dawes (2001) p131.

[60] Vaillant (1982).

[61] *"It is typical for adults who were neglected as children – and become unattached children – to deny that their mothers were cruel to them."* Magid (1987) p16.

[62] E.g. *"Jeremy has no conscious memory of the painful events that occurred when he was eleven weeks old, although bringing those events to a conscious level and dealing with the rage inside is the primary task of his therapist."* Magid (1987) p215. The brain of an eleven week old baby is so different to a fully developed brain that it is impossible to recall such events, but not impossible to believe you recall them.

[63] There are a number of scary books on this shameful and bizarre era of group hysteria in the counselling field, e.g.:
Nathan (1995), Crews (1995), Campbell (1998); Yapko (1994).

[64] Witches were accused of eating babies back in the Middle Ages. Early Christians were accused of eating babies by the Romans and Crusaders were similarly accused. Jews have been often accused at various times of eating babies from the middle ages up to Nazi Germany, this is known as the "blood libel."

[65] Pinker (2011).

[66] *"I do not think a week's holiday away from your child is worth the inevitable upset."* (Times Ed Sup, 14 Jan 1972).

[67] This outrageous claim was made in the aptly entitled, *"Beyond the best interests of the child"*, by Goldstein, Freud, & Solnit (1973). This book was until recently on lots of University reading lists. *"in infancy, any change in routine leads to food refusals, digestive upsets, sleeping difficulties and crying. Such reactions occur even if the infant's care is divided merely between mother and babysitter. They are all the more massive where the infant's day is divided between home and day care centre."* (p 32).

[68] Rutter (1993) p120.

[69] Weisner (1977).

[70] Henrich (2010).

[71] Scarr (1987) p71.

[72] Veenstra-Vanderweele (2004).

[73] Bettelheim (1967).

[74] Pollak (1997).

[75] Dolnick (1998) p184.

[76] Dolnick (1998) p194.

[77] Bettelheim (1967) p163.

[78] May (1958).

[79] Bateson (1956).

[80] *"the enormously influential double bind theory was based not on a large number of observations of schizophrenic patients and their families, or even on a small number, but on no observations at all."* Dolnick (1998) p122.

[81] Dolnick (1998) p165.

[82] Stattin (2000).

[83] Herzberger (1996) p15.

[84] McInnes (1995) p3.

[85] Brezina (1999) p418.

[86] Caplan (1981) p5/6.

[87] Somerfield (1989) p20.

[88] From UK Parentline report "Aggressive behaviour in children: parents' experiences and needs" 2008, p21.

[89] Hardyment (1995), Beekman (1977).

[90] There's a good review of all three in Hays (1996).

[91] Orme (2001).

[92] Holt, L. E. 1903 quoted in Beekman (1977) p117.

[93] Watson (1928).

[94] Ibid p 87.

[95] One notable exception was Arnold Gesell, one of the foremost child psychologists pre-War who preached democratic parenting, Gesell (1943).

[96] H. H. Goddard was one of the most influential in the American eugenics movement and his books were popular in Nazi Germany. He suggested that all 'the

feebleminded' should be castrated or have their ovaries removed and bemoaned the fact that the public had an 'irrational' aversion to this! Goddard (1912).

[97] Lykken (1999) p236.

[98] Harris (1998), Morgan (1975), Rutter (1982).

[99] Lomax (1978) p64, quoting Reid in *Parents' Magazine. 25: 44-45 May 1950.*

[100] Reid in *Parents' Magazine 1950 quoted in* Lomax (1978) p66.

[101] In 2000 a ten-year-old girl, Candace Newmaker, died as the result of 'rebirthing' by so-called 'Attachment Therapists'. *"The techniques used by attachment therapists to ostensibly remediate children's problem behaviour rare invasive and aggressive, often involving restraint, shouting, and humiliation. Some of the major attachment therapy techniques include 'holding therapy' in which therapists restrain children for minutes to hours at a time and shout threats and taunts at them; 'therapeutic foster care,' in which children stay full time with an attachment therapist who enforces military style ritualized discipline; and discipline techniques involving intense physical labor and deprivation of food, sleep, and education."* Lilienfield (2005) p197.
For a more detailed account see: Mercer (2003).

[102] Maier (1998).

[103] Beekman (1977) p xiv.

[104] Caplan (1981) p105.

[105] Dreikurs (1964) p14.

[106] Ibid p129.

[107] Ibid p137.

[108] Ibid p63.

[109] Ibid p63.

[110] Ibid p64.

[111] Ibid p66.

[112] Ibid p68.

[113] Ibid p239.

[114] Ibid p250.

[115] Ibid p250.

[116] Ibid p258.

[117] Ibid p185.

[118] Ibid p136.

[119] Nelson (1999) p153.

[120] Gordon (1970) p248.

[121] Bennett & Rowe (2003) p47.

[122] Maier (1998).

[123] Pollak (1997).

[124]

http://www.guardian.co.uk/books/2008/jun/01/mentalhealth.society?INTCMP=SRCH
A surprising number of male parenting gurus appear to have been pretty poor fathers.

[125] Dobson (1970): The part about hitting them for crying because you've hit them is page 38 of the 1980 Bantam edition.

[126] Leviticus 20:9: "If there is anyone who curses his father or his mother, he shall surely be put to death."

[127] *"Respondents consistently see others in their immediate environment as the cause of their anger."* Olatunji (2007) p80.

[128] *"The impression one gets from reading many ethnographies is that conflict and antagonism between adolescents and parents in most traditional societies are not, in fact, serious problems. Adolescents do not struggle to individuate themselves from the family to the degree that Western young people do: their dependency on their families, or their spouses, will continue even after they reach adulthood, and much of their economic well-being is likely to come from their contribution to group effort rather than from independent action."* Schlegel (1991) p62.

[129] *"It has been shown that people are so facile at making up explanations that they can use almost any event in a person's past life to explain why he did something later on. Subjects were given a genuine potted biography of a man and were then asked to explain something he did subsequently in terms of his previous history: for example they might be asked to account for his committing suicide, having a hit-and-run accident, joining the Peace Corps or becoming a politician. ... e.g. joining the navy earlier in life, if he was described as having become a politician then this was seen as a sign of a gregarious nature, if suicide this was seen as running away from his family and friends and wanting to punish them..., each subject thought on the basis of the biography that the event he had been asked to explain was the most likely."* Sutherland (1992) p153.

[130] Steinberg (1997) p20.

[131] Twenge (2014) p4.

[132] *"The isolation of adolescents from informal contact with adults outside the home, except for authority figures, is a modern phenomenon and is extreme in the US."* Alice Schlegel, Anthropologist, private correspondence 2 Jan 2016.

[133] Schlegel (1991).

[134] Brooks (2008) p9.

[135] Schor (2004) p20.

[136] Hamilton (2008) p4.

[137] Schor (2004) p170.

[138] Christakis (2004) found increased TV viewing between one to three years resulted in increased rates of attentional problems at age seven.

[139] Zimmerman (2005).

[140] Schor (2004) p183.

[141] *"survey of US social networking sites among an adolescent cohort aged 12-19, data indicated that they overwhelmingly chose negative rather than positive adjectives to describe how people act on social networking sites, including 'rude, fake, crude, over-dramatic and disrespectful'"* Greenfield (2014) p36.

[142] Narcisism: Buffardi (2008). Individualism: Greenfield (2014).

[143] I've been giving an attitude questionnaire to workers coming to my training sessions and only about a third agree that media has any influence on violence to parents, although 80% believe that violence to parents is increasing.

[144] Paris (2000) p59.

[145] O'Guinn (1997).

[146] Mayo (2005) p3.

[147] Murphy-Edwards (2012) p163.

[148] Linn (2004), Brooks (2008), Paul (2008).

[149] Nancy Shalek, president of the Shalek Agency, in Ruskin (1999).

[150] Linn (2004) p230.

[151] Both quoted in Douglas (2004) p277.

[152] Twenge (2009) p83.

[153] You can access a lecture on the Science of Greed by Berkeley Psychologist Paul Piff: http://truthseekerdaily.com/2013/10/take-two-normal-people-add-money-to-just-one-of-them-and-watch-what-happens-next/

[154] E.g. Levine (2006) *"So why are children from financially secure homes exhibiting epidemic levels of emotional distress?"* p 21. Yet another epidemic!

[155] Ambert (2001) p201.

[156] Schor (2004) p202.

[157] Schor (2004).

[158] In UK: Haste (2000) p7 In the USA: Greenberg/Quinlan Democracy Corps, 12/99. http://www.frameworksinstitute.org/toolkits/canp/resources/pdf/DisciplineAndDevelopment.pdf

[159] Cottrell (2004) p91.

[160] Koman (2002) p154.

[161] Hamilton (2008) p54.

[162] Hamilton (2008) p53.

[163] Garbarino (2006) p102.

[164] Dill (2009) p67.

[165] For a review see: Anderson (2003).

[166] Media Violence Commission (2012), Dill (2009).

[167] Anderson (2003).

[168] These figures are probably much higher by the time you read this. Senate Committee on the Judiciary. *Children, violence, and the media: a report for parents and policy makers.* September 14, 1999.

[169] Steinberg (1997) p22.

[170] Funk (2004).

[171] Dill (2009) p20.

[172] Pinker (2011) argues convincingly that society has become less violent. There are a number of factors, including parenting, less poverty, smaller families, less physical punishment, which are acting to lower the overall amount of violence. Acting against this are the influence of media and drugs.

[173] The Telegraph, 12 Sep 2006. http://www.telegraph.co.uk/news/1528639/Modern-life-leads-to-more-depression-among-children.html.

[174] Sommers (2005) p23.

[175] Rutter (2002) p15.

[176] Maccoby (1983).

[177] E.g. "During the half-century between 1880 and 1930, parent-child relations underwent a profound transformation. Middle-class family life grew more democratic, affectionate, and child-centered..." Mintz (2004) p215. This is the general impression I get from my reading on the history of childhood and families and from parent advice books.

[178] Those attending my workshops are probably focusing on control over misbehaviour and disrespect, given the topic. In terms of protectiveness many are no doubt more controlling than previous generations. There's a chapter on Overprotection later.

[179] Gill (2007) p12. The report mentioned was: Future Foundation, *The changing face of parenting* London: Future Foundation (2006).

[180] Jeffers (1999) p133.

[181] Baumrind 1971).

[182] Dornbusch (1987).

[183] Levine (2006) p129.

[184] Small (1999) p xv.

[185] Koman (2002) call these parents 'Flexible' in contrast to 'Inflexible' or Authoritarian parents. However, any style of parenting can be done in a more or less flexible manner.

[186] Baumrind (1996).

[187] E.g. Baumrind (1989).

[188] Gosman (1990) p144.

[189] Dornbusch (1987).

[190] Lamborn (1991).

[191] Levine (2006) p131.

[192] Mackay (1997) p130

[193] ibid p192.

[194] Olweus (1991) p425.

[195] Hinde (1998).

[196] Marano (2008) p4.

[197] Baumrind (1996) p412.

[198] Mackay (2007).

[199] Hays (1996).

[200] Arendell (2000) The link with social class appears to be getting weaker as these ideas spread down to less educated and poorer parents (e.g. Craig (2013).

[201] Rizzo (2013).

[202] Craig (2013) Also: *"Data from 20 industrialised countries from 1965 to 2003 show an overall cross-country increase in men's proportional contribution to family work from less than one fifth to more than a third"* Mahoney (2009) p4.

[203] Holt (2013) p68.

[204] Holt (1974).

[205] Honoré (2008) p8.

[206] Marano (2008) p4.

[207] Levy (1943).

[208] Skenazy (2009) p8.

[209] Honoré (2008) p5.

[210] Gill (2007) p77.

[211] *"although reported and recorded crime were generally falling and have continued to fall... larger and larger percentages appear to believe crime is increasing."* Squires (2005) p15.

[212] Skenazy (2009) p193.

[213] Ungar (2008) p106.

[214] Pinker (2011).

[215] Marano (2008) p12.

[216] Marano (2008) p180. *"Think of the cell phone as the eternal umbilicus. It is the new and pervasive instrument of overprotection."*

[217] Skenazy (2009) p19.

[218] See for example: Harris (1998).

[219] Marano (2008) p2.

[220] Skenazy (2009) p xxi.

[221] Marano (2008) p3.

[222] Levine (2006).

[223] The Japanese call stay-at-home young people Hikikomori and there are estimates of tens of thousands of their young people adopting such lifestyles. I believe we are seeing an increase in such young people in Australia and with greater internet connectivity and more addictive games, this is likely to get much worse.

[224] Honoré (2008) p12.

[225] Levy (1943) p161.

[226] Felson (1988).

[227] http://www.sylviarimm.com/article_protecting.html accessed Jan 2016.

[228] There is a very good, entertaining yet disturbing, book called "Perfect Parents" (Hardyment 1995) which traces the horrible history of advice to parents over the past hundred years or so.

[229] Kindlon (2001) p23.

[230] This is an example of a wider issue. You cannot say what is truly rational behaviour unless you first declare what are your goals. You can only be rational towards a goal and the selection of the goal is almost always an emotional and moral choice. Most of us would agree that it isn't rational to be totally greedy or totally hedonistic… but what about being totally self-sacrificing or totally devoted to the pursuit of knowledge. Is having kids ever rational? Why should we give up so much time and money just to produce another human when there are already billions more than are healthy for the environment? Applying science to human lives always entails political or moral choices and these are often taken for granted rather than made explicit. So most writers about parenting assume that they know what the goal of childrearing is without ever spelling this out.

[231] E.g. Harvey (1999).

[232] Caplan (1981) p25.

[233] Kindlon (2001) p24.

[234] Small (1999) p72.

[235] The term "good enough parent" is usually attributed to the English psychoanalyst David Winnicot. This is surprising as the idea seems to fly in the face of psychoanalytic theory and the approach of most analysts, who are consummate mother-blamers. However, Winnicot was less nutty than most of his colleagues and would have made a great psychologist if he hadn't fallen under the sway of the psychoanalytic cult.

[236] Marano (2008) p10.

[237] Quoted in Kanwar (1971) p141.

[238] McDonald (1995) p16.

[239] Coontz (1992) p230.

[240] Rutter (2002).

[241] Lewis (1987) p168.

[242] Singer et al. (1998).

[243] Leon (2002).

[244] Sharma (1998).

[245] Golombok (1995).

[246] Selwyn (2014).

[247] Ibid p183.

[248] Ibid p193.

[249] E.g Abramovich (1986) Found first-borns to be more aggressive with peers while Stoneman (1984) found that dominance by first-borns was only a factor within the

family. Such wishy-washy results suggest that birth order is not a major factor outside the family.

[250] Altogether these families contained seven hundred children, so 40% were first born.

[251] Kethineni (2004) p388 Most studies have not looked at this but Kumagai (1981) in Japan also found that parentally-violent children were often the eldest child or an only child.

[252] Dunn (1990).

[253] Lit review at http://www.psychology.org.au/Assets/Files/LGBT-Families-Lit-Review.pdf accessed Jan 2016.

[254] The research suggests that lesbian mothers tend to be child-focused, emotionally expressive and less likely to use physical punishment than other families.

[255] "Several studies show that it is a woman's degree of satisfaction with either the housewife role or paid work, and the continuity of her work experience when she does work, that best correlates with positive outcomes in her children." Coontz (1992) p217.

[256] Coontz (1992) p216.

[257] Schaffer (2000) p6.

[258] The idea that people should fit into neat categories, such as extrovert or introvert, remains very popular. There are vast numbers of books offering to show how you fit into a category based on your star sign, some numerical code based on your name, your year of birth, order of birth in your family of origin, etc. One of the most popular personality tests of the past fifty years has been the Myers-Briggs, which is based loosely on Jung's semi-mystical speculations (though Jung didn't approve of it and it was made up in an ad hoc manner). It divides people neatly into either extroverts or introverts (along with a number of other categories) even those who fall very close to the average. As all tests have a fair margin of error those close to the average might as well be pigeonholed by the toss of coin. It makes me embarrassed as a psychologist that such an unscientific test is still popular and is still used in job selection and occasionally even given as evidence in courts.

[259] *"Much as expected from previous studies, we did find that extraverts were more likely to bully and introverts to be bullied."* Rigby (2002) p159.

[260] Lippa (2002) p13.

[261] Kolvin (1988), Farrington (1988).

[262] Raine (2013).

[263] Lykken (1999) p223.

[264] Rothbart (1994), Diener (2004).

[265] Some writers have tried to apply "Strain theory" to violence to parents, using unreliable family violence surveys to suggest that these young people are more stressed than others, which is often the opposite of the truth, except as they stress themselves. Of course this does apply in families where there has been DV, but it is not the stress and strain that causes violence to parents.

[266] Apter (1992).

[267] "In four of the six of the categories tested – vocabulary, verbal memory, spatial orientation, and perhaps most heartening of all, inductive reasoning – people performed best, on average, between the ages of forty to sixty-five." Strauch (2010) p14. Middle aged brains are worse at perceptual speed and numerical ability.

[268] Dawson (2007).

[269] Farrington (2000).

[270] Baron-Cohen (2004) ch 5. De Wall (2009) p67.

[271] Konrath (2011).

[272] Greenfield (2014) p36.

[273] *"Conceptually, reactive aggression can be used as a synonym for 'defensive,' angry' 'hot blooded,' 'impulsive', emotional' or 'retaliatory' aggression'. Proactive aggression can be used as an instrumental means to secure goods from others or to dominate others. Synonyms for proactive aggression are 'offensive,' 'predatory,' and 'instrumental' aggression."* Vitaro (2005) p179. It is a bit confusing including 'defensive' aggression with expressive and I generally prefer to talk about expressive vs instrumental. Not everyone agrees that these are valid distinctions and it is often hard to tell how much an aggressive act is reactive and how much proactive. It is often a combination of the two.

[274] Garbarino (2006) p39.

[275] Baillargeon (2002).

[276] Archer (2005).

[277] There are logical evolutionary reasons why men are more aggressive than women. In the past being aggressive led to men having more children. The extreme of this is shown by the 'Genghis Khan effect'. Genghis has eighteen million living descendants. An Irish ancestor of mine, Niall of the Nine Hostages (not a nice man), has three million descendants. Being aggressive rarely gives women any such advantage in quantity of children but could make their children less likely to survive.

[278] For a review of the evidence on indirect aggression: Vaillancourt (2005).

[279] Gallagher (2002).

[280] Sibling assaults: 73% boys, 27% girls Krienert (2011).

[281] Martin (1990).

[282] Lloyd (1995), Simmons (2002).

[283] The common assumption seems to be that witnessing DV will make boys aggressive but girls may become passive or are less affected. This is generally not based much on evidence but on the assumption that children model same-sex parents. At least two studies found girls more affected than boys by DV (Sternberg et al, 1993 & Spaccarelli et al, 1994) and one found no gender differences (O'Keefe, 1994). Many other studies report that boys have more behaviour problems following DV, but then boys have more behaviour problems generally. DV increases the rate of behaviour problems in both boys and girls but it doesn't appear to increase gender difference. In my sample 46% of the girls (sixty-five of one hundred and forty) have had DV in their family compared to 45% (one hundred and forty-seven of three hundred and twenty-seven).

[284] Pinker (2002) p377.

[285] New York Times Feb 18 1986. 'Adopted child syndrome' is not an official psychiatric category.

[286] Pinker (2002) p175.

[287] Lewis (2015).

[288] Frances (2013).

[289] Ibid.

[290] Ibid p177.

[291] Ibid.

[292] Bancroft (2002) p9.

[293] Huggins-Cooper (2006) p39.

[294] E.g. Biddulph (1997).

[295] "Although puberty brings about significant hormonal changes, such changes are not the cause of teen turmoil. Tens of millions of teens in preindustrial nations around the world also reach puberty every year, but the mood problems we see in America are almost entirely absent in such countries. Moreover, physiological research shows that the hormonal changes that occur during pubertal maturation don't predict behaviour very well." Epstein (2007).

[296] Offer & Schonert-Reichl (1992).

[297] Bongers et al (2004), Brame et al. (2001), Nagin & Tremblay (1999)

[298] Van Goozen (2005).

[299] "Persons with a history of violent behaviour may have slight elevations in testosterone levels, but this effect is not large. The elevation may be a consequence of the behaviour or its antecedent." Volavka (1995) p76. Or see: Sapolsky (1997).

[300] Pinker (2011) p501.

[301] McBride Dabbs (2000).

[302] Schachter (1962).

[303] Arnett (1999).

[304] Epstein (2007).

[305] Arnett (1999), Coleman (2011).
"The results reveal that normal adolescents are not in the throes of turmoil. The vast majority function well, enjoy good relationships with their families and friends, and accept the values of the larger society." Offer (1984).

[306] We shouldn't assume that people always believe their own excuses (though the best liars are those who can convince themselves). Thus someone who says they couldn't help their behaviour because of some excuse or other may believe it, may *half* believe it, or may just be lying outright. Sadly some researchers on violence or other anti-social behaviour seem to believe everything they're told.

[307] Omer (2000) p82.

[308] Epstein (2007).

[309] Harris (1998), Paris (2000).

[310] Mednick (1884).

[311] Crichton-Hill (2006) p274.

[312] Frances (2013), Greenberg (2010).

[313] De Lange (2004).

[314] Grandin (2013) p105.

[315] The definition of intellectual disability includes not only a low IQ but some functional impairment. In practice this is vague, often ignored, and you can always find some impairment in some area if you look for it. Obviously school is the place where having a low IQ is most disabling so almost all those with an IQ below seventy are impaired in this setting.

[316] Bancroft (2002) p328.

[317] Molina (2009) in a large follow-up study (seven years) found that children on stimulant drugs were no better off than those who didn't have medication for ADHD.

[318] For example Healy (2004) illustrates the disturbing way the pharmaceutical industry distorts the evidence.
See the damning letter of resignation from the American Psychiatric Association by Loren Mosher: www.oikos.org/mosher.htm over this issue: "At this point in history, in my view, psychiatry has been almost completely bought out by the drug companies."

[319] Baumeister, Smart et al. (1996).

[320] Baumeister (1997).

[321] Twenge (2009) pl 27.

[322] Mackay, H (2006) 'So much love, but sadly it's the wrong kind' *Sydney Morning Herald* 16 Dec.

[323] Berne (1996).

[324] Twenge (2009) p34.

[325] Pioneered by the work of Diana Baumrind, e.g. Baumrind (1991).

[326] Twenge (2009) p17.

[327] Sutherland (1992) p66.

[328] I've been using the Piers-Harris test of self-concept, but have only scored twenty young people who were abusing parents. Although it's interesting to discuss this with young people, there are some problems, for instance a child who fights a lot and gets into trouble a lot will score low on 'behaviour' even if he is very proud of this. A child who believes he is a genius but hates school and truants and disrupts the class will score low on the Intellectual and School sub-scale even if he is genuinely either proud or indifferent to this. Thus truly arrogant kids with bad behaviour and who are disengaged from school don't come out as particularly high on self-esteem on this test.

[329] *"The great evil figures of religion and mythology do not have low self-esteem – on the contrary, they have always been inordinately proud, confident, and even arrogant."* Baumeister (1997) p69.

[330] Fiske (2015) p14.

[331] Baumeister (1997) p376.

[332] Hershman and Lieb (1994).

[333] Baumeister (1997).

[334] Lindberg (2013).

[335] Twenge (2009) p216.

[336] Olweus (1993) p34.

[337] http://www.psychologytoday.com/blog/pop-psych/201311/might-doesn-t-make-right-it-helps

[338] Twenge (2009) p74.

[339] A rare mention of false allegation in relation to violence to parents is in Routt (2015) p47.

[340] Twenge (2014) p291.

[341] Bancroft (2002) p64.

[342] Doherty (2003) p35.

[343] Bennett & Rowe (2003) p 46.

[344] Haste (2000).

[345] Palmer (2007).

[346] Frank Furedi, The Times, October 25, 2005.

[347] Balson (1981).

[348] Holt (1974) does argue that children have the right to have sex and take drugs. He's still highly regarded in some circles!

[349] Omer (2000) p63.

[350] Hamilton (2008) p43.

[351] Exodus 21:7-11 NLT.

[352] Jenkins (1990).

[353] Jenkins (1991) p186.

[354] Shaw (2003) p17.

[355] Bancroft (2002) p57.

[356] *"Optimism also explains why we spend so much and save so little… It's in the spirit of optimism that a person blithely builds up credit card debt on optional expenditures… And the ideology of positive thinking eagerly fanned this optimism and the sense of entitlement that went with it."* Ehrenreich (2009) p108.

[357] Gadoros (1990) p260.

[358] Levine (2006) p142.

[359] Epstein (2007).

[360] *The Times*, Saturday 4 February 2006, page 27.

[361] See Harris (1998).

[362] Paris (2000) p xi.

[363] Bruer (1999), Kagan (2010), Rutter (1993), Ambert (1992), Harris (1998), Morgan (1975).

[364] Parent quoted in Murphy-Edwards (2012) p174.

[365] Rigby (2002) p32 gives a number of examples though admitting that this idea "is not without difficulties. Many of these relate to the trickiness of the concept of power itself" he also uses a definition of bullying which includes a power imbalance.

[366] Definition from Concise Oxford Dictionary, 10th edition.

[367] Collishaw et al. (2004).

[368] Frances (2013) p178.

[369] Bancroft (2002) p44. The influence of Marxist theory in sociology and related disciplines has undoubtedly encouraged the myth of powerlessness.

[370] Routt (2011) p10.

[371] Crichton-Hill (2006) p120.

[372] The Boiled Frog metaphor has been applied to abuse before, e.g.: "We are not inclined to notice gradual changes. This is how most partners adapt to verbal abuse. They slowly adapt until, like frog number two, they are living in an environment which is killing to their spirit." Evans (1996) p111.

[373] Fiske (2015) p198.

[374] Omer (2004) p3.

[375] Bancroft (2002) p153.

[376] Ian Robertson in New Scientist 7 July 2012 p 28.

[377] Galinsky et al. (2006).

[378] Condrey (2007).

[379] Ambert (2001) p98.

[380] Shannon (2005) p64.

[381] Murphy-Edwards (2012) p189.

[382] Condrey (2007).

[383] Glick (2001).

[384] Hilton (1992) p82.

[385] Quote from NCA Action for Children report 'The Hidden Victims' 1995.

[386] I'm not going into the technical arguments here but they are available in my Master's thesis. Surveys of both DV and CPV suggest three things: very high rates of abuse, gender is not important, and most family violence is mutual. It is very common for writers to choose to believe one or two of these and ignore the other implications. With adult family violence many people know that the ideas that women are just as violent as men and that most violence is mutual are absurd (but they still quote the

survey incidence rates). However, with CPV people don't know enough to reject these ideas and the mutual violence idea fits in with parent-blaming assumptions.

[387] Often the female partner is either mentally ill or a drug abuser. I've also known two or three adult men with Asperger's who had been abused by their partners. My guess is that physical abuse by the male partner in heterosexual relationships is ten to twenty times more common than the reverse.

[388] Miller (2007) p235.

[389] Pinker (2011).

[390] See Hay (2005).

[391] Adult son, quoted in Hilton (1992) p80.

[392] O'Brien (1994).

[393] Bancroft & Silverman (2003: 11.

[394] Jasinski (1998) p86.

[395] Patterson (1988).

[396] Holden (1991), Jaffe (1990).

[397] Patterson (1982), Patterson (1989).

[398] Jaffe (1990).

[399] Davis (1987), Dodge (1994), Holden (1991).

[400] Levendosky (2000) p90.

[401] Smith (1996) p5.

[402] Jasinski (1998) p88.

[403] Bancroft (2002) p34.

[404] Levendosky (1998), Levendosky et al (2000).

[405] Joseph (2013).

[406] Wolfe (1985).

[407] *"The more the respondent observed parental violence, the lower his self-esteem."* Stith (1993) p197.

[408] Blanchard (1993) p33.

[409] PTSD is a rather vague diagnostic label and the symptoms seen in children exposed to long-term abuse are very different to those seen in adults reacting to a trauma. And is it fair to slap a psychiatric label on a child who is reacting normally to an extreme environment?

[410] Fojtik (1976), Roy (1977).

[411] Simons (1993).

[412] Fiske (2015).

[413] Bancroft (2002) p113.

[414] Bancroft (2002) p9.

[415] This was first spelled out by the researcher Finklehor, talking about sexual abusers.

[416] Koman (2002) p54.

[417] Rubin (1996) p89.

[418] E.g. McCord (1991).

[419] Leach (1986) p440.

[420] Balson (1981) p86.

[421] Gordon (1976).

[422] *"What is this discipline parents feel they need to use?... The key to the term discipline is the concept of power or authority – power to obtain* obedience, *to enforce orders – using punishment or giving rewards."* Gordon (1976) p181.

[423] Balson (1981) p89.

[424] Baumrind (1996) p413.

[425] Twenge & Campbell (2009).

[426] Festinger (1959).

[427] Sutherland (1992) p113.

[428] Heinrichs (2003).

[429] The term "unconditional love" is not one I find useful. If love is really unconditional then it is impersonal. If someone loves me no matter *what* I do then it has nothing to do with me as a person. It smacks of the sort of blind loyalty that sometimes sees parents backing up, and covering up for, murderers and abusers.

[430] Berkowitz (1993).

[431] http://www.theage.com.au/lifestyle/life/girls-get-less-pocket-money-than-boys-20130818-2s4pc.html.

[432] Absent?

[433] Ibid p59.

[434] Routt (2015) p125.

[435] Edenborough (2008), Holt (2011), Cottrell (2001).

[436] Cottrell (2004) p1089.

[437] http://www.secureteen.com/domestic-violence/parent-abuse-when-teenagers-turn-violent-on-their-parents/

[438] Writing about violence to parents, Wilson (1996) said that therapists who feel a family member is unsafe should, "provide immediate protection through insistence on separation." p119.

[439] Routt (2015).

[440] Bancroft (2002): first part p37, second part p60.

[441] Fiske (2015), Eller (2010).

[442] Baumeister (1997).

[443] Cited in Berkowitz (1993).

[444] Travis (1982).

[445] Clements (2005) p139.

[446] Caplan (1981) p26.

[447] This goes back to the Greek Stoic philosopher Epictetus who said: "We have two ears and one mouth so we may listen more and talk the less." There is another version suggesting we should listen twice as much as we talk. This is silly! If two people were both trying to do this it would eventually result in total silence.

[448] Fisher (1981) p54.

[449] Ibid p23.

[450] Epstein (2007).

[451] Ambert (2001) p85.

[452] Cottrell (2004) p107.

[453] Omer (2000) p x/xi.

[454] Eckstein (2002) p210.

[455] Regalado (2004) p5.

[456] Smart (1984) p305.

[457] Frizzell (1998) p78.

[458] Routt (2011) p10.

[459] Duncan (2013), similar results have been found in the USA.

[460] Omer (2004) p76.

[461] Kowalski (2008) p35.

[462] Rhule (2005).

[463] Between a rock and a hard place: how parents deal with children who use substances and perpetrate abuse." Adfam 2012. Http://www.adfam.org.uk/docs/Between_a_rock_and_a_hard_place_-_The%20executive_summary.pdf

[464] E.g. Evans & Warren-Sohlberg (1988), Ibabe & Jaureguizar (2010).

[465] Potter-Efron & Potter-Effron (1985).

[466] Barnard (2007) p13.

[467] Cottrell (2004).

[468] Rubin (1996) pxiii.

[469] Brook et al (1989) Similar conclusions about brothers having greater influence than parents comes from the longitudinal study by Duncan et al (1996).

[470] Kaufman & Straus (1987).

[471] See for example: Heyman (2009).

[472] Bancroft (2002) p117.

[473] Lewis (2015) p164.

[474] Alexander et. al. (1981).

[475] Lewis (2015).

[476] Parent quoted Edenborough & Jackson (2008).

[477] Barnard 2007 p 22.

[478] "… a label is not a diagnosis. Saying someone is 'depressed' or 'anxious' is a far cry from finding out what causes the depression or anxiety; it's comparable to a physician saying a child has 'spots'." Walker (1996) p5.

[479] Kotov R1, Gamez W, et al. (2010). 'Linking 'big' personality traits to anxiety, depressive, and substance use disorders: a meta-analysis.' Psychol Bulletin 136(5): 768-821.

[480] "Depression has not generally been linked with crime or violence (unlike other mental disturbances). The only exception was that there seemed to be some link to domestic violence, and even those findings were inconclusive or ambiguous. In particular, it seemed likely that depression was the result rather than the cause of family violence." Crichton-Hill (2006) p137.

[481] In trials, 3.4% of children on the drug experienced mood changes, tried to harm themselves or thought of committing suicide, compared with 1.2% on placebo pills. http://www.guardian.co.uk/science/2003/jun/11/sciencenews.medicineandhealth In another study of paroxetine (aka Paxil), 23% reported manic-like symptoms, which included hostility, mood swings, and nervousness. Keller et.al (2000)

[482] Bancroft (2002) p383.

[483] Boys born in Dec were 41% more likely to get ADHD meds and girls 77% more likely than those born in January Morrow (2012).

[484] Lebowitz (2011).

[485] Research carried out by Okayama University in 2002 quoted in Honoré (2008).

[486] Quint (2005) p325.

[487] One study found that autistic children were just as likely to be bullies as were other children. But if they had ADHD as well as autism they were four times *more* likely to be bullies than children without any disability (Montes & Halterman (2007). A study in Special Schools found that teachers classified a quarter of the children with autism as bullies, van Roekel (2010). It isn't rare!

[488] Clements (2005) p138.

[489] Attwood (2006) p170.
[490] Kanne (2010) p934.
[491] Ashton (2014).
[492] Ghaziuddin. (1991).
[493] DSM4 p100.
[494] DSM4 p 102.
[495] DSM4 p 102.
[496] Caplan (1994) p41.